Holistic Management

Holistic Management

A New Framework for Decision Making

Allan Savory

with Jody Butterfield

ISLAND PRESS

Washington, D.C. | Covelo, California

Library of Congress Cataloging-in-Publication Data
Savory, Allan, 1935–
    Holistic management : a new framework for decision making / Allan
Savory and Jody Butterfield. — 2nd ed.
        p.   cm.
    Rev. ed. of: Holistic management, 1988.
    Includes bibliographical references and index.
    ISBN 1–55963–487–1 (cloth). — ISBN 1–55963–488–X (paper)
    1. Environmental economics.   2. Sustainable development.   3. Human
ecology.   4. Natural resources—Management.   I. Butterfield, Jody.
II. Savory, Allan, 1935–   Holistic resource management.
III. Title.
    HC79.E5S2823   1999   98–42237
    333.7—dc21   CIP

Printed on recycled, acid-free paper

Manufactured in the United States of America
10 9 8 7 6 5 4 3 2

In memory of my father, J. H. R. Savory, O.B.E., a gentle soul whose love of nature and respect for wildness influenced me profoundly

Contents

Part IV   The Ecosystem That Sustains Us All

Part V   The Tools We Use to Manage Our Ecosystem

Part VI   Testing Your Decisions

Part VII   Completing the Feedback Loop

Part VIII   Some Practical Guidelines for Management

Preface

As a youngster my only aim in life was to live in the wildest African bush forever. Although I eventually did have that opportunity, I ended up forsaking it to work toward saving the wildlife that was my reason for being in the bush. Even in the wildest areas the land was deteriorating, in fact turning to desert, rendering it ever less able to support life of any kind. I was determined to find a way to reverse this process.

That quest took me in a direction I would never have anticipated, compelling me to work first with people who for generations had been caretakers of the land and whose management I believed was responsible for initiating the deterioration, then with those who were advising them, and eventually with many others as a member of parliament attempting to deal with land management at the policy level.

What I learned from these experiences was that the remorseless spread of deserts and the human impoverishment that always resulted *were* related to management, but more fundamentally to the way people were making management decisions, whether or not those people lived or worked on the land.

This book attempts to describe the way forward that emerged. It involves a new framework for decision-making that enables people to make decisions that satisfy immediate needs without jeopardizing their future well-being or the well-being of future generations. That, of course, requires that the actions ensuing from any decision also enhance the well-being of the environment that sustains us now and will have to sustain future generations. The greatest strength of the new decision-making framework is that it leads us to see that we serve our own interests best when we account for the environmental, as well as the social and economic, consequences of our decisions.

Holistic Management is the revised and updated version of *Holistic Resource Management* (1988), which was a first attempt to explain the development of the new decision-making framework and how it could be used. The change of title is only the most obvious difference. The book's ideas have been clarified and strengthened by those who have put the ideas into practice, most of whom care more for results in real life than well-sounding theories that are more interesting than useful. These people include many thousands who make their living from the land and are learning to restore it profitably through practices that mimic nature and many others who have merely sought a more rewarding personal or family life. They also include whole communities of people who have found the ideas useful in bringing their members together—even where conflicts divide them—to establish a common vision that reflects what they genuinely value and hope to accomplish.

Readers of this edition will benefit from what we have learned from all these people as they have struggled to incorporate the ideas—the problems they had, the mistakes they made, what worked, and what didn't and why. It also reflects the contributions made by my wife, Jody Butterfield, who rewrote hundreds of pages many times to simplify, clarify, and remove unnecessary jargon and who forced me to think more deeply than ever before on nearly every point. Because no amount of acknowledgment would have done justice to her effort, her name appears with mine on the title page.

The key differences between the first edition and this one are woven throughout the book as critical themes and will become apparent to anyone who reads both volumes. But perhaps the most significant is that we have worked to enlarge the readership to include those not directly involved in land management. Although our fate as a civilization is tied to the land and its health, and although millions of ordinary people in making their living from the land control that fate to a large degree, unless these people have the support of the hundreds of millions of others who depend on their efforts, they cannot succeed.

Equally important is a point made repeatedly in the following pages, that each of us, no matter what path we have chosen to follow in life, makes decisions that in one way or another impact the health of our environment and the quality of other people's lives. The simple technique described in these pages for determining what that impact might be goes a long way to ensuring that the outcome is life enhancing.

We have done our best to eliminate details that would confuse the general reader, but to eliminate them all would have made the book meaningless to the core audience it must reach. Some of the information that appeared in the first edition has been moved to a series of handbooks, currently under preparation and referred to specifically in later chapters. Throughout the book we have also noted chapters the more general reader might want to skim.

In the future, as we gain more experience in different realms of endeavor, new books will surely be written that address the specific concerns of these various domains. In the meantime, the issues raised in this one touch the lives of everyone and will do so increasingly in coming years.

Some months ago, after I gave a brief talk on Holistic Management to members of the Explorer's Club in New York, a man named Ron Brandes approached me. He suggested that without my having realized it, what I had done in my talk was to focus attention on what would surely become the outgrowth of the current Information Age—the Decision-Making Age. In the end, he said, all the information we have amassed in the past decades will serve little purpose unless we make intelligent decisions about how it is to be used. It is my hope that the framework we have developed helps to serve that end.

Allan Savory
Albuquerque, New Mexico

Acknowledgments

A nything we do in science is built on the work of thousands who have gone before us. Both from their successes and from their failures we learn and thus advance. I am deeply indebted to the many who have struggled to find better ways for us to live in harmony with each other and our environment and on whose work I have built.

From the time I departed from the conventional thinking of my training, I have been supported and helped by many people, and I welcome this opportunity to thank them. I am particularly indebted to the many farmers and ranchers in southern Africa, and later in North America, who loved their land and were prepared to work with me in those early years in the search for answers. I am no less indebted to those working in government agencies at the time who supported our efforts, despite considerable criticism from their peers. Without the courage and enthusiasm of all these people we would never have succeeded in finding a better way.

Since forming the Center for Holistic Management in 1984, my wife, Jody Butterfield, and I have been joined by many others equally committed to developing the ideas further, most notably our growing network of Holistic Management Certified Educators. Many of the changes reflected in this edition of *Holistic Management* are a direct result of the contributions they have made, based on what they have learned through their own practice and in assisting others. We are all indebted to the village-based facilitators who have worked so hard to bring Holistic Management to the Hwange Communal Lands of Zimbabwe. They have shown the rest of us how we could simplify and clarify concepts that people everywhere have struggled to learn.

A number of friends and colleagues read portions of the manuscript, providing invaluable criticism and correcting embarrassing errors. They are Dr. Paul Martin, Department of Geosciences, University of Arizona; Dr. Cliff Montagne, Department of Plant, Soil, and Environmental Science, Montana State University; Dr. R.H. (Dick) Richardson, Department of Zoology, University of Texas at Austin; Dr. Brian Sindelar, a range management consultant in Bozeman, Montana; Dr. Deborah Stinner, Department of Entomology, Ohio State University; and Dr. Ray Travers, a registered professional forester in private practice in British Columbia. In addition, the following persons read the entire manuscript helping to improve the overall structure, challenging points that were weak or vague, and greatly reducing the number of incomprehensible passages: Alan Carpenter; Bill Casey; John Cleveland; Frank Dawley; Ghislaine Keyzer; Hunter Lovins; Walt Ruzzo; Arne Vanderburg; and Tom Walther. Marce Rackstraw made a valiant attempt to liven up the illustrations, and Stephen Verzi lent timely assistance in three-dimensional design. To all these people I give my most sincere thanks.

Finally, Jody and I are grateful most of all to the staff of the Center for Holistic Management, who for close to three years were forced to make do with two less people to share an enormous workload. That they did so without complaint only adds to the admiration we feel for them all.

A grant from the 777 Fund of The Tides Foundation helped to make this book possible. Many thanks.

Part I

Introduction

1

Changing the Way
We Make Decisions

In 1948 I entered Plumtree School, a boarding school in the British tradition set in the African bushveld on the border of what was then Southern Rhodesia and Botswana. When not on the rugby or cricket fields we were encouraged to get out into the bush, a gesture of liberality that offset all my adolescent frustration with formal education. I became fanatic about the bush and its big game, and a passion to return to it drove me through a university education that qualified me for a Northern Rhodesian Game Department post at the age of twenty.

Once in the Game Department I began to realize that all I loved was doomed. Not for the commonly talked of reasons—poaching and overexploitation—but rather because of our own ignorance as professional bureaucrats. But professional people do not like to admit to ignorance or to raise the questions I did. It is more customary to blame others while calling for more money, research, and staff. So began a long struggle, often very lonely, to find solutions to the deterioration I saw everywhere. Along the way I learned that what I saw in the destruction of wildlife reflects the condition of humanity and all other life on this planet. The wildlife problems that I first grappled with were little more than advance gusts of the violent storms that ultimately threaten the whole world.

Now several decades later, much water has flowed under the bridge, and I can write about the way forward that I found and subsequently developed with the help of many others. It involves no elaborate or costly technology or specialized knowledge, but rather some new insights and a new decision-making process that gives us the ability to design and to plan the future we want while ensuring that the environment can sustain it. The decision-making process can serve to manage a farm, a national park, or a city's water supply, or one's personal life, a household, a corporation, or organization of any kind. It also can be used to diagnose the underlying cause of many problems, to assess a variety of policies, and to make research more relevant to management needs.

I would not have guessed in those early years that decision-making had much to do with the challenge of saving wildlife in an ever-deteriorating environment. But in the end I found that changing the *way* we make decisions was key to meeting that management challenge—and many others. One experience proved pivotal to my understanding.

I was preparing a teaching exercise to show that the causes scientists, politicians, and others most often blamed for the environmental deterioration in Africa were suspect. These causes included overpopulation; poverty; lack of education, capital, and technology; collective ownership of the land (by the state, rather than the individuals who use it); government corruption; poor farming methods, such as slash and burn cropping in the forests or the cultivation of steep slopes and unsuitable soils elsewhere; lack of agricultural extension services; and overstocking on the rangelands.

There appeared to be total certainty in the matter. The only aspect really debated in the scientific literature and in the voluminous government and development agency reports was the hierarchy of the causes. If one or all of these things were indeed the causes of the degradation, then the environment should be improving in places where the opposite conditions and practices prevailed. But was it? In the western part of Texas, where I was working at the time, and where the climate was similar to much of Africa's, the rural population was low and declining. The land was owned privately and the owners had access to good education, to plenty of capital, and to the latest technology. The government, although not perfect, basically served the interests of the people and had provided them with millions of dollars in financial aid and sophisticated agricultural extension services. None of the poor farming methods listed were practiced. The rangelands could hardly be called overstocked when animals were so few compared to what they had been only a century earlier.

Nevertheless, the soil and the agricultural economy of West Texas had degraded badly. Texas farmers were able to keep production levels high by using ever more fertilizer, pesticide, irrigation, and other technologies. However, vast areas of rangeland that had once sustained immense herds of bison and later cattle were hardly distinguishable from the most degraded rangelands on the fringes of the Sahara. Sand dunes were beginning to form in West Texas. The water table was falling, too, and rivers once filled with fish had been dry for decades except for the occasional flash flood. The Texas government had spent hundreds of millions of dollars to fight insects, weeds, and brush that were blamed for ruining the land, but they continued to thrive. All the while, the people, as in Africa, were leaving the land for the big cities, where crime and poverty continued to grow.

Logic told me there had to be a common denominator when the same results were produced under such different conditions and practices. Communities I had visited elsewhere in North America, in Europe, and in Asia were experiencing many of the same problems. And no matter how wealthy and developed or poor and underdeveloped the community, people said these problems were getting worse, despite all the money and effort they had poured into tackling them. Was there a common denominator in these situations? Was it the same? Probably so, and probably also in the many past civilizations that had bloomed and died when their environment could no longer support them.

This common denominator was unlikely to be related to systems of government or any particular technology because we had had all manner of these through the ages. Greed and ignorance, although certainly a factor, had not been common to every situation, nor had population pressure. Areas where human populations were low or almost nonexistent, such as national parks and wilderness areas, were also deteriorating.

The only common denominator, in past and present civilizations, and in Africa, West Texas, and communities everywhere, was that human management was involved, and that it had resulted in *decisions* that had led to the deterioration. The forms of management had changed, and often, but I began to suspect that decision making had not. Something was faulty about the way we were making decisions, and it had been faulty for a very long time. But where was it at fault, and how were we to find out? Decisions are made in millions of ways.

The answer does not become apparent until you first examine *how* we make decisions and identify what is fundamental to the process. In any situation we manage, whether that be a specific entity, such as a business, or something more general, such as our personal lives, our decisions usually emanate from the desire or the need to meet a variety of goals or objectives—ranging from those aligned with some sort of mission, to those that satisfy basic needs. To make sure our decisions are in line with the expected outcome of those goals or objectives, we—either individually, or collaboratively—will consider various criteria. Depending on the context and the actions contemplated, we might ask one or more of the following questions:

Who has expert knowledge and what do they advise? What does the research show? What does our intuition tell us about it? What past experience do we have to go on? Will it do the job? How quickly? Is it allowable under prevailing laws and regulations? Is it cost-effective? Is it ethical? Will it produce a positive cash flow? Is it profitable? What will our peers say? What will the neighbors say? Is it politically expedient?

Will it harm the environment? Will it have adverse social consequences? and so on.

If we are convinced the action we are contemplating will achieve the expected outcome, we'll go ahead with it. Generally, we assume we have made the right decision, although we can't be sure until we see what actually happens.

The major fault in this process—and thus, in the way we were making decisions—is that it lacks an organizing framework. In pursuing a variety of goals and objectives, in whatever situation we manage, we often fail to see that some of them are in conflict and that the achievement of one might come at the expense of achieving another. In weighing up the actions we might take to reach our goals and objectives, we have no way to account for nature's complexity and only rarely factor it in. Actions that are judged to be financially sound might prove to be socially or environmentally unsound, but how do we really know?

The need for such a framework has long been obscured because of the success we have managed to achieve without it. We have been able to develop ever more sophisticated forms of technology with which to exploit Earth's resources and to make life genuinely more comfortable, but we have not been able to do so without damaging our environment at the same time.

The earliest human populations would have had no cause to reflect on such matters as long as their technology did not surpass that of other animals that used stones to break eggs and shellfish. At that early level people could not distort their environment enough to upset ecological harmony much at all. But that soon changed.

By the time humans had acquired the use of fire, and our technology had grown sophisticated enough to enable us to reach and settle new continents or isolated islands, we were capable of inflicting enormous damage. Within 400 years of their arrival in New Zealand, the Maori had exterminated nearly all the flightless birds, including 12 different species of the giant (550-pound) moa, and decimated much of the seashore life. Following the arrival of the Aborigines in Australia 40,000 to 60,000 or more years ago, over 80 percent of the large mammalian genera* became extinct. The fires deliberately set by the Aborigines when hunting, or to limit the extent of uninhabitable rainforest, led to a dramatic increase in soil erosion, the abrupt disappearance of fire-sensitive plant species, and a dramatic increase in fire-dependent species, such as eucalypts.[1]

In North America, over 70 percent of the large mammalian genera became extinct following the arrival of Native Americans around 12,000 years ago. Mammoths, saber-tooth lions, horses, camels, piglike animals, and

---

*Genera is plural for genus. A genus consists of one to many closely related species.

members of the family that included goats, sheep, and cattle were among the species lost. Native American fires were also likely to have been responsible for the fire-dependent vegetation that dominates many American landscapes today. When horses were reintroduced to North America by Europeans in the seventeenth century, the Plains Indians quickly adopted them as a means of transport. That, combined with the readiness with which they also adopted the rifle, made them highly successful bison hunters. Given time, they might have killed out the remaining bison had European immigrants not intervened and conducted a wholesale slaughter of the animals themselves.[2, 3]

Scientists still debate whether these mass extinctions were the result of hunting alone. The profound changes created by human-made fires radically altered the environments that had sustained these animals for tens of millions of years and must also have played a role in the extinctions. Both hunting and fire were probably responsible for the more gradual extinctions that occurred in what is now the interior of the Sahara desert, where as recently as 10,000 to 50,000 years ago elephant, giraffe, buffalo, and hippo roamed savannas and marshlands.

The technology we wield today has greatly expanded the ways in which we can alter our environment and that, combined with the exponential increase in our numbers, has magnified our potential for causing damage. Now, more than ever, we require the ability to make decisions that *simultaneously* consider economic, social, and environmental realities, both short and long term. Given an appropriate framework for organizing management and decision making, we should be able to do this.

Creating such a framework has been the driving force in the development of Holistic Management, but as the next five chapters will show, we had much to learn before it took shape. Four key insights discovered over the last seventy years, when taken together, proved critical. The first insight made the argument for why such a framework was needed and the form it should take. The next three insights enabled us to understand why some environments rapidly deteriorate under practices that benefit others and added pieces to the new framework that proved vital for completing it.

This new management and decision-making framework is summarized in Chapter 7 and described at length in the remaining chapters of this book. In brief, however, one begins by defining the entity being managed in terms of the people responsible for its management and the resources available to them. These people then form what we refer to as a *holistic goal* that describes the quality of life they collectively seek, what they have to produce to create that quality of life, and a description of the resource base they depend on *as it will have to be,* far into the future, to sustain what they must produce to create the quality of life they envision.

All the decisions they make in planning how to reach the holistic goal, or in addressing problems or opportunities that arise along the way, will be evaluated according to the same criteria they have always used. In addition, however, they finally ask seven simple questions to ensure their decisions are socially, environmentally, and economically sound *and will lead them toward the holistic goal.* In other words, any action taken to deal with a problem, to reach an objective, or to meet a basic need should not only accomplish what is required, but also enhance progress toward the holistic goal. To ensure that this happens, a feedback loop is established so that if monitoring shows the decision is not taking you where you want to go, you can act immediately to correct it.

This might seem a lot with which to concern yourself just to make a decision, and it is. However, once the idea is grasped, and as people become increasingly committed to achieving their holistic goal, making decisions this way is no more time-consuming than before. In fact, the process often enables you to reach a decision more quickly, particularly when the decision is a difficult one.

Those working in leading-edge corporations today will find much in this process that is familiar to them. The quality of life portion of the holistic goal is similar to corporate mission statements when those statements genuinely reflect shared values. The next two parts of the holistic goal are just as critical and are a new development. Feedback loops are also used routinely in many quality-conscious corporations and have been written about extensively. One or two of the seven questions might also be familiar and, in some cases, routinely used in corporate decision making.

Much is genuinely new, however, largely because these ideas originated from a drive to restore deteriorating environments rather than to enhance the corporate bottom line. We soon found, of course, that it was impossible to make any real progress on the land unless we consistently examined the financial and social consequences of any decision, just as corporations increasingly find that black ink turns red when they don't consider the environmental and social consequences of their decisions.

This book does not address the corporate domain specifically, but it should prove enlightening to those working within it or to anyone else not specifically concerned with land management. If you are one of many who feel disconnected from the land, my hope is that this book will help to reestablish that connection. I can guarantee that after reading it you will never view the land the same way again. Most of what is reflected in this book, however, is based on experience gained in working with people living on the land and attempting to make their living from it. Much of what they struggle with in attempting to do that, is what people everywhere struggle with in making a living or a life together. In that sense, this book speaks to everyone.

Those who are looking for *the* way to solve the ever-escalating problems we face will not find it in Holistic Management. There is no one way and no one answer to any problem, and never can be. There are millions of answers and potential solutions, and these have to be worked out case by case, situation by situation, by people who are driven by a desire for something better. Holistic Management merely empowers people to identify and to achieve what is best *for them*.

Part II

Four Key Insights

2

The Power of Paradigms

H ad we concluded a hundred years ago that we needed to change
the way we make decisions, we could not have done so successfully. Our knowledge still lacked some vital pieces. Four new insights, taken
together, proved key to removing the obstacles in our path. They have all
been discovered separately over the last seventy years, but were either
ignored, forgotten, or bitterly opposed because they represented new
knowledge that went contrary to the beliefs held by most people—by no
means a new problem.

We could draw parallels to innovators such as Copernicus or Galileo
and have faith that one day the world will accept new knowledge readily.
The fact is that, although we would like to believe otherwise, even as
trained scientists people still approach new knowledge in much the same
way they did in Galileo's time. They will always judge new ideas in the light
of prevailing beliefs, or *paradigms,* according to Thomas Kuhn, in *The
Structure of Scientific Revolutions.* They can never be objective about new
information.

If a new idea is in line with what we believe, said Kuhn, we accept it
readily. But when a new idea goes against our experience, knowledge, and
prejudices—what we *know* rather than what we *think*—our minds either
block it out, distort it, or rebel against it.

None of us can escape this *paradigm effect.* If you don't agree, then take
a few seconds to read the following sentence, and as you do count the
number of times the letter F appears:

> Finished files are the result of years of scientific study com-
> bined with the experience of many years of experts.

Chances are, you probably counted two, three, or four. Few people count more. Now, take a few seconds to read the following sentence, and again count the number of F's:

> Strepxe fo sraey ynam fo ecneirepxe eht htiw denibmoc yduts
> cifitneics fo sraey fo tluser eht era selif dehsinif.

Chances are you counted six or seven. There were seven in both cases. You probably realize that the second sentence was the same as the first—only typed backward to prevent your mind from seeing the words. The way you were taught to read made you see words more easily than letters in the first sentence. When there were no words to see in the second sentence you could easily see the F's. I doubt you hold any deep beliefs about the existence of F's, or that you have a Ph.D. in that field, or that your self-esteem is tied to F's in any way. Had you been somewhat emotional, even subconsciously, about F's, there would have been an even greater disparity in the results.

When it came to understanding the causes of environmental deterioration, scientists already *knew* the answer. Their assurance that enough money and technology would put things right differed not at all from the conviction of renaissance theologians that God caused the sun to circle the earth and not vice versa, as Copernicus had suggested.

A photograph I took some years ago illustrates the point. On the left side of the fence in photo 2-1 hundreds of thousands of dollars had been spent on erosion control measures and other techniques to reverse the deterioration occurring on this land, a national park. On the right, nothing had been done. For several centuries Navajos had grazed their flocks of sheep and goats there, which scientists had blamed for causing the deterioration. In the national park livestock had been banned for over forty years, but even so the land was no better off. In fact, the land on both sides of the fence looks remarkably similar now. Clearly, no one really knew what was causing the deterioration in this case, and no amount of money or technology could change that lack of understanding or reverse the deterioration.

With the benefit of hindsight we can easily see what smaller revelations had to occur before people accepted Copernicus's theory. After people became truly comfortable with the notion of a round Earth, the theory of gravity, certain advances in mathematics, and the moons of Jupiter, the movement of the planets became a simple matter too. In the meantime a number of people went to the stake.

Four such bottlenecks of understanding impeded the development of Holistic Management. The insights that enabled us to move forward came late and painfully, however, because, although they were each rather simple

Photo 2-1 *Despite different management, the results, on both sides of the fence, are the same. Chaco Canyon National Park, New Mexico.*

to grasp, they only become obvious when taken together. Thus, it had been difficult to discover or prove any one of these concepts in isolation.

Earlier peoples had expressed occasional flashes of insight into the principles involved, but as "primitive" or peasant people their opinions were discounted by the scientific community. It took close to twenty-five years to discover their actual significance and to put them together successfully. As you will see, we had to understand their connection to the problem of environmental deterioration and to each other first in order to move forward.

The first insight overturned the notion that the world could be viewed as a machine made up of parts that could be isolated for study or management. In reality the world is composed of patterns—of matter, energy, and life—that function as *wholes* whose qualities cannot be predicted by studying any aspect in isolation. We would know very little about water, for instance, by making an exhaustive study of hydrogen or oxygen, even though every molecule of water is composed of both. Likewise, we could never manage a piece of land in isolation from the people who work it or the economy in which both the land and the people are enmeshed. As Chapter 3 explains, this insight led to the development of a framework for management and decision making. Defining the whole we were dealing with became the first step in Holistic Management.

The next three insights contradicted long-held beliefs about the causes of the environmental deterioration I had first witnessed in Africa and later found in America. As Chapter 4 explains, there were two broad categories of environment we had not recognized before that had evolved in different ways and responded differently when the same actions were applied to them. The types of animals associated with the two categories of environment also differed. As Chapters 5 and 6 show, much of the land deterioration that has occurred in the world was initiated by the severing of a vital relationship between herding animals and their pack-hunting predators. Armed with this new knowledge we could more accurately predict how any piece of land might respond to our management. And this in turn would influence the decisions we made in determining which actions to take.

The four key insights are:

1. A holistic perspective is essential in management. If we base management decisions on any other perspective, we are likely to experience results different from those intended because only the whole is reality.

2. Environments may be classified on a continuum from nonbrittle to very brittle according to how well humidity is distributed throughout the year and how quickly dead vegetation breaks down. At either end of the scale, environments respond differently to the same influences. Resting land restores it in nonbrittle environments, for instance, but damages it in very brittle environments.

3. In brittle environments, relatively high numbers of large, herding animals, concentrated and moving as they naturally do in the presence of pack-hunting predators, are vital to maintaining the health of the lands we thought they destroyed.

4. In any environment, overgrazing and damage from trampling bear little relationship to the number of animals, but rather to the amount of *time* plants and soils are exposed to the animals.

The next four chapters will introduce these four key insights one at a time, but an understanding of all four is essential to see why, despite all our efforts, the environments that sustain us continue to deteriorate. No doubt many other insights await discovery, but at this stage we know that these four represent a major advance.

3

The Whole Is Greater
Than the Sum of Its Parts

O f the four new insights, the discovery that a holistic perspective is
essential in management, is the most vital. Unfortunately it is also
the most difficult to understand and more difficult still to bring to bear in
actual practice. Nevertheless, we now realize that no whole, be it a family,
a business, a community, or a nation, can be managed without looking
inward to the lesser wholes that combine to form it, and *outward to the
greater wholes of which it is a member.* Each day we put the utmost concentration and energy into our chosen tasks, seldom reflecting that we work
within a greater whole that our actions will affect, slowly, cumulatively, and
often dramatically. In our culture it is mainly philosophers who concern
themselves with this larger issue because it is hard to see how individuals
caught up in daily life can take responsibility for the long-term consequences of their actions, but they can. We can.

The need for a new approach to the challenge of making a living without destroying our environment goes back to prehistoric times, to the
moment humans acquired fire, spear, and axe, and thus the ability to alter
our environment in ways other animals could not. The sheer bounty of
Earth's resources, however, has enabled us to keep the old caveman attitude
to any challenge: If you have a problem, get a rock and smash it.

In the last 400 years our knowledge and the technological power to
respond to any challenge have increased more rapidly than in all of the one
million or so years of human existence. Over the same few centuries the
health of our natural resources has entered a breathtaking decline. The parallel is no coincidence, as figure 3-1 helps to illustrate. The first column
shows areas of technological success, while the second shows areas of fail-

Mechanical	**Nonmechanical**
Development of	*Management of*
Transport: air, land, water	Agriculture
Communication: radio,	Rangelands
television, telephone,	Forests
satellite	Air quality
Weapons: conventional,	Fisheries
nuclear, laser	Water supplies and quality
Space exploration	Erosion
Computer technology:	Economies
artificial intelligence,	Wildlife (including insects)
robotics	Human relationships
Home building and home	Human health
appliance technology	*(Ever-increasing problems testifying*
Energy plants: nuclear,	*to our lack of understanding)*
hydroelectric, etc.	
Medical technology: brain	
scanners, eyeglasses/contact	
lenses, medicines, etc.	
Genetic engineering	
Chemical technology:	
synthetic fertilizers	
(Ever-increasing success story	
testifying to the marvels of science)	

Figure 3-1 *Areas of human endeavor at which we have excelled are limited to those of a mechanical nature, and are listed in the left column. We continue to face innumerable challenges in nonmechanical areas of endeavor (right column), where our successes have been fleeting.*

ure, although a few might contain apparent short-term successes. It takes no special insight to generalize about these two realms of endeavor. Every item on the left is of a mechanical nature and involves some form of technology. Each one on the right involves the nonmechanical world of complex relationships and wholes with diffuse boundaries. A deeper analysis of this difference sheds some light on our failures.

The modern scientific approach to the areas in both columns goes back to the thirteenth-century work of Roger Bacon, who first distinguished experimental science from the unqualified belief in scripture and tradition. This idea developed into the formal scientific method wherein one seeks to test a hypothesis by controlling all variables of a phenomenon and manipulating them one at a time. By the seventeenth century, scientists began to view the whole world as a machine made up of parts that could be isolated and studied by the scientific method, and their success in areas that are in fact mechanical seemed to confirm this as fundamental truth.

However, in studying our ecosystem and the many creatures inhabiting it we cannot meaningfully isolate anything, let alone control the variables.

The earth's atmosphere, its plant, animal, and human inhabitants, its oceans, plains, and forests, its ecological stability, and its promise for humankind can only be grasped when they are viewed in their entirety. Isolate any part, and neither what you have taken nor what you have left behind remains what it was when all was one.

In the 1920s this new worldview was given a name, *holism* (from the Greek *holos*), and a theoretical base by the legendary South African states-man-scholar Jan Christian Smuts (1870–1950); (photo 3-1). In the years since, others have further elaborated on Smuts's original theory. However, it is Smuts who most influenced my own thinking.

In *Holism and Evolution* (1926), Smuts challenged the old mechanical viewpoint of science. Like modern-day physicists, Smuts came to see that the world is not made up of substance, but of flexible, changing patterns. "If you take patterns as the ultimate structure of the world, if it is arrange-ments and not stuff that make up the world," said Smuts, "the new concept leads you to the concept of wholes. Wholes have no stuff, they are arrange-ments. Science has come round to the view that the world consists of pat-terns, and I construe that to be that the world consists of wholes."[1]

Individual parts do not exist in nature, only wholes, and these form and shape each other. The new science of Smuts's day, ecology, was simply a

Photo 3-1 *Jan Christian Smuts (courtesy* The Star, Johannesburg*)*

recognition of the fact that all organisms feel the force and molding effect of the environment as a whole. "We are indeed one with Nature," he wrote. "Her genetic fibers run through all our being; our physical organs connect us with millions of years of her history; our minds are full of immemorial paths of pre-human experience."[2]

Without realizing it, American biologist Robert Paine provided dramatic evidence of the holistic nature of communities in a study he did in a seashore environment. When he removed the main predator, a certain species of starfish, from a population of fifteen observable species, things quickly changed. Within a year, the area was occupied by only eight of the original fifteen species. Numbers within the prey species boomed and in the resulting competition for space, reasoned Paine, those species that could move left the area; those that could not simply died out. Paine speculated that in time even more species would be lost. His control area, which still contained the predatory starfish, over the same time remained a complex community where all species thrived.[3]

Viewed from the old paradigm that nature can be viewed as a machine made up of parts, the results of this study were interesting, but not surprising. When a critical part (the starfish) was removed, the food chain was dramatically affected because all those species (or parts) were interconnected. Looked at in Smuts's terms, Paine's findings are more dramatic. Although there were fifteen observable species in the environment studied, they were more than a collection of interconnected species. They were a whole, just as algae and fungi that cling so closely to one another have become lichens, or hydrogen and oxygen have become water. And just as billions of nerve, muscle, skin, blood, and bone cells have become you. You do not see yourself, or your parents, or your children as communities of interconnected cells, you see them as whole persons. Removing one element in the whole, as Paine did, severely disrupted the whole community. Given that there can be up to a billion organisms in a teaspoon of water, we really have no idea how much more deeply the whole in Paine's study was affected.

I witnessed a similar disruption in two much larger communities in Africa. For a period in the 1950s I worked as a game department biologist in the Luangwa Valley in Northern Rhodesia (today Zambia) and the lower Zambezi Valley of Southern Rhodesia (today Zimbabwe). Both areas contained large wildlife populations—elephant, buffalo, zebra, more than a dozen antelope species, hippo, crocodiles, and numerous other predators. On more than one occasion I saw more than forty lions in a day's walk, which gives a good indication of just how large the populations were that they preyed upon. Buffalo herds were so thick that one day when a friend shot one buffalo with a light rifle, twenty-seven adult buffalo were trampled to death in the resulting stampede. Yet despite these numbers, the river banks were stable and well vegetated (photo 3-2). People had lived in these

Photo 3-2 *In the 1950s the banks of the Zambezi River were stable and well vegetated, despite the high numbers of game and the presence of hunting, gardening humans. Zimbabwe.*

areas since time immemorial in clusters of huts away from the main rivers because of the mosquitos and wet season flooding. Near their huts they kept gardens that they protected from elephants and other raiders by beating drums throughout much of the night or firing muzzle-loading guns to frighten them off. The people hunted and trapped animals throughout the year as well.

But the governments of both countries wanted to make these areas national parks. It would not do to have all this hunting going on, and all the drum beating, singing, and general disturbance, so the government removed the people. Like Paine, we, in effect, removed the starfish. But in our case we put a different type of starfish back in. We replaced drum beating, gun firing, gardening, and farming people with ecologists, naturalists, and tourists, under strict control to ensure they did not disturb the animals or vegetation.

Just as in Paine's study, the results were quick and dramatic. Within a few decades miles of riverbank in both valleys were devoid of reeds, fig thickets, and most other vegetation (photo 3-3). With nothing but the change in behavior of one species these areas became terribly impoverished and are still deteriorating seriously as I write. Why this resulted will become clearer in the following chapters. For now, let me just say that the change in human behavior changed the behavior of the animals that had naturally feared them, which in turn led to the damage to soils and vegetation.

Photo 3-3 *By the 1980s the banks of the Zambezi River within the national park were nearly devoid of vegetation, even though game populations had been culled heavily and the hunting, gardening humans removed. Zimbabwe.*

Had I better understood what Smuts was saying, I might have seen the danger in what we had done before it was too late. It was years, however, before his message finally made sense to me.

Like many young boys growing up in Africa during the Second World War, I had idolized Jan Smuts for his exploits as a field marshall in the British Commonwealth forces but his philosophy had lain far beyond my grasp. Even though I used the word *holistic* for years, I had to go through a long and intellectually unsophisticated school of hard knocks before I could even read his book, let alone understand holism well enough to put it to practical use. That experience is nevertheless probably worth relating for what it shows about the biases that must be overcome in our culture because of the paradigms we hold.

I received my scientific training in the conventional approach that viewed events in isolation. My professors discouraged any attempt to combine what we learned in one discipline with what we covered in another, and the sanctity of research was held inviolate, even when it offended common sense.

Once a visiting lecturer from Cambridge informed us that research had shown no use for the flap of flesh behind a crocodile's ear and that despite having the musculature to move the flap, the croc never did so. As I had kept a tame croc myself I knew I could make him move his ear flaps any day just by teasing him. When I ventured that crocs raised their flaps in response to a threat, the lecturer quickly put me down. My observations just could not tip the scales against years of experiments in a controlled environment.

Small as this incident was, it fueled a growing disillusionment with the artificiality of any approach that isolated parts of nature for study. The crocodile isolated from his environment was not the same animal.

Later, as a research officer in both the Game and Tsetse Fly Control Departments, the same kind of ambivalence led me to greatly disappoint my superiors. I never managed to set boundaries for any of the research projects I was expected to design. Common sense told me in each case that the very limitations that would make a research project acceptable scientifically would also make the results meaningless. The Department of course needed research reports to justify its existence, but even under extreme pressure to do something, I could not commit myself to work that in my opinion could never lead to realistic answers to our management problems.

Later still, as an advisor to private ranchers on land management, I encountered the same dilemma again. They listened well to my opinion on techniques that would improve their land, but several, while making great progress toward that end, still went bankrupt after committing scarce funds to government-sponsored irrigation schemes. From my own farming days I knew the risk of tying up capital in government incentive programs to build irrigation dams, as these ranchers had done, but as I was an ecologist, not a financial advisor, they ignored my friendly warnings.

That taught me that to help any rancher to manage his or her land, livestock, and wildlife, I had to become involved in the financial planning to some extent. That involvement helped, but frequently other troubles cropped up that expertise in financial planning did not address. Otherwise sound operations could also flounder because of communication problems among the people involved or because of their blundering along without long-range goals. This led me to add organizational management to the specialties I studied.

By this time I was calling my work holistic ranch management, but in reality it was anything but holistic. I still had not read Smuts and saw no need, assuming myself to have advanced beyond anything he might have written in 1926. I had a record of good results on the land to support this opinion and had spent two five-year periods in partnership with consultants from whom I had learned much about the latest economic thinking. Nevertheless I still got sporadic results and clearly something was missing.

Other scientists, encountering similar frustrations, had concluded that we often aggravated management problems by approaching them from the perspective of narrow disciplines. No animal nutritionist, soil scientist, economist, or any other specialist alone had meaningful answers. Where I had accumulated knowledge in several fields and had even teamed up with other experts, others formed interdisciplinary teams of various kinds but fared no better.

Why these teams, my own included, did not work deserves a close look because increasing numbers of people are calling their work holistic, as I once did myself, when clearly, or not so clearly, it is not. Their fundamental weakness was described in the book *Landscape Ecology* by Zev Naveh and Arthur Lieberman (1983):

> In a computerized simulation game, Dorner (a researcher) asked 12 professionals from different relevant disciplines to propose an integrated development plan for the overall improvement of an imaginary African Country, Tana. The results achieved were very disappointing: if these proposals were carried out they would worsen the lot of the people, destroy the agricultural-economic base, and create new, even more severe problems.[4]

My only criticism of this work was the need to invent an imaginary country. "Tana" could have been any one of my clients or any state in America or any developed country in the world using integrated planning teams. What Dorner simulated with a computer was what I had seen and experienced repeatedly in practice.

First of all, specialists often communicate poorly, not only because they have different perspectives but also because they speak different languages. Often the same words in one jargon mean something else in another. Even where team members have training in several disciplines, as I myself did to some extent, the tendency is to simply swap hats and keep talking without ever being able to stand back and see the whole. In such cases, opinions acquire weight and conclusions are negotiated according to criteria that may have no relationship whatever to overall need.

I, however, did not see any of this until many years later when I undertook to explain my approach to management in training courses I was asked to provide for professionals in U.S. government agencies. It is a great credit to the openness of America that this happened because my ideas departed radically from those given in the training most of these people had embraced for years. Nonetheless, the courses were very stressful events, and in struggling to teach what I knew of holism to an audience of very skeptical peers, I came to realize I didn't understand it myself.

Finally, I read Smuts and realized wherein the holistic worldview differed from everything prior. It became obvious to me that not only are there no parts in Nature, there are no boundaries either. Your skin could be viewed as the boundary between the community of cells that compose you as a person and the outside world. Yet, skin is permeable and the traffic passing through it in both directions is heavy. Viewed at the molecular level, skin is more space than substance.

Any time we talk about interconnectedness we are implying that boundaries exist between whatever is being connected. To more accurately view the world, one has to accept that *in reality* there are no boundaries, only wholes within wholes in a variety of patterns. And to understand the world, according to Smuts, we must first seek to understand the greater whole, which has qualities and characteristics not present in any of the lesser wholes that form it.

The design in photo 3-4 shows this well. Take a close look at it and think of it as depicting our ecosystem. This is the sort of confusing picture we saw when first trying to understand ourselves and our environment. According to scientific custom we isolated the individual squares for study, believing that if we could learn enough about each of them we would understand the whole. However, in the case of nature, as in this pattern of squares, this leads nowhere.

Now stand well back from the pattern, squint your eyes so the squares blur into each other and the picture appears as a whole. It is a face, and a

Photo 3-4 *This is the sort of confusing picture we saw when first trying to understand ourselves and our environment (courtesy AT&T Bell Laboratories).*

familiar one to many of us (Abraham Lincoln's). If you had set out to somehow manage this design by paying attention only to the individual squares, anything you might have learned would have made you seem foolish, for no square has any meaning in isolation from all the rest.

Of course, once you see the whole in the pattern, detailed knowledge of the squares does become useful. You would need a great deal of such knowledge to reproduce, enlarge, preserve, market, or modify the work in any way, but only having first seen the whole could you even ask the right questions about the details.

I personally had tremendous difficulty in seeing why the fact that wholes have qualities not present in their parts, causes the interdisciplinary approach to flounder, until I actually could work it out with my own hands as a young child might.

I took four balls of kindergarten-type modeling clay in red, green, yellow and blue, and began kneading them together until they slowly blended into a fifth color, gray. Mentally I let gray represent the world we originally set out to understand. Close inspection of my gray ball revealed traces of the four colors I had begun with. So to understand this world of gray I would study the colors I knew to be in some way involved in it, in much the same way our earliest scientists broke our natural world into what they perceived as parts for study. Today we have thousands of disciplines, but for simplicity I used four, represented by the four colors, to make my point as shown in plate 1 (following page 46). Although a few hundred years of intense effort have greatly increased our knowledge of the four colors, we still had not studied gray. No matter how great our knowledge of any or all of the four colors, we could never understand, and thus manage, gray as we had no knowledge of gray itself.

Next I pulled the four colors together as shown in plate 2 to represent a multidisciplinary team. Immediately I could see that the problem was a lack of knowledge of gray, not a lack of communication between disciplines as was previously thought.

Next I mixed, or *integrated,* the four colors until I had four balls, each of which contained equal divisions of green, red, yellow, and blue to represent interdisciplinary teams with knowledge of each color, as illustrated in plate 3. Still no knowledge of gray! Now I could see why the interdisciplinary approach could not succeed.

In practice, I realized, all management decisions had to be made from the perspective of the whole under management. If we based our decisions on any other perspective, we could expect to experience results different from those intended because only the whole is reality. First, however, the whole had to be defined, bearing in mind that it always influenced, and was influenced by, both greater and lesser wholes—and we had to know what we wanted to do with it: we needed an all-encompassing, *holistic* goal. Last, we needed a means of weighing up the many ramifications stemming from our actions. Thus, a framework for management and decision-making had emerged. In using that framework we can now take the perspective of the whole by reversing the arrows and weighing up management or policy decisions, as depicted in plate 4.

The rest of this book will deal with what this means in terms of what you will do after breakfast this morning, but before moving on, there is a final point. Any number of people have suggested that, given the complexity of our world, computers are more capable than most of us in weighing up the consequences stemming from any particular decision we make. Yet, powerful tools as they are for solving specific mechanical problems, computers cannot think holistically. In particular they cannot evaluate emotions and human values, which are vital components of the whole. The human mind, by contrast, can see patterns and make decisions out of a deep, even unconscious, sense of the whole, and given an awareness of the necessity, and the mental crutch of a framework for decision making that keeps our focus on the whole, far-reaching changes can be brought about by the likes of you and me.

Because you are incorporated in the wholes you manage, only you and others directly involved in those wholes command the outward-looking perspective vital to your particular management needs.

Conclusion

Although still in the infancy of its development, this holistic decision-making process already enables us to look outward and to choose from all the available knowledge that which promotes our holistic goal and ensures that our environment can sustain it. It also lets us predict results ahead of time. With a bit of practice, almost anyone can use the process to solicit advice from specialists and judge when such advice does or does not serve the holistic goal.

Frequently, advice that appears perfectly sound from an economist's, engineer's, or any other's point of view proves unsound holistically in a particular situation at a particular time. This has spelled disaster, as Dorner's study predicted, for many a foreign aid project and national policy, but also for families, communities, and businesses large and small. As a culture we have acquired such an awe of experimental science that we have trained ourselves simply to phone any certified expert whenever adversity arises. Great difficulties lie ahead until a new generation can be trained to think holistically for themselves and then weigh and select expertise that really fits the case.

The first key insight then, is that a holistic perspective is essential in management. If we base management decisions on any other perspective, we are likely to experience results different from those intended because only the whole is reality.

4

Viewing Environments
a Whole New Way

The first key insight enabled us to develop a framework for management and decision making, but we still lacked certain insights that were key to reversing the environmental deterioration that had accompanied the rise of numerous civilizations, including our own, and without which that framework would not be complete.

The second insight overturns the belief that all environments respond in the same manner to the same influences. They don't. The standard classifications of environments by vegetative features—desert, prairie, or rain forest—accurately describe major variations within our global ecosystem, as do such climatic categories as arid, semi-arid, temperate, and so on. Nevertheless, in looking at why some deteriorate to the extent that deserts form while others don't, leads to a new way of classifying them. More specifically then, the second insight is the new principle that environments may be classified on a continuum from nonbrittle to very brittle according to how well humidity is distributed throughout the year and how quickly dead vegetation breaks down.

We have long recognized that some environments readily deteriorated under human management. Herodotus, for example, described Libya in the fifth century B.C. as having deep, rich soils and an abundant supply of springs that provided a highly productive agricultural base for a large population. Today only desert remains. Those who chronicled this sort of deterioration, believed that such regions were vulnerable to desertification because they were arid or semi-arid.

The bulk of the world's arid and semi-arid regions are in fact predominantly grasslands of one form or another where livestock production has long been the chief occupation. When livestock management practices produce bare ground, a critical share of available moisture either evaporates from the exposed surface or runs off it. Springs dry up, silt chokes dams, rivers, and irrigation ditches, and less water remains for croplands, industry, and people in nearby cities.

Going back even beyond Herodotus, common sense has always assumed that, once the land is damaged, the best remedy is to rest it from any form of human disturbance, including domestic stock. But despite the application of this wisdom, the croplands and rangelands of Libya and its neighbors have desertified anyway, as much of America is now doing. The old assumption that resting land will restore it to its former productivity and stability appears logical. Moreover, it does apply to the stable environments of northern Europe and the eastern United States where modern agricultural science has its roots.

I worked under the old belief that resting land restored it in my early game department days, but a unique experience led me to suspect a fundamental flaw in this belief. For many years, Zimbabwe had a practice of eradicating all game animals over vast areas to deny the tsetse fly a source of blood—its only source of nourishment. Once the tsetse fly was gone, and the fatal human and livestock diseases it carried, livestock could safely be introduced. As a research officer for both the Game Department and later the Department of Tsetse Control, I worked often in these areas. I witnessed environmental damage I could not explain and that did not fit the neat scientific theories I had learned. The land in tsetse fly areas deteriorated seriously once the original game populations were decimated and the incidence of fires, to make the hunting easier, increased. At that time we *knew* that fire helped maintain grassland. The only other influence we *knew* could cause such damage was overgrazing. However, neither game nor domestic animals were present, and so there was no overgrazing. It was very puzzling.

Yet another experience added to my confusion. We had a massive buildup of animal numbers in a game reserve on the Botswana border known as the Tuli Circle, and as a result, thousands of animals starved to death. I, and the wildlife biologists working with me, believed that with dramatically fewer animals living there, the area would naturally recover, but it continued to deteriorate. Most of our scientists blamed drought, but in the year of worst so-called drought the records showed one of the best rainy seasons ever, in both volume and distribution. I published a paper at the time in which I concluded that once land was so badly damaged, it had reached a point of no return and would never recover. I didn't realize how wrong I was until years later.

Another shock to my conviction that low rainfall and overgrazing inevitably produced desert came out of my first visit to northern Europe.

There I saw areas that had as little as 15 to 20 inches (375–500 mm) of rain per year that were not desertifying, despite hundreds of years of overgrazing and poor management. Areas in Africa and the Middle East that received as much as 40 to 50 inches (1000–1250 mm) of rain annually, however, had desertified rapidly under the same practices. Even when we had greatly reduced the animal numbers in these areas, cleared the brush and planted grass, at considerable expense, they continued to deteriorate. No matter how scientifically advanced we were, our knowledge still lacked a vital piece.

Finally in the vast and relatively unused lands of North America I discovered what had eluded me in the highly populated and much used lands of southern Africa, and in the different environments of Europe—that we had in fact two broad types of environment that had not been recognized. At their extremes, these react differently to management. Practices that benefited the one type of environment damaged the other. The terms *brittle* and *nonbrittle* come from that insight.

No clear break exists between the extremes that range from nonbrittle to very brittle. On a scale that classifies true jungles as a 1 and true deserts as a 10, all other environments range somewhere in between. A single vegetative category may cover a wide range on the brittleness scale. Grasslands, for instance, may lie anywhere from 1 to 9 or 10 on the scale; forests from 1 to 7 or 8.

Brittleness is not the same as fragility. Within many environmental classifications are areas that are very easily upset by a variety of forces and robust communities that withstand much more abuse. However, fragile communities may exist in a nonbrittle environment (e.g., a delicate fern-dominated glade in a forest), and some fairly brittle environments may be nonfragile (e.g., the African savannas and the American prairies).

Because the two extremes on our 1 to 10 scale show such a clear correlation to total rainfall, it is easy to see in retrospect why we linked an environment's vulnerability to desertification to low rainfall. The degree of brittleness determines this vulnerability, however, more than total precipitation. The closer we get to 10 on the brittleness scale, even with high (30–80 inch/750–2000 mm) rainfall, the faster the land will deteriorate under modern agricultural practices. This is not to say that nonbrittle means nonvulnerable to deterioration, as the massive clearing of tropical rain forests makes clear.

The features that distinguish any environment's position on the brittleness scale derive not so much from total rainfall as from the distribution of precipitation and humidity throughout the year. Toward the very brittle end of the scale, environments characteristically experience erratic distribution of both precipitation and humidity during the year. The pattern determines the degree of brittleness. A 30- to 50-inch (750–1250 mm) rainfall area that typically has very dry periods in the middle of its growing season and a long dry season, is likely to be very brittle. Toward the nonbrittle end of the scale environments characteristically experience increasingly reliable moisture in the growing season. Even though total precipitation may seldom top 20 inches (500 mm) a year in some of them, the distribution is such that throughout the year, atmospheric humidity does not drop severely. In completely nonbrittle environments both precipitation and humidity would be constant and high.

The distribution of the precipitation, as well as the elevation, temperature, and prevailing winds, clearly affects the day-to-day distribution of humidity and this links very closely to the degree of brittleness. The poorer the distribution of humidity, particularly in the growing season, the more brittle the area tends to be, even though total rainfall may be high, as shown in figure 4-1. Very brittle environments commonly have a long period of nongrowth that can be very arid.

The brittleness scale can perhaps best be understood by looking at how environments at either end of the scale functioned prior to the development of fire-lighting and tool-making humans. In the perennially humid nonbrittle environments, as illustrated in figure 4-2, a mass of evergreen vegetation was produced throughout the year; there was no period of dormancy. Plants died throughout the year as well, but decomposed quickly due to the high numbers of insects and microorganisms whose populations remained high and active throughout the year.

This was not the case, however, at the other end of the scale where humidity was erratic and the environment very brittle. Here, as figure 4-3 shows, vegetation and insect and microorganism populations would build up during the rainy months of the year. However, when the rains stopped, humidity dropped, and as the soil dried out, most of the aboveground vegetation died—only trunks, branches, and the bases of perennial grass plants remained alive. At the same time, insect and microorganism

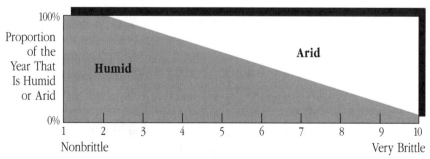

Figure 4-1 *Humidity and the brittleness scale. Humidity is high over a greater portion of the year the closer an environment is to the nonbrittle end of the scale.*

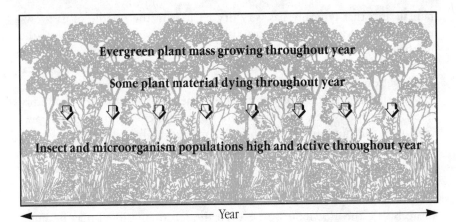

Figure 4-2 *In the perennially humid nonbrittle environments, vegetation is evergreen and plants die throughout the year. Any plants that die will decay quickly due to the presence of insects and microorganisms that remain active throughout the year.*

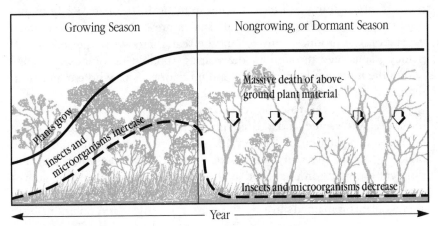

Figure 4-3 *In the seasonally humid brittle environments, most above-ground vegetation dies at a certain point in the year. At the same time, populations of insects and microorganisms that would normally assist in the decay process decrease or become dormant.*

activity was drastically reduced as these organisms went into dormancy, died off, or survived only in the egg or pupal form, through the dry period. Photo 4-1 was taken in a high-rainfall (35 inches/875 mm) very brittle environment many months after the last rainfall of the growing season. The stems and leaves of these grass plants are now dead and of no use to the plants. In fact, the mass of material remaining on the plants is a liability because it will block sunlight from reaching the plants' ground-level

Photo 4-1 *The stems and leaves produced in the last growing season by these grass plants are now dead and will block sunlight from reaching the plants' ground-level growth points. Unless this old material is removed before the coming growing season these plants will produce very few new leaves. Very brittle 35-inch (875-mm) rainfall environment, Zimbabwe.*

growth points. When the rains come again these plants will produce very few new leaves.

So how did all that dead vegetation break down every year over millions of years in the past? Lightning, then as now, would have sparked fires and consumed some of the vegetation, but relatively few areas would have been affected in any one year. There was a much more powerful and pervasive influence, however—grazing animals, and lots of them. Bison, elk, pronghorn, kangaroos, saiga antelope, the many species of African antelope, elephant, buffalo, zebra, and so on, all evolved in these environments. Their presence was significant because they consumed a fair amount of plant material while it was still green and growing, *and* they continued consuming it long after all growth had stopped. In the moist digestive tracts of these animals, a mass of microorganisms continued to thrive, and managed to reduce the large volume of material consumed to dung. In the following rainy season when insect and external microorganism populations once again became numerous, they would consume the dung, as well as the dead vegetation that had been trampled onto the soil, and complete the cycle of decay.

Today, of course, the vast herds have disappeared from these environments (they never did occur in nonbrittle environments). In their absence, only a small proportion of the vegetation produced is able to decay. Most is left to break down chemically through oxidation—the same process at work on rusting metal, although dead plant material turns gray and then black, rather than reddish-brown—or physically through weathering, where wind, rain, and hail very gradually wear them down. Humans of course also assist the breakdown by burning the dead vegetation, which is why we needed to go back to the time before humans had the ability to light fires to examine the differences in the two broad types of environment.

As the ability of plants to decompose and recycle their nutrients is crucial to the health of the whole environment, determining the degree of brittleness becomes a prime factor in the management of any environment. Nonbrittle and very brittle environments react quite differently to many of the management practices we engage in daily, yet we have failed to make this distinction. I could not have made this discovery myself had I not simultaneously arrived at the brink of articulating the other three insights. The full ramifications of the brittleness scale do not become clear without them all.

At this point let me just say that the old belief that *all* land should be rested or left undisturbed in order to reverse its deterioration has proven wrong. Environments lying close to the nonbrittle end of the scale do respond in this way. When ancient cities were abandoned in these environments, biological communities recovered and buried the ruins in vegetation as shown in photo 4-2. In environments leaning toward the very brittle end of the scale, prolonged rest will lead to further deterioration and instability. Ancient cities that were abandoned in these environments are now buried under desert sands, as shown in photo 4-3. Since over half of the earth's land surface is more, rather than less, brittle, it is no surprise that desertification is spreading at the rate it is.

Once we understood the brittle and nonbrittle distinction and had identified the characteristics associated with both types of environment, my puzzling observations of the past became clear. The Tuli Circle, where so much of the game had died off and where so much soil lay exposed, could not recover if left undisturbed because it was a very brittle environment. It required some form of disturbance at the soil surface, similar to what the formerly large herds provided, to get more plants growing, as the next chapter explains. In the tsetse fly areas, the increased use of fire had exposed soil, and though old grass plants remained healthy, nothing disturbed the soil sufficiently to allow new ones to grow. Thus, communities declined and soil became unstable.

All environments lie at some point along the scale of 1 to 10. The easiest way to determine where is to look at various sites and to assess how the bulk of the vegetation is breaking down. At the nonbrittle extreme it

Photo 4-2 *When ancient cities in nonbrittle environments were abandoned, biological communities recovered and buried the ruins in vegetation. Palenque, Mexico.*

Photo 4-3 *Ancient cities that were abandoned in very brittle environments are now buried under desert sands. Marib, Yemen.*

will be 100 percent biological, that is, decay. This decreases steadily as an environment moves toward brittleness when chemical and physical breakdown begins to appear and steadily increases with the degree of brittleness. *It is how the bulk of the material has broken down by year's end that should concern you most.* During the growing season in a high rainfall area of the tropics, for instance, the breakdown might be predominantly biological. But in the long dry season that follows it is likely to be chemical and physical. In that case, the environment would be closer to the very brittle end of the scale. Outside the tropics, where many plants lose their leaves or die off because of the cold, microorganism populations may still be active throughout the dormant season, given the high and constant humidity, and material would continue to be broken down through biological decay. In this case, the environment would be closer to the nonbrittle end of the scale.

The presence of bare ground is another indicator of brittleness. At the nonbrittle end of the scale, it is extremely difficult, if not impossible, to create large areas of bare ground and to keep them bare. New plants will colonize exposed surfaces fairly rapidly. As you move across the scale this picture changes dramatically until at the very brittle end, bare ground is easily created. New plants can only establish with difficulty, and algae and lichens commonly dominate.

Conclusion

The second insight then, is that environments may be classified on a continuum from nonbrittle to very brittle according to how well humidity is distributed throughout the year and how quickly dead vegetation breaks down. At either end of the scale, environments respond differently to the same influences. Resting land restores it in nonbrittle environments, but damages it in very brittle environments.

Taken by itself, this second insight raises the practical question of how grazing animals might provide the disturbance necessary to the health of an environment that is brittle to any degree—without overgrazing. Fortunately the answer lies in the remaining two insights.

5

The Predator–Prey Connection

In my university training I learned, like all scientists of that era, that large animals such as domestic cattle could damage land. Only keeping numbers low and scattering stock widely would prevent the destructive trampling and intense grazing one could expect from livestock.

Once I left university and went into the field as a biologist, my observations led me to question that dogma. I now defend the exact opposite conclusion. Relatively high numbers of heavy, herding animals, concentrated and moving as they once did naturally in the presence of predators, support the health of the very lands we thought they destroyed. This revelation came slowly and only after experience in a large variety of situations, because herding animals, like others, have more than one behavior pattern, and the effects on land are often delayed, subtle, and cumulative.

In the mid-1960s Zimbabwe erupted in civil war and I was given the task of training and commanding a tracker combat unit. Over the next few years I spent thousands of hours tracking people over all sorts of country, day after day. This discipline greatly sharpened my observational skills and also taught me much about the land, as although I was hunting humans, my thoughts were constantly on the state of the lands over which we were fighting. I doubt many scientists ever had such an opportunity for learning. I tracked people over game areas, tribal areas, commercial farms and ranches, and over all different soil and vegetation types in all rainfalls. Often I covered many different areas in a single day as I flew by helicopter from one trouble spot to the next. Everywhere I had to inspect plants and soils for the faintest sign of disturbance by people trying to leave no hint of their passage.

Gradually I realized that vast differences distinguished land where wildlife herded naturally, where people herded domestic stock, and where stock was fenced in by people and not herded at all. And compared to areas without any large animals, such as tsetse fly areas in which all large game had been exterminated, the differences were startling indeed. Most obvious was the fact that where animals were present, plants were green and growing. In areas without animals they were often gray and dying—even in the growing season—unless they had been burned, in which case the soil between plants was bare and eroding and tracking was easy. When I compared areas heavily disturbed by animals, where soil was churned up, plants flattened, and tracking was difficult, it became clear that the degree of disturbance had a proportionately positive impact on the health of plants and soils and thus the whole community.

I began to pay particular attention to the way animals behaved in different situations, as different behavior and management patterns produced different effects. In tracking large buffalo herds on my own game reserve, for instance, I noted that when feeding they tended to spread out, although not too far for fear of predation, and to walk gently and slowly. They placed their hooves beside coarse plants and not on top of them. They also placed their full weight on their hooves, compacting the soil below the surface but hardly disturbing the surface itself. While thus feeding they had remarkably little impact on the plants and the soil, other than the obvious removal of forage and the soil compaction.

Once feeding was over, however, and the herd began to move, or when predators were about, the animals behaved differently. They bunched together for safety and in their excitement kicked up quite a bit of dust. I noted that while bunched as a herd animals stepped recklessly and even very coarse plants, containing much old material that would not be grazed or trampled normally, were trampled down. That provided cover for the soil surface. In addition, the hooves of bunching and milling animals left the soil chipped and broken. In effect, the animals did what any gardener would do to get seeds to grow: first loosen the sealed soil surface, then bury the seed slightly, compact the soil around the seed, then cover the surface with a mulch. I also noted that where the grazing herd had kept off the steep, cutting edges of gullies, the bunched herd now beat down the edges, creating a more gradual slope that could once again support vegetation.

I became convinced that the disturbance created by the hooves of *herding* natural wild animal populations was vital to the health of the land and that humankind had lost this benefit when we domesticated cattle, horses, sheep, and goats and protected them from predators. Even where people herded livestock, as opposed to merely fencing them in, they did not behave as they would do if naturally herding under the threat of predation.

In the more brittle environments, the large predators differed from those in nonbrittle environments in one important respect: they hunted in packs and they ran down their prey. Wolves, lions, cheetahs, wild dogs and hyenas all fall in this group. In the nonbrittle environments the predators, such as tigers and jaguars, were a different type: they hunted singly and ambushed their prey. They had their counterparts in the more brittle environments, such as leopards and mountain lions, but these predators generally did not associate with large herds. It was the pack-hunting predators who were mainly responsible for producing the change in behavior of their herding prey. Bunching up tightly in large numbers became the herd's chief form of protection, particularly of females and young, because pack hunters are confused by a crowd and thus fear it. They can only kill successfully when the herd strings out and they can isolate an individual.

This relationship between pack hunters, their herding prey, and the soils and plants they trampled and grazed developed over millions of years, long before humans themselves became pack hunters with the aid of fire and spear. There was no other influence that could realistically have both created the necessary soil disturbance to provide a good seed bed for new plants and protected bare soil by trampling down old plant material. Both functions appear critical to the health of environments at the more brittle end of the scale.

My understanding of the tremendous significance of these relationships evolved slowly. In Africa I dealt with very large game herds and numerous predators, including enormous prides of lions. It was not until I came to the United States, where predators no longer had significant impact on the wildlife populations that I realized how much they contributed to creating the kind of soil disturbance needed in the more brittle environments.

In the United States massive destruction of predator populations and wild herds precipitated the decline in the environment we see today throughout most of the western states. We have only exacerbated it by spreading relatively few domestic animals over large areas. This perhaps explains why land deterioration in North America has occurred more rapidly than in Africa.

In North America the problem is compounded by the annual freezing and thawing which creates air pockets in the soil. If the environment is very brittle then not only has there to be some agent of disturbance that will remove old oxidizing material from perennial grasses and chip soil surfaces, but that agent has also to provide soil compaction to increase grass seedling success.

I was not by any means the first to make the connection between the hooves of animals and the health of land. Many centuries ago shepherds in the less brittle environment of Scotland referred to the "golden hooves" of sheep. In the 1930s Navajo medicine men in the very brittle environment of the American Southwest warned government officials who were drastically reducing their livestock numbers that a link existed between the hooves of the sheep and the health of the soil. In southern Africa the old-timers of my childhood had a saying, "Hammer veld to sweeten it." They meant literally hammer the land with herds of livestock to improve forage quality. Unfortunately none of these earlier observations were fully understood because too many of us believed that plants and soils needed protection from the damaging effects of animals. My own early observation of the vital relationship between natural herds, soils, and plants met violent rejection and ridicule from my fellow countrymen and the international scientific community—and still does from an ever-dwindling few.

In the 1980s thanks to some careful research done on the herding wildlife populations in East Africa's fairly brittle grasslands, a relationship between these animals and the plants they feed on was documented independently.[1] Gradually scientists are becoming more comfortable with the idea. Further research should soon confirm beyond doubt the role of pack-hunting predators in the equation.

Conclusion

The third key insight then, was that in brittle environments, relatively high numbers of large, herding animals, concentrated and moving as they naturally do in the presence of pack-hunting predators, are vital to maintaining the health of the lands we thought they destroyed. Acceptance of this insight will help to reverse the millennia of damage humankind has inflicted on the land in the more brittle environments by trying to protect it from the effects of trampling that were perceived as evil. As bare ground increased and the environment deteriorated in response to the lack of *herd effect,* we attributed it to overgrazing, which we in turn blamed on too many animals. As a result, we decreased animal numbers and thus increased the bare ground and the deterioration. That overgrazing is not in fact a function of animal numbers is the fourth insight.

6

Timing Is Everything

A fundamental belief, embraced throughout the world, holds that overgrazing, overtrampling, and the resultant destruction of land are caused by the presence of too many animals. Despite massive and sophisticated research on plants, soils, and animals, virtually all land improvement schemes before now have rested on this very unsophisticated bit of apparent common sense and have called for the reduction or removal of animals.

Until very recently no one truly explored the question of *when* animals are there as opposed to how many there are. My own experience illustrates how elusive an obvious principle can be. As a child in Zimbabwe I, too, learned of the destruction caused by too many animals when I accompanied my father into the native reserves. He, a civil engineer, had the task of improving water distribution for the people and their stock. Overgrazing and overtrampling had devastated the areas surrounding the few existing water points, and the theory ran that creating more water points would scatter the stock and reduce the damage. The hot and dusty hours spent amid the rabble of cattle, goats, and donkeys on that barren land, together with what others told me, certainly convinced me that my father's work and the government policy that supported it made sense.

I did not question this assumption for a decade or so, until as a young man I encountered historical records that showed what enormous herds of wild animals had existed on the land before people and their domestic stock replaced them. As pioneers made their way into the interior of South Africa they apparently recorded herds of springbok (a pronghorn-size antelope) so vast that when they migrated through settlements they trampled everything in their path, including yokes of oxen that couldn't be unhitched from wagons fast enough.

Such herds together with all the millions of other animals on the southern African veld vastly outnumbered the cattle and sheep herds that came later and yet for millennia they had enjoyed an environment more abundant than anything the descendants of those pioneers can imagine. One sign of that former abundance is the animal names borne by villages and towns of today linked to the springs they watered at: "Elands*fontein*," Springbok*fontein*," and "Buffels*fontein*" from the Dutch word for fountain or spring. No hint of free-flowing water exists in those places today. The weather, according to record, did not change, yet the "fountains" disappeared together with the healthy grasslands and the vast herds. As the memory of the wild herds also vanished, people blamed the disappearance of the water and the grasslands on the overgrazing and overtrampling of their own livestock, although fewer in number.

This riddle confused me, but I still could only conclude that overgrazing and overtrampling were related to animal numbers. The most obvious deterioration was occurring on the most heavily stocked tribal land, and in certain national parks and game reserves where wildlife numbers were also high, which tended to support the prevailing wisdom. As a research officer in the Game Department I found myself recommending, despite my questions, a drastic culling of elephant and buffalo to arrest the damage done by trampling and overgrazing. The decision was made in anguish because by this time I had already noted that the extermination of game in the tsetse fly areas had not in fact brought improvement of the land. Only later did I begin to penetrate the riddle.

I had observed that very large buffalo herds moved constantly and seldom occupied any area longer than two or three days, after which the land had an opportunity to recover. Could the time they stayed be an important factor? It also began to dawn on me that a lot of game confined to a small area—as happened in some of our newly forming game reserves surrounded by human settlement or tsetse fly areas—produced *too many herds* in too small an area. Though each herd moved frequently, plants and soil had little time to recover after being grazed or trampled. I did not yet see *time* as the crucial element, but I was beginning to think that the reduced size of home ranges and territories on which the animals could move lay at the bottom of the problem.

I studied elephant herds. Did they shift location every few days? Did it matter? Did another herd move into areas only recently vacated? I decided to find out, but immediately struck an obstacle—I couldn't tell one herd from another as I was on foot and in dense brush. In those days before methods were refined for drugging and tagging animals, I stalked unsuspecting elephants with homemade paint bombs which I threw from close range. Such work, however, generated minimal enthusiasm among potential helpers, and I simply couldn't paint enough elephants singlehandedly. I also lacked sufficient staff to conduct observations over enough area to support any conclusions.

For some time I had possessed a book entitled *Grass Productivity* by French researcher André Voisin. I had bought it because the title interested me, and I thought it might help to clarify what was taking place in our wildlife areas. Voisin, however, had worked mainly with cattle on pastures in Europe. After browsing his book I could see no connection between dairy cows on lush French pastures and elephant and buffalo on dry African ranges. The book stayed unread on the shelf.

In the meantime a loathing for cattle, which I believed were destroying the land, prompted me, along with some others, to begin promoting a new concept I called "game ranching." If ranchers could substitute game for livestock, and if we could find ways to effectively market the product and give wild game a financial value, perhaps we could get rid of the cattle and save the game and the land. Ranchers would come to see wildlife as an asset (by custom they considered it vermin), and wildlife would not wreak nearly the damage of domestic stock, or so I thought.

Neither the development of game ranching nor the business of culling the buffalo and elephant proved very popular in the early 1960s, and I was forced out of my Game Department job by those not-so-subtle pressures bureaucracies apply to the dissenting. However, I turned to farming, game ranching, and consulting as a livelihood and continued my work with private landowners in Zimbabwe and other countries in southern Africa.

At the time, governments in southern Africa, my own included, acknowledged that overstocking was probably causing the land to deteriorate, but ascribed a greater share of the blame to a series of droughts that had occurred. I created somewhat of a controversy when I publicly challenged the latter view by suggesting that our droughts were becoming more frequent *because* our land was deteriorating. To my surprise, several cattle ranchers approached me—a known enemy of their industry—because they believed I was right and wanted to do something about it. I agreed to work with them, but only after I was sure they understood I had no answers myself and that it would be a case of the blind leading the blind.

The many sophisticated schemes for preventing overgrazing on ranches always began by limiting livestock numbers. One of the most common sought to regulate numbers so that animals would not graze off more than half of certain "key indicator" plants in the community. Research indicated that many perennial grasses suffered root damage with the removal of more than 50 percent of their growing leaf area.

The theory, however, had to fail, as wild or domestic severe-grazing animals, given the mouth and teeth structures they possess, aren't able to nibble individual leaves, or limit themselves to taking half the plant. They tend to feed by the mouthful and will commonly graze perennial bunch grasses, in particular, right down. Fortunately, these grasses, having coevolved with grazing animals, have their growing points, or buds, at the base of the plant where they are out of harm's way. As land continued to deteriorate under various attempts at take-half–leave-half management, government researchers began to doubt that the ranchers had tried seriously. Since my own clients were among them, I paid a visit to the research stations in Zimbabwe and South Africa where things were done "right" to learn what I could.

The research stations measured their success by the bulk of forage, the presence of a few species considered desirable, and the general appearance of the land as one glanced at it. By these criteria their ideas had indeed proved successful in practice. By my own criteria, however, even their research plots were desertifying. The soil between the plants was bare and eroding seriously—something not always visible to the person who didn't look for it. Plants were overgrazed severely in some patches while in others they had grown old and excessively fibrous and were smothered with gray-to-black oxidizing material. The researchers had attempted to resolve the uneven grazing pattern by burning about once every four years; the burned areas were quite visibly eroding. But the most shocking characteristic was the almost complete absence of new seedlings, despite massive seed production on parent plants. Desirable species were indeed present, but very few other species.

The bulk of forage produced by the "key indicator" plant species and the high individual production, in terms of weight gain and conception rate, on the few animals present had masked the evidence of degradation. Production per animal was high and increasing, along with supplementation costs, even as production per acre remained low and declining. For the first time I began to realize the extreme danger in considering short-term high production, or, for that matter, species composition, a measure of success. For the ranchers and my country, blinded by such apparent success, I could only foresee ruination.

Continually seeking answers, I began reading the range management research from various countries, but all appeared to follow the same thinking: excessive animal numbers cause overgrazing. Then one day while assisting a rancher in starting up a game ranching operation, I glanced at a South African farm magazine that lay on his coffee table. In it was an article by a man named John Acocks who described a grazing system he claimed would heal the land. It made more sense than anything I had read before, so I went to South Africa and tracked him down.

I found Acocks a delightful old botanist and very knowledgeable indeed about the extent of the land deterioration that had taken place in South Africa. He believed it came from the selective grazing of the livestock that had replaced the original large and diverse game populations. Livestock, he said, overgrazed the species they preferred until those species disappeared. They then overgrazed another until it, too, disappeared. Gradually only the least desirable species remained. Thus he explained how areas dominated two or three hundred years ago by perennial grasses had become the domain of desert shrubs. He had plotted the steady movement of these shrubs across southern Africa as the desert spread over the years.

Acocks theorized that as overgrazing weakened or killed plants of a particular species, other species replaced them that appealed less to livestock and thus held an unfair advantage over the grazed plant in the competition for light, water, and nutrients. He concluded that the actual numbers of livestock mattered less than their repeated selection of species that were thus handicapped and eventually replaced in the community. The diverse game species of old, reasoned Acocks, used all plants equally because each species selected a different diet. Thus, no plant type had an advantage over another, and many thrived side by side on an even playing field. Based on these observations and interpretations he made the remarkable statement that South Africa was "overgrazed and understocked."

His remedy called for concentrating livestock on to a small portion of land and holding them there till they had grazed down all the plants evenly. Once they had done this, they could be moved to another area to do the same thing. Each grazed area would then be rested so all the equally grazed plants could recover without unfair competition among them. Acocks's theory did not answer all my concerns by any means—the deterioration of tsetse fly areas that had no grazing being one—but it had merit and offered a new direction. Before leaving he introduced me to a nearby farming couple who were practicing his ideas.

Len and Denise Howell had a deep concern for the land degradation occurring all over the country and were excited by the results of applying Acocks's idea. So was I. The Howells looked on in bewilderment as I fell to my knees and probed my fingers into the soil, pointing out excitedly what had happened where their stock had accidentally trodden in very high concentration for a short time in one corner of a paddock. The surface was broken; litter lay everywhere; water was soaking in rather than running off; aeration had improved; and new seedlings grew in abundance. John Acocks, and the accidental bunching of the animals that had occurred on the Howell's farm, had given me a vital piece of knowledge—that livestock could simulate the effects of wild herds on the soil. Here in one area was the heavy trampling I had seen following game but now done by livestock and without the damage to the land we had come to expect.

I rushed back to Zimbabwe eager to persuade some of my rancher

clients to concentrate their livestock. The first one to do it rapidly produced the desired effects. Unfortunately, as fast as the land responded, his
cattle fell off in condition. In fact they nearly died. Others who followed
my advice reported the same results. As disappointing as this was, I still
believed we were at last approaching the answer, and much to their credit
a handful of ranchers who loved their land decided to stick with me until
we had it. We had no other allies in the quest. Under a barrage of criticism
and ridicule we confronted the new riddle of poor livestock performance.

The cattlemen and our government extension officers believed in scattering cattle so they could select the grass species they needed to perform
well. Acocks believed in concentrating the animals to keep those very grass
species from getting selected out of existence. Both arguments had obvious merit and somewhere between them the clues to good livestock and
land management had to lie. Now, indulging in the perfect vision of hindsight, I can see that *time* was the factor staring us in the face and always
overlooked.

As the problem now involved cattle, I once again dusted off André
Voisin's book, and there it was. He had established that overgrazing bore
little relationship to the number of animals but rather to the *time* plants
were exposed to the animals. If animals remained in any one place for too
long or if they returned to it before plants had recovered, they overgrazed
plants. The time of exposure was determined by the growth rate of the
plants. If plants were growing fast, the animals needed to move on more
quickly and could return more quickly. If plants grew slowly, the opposite
was true. Suddenly I could see how trampling also could be either good or
bad. Time became the determining factor. The disturbance needed for the
health of the soil became an evil if prolonged too much or repeated too
soon.

If this was so, then how had time figured in the grazing and trampling
of the vast wild herds of the past? This, too, could be reasoned out. Animals
that bunch closely to ward off predators also dung and urinate in high concentration and thus foul the ground and plants on which they are feeding.
No animals normally like to feed on their own feces, as anyone who has
kept and observed horses will know. Thus, to be able to feed on fresh plants
the herds had to keep moving off the areas they had fouled. And they could
not, ideally, return to the fouled area until the dung and urine had weath-
ered and worn off. This meant that plants and soils would have been
exposed to massive disturbance in the form of grazing, trampling, dunging
and urinating, but only for a day or so, followed by a period of time that
gave the soil and plants an opportunity to recover. This pattern would have
been repeated again and again over millions of years. Even in the age of the
dinosaurs, there were pack hunters and thus presumably herding grazers

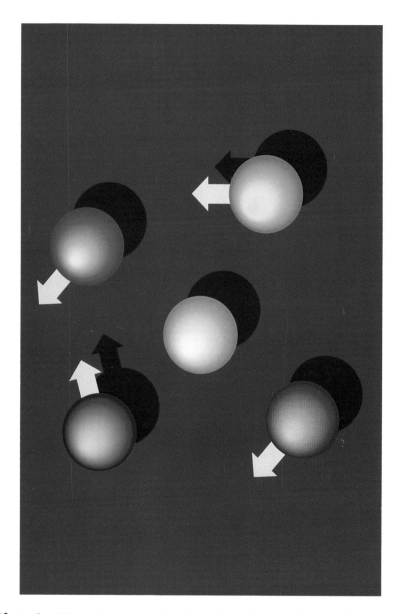

Plate 1. *Although they have considerable knowledge of green, yellow, red, and blue, people in single, isolated disciplines are unable to manage gray (the "whole") of which they have no knowledge. Management is not even focused on gray, as the arrows indicate. This single-discipline approach to management was generally recognized as a failure many years ago.*

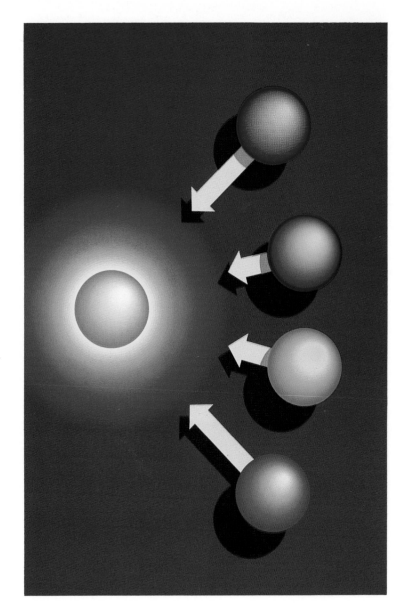

Plate 2. *People in a multidisciplinary team are focusing on gray from their perspective, as arrows indicate, but still with no knowledge of gray. The lack of success arising from multidisciplinary management was attributed to poor communication owing to the jargon associated with the various disciplines, rather than a lack of knowledge.*

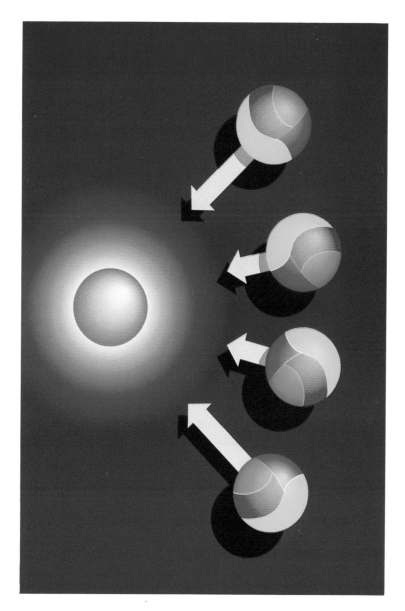

Plate 3. *To overcome communication problems, people trained in several disciplines form interdisciplinary teams that then focus their attention on gray, as the arrows indicate. Knowledge of gray is still lacking, however. The lack of success arising from the interdisciplinary approach to management has only recently been acknowledged.*

Plate 4. *We now take the perspective of the whole (gray), first of all by defining the limits of a "manageable" whole, then determining what that whole must become based on the needs of the people within it and the environment that must sustain their endeavors (the holistic goal). Now the people making decisions within the whole can look outwardly at all available knowledge to detemine which best serves their needs and takes them toward the holistic goal.*

and browsers. Recovery times for soils and plants would have varied because there were so many different species feeding in an area and each was only trying to avoid the fouling of their own, or closely related, species, not necessarily that of others.

I now went back to my clients and suggested that we combine the ideas of Acocks and Voisin, concentrating the animals, but not forcing them to graze all plants evenly, and timing the exposure and reexposure of plants to the animals according to the rate at which the plants grew. Again, we were very enthusiastic and this time certain of success. We did in fact improve animal performance somewhat, but in many important respects we fell flat on our faces once more.

Voisin had done his work in a fairly nonbrittle environment, and we had not yet discovered the fundamental differences between nonbrittle and very brittle environments. Thus, we did not immediately see how to fit our highly erratic growing conditions into his systematic accounting of time and growth rates. Neither, of course, did we know then that the solution in our fairly brittle region also depended on the actual behavior of the cattle—the herding behavior, not merely the concentration of animals which, unless extreme, does not change behavior. We also encountered variables that Voisin, managing planted, fertilized, and well-watered pastures, did not. Our rangelands had a tremendous variety of grasses, forbs, brush, and trees—all growing at different rates. And they had a variety of soil types that produced varying results. We also had wildlife running on the same land as our stock, seriously affecting our time calculations. Whatever we suspected about time, we could not manage it effectively.

We would not unravel the whole mystery for a long time, but we knew at least we had discovered the right path. Politics as much as ecology forced us to keep learning. By the early 1970s Zimbabwe, then Rhodesia, had become a pariah among nations because the white-led government, to which I was by then leading the opposition in Parliament, refused to give in to the demands of the black majority. The tragic civil war that had erupted in the mid-1960s had grown increasingly fierce, and to force an end to it the rest of the world raised economic sanctions against us. To survive under the embargo, our ranchers and farmers had to greatly diversify their operations and manage great complexity and constant change on a day-to-day basis.

Livestock operations added new crops, and farmers, who had previously specialized in one or two cash crops, added many others and began to rotate crops and pastures to maintain the livestock they had also added. To handle the difficulties inherent in such diversity, I developed a thorough, but simple, planning procedure based on military planning concepts I already knew. It proved successful, and within a few years it was being applied on over a hundred farms and ranches throughout the country. The experience gathered from such varied situations, gave birth to many new insights.

For one it showed us that John Acocks's statement that South Africa was overgrazed but understocked was true, *but not for his reasons*. Selection of the most palatable plant species by livestock and a consequent unfair competition against less handicapped ones did not explain the deterioration in southern Africa. Nor was the remedy to force livestock to eat off all plants equally, which we found caused stock stress. We realized that livestock do not select species but rather select for a balanced diet, regardless of species. Wild herding animals also select for balanced diets; they never graze all plants equally, and never has this been necessary.

The overgrazing Acocks observed reflected the *time* plants were exposed to livestock, not the low numbers of animals grazing selectively. The understocking he observed did not damage the land by allowing less palatable plants to escape punishment. In fact, lack of grazing allowed good perennial grasses to die from overrest in the more brittle environments, as old material accumulated on them and blocked adequate sunlight from reaching their growing points. Understocking also meant that too few animals scattered too widely in an unexcited, non-herding manner failed to provide the soil disturbance so necessary in brittle environments.

We only discovered all this because the planning procedure allowed us to control the time dimension more subtly than ever before. We found we could minimize overgrazing and overtrampling while still allowing animals to select the plants and nutrients they required. We could also induce adequate disturbance on the soil surface in small areas by briefly attracting the livestock to them, with a bale of hay, for instance, so that new plants could establish. We were able to plan for crops and hay cuttings, as well and manage habitat critical to wildlife in particular seasons. All this became possible once we understood the time factor and had a planning procedure that left a good record of what we had done and what result followed.

Taken together the last three insights provide an explanation for why, despite all our efforts, so many environments have continued to deteriorate under human management. The discovery of the brittleness scale and the vital role of herding animals and their predators in maintaining the health of the more brittle environments showed why these environments were prone to desertification. This is significant because desertification has ultimately destroyed more civilizations than war and currently, according to the United Nations, adversely affects over 900 million people in over a hundred countries. The problem is not limited to developing countries, either, as a group of scientists pointed out at an international conference in Tucson, Arizona, in 1994 entitled, "Desertification in the Developed Countries: Why Can't We Stop It?"

That we have been unable to stop it anywhere is not surprising, since approximately two-thirds of the earth's land surface is brittle to some degree and our management has not catered to that fact. Nor until now have we known what to do. Only those actually managing land can implement the changes necessary to reverse the desertification process, but they need the support of the rest of us to do this effectively. None of us can afford to ignore the importance of the brittle/nonbrittle distinction and of how it affects the management of different environments, any more than we can afford to remain indifferent to the need for a holistic perspective in all the wholes we manage.

In years to come we will look back on the time before the discovery of these four new insights as truly the dark ages of humankind's whole attitude toward the greater ecosystem that sustains us. The time for change of course is now, lest ours go the way of other sophisticated civilizations that rose and then destroyed themselves in the brittle environments of the world.

7

A New Framework
for Management and
Decision Making

U ntil we had arrived at the four key insights and understood their significance, we could not address what was faulty in our decision making, nor did we even see that it was flawed. The first insight enabled us to develop the framework that had been lacking; the next three only became obvious when the first was understood, and enabled us to complete that framework.

The framework is summarized in figure 7-1 in what we refer to as the Holistic Management model. It falls short of what we conventionally think of as a model in that it does not illustrate the flow of a process, merely the elements within it. To illustrate the relationships shared among the various elements—which would vary depending on the management or decision-making context—would require so many loops, lines, and arrows that we have merely stuck with the skeletal structure, the framework for holistic decision making and management. As later chapters will show, this same framework can be used for diagnosing management problems, creating sound policies, and designing or utilizing research that is relevant to management needs.

Some of the rows in the model will have little meaning to you at this point and will not require much attention later on if you are not engaged in land or resource management. The *tools* of rest, fire, and grazing, for instance, are unlikely ever to be required in managing a household, a law office, a bank, or any number of other endeavors, and neither would many of the management guidelines listed. We could of course have developed one model, or framework, for land managers and one or more for everyone else, but I have long resisted doing so because the land manager's

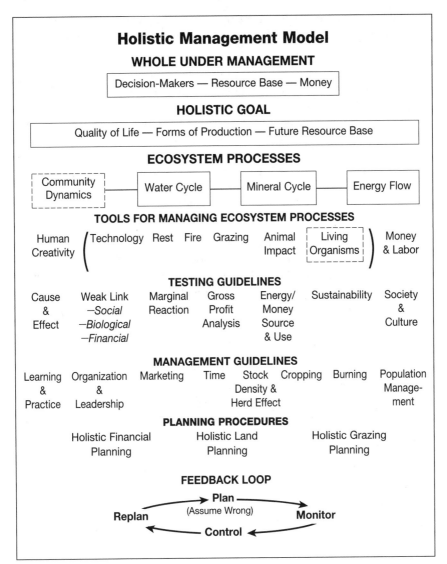

Figure 7-1 *The Holistic Management model.*

concerns are ultimately everyone's concerns if we are to sustain our economies, our civilization, and our planet.

Be assured that you do not have to be managing a piece of land to practice Holistic Management or to engage in holistic decision making, but you do need to have an understanding of some basic ecological principles because many of the management decisions you make will affect the land at some point, as you will see. A brief run through the model will give you a fair idea of what to expect in the upcoming chapters, which more or less follow it, so you can decide which are most relevant to your situation:

- *The whole under management.* All management decisions have to be made from the perspective of the whole under management, bearing in mind that it always influences, and is influenced by, both greater and lesser wholes. As Chapter 8 explains, the minimum a whole would have to include to be manageable is the *decision makers*—those directly involved in its management; the *resource base,* which refers to the physical resources—land, buildings, equipment, and other assets—from which you will generate revenue or derive support, plus the people who influence or are influenced by your management; and finally the *money* available or that can be generated from the resource base.

- *The holistic goal.* The ideas underlying Holistic Management take on meaning and power only in relationship to a goal, but in this case it is specifically a *holistic goal*—one that is based on the whole you have defined, created by those responsible for managing it, and expressing their collective needs and aspirations, both short- and long-term. It is written in three parts: (1) *quality of life*—an expression of the way people want their lives, in this particular whole, to be, and what they ultimately want to accomplish together, based upon what they value most; (2) *forms of production*—what the people need to produce to create that quality of life and to run the business or entity; and (3) a description of the *future resource base*—what the resource base must be like far into the future to truly sustain the forms of production specified. It will take a couple of chapters (9 and 10) to develop the logic of defining a goal in this way. Suffice it to say here that the holistic goal drives Holistic Management and guides every significant decision.

- *The ecosystem processes.* To work with the complexity inherent in the greater ecosystem that sustains us all, we focus on four fundamental processes, each representing vital functions within it: water cycle, mineral cycle, solar energy flow, and community dynamics (the patterns of change and development within communities of living organisms). We recognize that any action taken to affect one of these processes automatically affects them all, as Chapters 11 through 15 explain. Where we once viewed our global ecosystem—everything on our planet and in its surrounding atmosphere—mainly as a source of raw materials, we now view it as the foundation on which all human endeavor, all economies, and all life are built. Even in situations where people may have little power to influence the environment directly, they will, through the cumulative effect of their decisions, have an impact on it and must specify in their holistic goal what they want that impact to be, a subject we will cover in Chapter 9.

- *The tools for managing ecosystem processes.* In conventional management, the tools available for altering any one of the ecosystem processes were limited to four broad categories: *rest, fire, living organisms,* and *technology.* (Human creativity and money and labor bracket the other six tool headings because neither of them can be used on its own to alter ecosystem processes, and one or both are always required in the use of the other tools.) In the more brittle environments, however, these tools alone were inadequate to maintain or improve the functioning of the four ecosystem processes. We found a remedy to this shortcoming in the behaviors of the large herding and grazing animals that had helped to maintain these environments for eons. Although the value of their dung for increasing soil fertility had long been recognized, most people had rejected the most vital parts of the animals (their hooves and mouths) which could be harnessed as tools (*animal impact* and *grazing*) for improving water and mineral cycles, energy flow, and community dynamics. (See Chapters 16 through 24).

- *The testing guidelines.* In deciding which tool to use to alter any one of the ecosystem processes, or in deciding whether or not to take an action *in any situation,* we use all the information that helped people to make decisions in the conventional manner. But now we also pose a series of questions based on seven guidelines that test for economic, environmental, and social soundness relative to the holistic goal. Chapters 25 through 32 cover these guidelines in detail. In brief, the questions are: Does this action address the root cause of the problem? The weakest link in the situation? Does it provide a greater return, in terms of time and money spent, than other actions? Which of two or more possible enterprises provides the best gross profit (if choosing among enterprises)? Is the energy or money to be used in this action derived from the most appropriate source, and will it be used in the most appropriate way, in terms of your holistic goal? Will this action lead toward or away from the future resource base described in your holistic goal? Finally, how will this action affect your quality of life and what will it do to that of others?

- *The management guidelines.* The management guidelines reflect years of experience in a variety of situations and will help shape a number of the decisions you test. Some of them depart considerably from guidelines used in conventional management and therefore require some study. The first three guidelines, covered in Chapters 35 through 37, apply most generally. The remaining five, Chapters 38 through 42, apply more commonly in land management situations.

- *The planning procedures.* These procedures were developed because Holistic Management enabled us to depart substantially from conventional practice in three areas. Holistic Financial Planning, Chapter

44, applies to any situation in which income is received or spent. Unless you are actually managing grazing animals and large tracts of land, you are unlikely to require Holistic Land Planning, Chapter 45, or Holistic Grazing Planning, Chapter 46.

- *The feedback loop.* In Holistic Management the word *plan* has become a 24-letter word: *plan-monitor-control-replan.* In the model these words are incorporated into a loop because this effort is a continuous process. Once a plan is made or any action taken, you need to *monitor* what happens from the outset because unforeseen circumstances always lie ahead. As Chapter 33 explains, when the feedback from your monitoring indicates the plan or action is causing you to deviate from the intended path toward your holistic goal, you must act quickly to *control* the deviation. Occasionally events go beyond your control and there is a need to *replan.* If an action, or a plan outlining several actions attempts to alter ecosystem processes in some way, then, despite having tested the decisions that led to it, you assume from the outset that, given nature's complexity, you could be wrong. Then you monitor, *on the assumption you are wrong,* for the earliest possible warnings so you can replan before any damage is done.

Conclusion

To summarize now how the Holistic Management process works, suppose I want to build a house custom-designed for my family and able to stand forever—that is my goal. I intend to build it on a solid foundation, in this case the four ecosystem processes. To build my house I may choose any of the tools at my disposal and will enlist all my ingenuity and brainpower to make efficient use of labor and capital. Not being entirely familiar with all my tools, or of how best to organize my labor force or manage my capital, I turn to a set of instruction books—the management guidelines and planning procedures—to learn more. A second set of instruction books—the testing guidelines—helps me to assess which tools will be best for the job. I work to a plan using the tools selected and monitoring my progress to stay on track. When events demand it, I replan, changing the way I'm using the tools or substituting different ones—whatever it takes to finish the building and achieve my goal. While learning about Holistic Management many people say, "This is just common sense." And so it is.

Some years ago I attended a conference sponsored by the International Society for Ecological Economics at the World Bank in Washington, D.C. During the plenary session one man was widely applauded for making a statement that reflected the frustration felt by most of those present: "Despite all our attempts to manage ecosystems and economies, we keep finding that we always end up being precisely wrong. Can't someone find a way to be at least approximately right?"

I believe Holistic Management enables us to answer that question in the affirmative. In testing our decisions toward a holistic goal we are generally assured of being approximately right, but we still complete those essential feedback loops—planning, monitoring, controlling, and replanning—to make sure.

Nearly every chapter in this book so far repeats in some way the notion that Holistic Management can exist only in the context of a journey toward a holistic goal. How we go about forming one is the subject of the next three chapters.

Part III

The Power Lies in the Holistic Goal

8

Defining the Whole: What Are You Managing?

The holistic goal, the subject of Part III, is the driving force in Holistic Management and will guide every significant decision you make. That is why the utmost consideration should be given to forming one. Before you can begin, however, you first have to define the whole your management encompasses.

But how does one define a whole, given Smuts's point that wholes have no defined limits? All wholes, he said, are comprised of wholes, and in turn make up yet greater wholes in a progression that extends from subatomic structures to the universe itself. No whole stands on its own, and, in management especially, many wholes overlap. To isolate a lesser whole by giving it a sharp and arbitrary definition such as household, business, watershed, or national park, would appear to thereafter cripple the management of it.

Yet there is a minimum whole at which point Holistic Management becomes possible. In any of the wholes just mentioned, this would include the people directly involved in management and making decisions, the resources available to them—physical assets, as well as people who can assist, influence, or will be influenced by their management; and the money on hand or that can be generated. At the outset you will always start with an arbitrary definition of the entity you want to manage. If that happens to be a bakery, then the whole might include the owner-manager and her staff; the building itself and the equipment in it; the customers, suppliers, service providers, and advisors; plus the money the business has available as cash on hand or a line of credit at the bank, or that it can generate from product sales. This minimum whole is then viewed as one entity for management.

Defining the boundaries of the whole your management encompasses is critical because in doing so you are identifying *who* will form the holistic goal and what they will be responsible for managing. You can do this and still acknowledge that any whole you define includes lesser wholes and also lies within greater wholes, both of which will influence your management.*

In training sessions people have argued that some wholes are unmanageable. But I have yet to learn of a single case. Theoretically a whole atom or molecule could be an unmanageable whole, but that is not the sort of thing one would attempt to manage. And, theoretically, the universe would be an unmanageable whole because we could never hope to learn all that we would need to know to tackle such a project.

If a whole is said to be unmanageable, generally it is either one that needs to be broken into smaller wholes, a subject covered later, or more commonly, one that has not been defined properly—it lacks the minimum criteria. Some people, for example, only loosely define the whole in terms of the land—a national park, a farm, a wilderness area, and so on—without mentioning the people who manage it or derive benefit from it. The fate of the land is so tied to the attitudes and beliefs of these people that only managing people and land together offers any hope of success. Likewise, no family, business, or community can be managed in isolation from the land that provides the raw materials for life and the repository for wastes. Now you begin to see where most economists fall short when they advise on the management of a whole economy, which in their eyes is divorced from the land and the attitudes and beliefs of the people in all but the most superficial sense. A more detailed look at the three parts that make up a minimum manageable whole will enable you to appreciate their importance.

The Decision Makers

Decision makers are the people who will form the holistic goal. They should include anyone making day-to-day decisions in the family, business, corporate division, or whatever entity your whole is based on. They should range from those who make the most profound, far-reaching decisions, to those making the most mundane decisions—from the owner of the coffee shop to the person who serves across the counter; from the owner of the ranch to the cowboys handling the cattle; from the trustees and faculty of the college to the secretary in the admissions office; from the senior partners in the legal firm to the person answering the phones. Make a list of

---

*Some people use the term *holon* to refer to the lesser wholes existing within a greater whole.

them all, trying to be inclusive rather than exclusive. If there are people who, while not making decisions can veto them or in some way alter them, they too should be included in this part of the whole, a point we will return to. Be prepared to redefine this part of the whole if you later realize that people who should have been included in forming the holistic goal were left out. Not doing so can lead to problems down the road.

The Resource Base

Next, list the major physical resources from which you will generate revenue or derive support in achieving your holistic goal: the land, the factory and its machinery, the office building, your home, or whatever is relevant in your case. These resources need not be owned, but must be available to you. You are not after a detailed list of every asset you have, only a very general one. You may later decide to sell some of the assets you own anyway, particularly the liquid or movable ones.

Now make a list of all the people you can think of who will or can influence or be influenced by the management decisions you make, but won't have the power to veto or alter them—clients and customers, suppliers, advisors, neighbors, family, and so on. If the entity you are managing includes something as large and complex as state lands or a national park, the people in your resource base could number in the millions. To overcome the dilemma of how to include them all, list instead groups of people representative of the larger public, for example, environmental groups, community organizations, and others concerned about how that land or wildlife is managed.

In earlier days we failed to include mention of *any* people in the resource base. We were dealing mainly with ranchers and farmers at the time and thought of the resource base strictly in terms of the land. In the early 1990s, however, when attempting to assist an agricultural research station in Mexico to define their whole, I realized something was missing. The decision makers included its board of directors and staff. The resource base included the land managed by the research station. The money included funds provided by the government and whatever revenue the staff could generate from the land. In short, we defined the whole much as we would have for a family ranch in those days.

When I paid a second visit, the board and staff were still struggling to form a holistic goal and not making any progress. After considerable discussion, it dawned on me that the problem lay in how we had defined the whole six months earlier, the resource base in particular. The research station had been created to do more than manage or conduct research on its own land—it had to serve the public in the state as well. The public included urban as well as rural people because, in addition to contributing to the research station's budget as taxpayers, urban businesses were being adversely affected by the land deterioration occurring in their state. Until it was clear that the research station's resource base also included the people in the state it served, it was impossible to form a holistic goal that made sense. It did not take me long to realize afterward that no matter what the entity being managed, identifying the people in the resource base was critical. As you will learn in the next chapter, these people are no less important than the decision makers included in the first part of your whole. In fact, they are often vitally important to the whole even though they do not make management decisions within it. Their views and concerns and how you want to relate to them should be reflected in your holistic goal. Many of these people, although not forming the holistic goal with you, will prove helpful in achieving it. Some, like customers or clients, will be essential.

Money

Money will be involved in most wholes under management; for better or worse, today it is the oil that makes the cogs of life go round. Thus, in defining the whole, make a note of the sources of money available to you. This might include cash on hand or money in a savings account or available from relatives, shareholders, or a line of credit at the bank. And it would almost always include money that could be generated from the physical resources listed in your resource base. Don't be sidetracked here by long and involved discussions on the meaning of money and wealth. Just think of money in terms of what you require to live on, or to run the business, institute, government, or whatever entity you are dealing with.

Keep Your Focus on the Big Picture

Remember the picture in Chapter 3 that became visible (as Lincoln's face) only when you blurred the detail of the squares? In defining the whole, you are attempting something similar. You do not, at this stage, need to reflect on the detail of the squares because if you do, you may lose sight of the whole you are dealing with. Try to keep your lists and notes brief. Great detail is not needed now, only big-picture clarity. Below I give a selection of examples. In each case a person or group of people have identified an entity they want to manage holistically—their lives, a business, an agency, and so on. Now they're ready to determine what the minimum, manageable, whole would be:

- A single, employed person seeking to manage her life holistically would conclude that there is only one person making decisions—herself. Her resource base includes her home, her job and work associates, her friends, neighbors, and mentors (many of these people would be named). Actually, any number of people could be regarded as a resource for her. For money she would have what she earns and can save or invest profitably.

- A family seeking to manage a farm holistically might say that the decision makers include the members of their immediate family and their two employees. Their resource base includes the land they own, plus the 200 acres they lease, their home, their extended family in town, their customers, their suppliers, the county extension agent, their soil testing laboratory, their local study group. For money they have only what they can earn from the farm.

- A group of accountants seeking to manage their firm holistically might say that the decision makers include the partners and staff. Their resource base is their office building and equipment, their clients, the people who supply professional and other services to them, and their families. For money they have what they earn from their services and, if needed, a $50,000 line of credit from the bank.

- Leaders in a large industrial corporation seeking to manage the corporation holistically might say that the decision makers include the board of directors and their staff. Their resource base would include their factories and the land on which they are located, their families, their shareholders, their customers, suppliers, the university (named specifically) they collaborate with on research, various regulatory agencies (named specifically), and various environmental groups (named specifically). For money they have their earnings, interest on those earnings, government grants for research, and share capital.

- A town council seeking to manage the local government holistically might say that the decision makers are the council members and staff. The resource base includes the physical structures within the town, as well as the parks and other recreational amenities, the businesses and cultural and other public institutions, the tourists and other visitors, and the people living in town and in the surrounding rural communities. They would have the money raised by taxes, which depends on the money all the people and businesses earn, interest on that money, and grants from state and federal agencies.

- The people in an African village seeking to manage the village holistically might say that the decision makers are those who live in the village, as well as extended family members working on nearby farms, mines, or in faraway towns or cities (all of whom make decisions at various times and levels). Their resource base would include the land within the village boundaries, plus the grazing lands they share with other villages, their homes, the school, and the clinic, the people with whom they trade (or buy and sell) goods or services, various government agents (veterinary, agricultural extension, medical, educational), various church groups, and nongovernmental organizations. They would have the money they can earn or that extended family members send.

I hope you appreciate the level of simplicity in this cross section of examples. Go much beyond this level and you risk clouding your picture of the whole. No amount of detail will help you to make holistically sound decisions if you do not have a clear picture of the whole. All the detail imaginable will come into play later.

Including the Right People in the Right Place

Occasionally, it may be difficult to determine whether some people fall in the first part of the whole, as decision makers who will form the holistic goal, or the third part—as resources in achieving the holistic goal. This is an easy mistake to make when the people concerned are not involved in day-to-day management, yet can veto some decisions.

A lesson we learned in this respect involved two eight-year-long "trials" of Holistic Management conducted by the U.S. Forest Service in cooperation with two ranching families permitted to graze livestock on forest lands. In forming the whole we included only the families in the first part of the whole because they were the ones directly involved in management and making the decisions. We put the Forest Service people in the resource base, along with various environmental groups and a host of others.

Neither of these trials succeeded, in large part because the Forest Service people were not included in the first part of the whole. Although they were not directly involved in management, the Forest Service did have veto power over major decisions. Their regulations in fact overrode some crucial decisions that then made it impossible for us to manage, and thus for the trials to succeed. In subsequent efforts elsewhere, we did include government agency representatives in the first part of the whole and had them form the holistic goal with us. When we again made some decisions that could have been vetoed, they worked with us to find a way around their own regulations, because those regulations were standing in *their* way too.

Don't be put off defining the whole for fear you won't get it right. You will have plenty of opportunities to further refine it. Initially, those defining the whole—it could be you alone—may have only a limited understanding of Holistic Management and will need time to deepen it. As others become involved, changes are bound to be made. You will make mistakes, but should be able to rectify them before any serious damage is done.

In your first attempt then, do your best to define your minimum whole. The result, no matter how rough, should be adequate to enable you to get on with forming your holistic goal, which initially will only be temporary anyway. As you work at refining your holistic goal, you will be obliged to reconsider your whole.

Wholes within Wholes

If the group of people you have included in the first part of your whole is very large, and if the enterprises engaged in are very diverse, or if members are separated from each other geographically, it often becomes impractical to manage the entity as a single whole. One reason why is that it becomes more difficult to make the holistic goal specific enough, even over time, to inspire the degree of commitment needed by everyone to bring it about. In these cases, it makes more sense to create smaller, more manageable wholes within the greater whole. Each of these smaller wholes would have to meet the minimum whole requirement—that is, include people who are directly responsible for making management decisions at that level, an identifiable resource base, and money available or that can be generated from that resource base.

In the large industrial corporation mentioned in the list of wholes earlier, the leaders would have recognized immediately that trying to manage the corporation as one whole would become a nightmare of a task. The people that would need to be involved in forming the holistic goal might well number in the thousands. We know there was more than one factory, and there is perhaps more than one manufacturing division with its administrative, personnel, and accounting departments and perhaps a research and development division. In each of these factories and divisions people would be directly involved in management and making decisions. They would have a resource base that was fairly distinct and included its own clients and suppliers, which would likely include other divisions in the corporation. Each factory or division would have money available, either through the parent company or greater whole, or through revenue the division could generate. Thus, each factory or division could be seen as a smaller whole within the greater whole and be managed that way.

As the decision makers in each of these smaller wholes form their own holistic goal, the goal can address their needs, desires, and responsibilities more specifically, yet still be in line with the holistic goal formed by those managing the greater whole. Chapter 10 includes guidelines for ensuring that core values and cohesion are maintained within the holistic goals formed in each whole.

If having these smaller wholes managed by their own people eases management of the greater whole and leads to people having greater motivation and greater freedom for creativity, it would only make sense to create this opportunity, as many quality-conscious corporations have already found. Although the organizational structure would not be radically different from that of most well-run companies, the attitudes and commitment of the people would be.

Don't let this example give the impression that only large, complex businesses need to think about defining wholes within wholes. A fairly small business could have a branch some distance away that would be more effectively managed as a whole on its own, although still linked closely to the main branch. If you are managing a business and a family as a single whole, as many farmers and ranchers do, there may be a need to define two wholes, particularly if some family members have no wish to be involved in the business.

If you have doubts about whether your management would benefit by forming a smaller whole within the whole you currently manage, it helps to remind yourself of what you are trying to accomplish. The primary purpose in creating separate wholes within a greater whole is to give the people within these smaller wholes the opportunity to form a holistic goal that relates to their specific management needs and the resources available to them. *The more specific a holistic goal can be, the greater the commitment of the people will be.* Once you have defined your whole and identified the people who need to be involved in forming the holistic goal, those whose concerns it needs to address, and the resources that will enable you to bring it about, you are ready to form a holistic goal.

9

Forming a Holistic Goal: What Is It You Really Want?

F rom time immemorial human goals have driven human actions: to make a spear, build a dwelling, buy a car, get an education, reach the moon. Yet when these goals were met, it was often at the long-term expense of other factors we failed to consider. None of our goals seemed to provide the guidance needed when it came to managing the whole of a situation. *What was really needed was a goal that catered to immediate and long-term needs, human values, economies, and the environment.* And science, or theology for that matter, provided little direction in that quest. Thus, the concept of a holistic goal developed slowly, winding its way through many wrong turns and dark passages. It would prove to be more difficult to articulate than any other aspect of Holistic Management, and it continues to evolve to this day.

This chapter retraces some of the steps taken along that path in the hope that they prove illuminating. Then it covers each of the holistic goal's components in some detail. The next chapter discusses some of the pitfalls one should seek to avoid in forming a holistic goal and guidelines for refining it until it truly expresses what you want. Read through both chapters to gain a sense of how the process works before you attempt to form a holistic goal yourself. But also be aware that a genuine understanding of what is said here will probably come only as you begin to put your own holistic goal into words.

Development of the Holistic Goal

The earliest version of the Holistic Management model (see Figure 7-1), did not even include a goal. Originally one began practicing Holistic

Management by first analyzing ecological processes in an attempt to improve their functioning and thus to restore the land to health. With experience came the realization of the futility of manipulating these processes without some idea of what we wanted to produce, and thus a production goal was defined. Soon after, we encountered the problem that afflicts so many businesses, particularly agricultural ones, of production goals achieved at the expense of the environment that supports them and the people whose lives were supposed to improve.

Including a landscape goal was a major step forward, but still the people involved often argued to a standstill over production goals, and thus the desired landscape. Some time passed before it appeared that such conflict could only be resolved by finding a common vision, in terms of quality of life, from which to proceed.

For a number of years some people had been saying that "religion" needed to be in the goal, but that idea made other people uncomfortable. One day, however, a rancher made the point in another way. What needs to be in there, he said, is a reflection of people's values—spiritual and otherwise—the things people live for, the things that make them want to do anything. He was right, of course. Include a quality of life statement in the goal that reflects what is most important to you, and you would gain the personal commitment needed to achieve whatever else you had to achieve. Once such a statement was formed, you would begin to know what you had to produce to create the outcome envisioned. Once you knew what you had to produce, you could begin to envision the sort of landscape that would sustain what you produced. Thus, an order was given to the formation of the holistic goal, as each aspect naturally led to the next.

"Production" became "*forms* of production" when we saw that people were including only products that could be sold or consumed and forgetting to include things like "meaningful work" or "an aesthetic environment," which would have to be produced to create the quality of life they envisioned. Landscape became the *future* landscape when we found that people were describing the land as it was, not as it had to be if it was to sustain them several generations hence. In clarifying the definition of a manageable whole, we realized that future *resource base* better described the third part of the holistic goal. The new heading still encompassed the idea of a future landscape, but the land manager now also needed to describe his or her land in terms of how water and mineral cycles, energy flow, and community dynamics would have to function. Others required only a general description of the environment surrounding them. The future resource base in any situation would also need to include some reference to the people who, when the whole was defined, were listed as resources to achieving the holistic goal. Finally, after considerable trial and error, we realized that quality of life, forms of production and future resource base goals had to be combined into one comprehensive, holistic goal. Otherwise decisions could be made in support of one aspect, while damaging another.

Weighing all decisions against this holistic goal increases the chance of success in both the short and the long term. Much of what is expressed in the first two parts—quality of life and forms of production—speaks to immediate needs: people want a better life now and to produce the things that lead to it. But both parts also contain idealistic elements that may not be achieved in a single lifetime. The future resource base always speaks to the long term, as it must if it is to sustain the rest of what the holistic goal encompasses.

On first exposure to a holistic goal, which often takes up to a page to express, many people will argue that it is not one goal, but several. The very idea of a goal that embraces human values and links them as one indivisible entity to economies and the environment is a foreign concept, particularly to those adept in the development of sharply defined objectives—which do have their place once a holistic goal has been formed. When conceived without reference to anything resembling a holistic goal, objectives along the lines of "By 2005 we will capture 40 percent of market share," have led to a host of problems. Such objectives are often met without our noticing until much later what they cost in human terms, in environmental terms, and in damage to a country and the long-term future of its children.

The Statement of Purpose

Many an institution is formed for a specific purpose but later loses sight of it and becomes ineffective or self-serving. If the entity you manage was formed for a specific purpose that you are *legally or morally obligated to meet,* you will need to ensure that your holistic goal addresses this purpose. The best way to do this is to create a statement of purpose as a preface to your holistic goal.

In some cases, the purpose for which you were formed will be well known and perhaps recorded in writing. But more often, the purpose has either been forgotten or was originally expressed in such vague terms that it was open to interpretation. Occasionally, because times change, and with them the context and situations that may have prompted the formation of an organization, the original purpose is no longer valid. If you find this to be true in your case, you need to do something about it.

In stating your basic purpose, you want to get at the heart of the matter. The statement should reflect, in very few words, what you were formed to do. If it takes you more than a sentence or two, you have not thought carefully enough, or, more commonly, you have gone beyond a statement of purpose into *how* you see yourselves doing whatever it is you are supposed to do.

The board, faculty, and staff of one private college I was assisting were guilty of the latter. They labored for hours over a whole paragraph of flowery words describing the services they would provide and how they would attract students—the sorts of things that would have to be tested *after* the statement of purpose was created and the holistic goal formed. In frustration, after repeated attempts to steer them away from fussing over words that had little to do with the task at hand, I finally blurted out, "Damn it, I feel like calling you a bunch of bloody academics, but I can't because you are!" They got the message, and soon after came down to a simple statement that expressed what they had been formed to do: "To provide exceptional education that is relevant to the future."

It took the staff and board of the Center for Holistic Management some time to clarify our purpose. The Center had originally been formed "to promote Holistic Management and coordinate its further development." But this proved to be too vague and the resulting lack of focus caused us to flounder. We got the word out about Holistic Management, but it didn't seem as if we were accomplishing much. It wasn't until we realized that what we had been formed to do was "to advance the *practice* of Holistic Management," as well as coordinate its development, that we began to make headway. The second part of our holistic goal, the forms of production, gained needed direction, and our management and monitoring really began to focus.

The statement of purpose will be reflected in your holistic goal, specifically in the quality of life statement, where you will refer to the outcomes that correspond to your purpose, and in the forms of production, where you will specify what you must produce to ensure those outcomes. Revisit your statement of purpose periodically, just to make sure that the purpose for which you were formed continues to be relevant.

Quality of Life

In forming the first part of your holistic goal, you are attempting to express how you want your life to be, *in the whole you have defined,* based on what you most value. If the whole you have defined includes only yourself, and you are merely seeking to manage your personal life holistically, then the quality of life you express would be limited to your own personal desires. But in most cases your whole will include more than one decision maker, and you will be managing something jointly—your life as a couple, your family and household, a small business, or a large corporation. Then the quality of life statement becomes an expression of the desires and aspirations *of all the decision-makers*—a reflection of your *shared* values.

The quality of life portion of your holistic goal expresses the reasons you're doing what you're doing, what you are about, and what you want to become. It is a reflection of what motivates you. It should excite you. It speaks of needs you want to satisfy now, but also of the mission you seek to accomplish in the long run. It is your collective sense of what is important and why.

Getting Down to What You Value Most

No one can specify what is or is not appropriate to include in your quality of life statement because what needs to be included is unique to each situation and the values of the people within it. However, there are four areas you might want to consider in thinking about quality of life.

ECONOMIC WELL-BEING

This is essential for meeting basic human needs for food, clothing, shelter, health, and security. The entity as a whole must be prosperous, but so should the individuals within it. How you define economic well-being will always depend on your circumstances. If your business is deeply in debt now, your greatest desire might simply be to be debt-free; a villager in Africa might place highest value on food self-sufficiency. In many organizations ensuring fair and adequate compensation is a consideration, or creating opportunities for individual economic advancement.

"Making a lot of money" is rarely as useful in a quality of life statement as naming instead what you gain from having money: security, comfortable surroundings, enough to eat, and the wherewithal to do what you want to do. The same can be said for any material object. Ask that person, commonly a teenager, who insists that a new car is essential to the life he wants to lead, what he gains from owning a car of his own. Freedom to come and go? Adventure and travel? Recognition and respect? The car may well be the *means* to achieve some of these ends, but its purchase is something that should be subjected to testing toward the holistic goal, as will be the case with most material objects.

The practice of expressing what you hope to gain from a thing, rather than the thing itself, can lead to some surprising revelations. A young couple once asked me to help them to locate a game ranch in Africa. They had recently come into some money and wanted to leave their urban professions to go game ranching. It was especially important, they said, that they own the ranch. I agreed to help, but first sat them down and asked them to talk about why they wanted to own a game ranch, what their family needs were, and in general the kind of life they were seeking. Without this information, I wouldn't know what sort of place to look for. But after hearing them talk about how they loved the bush, the hunting, camping by a campfire, and so on, I recommended they seek jobs on someone else's game ranch.

Not once had they mentioned anything that came close to describing the life of a game ranch owner in those early days of the industry. They had said nothing about the long hours they would have to spend trying to create a financial plan that would keep them in the black or about battling Game Department bureaucrats who were opposed to the idea of private individuals managing game and were responsible for issuing the permits to hunt, transport, and market it. Nor had they mentioned the days and nights on the road and in city hotels that were required to develop markets for their products, nor any of the many other tasks that occupied most of a game ranch owner's time. All that they had described as important to them was all that the life of an employed hunter offered.

I later struck similar cases where, for instance, a young couple was certain that owning their own farm was more important to them than nearly anything else in life. And they had used all their working capital plus a loan from the bank to finance the purchase of one. Now they struggled to make ends meet and the financial stress was beginning to take its toll on their relationship. Not the sort of life they had envisioned owning a farm would give them.

Had they instead at the outset discussed what they wanted to gain in their lives by owning a farm, they might have realized that ownership was not what was important, it was the way of life that was. They then could have leased a farm, leaving them with enough working capital to make a comfortable living for themselves and create the way of life they had envisioned. Later, when they could afford the luxury of ownership, and didn't have to borrow high-interest money to achieve it, they could purchase that or another farm—a decision they would test toward their holistic goal.

RELATIONSHIPS

Humans are social creatures. When we feel alienated or alone, we rarely function as well as when we feel we belong, that "we're all in this together." It becomes important then to ask yourselves how you want to behave with each other and with those listed in your resource base. Your behavior will influence the level of trust that exists among you, and thus your ability to communicate. Depending on the circumstances, you might also consider the qualities of the people you want to associate with or enlist in support of your efforts—future co-workers, organization members, clients, suppliers, advisors, and so on. In the end, the quality of your relationships will greatly influence your ability to achieve all that you set out to achieve.

You want to have a collective sense of what you expect to give and receive from the relationships that are most important to you.

CHALLENGE AND GROWTH

Humans have a need to experience challenge; without it we fail to grow and develop. Where is the challenge in what you do? Try to think in terms of what you find stimulating, what requires all the resourcefulness and creativity you can muster. Is it important to you to have opportunities to further develop your skills or to enhance the knowledge and talents you already possess? If it is, then is everyone able to explain why? Think about what kind of atmosphere and environment you might create to ensure that everyone remains enthusiastic, yet no one feels overwhelmed.

PURPOSE AND CONTRIBUTION

People will give their best to an effort only when it has meaning for them. Meaning, in any kind of organization, is not something that can be created by a leader and handed down; it has to be a shared discovery. Ask yourselves, "What are we about?" "What do we want to be?" and "What do we ultimately want to accomplish?" The answers will help you discover the meaning in what you are doing and the reason for your existence as an organization, family, company, or whatever.

If you are the type of organization that required a statement of purpose, you will have defined what you were specifically formed to do, but that may not cover all you are about, and certainly not all you want to be. What you ultimately want to accomplish will be tied to the outcomes you envision in meeting your purpose. In our case, as mentioned, we are working to advance the practice and to coordinate the development of Holistic Management, but what really inspires and drives us are the results we envision from such an effort: a world in which people live well and in harmony, where deserts are healing, wildlife abundant, and the fishing's good and getting better.

Any group of people working or living together does so for a reason, though often unexpressed. What is it that you are able to achieve collectively that you could not achieve individually? The answers may be fairly obvious when the whole is limited to a family, but are often less so when the whole involves a business. In the latter case, another way of thinking about why you exist, and for what purpose, is to consider what the founder's aspirations might have been in setting up the business, or the reasons your industry or line of work came into being. This sometimes provides a clue that eventually enables you to articulate an answer.

In asking yourselves these kinds of questions, you should begin to form an idea of what you contribute to the world through your efforts.

Knowing that we are contributing to something greater than ourselves is a strong motivating force, and also, I believe, a need most people share. Some may argue that those engaged in a struggle for survival have no time to give to such notions. But even those living in the most impoverished and appalling conditions nourish the desire to make the world a better place for their children.

Creating a quality of life statement requires a good deal of reflection and numerous conversations, and it may be several months—a year or more in large organizations—before it begins to express what you want it to express. In the interest of moving on, however, start with a very rough statement that indicates the general direction in which you want to head. Then you can form the remaining two parts of your holistic goal and begin making decisions that lead you toward it.

Crafting Your Statement

In recording everyone's thoughts initially, it is important that you capture them in simple phrases, rather than well-worded sentences. You will have plenty of time to edit the results into a unified statement. On the other hand, resist the temptation to break the phrases down into the values they represent, ending up with a long list of values with no context. Although there is nothing wrong with a list of values, they won't adequately express how people want their lives to be, and that makes testing future decisions difficult. So don't just write: "prosperity, security, family values, and health" when what you really want is "to have stable and healthy families where all generations feel secure and are cared for."

In general, people will want many of the same things, regardless of their position in the business, institution, family, or whatever. But the specifics may vary, and in some cases conflict. A married couple might discover that one partner finds a life of travel and adventure most rewarding, while the other finds the greatest enjoyment in a quiet life at home. The partners and staff of a law firm might discover that some find the greatest reward in working with the poor, while others relish the challenge of working with wealthy corporate clients. In either case, there is a good chance that each can accommodate the other as long as the difference has not already caused conflict and hurt.

I deliberately use the word *accommodate,* rather than compromise. Anyone forced to compromise on something very important to him or her will not have much commitment to achieving the holistic goal. The same applies when differences arise over how an idea is worded. When this happens, keep talking until you find the words that best express your collective meaning.

In editing your quality of life statement, take care that you do not lose anything. In a training session a few years ago, one group of participants drew up a lengthy list of phrases and, as they had finished early, sought to smarten the English by bringing the phrases down to a few well-written sentences. On presenting the resulting statement to the others, however, they had lost some important thoughts expressed in the original rough phrases.

This holistic goal you are forming is primarily for your own internal use. You do not have to show it to anyone else, so don't worry about how well it reads. All that matters is that the words capture how you want your life to be in that particular whole, *and* that those words mean the same thing to each person. Once you have a rough draft of your quality of life statement, you will be ready to describe all the things you have to produce to create it.

Forms of Production

The things you have to produce will take many forms, and thus we refer to this second part of the holistic goal as "forms of production." Some of these "products" will be derived from the resource base defined in your whole as well as from the money you have or can generate. Others will be derived solely from the creativity and skills of the decision makers.

In describing what you have to produce to create the way of life envisioned, you will naturally come to describe what you have to produce to effectively manage the whole, as you will see shortly. If yours is an organization with a specific purpose, you also need to make sure you include what you have to produce to accomplish the stated purpose.

Meeting Quality of Life Needs

Each of the needs or desires expressed in your quality of life statement will have to be met by some form of production. This doesn't mean that you merely go through each phrase in your statement and create a "product" to match it. It takes a little more thought than that. It becomes helpful if you ask the question: "What don't we have now, or what aren't we doing now, that is preventing us from *achieving* this?" Rephrase the answer in positive terms and you will know what you have to produce. One form of production might meet several of the needs described, and vice versa. If one of your desires was "to enjoy what we do everyday," that could be met in part by producing "a balance between our work and personal lives," "sufficient time for strategic planning," or a host of other things. If one of your desires was for "financial security" that could be met in part by producing "a retirement or pension plan" or "an estate plan that ensures an orderly transfer of assets to our children and adequate income for us." By asking the question, you will discover what areas are currently weak and prevent you from meeting those needs.

Some have questioned the necessity of including such things as "a balance between our work and personal lives" or "a retirement plan." But *only* by including them are they likely to be produced. The following example illustrates the point. Near a home I once had in Harare, Zimbabwe, is a large *vlei,* or meadow. Every year during the rainy season the grass grows very tall in this meadow and in the many other meadows running through the city's residential suburbs. Several times a year the city council sends fleets of tractors out to mow the grass, which becomes a fire hazard in the dry season and also looks untidy. This is an expensive exercise since the country has to import, at high cost, all the tractors and the fuel to run them. And, since the ground is uneven, the tractors do a rather poor job of the mowing. The people these machines replaced used to do a far better job slashing the grass by hand. They have since joined the ranks of the unemployed in a city where unemployment is approaching 50 percent, poverty is endemic, and crime and violence are escalating.

If the mayor and city council were to express what they wanted in terms of quality of life for the city they manage, their list would probably include greater prosperity, aesthetic surroundings, and physical security. The latter would likely appear at the top of their list, as a decrease in physical security generally parallels an increase in poverty and joblessness. Undoubtedly, one of the things the mayor and councilors would want to produce that would lead to this quality of life would be "full employment." With only this much of a holistic goal formed, you can already see that in testing the decision of how to cut the grass each year, people rather than tractors would be selected.

If any of the desires included in your quality of life statement will require money to produce—"to be debt free" for instance, or "financially secure"—then *profit* from whatever source(s) you specify will need to be a form of production in most cases. In specifying the sources for that profit, it is important to do so in very general terms. A farm might produce profit from livestock and profit from crops. Specifying the kinds of crops or the breed and class of livestock is unwise because markets and attitudes are constantly changing and because this sort of detail involves decisions that should be tested toward the holistic goal. For the same reasons a toy manufacturer would produce "profit from toys," rather than profit from Hoola Hoops and Barbie dolls. The accounting firm would produce "profit from the services we provide," rather than profit from tax returns and corporate audits.

If the whole being managed was a household and the money required to run it was produced from the salaries of one or two people, there would still be a need to produce an excess of income over the costs of running the household if you wanted to be financially secure or debt free. Some couples have expressed this as "to produce a 'profit' from our salaries" or "to produce a surplus in our household budget."

Meeting Your Stated Purpose

If yours is an organization formed for a specific purpose, you will need to ensure that what you must produce to meet that purpose is included here. At least one of your forms of production will be to produce what you were specifically formed to produce, but many other forms of production will be influenced, and clarified, if your stated purpose is taken into account when expressing them.

This was certainly true when we listed the forms of production for the Center for Holistic Management. Before clarifying our statement of purpose, one of the things we knew we had to produce was "a collaborative network of educators." Once we realized that advancing the *practice* of Holistic Management was critical, we revised our original phrase to "a collaborative network of educators *able to produce Holistic Management practitioners.* A seemingly minor addition, but it made a world of difference when we later came to test some decisions about the educational programs we offer.

Creating Your List

In gathering together the notes from all of the above discussions, check to be sure that you have avoided some fairly common errors:

- Are all of the ideas expressed in the quality of life statement covered?

- Have you included what you must produce to achieve your stated purpose (if applicable)?

- Are there any "how to's"? You only want to list *what* has to be produced, not *how* it will be produced. *How* something is to be produced is a decision that needs testing.

- In determining what you need to produce did any conflicts arise? If so, then again it is probably because you were beginning to discuss how to do something.

Here's how a rough draft of these first two parts of the holistic goal might look if formed by the staff and partners of a small law firm.

Quality of life.

- We want our work to be enjoyable and meaningful; to be proud of what we do; to be of service to our community and to be recognized and respected for our services by our community and families; to be prosperous and financially secure; have balance between our work and family lives; respect for each other's views and each other's private lives; to work in a place where every day is fun and free from interpersonal stress; and to create through our work a more just and humane society.

- *Forms of Production.* Profit from our services; pension and health plans for all our staff; a tradition of, and a reputation for, ethical behavior that is never violated or compromised; services that are broad, but backed up by internal expertise; an open, friendly, collaborative work environment; offices that reflect our values and are clean, spacious, and tastefully designed. Professional work that we can always feel proud of.

As mentioned, these first two parts of the holistic goal speak largely to immediate needs in that you want these results as quickly as you can begin to achieve them. This is particularly the case if you are a business facing imminent bankruptcy or Caribbean islanders felling your last trees and justifying the action because you have to survive. Now we move on to the final part of the holistic goal, which addresses long-term needs—looking to the future and largely ignoring the present situation.

Future Resource Base

In describing your future resource base you need to consider how it must be many years from now if it is to sustain what you have to produce to create the quality of life you want. When you later make decisions that deal with some of the immediate needs described in the first two parts of your holistic goal, you will be weighing them also against this long-term vision.

When land is included in the whole you defined—a farm, ranch, forest, national park, and so on—you need to think of your future resource base over the very long term, describing it as it would have to be 100, 500 or 1,000 years from now. It may take hundreds of years to produce a forest in which all stages of growth occur and only somewhat less time to build a biological community that will sustain certain wildlife species.

There are several different elements to consider in describing your future resource base. Two that always should be addressed are the *people* you included in the resource base when defining your whole and the *land,* even if you did not make reference to it when defining your whole, and even when you operate a business that has no direct connection to the land. Other elements that may need to be considered are the *community you live or work in* and *the services available in that community.* There are likely to be more depending on the circumstances and the whole defined.

The People

Most businesses and organizations, with few exceptions, will have clients, customers, suppliers, supporters, members, advisors, and others who in one way or another are critical to the health and future of that concern. Many of these people will have been listed in the resource base defined in your whole. Those were the people who, you'll remember, make no management decisions, but can greatly influence them or be influenced by them. You may now need to add others as well.

Farmers and ranchers whose products are sold as commodities—milk, beef, grain, and so on—rarely meet either the retailer or the consumer of those products and thus give little thought to the concerns of either. "Customers and clients" rarely figure in their future resource base. But other people will: buyers, suppliers, extended family, extension agents and other advisors, neighbors, and so on. If, on the other hand, you are a farmer or rancher producing products identified with you and that you are proud to be associated with, then you will want to mention in your future resource base the customers who purchase those products and the particular suppliers who enable you to produce them efficiently. You *want* your customers to know you, like you, respect you, and promote your products. You *want* your suppliers to be trustworthy, loyal, and committed to serving you well.

How can you describe such people far into the future? You can't. Would it help you to make better decisions if you could? Not really. The way we overcome this dilemma is to describe how *we* must be far into the future, not *them.* So, in describing the people in your future resource base you describe how you and your business, organization, or whatever will have to be seen to be, far into the future, for these people to remain loyal to you, respectful, or supportive, or whatever is required. Vary the attributes according to the people you are concerned about, whether they be clients and suppliers, extended family, environmental groups, or a representative from a regulatory agency.

If you were considering your clients for instance, people whose loyalty and patronage you want to maintain, you would describe yourselves as you would have to be in the future: honest, professional, prompt, reliable, caring, producing nothing but the best quality, up-to-date, environmentally and socially responsible, and so on. This is not difficult to do if you just try to think from their point of view. Or better still, invite some of these people in as you are discussing this part of your holistic goal and get their opinions firsthand.

Remember, the words you finally use here are not meant for public consumption, so don't worry whether outsiders might misinterpret them. You will be judged by your behavior and actions, not by your words. If you test decisions genuinely toward how you will have to be, this will lead to behaviors and actions that are consistent with how you have said you will be.

The Land

When what you produce to meet your quality of life or stated purpose does not come directly from the land, or when the whole defined does not include land under your management, you may wonder why land should figure at all in the description of your future resource base. It needs to be included simply because in the long term, the well-being of any family, business, or community depends on the stability and productivity of the land surrounding them. When I say "land" I am referring to it in the broadest sense meaning soils, plants, forests, birds, insects, wildlife, lakes, streams, and, ultimately, the oceans as well.

All households and businesses—even those that are service oriented—at some point tie back to the land and its waterways and affect ecological health. For example, most businesses use paper and inks as well as detergents, and these, in both their production and their final disposal, came from and return to the land, with consequences. Banks provide loans for myriad enterprises that impact ecological health in both small and large ways.

Arising from almost every financial transaction there is an effect on the land that is experienced months or years later and generally far removed from the site of the original transaction. For example, the cotton T-shirt you buy for your child is likely to have been produced from plants grown on deteriorating soils, and dyed with chemicals that adversely affect water quality and human health. The pesticide you spray on your lawn can be tracked into your home, and can also end up in the water system where it accumulates in shellfish which in turn are eaten by another family many miles away.

The average citizen generally assumes that someone somewhere is going to do something to ameliorate these effects. That *someone,* as it turns out, is going to have to be ordinary folks like you and me. By including a description of the land around us, as it will have to be far into the future, we give the holistic goal a much-needed dimension. When we later test our decisions toward it we will always be reminded to consider the effects of those decisions on our environment.

Some people might hesitate to describe the land around them as it would have to be far into the future, feeling they don't know enough about it to do so. That is understandable when you aren't actually managing land. But you don't need a scientific background to be able to express a need for surroundings that are stable, productive, and healthy, with clean and clear-running rivers, covered rather than bare soils, and prosperous rural communities. And this would be enough of a description to begin testing decisions toward.

When what you have to produce to create the quality of life you envision comes directly from land you manage, you need to provide a fairly detailed description of what that land must look like far into the future and how the fundamental processes at work in any environment—water and mineral cycles, community dynamics, and energy flow—will have to function.

In any living community we manage, water will cycle. Since almost all the life forms we depend on will require water from the soil, we must ensure that water is in fact adequately present in usable form. A water cycle characterized by flood-causing runoff or excessive soil surface evaporation, would generally undermine production.

Similarly, the community always has a mineral cycle functioning at some level. Again, the life forms we depend on will require mineral nutrients from the soil and air, and to maintain them we must ensure that those nutrients cycle appropriately. If nutrients are trapped in dead vegetation that is not breaking down (unless burned), production will suffer. Likewise, if we have to depend on the constant reintroduction of major nutrients, something is wrong.

All living communities are dynamic, undergoing continuous change, becoming ever simpler or ever more complex. Some forms of production will require a certain level of complexity in the communities being managed. In the future you will want these desired levels to be self-sustaining.

Last, self-sufficient life depends on the conversion of solar energy through green plants and into the stuff of life—food, fiber, and so on. Most of what we produce from the land will require that the maximum energy be converted both to maximize production and to sustain it.

Your task as a land manager is to describe the land in terms of these four processes, not as they now are functioning, but as they will have to be functioning in the future if you are to sustain what you have to produce, and the quality of life you want to create, over many generations. In many cases you will be dealing with several environments, such as rangelands, croplands, wetlands, riparian areas, or forests. Because each will have different requirements, you should create separate descriptions for each of them. When extensive land areas are involved, it is generally helpful to map these descriptions as well, a subject dealt with in Chapter 45 on land planning.

One of the most common mistakes is to describe a future landscape that is not much different from what you have today, when it needs to be. The mistake is understandable in many cases, because people have trouble visioning something they've only heard about but have never seen. I have struck this in both developed and developing countries.

A Louisiana sugarcane farmer, for instance, had in all his life only seen enormous fields of sugarcane and found it terribly hard to envision anything different. He realized that his large fields had to be broken up into smaller ones in which several crops were mixed, and that he needed plenty of "edge" to increase the diversity of insects, birds, bats, and other wildlife. But when it came down to actually describing this on his own land, he found it impossible to do.

Young people in an African village surrounded by bare ground and starving goats and cattle found it hard to picture grassland with their livestock herded amongst zebra, sable, impala, and other game. Having hunted big game as a young man over the same land they now occupy, this seemed simple enough to me. I couldn't understand their struggle until they pointed out that they could not picture something that had disappeared before they were born. If you are faced with a similar situation, visit other areas to help to expand your vision or talk to a few old timers who have a good memory of what your area was like long ago, although sometimes changes have occurred so slowly they may not have noticed them.

As with the rest of your holistic goal, how you describe the land in your future resource base will be refined over time as you learn more about that land and what it is capable of producing, and as testing decisions forces you to become more specific.

The Community You Live In or Work In

Sometimes you might want to describe the type of community you want to live in or in which your business is located since many of your future resources may be derived from that community and what you produce may depend on them. Even though your community may be impoverished, racially divided, or lacking in cultural amenities today, describe it as it will have to be to sustain what you have to produce to create your quality of life. Although many of the decisions you make will not have a direct bearing on the future of your community, many will indirectly, and cumulatively they will be felt.

Don't underestimate your power as an individual person or business to generate change. In describing a community that is prosperous, racially harmonious, and rich in cultural amenities, you can begin making decisions that take you toward that. This might mean finding local suppliers or local customers so you can keep the dollars cycling longer in your community, or it might mean engaging in some type of community service. You won't change things overnight, and you don't have to. You just want to ensure that the decisions you make lead you away from what is undesirable and toward the future community you envision.

The Services Available in Your Community

A related element worth considering in some cases are the services that would need to be available in your community. Although you may lack the bank or other lending institution, the library, or the medical services you need today, you know that the future health and well-being of your community, your business, and family depend on them. What you have to produce may depend on these services as well or be unable to be sustained without them. This aspect of life is generally more a concern for those in rural communities, although even some urban communities lack essential services. Think carefully about your situation, and if you can see that there are services your community will have to have available to sustain what you produce, list them.

Once you have thought through and described all the elements that make up your future resource base, you will have a holistic goal. Case 9-1 is an example of a holistic goal that a middle-aged couple might form to manage their lives. Case 9-2 is one the decision makers in a government agency might form as a temporary measure to get them started in managing a forest holistically. Both goals are hypothetical, but they do give an idea of the form a holistic goal often takes. Be wary of the temptation to let them influence your own.

Case 9-1. Holistic Goal Formed by a Middle-Aged Couple to Manage Their Lives

Quality of Life

To be engaged in meaningful work for the rest of our lives and to be excited and enthusiastic about what we have to do and get to do each day. To be secure financially, physically, and emotionally into old age; to be known for our honor, integrity, chivalry, and spirit. To maintain robust health and physical stamina; to enjoy an abundance of mutually satisfying relationships. To explore and experience wild places and to ensure those places will still be there when our grandchildren's grandchildren seek to find them. To live simply and consume sparingly.

What We Have to Produce (Forms of Production)

- Profit from meaningful work.

- Work or leisure time in wild places.

- Time for learning, meaningful discussion, companionship, and exercise.

(continues)

- A warm and hospitable home environment—wherever *home* happens to be at any time—in which friends, family, and colleagues always feel welcome.

Future Resource Base

- *People.* We are known to be compassionate and thoughtful, well-informed, good listeners, fun to be with, adventurous, and supportive.

- *Land.* The land surrounding and supporting our town will be stable and productive. Wildlife will be plentiful—we'll be able to see animals, or signs of them, anytime we venture out. The river will run clear and be full of life, and eagles will nest in the trees alongside it once again.

Case 9-2. Temporary Holistic Goal Formed by a Government Agency Managing a National Forest

(*Note:* Like most government agencies, this one was formed for a specific purpose that it is obligated to fulfill.)

Statement of Purpose

To ensure that the forest is managed sustainably and for the benefit of the nation.

Quality of Life

To be proud of our work and respected for it. To be so good at what we do that other agencies want to emulate us. To work in a caring and collaborative environment in which we have opportunities to further our learning and in which our special talents and capabilities are acknowledged and utilized. To have opportunities to share what we do with our families and with the people in the surrounding communities so they can better support us—especially during fire season—and so we can better support them. We want to manage this forest so that it provides an excellent financial return to the nation and an even greater return in "biological capital."

What We Have to Produce (Forms of Production)

- An environment in which all feel free to speak up and are heard when they do.

- Effective educational programs for the public and our families.

- An effective public volunteer program.

- Regular forums in which we have opportunities to solicit public input.

- Time to engage in community activities, to attend conferences, and to visit other forests and research sites.

- Opportunities for furthering our education and skills.

- A long-term forest management plan.

- An effective fire prevention plan.

- A safe and effective fire management plan.

- An effective financial plan each year in which the public is assured of maximum return on their investment in our services.

Future Resource Base

- *People.* The public will see us as innovative, knowledgeable, professional, friendly, and helpful, and, above all, as serving the public's interest.

- *Land.* Many generations hence, this forest will be healthy and rich in biological diversity, from the trees—in which all age groups are represented—to the abundant birds, mammals, insects, and microorganisms. The soils will be covered throughout the year and remain where they form. Streams will flow perennially and clear and be healthy enough to drink from. Water and mineral cycles will be maximized and energy flow optimized for all life forms.

Conclusion

Given that the development of the holistic goal was such a lengthy and difficult process, it is no surprise that for many people forming one that truly serves their needs is the most difficult aspect of Holistic Management and generally takes a fair amount of time. That is why, as the next chapter explains, you should start with a temporary holistic goal.

10

Developing a Sense of Ownership: Are You Sure That's What You Really Want?

B ecause it takes time for people to feel comfortable enough to express more than superficially what they want in terms of quality of life—even when those people live in the same family—to gain clarity on what needs to be produced, and to fully envision a future resource base, forming a holistic goal to which people are deeply committed can take several years. But few want to, and some cannot afford to wait this long to begin putting their situation right. We overcome this dilemma by first forming a temporary holistic goal and starting toward that, much as a military pilot might head generally toward the action before knowing the precise destination. To wait on the ground for perfect intelligence or to burn up fuel circling randomly would waste his chances, his resources, or both. Like the pilot, as you obtain more information and a clearer picture, you can refine your holistic goal so that by the time you know the target, you are well on your way without having wasted time or fuel.

Form the temporary holistic goal fairly quickly, in a matter of hours, rather than days, and then use it to make real decisions right away, preferably on the same day, so people begin to see its value. The use of the word *temporary* indicates to everyone that this initial attempt at forming a holistic goal is open to discussion and improvement. Yet, it provides the needed direction and buys time to sharpen your understanding of Holistic Management, to more fully involve the people who need to be involved, and to gain the level of comfort needed for free and unhindered expression.

Until the holistic goal expresses what people genuinely desire and want to accomplish, they will tend to go back to arguing about tools and actions because they have more invested in their knowledge and areas of expertise than in the holistic goal. They are likely to find holistic decision making, planning, and management "too difficult" or "too much trouble" and to be tempted to return to the old, more familiar, ways. Don't be too discouraged by this. Over time, as the holistic goal comes to reflect what they truly want, people will begin to do what it takes to achieve it, and the rest of Holistic Management becomes a relatively easy task. Although it may take several years before you have a holistic goal in which all feel a deep sense of ownership, you will in the meantime begin to achieve some of what you set out to achieve and develop an appreciation for the power the holistic goal gives you.

The case of Canadian ranchers Don and Randee Halladay is a typical one. The temporary holistic goal they initially formed with their two children was enough to get them started in 1986. But it took six years of refining before it truly reflected who they were and what they wanted to achieve. As case 10-1 shows, what they wrote down in 1986 was vague and tentative and full of "how-to's." But by 1992, after numerous decisions had been tested and their communication had improved as a family, what they wrote was strikingly different.

Case 10-1. The Evolution of a Holistic Goal

Don and Randee Halladay and their two children struggled over a six-year period to create a holistic goal that truly reflected who they were and what they wanted to accomplish on their ranch. Below is a sampling of some of the statements that appeared in their temporary holistic goal in 1986, followed by the revisions made in the more permanent goal developed by 1992.

Quality of Life

1986:

We want to live well, with money available for recreation; earn our living without back-breaking work; provide education, or whatever, for kids.

1992:

We want to be debt-free; we want to be excited and enthusiastic about what we are doing and have to do on a daily basis; we want to

(continues)

leave this world (when we are very, very old) with our family happy, knowing that we led productive, happy lives, left the land in a better condition than we found it, and be recognized for this achievement; we want Laurel and Jayson [their children] to be happy and productive, and we want to be able to help them reach their full potential.

Forms of Production

1986:

Use either cows or yearlings to maximize production, but don't rule out things like sheep; get enough cows so Randee doesn't have to work off the ranch; keep costs as low as possible.

1992:

Profit from livestock and crops and anything that doesn't interfere with our values and that complements what we do and who we are.

Future Resource Base

1986:

Complex, stable environment with permanent pastures, including microorganisms, birds, small animals, and wildlife; absolutely no erosion and no bare soil; lots of flowers, trees, shrubs, and tall grass.

1992:

Community Dynamics: Very complex grassland not allowed to advance to forest except in the areas mapped. Different species and varieties of plants in the form of shelter belts that could have harvestable products within; a great variety of animal life with considerable emphasis on birds; great complexity in soil organisms; including fungi and molds.

[Water cycle, mineral cycle, and energy flow also include similarly detailed descriptions].

Although it was very rough initially, their holistic goal covered most of the needed elements, and they did get it down on paper. Merely by mentioning in one of their early revisions the desire to be debt free, they, like many others, found they were able to reduce their debts fairly drastically, even though their testing of financial decisions was a little shaky. They began to prioritize their commitments, dropping those that were not important, and life immediately became more enjoyable. They found that they had the funds for the education and travel that were so important to their quality of life. Today, they attribute this turnaround to the power their holistic goal has given them: "Without a holistic goal we had no way of knowing whether our actions were taking us in the direction we wanted to go, because we didn't have a direction."[1]

The temporary holistic goal and the more permanent holistic goal that develops from it will have much in common. The main difference between them will lie not in the wording but in the degree of commitment people have to achieving them. Commitment is not something you can force. If you try, people will only pay "lip service" to the holistic goal and it will lose its power.

Common Mistakes

Many years' experience in forming holistic goals myself and in working with others to form theirs have convinced me that the mistakes made in forming a holistic goal are fairly common, if not universal. One of the first mistakes people make is to begin from the standpoint of today's problems or issues—various conflicts, poor communication, a loss of production, and so on. When a goal focuses on a problem it provides no incentive to go beyond the problem to what people really want. If your goal becomes "to end the conflict," you may be ending conflict the rest of your lives. You need instead to describe what lies beyond the conflict, that is, how it will be when the conflict is over. Then you know where you need to be heading and have an incentive to get there.

Some groups have been tempted to start by describing the future resource base first, believing they were in too much conflict to start anywhere else. This generally only exacerbates the conflict and results in deadlock. You will find that across most cultures in most of the world, there is far greater similarity in the values underlying the quality of life desired than in anything else. Who does not want stable families, prosperity, security, health, and clean and abundant food, water, and air? Thus, in forming a holistic goal, you always begin by expressing the quality of life you desire. As you begin refining your temporary holistic goal, you can avoid many of the more common mistakes if you take note of the following do's and don'ts.

- *Do* make your holistic goal 100 percent *what* you want and have to produce and 0 percent *how* it is going to be achieved. This can be surprisingly difficult, given the fact that we are so used to stating the means rather than the ends. Far too many present-day conflicts owe their origins to this shortcoming. If those involved first sat down together and discussed what they genuinely wanted, rather than the tools or actions employed in what they do or don't want, they would find much to agree upon.

The enormous conflict between ranchers and environmentalists in the western United States is just such a case. Ranchers are fighting for the right to graze their livestock on public lands (an enormous area, the majority of land in many of these states), as some have done for generations, while environmentalists are fighting to deny them that right. The land should be rested, they say, because it is deteriorating under livestock grazing. Both are right and both are wrong for reasons that will become clear in later chapters. The point is that if both sides were to sit down and discuss it, they would find they wanted the same things: thriving grasslands and forests, clear-running streams, abundant wildlife, thriving communities in a stable country, and so on. If they wanted those things badly enough, they would then determine how they could achieve them, which is entirely possible with Holistic Management.

- *Don't* allow any prejudices against future tools or actions to appear in the holistic goal. You wouldn't, for example, mention "organic farming" in your holistic goal because it is a prejudice against chemicals. There may come a time when the only way to save the situation is through the use of a chemical and thus the use of any chemicals should be left where it belongs—in the testing of decisions. It is perfectly all right, however, even necessary, to reflect how you want to live based on the values expressed in the word *organic*, such as clean air, water, and food, healthy bodies, or land that is rich in biological diversity.

- *Don't* attempt to prioritize the ideas expressed in the quality of life statement. Decisions will be tested toward all of them, and thus there is no need to order them. If you prioritize, you invite unnecessary conflict.

- *Don't* quantify the forms of production in any way. How much of anything you have to produce is a decision that should be tested. Nothing requiring testing should be in the holistic goal.

- The holistic goal should be formed by the people who will be living it, not by outsiders. As you learned in Chapter 8, those directly involved in management are the ones who must form the holistic goal because they will be responsible for making the decisions that take you toward it. Reexamine the whole you described to be sure no one was excluded who should have been included. If yours is a family business, don't forget to include the children, even younger children who can often be involved in management to some degree. Leaving them out generally has adverse effects on the business and/or the children sooner or later. Facilitators engaged to assist a group in forming its holistic goal need to be careful not to influence the holistic goal in any way. They can coach you and guide you and point out where you might be infringing on any of these guidelines, but that is all.

- Recognize that different levels of commitment will almost always exist when some of those who formed the holistic goal are somewhat removed from day-to-day management. This situation is rather common in organizations or corporations that operate with a board of directors, or in any business where absentee owners are involved. You cannot expect the commitment of these people to equal that of those who must live with and respond to management challenges on a daily basis.

Common Challenges

A problem many groups encounter when refining their holistic goal is a tendency to get so specific in accommodating everyone's needs and desires that the holistic goal takes pages to express. The holistic goal then becomes something you have to keep reading to remember, rather than something you carry inside you. Many groups have to go through this experience, however, in order to distil the essence of what it is they genuinely want to create, and they may struggle to maintain the momentum they initially had. Two of the greatest challenges in forming and refining a holistic goal lie first of all in the reluctance or inability many people have to express what they value most, and second, in trying to develop a holistic goal in a group that is not functioning well.

Expressing Personal Values

Common sense tells us that making a decision that is not in line with our values is illogical. But that is precisely what humans have done throughout history. A well-to-do family might buy a beautiful adobe home under the cottonwood trees in a rustic village along the Rio Grande because they are captivated by the beauty of the area—the charm of the small, country lanes, the grand old trees in the dry, desert country. Months later when it rains, their Mercedes is splashed with mud on returning home along one of those charming, tree-lined lanes, and the next week the family petitions the local government to pave the lanes. Little do they realize that in making the decision to have the lanes paved they are destroying much of the character of the village, which led to their moving there in the first place. Had their values—why they chose that place—featured in a holistic goal and all decisions been made toward that, they would have thought twice, and perhaps taken pleasure in washing their car three or four times a year.

Most of us want to live our lives in a manner that is pleasing and rewarding to us and based upon the things we value most. As one Holistic Management educator, Noel McNaughton, expressed it: "Since we are all striving for quality in our lives, we might as well figure out just what that is for us, and make sure that what we do delivers it." Unfortunately, that is easier said than done. Many people, even within closely knit families, find it difficult indeed to talk about what they value most, let alone write down a holistic goal that expresses how they want their lives to be.

Men, more so than women, in my experience, find it difficult to express what they truly want. We have spent countless hours trying to ascertain why this is—fear of commitment, peer pressure, upbringing in cultures where it was not okay for men to talk of feelings. Round and round the discussions go, never arriving at any conclusion other than that exposing one's deepest desires is a little like walking around naked, and people might laugh. However, as the first step in forming a holistic goal is to identify what is most important to you, and because the rest of the holistic goal builds from that, ways must and can be found to make this easier. The last chapter suggested a number of questions one could ask to start the discussion rolling.

Some businesses have developed mission statements that their owners insist express the values of the company and its employees and can serve as the quality of life statement in their holistic goal. In some cases this is true. However, all too often mission statements are written by the leader or a committee and are more or less imposed on everyone else. Such statements tend to express superficial, often politically correct values for public consumption, morale boosting, or marketing the company. Watch the performance of the employees, and their lack of commitment to the mission is obvious. By contrast, the wording in a holistic goal will initially be rough and unrefined, but if formed properly will have meaning for all who produce it and are going to live or work by it. I would not be prepared to devote my life to a mission statement created by someone else, but I would to a holistic goal I was involved in forming because it would reflect so much that was dear to me.

Many corporate leaders are now well aware that developing a corporate mission or vision statement is a shared responsibility that must include everyone concerned, and there is an abundance of literature that addresses ways to do this effectively. A number of books discuss ideas and techniques that would also prove helpful in forming a quality of life statement. Several are mentioned in the references at the end of this book.

Dealing with Dysfunction

There are no easy answers for the problem many experience in trying to form a holistic goal in groups that are not functioning well. I have grappled with it in a number of situations and have never yet found an easy solution. Rare indeed is the group that does not contain one or more individuals suffering to varying degrees from low self-esteem, a lack of trust, fear, or unexpressed anger, and more. And in my experience it only takes one such person in a group of ten or twenty to make the whole group dysfunctional to a degree. It can take a long time to locate the source(s) of trouble, and even when found, if others take the decision not to react, they *are* reacting. Thus, dysfunction in any group leads to confusion and frustration.

There are mainly two schools of thought on how to proceed in forming a holistic goal in these situations. One view is to do a lot of work beforehand on team building, trust building, conflict resolution, personal growth, and so on. If the dysfunctional people can be identified, they can be encouraged or required to get counseling and professional assistance. Once the team is more functional (less fearful, more trusting) then proceed with forming the holistic goal. The disadvantage of this approach is that it may be years before you have a well-functioning group and you may never get around to forming a holistic goal.

The other view is to form the holistic goal first, acknowledging upfront that the people in the group are not yet comfortable with one another. Then address the problems that almost certainly will emerge as you begin to manage holistically. Many of the issues, problems, and pressures that have promoted low trust, low self-esteem, conflict, and so on, may in fact be symptoms produced by the way decisions were made in the past. If this is so, then there is little point in treating the symptom with workshops on team building, conflict resolution, and so on without first eliminating the underlying cause.

Thus, I lean increasingly to forming the temporary holistic goal right away and beginning to make decisions toward it. If you are one of the leaders of such a group, you will be on thin ice until people begin to get beyond their fears and to trust the process and themselves. You may in fact lose some people. But you may likewise be surprised at how quickly their confidence grows.

In very large companies or communities, you generally have no option but to start by forming the holistic goal. A few years ago, I would have said this with some trepidation. Now, having worked with a number of very large groups, I have few reservations, particularly when people are in conflict, as long as you can get them to stop fighting long enough to form a temporary holistic goal, beginning with how they want their lives to be. It is essential, in such cases, that a facilitator be present who is knowledgeable in Holistic Management and also very helpful if that person has skills in conflict resolution and consensus building.

Some years ago I was asked by the U.S. Fish and Wildlife Service to provide a workshop on one of their refuges in South Dakota. Refuge managers were trying desperately to save a rapidly dwindling duck population but were getting little cooperation from people in the local community who shared use of the land. I asked the refuge managers to also invite these people.

On arriving, I found a rather hostile group of men who had left their families home expecting our session to be rather unpleasant. And initially it was. When I spoke to them about the need for a holistic goal in their community, they ridiculed the idea. They assured me that forming one would be an impossible task and suggested not too politely that I go back to where I had come from. Realizing that trying to get this group of men to talk about the things they valued would only invite more ridicule, I agreed with them that forming a holistic goal for their community would be impossible. I suggested they go home and continue fighting one another, wasting energy and money and getting nowhere. Alternatively, I said, they could stay and work with me for an hour or so and prove me wrong, rather then merely telling me I was wrong. This they agreed to do.

To start them off, I had them complete an exercise. I told them they were all going to die, and, by the look of them, within about twenty years. Knowing that to be the case, I asked them to be totally selfish in thinking of what they would like to see in their community if they were to come back a hundred years later. Each man took a piece of paper and went off on his own to complete the exercise.

When they handed in their sheets of paper, we recorded the contents on a blackboard for all to see. Not too surprisingly, you couldn't distinguish the comments of a rancher, farmer, or local business owner from those of the refuge staff. They apparently all wanted to see the same things. With minimal discomfort, we had brought out what these people most valued and could now create the first part of the holistic goal, the quality of life statement. We formed the rest of the temporary holistic goal without a murmur of disagreement over any aspect.

Wholes within Wholes

In Chapter 8 I mentioned that in larger or more diverse companies or organizations, defining the whole becomes an exercise in defining manageable wholes within wholes. Suppose you had defined two smaller wholes within a greater whole and that the decision makers in each had formed a holistic goal for their entity. How would you ensure that the three wholes remained cohesive and committed to the well-being of one another? What if one holistic goal included statements that conflicted with statements in another? How would you ensure that the channels of communication remained open? All of these questions are addressed if, when defining smaller wholes within a greater whole, you follow these guidelines:

1. *Make sure that some of the decision makers in the greater whole also make decisions in the smaller wholes,* and thus help to form the holistic goal in each entity. This crossover is essential for establishing the core val-

ues that unite the various wholes. And without it communication will be compromised.

2. *Create a statement of purpose for each smaller whole.* When you are forming a whole within a whole, you are doing so for a specific purpose and that needs to be expressed clearly (in writing) and understood by everyone. Each smaller whole has roles to serve and tasks to perform that support the greater whole, which the statement of purpose helps to clarify. When the decision makers in the smaller whole come to define their holistic goal, one or more of the forms of production they focus on will relate specifically to their statement of purpose.

3. *Make sure the future resource base described in each entity's holistic goal addresses client–supplier relationships.* The smaller wholes figure prominently in the resource base of the greater whole, and the greater whole figures strongly in theirs. *At one time or another each is a client or supplier of the other.* If you want those relationships to remain smooth and productive, then in forming their holistic goal, the decision makers in each whole will need to describe their behavior *as it will have to be* to maintain smooth and productive relationships.

4. *Clarify financial arrangements.* The money on hand or that can be generated in each whole will often overlap. In defining a smaller whole, for instance, some of the money on hand might include amounts made available by the greater whole. The smaller whole might in turn be generating cash from an enterprise made possible with expertise provided by the greater whole. If the greater whole invests capital (cash or assets) in the smaller whole and expects some sort of return on that capital, this needs to be clarified upfront. Numerous other financial transactions will take place within and among the various wholes, all of which will proceed more smoothly if some parameters are established at the outset.

Our own case helps to illustrate these points. The Center for Holistic Management includes three additional wholes that are managed separately within it: Holistic Management International, our for-profit subsidiary; the Africa Centre for Holistic Management, our sister organization based in Zimbabwe; and the Regional Training Centre (for English-speaking Africa) we jointly own with the Africa Centre. Figure 10-1 shows the relationship of these smaller wholes within the greater whole. The Regional Training Centre is linked administratively to the Africa Centre but engages in special projects and receives some funds directly from us (the Center), thus the overlap in the diagram's circles.

Our purpose in forming Holistic Management International (HMI) was to create an entity that would engage in activities providing a financial

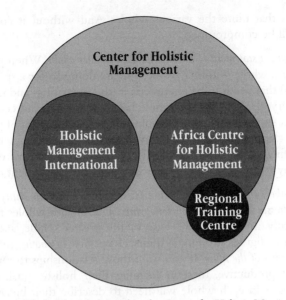

Figure 10-1 *The wholes within the Center for Holistic Management.*

return to the Center while expanding the awareness and practice of Holistic Management outside our traditional circles of influence. Some of the Center's decision makers serve on the board of HMI and took part in forming its holistic goal. The Center is currently a major supplier of expertise and contract labor to HMI.

HMI's holistic goal differs considerably from the Center's. The quality of life statement reflects the core values we share, but stands apart in its details because different people are involved. The forms of production have an entirely different focus because HMI is engaged in a different type of business. The statement of purpose, however, ensures that what HMI strives to produce enhances the Center's own efforts. The future resource base again has similarities in general but differs in the particulars. Despite these differences, HMI's holistic goal is not in conflict with the Center's. HMI's statement of purpose and the overlap of decision makers between the two entities has helped to ensure this.

The Africa Centre for Holistic Management (ACHM) was formed in 1992, with capital provided by the Center, for the purpose of expanding awareness and the practice of Holistic Management in Africa. As in HMI's case, some of the Center's decision makers serve on ACHM's board and helped to form its holistic goal. The Center again serves as a supplier of contract labor and expertise.

A few years ago we found it necessary to carve another whole, the Regional Training Centre, out of ACHM to facilitate its management.

ACHM's office and the Regional Training Centre are separated by 300 miles (a twelve-hour drive) and sporadic telephone service. The ACHM office is located in the capital city, Harare, where facilities are available for running an international organization. The Harare-based staff are chiefly involved in designing, implementing, and raising funds for a variety of educational programs; producing publications; and networking with other organizations. Much of the training they do, however, takes place at the Regional Training Centre, which includes not only all the facilities needed, but also a 7,000-acre "learning laboratory"—grasslands, woodlands, a large wildlife population, and a herd of cattle.

The Training Centre staff obviously required a holistic goal that was more specific to the enterprises they were managing—training facilities, a catering service, livestock, and wildlife—and to their circumstances. Among other things, the staff and their families were living on site.

When the staff of the Regional Training Centre formed their holistic goal, decision makers from the ACHM and the Center participated in forming the quality of life statement to ensure that the core values among us were truly shared, but left the on-site staff to describe other aspects relating to the day-to-day realities of their own living and working environment. It was much the same in describing their forms of production. We needed to make sure that everyone understood the meaning of the phrases that resulted, particularly those that addressed the statement of purpose. Because both ACHM and the Center are clients and suppliers in the Training Centre's whole, when it came to describing the future resource base, we also made a point of describing the qualities in our relationships with the Training Centre staff that were important to us. These were then reflected in their description.

Again, the Regional Training Centre's holistic goal reads quite differently from the Center's and ACHM's, but it is in line with both. And now it has as much meaning for the herdsmen and the catering manager working at the Training Centre as ACHM's holistic goal has for the secretary and the training director working in the Harare office.

If you heed the guidelines given you are unlikely to create holistic goals that conflict or lead to a lack of cohesion. As those in the smaller wholes make progress in achieving their holistic goals, they will move those in the greater whole closer to achieving theirs.

Conclusion

Form your holistic goal properly, as described in this and the previous two chapters, and even though you might muddle your way through the rest of Holistic Management, you will begin to see a change for the better. But muddle through forming the holistic goal—drop one or more parts of it, don't write it down, or don't bother to check for agreement—and do the rest to perfection, and you may eventually give up in despair.

Don and Randee Halladay, who struggled, along with their two children, to express the dreams and ideas that were gradually incorporated into their holistic goal, often talk about how worthwhile that struggle has been:

> After our first course in Holistic Management, we went home and set about working on our holistic goal. We each took a blank piece of paper and went to separate rooms to write down what was important to us. When we exchanged papers we found that each of us had made some nice-sounding, fairly general statements. It was a start, but we realized that before we could form a holistic goal as a team, each of us would have to have a clear idea of who we were and what our dearest values were.
>
> Without this individual clarity it was easy to accept what the other family members put forth as there were no real grounds for objection. There were also no grounds for ownership. We found that without a strong feeling of ownership in the holistic goal, the motivation to carry out decisions dissipated and general apathy set in.
>
> Those vague yearnings and desires written down in our first goal-writing session have been nurtured like a fine garden over the past six years until we finally have a holistic goal that speaks to our very being. When we share it with others, as we sometimes do, simply reading our intentions under Quality of Life evokes a deep emotional response in us. It was when our holistic goal truly reflected who we were that things started to happen. It was only after we got deadly serious about what we wanted and committed that to paper that we really started moving in the direction we wanted to go.[2]

Part IV

The Ecosystem That Sustains Us All

11

The Four Fundamental
Processes That Drive
Our Ecosystem

M any scientists today speak of different ecosystems—riparian ecosystems, grassland ecosystems, wet tropical forest ecosystems, and so on. I have personally resisted doing so because in managing them, too many people fail to remember that the boundaries that define an ecosystem are artificial. A riparian ecosystem, for instance, cannot be managed separately from the grassland or forest ecosystem surrounding it, but time and again I have found that in practice it is. Each of these ecosystems exists only in dynamic relationship to the other and as members of a greater ecosystem.

Although most ecologists appreciate this fact, so many managers don't that I find it more helpful to refer to one ecosystem, which encompasses everything on our planet and in its surrounding atmosphere, and probably more than that as well. Rather than distinguish lesser ecosystems within it, I have found it more practical to speak in terms of different *environments*, each of which functions through the same fundamental processes: water cycle, mineral cycle, community dynamics, and energy flow.

The word *environment* does not, in my experience, seem to promote the idea of boundaries to the same extent that the word *ecosystem* does. When people talk of managing a riparian *environment*, I mostly find that the boundary between the riparian area and its surrounding catchment becomes seamless in their minds, and this is reflected in their actions. The idea is reinforced, of course, by their focusing on the four fundamental processes that are common to all environments, and through which the greater ecosystem—our ecosystem—functions. Ultimately these four processes are the foundation that undergirds all human endeavor, all economies, all civilizations, and all life. That is why they appear near the top of the Holistic Management model, serving as the foundation on which the holistic goal rests.

Consciously modify any one of these processes, and you automatically change all of them in some way because in reality they are only different aspects of the same thing. It helps if you think of them as four different windows through which you can observe the same room, our ecosystem as it functions. You cannot have an effective water or mineral cycle or adequate energy flow without communities of living organisms, because you would then have nothing to convert sunlight to a form of energy useable by life. If you were managing a piece of land and wanted to change the water cycle to bring it closer to what you envisaged in your holistic goal, you would plan which tools to use and how to use them. But before going further, you would also consider how those tools would affect the mineral cycle, energy flow, and community dynamics.

To perceive the unity of our ecosystem requires no scientific training or specialized education. The spread of acid rain across wide areas, the buildup of carbon dioxide and the breakdown of ozone in the stratosphere, the worldwide implications of a nuclear power plant disaster all demonstrate that isolated ecosystems do not exist. However, it is less obvious that if we are to head off the environmental disasters looming ahead, all of us, not just scientists, or farmers, foresters, and others managing land, must begin to acquire a basic understanding of the fundamental processes through which our ecosystem functions. It will soon be unacceptable for any economist, politician, or corporate CEO to remain environmentally illiterate and thus ignorant of these processes and our connection to them.

You can read these words only because the sun shone on the leaves of a plant somewhere and the leaves converted that sunlight energy to food and oxygen. You ate the food and inhaled the oxygen, both of which enabled you to read these words and understand them. The living organisms in our ecosystem are responsible for keeping atmospheric gases in balance so that the air we breathe remains conducive to life as we know it. Oxygen, for instance, makes up 21 percent of the atmosphere's gases. If it were to increase by 4 percent, the world would be engulfed in flames; were it to decrease by 4 percent, nothing would ever burn. Any time oxygen is exposed to sunlight, it reacts chemically with other gases and binds to them, thus free oxygen is constantly being depleted. To ensure that atmospheric oxygen remains at 21 percent, living organisms—the whole complex of plants, animals, insects, and microorganisms—must keep supplying it. Bear in mind that there was no free oxygen to support humans and other higher life until living organisms, of one form or another, created it.

Tragically, we are now less aware of our dependence on a well-functioning ecosystem than we were in earlier, less sophisticated eras. Economists now have more leverage in the U.S. government than the farmers who formed it ever did. Accountants and lawyers serve as the chief advisors to the business world in which some corporations now wield larger budgets and more influence than many national governments. To be the specialists they are, most economists, accountants, and lawyers have considerable training in the narrow confines of their professions but less of an education in the broader sense, with some exceptions, ecological economists being one. As a consequence, most of these specialists exhibit little knowledge of the natural wealth that ultimately *sustains* nations, the quantity and quality of which is determined by how well our ecosystem functions.

All of us, however, have played a part in creating the environmental problems we now face simply because all of us at one time or another have made decisions that contributed to them. The decision to burn a field, poison the cockroaches, or buy a bar of soap often appears to be correct because the objective is accomplished. The field is cleared, the cockroaches are dead, and you are clean. But in the longer term, the decision can prove wrong, particularly in terms of how it affects the four processes through which our ecosystem functions.

If the whole you have defined includes land under your management, you must become intimately acquainted with water and mineral cycles, energy flow, and community dynamics; otherwise you will not be able to monitor the results of decisions you make that affect the land. Managing a piece of land in terms of these four processes may seem a daunting task, but it is simpler than first appears. An analogy provided by Sam Bingham, my coauthor on a previous book, helps to make the point. It is one he borrowed from the German writer Heinrich von Kleist who, sometime in the early 1800s, interviewed a famous puppeteer.

How, von Kleist wanted to know, can a normal person possibly manage the body and each individual limb of a marionette so it moves harmoniously like a real person instead of like a robot? How does the puppeteer learn that when he moves the puppet's leg forward, he also has to tilt its head slightly, bend the torso, and shift both arms in opposite directions? The puppeteer answered that von Kleist had not understood the actual challenge, which was both simpler and more elegant. Of course, no human could produce natural gestures by pulling any number of individual strings. No matter how skilled the puppeteer, the result would still look mechanical. On the other hand, a skillfully designed marionette had a center of gravity, and simply moving that center of gravity would bring about all the other gestures automatically, just as a human when taking a step automatically moves all the other parts of his body to stay in balance.

In Holistic Management, the four fundamental processes are the center of gravity. The land manager who formulates a holistic goal that describes a future landscape in terms of these four processes will find that in moving *them* in the direction of that vision, the land will come right.

12

Water Cycle: The Circulation of Civilization's Life Blood

As far as we know there is a fixed amount of water on the planet that constantly cycles from the atmosphere to the surface and back to the atmosphere. Much of this water is seawater, too salty for most uses until it evaporates and returns as rain or snow. Some of it becomes locked for vast periods underground or in polar icecaps before rejoining the cycle. But most water remains constantly on the move, becoming now liquid, now ice, now vapor.

Because water is fast becoming a limiting factor to the growth of cities, agriculture, and industry, there is an urgent need to understand how it cycles and thus becomes available for use. I have drawn the basic pattern of the water cycle in figure 12-1. It shows the various paths taken by water falling on the land as rain, hail, and snow. Some evaporates straight away off soil and plant surfaces back into the atmosphere. Some runs off into streams, rivers, dams, lakes, and eventually the sea before evaporating. Some penetrates the soil, and of that a portion sticks to soil particles. The rest flows on down to underground supplies. There it may remain for millennia or find its way back to the surface in river bank seepage, springs, and bogs, or possibly through deep-rooted plants that pick it up and transpire it back into the air, or in some cases leak it out through surface roots that shallow rooted grasses take up and transpire. Of water held by soil particles, a small portion remains tightly held, but the bulk is either attracted to drier particles or drawn away by plant roots and transpired. Thus, one way or another all the water eventually cycles between earth and air.

Because the time water spends in the soil is critical to the growth and reproduction of plant life, which in turn is essential to most animal life,

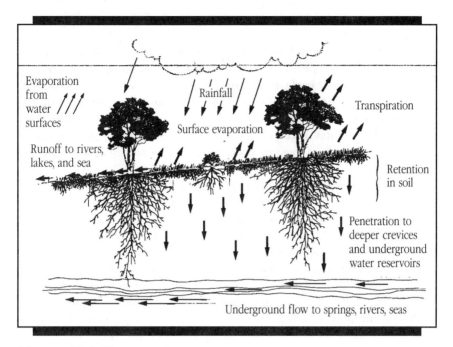

Evaporation from water surfaces

Rainfall

Transpiration

Surface evaporation

Runoff to rivers, lakes, and sea

Retention in soil

Penetration to deeper crevices and underground water reservoirs

Underground flow to springs, rivers, seas

Figure 12-1 *The water cycle.*

including humans, it is important to understand this stage of the water cycle in more detail.

Any water that penetrates the soil will be strongly attracted to drier soil particles. This is why, after a while, no sharp edge between wet and dry soil remains, but rather a gradient from wetter to drier particles. The water will keep moving until all of it has adhered to soil particles or passed on to underground reservoirs of free water. Short of drying soil in the sun or in an oven, it is hard to remove the final film of water from a soil particle. As water is drawn away from a particle by any means, that particle tightens its hold on whatever remains. However, particles hold each added increment of water more feebly than the last, just as you, if mugged on the street with an armload of parcels, will defend the last one you hold better than the first ones taken.

Plants absorb water and the essential nutrients dissolved in it through root hairs. They can do this as long as their ability to draw water can overcome the grip on the water exercised by soil particles. As drying particles yield less and less water, the plant slows its growth rate. Eventually it begins to wilt in the heat of the day or curl its leaves to conserve moisture as its ability to obtain water from the soil is reduced. Much can be done, however, to retain more moisture in the soil and thus extend the time during which plants can grow vigorously before wilting point is reached.

To sustain humans and the maximum amount of life, in all but wetlands and true deserts, we need to maintain what we call an *effective water cycle*. In an effective water cycle, plants make maximum use of rainfall or melting snow. Little evaporates directly off the soil. Any water that runs off the soil tends to do so slowly and carries little organic matter or soil with it. A good air-to-water balance exists in the soil, enabling plant roots to absorb water readily, as most plants require oxygen as well as water around their roots to grow.

In a *noneffective water cycle*, plants get minimal opportunity to use the full amount of precipitation received. Much is lost to surface evaporation or runoff, and what soaks in is often not readily available to plants because air and water are not in balance. Too much water, and the soil becomes waterlogged. This can occur on rangelands, croplands, and of course in all wetlands, where an impervious layer of subsoil prevents the downward movement of excess water. The water actually displaces air in the soil, and thus only plants adapted to a lack of oxygen around their roots can grow. Some, such as mangroves, which grow around coastal wetlands, surround themselves with roots thrust up a foot or more above the water in order to breathe.

As a sugar cane farmer in Africa, I experienced firsthand just how critical proper aeration can be. I had my crops under overhead irrigation and was told by the local extension service to plant my cane in hollows between high ridges made with a ridging implement. I questioned this advice and sowed a test plot of cabbages claimed by the seed company to produce two-pound heads.

I got the answer I sought very quickly but let the crop mature in order to sell it. Heads planted in the furrows averaged one pound. Those on flat ground averaged two pounds. Those planted on ridge tops averaged eight pounds. Clearly several factors operate in such a situation, but most obvious was the fact that the soil in the ridges was never waterlogged and always well aerated; in the ridges the water cycle was always effective.

An effect very similar to waterlogging—too much water and not enough air—can also occur when soil is exposed and has become sealed over with a crust, or "cap." This allows some water to eventually soak in but not enough air. Once the cap is broken, the situation can be remedied as I'll explain shortly.

When forming your holistic goal you should describe the water cycle on the land you manage as it will have to be functioning in the future to sustain what you want to produce on that land. If you are not actually managing land, but merely describing the land surrounding the community in which you live, this is not imperative, but it is desirable. In most cases you will want to have an effective water cycle, but perhaps not everywhere. You may be dealing with a wetland, or perhaps rice paddies, or with a semi-desert plant, or animal species that might require a landscape produced by a less effective water cycle. If you are managing such a piece of land, the careful application of available tools (see Chapters 16–23) and constant monitoring should produce this.

Whether or not you are actually managing land, it is important that you have a deeper understanding of effective and noneffective water cycles and what produces them in different environments.

Effective Water Cycles

Most land managers know the average rainfall their land receives and manage accordingly. Unfortunately, averages often mean little, particularly in the more brittle environments. In areas of erratic precipitation, as these environments are, the average seldom occurs. Nearly every year the rain will be higher or lower than average. Even when it is average the distribution can be very different from the last year of average rainfall. Fortunately, an effective water cycle tends to even out the erratic nature of the rainfall in any environment by making rain that does fall more effective.

Effective rainfall is that which soaks in and becomes available to plant roots, insects, and microorganisms or that replenishes underground supplies with very little subsequently evaporating from the soil surface. To make precipitation as effective as possible means producing a cycle that directs most water either out to the atmosphere *through plants* or down to underground supplies. In all the more brittle areas of the world where I have worked, rarely have I seen an effective water cycle. Typically of, say, 14 inches (350 mm) of rain received, only 5 or 6 inches (125 or 150 mm) is actually effective. In very rough figures it takes approximately 600 tons of water to produce one ton of vegetation, so one cannot afford to waste any of the rain that falls.

In less brittle environments, effective water cycles tend to be more common simply because it is so much more difficult to create and to maintain vast areas of bare soil. However, where soils have lost a large proportion of their organic matter, they are unable to absorb much water, which runs off, and a less effective water cycle results. This problem is compounded on croplands, where much of the soil surface is deliberately exposed, and kept exposed, leading to even more runoff, and, depending on the humidity, higher surface evaporation rates.

Capping

From these remarks you can see that the nature of the soil surface is vital to the water cycle. On bare and exposed ground, the direct impact of raindrops tends to destroy soil crumb structure.* The amount of damage is actually governed by the size and velocity of the drop. Evidence of this shows up on bare ground under tall trees as large drops tend to come off the leaves and to reach terminal velocity in about 22.5 feet (6.75 meters) of fall.

When raindrop impact breaks down the surface crumb structure, it frees the organic and lightweight material to wash away while heavier fine particles settle and seal, or cap, the soil. The importance of surface crumb structure to water penetration is easily demonstrated by comparing a bowl of wheat grains and one of flour. Neither has a hard cap at the outset, but one has large particles, and the other has lost that structure. Pour a jug of water on each bowl and watch. Most of the water soaks into the grains, but it seals the surface of the flour immediately and runs off.

A capped surface not only reduces water penetration but also prevents oxygen from getting into the soil and carbon dioxide from getting out. This in turn leads to a number of problems, one of which is nutrient deficiencies that show up in plants and the animals that feed on them, even though the nutrients may be abundant in the soil. The air imbalance appears to affect the activity of the millions of soil organisms responsible for releasing nutrients in a form plants can use.

The initial capping is subsequently enhanced by a vast array of microorganisms and fungi that develop in it, providing more strength. You can see this if you lift a bit of the capped layer and inspect it closely. Even very sandy soils will develop a cap with this form, although to a lesser degree. Some soils, particularly in the tropics where there is no freezing and thawing action to loosen the soil, develop a cap so hard it is difficult to break without a knife or some other hard object. If you tap such a severely capped soil with your fingers you will hear a hollow, drum-like sound created by the air space beneath it.

It is well known that soil cover protects the soil surface from the impact of raindrops and thus preserves the crumb structure and prevents capping. Soil cover generally comes in two forms: low-growing plants that intercept rainfall so that drops hit the ground with less energy; and dead, prone plant material, or litter, that not only stops rain from hitting the surface, but also effectively slows the flow of water across the land. (Water can flow quite

---

*Crumb structure refers to presence of aggregated soil particles held together with "glue" provided by decomposing organic matter. The space around each crumb provides room for water and air, and this in turn promotes plant growth.

fast between plants where no litter impedes it.) Snow also provides soil cover and can help to lay dead standing plant material on the ground for faster decay.

In less brittle environments, maintaining soil cover is seldom a problem as plant spacings are naturally close and tend to hold litter in place and also because plant life establishes quickly on exposed surfaces. It is almost impossible to create thousands of acres of ground with a high percentage of bare soil between plants unless you use machinery and herbicides constantly, as many crop farmers do.

The more brittle the environment, the more the opposite is true. Bare soil develops easily between plants and over millions of acres. Plant spacings tend to be wider apart, allowing wind and water to carry litter away.

Creating an Effective Water Cycle

To enter the soil, water must first penetrate the soil surface, and this depends on the rate at which it is applied and the porosity of the surface in particular. Management tools that break up a capped surface or increase the soil's organic content and crumb structure speed up penetration. Tools that create a surface that slows the flow of water slow the rate of application and allow more water to soak in before running off. A loosened, rough surface or one covered by old, prone plant material achieves this.

More than any other single factor an effective water cycle requires management that maintains soil cover, followed by organic matter, aeration, and drainage, the last often more a challenge in less brittle croplands and pastures than in forests or on the more brittle rangelands. As soil cover is the key to an effective water cycle, let's first look at the management tools available to us that can either destroy or promote it.

In the less brittle environments there is almost no tool whose application causes soil exposure over large areas other than technology—the repeated use of machinery or herbicides on croplands, as mentioned. In the more brittle environments, however, which cover most of the earth's land surface, a one-time use of machinery or a dose of herbicide can cause the majority of the surface to remain exposed for years. On rangelands, forests, and in national parks that lie closer to the very brittle end of the scale, millions of acres of soil have been exposed between the plants through the application of three tools: rest (partial or total), fire (periodically), and to a lesser degree overgrazing (the tool of grazing misapplied). No other tools available can expose soil on such an extensive scale. Because these three tools are applied nearly universally in the more brittle environments, the staggering amount of bare ground comes as no surprise. Even nomadic herders used the same tools before being forcibly settled in various development projects. They tended to overgraze fewer plants because of constant movement but still partially rested the soil and used fire much too frequently.

In environments leaning toward the nonbrittle end of the scale, rest (partial or total) is the main tool available that can *produce* soil cover. On croplands, farmers use rest to increase soil cover by leaving crop residues on the soil surface and using minimum tillage. On land put to other uses, other managers do much the same. To increase soil cover, they disturb the soil as little as possible, if at all.

In more brittle environments, the only tool that can provide adequate soil cover over large areas is animal impact. On both rangelands and croplands animals can be used to trample down old standing vegetation or crop residues to provide litter. Their hooves can be used to break up bare, capped soil surfaces, preparing a seedbed in which new plants can germinate. On the very hard-capped soils in the tropics, mentioned earlier, large hoofed animals are only able to break up soil surface capping progressively or when concentrated in large numbers at very high densities.

Aeration, organic matter, and drainage all somewhat depend on soil cover. If the soil surface remains bare, no matter what type of environment, aeration, organic matter, and drainage will be adversely affected. All three are also affected by the root structure of the plants inhabiting an area. If roots are healthy, they will help to aerate the soil, to add to the organic matter present in it, and to pump a greater amount of water upward. Root health is damaged when plants are overgrazed (in any environment), but it is enhanced when plants are properly grazed (in any environment). Most of the damage occurs, however, in the more brittle environments due either to overgrazing or to *overresting* of perennial grass plants whose network of shallow roots are the main soil-stabilizing force in moderate- to low-rainfall areas.

Aeration, organic matter, and drainage also depend on the activity of small animal life forms in the soil. While there are billions of organisms living in the soil that we have yet to identify, let alone understand the roles they play, we do know quite a lot about some of them. Earthworms, for instance, play a vital role in developing good soil structure and aeration. A number of studies in several countries have compared similar soils on adjacent sites with and without various species of earthworms and the results in every case suggest that when earthworms are present there is greater water penetration and retention. To encourage earthworm populations you should avoid plowing or the use of pesticides and ensure that litter covers the soil surface.

When you have an effective water cycle, floods and droughts become fewer and less severe, even where rainfall is very erratic. Those floods that do occur, as they will in very high-rainfall years or years of rapid snow melt, tend to rise more gradually and to subside more slowly. The floodwaters tend to be clear, as they carry far less soil and debris. In one such flood in Africa I was working from a canoe and dropped my pen into the water. Although the river was flooding far over its banks I was able to dive and retrieve my pen which was still visible under several feet of water.

The effects of droughts that do occur, as they will in a year when there is little or no rainfall in the growing season, are far less severe because moisture received in the previous year has likely been stored in the soil, and any received during the drought penetrates the soil surface more readily. In general, an effective water cycle will ensure that far more water is available over a longer time for plant growth. Plants will start to grow earlier in the growing season and more profusely, and will continue growing longer, even into the fairly long dry periods that can be present in the growing months. And there is of course far more water available to be released gradually to stream flow, bogs, springs, and underground aquifers.

What would it be worth to you as a rancher, farmer, or even a city planner concerned about urban water supplies, to be able to double your rainfall? No doubt quite a lot. Fortunately, with a little understanding, you can double the *effectiveness* of your rainfall. And this, as I illustrated with the cabbage plants I grew, has an even greater effect than doubling the rainfall.

Noneffective Water Cycles

When you have a noneffective water cycle, droughts occur more frequently and are much more severe because so much water is lost to evaporation or runoff. Good plant growth only takes place in short bursts, often a few days after rain. Soon thereafter the plants begin to wilt and growth comes to a standstill until it rains again. Plants start growing later in a new season since moisture from the previous season has not been stored in the soil. At the end of the growing season plants stop growth earlier, often before temperature would slow or stop growth, simply because no moisture remains in the soil. Thus, on rangelands or pastures far less forage is produced in the year, and on croplands crop yields are less than they could be.

When rainfall is high or snow melts rapidly, floods often occur, but when you have a noneffective water cycle, they are more severe than they would be otherwise. This is certainly the case when you have large areas over which a high proportion of the ground is bare, as you do on many croplands and rangelands. The greater the amount of bare ground, the higher the rate of water runoff—bare soil can shed more than half the water falling on it. If 30 inches (750 mm) of rain were to fall on an acre (0.405 hectares) of land, that would total 814,625 gallons (3,038 cubic meters) of water. Over a million acres (405,000 hectares), which is a more representative scale in the context of the more brittle rangelands, that figure would be over 814 *billion* gallons (over 3 *billion* cubic meters) of water. If half of that were to run off, it would constitute an amazing flood. Even in the less brittle Midwest of the United States there are millions of acres of cropland that contain a high proportion of bare ground. You won't see it, though, unless you get out of your car, walk into the fields, and look straight down at the soil. Even though a forest of corn plants may tower above you, over 80 percent of the soil is often bare.

If the amount of water lost through runoff is alarming, the amount lost through evaporation in the more brittle environments is equally or more so. Some time ago I visited a research station in Pakistan that had received heavy rains that wet the bare sandy soil more than a meter (three feet) deep. When the researchers measured again a few days later, they were amazed to find no trace of moisture left.

Far too little attention is paid to the amount of water lost to the cycle through soil surface evaporation. I was once asked to participate in a lengthy symposium in Nevada to which experts on various aspects of water conservation and management had been invited. Each expert was to provide suggestions on how to deal with the serious water shortages developing in the state's fast-growing cities. Throughout the day not one expert mentioned the greatest source of water loss in Nevada, or what to do about it. That of course was the high rate of evaporation occurring from the exposed soil that is visible over nearly all of the state. If that water were to remain in the soil, more plants would grow, covering more soil, and more water would seep into springs, rivers, and eventually down to aquifers, thus adding to the supply available to the state's cities.

A lot of the ignorance about water cycles in the more brittle environments is understandable because few people pay attention to the tremendous amount of soil that is exposed between plants. Even scientists assume that rangelands in such a state are "natural." But humans, rather than nature, created these landscapes when humans learned to use fire and spear, eliminated most of the wild grazers, and domesticated a few.

Because so little attention is paid to the amount of bare ground between plants, which adds up to billions of acres in the world's more brittle environments, and because the amount of evaporation this leads to is often ignored, I like to use a simple example to illustrate the impact this has on the water cycle. Imagine an area of rangeland in a more brittle environment that receives a rainfall of one inch (25 mm) per month over the next three months. The land is level and light regular showers produce no runoff. In figure 12-2 we have an effective water cycle on the left. The soil is covered and plants have healthy roots and are plentiful. On the right we have a noneffective water cycle where there are fewer, less healthy plants and a great deal of bare soil between them.

Assume that the first inch (25 mm) of rain has fallen and all the water in both cases has soaked into the soil down to level A. We have an inch

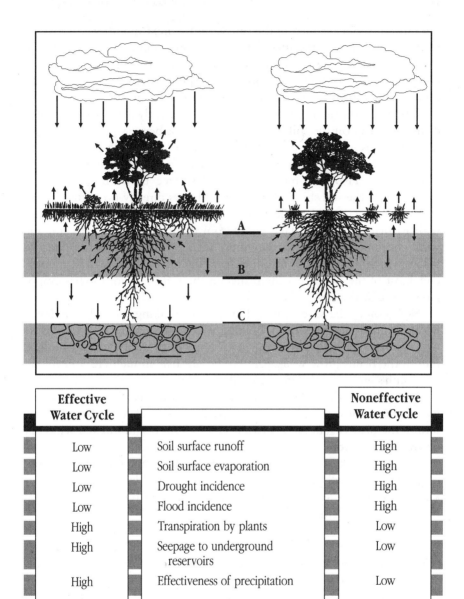

Effective Water Cycle		Noneffective Water Cycle
Low	Soil surface runoff	High
Low	Soil surface evaporation	High
Low	Drought incidence	High
Low	Flood incidence	High
High	Transpiration by plants	Low
High	Seepage to underground reservoirs	Low
High	Effectiveness of precipitation	Low

Figure 12-2 *Effective and noneffective water cycles. Over three months, three rainfalls of one inch (25 mm) each will wet soil layers all the way down to level C on the left where the water cycle is effective. The excess will trickle through decomposing rock fragments to join underground supplies. In the noneffective water cycle on the right, most of the moisture will evaporate after each rainfall and will never wet soil layers deeper than level A. Ground water will receive no recharge at all this season.*

(25 mm) of water retained in the soil. Over the next month we receive no further rain and the sun shines, temperatures are good, and plants grow. On the left they grow well, drawing out half an inch (12.5 mm) of water in the process. No further water losses take place, and by the end of the month half an inch (12.5 mm) of water still remains in the soil.

The plants on the right have their roots in poorly aerated soil because of the hard cap on the soil surface and have not been as productive. They have grown as well as they could, using a quarter inch (6.25 mm) of water. Theoretically then, three-quarters of an inch (18.75 mm) should remain at month's end. However, most of the soil surface between the plants is exposed, and the sun shines and the wind blows directly on it, thoroughly drying the surface soil particles. The surface particles, directly in contact with particles below, can take water from them, and they do. As sun and wind continue to dry them, they draw yet more water from the particles below, which in turn draw moisture from the next layer down. At month's end, most of the water that the plants on the right did not use has evaporated through the soil surface.

Now comes the second inch (25 mm) of soaking rain. On the left it flows through particles already holding water and penetrates to level B, so we now have an inch and a half (37.5 mm) in the soil. During the next month the plants grow well, again taking out half an inch (12.5 mm), but by month's end an inch (25 mm) still remains.

The water on the right has soaked in, but the dry particles near the surface retained most of it, so it again only reaches level A. In the following month the plants again use a quarter inch (6.5 mm), and sun and wind dry up the rest as before.

When the same processes repeat after the third rain, the inch (25 mm) of precipitation will penetrate all the way to level C in the left-hand picture, and there the excess trickles through larger decomposing rock fragments to join underground supplies and/or eventually stream flow.

The water on the right has still not pushed beyond level A. Groundwater will receive no recharge at all this season. The soil has only an inch (25 mm) of water to carry plants through the long dry season to follow and all of that will be lost soon through plant use and surface evaporation. Growth could well end before reduced temperatures limit it. In the following season, when temperatures rise again, growth will have to await rainfall. People attempting to manage land such as this will say that "the rains aren't what they used to be."

The soil on the left has almost two inches (50 mm) of water in it at the start of the nongrowing season. Plants will continue to grow until temperatures fall. The following year they will still have moisture enough for an early start when the weather warms, even though rain may not fall for another month.

I have deliberately devoted considerable space in this chapter to water cycles in the more brittle environments simply because these environments cover the majority of the earth's land surface and they are characterized by noneffective water cycles. Some of the world's largest cities also lie in these environments and are rapidly running out of water because of noneffective water cycles on the land surrounding them. The planners of one such city attempted to maximize the amount of water that flowed into the dams supplying their city by encouraging a high level of overgrazing in the dams' catchment area. They rightly observed that by keeping vegetation off the hills more water would run off into the dams. And so it did, carrying a large amount of silt with it. Before too long that silt is going to fill those dams and the city will lose its water supply altogether, as well as its dam sites.

This problem is an ancient one. The first large dam ever built (by humans) was located on the Arabian peninsula near the city of Marib, reputedly mentioned in the Koran as the original Garden of Eden. Built in 400 B.C., the dam filled with silt and burst. It was rebuilt in 200 B.C., but burst again soon after as the dam bed was still full of silt. The remains of the dam wall are still visible today and the silt behind it remains, the river that fed the dam having carved a deep channel through it.

Dam sites can really be used only once. So, before we make use of them we should first ensure that the water cycle in their catchment area is effective. Ironically, in the more brittle environments noneffective water cycles so reduce the amount of water available to cities that citizens demand dams be built. And we build them, rendering the few available sites useless for future generations who might in fact get beyond our ignorance and begin to produce more effective water cycles.

There is much that cities in these environments can and need to do to improve the water cycle within their city limits, as I'll cover later, but unless something is done to put the water cycle right on the land surrounding them, they are doomed.

Consequences of a Noneffective Water Cycle

To summarize, a noneffective water cycle results in the following to varying degrees:

- Increased runoff wherever the land slopes. More water runs faster and carries more silt. Trickles join to form rivulets, and these form streams that lift rivers into full and damaging floods. Noneffective water cycles lead to increasingly frequent and severe floods.

- Decreased water penetration and increased losses through evaporation that increase the frequency and severity of droughts, particularly in more brittle environments. Commonly both scientists and lay people conclude that "the rains aren't what they used to be."

- Less forage or crop production on the land in all years, together with greater instability and fluctuation in forage/crop volume.

- Slower plant growth rates in all conditions, which leads to reduced production.

- Falling groundwater supplies; drying up of springs, bogs, and wells. Pumping of groundwater that is not being replenished, of course adds to this problem.

- Unstable rivers, prone to flash flooding and intermittent flow. Pools silt up.

- Silted dams and eroding catchments.

- Detrimental effects on the other ecosystem processes.

Many countries have undertaken extensive engineering feats to overcome problems caused by noneffective water cycles. But no extravagant technology will ever achieve what simply putting the water cycle right does at a fraction of the cost. When we intervene with our earth moving, we are dealing with water that has already started to flow. Dams hold only a fraction of it. Likewise contour ridges serve only to spill the water on a more gradual gradient into the drainage pattern. The "keyline" contouring system developed in Australia by Keith Yeomans at least spills that water back toward the ridges to allow more time for it to soak in instead of leading it into the drainage and thus off the land.[1] Far better than any of these interventions is to prevent the loss of water from the land at the outset.

How Do You Recognize a Noneffective Water Cycle?

The signs of a noneffective water cycle are basically identical across the brittleness scale, but most easily seen toward the very brittle end where noneffective water cycles are more common. On conventionally managed croplands, even in less brittle environments, excessive soil exposure, breakdown of organic matter and crumb structure, and a lack of diversity in root structure and depth combine to produce water cycles that are less effective than they should be.

First and foremost, get out and walk on the land. The earliest possible warnings of a noneffective water cycle are evident on the surface on which the rain is going to fall. There is no need for expensive gimmicks or satellite photos to tell you when things have gone wrong. You want the information early on when it is easier to correct the situation.

When you look at the soil surface, get down and look between the plants at their bases. Is the soil bare or covered with fallen plant material? Bare soil means that any rainfall received is going to be less effective than if the soil were covered. This will give you the first warning.

Other signs include:

- Litter banks where litter has been washed and caught against vegetation.

- Signs of water flow, such as rills, exposed grass roots sticking up into the air in the spaces between plants, silt deposits, coarse pebble layers left on the bare surface.

- Rivers that once flowed all year now only flowing in periodic floods and not at all through the nongrowing or dry seasons.

- Water levels lowering in wells or springs drying up.

The evidence of poor water cycles is so obvious in the more brittle environments that many people, perhaps most people, assume that a poor water cycle is natural. In the mid-1980s scientists in Zimbabwe were puzzled when their measurements showed a 40 percent increase in water flow over the Victoria Falls since 1948, with no change in rainfall. Having done some of my early work in the catchment areas of the Zambezi River, which feeds the Falls, I have no doubt that this was due to the damaged water cycle existing in those catchments.

Some years ago in Zimbabwe a rancher who had just received an award for "The Best Managed Ranch of the Year" by the Natural Resources Board asked me for a second opinion as he wasn't sure that his ranch was really as good as the officials said. The ranch was stocked at a very low level to avoid overgrazing and was being "maintained as a grassland" by the use of fire. I ran a number of transects in the best grassland on the ranch. These showed that 97 percent of the soil was bare and eroding. Because the bare ground lay between tall grass plants, which at a glance appeared to be a sea of healthy vegetation, it wasn't visible unless you looked down and examined the soil surface itself.

In another instance I was asked to assist a rancher in Namibia whose land was being expropriated by the government of the day at what he thought was an unfair price. His land was being compared to a ranch that authorities claimed in court had no trace of erosion and in fact was managed to perfection. Court was adjourned for me to spend a day on the perfectly managed ranch taking random measurements and photographs. Bare and eroding soil dominated the ground between grass plants; 95 percent of the perfectly managed ranch was in fact bare ground.

These cases are not unusual. I believe we would find serious erosion anywhere in a more brittle environment where land is either rested or managed under prolonged grazing with animals at low numbers and widely scattered. What often appears as a sea of grass has fooled many an observer into thinking all was well. Typically, rangelands in the western United States are classified as being in "good condition," even though more than 50 percent of the soil is bare.

Water Cycles in Cities

The importance of water cycles does not apply only to rangelands, croplands, pastures, forests, and fisheries, but also to cities, industry, and all of humankind's activities that depend on good healthy water supplies from healthy catchments. Urban dwellers are generally unaware of the importance of an effective water cycle even when forced to evacuate their homes, schools, factories, and businesses as floodwaters swirl over valiant efforts to shore up the banks of the local river. Or when they face water rationing or ever-rising water bills.

Apart from the need to be concerned about the water cycle on the land surrounding their cities, urban residents also must concern themselves with the water cycle within their cities. Simply by increasing the effectiveness of the water cycle in urban areas, we can decrease the amount of water that has to be transported to them, at great cost, and decrease the vast amounts of water that go to waste.

Look down on most cities as though you were a falling raindrop and you will find that about all you can land on are impervious roofs, pavements, and roads. Even the lawns would likely be chemically manicured biological deserts with roots amassed in a few inches of topsoil and sterile subsoil below. Because there are so few places rain can soak into, the runoff from cities is extremely high. A mid-size city spread over 50 square miles (130 square km)—about 7 miles (11 km) long by 7 miles wide—will have to deal with 26 billion gallons (98 billion liters) of water if it receives 30 inches (762 mm) of rain. Very little of this water is utilized where it falls, but rather is channeled into storm sewers and emptied into lakes, streams, or wetlands. Much of this runoff includes excessive amounts of toxic substances—pesticides and other chemicals used in households and gardens and stored on vacant lots, in garbage dumps, or industrial yards. These contaminants are returned to us in the food we eat and sometimes in the water we drink. Runoff from urban areas can also destabilize river banks, adding silt to the flow that damages towns, croplands, bridges, and other structures downstream.

Rather than take advantage of the precipitation that falls on the city itself, city planners instead tap underground sources or transport water from dams, lakes, and rivers, with little consideration of the long-term consequences or costs. Imagine what would happen if a city were to make all building, road, and pavement codes meet standards that more closely imitated nature's water cycle. Roofs, for example, could be catching water and running it into cisterns for use in homes and offices, thus saving billions of gallons from being pumped into the city at great cost.

I once had a home on a small island in the West Indies where our only water supply was what we could catch off our roof and store in a cistern. The water kept beautifully year round, aided by frogs that helped to keep it clean. The water tasted better than any I've ever had in a city. The air pollution in some urban areas might make roof water undrinkable, but still useable as "gray water."

Paving and road materials that allow the immediate penetration and absorption of the water falling on them could be utilized. Porous concrete blocks honeycombed with gravel provide a highly permeable, nonslip surface that's being used on some city streets and walkways. There are numerous alternatives. Roads and parking lots could be periodically treated with oil-eating bacteria so that less rubber and oil are carried into underground aquifers and rivers. Many other strategies and technologies exist or are under development that would enable rain to soak in or be utilized where it falls. In the end we will be forced to make use of them to mimic nature in our cities. The sooner we learn to do so, the better.

Conclusion

In terms of your holistic goal, you can see why it is important to consider how the water cycle functions on the land surrounding your community, even when you do not manage that land yourself. If your community, town, or city is prone to flooding or water shortages, the water cycle is probably not functioning well on the surrounding land. Having read this chapter, you now know what land generally looks like when the water cycle *is* functioning well. Bare ground is covered in vegetation, for instance, and rivers and streams run clear—even when in flood—because soil, rather than being carried into them, stays where it forms.

If you *are* managing land, you will need to describe how the water cycle must function on it if you are to sustain the forms of production specified in your holistic goal. In most cases, you will want to describe what the land looks like when the water cycle is effective, and if you are managing larger tracts of land, will need to include separate descriptions for the different land types—croplands, rangelands, riparian areas, woodlands, and so on. If you want to maintain a wetland environment, you will in effect be describing a noneffective water cycle where soils remain waterlogged.

13

Community Dynamics: The Ever-Changing Patterns in the Development of Living Communities

From the moment living organisms establish residence on bare or recently disturbed soil, a rock, or in a newly formed pool of water, things are never the same again. Change begets change as the organisms interact with one another and with their microenvironment (the environment immediately surrounding them). Eventually a complex community* made up of a great many life forms develops and functions as a whole in an apparently stable manner.

Once any community has reached the highest level of development achievable in any environment, be that environment grassland, river, lake, coral reef, or forest, it can appear to remain in that stable state for many years. However, closer inspection reveals a kaleidoscope of changing patterns even within the mature community. Species composition, numbers and age structure, as well as numerous other factors are in a constant state of flux. Individual plants and animals are continually dying and being replaced, and varying weather conditions promote the well-being of some species and diminish that of others. Because communities remain dynamic at every stage, we refer to the process of their never-ending development as *community dynamics*.

Precisely what is taking place in any community at any one time is currently beyond human understanding and may always remain so. It is only relatively recently with the invention of high-power electron microscopes, that up to a billion or more organisms were found to be present in a cubic inch of soil or a spoonful of water. Most of these organisms have not even

---

*The collection of organisms that exists in any locality.

120

been named, and their relationships to one another and how they function within a community of organisms, which is far more important, is barely understood and difficult to imagine.[1]

In *The Redesigned Forest*, ecologist Chris Maser offers a glimpse of the complexity inherent in a northern temperate forest when he describes a relationship that exists among squirrels, fungi, and trees. The squirrels feed on the fungi, then assist in their reproduction by dropping fecal pellets containing viable fungal spores onto the forest floor. There new fungal colonies establish. Tree feeder roots search out the fungi and form an association with them that enables the tree roots to increase their nutrient uptake. The fungi in turn derive sustenance from the roots.[2]

Of the four ecosystem processes, community dynamics is the most vital. Water and minerals cannot cycle effectively and solar energy cannot flow through life unless plants of some form—algae to trees—first convert sunlight to useable energy for life and cover the soil. For this reason it is imperative that we learn to maintain healthy biological communities whether they be associated with grasslands, forests, rivers, lakes, coral reefs, or oceans.

Although we still have much to learn about the dynamics of living communities, a few general principles have emerged based on the work of a great many ecologists and on the four key insights. Those mentioned below do not make up a comprehensive list, but they are the ones that bear most directly on day-to-day management decisions. (My apologies to any ecologists offended by my simplification of some very complex concepts.)

There Are No Hardy Species

If we take *hardy* to mean that an organism is able to withstand very adverse conditions, then there are few hardy species. All living things are adapted to specific environments in which they can establish and thrive. Even though we may label a certain plant or animal "hardy" there is no evidence that it is. You might think that a teenager from one of the toughest neighborhoods in Chicago is hardy because he thrives in an environment of crime, gangs, guns, and violence. But place him with a hunter-gatherer bushman family in the Kalahari desert and he probably would not survive a season. Take a teenage bushman out of the Kalahari and place him in a four-star hotel with hot showers, television, air-conditioning, and three meals a day, and he would fail to thrive. The same applies to those so-called hardy plants that invade bare, baked, and cracked ground. That is the environment that suits them. If it was covered, damp, and cool, instead of being bare, baked and cracked, they would have difficulty establishing themselves.

When an organism establishes in a community, it will inevitably alter the microenvironment surrounding it. Even though the environment may be hot and dry, for instance, an incoming plant will create a little more shade and hold a little more dew and that might make the microenvironment hospitable for a new insect or microorganism, both of which in turn subtly alter the microenvironment as well. The germinating and establishment conditions may eventually become less favorable for that original plant and more so for other plant species, which begin to establish themselves. As these new species change the microenvironment, this change influences the types of animals, birds, insects, and so on that find this habitat ideal, and their populations change too. Thus, some species increase and others decrease as the composition of the community and of the microenvironment make it more or less suitable for them over time.

Nonnative Species Have Their Place

Biological communities develop as wholes over time as numerous species join them, interact with and change them, and depart them. But sometimes communities can be altered catastrophically within a short time by the accidental or deliberate introduction of a new species. We see this most noticeably on islands, particularly when the introduced species are predators or grazers. Cats, rats, goats, rabbits, mongooses, snakes, and humans have all wreaked havoc on islands where they were let loose, and on a number of continents as well. Many species in the community, having no defenses to ward off the introduced predator or grazer are quickly killed out, and many species that depend on those species die out with them, leaving an impoverished community for years to come.

East Africa's Lake Victoria was wonderfully productive and stable until British colonists, hoping to attract tourists through sport fishing, introduced the Nile perch. This huge, voracious predator spread to every corner of the lake within 20 years, sending some 350 species of native fish into a tailspin. Algae began to flourish in the sunny upper waters as the fish that once grazed it were consumed by the perch. As the algae died, it sank to the bottom and rotted. The bacteria that decayed the algae used so much oxygen in the process that bottom waters became uninhabitable by fish attempting to evade the perch. Even more fish species became extinct. The people who had fished the lake from time immemorial shifted their harvest from native species to Nile perch. But because the perch were too big and too oily to dry in the sun, unlike the smaller native species, the people were forced to smoke the perch over charcoal fires. To feed the fires, they cut down much of the surrounding forest, extending the ecological tragedy out of the water and up the slopes around the lake.[3]

Within a matter of a few decades a once-thriving community was decimated, largely because of the introduction of a single species. Given geological time, communities such as this one would in all likelihood recover much of the diversity and stability that once characterized them, although the species composition would undoubtedly change. We cannot, however, afford to rely on geological time frames to heal our errors.

From such experiences we know today what we tragically did not know when we first introduced new species, including ourselves, to long-established communities. That is not to say that all introductions have been catastrophic. On the contrary, species *appear* to have been introduced successfully on many continents. One of the better known was the honey bee introduced from Europe to North America nearly 400 years ago. That we regard this bee as a benign introduction might of course be a reflection of our ignorance.

Although I have focused on animal species, introduced plant species have followed a similar course, though those that have created havoc in the communities to which they were introduced don't seem to be of a certain type (like predators). Humans tend to refer to them, however, as weeds. Successful plant introductions have in many cases been so successful that we no longer think of them as nonnative: corn from South America has become the staple of Africa and potatoes the staple of northern Europe, and coffee from Ethiopia and tea from China have spread to every continent on which they can be grown.

The number of new species introduced to long-established communities by humans pales in comparison to the species dispersed by nature. Plants, birds, and insects in particular have been spreading around the world unaided by humans for millions of years. Once any species establishes in a community the species becomes a part of it, although the community always changes and over time the species itself can change. If a new species causes major disruption, then it may take a very long time for the community to rebuild its former complexity and to stabilize. Fortunately, most introduced species are either absorbed into the community without major catastrophe or die out altogether.

I mention these examples because there is today an unhealthy fixation on non-native species in the United States that is rapidly spreading to other countries. I believe the term *nonnative* in most instances is purely bureaucratic, because those who use it assume that species that arrived after a specified date, often in the last century, do not function naturally in their new communities and should thus be destroyed *at any cost*. If a species arrived even shortly before the specified date, it is often considered legitimate; after that date it is nothing less than an illegal immigrant. Some animals, such as the elk of North America, pose problems for the classifiers. Because the elk arrived on this continent at roughly the same time as the first humans, they are accorded legal status, as are "Native" Americans. Yet horses, whose ancestors were present in North America prior to the coming of humans and were probably killed out by them, are now considered nonnative, or illegal, immigrants.

Once an illegal immigrant arrives it will, like the legal immigrant, fill any vacuum nature or more commonly, mismanagement provides. In the United States snakeweed, mesquite, sagebrush, cedar, a number of rodents or grasshoppers (all legal immigrants) may fill the vacuum just as successfully as knapweed, leafy spurge, and fire ants (all illegal immigrants). No one has managed to annihilate either the legal or illegal immigrants, despite the expenditure of billions of dollars, nor has this been necessary.

Laws have been passed in various U.S. states that require landowners to poison or otherwise "control" some of the nonnative plant immigrants. If the landowners refuse, the state will do it for them and send them the bill, even when the landowners can point out that the species in question is not causing any harm, is useful as forage for wildlife and livestock, provides ground cover, cycles nutrients, and generally plays nothing but a beneficial role.

With greater enlightenment those managing holistically are finding a way to live productively with both legal and illegal immigrant plant and animal species, all of which at one time or another were "nonnative." The landscape you describe in your future resource base, when you reach it, may still include immigrant species you once considered pests, but in reduced numbers, and likely as not in a beneficial role as they contribute to the complexity, health, and diversity of the communities they inhabit.

None of what I have said here is meant to encourage the introduction of new species, including genetically engineered ones. We are right, I believe, to do our best to prevent the accidental introduction of species to new areas. However, once a species has established itself in a community, we are better off managing for the health of the whole community. I believe it is futile to spend the vast sums we generally do to try to eradicate it, particularly when an introduced species invades a monoculture community, where it tends to become virulent. Our main option then is to drench the invader with poisons that damage other soil life and further simplify the community, making repeated treatments inevitable, as will become clear shortly when we· look at the link between simplicity and instability in communities.

Collaboration Is More Apparent Than Competition

There is far more collaboration than competition in nature. What I am referring to as *collaboration* most scientists call *symbiosis*, the mutually beneficial relationships that occur among species in a community. The relationship among the squirrels, fungi, and trees mentioned earlier is a good example. There are many others. For instance, there are apparently some nine hundred species of figs in the world, and each is dependent on a different species of wasp for reproduction. Lichens, a marriage of algae and fungi, are so bound together that for all practical purposes we think of them as one plant. Over the millennia in Africa a partnership has developed between two honey-eating species, honey guide birds and humans. One has the ability to locate beehives and the other to break them open. The bird signals the human, who has learned to recognize its call and follows it to the beehive.

Many educators, based on an oversimplification of Darwin's ideas, continue to push competition as the driving force in nature, despite increasing evidence to the contrary. Studies of island communities, dating from the earliest observations of Darwin and his contemporary, Alfred Wallace, have revealed that over time the new species will develop from existing species in an attempt to *avoid* competing for the same ecological niche. Personally, after years of working on several continents, I have been unable to find any *clear* evidence of competition in nature. Where problem plants are said to be outcompeting other plants and taking over, closer observation usually turns up evidence that shows that mismanagement has created ideal conditions for the establishment of the offending plants, and less than ideal conditions for more favored plants. In many cases management had resulted in bare ground and the problem plants were merely establishing on ground unoccupied by *any* plants. Being the only plants growing on the bare ground, however, they are automatically assumed to have caused the ground to become bare.

Many animals appear to compete for food, but that relationship is probably more complex than it seems. Wildlife are said to compete with livestock for forage, yet when the same land is properly managed we find there is abundant food for all. Hyenas may take prey from a lion when under stress because of human intervention (fences, fires, roads, and so on) and vice versa, but I have not seen that occur when the community was healthy and neither species was stressed. Some birds do take over the nests of others or lay their eggs for unwitting foster parents to hatch and raise, but both the parent and foster parent species have continued to thrive in many places so something more than competition is at work here.

When you view competition as the driving force in nature you are compelled to take actions that may have ramifications you do not expect. The rancher who views the coyote, dingo, or jackal as a competitor (for calves and lambs) and shoots them out, may later find that the predator helped to keep small animal populations in check. With the predator gone, their numbers explode. In some parts of Africa where we believed crocodiles were competing with people for fish, we killed out the crocodiles but found to our surprise that fish populations then plummeted. We now suspect that while young crocodiles fed on insects, amphibians, and then fish, crocodiles of older ages had all along been limiting the numbers of fish predators. If your paradigm is competition, then you tend to see competition everywhere. But if you begin to think in terms of functioning wholes, collaboration, and synergy, you interpret events differently.

Stability Tends to Increase with Increasing Complexity

When biological communities are in the early stages of development or when they have lost biodiversity★ because of natural catastrophe or human actions, they are prone to major fluctuations both in the composition of species and in their numbers. Disease outbreaks in plants, animals, and humans occur more frequently, as do outbreaks of weeds, insects, birds, or rodents.

This instability often correlates with weather patterns. In a high-rainfall year a mass of annual plants may germinate; in a low-rainfall year few plants may germinate at all. If the rains come early in the growing season one year, a particular weed may dominate; if they arrive later in the season the next year, another weed may dominate. Several seasons may go by when rodents or grasshoppers are not a problem and then in the next become a terrible plague. Above-average rainfall years tend to become serious flood years; below-average rainfall years tend to become serious drought years. Inevitably we blame these conditions on the weather, rather than a loss of biodiversity that has probably occurred as the result of our management.

The more complex and diverse communities become, the fewer the fluctuations in numbers within populations of species, and the more stable communities tend to be. As the number of species increases, so does the web of interdependencies among them, as illustrated in figure 13-1. In both higher and lower rainfall years, there are fewer outbreaks of any one species and lesser fluctuations in the mass of life, or *biomass*, present. An exception occurs in the true deserts, where communities may be simple, but because the weather is consistently dry they appear remarkably stable. Even so, when the desert does get rain, a mass of flowering annuals may suddenly appear or swarms of locusts may develop and take flight.

When grasslands in the more brittle environments begin to die out—usually through overrest—some argue that this is a case where increasing complexity does *not* lead to stability. They are ignoring of course a major

---

★Biodiversity is the diversity of plant and animal species—and of their genetic material and the age structure of their populations—within a given community.

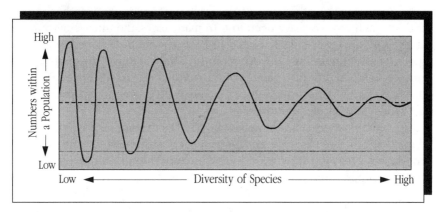

Figure 13-1 *The more complex and diverse communities become, the more stable populations within them tend to be.*

component of that complexity—the grazing animal species and their predators that have either become extinct or remain in far fewer numbers.

Scientists have long believed that complexity in a biological community leads to greater stability, although they have had difficulty proving it. In 1996, however, a group of researchers managed to provide convincing evidence. Their well-replicated field experiment in the American Midwest, involving 147 grassland plots, established a significant connection between diversity of species, productivity, and stability.[4]

Most of Nature's Wholes Function at the Community Level

If we consider the world to consist of, and function as, wholes within wholes, it helps us to understand certain important relationships. Each individual plant or animal is a whole composed of billions of cells, each of which is itself a whole. Individual plants or animals, in turn, belong not to a whole population, but to a whole community composed of many species. I make this distinction because a *population* of any one species would not constitute an ecologically functioning whole, although we often attempt to manage some populations as if they were. The members of any one species cannot exist outside their relationship with millions of other organisms of different species.

The fundamental importance of the whole community, including the functioning of the four ecosystem processes within and surrounding it, can too easily be overlooked when we focus on rare, endangered, or preferred species. Some rangelands are still classified as being in good condition if the "right" (useful to humans) species are present. Many of those areas, however, belong at the other end of the scale because so many other species and so much biomass have been lost. In many cases, the microenvironment at the soil surface has deteriorated to such an extent that perennial grass species, although still present, can reproduce only asexually through surface runner stems or stolons (underground running stems). Plants establishing through runners or stolons, rather than seeds, lack genetic diversity as they are merely clones of the mother plant.

Our inability to think in terms of whole communities is reflected in our efforts to save rare and endangered species through increasingly draconian laws that pay little heed to the biological (and human) communities that support these species. In a few cases where slow-breeding, easily hunted species, such as rhinos, are involved, these laws can serve as temporary Band-Aids, but no more. Our ignorance is understandable, however, because it is based on some long-standing beliefs and widespread misunderstandings.

When I attended university in the mid-1950s, we studied ecology strictly in terms of animal communities or plant communities, but not as biological communities. The separate disciplines of zoology and botany established to increase our understanding of nature had successfully divorced two obvious partners. Soils were barely considered in the scheme of things other than as a physical base to hold plants upright.

We now know that biological communities include all living organisms—from the most simple virus or unicellular organisms to elephants, humans, trees, whales, and corals. This of course includes the microscopic world in our soils, where a complex web of life dwells among decomposing particles of rock, sand, clay, and "dead" organic material. And they include the near-invisible world of our atmosphere as well. Many complex and mutually dependent relationships exist among all levels—below ground, above ground, and into the atmosphere.

Some scientists suggest with good evidence that our whole planet is a living organism that modifies the atmosphere surrounding it through the activity of biological communities on land and sea. The composition of Earth's atmosphere, on which all life depends, can change gradually in conjunction with Earth's life forms as the two, life and environment, influence each other, but it cannot change rapidly without catastrophic consequences. Billions of years ago the very earliest communities would have been suited to a totally different environment from that of today, as there was little free oxygen until it was formed by living organisms. We have remnants of these earliest communities in the anaerobic life forms (those that do not use oxygen), such as some species of bacteria, which still exist in a variety of environments, including the stomachs of many animals.

In ignorance over the last few thousand years we have overloaded our planet's respiratory system by greatly increasing our use of fire over what occurred naturally (before humans could light fires), and by consuming fossil fuels in massive amounts once we discovered how to exploit them. In addition, over the last 50,000 or so years we have, through the decimation of numerous herding species and their predators, greatly reduced the ability of the rangelands and savannas that cover so much of the world to trap carbon in plants and soils. Our attempts to replace the role of the animals with fire, which started many thousands of years ago and continues today is, I believe, the most profound environmental error we have ever made. Our planet's ability to balance the gases in the air pocket surrounding it took billions of years to develop, and we cannot expect it to adapt to this relatively sudden change of circumstances without fairly dramatic weather and climate changes.

Even though the emphasis here is on whole communities (the collection of organisms that exist in any locality), to be practical you can see that I often describe the environments they occupy in terms of the most obvious plants, such as grassland or forest, for the obvious reason that vegetation is most visible. This unfortunately fosters the misconception that plants, and sometimes only certain plants at that, are more important than the whole. In reality the insects that pollinate the plants are just as crucial to the survival of a community. So are many unseen species, as well as species that may visit only once every few years.

Most Biological Activity Occurs Underground

Any changes brought about above ground are likely to cause even greater changes underground, simply because there is generally more life underground than above ground. Figures vary widely with different soils, but on average, upper soil layers contain 7.75 tons of microorganisms, such as bacteria, fungi, earthworms, mites, nematodes, or protozoa, *per acre* (17.5 metric tons per hectare). The richest soils can contain up to fifteen tons of microorganisms per acre (33 metric tons per hectare).[5] Healthy European pastures carrying large numbers of cattle have been calculated to contain earthworm populations alone that are double the weight of the cattle.[6]

Plant roots also contribute to the biomass underground. The roots from a single tallgrass plant in the American prairie continue downward for anywhere from 12 to 20 feet (4 to 6 meters), spreading through an area the size and shape of a tepee. If placed end to end, they would run for miles, with the roots of one tallgrass plant developing as many as 14 billion fine root hairs. Scientists estimate that a full 75 to 85 percent of the prairie's biomass is underground.[7] Even when as many as 60 million bison may have roamed the prairies, and millions more elk, deer, and pronghorn, the underground organisms would likely have outweighed them by a considerable amount.

Knowing that so much life exists below the soil surface, you begin to understand that if by excess compaction of the soil, exposure and capping of the soil, inadequate drainage, fertilization, pesticide poisoning, or any other action, you alter the underground community, change will inevitably follow above ground. My experiment with the cabbages mentioned in Chapter 12 is a good example. The cabbages planted on the ridges where the soil was well aerated grew to an enormous size, while those planted in the furrows, where the soil remained waterlogged for several days following each irrigation, were small and stunted.

Change Generally Occurs in Successional Stages

The process of change in biological communities from bare rock or new pool to mature grassland, forest, or lake is a gradual, often staggered, buildup of species diversity and biomass along with changes in the microenvironment. I like to compare this movement from simplicity to ever increasing complexity to a coiled spring, which, whenever pressed down by human intervention or natural catastrophe, will, by its nature, rebound as soon as the pressure is taken away. Thus grass reclaims old battlefields. Jungle climbs the slopes of dormant volcanoes. And weeds invade fallow ground.

This relatively orderly process of change has been given the name of *succession*. The word entered the vocabulary of science through the work of botanists who observed that disturbed areas revegetated in successional stages—from bare ground to simple algae/lichen/moss, to grasslands, brushlands, and forest. Later insight took account of the fact that plants cannot exist in isolation, and thus we now think of succession in terms of entire communities. A simple understanding of the basic idea of succession is easy to grasp if you visualize it in process on a tropical island lava flow.

After the lava has cooled and hardened, its surface remains a very harsh microenvironment. In rain it is very wet, minutes later it is extremely dry. At dawn it may be quite cold, but by midday too hot to touch. Only a few species find an environment of such extremes ideal, and thus initially establish. Other species will try and fail. The mobile ones will merely pass by.

Without soil, only algae, lichens, and minute organisms dependent on them, will establish. The moment they do, however, the microenvironment becomes different. The meager collection of life will hold moisture a bit longer and reduce the daily temperature range ever so slightly, and moisture retained at the surface will now have time to begin dissolving the rock. When a few fine particles of dust catch on the algae and lichens, moss and other organisms are able to establish and the creation of simple soil has begun.

Gradually other organisms join the community as the microenvironment begins to favor them and their offspring. They further change the microenvironment. Succession accelerates. Moisture is retained longer. That breaks down the parent rock faster to join with living organisms in forming yet more soil. Anywhere physical weathering cracks the surface, the process speeds up in the microenvironment of the crack, which in turn affects the immediate neighborhood.

Complexity, productivity, and stability increase, and the microenvironment changes until something limits the successional process, typically climate or some obstruction to further soil formation. A subsurface rock layer, for example, might cause a patch of ground to remain at the grassland level. Otherwise, the lava of the tropical volcano will eventually advance to a rain forest community complete with its soil and the millions of organisms forming the whole forest complex. Elsewhere dry seasons, hard winters, limited sunlight, and the pattern and volume of precipitation will define the kind of landscape unfettered succession can produce. But whether the outcome be jungle, desert, savanna, healthy productive lake, or coral reef, the community is always dynamic as deaths, decay, and rebirth foster ongoing change within it.

The full implications of succession become clearer through an understanding of population dynamics at various successional levels—when do certain species thrive, in what numbers, and why? Typically a particular species will begin to appear and its population to build up as its requirements for establishment within the community are met. The community will be made of populations of many other species, each with specific requirements for their survival and each with specific contributions to the ever-evolving community. These populations will tend to build in numbers as their requirements become optimized through the changes in the microenvironment brought on by the growth of the whole community. But as the community advances, a population may find its requirements for successful reproduction are no longer ideal. It will decline in numbers and may even disappear as the successional process advances beyond it. The range of conditions that are favorable to any one species varies greatly. The eland antelope of Africa, for instance, can thrive from the snowline to the deserts, while many other African antelope species are restricted to areas with specific vegetation patterns. Elephants or cattle can feed across a very wide range of plants, but koalas apparently derive nourishment only from the leaves of a few species of eucalyptus tree.

Defying Succession

Succession is never a smooth or straightforward progression from simplicity to complexity. Some species appear to actively try to maintain their own ideal environment against the tendency of succession to advance the community beyond it. Others have developed adaptations that limit the success of species that graze, browse, or prey on them.

Prairie dogs create open country around their towns to make their predators more visible. Certain harvester termites maintain open ground, and thus a reduced water cycle and low successional community, around their mounds. Many creatures have developed skin, coats, or feathers that camouflage them, mimic other more dangerous or poisonous species, or exude chemicals that produce a foul smell or bitter taste. Some grasses are said to exude chemicals from their roots to prevent woody plants from establishing nearby, and some woody plants allegedly do the same. Some woody plants, when browsed, send chemical messages to their neighbors who release repellents to ward off the browsing animal. Other woody plants have spines or thorns to reduce browsing. And both grasses and woody species can develop a hedged form to protect themselves from grazing or browsing animals. Of course we humans, who have learned to modify our environment and behaviors to maintain higher numbers of our own species, provide one of the best, but least successful, examples of self-preservation because in doing so, unlike other animals, we destroy our environment.

Other cases are more subtle. For example, algae, lichen, and moss in more brittle environments are often the last plant life left in a deteriorating biological community, even though thousands of years ago they were probably the first life to establish in that community. Once they encrust soil surfaces in the more brittle environments, succession stagnates unless the crust is broken on a large enough scale. Once it is, other species will begin to establish and succession advances once more. In less brittle environments breaking the crust is generally not necessary, other than on croplands. Succession will advance of its own accord in reasonable time.

In several national parks and monuments in the western United States signs have been posted informing the public of the value of these "early successional" algal crusts. They explain that the crust protects the soil, provides nitrogen, and creates rough surfaces on which grasses and other plants can establish, *as long as the crust remains undisturbed.* This is true in less brittle environments, as mentioned, but not in very brittle environments, as these are. Not surprisingly, because of the protection these areas have received (large animals have not disturbed the crust for close to a century in some parks), it is the *lack* of grass plants and more complex communities that is most obvious. (See photo 13-1.)

That the park officials subconsciously question their own wisdom is illustrated by their attempts to assist grasses to establish by placing a wood–wool mulch encased in nylon netting over certain areas, as shown in photo 13-2. Surely, if these crusts were early successional, by their reasoning plants should be able to grow on them unaided by humans.

Photo 13-1 *Typical rested soil surface dominated by algae and lichens and roughened by freezing and thawing. Natural Bridges National Park, Utah.*

Photo 13-2 *Unsuccessful attempt to get grass established with nylon netting and woodwool as litter. Dead sticks are holding down netting (not visible). Canyonlands National Park, Utah.*

However, a year later all you can see are the oxidizing remains of the mulch. The hoped-for grass communities have not even begun to develop, nor will they until the artificial human-made concept of rest in such environments is removed and the soil surfaces periodically disturbed and sufficiently compacted to provide seed-to-soil contact.

Succession and the Brittleness Scale

In very brittle environments the microenvironment on exposed soil surfaces is subject to such daily and seasonal extremes that the successional process starts with the greatest difficulty. On smooth surfaces that are steeply sloped or vertical, the process might never get beyond frail algal communities that are easily lost as a result of the physical action of rain, hail, wind, and animal life, or the movement of eroding soil. This is why the walls of the Grand Canyon cannot really stabilize with higher communities, although some plants and animals establish in odd niches.

In the more brittle environments, the process starts more easily on soil covered by old material and on ground cracked by weathering or broken by the physical impact of animals, or machinery that "chips" the surface. In both cases a better microenvironment results, with two notable exceptions.

If fallen material all lies in one direction, as in the case of lodged wheat, grass, or pine needles, it suppresses plant growth. The reason is not yet well understood, although farmers have long known that a straw mulch has to be scattered to be effective. On rangelands snow and wind will lay old, moribund bunch grass in one direction, suppressing growth. Hail and animal impact tend to scatter it, encouraging growth. In forests a carpet of undisturbed pine needles may suppress plant growth. But new plants establish when animal impact (or some other action) disturbs the pine needles. Earthworms and a variety of insects help disturb deep litter surfaces. Turkeys, guineafowl, or baboons often do so extensively.

The other exception concerns areas outside the tropics where certain soils become puffy and soft from alternate freezing and thawing. As photo 13-1 shows, they may have very broken and rough surfaces, and yet succession does not progress easily due to lack of soil compaction. Photo 13-3 shows broken, cracked, but very puffy, soil that has been heaved and broken by freezing and thawing but has not been compacted by any physical disturbance. The plants trying to establish are tap-rooted forbs, considered weeds, and strongly associated with cracks as establishment sites. Not a single grass seedling can be found, although millions of seeds were produced locally. Photo 13-4 is the same soil on the same day five paces away, but across a fence where cattle milling around have broken the surface and firmed up, or compacted, the ground somewhat. Thousands of new plants have sprouted, all of them perennial grasses. This is a low-rainfall (9

Photo 13-3 *Broken, cracked, but very puffy soil (due to freezing and thawing) that has not been compacted by any physical disturbance. The plants trying to establish are tap-rooted forbs, considered weeds, strongly associated with cracks as establishment sites. No grass seedlings have been able to establish. New Mexico.*

Photo 13-4 *The same soil on the same day five paces away, but across a fence where milling cattle have broken the surface and firmed up, or compacted, the ground somewhat. Thousands of new plants have sprouted, almost all of them perennial grasses. New Mexico.*

inch/225 mm) area where nothing but grass could grow densely enough to stabilize the soil.

Such examples highlight once more the need for viewing the community as a whole. Managing plants or animals in isolation is meaningless and, as in this case, likely to be damaging. Any brittle environment community that lacks large grazing animals is unlikely to be able to develop to its optimum level of complexity and stability. The presence of grazing animals will be necessary if we are to facilitate the healing of the world's human-made deserts.

By contrast, in nonbrittle environments succession starts with ease from any bare surface and plants will establish even on vertical slopes. The nature and distribution of temperature and humidity allow the rapid advance of succession nearly anywhere without the aid of some physical disturbance. It will start on the back of a shower curtain, the abandoned bicycle seat in the garage, or the clapboards of the house.

Photo 13-5 shows a once-smooth concrete mantlepiece where a community rapidly developed to the point of supporting perennial grass, obviously without benefit of disturbance from fire, machinery, or herding animals. I have even seen succession start within a few weeks from algae on the sloping glass of a greenhouse window in the English countryside. In a more brittle environment the glass would remain bare for years, perhaps forever.

Photo 13-5 *Community establishing on a concrete mantlepiece in a less brittle environment. Oregon.*

In environments leaning toward the nonbrittle end of the scale it is hard to stop the rise of succession. The coiled spring is powerful and hard to hold down. Clear a jungle or rest a pasture and watch how fast the community regains complexity. If a jungle has been cleared for farming and the soil structure and fertility destroyed or badly damaged, as past civilizations did in such areas, the return to full complexity as jungle may take decades, but the successional advance from bare to covered soil will proceed very fast indeed.

The successional process in nonbrittle environments is highly resilient to periodic drastic disturbances, be they weather or human induced. The coiled spring expands with such force. Without major disturbance, the community retains great stability while minor fluctuations in populations within it continue to occur.

Community Dynamics and Management

Obviously an understanding of community dynamics opens all kinds of possibilities for better management of land, water, and all life. In the Holistic Management model (figure 7-1 on p. 51) a dotted line surrounds both the ecosystem process Community Dynamics and the tool Living Organisms to indicate that they are in fact the same thing. All life is successional and dynamic, and therefore the future resource base described in a holistic goal revolves around community dynamics. Our food comes from living organisms and so do most of our diseases. Our landscapes include living organisms. But to date we have too often managed living organisms in ignorance of the community as a whole. If we continue to ignore it, we will endanger all higher life forms.

If you seek profit from livestock or game, you may want a landscape that includes productive grassland. In one case that may mean advancing succession from desert scrub. In another it may mean preventing your pastures from returning to forest. Either way, certain plants, insects, predators, and other forms of life may become either allies or foes, depending on how you understand their place in succession.

If you wish to favor a species—game animal, plant, reptile, insect, or bird—then you must direct the successional movement of the community toward the optimum environment for that species, not by automatically intervening with some technological tool, but by applying whatever tools produce an environment in which that species thrives. Simply protecting the species, desirable as that might be, will not save it, although protection may be a necessary interim step.

If you start with a landscape that contains problem numbers of an undesirable species, the future landscape in your holistic goal will specify a community that is less than ideal for that species and more suited to what you want to produce. To achieve this in practical terms you will need to know something of the basic biology of the species. What stage in the life cycle of the organism is its weakest point? What precise conditions does it require to survive at that weakest point? A little effort toward providing the appropriate conditions at that point will greatly influence whether the population of that species increases or decreases.

As mentioned in Chapter 4, in Zimbabwe we eradicated big game from tsetse fly areas to deny the fly its source of blood food. To aid the hunters, we burned the brush. That, however, exposed soil, damaged the water cycle, and greatly increased the fly's egg laying sites. With decreased blood supplies, but increased egg laying sites and reduced enemies (by spraying DDT), the tsetse flies advanced right through the hunting areas designed to stop them. They continue to advance to this day as the conditions for the fly's survival at the weakest point in its life cycle have continued to be met.

Similarly, for the grasshopper that lays its eggs in bare ground and requires a dry, warm, soil for their survival, damaged water cycles ensure higher breeding success than poor weather alone could. How many entomologists, however, consider the effectiveness of the water cycle in their predictions? It is partly because this principle is not understood that insect damage to American crops has doubled since the massive use of pesticides began in the late 1940s.[8] The more chemicals are used, the simpler the community becomes and the greater the tendency for outbreaks of problem species. When a few fast-breeding organisms develop an immunity to pesticides, the problem is made much worse. It is compounded when the frequency of good breeding seasons is increased by the creation of a less effective water cycle.

In seeking to increase or to decrease certain species, you must not fall into the trap of seeking a monoculture of whatever plant appears most beneficial. Even if you want a less than maximum advance in succession, as in the case of a pasture in a less brittle environment that could advance to forest, you will probably need complexity. To achieve a monoculture of your favorite perennial grass would probably require large-scale technological intervention. This in turn would reduce soil communities to a level that would not allow your grass to reproduce without constant technological support. Modern range science has given us many examples of this.

A successful approach to management should rest on the concept of the coiled spring. By *nature* succession moves upward, as does the coiled spring, toward greater stability and complexity. All prolonged downward shifts, or compressions in the spring, that I have experienced—and they are many on five continents—could be traced to human intervention in the process by the purposeful or accidental application of one or other of the tools listed in the tools row of the Holistic Management model. The moment we reduce or cease that pressure on the spring, it rebounds, and the community gradually regains its complexity and stability.

This is a *very* important principle as we currently spend billions of dollars annually worldwide on actions that compress the spring while chasing objectives that small advances in succession could produce. Attempts to eradicate a so-called pest plant or animal species with traps, guns, or poison generally symbolize our tendency to ignore the force of succession and deal only with its effects. Theoretically these direct measures could occasionally work if our intervention did nothing to other species, but that rarely happens. Most intervention compresses the whole spring by damaging many species, when a real solution depends on letting the spring expand.

Some fluctuation of species is natural within a community, especially among short-lived organisms with high reproductive rates, which often characterize lower successional communities. Prolonged downward movement to lower successional levels of a whole community is unnatural, however, and excepting the occasional natural catastrophe virtually always betrays human intervention.

The cultivation of large areas of uniform crops is believed by modern agroeconomists to be the most efficient and most economical method of farming. This is a myth. Management is eased to the extent that larger machines save labor, but the amount of chemicals necessary to keep these monocultures productive leads to a dependency and financial commitment that becomes ever greater. Economists, who do not understand this, have promoted measures to reduce a farmer's hours of labor but caused him to lose the farm. It is my belief that if humans are to survive, our cropping practices will need to mimic nature. That means increasing the use of perennial and deep-rooted crops, and creating ever more complex communities. And it means using grazing animals when the environment leans toward the very brittle end of the scale.

Leaving It to Nature

There are those who would prefer to leave the management of biological communities to nature, based on the assumption that nature knows better how to manage them than we do. Left to nature, I believe all communities would eventually regenerate. In less brittle environments that could occur fairly quickly, because rest is such a powerful tool for restoring biodiversity. In the more brittle environments, which cover most of the earth's land surface, the time scale for regeneration would not be a human one but a geological one. Lands surrounding cities that were abandoned and left to nature centuries ago in these environments are still deteriorating. They won't recover, at least on a human time scale, unless we use the animals still available to us that can simulate the effects produced by the herds and predators that once made these environments functioning wholes. The alternative is to wait several million years for new species to develop, which is of course impractical. We have no option but to take responsibility.

Conclusion

If, in forming your holistic goal, you are attempting to describe the land surrounding your community, you now have a better idea of how biological communities function, and you can begin to describe what is needed: mainly, communities that are rich in plant and animal species, or *biodiversity*. If you are a birdwatcher or like to fish, it may be important to you to describe, in general, the habitats that support a variety of birds and fish.

If you are attempting to describe a future landscape for land you manage, then, again, you will need to be more specific, but would likely describe all the environments you manage as complex biological communities in which many species thrive, both above and below ground. Occasionally, you will need to describe communities that are less diverse to maintain a particular species—one that thrives on bare soil, for instance, such as prairie dogs. When managing diverse wildlife populations, quite often you need to describe a patchwork of different environments, which might again include bare soil areas where game birds can take dust baths, or that larger mammals have kept bare because they are highly mineralized and serve as salt licks.

14

Mineral Cycle: The Circulation of Life-Sustaining Nutrients

L ike water, minerals and other nutrients follow a cyclical pattern as they are used and reused by living organisms. Nevertheless, because we don't see these nutrients so conspicuously in motion, we tend to ignore the extent to which our management can drastically alter the speed, efficiency, and complexity of their circular journey within our ecosystem.

A good mineral cycle implies a biologically active *living* soil with adequate aeration and energy underground to sustain an abundance of organisms that are in continuous contact with nitrogen, oxygen, and carbon from the atmosphere. Because soil organisms require energy derived from sunlight, but many do not come to the surface to obtain it firsthand, they rely on a continuous supply of decomposing plant and animal residues to provide their energy needs. A good mineral cycle—one that provides a wide range of nutrients constantly cycling—cannot function in a dead soil, a fact often forgotten in our modern obsession with chemical fertilizers and other technology.

On farms, agricultural chemicals may temporarily help to produce higher crop yields, but destroy many soil organisms and inhibit others, such as those that fix nitrogen from the atmosphere. The net result is the destruction of soil, something humans cannot afford to do. Turning over deeper soil layers, as we do when plowing, leads to the breakdown of organic material and destroys millions of soil organisms. The planting of crops as monocultures results in a less diverse root system and an environment that discourages diversity in microorganism species. All the same problems and possibilities for damaging soils and mineral cycles also exist on rangelands and in forests.

To produce anything from the land at low cost on a sustainable basis, soil and air should provide almost all the nutrients required by plants and animals, including humans. Some nutrients come in the form of minerals from newly decomposing rocks. Some nutrients come from the atmosphere via falling raindrops or organisms that convert gaseous substances such as nitrogen and carbon to usable form. For most holistic goals involving crops, wildlife, livestock, and timber we *strive to keep nutrients from escaping the cycle* and to steadily *increase the volume of those cycling in the soil layers that sustain plants.*

This concept of high and increasing volume of nutrients cycling and available for use near the soil surface is easy to visualize (figure 14-1). To achieve it, however, requires a grasp of the natural processes that produced healthy growing conditions for eons before anyone thought of plows, chemical fertilizers, or pesticides. These processes are incredibly complex, but here we will look at the basic principles we need to know about to manage any mineral cycle well. Remember as we do that the mineral cycle does not function independently of the other three ecosystem processes. It is totally dependent on living organisms and the dynamics of the communities they inhabit and inextricably linked to the water cycle and energy flow.

To benefit humans, wildlife, and livestock, mineral nutrients have to be brought above ground in living plants. To obtain maximum nutrient supplies in the active soil layers, minerals must continually be pumped up to the surface from deeper soil layers. Then, after use above ground by plants and animals, they must be returned underground. There they will be held in the active root zones until used again or lost down to greater depths.

Minerals to the Surface

Plant roots are the main agents for lifting mineral nutrients to surface soil layers and enabling plants to take a proportion of them above ground. For a good mineral cycle then, we need healthy root systems with many of those roots probing as far as possible into the lower layers of soil and decomposing rock. In addition, we need a wide range of plant species to have many root structures. Just as you recognize plants above ground by their appearance, so underground you could know them by their wide variety of rooting patterns. Some have abundant surface roots while others probe deep, sometimes reaching below the soil itself into rock crevices and cracks, to seek water and nutrients, which then move upward through the plant.

Where shallow-rooted plants such as grass, corn, or wheat are the main line of production, some deep-rooted plants may be essential to the health

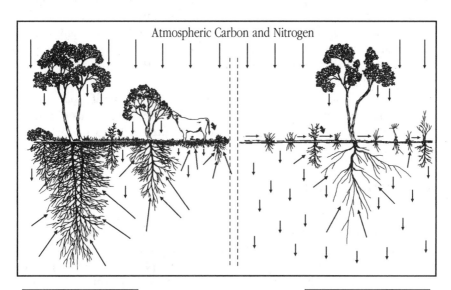

Good Mineral Cycle		Poor Mineral Cycle
High	Percent surface litter cover	Low
Mature, decaying	Nature of litter	Immature or oxidizing
Many	Surface insects/ microorganisms	Few
Close	Plant spacing	Wide
Porous	Soil surface	Capped and sealed
Abundant	Plant roots	Reduced
Many levels	Root penetration	Mainly shallow
Porous with good crumb structure	Soil underground	Poor or no crumb structure, compacted
Abundant	Underground life	Reduced
Low	Surface mineral loss	High
Low	Mineral loss to leaching	High
High	Mineral turnover rate	Low

Figure 14-1 *Good and poor mineral cycles.*

of the whole community. Incredibly small amounts of many trace minerals are critical to plants and animals, including humans, and they may lie beyond reach of shallow roots. If you have ever noticed the many colors and textures in soil layers revealed by a highway or railway cutting, you have an idea of the variety of essential nutrients that might be found at widely varying depths.

Although plant roots are the main agents in mineral uplift, many small animals play an important role too. Earthworms are the obvious example, but in drier areas termites and other insects often help to perform this function.

Above Ground to Surface

Plant material, having obtained nutrients from the soil and in certain cases air, finally returns to the soil surface in the form of dead leaves, stems, bark, branches, seeds, flowers, and crop residues. This may happen quickly or over a period of many years in the case of some plant parts, although the feeding and other activity of animals, birds, and small organisms generally speeds up the process.

Returning plant material to the surface, however, does not yet make it available for reuse. To be reused, nutrients have to move underground, and this does not happen until the dead material is broken down into fine particles, preferably by mechanical forces, such as rain, wind, hail, or trampling, or through consumption or decay by surface-feeding insects and other soil organisms. When plant material is broken down by fire or oxidation, many of the nutrients are rendered into gaseous form, and their residue or ash is blown or washed away. At the same time, soil is also exposed, which in turn reduces biological activity both at the surface and underground.

Biological, rather than chemical or physical, activity ideally should play the lead role in the breakdown of old plant material in all environments right across the brittleness scale, with one major difference. In the less brittle environments, the generally moist microenvironment at the soil surface typically supports extremely active communities of small organisms throughout most of the year that can break down old plant material without any contribution from larger animals. In the more brittle environments large animals become critical because over the short period of the year when 50 to 95 percent of the above-ground plant material dies, the microorganism and insect populations also die down. In such environments, large animals are needed either to trample the material down to the soil surface where it will break down more quickly or to reduce its bulk by grazing and digesting it. The gut of the grazing animal is one place microorganisms do remain active year round.

As you will see in later chapters, without adequate large animal impact, the spacing between plants in the more brittle grassland environments enlarges and soil becomes exposed. This decreases biological activity even in the humid months. Some mobile organisms, such as termites, will build their earth structures out over the bare soil to reach animal droppings or leaf fall, but this activity alone cannot sustain a good mineral cycle. In an environment where plant spacings are wide and soil easily exposed, it becomes difficult to hold plant litter in place against the forces of wind and water.

Fire drastically alters plant material, of course, and this may not always be bad, although we need to be aware of the pollution it creates and its tendency to ruthlessly expose soil. As Chapter 19 explains, fire converts many nutrients that are vital assets when contained in the soil, to gases that become harmful when released into the atmosphere—hence its polluting effect. Soil exposure becomes increasingly important in very brittle and low-rainfall environments where soil cover is so fragile at the best of times and takes so long to rebuild. For years I have flown in a light plane over much of the western United States and southern Africa where large expanses of very brittle grasslands are turning to desert. From the air it is possible to see the scars of fires that swept through them many years before. These scars are only visible because soil-covering litter takes so many years to rebuild.

Physical weathering also functions differently across the brittleness scale. In the less brittle environments, where humidity tends to be higher and more consistent, weathering may play little part as biological decay proceeds so rapidly. Most plants, even the largest of trees, tend to rot at their bases first, fall over, and then continue to decay on the ground. By contrast, in more brittle environments, even those with high rainfall, most dead plant material breaks down slowly through oxidization and weathering in the absence of large animal populations. Because weathering occurs from the top down, dead grass, brush, and trees do not readily fall to the soil surface where microorganisms could help speed their breakdown. Dead trees in such environments can stand for a century or more. The dead leaves and stems on perennial grass plants can stand for many decades. This can create a bottleneck in the cycle as nutrients remain tied up in dead plant material above ground.

Large accumulations of unrecycled plant parts also suppress plant growth, especially in those perennial grasses that depend on severe grazing or fire for their existence, and renders these plants less able to absorb those nutrients that do eventually get below the soil surface. When the plants have growth points, or buds, elevated above the undecayed material, as most trees and shrubs, and some perennial grasses do, growth is generally unimpeded. Such plants are not as dependent on fire or severe grazing or browsing for their existence

In more brittle environments, the slow weathering that occurs in the absence of large animals can lead to the premature death of most perennial grass plants as sunlight is unable to penetrate the accumulated old growth to reach the plants' growing points. This is seen mostly in bunchedgrass species with growth points at ground level, out of the way of the grazing animals with which they coevolved.

In environments that are brittle to any degree, therefore, animal activity in various forms speeds the breakdown and cycling of the plant material essential to building mineral supplies in the top layers of soil. Also, in contrast to fire, animal activity achieves this effect without exposing soil or polluting the atmosphere. I am fully aware that in the United States and Europe in particular, animals are also creating a major pollution hazard. Livestock confined to feedlots where they stand shoulder to shoulder in their own feces while being force-fed high-energy grain, are the primary example. These animals will eventually have to be returned to the land, where they are desperately needed and where their excretions are a valuable asset, rather than a costly liability.

Surface to Underground

Once biological action, fire, oxidation, or weather has broken down plant material, how do the critical nutrients move underground? Two agents, water and animal life, bring this about naturally. That explains why when managing to enhance the mineral cycle you will tend most often to apply tools that encourage water penetration and animal activity.

One further danger remains, however. The same water that carries nutrients underground can carry them on down below the root zone of plant types you hope to encourage. This is called *leaching*, and it is what, I believe, more than any other factor, caused the demise of many civilizations in nonbrittle environments. The main factor that impedes leaching is organic matter in the soil. (Many tropical forests actually grow on poor underlying soils and are only lush and productive because a mass of organic material is held in upper soil layers.) The chemistry by which organic molecules bind mineral elements is extremely complex but derives from the same principles that allow organic matter to create the beneficial crumb structure referred to in Chapter 12. The less organic material provided by dead plants and animals, and the less biological activity, the greater the tendency for leaching to occur.

Therein lies one of the great dangers of synthetic herbicides, pesticides, and fertilizers to our soils. The more we apply, the more we destroy organic material and living organisms in the soil, and the more we decrease the soil's water-retaining capabilities, the more we increase the loss of nutrients to both leaching and surface runoff. This is why farmers who add soluble nitrogen in various forms to their land have to keep applying it in ever-increasing amounts. By damaging the natural mineral cycle, nutrient balance, and in turn soil life, they must spend increasing amounts to replace the nutrients that leach out of it. The leached minerals not only become unusable on that particular piece of ground, they may become highly dangerous pollutants as groundwater flow carries them to places they were never intended to be.

The Importance of the Soil Surface

The key to the health of the mineral cycle, like both the water cycle and community dynamics, ultimately lies in the condition of the soil surface. An exposed surface, capped by the effects of rainfall, is a harsh microenvironment in which biological breakdown occurs slowly at best. Such a capped surface also limits air exchange between the soil and the atmosphere leading to reduced oxygen and excessive carbon dioxide, which generally inhibits root growth. As aeration decreases, so does life. As life decreases, so does organic material. As organic material decreases, so does soil structure. As soil structure decreases, so does aeration. As this chain reaction ripples through the ecosystem, fewer plants produce less soil cover and more bare, capped soil results.

Although this syndrome occurs seldom in the less brittle environments, where new communities readily reestablish on bare soil surfaces, it is ever present in the desertification of more brittle ones. In the more brittle environments, too, the interconnections among the four ecosystem processes, although present everywhere, show most clearly. So much so that, whenever possible, I try to introduce students to these fundamental processes by conducting the initial sessions in a more brittle environment.

Conclusion

In terms of your holistic goal, then, if you are attempting to describe the land surrounding your community as it must be in the future, you would describe it much as you did to indicate an effective water cycle. But if that land is now characterized by miles and miles of monoculture cropland, or grassland, you might want to describe it as also including trees, brush, and forbs—all of which tend to have deeper roots than annual crops or grasses and thus enhance mineral cycling.

The same applies if you are managing land, although your description would be more detailed and could vary according to land type. If cropland, rangeland, or forest soils are sterile now, you will want to describe them as biologically active. If you are in a brittle environment, you will want to be sure that minerals do not remain trapped in dead, oxidizing material and may want to describe what the land looks like when minerals are cycling rapidly (very little gray is visible by the end of the nongrowing season).

We have explored the relationships between water, soil structure, mineral availability, and communities of living organisms. The next chapter discusses the flow of energy that animates all these relationships.

15

Energy Flow: The Flow of Fuel That Animates All Life

A ll organisms require energy to live. And all of them, apart from a few organisms dwelling near thermal springs deep in the ocean, depend on the ability of green plants to capture that energy from the sun and convert it to a form they can use. This chapter addresses both how that energy is employed as it moves through our ecosystem and what can be done to increase its availability.

The energy flow in our ecosystem is considered by some as synonymous with the carbon cycle, because the storage of energy in most living organisms involves carbon. But where carbon is constantly moving between Earth and the atmosphere, energy from the sun is a one-way flow. Those who focus on the energy–carbon relationship miss the point most relevant to managing the four ecosystem processes: that the natural living world runs on solar power and our management decisions drastically affect how much is captured and put to use.

Because all life depends on the plant's ability, through photosynthesis, to convert sunlight energy into edible form, so does every economy, every nation, and every civilization. The importance of this statement warrants a little reflection in today's world of electronic marvels, corporate takeovers, and drive-up banking. Most economists, not to mention the rest of us, have all but lost sight of our dependence on the plant's ability to harness sunlight.

Photovoltaic, hydroelectric, wind, and tidal power sources also convert energy for practical use, but not directly into forms usable as food for life. Nor do geothermal and nuclear power plants produce food for living organisms. Fossil fuels, which represent solar energy converted by green plants long ago, can be used to produce a variety of products, but the fuels themselves are nonrenewable and inedible to all but the simplest bacterial life forms.

The Energy Pyramid

Traditionally, the flow of sunlight to food for life is represented conceptually as an energy pyramid, as shown in figure 15-1. Of the sunlight striking land and water, some is reflected back immediately, some is absorbed as heat to be radiated back later. A very small portion is converted by green plant life into food for their own growth and that of other organisms in the food chain. Thus green plants form the base, or Level 1, of the energy pyramid and support almost all other forms of life, including, of course, humans.

On land all of Level 1 energy conversion is at or above the soil surface where algae and the green parts of plants convert the energy. In aquatic environments it is slightly different. Around the shallow edges where plants can grow and protrude above the water's surface, energy conversion still takes place as it does on land. But over the rest of the area covered by a body of water, energy is also converted by plant life below the surface at depths sunlight can reach. Other than this difference, the concept of the energy pyramid is similar in all environments.

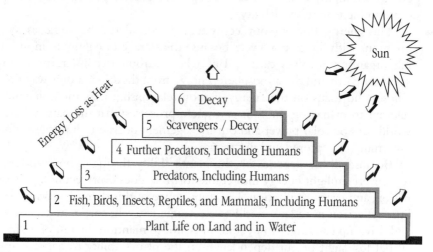

Figure 15-1 *Basic energy pyramid. Sunlight energy must first be converted by the plants at the base of the pyramid (Level 1) before it can be utilized by other life forms. Therefore, to increase energy flow through the ecosystem you first need to expand the base of the pyramid.*

Level 2 represents the energy stored by animals that eat the plants of Level 1—fish, mammals, insects, birds, reptiles, and humans. It is smaller by the amount of energy expended as heat in the living processes of the feeders. This is no small amount. Roughly 90 percent of the energy is lost as heat as you move from one level to the next.

Level 3, the realm of predators, again including humans, which eat the eaters of Level 1, is smaller still for the same reason.

At Level 4 we again find humans and some other predators dining on fish and the other predators that fed on Level 2. Once more the living processes of the feeders has diminished the bulk of energy remaining in usable form by a further 90 percent.

By Level 5 humans drop out of the pyramid. Scavengers and organisms of decay reduce the bulk of stored energy yet further, and beyond that perhaps another level or two of decay organisms will use and convert to heat the last remaining useful energy. The last of the complicated organic molecules assembled by the original green plants will finally have been broken down, having made energy from sunlight available to many organisms.

At all levels, of course, a portion of the energy passes straight on to decay levels through feces or urine in the animals and through microorganisms that feed on the plants. Thus in real life the energy pyramid is not exact or tidy. And its form, because of the high loss of energy between each level, is much flatter than shown in figure 15-1, which is vertically exaggerated to get it on one page. However, the concept of ever-decreasing volume in usable energy holds throughout. None of this energy is actually destroyed or used up; its form merely changes to heat that is nonusable as food for life.

Humanity's position in the pyramid covers three possible levels. One person can actually dine on all three in a good fish chowder, in which the potatoes represent Level 1, the piece of grain-fed salt pork Level 2, and the boiled cod Level 3. Where high human populations exist on restricted land, people tend to feed directly off Level 1 rather than sacrifice the energy lost by first passing the food through the animals in Level 2. The animal protein they do consume probably comes from animals that do not compete with them. Fish or other animals may feed at the same level but off plants that humans cannot eat or at higher levels from animal (including human) wastes. In some of the so-called developed countries the pyramid becomes messy when animals that would normally only feed at Level 1, the herbivores, are fed offal (waste meat and blood) to supplement the protein in their rations and are thus forced to dine on animals at their own level or higher.

The energy pyramid also extends below ground where the energy flow greatly affects the health of the other three ecosystem processes—water cycle, mineral cycle, and community dynamics. All three require a biol-

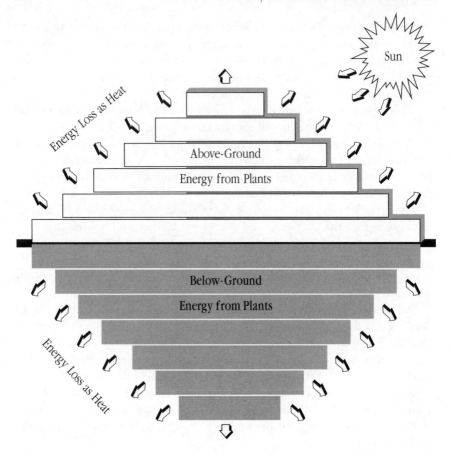

Figure 15-2 *Energy flow above and below ground.*

ogically active soil community that in turn requires solar energy to be con-
veyed underground mainly by plant roots or surface-feeding worms, termites, dung beetles, and others (figure 15-2).

The Energy Tetrahedron

The four key insights have enabled us to see that the old two-dimensional pyramid diagram does not reveal the possibility of much sophistication
in the management of energy flow. Clearly the broader the base of the tri-
angle, which the face of the energy pyramid represents, the larger the
whole structure, and the more energy available for use at every level. This

two-dimensional view, however, suggests very few ways of broadening the base. On cropland, we have done it by increasing acreage, producing better yielding crop strains, irrigating, planting two or more crops on the same land, and so on. On rangeland, we have attempted to do it through such technologies as brush clearing, range reseeding, and so on. In forests, we have attempted to do it with fire and machinery to regulate timber stands. In aquatic environments, we have all but ignored the energy base by creating an artificial one in fish hatcheries and shrimp farms. In each case, especially in industrialized countries, we have accomplished this through heavy use of resources in a nonrenewable manner to fuel machinery and manufacture fertilizers and chemicals to kill unwanted life.

Even discounting the fact that many of these methods tend to damage natural water cycles, mineral cycles, and biological communities to the extent that only increasing outside energy input can compensate, most present technology quickly reaches the point of energy debt: broadening the base requires more energy than it returns in captured sunlight. As long as fossil fuel remains abundant and cheap and we ignore the long-term effects of our heavy consumption, this fact may appear academic. However, in countries where inputs are costly it is already a question of life and death. It underlies much of the continuing American farm crisis manifested in ever fewer family farms and an increasing reliance on heavily subsidized corporate agriculture. In the case of the vast, but minimally productive, rangelands, it already prices technical solutions far out of reach. The problems can only get worse until humanity understands and starts to manage energy flow as an integral part of community dynamics, water, and mineral cycles.

Based on what we now know through the four key insights, we have come to view the energy pyramid as multidimensional, above and below the surface, that is, as two tetrahedrons (figure 15-3) joined at their bases. In applying this concept we now have opportunities for increasing energy flow at the vital first level—the soil surface—greatly. Level 1, in this three-dimensional diagram, now has three sides, which I call time, density, and area as indicated on the cross section of the double tetrahedron shown in figure 15-3.

On land, the right management can increase the volume of energy stored at Level 1 by increasing not only the *density* of standing vegetation on a unit of ground, but also the *time* during which that vegetation can grow and increasing the rate at which it can grow and the leaf *area* of individual plants to capture more energy. In aquatic environments we have still to learn how we might use some of this new thinking.

Clearly the more we can extend any of the three sides of the base, the greater the volume of energy humans can harvest at levels 2, 3, and 4.

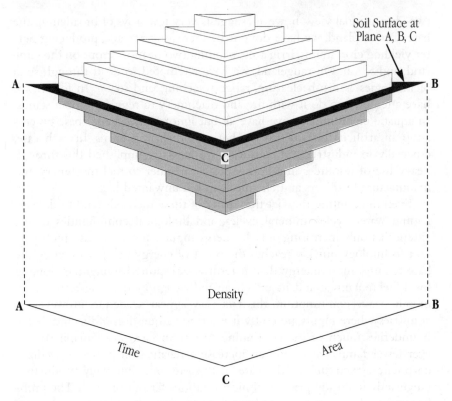

Figure 15-3 *Energy flow seen as two tetrahedrons joined at their bases (labeled A, B, C). We can increase the amount of energy stored in the above- and below-ground bases (shown in the cross section) in three ways: by increasing the* time *during which that vegetation can grow and the rate at which it grows; the* density *of plants on a unit of ground; and the* leaf *area of individual plants.*

On the other hand, shortening any single side decreases the volume of energy we can harvest all the way up, and the same effect ripples underground.

Before going into detail about how this works in practice one example should illustrate what attention to energy flow can mean in land management. Once while consulting on a ranch struck by a serious drought, I found that my explaining the importance of increasing energy flow appeared to bore the rancher to distraction. He wanted to discuss less theoretical questions, such as the hay he would have to buy and the animals he would have to sell. But in fact his problem really was a matter of energy flow, and his exasperation forced me to state it in less theoretical terms.

We went out onto his land where I broke the capped soil with my fingers, and pushed down some of the dead and oxidizing grass to cover the surface, much as any gardener would do to prepare a seedbed. I asked him if he thought an extra once (28 grams) of grass could grow on this small bit of "prepared" ground if it received only one inch (25 mm) of rain. He said he did. Then I asked him to calculate the amount of hay he would have to buy to replace the one extra ounce (28 grams) of grass per square yard (or meter) that he could grow if he had his animals prepare the ground for him. Multiplied by the area of his land, that ounce (28 grams) represented 15 million pounds (6.7 million kg) of grass. We grew that and more at no extra cost simply by grouping all herds into one much larger herd that in concentration could more effectively break the capping and trample the old grass down. This also enabled us, as Chapter 38 explains, to reduce the time the animals remained in any one area so that all plants had more growing time. The increase in energy flow that resulted saved him thousands of dollars in hay purchases and herd reduction. Perceiving the full ramifications of energy flow requires a thorough understanding by the land manager, so let's look at the three sides.

Time (Duration and Rate of Growth)

The energy converted by plants while they are green and growing must support all life both above and below the surface throughout the year. The longer plants are growing, the more productive the community as a whole. We can increase the growing time—the *time* side of the base—by lengthening the growing season or by increasing the growth rate within a given time.

In practice, producing a better mineral cycle and water cycle and greater complexity in the biological community will extend growing time in both ways. In the management of grasses, the growing time can also be used more efficiently if the bulk of the grazed or cut plants is not taken down too far. The less taken from a plant during its active growth, the faster it regrows, as it has more leaf area with which to convert sunlight immediately.

In Chapter 6, I described my frustrations in learning about time as a dimension in grazing on brittle rangelands and how we had to plan its manipulation to neither overgraze plants nor depress the performance of the animals. Later, under the management guideline of time (Chapter 38) we will see how to actually prevent severe grazers from reducing the energy flow on pastures and rangelands, although they graze some plants severely within the first hour or so on the land as they select their diet.

Taking rangeland as an example, naturally anything that creates better growing conditions through improvements in water and mineral cycles will allow plants to grow more rapidly. The role of the water cycle, however, deserves special attention. Under good management of the four ecosystem processes, moisture will remain available in the soil after falling temperature and diminishing daylight hours end the growing season. As explained in Chapter 12, this enables plants to start growing the instant the new year restores those conditions. Given a noneffective water cycle, growth won't start until the first rain. Given a more effective water cycle, plants can also continue to grow for much longer during dry spells in the growing season because less moisture is lost through soil surface evaporation.

The opposite problem—too much water due to overirrigation or poor drainage and aeration—also occurs, cutting time out of the growing season. Every hour with adequate temperatures in which plants cannot grow at their best potential rate because of poor aeration means lost energy conversion on croplands or pastures under rainfall or irrigation, as I illustrated with the example of the cabbages in Chapter 12.

The degree of species complexity in a community also has a fundamental relationship to growing time. The most obvious examples are rangelands that support both cool-season and warm-season grasses. A complex healthy rangeland will include enough of both to ensure that some part of the plant community will be growing as long as any growth is possible. The annual grasslands produced by poor management such as we find over most of California and in many parts of Africa and in southern Australia illustrate this clearly. On these rangelands where the dominant grasses are now annuals, there are prolonged good growth periods in every year in which no growth at all is taking place as the perennial grasses that could and should be converting energy have for the most part disappeared as a result of the management practices used.

Photo 15-1 shows some of the few remnant patches of perennial grassland that still survive on one California ranch. Even as they continue to grow actively and convert energy to fuel the rest of the life in the community, the annual grasses that have come to dominate the surrounding land have long since finished their cycle, dried off, and died. A change in management, using the knowledge now available, could bring back the perennials that once covered the land and restore months of productivity to the area.

The same principles for extending time apply equally well on croplands and offer even more management opportunities. Photo 15-2 shows the poor growth of plants in an overirrigated field in New Mexico alongside excellent growth in the same plants on the edge of the field where aera-

Photo 15-1 *Remnant perennial grass patch in annual California grassland (courtesy Richard King).*

tion is accidentally good. The plants on the edge reached cutting stage a month before the main crop.

Many farmers are aware of the difference in time efficiency rendered by applying nitrogen fertilizer in periodic light dressings as opposed to a single large dose. Good selection of heat- and cold-tolerant crops and planting dates can also extend effective growing seasons and thus the time base of the energy tetrahedron. Some of the same principles could well apply in aquatic environments.

Density (of Plants)

The density side of the base refers to the number of plants growing on each square yard (or meter) of land. Ten plants growing on the average square yard (or meter) of ground can probably convert more solar energy than three. Farmers have long recognized that plant spacing, or density, can greatly affect energy flow in their fields and have planted accordingly— striving for the density that produces the highest yields.

In environments that lie closer to the nonbrittle end of the scale, the spacing between plants growing in the wild, which is close, is a reflection of climate. Management can affect it, but plant density is naturally high. By

Photo 15-2 *Sparse growth of grass in an overirrigated hay field but with excellent growth in the foreground on the accidentally well-drained edge of the field. Albuquerque, New Mexico.*

contrast, the more brittle the environment, the more plant density is affected by the disturbance, or lack of disturbance, from large animals. Over time the use of fire and animals, animals alone, or some of the machines developed by range scientists to imitate animal disturbance, can lead to close plant spacings. Incorrectly applied, any one of them can expand the bare spaces between plants. Fire used on its own has a marked tendency to do so.

Photos 15-3, 15-4, and 15-5, taken on a ranch in west Texas, show the difference disturbance by animals can make in a fairly brittle environment. Photo 15-3, taken in 1982, shows the bare spaces on a piece of land within the ranch boundaries that was fenced off and thus undisturbed for some years. A series of fixed-point photos, including photo 15-4 (taken in 1985), reveal that these plant spacings have widened continually as old plants stagnated from overrest and new seedlings failed to establish on the bare capped soil. Photo 15-5, taken in 1984, shows nearby land where the same rancher has planned the grazings and periodically subjected the land to disturbance in the form of high animal impact. Its proximity to a livestock watering point intensifies the animal impact. As you can see, plant densities show a very positive correlation to this periodic disturbance. Our measurements confirmed that where animal impact was highest, close to

Photo 15-3 *A long-rested site fenced off from grazing animals showing sparse grass and some bare ground between plants, 1982. Texas.*

Photo 15-4 *Identical view as in photo 15-3 but taken three years later in 1985. Grass has become more sparse and bare ground increased under continued rest. Texas.*

Photo 15-5 *View on same ranch and close to the site shown in photos 15-2 and 15-3. Here, where very heavy animal impact has been applied periodically close to the waterpoint (on left), the grass has thickened up considerably and the bare patches have disappeared, 1984. Texas.*

the water, plant spacing was closest and that spacing widened the further we went from the water where the same periodic impact was lighter. Generally, more energy can be converted where more plants grow.

Traditionally people have believed that such plant spacings were a function of climate and soil, which is correct if the environment tends toward the nonbrittle end of the scale, and thus lay beyond their control. However, in more brittle environments, management can be crucial as these photos show. Chapter 22 describes animal impact and its management in more detail. Suffice it to say here that animal impact does provide a means of increasing the density of plants per unit area of land, particularly in grassland environments that are brittle to some degree.

In aquatic environments one needs to be wary of promoting too high a plant population when adding nutrients to water, as we do every day when we dispose of detergents and other wastes. When these nutrients arrive in large quantities, plant populations can explode, consuming so much oxygen in the process that little or none is left to sustain other life forms.

Area (of Leaf)

Area of leaf matters because a very dense stand of narrow-leafed plants may trap less energy than a moderately dense stand of broader-leafed plants. So to expand the area side of the base, you would have to increase the number of broad-leafed plants.

Plants adapt themselves in three major ways to suit different growing conditions. *Hydrophytic*, or wet-environment, plants thrive in soggy, poorly aerated ground. *Mesophytic*, or middle-environment, plants grow best when air and water are balanced in the soil. *Xerophytic*, or dry-environment, plants survive where water is scarce, though aeration may be good.

In some ways the wet- and dry-type plants resemble each other more than they do the middle-type plants. Both often have cuticles or fairly impervious skins over their leaves, and adaptations surrounding their breathing pores that result in them passing little water through their systems. Both may have narrow leaves or leaf stems (green stems that convert energy), which reduce the area exposed to sunlight and thus the area transpiring water. Some dry-type plants may have broader leaves, but they are often tightly rolled for the same reason.

The wet-type plants such as water lilies, bulrushes, cattails, many sedges, and some grasses are generally found in sites that remain wet because of high rainfall or poor drainage. They can also be found in sites that, in terms of rainfall and soil depth, should be occupied by the middle-type plants, but where severe soil capping has caused poor aeration. Likewise, dry-type plants such as cacti, euphorbias, and some grasses are generally found in sites where moisture is minimal. However, they can also be found in sites where rainfall is high but quickly shed or evaporated from a capped surface. Among the dry-type plants, many of the perennial grasses often stand out clearly in the dormant season when they dry off to a white or very pale color. Both wet- and dry-type plants tend to grow slowly and thus store a limited amount of solar energy in a given time.

The middle-type plants are very different. They produce generally open, flat, and broad leaves that curl only when wilting under moisture stress. They do not have thick protective skins or well-developed mechanisms to shut off breathing pores. They also tend to grow rapidly when moisture and temperature are favorable. In contrast to their cousins in the dry category, many of the middle perennial grasses cure to red or gold in the dormant season, which happens also to reflect more nutritious dry forage for animals.

Oldtimers in South Africa made the distinction between "witveld" and "rooiveld" (white range and red range), the latter being far more productive. In America this difference can also be seen along many western highways. Protected from overgrazing and kept alive by severe defoliation as a result of periodic mowing, these roadside grasses when dormant often have a definite reddish or deep gold tinge. Yet, just over the fence, where plants are overgrazed and soils insufficiently disturbed, the grasses show pale or dead white in color. The sharp change from red or gold to white along the fence line shows up for miles.

Obviously, to increase the area side of the energy tetrahedron on land in more brittle environments you need to shift the community to the middle plant that spreads broad leaves to the sun and grows fast. As in the case of plant spacings, most people have always felt that plant type depended on soil type and lay beyond their control. Occasionally something like an impervious layer of clay or rock below the surface can indeed kill any chance for the middle plant, but generally poor water-to-air balance results from sealed or capped soil and poor water cycles, which management can change.

In less brittle environments where soil capping is far less a problem, the maintenance of more broad-leafed plants can often be improved by drainage. In Zimbabwe I have seen, in the course of twelve years, a patch of 84 percent *Loudecia* grasses, known for their fibrousness, poor forage quality, and association with badly drained ground, change to an 80 percent mix of productive middle grasses associated with good drainage. We had used animal impact to break up the hard soil capping and create closer plant spacings and planned the grazings to prevent overgrazing. The change in species was an unexpected by-product and led to more observations of the same kind.

In addition to causing grass plants in more brittle environments to grow closer together, animal impact and severe grazing (without overgrazing) cause many species to produce more leaves and less fiber, which in turn increases the flow of available energy to animals and humans. The same holds true for grasslands and pastures in less brittle environments.

Using Technology to Increase Energy Flow

We can also increase energy flow through direct use of technology in many forms—machinery, drainage, irrigation, chemicals, and genetic engineering to name a few examples However, in doing so we need to be particularly alert to the fact that such direct intervention in one of the fundamental processes can be extremely dangerous because we are dealing with complex interrelationships of which we understand little. We should intervene with technology only in ways that allow for simultaneous development, but never damage, of the water cycle, mineral cycle, and biological communities.

No one ecosystem process can safely be bolstered at the expense of the others. As mentioned, enhancing energy flow through heavy inputs of fossil fuel products, which damage biological communities and water and mineral cycles, has been the cornerstone of American agriculture, but we are paying a heavy price for our ignorance: increasingly severe floods, food and water riddled with life-threatening chemicals, rising rates of reproductive disorders, cancer and other diseases, accelerated erosion destroying millions of years of biological capital, millions in public funds spent yearly to kill insects and other increasingly resistant pests, and ultimately thousands of farmers and ranchers leaving the land, followed by once-healthy small businesses and rural communities.

Conclusion

In terms of your holistic goal, if you are attempting to describe the land surrounding your community as it must be in the future, describe what it would look like if energy flow were high: soil would be covered in vegetation, plants would stay green and continue to grow much longer than they do now, and there would be a variety of them. Wildlife would reap the bounty and be more plentiful as a result. In essence, if water cycles are effective, minerals are cycling rapidly, and biodiversity is high, then energy flow would tend to be maximized.

The future landscape that land managers will describe to sustain their forms of production will generally require the highest energy flow possible, whether rangeland, cropland, or forest be their concern. In most cropland situations, we should strive to manage for an effective water cycle, good mineral cycle, a highly complex biological community (above and below ground) and thus a high and sustainable energy flow. We will seek to maximize the time side of the energy tetrahedron's base by ensuring good daily growth rates and lengthening the season through polyculture cropping or at least two or more crops per year whenever possible. We will maximize density by planting with close spacings. We will maximize the area of leaf open and exposed to sunlight by creating good drainage, crumb structure, and abundant organic matter in the soil and providing adequate soil cover. In the future, we will be better able to manage our cropland soils and increase the energy flow to the microorganisms that populate them by planting perennial grain crops, some of which are currently under development, and in the more brittle environments, by incorporating animals into cropping strategies.

In most forest situations, we should strive to maximize energy flow by improving water and mineral cycles and by increasing the diversity of plant and animal species, particularly in forests that have been simplified through industrial-style forestry practices. And in aquatic environments, we will maximize energy flow by reducing pollution and sustaining highly com-

plex biological communities, and by ensuring that on the land that surrounds them and that catches much of the water that feeds them, water and
mineral cycles and biological communities are healthy.

In most rangeland situations, we will increase energy flow by manipulating the tools of grazing and animal impact, with both livestock and
wildlife, to produce and maintain maximum growing time, plant density,
and leaf area. The amount of energy we might have to buy from other producers on other land to supplement what our own land does not provide
would be the measure of success or failure.

The chapters in the next section describe in detail the tools we can use
to alter any one of the four fundamental processes. An understanding of
how each tool affects their functioning is essential to the land manager and
will influence many of the decisions he or she makes. The nonland manager also utilizes some of these tools and, although not doing so to influence the ecosystem processes directly, does so indirectly. Thus, before moving on to the testing guidelines that will enable you to find the quickest
route to your holistic goal, we first need to learn more about these tools so
we can plan to use them wisely.

Part V

The Tools We Use to Manage Our Ecosystem

16

From Stone Age
Spears to Genetic
Engineering

B elow the row of Ecosystem Processes in the Holistic Management model stands the row of tools, but the word here gets a broad definition. It includes everything that gives humans the ability, which most organisms lack, to significantly alter our ecosystem in order to enhance or sustain our lives. Many of the decisions you make will not involve the use of any of these tools specifically, and you may well feel you need not concern yourself with them. But many other decisions will involve their use, either directly or indirectly, even if the whole you have defined is limited to your own personal life. For this reason, among others, you need to be aware of the effects these tools can produce.

All tools available to humans, from stone age spears to computers and genetic engineering, fall under one or another of the headings in the tools row. Whether you are a politician, economist, engineer, housekeeper, gardener, widget maker, or whatever, you will not find a tool currently known to humanity that is not included within these eight general headings.

Human creativity as well as money and labor bracket the other six tool headings in the model because both come into play in the use of the other tools. We list money and labor together because the once simple combination of labor, creativity, and resources frequently operates through the agency of money. The capitalist's investments, the labor of a commune, or the unpaid children on a family farm all function according to similar principles to be covered in later chapters.

Of the six tools listed between the brackets, technology alone is the prime tool employed in urban or industrial businesses and professions and by most households, few of which attempt to modify our ecosystem through the use of technology, either directly or deliberately, but often do nonetheless. Chapter 24 elaborates on this theme. If you are not managing land, then do you need to concern yourself with the chapters on fire, rest, grazing, animal impact, and living organisms? Not necessarily, but you would be the poorer for it. I suggest you at least skim through these chapters (19 through 23), particularly if your home or business lies in a more brittle environment, because the information in them will be critical to sustaining your business and your community. Likewise, if you support nonprofit organizations and their programs to save threatened wildlife populations, alleviate hunger, or assist environmental refugees, it would be helpful to know more about how these remaining tools can be used to eliminate or exacerbate such problems.

In any land management situation, *fire* and *rest* are included with *technology* as the standard tools for modifying our ecosystem. But none of these tools can begin to reverse the desertification occurring in environments that lean toward the more brittle end of the scale—the majority of the earth's land surface.

A typical example is the civil engineer commissioned to stabilize an eroding catchment to save an important dam or irrigation project from silting up. The average engineer's tool kit contains only technology. Thus, the average engineer may contour all the slopes, build silt traps in all the valleys, or try to channel rivers to no avail because in the more brittle environments, where most dams and irrigation projects are developed, that can never constitute more than a Band-Aid on a dying patient. The catchment in question has, in all likelihood, been subjected to the influence of three tools whose damaging influences the engineer was unaware of, rest (as partial rest), periodic fire, and grazing (as overgrazing), all of which tend to expose soil and increase the amount of water that runs off it. Inevitably, the dam will silt up, as I, the son of a civil engineer, have seen repeatedly and as past civilizations have illustrated abundantly.

Were engineers to expand the number of tools in their kit, they would greatly increase the possibility of success. The more brittle the environment, the more the need for some form of periodic disturbance over millions of acres of the catchment and for assistance in breaking down billions of tons of plant material every year without using fire. There is no technology, and likely never will be, that can do this in a more environmentally friendly way than the animal impact and grazing provided by herding animals. And as they perform these tasks they remove the cause of the erosion on the catchment that leads to the silting of the dam. Fire and rest cannot do this. In most cases they will only make matters worse.

Sociologists, economists, environmentalists, and politicians can similarly move beyond the tools traditionally available to them within their professions. But this becomes possible only when they begin to work together with others outside their professions—something more and more people are attempting to do as they find that very few problems can be solved within the confines of individual disciplines. These multidisciplinary teams can overcome major hurdles by sharing knowledge of the various tools available within their professions, but success will still elude them, as I emphasized in Chapter 3, if they fail to see the whole first.

The tools of the future will undoubtedly incorporate many technological wonders, including, hopefully, benign sources of energy. And broad thinking might lead to tools outside technology that break new ground. A young cousin of mine, after watching a television program where Israel's Uri Geller bent iron with his "mind" and a light stroke of his fingers, picked up a steel nail file and did the same thing himself. He was of course too young to know, as we all do, that "you can't do that."

For most of us, such mind-over-matter phenomena fall completely outside the tool chest, and just reading the last paragraph may make us wince. Nevertheless, that is just the attitude we must avoid at all costs when looking at the tools row of the Holistic Management model, which may well be expanded in the future.

When managing holistically, all tools are equal. No tool is good or bad, and no judgments on any tool or action should be made outside the context of the whole under management. Only when the holistic goal and the degree of brittleness of the environment are known, together with the many other factors having a bearing on the situation, is any tool finally judged suitable or unsuitable in that particular situation at that time. Fire, for instance, is good when it keeps my hands warm on a cold morning, but it is bad when it is burning down my house.

In Chapters 19 through 22 we'll examine how fire, rest, grazing, and animal impact *tend* to affect each of the four ecosystem processes relative to the brittleness scale. Analyzing the impact of a single tool when many other processes and other tools may be at work at the same time would appear to be an impossible task. Where a cow places her hoof today, for instance, begins a chain of reactions that ensures that spot will never be exactly the same again. A solution to this dilemma rests on the hypothesis that the tendencies of these four tools, when chosen and applied in a certain way, function in the ecosystem like the ripple patterns of pebbles thrown into a still pool.

It is a fact of physics that even though multiple ripples appear to create disorganized chaos on the pool's surface, the orderly ripples produced by pebbles thrown individually still exist. Each pebble does in fact impart a predictable *tendency*. If we throw in two pebbles of very different sizes, we can, in fact, see what each pebble's ripples tend to do. A larger pebble may overcome a smaller one's ripples but the smaller ones's ripples will still have a visible effect.

In considering which tools to apply, either singly or in combination, we think of them like those pebbles and ask ourselves, "Will it start a ripple that pushes the community toward more complexity? How will its ripples tend to change water and mineral cycles and energy flow?" Although there may be countervailing ripples that diminish and partially obscure the force of the ones we start, it is not likely that the power of two ripples moving in the same general direction will combine into an entirely new and opposite force.

Once these tendencies are acknowledged, a careful consideration of the testing and management guidelines covered in later chapters helps us then to judge which tools are best to apply now. Even then we always assume we could be wrong and monitor to ensure the tools selected achieve what we want them to achieve.

17

Money and Labor: One or Both of These Tools Is Always Required

Once upon a time people supported themselves by applying creativity and labor, or brains and brawn, directly to the raw resources of our ecosystem. Many societies still do this, as do many farm and ranch families not actually paying for the labor of family members. Both then and now we used our creativity to obtain the maximum effect with as little labor as possible.

Because money and labor are often linked (e.g., cash can be exchanged for labor) and because neither can be used other than through another tool, we group them together in the Holistic Management model. Ideally, our natural tendency to economize on labor should apply equally to money. But money is a more complicated matter and this isn't often the case.

A few years ago, I spoke to a group of economists from various universities and asked them to define wealth. To my surprise they grappled over that question a long time and in the end only defined wealth as money. Well, once upon a time money probably did perfectly represent wealth, but that was a long time ago, and the fact that many experts still believe it is a disturbing aspect of modern times.

The distinction between wealth and money has taken a few millennia to develop. Humans in a primitive state organized around small family units had no money but did have wealth. If we had bothered to measure that wealth, we would have tallied up the natural resources available for use in our group's home range or territory, our tools and weapons, the protective quality of our cave, and perhaps the closeness of our ties to one another.

There is some controversy over whether family groups evolved into urban societies after discovering how to domesticate certain plants and animals or after discovering excellent hunting grounds that included sites rich in the resources needed for making tools and weapons. Whichever it was, at some point very early on, human communities developed to the extent that individuals could share the tasks of survival and specialize in what they did best. Until this point was reached there was no pressing need for a medium of exchange.

Following settlement and specialization the need became urgent. If I had been crippled in the hunt but could make excellent spear points, and you were an excellent hunter, not so good at making spear points, we could begin to trade spear points for meat or hides. If I grew a good crop but elephants flattened yours, we could do a trade this season. I would help feed your family in return for you doing the same for mine should a similar fate befall me.

While our community was still very small such exchanges could be memorized or recorded as marks on a stick or bone. We would all know each other well and thus trust that our simple deals would be honored. (As communities became larger, and deals more complex this might no longer apply.) I might have become an expert sandal maker by this time who traded pairs of sandals for half a sheep or a basket of grain. However, I didn't always want the sheep or grain immediately and those needing the sandals might not be ready to slaughter or harvest. So they gave me a token representing the trade, which I could redeem later. This worked well until I needed a blanket from the man most expert at making them, but he needed no sandals. We overcame this impasse by creating money. I got my blanket by giving the blanket maker a token given to me by the grain farmer. The blanket maker then collected the basket of grain that he did need. In fact he needed more than one basket of grain to feed his family and he got two more baskets by giving the grain farmer two blanket tokens, which he promised to honor before winter.

Such tokens would have been extremely convenient, as they still are, to carry and store or accumulate for later use, in exchange for some service (labor) or goods (grain, blanket, sandals).

Once such tokens were established as a trusted means of exchange, they inevitably began to be distributed through the population in an uneven manner. I might begin to accumulate more than my family required for services or goods. One day a close friend approaches me as he has cut his hand badly and is unable to make the hoes on which his family's livelihood depends. He is out of tokens and needs food. I know him and trust him and I realize he will be better soon and able to earn tokens in exchange for the excellent hoes he makes, so I lend him some tokens. However, for this favor we agree that he will return one more token than he borrowed. At this point my tokens (money) began earning me simple interest.

As our community grew, we established trade with a community in the next valley. Since we didn't always know or trust the individuals, we were hesitant to exchange tokens in lieu of goods or services. Early people would inevitably have asked, was this a token that I made and exchanged for grain a year ago, or has someone cleverly made it to look like mine? Thus for a long time bartered goods would have been the only acceptable currency between distant communities. Trust in tokens would take time to develop as we see even today where the tokens (currency) of only a few nations are acceptable internationally.

In my Game Department days in Zambia, I had the task of paying out a government bonus on bushpigs killed by villagers over and above those my staff killed in control work. These bonuses were paid out on my behalf by the District Commissioners in each district as the country was so large. Once a year I visited the District Commissioners, counted the tails collected as tokens of payments made, and then reimbursed their department from mine. At one station I found that the District Commissioner had paid out a very large sum to the local villagers. Indeed, he had an enormous pile of tails to prove the number of pigs killed and paid for. Much to his dismay, I and my game scouts, sat down and inspected each tail carefully as we counted. Slowly we sorted out a small pile of genuine tails from a mountain of clever counterfeits. The villagers had economized on labor and found it paid better to spend their time making tails from parts of the hide which they twisted, trimmed and dried, than to actually hunt pigs.

Those Zambian villagers were not the first to make their own tokens. At some point in the past one source for making tokens in a way that made counterfeit difficult would have had to be agreed upon. Otherwise, we would not have retained our confidence in the value of tokens, or money as they had now officially become, and we would find distant trade cumbersome.

Up to this point, tokens represented actual wealth, goods, or services, but once there was one source for the manufacture of money there was also the possibility that more could be made and put into circulation than represented actual services or goods exchanged. Thus was primitive inflation born.

From here it was easy for one of us who had accumulated money and was lending it periodically, to develop a safe place to keep it from thieves. Others might ask if they could also store their money with this person when they were away. Soon this storer-of-money would find that he could lend your money too and earn interest as long as he had enough money available when you got back. In fact, he would increasingly find that he could do this even if you did not go away, as long as we all had confidence in him and did not all ask for our money back at the same time. Thus was primitive banking born.

Now, you as a grain producer find that you want to build a larger house before winter and need several people to help you. Your grain will not be ready to harvest for several months, so you borrow the necessary money from the banker to pay for this labor. It is going to take more than he has in safekeeping and to still allow for some who might come to get their money. He does not have enough to lend you, but at the same time he does not want to lose this opportunity to earn interest. He is creative and agrees to let you have *credit* up to the amount you require. He will honor pieces of parchment with his mark on them, up to a certain amount, when your laborers present them to him. Now, not only can the central manufacturer of the money cause inflation, so can the lender of money.

Money has been the oil that has kept the wheels of society turning and allowed the complexity of our present civilization to develop, but credit, the centralized creation of money, interest, and particularly compound interest, have seriously destabilized the relationship between money and the goods and services, or wealth, it originally represented.

In my lifetime alone, the distinction between wealth and money has probably become more blurred than at any time in history. High interest was usurious when I was a child; now that's seen as quaintly old-fashioned. Major banks move headquarters to states with more lenient usury laws and still retain customer confidence. Where it was once unacceptable for lenders to advertise or engage in aggressive promotion, it is now commonplace. Money itself has become a commodity, like grain or oil, that earns money and can be traded internationally. The use of credit cards and the electronic speedup of monetary transactions have blurred the distinction even further.

Today fortunes can be made overnight on the international trade in money, or currency speculation, where real goods or services play no part at all. The amounts of money involved in this trade in any one day exceed that of most nations' annual budgets. Compounding interest—where interest is computed on principal and accrued interest—has only encouraged the trade in money as a commodity and is responsible for much of the enormous increase in the money supply, or inflation. In fact, according to the World Bank, the world's money supply is now fifteen to twenty times greater than the value of the goods and services produced in the world economy.[1]

It becomes easy as one stands in a plush, air-conditioned bank, humming with electronic activity, to lose sight of the underlying reality of wealth in the financial resources we manage. Whatever the source of the money—real goods and services, including information, or corporate takeover—it all looks the same as we stare at the dollar bills or the computerized spreadsheet.

Primitive societies did not make this mistake as their wealth and reality were one and the same thing. But for us the *token* that our ancestors created to facilitate the exchange of goods and labor has become our *real-*

ity. The urban life of most people seldom challenges this misconception, as we fill all our basic and not so basic needs with cash or credit, and it does not seem to matter much where either comes from.

Most of the holistic goals we form, whether they apply to us as individuals or to a nation as a whole, should involve a sustainable source of wealth, as the reality (wealth) is more vital than the symbol (money) in the long haul. However, to manage wealth as it has become today, where a dollar (pound, franc, or rupee), regardless of source, can purchase the same things as any other dollar, we must first understand the three most basic sources of wealth the dollar represents: mineral dollars, paper dollars, and solar dollars.

Mineral Dollars

I call money derived from a combination of human creativity, labor, and raw resources (soil, timber, dung used as fuel, water, oil, coal, gas, gold, silver, uranium) mineral dollars. Mineral dollar wealth has certain characteristics. First, the raw resources from which it is derived can be used *cyclically*, over prolonged time. This would include paper, plastic, or metals that are recycled—with further input of energy that itself involves mineral dollar wealth. It also includes soil, timber, and dung that can be constantly regenerated with inputs of free solar energy. Money so generated can be used to develop infrastructure to generate future wealth (e.g., education, buildings, factories, farms, railroads, highways).

Second, the raw resources can also be used *noncyclically* (i.e., consumed in a single use). Soils in mainstream American agriculture are being mined in a consumptive, noncyclical manner, when they could be regenerated if used cyclically. Oil and gas are always used noncyclically when burned as fuel, but cyclically when converted to products that are recyclable. Water can also be used either way. If, after use, water is too polluted for reuse, it is being used noncyclically in terms of human use. In either case, energy derived from these raw resources can also produce by-products that are potentially destructive to our ecosystem. We have abundant evidence that the present consumption of coal, oil, gas, and uranium/plutonium may soon endanger life as we know it.

Paper Dollars

Many of us acquire money through human creativity and labor alone. I refer to this source as paper dollars. The beauty of such income is that it consumes no other resources. All we have to do is apply our creativity in thousands of different ways to the many avenues open for investment: speculation in futures markets, stocks, bonds, corporate takeovers, and so on.

On the other hand, various services—many of them essential—also fall into this category. Lawyers, consultants, educators, accountants, civil servants, armies, and so on do not actually make anything or produce the kind of elemental wealth that supports life. But they do enhance and protect that wealth, and life without them would be inconceivable today. Professional speakers, entertainers, athletes, and many others also reap paper dollars for the services they provide, and although they produce no tangible goods, they make life genuinely more pleasurable.

In some cases the money generated in this category has the fascinating characteristic of apparently instant and unlimited accessibility. We can make fortunes in a day with nothing but our creativity and minimal effort in the stock market. On the other hand, this money can vanish as quickly as it appeared. Paper dollars are backed by confidence in the government and the banking system, and when that confidence is lost, paper dollars can lose their value overnight.

Solar Dollars

Third, we can generate income from human creativity, labor, and such constant sources of energy as geothermal heat, wind, tides, wave action, falling water, and most of all the sun. I call this last class of money solar dollars. Such energy as a source of wealth is noncyclical, but it is apparently inexhaustible. A characteristic of wealth derived from this combination is that it tends not to damage our life support system or to endanger humankind as far as we know today. Not long ago, however, we thought the same of fossil energy and firewood.

A further characteristic is that wealth in this category is the only kind that can actually feed people. Unfortunately, this requires the conversion of solar energy through plants that themselves depend on water and biologically active soils. Both plants and soils fall into the first category, mineral resources that can be mined in a consumptive manner or managed on a sustained basis, depending on the treatment. *Only when soils are managed on a sustained basis would the money earned from a crop or forage qualify as solar dollars.*

Keeping the three categories of money in mind enables us to see the extent to which failure to do so governs our society now. Economists daily engage in juggling paper dollars, sublimely unaware of what those dollars actually represent in terms of real wealth. On the advice of these same economists, farmers diligently pursue mineral dollars while consumptively mining their soils to do so. Some 24 billion tons of soil erodes from the world's agricultural lands each year, enough soil to fill a train of freight cars stretching from Earth to the moon and back again five times.[2]

Conclusion

Sooner or later the underlying basis of a nation's or an individual's quality of life asserts its nature. A country rolling in oil revenue today must ask itself to what end the cash flows in. The nation that thrives by burning the oil must ask what that does to the greater ecosystem that sustains us all. What will happen to the nation's long-term quality of life and productive base? If the wealth from oil goes to accumulating paper dollars and to support unproductive legions of bureaucrats, accountants, soldiers, and others who consume and keep transactions going, but do not enhance the nation's ability to increase or to maintain its biological capital, is that sound? In other words, is it sound if the nation's resource base deteriorates while it wallows in paper dollars? Shouldn't some of the dollars from nonrenewable mineral wealth go to develop ways to reap solar and mineral dollars on a sustainable basis?

One of the seven tests included in holistic decision making asks you to consider the source and use of the money involved in implementing a plan of action. If you are a land manager, this is a reminder to consider whether that action will lead to the production of solar dollars gained by enhancing mineral resources. All forms of money will figure in your plans, but only solar dollars combined with resource-enhancing mineral dollars will enable you to produce the biological capital that sustains your efforts in the short run, and the rest of humanity's in the long run.

Whatever forms of wealth you control, success in achieving your holistic goal depends on how creatively you use them. Thus we look at *human creativity* next.

18

Human Creativity: Key to Using All Tools Effectively

When Holistic Management was in its infancy we needed a name for the reasoning and judgment attendant on any use of labor and resources. I first used *brainpower* but soon realized that word didn't cover the ground. A man who adds up six-digit numbers in his head may have great brainpower but no common sense or humanity.

Just as notable in Holistic Management is that an idea that enables one person to attain maximum effect from his or her labor and money may not work for another, or even for that person in the following year. A small family farm, for instance, is as unique as your fingerprint—it cannot be duplicated anywhere in the world. However, where your fingerprint keeps the same unchanging pattern every day of your life, the small family farm changes continually: the people change as individuals and as a family over time, members are born, then grow, mature, marry, divorce, or die; the land is never the same two years in a row; and markets can vary from day to day.

Thus, *every situation requires management that must be an original product of human imagination, and even that must evolve as the situation changes.* Creativity, not brainpower, is the crucial element and it is needed constantly.

This unique character of any whole we manage is why I believe no formula or management system can work other than short term. And it is why different persons in different situations have to learn to think creatively for themselves and their situation. In *Meeting the Expectations of the Land*, farmer-essayist Wendell Berry noted that a whole generation of farmers has been brought up to use their heads to advertise others' products (on their caps) and to phone the extension service to be told what to do. The extension service in turn employs a generation of advisers whose university education trained them in how to do rather than how to think. This problem is not limited to farming, but has become increasingly common in all fields, particularly in developed nations.

In my early years as a consultant, I played a role much like an extension agent and merely advised my clients what to do. When things went wrong, I advised them to do something else. Using my head to design their management always produced imperfect advice because I was an outsider looking in at something very complex. Although superficially results were good, depth and sustainability were lacking because I, not my clients, did the planning. Had I first given them my knowledge and then let them do the thinking for themselves, they could have developed management that was far superior and more holistic. My role should have been to bring in outside experience to stimulate their thinking. They would have known which bits of knowledge would fit their case and which would not.

As it was, I did none of this. Many who became heavily dependent on me went seriously adrift when I suddenly had to flee my country as a political exile. Some of their mistakes had serious consequences for which I was really to blame. Some years later, I realized that any consultant consistently has a much higher than average chance of being wrong, as I was, no matter how knowledgeable or dedicated, because he or she is always an outsider looking in. To manage holistically, it has to be the other way around. To correct this I subsequently only agreed to work with people who would first learn how to make decisions holistically and how to plan for themselves. Then my counsel could become a matter of suggesting ideas and collaboratively thinking through them. We could proceed from the client's point of view, not mine, using the holistic goal and the testing guidelines to make sure we always steered in the right direction.

The Holistic Management testing guidelines have been developed to help us to assess the possible consequences, both good and bad, relative to our holistic goal, of using any available tool. As many of the consequences are not quantifiable, this is not a task for a computer. Any human responsible for management will have certain feelings about it and will encounter the feelings of others. Love, fear, hopes, dreams, and interpersonal conflicts very much affect any management situation in ways no computer yet devised can understand.

The Holistic Management framework itself, however, is nothing more than a bit of software to help organize thinking and planning. Its successful application depends entirely on your ability to think and to be creative. Fortunately, creativity is not simply a genetic endowment. It depends on your mental, emotional, and physical health, your environment, and most of all on the commitment you have to achieving your holistic goal.

Although individuals can and should ideally manage their lives holistically, resources are rarely managed by one individual. More often a family, a company, a tribe, or a nation has some kind of institutional responsibility. Relationships between the people involved can be at all points along a continuum from very stressful to very caring, and the state of these relationships has a bearing on the creativity of each individual and the group as a whole. However, it is the person at the top—the owner, manager, chief, etc.—who sets the tone. His or her beliefs and behavior have the greatest impact on the creativity of the group.

The most vital responsibility any manager ever has is to create an environment that nurtures creativity. Research since the 1960s has shown that the living and working *environment* is key to the release of creative potential, whether it be within a small, family-run operation or in our largest corporations. Creativity of the group, no matter its size, tends to be greatest when the leader's everyday actions display trust and confidence in his or her people, when the work is meaningful, when all feel free to express ideas and to be creative, and when all feel valued.

Such a spirit cannot be faked. The person at the top really must value his or her coworkers as human beings and not mere tools for making profit. Corporations that saw profits rise when they treated employees as their prime resource, saw them tumble when employees sensed they were merely being manipulated.

At present the majority of us take human creativity for granted and do not see it as something that must develop through the family and social and work environment. We rarely see it as a tool that governs our success or failure. The male head of a small farming family leaving the land in America today, as hundreds of thousands are doing, no doubt blames the banks, the interest rates, the prices, the government, the weather, and looks to society to help him and his family. It is difficult indeed for him to see that while he labored long and hard with his hands, using his head and the creativity of family members and friends might have helped him to survive.

Subconscious worries and stresses all too often completely sap our creative energies. Unfortunately, this is a common and subtle factor that affects many of us, but fortunately it is entirely within our control. Many of our stresses are allied to crisis management—where one crisis after another hits and drives your management—which in turn is closely allied to the way people make decisions. Holistic decision making will help to circumvent any tendency toward crisis management and reduce the stress associated with it.

Poor time management also leads to crisis management and a stifling of creativity. It has certainly proved to be a serious obstacle in many of the situations where I have consulted. Typically, a person would call on me to help stave off impending bankruptcy. Within a very short time I would realize that my talk of planning for the future was meaningless, because my client's mind was on the tractor that needed a new clutch, the pickup that needed new wheel bearings, the boundary fence that was down, or the dam that had burst the night before. To get him out of the crisis he needed all the creativity he could muster to carefully plan the next crucial months. But his worries prevented him from planning his time or anything else.

Over many years I had perfected a good system for managing my time that had served me well and that I shared with clients in these sorts of cases. I would assist the person in plotting ahead and allocating his time for all the concerns that had piled up and were believed to be of equal importance, so much so that nothing at all was being done because everything, he thought, had to be done today. Once we established priorities, including family time and holidays, and allocated more than enough time over the next few months to complete them, there would always be many days left with nothing to do! The person would be immensely relieved. But this plan inevitably was not followed because the person lacked the self-discipline, or so I thought. On reflection, I realized it was deeper than that. What was lacking was an established routine, or habit, which could be learned.

Whatever time management system one uses, the keys to its success are *habit* and *trust*. A habitual procedure must be established whereby all the ideas that come to mind and all the commitments made are immediately recorded in one place, rather than on scattered scraps of paper, so they can later be retrieved (and understood) and acted on. Once this habit is formed then you cease to worry about commitments or ideas you might forget and you begin to *trust* the procedure and let go of your subconscious, or conscious, worries. This then frees up the mind for creative thought.

Conclusion

Most of us complain that we just don't have enough time for creative thought or in fact to do all that we want to do, and we marvel at those who seem to find it. Often we feel others have less to do while in fact they achieve far more than we do. In truth, every person in the world has exactly the same amount of time. How we manage it makes the difference in the quality of our lives and in what we achieve through our creativity.

Human creativity will turn up again in Chapter 36 when we discuss the guidelines for creating a nurturing work environment in order to unleash the creativity inherent in us all. For the present, however, think of it as the key to using money, labor, and the other tools of management successfully and as being the *only* tool that can produce a holistic goal and be used to plan its achievement.

19

Fire: The Most Ancient Tool

B e wary of the argument that says fire, because it occurs naturally, can be used as a management tool without adverse consequences. Its effects will vary greatly depending on how frequently an area is burned, what other tools are associated with its use, and how brittle the environment is.

Although fire has existed ever since green plants amassed pure oxygen in our atmosphere millions of years ago, its use as a tool by humans for modifying our ecosystem is a relatively recent phenomenon. Nevertheless, we have used it with such abandon that on any given unit of land, the frequency of fire has almost certainly undergone a geometric increase against the background of the millions of years it took many biological communities to evolve.

Natural fires started by lightning, spontaneous combustion, or volcanic activity occur infrequently in comparison to the number of human-made fires. In addition, most lightning fires occur with rain and thus spread less than those lit by humans, who often burn well before rain is expected. Although humankind has had the ability to make and use fire for the last 80,000 to 100,000 years, and there is some evidence that it might be as long as a million years or more, booming populations and, more recently, matches and government agencies that advocate using them have radically increased the use of fire in modern times.

It is my firm belief that this increased frequency of fire, combined with a reduction in the disturbance to soil surfaces and vegetation caused by dwindling animal herds and their predators, is one of the prime factors leading to desertification in the world's brittle environments. In discussing water cycles in Chapter 12, I mentioned the reported increased flow of water over the Victoria Falls in Africa since 1948. To me the bigger mystery would be if water flow were *not* increasing because, in most of the catchment areas above the Victoria Falls, the use of fire has increased, and the once prolific big game herds have continued to decrease. This has led to an increase in bare ground, and thus an increase in the amount of water running off it.

We know that in North America the earliest people used fire a great deal and that they significantly altered the landscape by doing so. This, together with the decimation of most of the large animal populations some 10,000 years ago, would have produced profound change. Where large numbers of animals did survive the earlier human onslaught, as in the case of the bison on the prairies, their presence would have diluted the damaging effects of fire. In fact, it was that combination of factors—fire, grazing, and predator-induced animal impact—that produced the lush grasslands found by early Europeans on the American prairies, *not fire alone*, a point we will return to. The same could be said for much of Australia as well. Today, enormous areas of Australia, like Africa and North America, are dominated by vegetation that is fire dependent because of the frequent burning by humans that caused previously abundant fire-sensitive species to disappear.

For millennia fire has played a vital role in human life, touching not only our hunting and agriculture, but also our religions and rituals. This has made it difficult to consider this tool objectively. In parts of Africa, for instance, people believe that if some hills are not burned off each year, poor rains will follow. Visible damage to the water cycle at the source of many streams and lack of any evidence that fire brings rain make no difference to the belief.

Some years ago I encountered a similar absence of scientific curiosity at a U.S. Soil Conservation Service training session on "prescribed burning" for the purpose of eradicating woody vegetation. Discussion centered on such things as time of day to burn, appropriate wind velocities and temperatures, and safe widths for firebreaks. We learned how much warning to give neighbors to avoid litigation, argued whether legally the rancher or the civil servant should hold the match, and probed the legal fallout of fires that get out of hand.

Throughout the day not a word was uttered about the effects of fire on the four ecosystem processes, about its contribution to atmospheric pollution, or about how burning would affect the long-term future landscape a manager might be attempting to produce. No one brought up the troublesome fact that fire invigorates many woody shrubs in the adult form. Every supporting argument rested either on ancient beliefs or short-term research that had focused on plant species at the expense of soil and biological communities as a whole.

My own introduction, as a biologist in training, to the beliefs of game management was while bouncing along in a Dodge Power Wagon through Zambia's Kafue National Park, flicking lighted matches into the grass under instruction of a superior. We wanted the game to have green flushing grass but gave no thought at all to the long-term consequences for the game we intended to help or the environment we meant to improve. In the United States overreaction appears to be the controlling national trait in this matter. The majority of people are pro-fire for a few years and then turn sharply against it for a few more, swinging back and forth like a pendulum.

The use of fire has so many ramifications, however, that the majority opinion, whether for or against, can seldom be right. Fire, like any other tool, *can be judged only in the context of a clearly defined holistic goal* and the current state of the four ecosystem processes relative to what is desired in that holistic goal. I find any discussion about the use of fire without this basic information to be academic and as likely as not to end up in pointless argument.

Effects of Fire on Biological Communities

Deciding whether or not to use fire in any year requires an objective understanding of what it does and does not do and the effects it tends to produce in any biological community. Those effects will always vary depending on how brittle the environment is and how high or low the rainfall.

Soil Surface

First and of primary importance, fire tends to expose soil surfaces. As soil surface management is central to the management of all four of the ecosystem processes, this tendency must be kept in mind before all others. Bare ground is conspicuous right after a fire and until new growth appears to hide it. More critical, however, is the time it takes to build up the litter between plants. That depends on such things as the brittleness of the environment, the amount and pattern of rainfall, the amount of grazing or overgrazing by livestock or wildlife concentrating on the burned area (as they tend to do), the amount of rest, or the degree and timing of animal impact.

Fire appears to have the most lasting impact where soil cover takes longest to form, the lower-rainfall, very brittle environments. The lower rainfall produces less vegetation that might restore cover, but the fact that bare soil makes rain *less effective* compounds that effect. The effects of fire on low-rainfall grasslands can persist for years, creating scarred patches of land that are clearly visible from the air. While flying across Botswana in a light plane years ago, I drew these scarred areas in on my otherwise featureless maps and navigated by them for nearly a decade. If fire is followed by total rest, as it is with most prescribed burns, or low animal impact (partial rest), soil cover accumulates even more slowly. The guidelines for burning detailed in Chapter 41 discuss using other disturbances with fire instead of the unnatural two years' total rest so commonly recommended.

Plants

Fire affects plants in different ways. Some sensitive perennial grasses disappear if burned. The majority, at least as mature plants, thrive when burned as burning removes all of the old material that prematurely kills grasses when allowed to accumulate. Some plants may in fact depend on periodic fire for survival. Many have specially adapted for establishing after fire. A number of grass seeds have awns, or tails, that actually twist and drill the seed into exposed soil when they become moist, suggesting an association with fire, which exposes soil.

   Woody plants, too, may respond in many ways. Some are extremely sensitive, others resilient. In many countries I have observed that most of the trees and shrubs considered problem species are resilient when burned. Although they may appear dead immediately afterward, they soon resprout more stems than before, as photo 19-1 shows. This plant in the Arizona

Photo 19-1 *Burning killed off the main stems of this shrub, but a great many new stems have sprouted. Arizona.*

chaparral once had about six stems, but after burning has thickened up to a great many more.

Many tree species are damaged by fire, yet some can still survive in the shrub form where burning is prolific. Mopane trees, common in the southern African tropics, once carpeted land I wanted to irrigate for sugar cane. I easily cleared the forty-foot trees by building a small fire at the base of each tree and leaving it undisturbed for several days. The whole tree burned down, and as long as the fire was left undisturbed so that blow holes in the ash were not closed, the roots burned out far underground. Yet where frost and many past fires had kept the mopanes down to three-foot shrubs, the same trick failed, as they were completely fire-resistant, and a bulldozer had to pull out enormous root systems.

Fire that is not followed by any other soil disturbance tends to cause major changes within a community because any influence that creates essentially the same microenvironment over large areas favors the establishment of the few species of plants, insects, and other organisms adapted to it. In a community of mature organisms that survive the fire, initially the new species brought into the burned area usually add complexity. Frequent repetition of the burning, however, will provide a largely similar microenvironment over large areas for so long that complexity diminishes. Gradually, the original community of diverse populations is replaced by those adapted to the fire-maintained uniform microenvironment. Thus, where a periodic fire can create greater diversity, frequent fires alone tend to do the opposite. A uniform microenvironment leads to fewer species generally, and often a near-monoculture of low stability. Test plots in both Zambia and Zimbabwe that were burned annually for over forty years were eventually dominated by one or two species of grass with self-drilling seeds adapted to charred, cracked, and bare ground.

A noteworthy corollary to this effect stems from the tendency of boundary areas to support particularly complex communities. Thus a healthy diversity may thrive on the edges of burned areas, and the impact of fire that produces a mosaic of patches and tongues through unburned land may differ significantly from the effect of a uniform burn.

Managers often choose to use either a hot or a cool burn, depending on the effect they want to produce. Chapter 41 gives guidelines for using both. Hot fires imply a lot of dry material that burns fiercely with large flames. Limited dry material produces a slow, creeping "cool" fire with small flames. The different immediate effect a hot or a cool burn has on certain plants sometimes obscures similar long-term effects.

Cool fires were used widely by managers in the teak forests on the Kalahari sands of Zimbabwe, Botswana, and Zambia to prevent hot fires later in the season. This policy appeared so successful in protecting large, mature trees that its impact on the forest floor went unnoticed.

The greatly altered microenvironment at the soil surface was now inhospitable to teak seedlings or to seedlings from the other hardwood species of commercial value, the protection of which was the aim of the forest managers.

To convince foresters in Zimbabwe that this was indeed the case, I suggested they see if they could find any teak seedlings over the thousands of acres they managed. When they were unsuccessful, I took them to a small area in one of the forests alongside a railway line where for many years large numbers of cattle had been offloaded from the trains for watering. On the ground where the cattle had trampled and milled around, fire had not occurred for many years and hundreds of teak seedlings had established, as well as seedlings from other species that were dying out in the areas burned to protect those species.

Forestry provides many variations of this example. Experts have argued that the slow burning of "useless" dead wood on the ground cuts the risk of hot fires and allows nutrients to cycle faster as ash than they would through decay.

Animals

Animals, like plants, also vary greatly in their response to fire. Many do not escape easily. Many others do. Some are attracted to fires for the easy pickings of food from fleeing insects. It is a myth to think the larger game animals of Africa always panic and flee from fire. Although people may drive them to panic with flames and noise, left alone and undisturbed they usually just get out of the way calmly. Once during a three-day battle against a grass fire in the Rukwa Valley of Tanzania, three companions and I barely escaped encirclement by plunging through a weak point in the line of fire. Only yards beyond the fire line we found a group of reedbuck who had just had the same experience and had lain down calmly on the warm ground to watch. Some animals will seek out burned areas very soon after the passage of the fire, especially when the first green regrowth appears.

Throughout history we have made the mistake of noting only the immediate impact of fire on the adult populations of plants and animals. The teak forests of the Kalahari sands were a case in point, but we tend to treat grass, trees, birds, reptiles, game, and other organisms in the same way. We only ask, were they hurt by fire, invigorated by it, or attracted to the green regrowth? Did food supplies increase? We have not watched and formed opinions on what happened to the ecosystem processes in terms of what these things we value need in order to reproduce over prolonged time.

A short-term benefit for adult populations can encourage further burnings that may destroy that population in the long run. I strongly suspect that the dwindling of roan antelope in Africa, usually blamed on disease, represents such ignorance.

For years I have watched totally protected roan herds decrease and die out wherever frequent burning caused the complex savanna communities they favored to deteriorate. Meanwhile we concentrated on the actual diseases that affected the impoverished animals as the cause. That seems a bit like citing pneumonia as the major cause of death among Russians left homeless by World War II, but the mistake is understandable. Roan antelope will come on to burned ground while logs still smoulder. Knowing they liked burns, we did our best to oblige, but our fires decreased the complexity of the community as a whole, particularly among the grass species that were necessary for the roan's survival. Both the animals and the plants of grasslands provide many examples of destruction following too-frequent burning. A great many game species are grassland community components, and their fate ultimately hangs on our more intelligent use of fire.

Fire Alone Does Not Maintain Grasslands

All those observations add up to debunk the old myth that fire maintains grassland. Like many myths it is easy to see how it arose, for cursory observation and research will find it borne out in the short term. However, the development and maintenance of the stable and highly productive grasslands of bygone days is much more complex than the myth implies.

In Chapter 4, I mentioned my first questioning of the beneficial fire myth when we used it in a government-sponsored program to help clear big game from tsetse fly areas in Africa so people and livestock could be settled there. We had wiped out the large game herds, had not eliminated the tsetse fly, and not introduced cattle. Yet the grasslands, which looked lush enough from the window of a Land Rover traveling 30 miles per hour, were deteriorating seriously, as a close consideration of the four ecosystem processes plainly showed. We were only using the tool of fire, having eliminated grazing and animal impact by shooting out the game. The temporary grassland we made masked a serious long-term desertification process, as time proved dramatically.

By the time the once-complex and healthy grasslands were ready for occupation by people with cattle, they were in a bad state of degradation. Active erosion between plants had set in, seedlings of many perennial grasses had become scarce, monocultures of mature plants abounded, and solar energy flow had dropped severely. While periodic fire in the past had contributed to the necessary disturbance in these fairly brittle grasslands, the animals had also played a major role in reversing fire's adverse effects and maintaining healthy communities. Ironically, it is now my belief that the fires we used in the tsetse fly operations were probably one of the main causes of the tsetse fly's spread, as the fire-induced, less effective water cycles led to a dramatic increase in the breeding sites for this slow-breeding insect.

The extent of the destruction caused by fire alone is symbolized for me by the oil sump of a Land Rover. In 1959 while in charge of the government burning and shooting operations in southeastern Zimbabwe, I drove out daily from my bush camp. After some months I was under the vehicle changing the oil and could not help noticing that the grass had polished the underside clean. In fact the front side of the brass sump plug had worn down so far and so smooth it would scarcely hold a wrench.

Six years later, because of the enduring fly, the area still lay largely unoccupied by large game, livestock, or people, although the burning had continued, so I made my old camp a base for training army trackers. After three months of continual driving over the same ground and remembering my past experience, I checked under all our vehicles and found the oil sumps caked with dusty grease. On level ground the grasses persisted weakly, but on slopes and where soil had been shallow before, naked earth and exposed pebbles characterized the scene. Such profound changes, when gradual, escape notice unless an observation like this forces us to think.

The Kruger National Park in South Africa is perhaps one of the best conventionally managed national parks in the world. Tragically, fire is now used every two to three years on average as managers attempt to maintain grasslands that are turning to brush due to partial rest. Because park managers believe that the overgrazing and overbrowsing that are also occurring are due to too many animals, they are culling large numbers of animals each year. This of course only increases the amount of vegetation that is overrested and subsequently burned. I know of no soils anywhere that can withstand burning of this frequency.

Tragically it is not only Kruger National Park that is shooting animals and then, in effect, using fire to replace the role the once-abundant animals played. In Zimbabwe, where elephants are destroying magnificent centuries-old baobab trees (photo 19-2), park managers are shooting them by the thousands. No one appears to be asking why even greater numbers of elephants in the past did not destroy the baobabs in these same areas. Why have elephant feeding patterns changed? I strongly suspect they have because of the increased use of fire throughout Zimbabwe and the surrounding countries, which has greatly increased the amount of bare ground, simplified the communities from which elephants derived their sustenance, and gradually transformed the vegetation they once favored into more fibrous, sharp-seeded, less nutritious grass species. Elephants are by nature mainly grazing animals, which most people today find hard to believe, so changed is their diet.

Photo 19-2 *For centuries undamaged by vast elephant populations, magnificent Baobab trees are now being tusked to death, most likely because frequent burning has caused the grasses elephants once favored to be replaced by more fibrous, less nutritious varieties.*

Fire and Atmospheric Pollution

Recent studies on the atmospheric pollution created by forest and particularly range/savanna fires in Africa and North America add good reason to seriously look at alternatives to fire wherever possible. Until quite recently, most atmospheric pollution was attributed to products or by-products of the petrochemical industry. Now, data gathered by researchers via satellite and fieldwork indicate that biomass burning is a significant contributor as well. Scientists have calculated that the emissions *every second* from a vegetation fire covering 1.5 acres (0.5 hectares) is equivalent to the carbon monoxide emissions produced per second by 3,694 cars and the nitrogen oxides produced per second by 1,260 cars.[1]

Today, half the world's savanna land (1.85 billion acres/750 million hectares), is deliberately set on fire each year, releasing about 3.7 million metric tons of carbon into the atmosphere. This is three times more carbon than is released through forest burning.[2] While the burning of grasslands is common wherever vegetation is dry enough to burn, most inevitably occurs in Africa, owing to the sheer size of the continent (the whole of the United States, China, India, Europe, Argentina and New Zealand would fit inside the boundaries of Africa with land to spare). In

Africa three-quarters of the savanna grasslands go up in smoke every year. Pollution—ozone, carbon monoxide, and methane—from grass fires in southern Africa, drifts thousands of miles within weeks to Australia and Antarctica where atmospheric pollutants have already created an ozone hole.[3]

Some scientists argue that the amount of carbon dioxide produced by these massive grassland fires is not an issue because once plants regrow they will absorb the same amount. But they fail to consider the adverse effects of fire on plant spacing, composition, soil cover, water cycles, and so on, which generally lead to the production of less biomass, as I found when the burned areas no longer grew enough grass to wipe our vehicle oil sumps clean. When less biomass is produced, less carbon dioxide is absorbed.

In 1994 scientists at Germany's Max Planck Institute found that disturbingly high levels of methyl bromide were also being produced by fires in Siberian forests, Californian chaparral, and South African savannas. The bromine in methyl bromide is potentially 50 times more efficient than the chlorine in chloroflurocarbons (CFCs) in destroying upper-level atmospheric ozone.[4]

While there is still much to learn, and the sheer scale of biomass burning makes accurate estimates impossible, we should not ignore the warnings provided by these studies. In the United States, where the pendulum has once again swung back in favor of fire, prescribed burning is heavily promoted with little or no consideration given to its effects on the atmosphere.

Few indeed are the people interested or even willing to explore alternatives to fire. On a ranch we manage as a learning site in New Mexico, we initially struck all the problems one would expect to find on land that for years has been subjected to partial rest and overgrazing of plants. Over 80 percent of the ground was bare, and the few perennial grasses that had survived were mainly of three varieties that could withstand high levels of rest. Most of these plants were dense, dark-gray-to-black masses of old material surrounded by eroding soil. To begin putting the situation right we needed to knock down the old dead material so the plants could again grow freely, and the soil could be covered. Naturally we wanted to use animals, rather than machinery or fire because their trampling would also churn up the capped surface so new plants could establish.

However, we immediately ran into problems because the majority of the land was leased from the government and regulations prohibited us from running animals at the density and with the numbers required. We could only use fire. Using fire would, of course, remove almost all of the plant material, expose even more soil, and do nothing to break the capped surface. At the same time it would release carbon into the air when we wanted to keep it cycling through plants and soils. We eventually worked with the government agency concerned to find a way around the regulations, but it caused us several years of delay.

Conclusion

When considering whether to use the tool of fire, keep your holistic goal in mind—know what you are trying to achieve. If other tools could achieve what you want without exposing soil or polluting the atmosphere, then consider them, too. Remember that the viability of the whole population structure, *not* merely adult plants and animals, is critical.

There will be times when fire is the best tool to use for the job. The guidelines for burning outlined in Chapter 41 will help you create a plan. Once your plan is made, of course, you must monitor to make sure that the results you expect do materialize.

Fire produces different effects depending on where an environment falls on the brittleness scale. I have tended to use examples from either extreme to illustrate those differences, but bear in mind that most environments will lie somewhere between the two extremes of nonbrittle and very brittle. Thus, if you are dealing with land at 7 or 8 on a scale of 1 to 10, it would tend to have most of the features of the very brittle extreme. Land at 2 or 3 would tend to have most of the features of the nonbrittle extreme. Here is a summary of the effects of fire on the four ecosystem processes at either extreme.

Very Brittle Environments

COMMUNITY DYNAMICS

Fire exposes soil. In low-rainfall areas where plant spacings are wide, new cover develops very slowly. In the short term, fire tends to increase the diversity of species in grassland and woodland. Repeated fires reduce diversity. Fire stimulates the growth of most woody plants that have grown beyond the seedling stage and kills only a few. Fire can produce mosaic patterns within a given area of vegetation, creating an edge effect, where two or more types of habitat meet and create a zone of greater biological diversity. Over time, fire reduces the ability of grasslands to remove carbon from the atmosphere.

WATER CYCLE

Fire generally reduces the effectiveness of the water cycle as it exposes soil and destroys the litter that slows water flow and maintains soil surface crumb structure and aeration. The lower the rainfall and the more frequent the fire, the greater this tendency.

MINERAL CYCLE

Fire speeds the mineral cycle in the short term by converting dead material to ash. But it also spews carbon and other pollutants into the air as it rapidly oxidizes vegetation. Because it exposes the soil and changes the soil surface microenvironment that supports the organisms of decay, fire, if used repeatedly, tends to slow the mineral cycle in the long run. Once more, the drier the area and the more frequent the fire, the greater this tendency.

ENERGY FLOW

In grasslands and savanna-woodlands fire may produce an immediate increase in energy flow by removing old material that hinders the growth of both grasses and brush. However, the consequent soil exposure leads to less effective mineral and water cycles and changes in the plant community that could reduce energy flow in the long term. The drier the area and the more frequent the fire, the greater this tendency.

Nonbrittle Environments

COMMUNITY DYNAMICS

Fire appears to have a short-term effect with little long-term consequence other than to the atmosphere. The generally higher humidity inhibits fires, and after a burn the return to complexity is typically rapid on undisturbed land. The close plant spacing in nonbrittle grasslands helps to minimize soil exposure.

WATER CYCLE

Fire tends to damage the water cycle by exposing soil, but with the better annual distribution of humidity and the more rapid advance of succession on bare surfaces, the effect is temporary.

MINERAL CYCLE

Fire appears to speed up the cycling of nutrients, but this effect is often an illusion. The biological decay so necessary to maintaining carbon in soil organic matter gives way to rapid oxidation and the air and atmospheric pollution associated with it. Mineral cycles, however, *appear* to recover fast after a fire. For thousands of years fire was of course the main tool in slash and burn agriculture. Although the fire freed many nutrients in the community for human use by growing plants in the ash, the effect was temporary. Such agricultural systems, sound as they appeared, broke down fast unless there was a rest of at least twenty years between fire use periods.

ENERGY FLOW

Fire disrupts energy flow in the short run, but like the plant community, energy flow also recovers quickly after fire. In slash and burn agriculture, more energy is temporarily directed to immediate human use. Frequent fires, even in a completely nonbrittle environment, will tend to damage all four ecosystem processes. In parts of Africa, and probably elsewhere, less brittle environments at about 3 to 5 on the scale with seasonal rainfall from 30 to 80 inches (750 to 2,000 mm) have been converted from forest to savanna through the repeated use of fire and have taken on the characteristics associated with more brittle environments. The loss of the tree canopy, which had kept humidity fairly constant at ground level even through long dry seasons, has led to a sharp reduction in microorganism populations over the dry period. Thus, the perennial grasses that replaced the trees now lack the organisms that can decay the mass of material left on them at the end of the growing season. As they lack enough animals to graze or trample down the old material, and thus assist in the decay process, the people in these areas have been compelled to burn the grass to keep it alive and fresh enough for animals to eat. When these same areas have been rested (from fire and livestock) for several years, however, they have returned to dense woodland or forest and once again assumed the characteristics of a less brittle environment.

This summary of the effects of fire in very brittle and nonbrittle environments generally assumes that the fire is followed by a period of rest, as is common practice. Many make the conscious decision to apply rest following a burn, but some also apply it unintentionally by making no decision at all. Depending on your holistic goal, fire followed by rest may not be the best thing to do. Because it is impossible to use fire as a tool without also using one of the other tools—rest, grazing, animal impact, or technology—read on.

20

Rest: The Most Misunderstood Tool

When speaking of rest as a tool that can be used to modify the four ecosystem processes, I am referring to rest from major physical disturbance that applies mainly to plants and soils. Disturbance comes in many forms. Large animals, domestic or wild, but particularly those that exhibit herding behavior, impact both soils and vegetation. So can machinery. Fire disturbs vegetation, but disturbs the soil only slightly; on occasion, hailstorms and natural catastrophes disturb both. A policy of withholding all of these forms of disturbance completely for a considerable time amounts to applying the tool of *total rest. Partial rest* is applied in the presence of livestock or large game, but with such calm behavior in the absence of pack-hunting predators that a large proportion of the plant life and soil surface remains undisturbed despite their presence and grazing.

Partial rest is a new concept that many find hard to grasp. How can the land be resting while high numbers of livestock or big game are grazing on it? Its effects, however, are evident anywhere livestock or large game animals seldom bunch; the more scattered they are, the greater the degree of partial rest. That includes most rangelands and many forests and national parks.

That rest in either form (total or partial) might function as a tool of the same order as a fire or a plow comes as a new concept. We considered rest natural until we registered the fact that brittle and nonbrittle environments react to it in very different ways and that the major grazing areas of the world, particularly before humans developed the ability to use fire and spears, seldom, if ever, experienced rest on a large scale.

Once humans could light fires, fell trees, domesticate animals, and plant crops, they had to bear responsibility for their impact on nature. The choice to give or withhold rest from a piece of land only amounts to another aspect of the powers we can exercise consciously. Our unconscious wielding of this tool, especially in the form of partial rest, in combination with the misguided use of other tools, such as fire, has had the most devastating effect on the brittle environments of our probable origin as a species.

When humans first settled in permanent villages and thus drove wild herds from the surrounding area, they unintentionally but decisively subjected those lands to rest. We now intentionally rest land in the hope that it will recover from the effects of fire, overgrazing, or overtrampling. Although we justify this as "leaving things to nature," we have changed natural relationships no less than those first settlers did. To understand why, we must look at the different effects produced by rest at either end of the brittleness scale.

Effects of Rest in Nonbrittle Environments

In nonbrittle environments (1 or 2 on a scale of 1 to 10) old plant material *by definition* breaks down quickly through biological decay. Such "rotting down" starts close to the ground where the microenvironment supports the highest populations of insects and microorganisms engaged in the decay process. Initial decomposition close to the ground particularly suits the bunched-type perennial grasses, because dead leaves and stems weaken at the base and quickly fall aside, allowing light to reach new, ground-level growing points. Photo 20-1 shows an example of this. Last season's leaves and stems have toppled, and new growth only awaits the right temperature and moisture.

This rapid, bottom-up decay process on dead woody vegetation as well as grasses allows nonbrittle biological communities under total or partial rest to maintain a high degree of stability and complexity of species in grassland or forest. Water, if it runs off soil surfaces at all, carries little silt or other debris. Even very prolonged rest from the rare fire or physical impact by machinery or large animals has little or no adverse effect on the water cycle, mineral cycle, community dynamics, or energy flow.

Nonbrittle environments reduced to bare ground by some natural or human-made catastrophe respond rapidly to rest and return relatively quickly to their former complexity and stability, whether jungle, forest, or grassland. Desertification is seldom a long-term danger, although deforestation can cause enormous damage in the short term.

Whether or not you use the tool of rest in such environments depends entirely on your holistic goal. Although rest does not prematurely kill perennial grasses in nonbrittle environments there is generally a tendency for rested grass communities to move on to shrubs and eventually woodland or forest unless some soil- or weather-related factor limits the succes-

Photo 20-1 *Less brittle grassland showing last year's old growth of leaves and stems (pale color) already fallen and decaying and not choking new growth. Alaska.*

sional process at the grass level. Thus if your holistic goal describes a future resource base that includes stable grassland and you suspect that natural succession will proceed toward forest, you should avoid rest in either form. Any oldtimer in such a place will explain how the fallow field goes first to weeds, then to briars, then to scrub, and finally to woods. To retard such advances, particularly in managed pastures, it becomes necessary to graze perennial grasses severely, but not overgraze them, to maintain a vigorous root system that is difficult for immature tap-rooted woody plants to penetrate. Your only other options for keeping grass roots vigorous and profuse are to use fire if the vegetation will burn or some form of technology, such as mowing. You could create a mosaic of grass and woodland by partially resting certain areas and not others, and if the environment could support solid jungle, you could get that, too, through rest.

That all this works so straightforwardly in nonbrittle environments has obscured the fact that it does not in very brittle ones. Some of the greatest environmental tragedies in human history have ensued from the false assumption that all environments respond the same way to rest. The key to land management is always the state of the soil surface. Remember that in environments leaning toward the nonbrittle end of the scale, it is virtually impossible to expose vast areas of soil and keep them bare. You can burn vegetation, poison it, bulldoze it, or overgraze all of it, and the soil surface will still cover over again quickly if rested. In a nonbrittle environment rest is, I believe, the most powerful tool available to us to restore and sustain biodiversity and healthy land.

Effects of Rest in Very Brittle Environments

In very brittle environments (9 to 10 on the scale) *by definition* old plant material breaks down slowly and the successional process advances slowly, at best, from bare soil. Most organisms of decay, especially in communities that have lost biodiversity, are scarce and present in high numbers only intermittently when moisture is adequate. In some arid areas, termites help to break down plant material and thus play a vital role. However, when fire and partial rest combine to produce the bare soil that favors many termite species, termite numbers can increase to such an extent that they consume all the soil-covering litter.

Under conditions of either partial or total rest, if animal numbers are also low most old plant material breaks down through oxidation and physical weathering. Being most exposed to the elements—wind, raindrops, and sun—the tips of leaves and stems break down first. While this top-down breakdown has little adverse effect on woody plants, it severely hinders perennial grasses with ground-level growth points that often remain shaded and obstructed for years. Old plant material that lingers through the next growing season weakens most perennial grass plants, and several years' accumulation can actually kill them. It also adversely affects the feeding of grazing animals who are always trying to balance their diets and to avoid old oxidizing plant material.

Some perennial grass species can withstand high levels of rest. Commonly these will have growth points above ground, reflected in branching stems, and this allows enough growth to keep the plant alive even when a mass of undecayed material chokes most of the plant. Tobosa grass, common in the western United States, is a good example. Other rest-tolerant species can be very short in stature, such as the grama grasses, or can have sparse thin leaves that, despite an accumulation of old growth, allow some light to reach ground-level growth points. Many of the species from the *Aristida* genus have this characteristic.

In the sparsely populated brittle environments of the western United States, where there are so few animals on the land, a few perennial grass species with a high tolerance for rest dominate the scene. In contrast, in the densely populated brittle environments of India, where there are millions of animals, particularly sacred cows, on the land, grasses that can withstand high levels of overgrazing dominate. In both cases, however, on similar type land, the amount of bare ground between plants remains about the same, as both are using partial rest to a greater extent than any other tool, and rest generally promotes bare ground—the more so, the more brittle and the more arid the environment.

When the soil surface remains undisturbed, as much of it is in the brittle environments of India and the western United States, new plants do not easily replace those that are dead or dying. The capping that usually forms on rested soil offers poor opportunities to the germinating seed. Outside the tropics, prolonged rest allows freezing and thawing of the upper layers of exposed soil to create a puffiness that also inhibits the establishment of young, fibrous-rooted grasses.

Very brittle, low-rainfall environments subjected to extended periods of rest (partial or total) characteristically have wide bare spaces between vestigial perennial grass plants. The remaining plants survive because light can reach the ground-level growing points around the edges of each plant, but the centers may already be dead. Photo 20-2 illustrates these symptoms on a once-healthy, but now totally rested perennial grassland on the Sevilleta Wildlife Refuge, which lies in a very brittle 9-inch (225-mm) rainfall environment of New Mexico. Most remaining grass plants are barely alive, having only a few green leaves round the edges of the dead stems. Despite many years of seed production no seedlings at all have established on the bare, undisturbed soil surface. What seedlings are present are all forbs.

After adequate disturbance of the soil surface, closely spaced perennial grass plants often do establish. If such land is then rested, however, the closely spaced plants kill one another off prematurely, as old growth that has accumulated on them shades even the edges of the neighboring clump.

Photo 20-2 *U.S. Fish and Wildlife Service officials inspecting rested and dying grassland with large, bare ground spaces opening between plants. All seedlings within view are forbs, not grasses. Sevilleta Wildlife Refuge, New Mexico.*

Photo 20-3 shows such a grassland in a 15-inch (375-mm) rainfall brittle environment in northern Mexico. Whole handfuls of dead grass can be pulled out by the roots with ease. Photo 20-4 shows the same thing in a 30-inch (750-mm) rainfall brittle area of Zimbabwe.

If the landscape described in your future resource base requires woody plant species and the animal organisms associated with them, then you would consider continued rest for these lands if they received enough rainfall to support good stands of woody plants. The dead clumps of grass provide a good microenvironment for seed germination and the dead roots lacing the soil make an excellent medium for penetration and establishment of the woody plant seedling's tap root. Photo 20-5, taken on the same ranch as photo 20-3 in Mexico, confirms that woody species, in this instance, mesquite, have already found their niche on this land with high levels of partial rest. Note the correlation of mesquite and dead grass clumps. If your holistic goal does not involve this kind of change, don't apply either partial or total rest. Most of the brush and tree encroachment we consider a problem today owes its existence to heavy doses of the tool of rest, mainly partial.

Continued rest in very brittle, low-rainfall environments can eventually destroy even the woody species, however. Once all remaining grass plants have oxidized and blown away, the bare surface becomes capped,

Photo 20-3 *Brittle environment grassland, which had developed close spacing under the influence of previous animal impact, now showing mass deaths under rest. Most plants are gray and oxidizing and can be pulled up easily. Coahuila, Mexico.*

Photo 20-4 *Perennial grassland in a 30-inch (750-mm) rainfall, very brittle environment rested one year. All plants are smothered by a mass of gray-to-black oxidizing material that is preventing light from reaching growth points. To the right, the same species are kept healthy by periodic mowing (performed by road crews). Zimbabwe.*

Photo 20-5 *Brittle environment community shifting from grassland to forbs and mesquite trees in overrested patches (background), while overgrazed patches (foreground) show excessive erosion. Coahuila, Mexico.*

and, lacking the old grass root systems, the once friable subsoil closes up. New seeds can establish only in cracks, if there are any, and growth proves difficult after that unless some form of disturbance is applied.

Photo 20-6 shows a piece of land within the very brittle Chaco Canyon National Monument in New Mexico, which has been rested for over fifty years. Most grasses are dead. The shrubs, too, are now dying and are surrounded by bare, eroding soil. In a few places where the land is flat enough, algae and lichens persist as the last life left.

Towns and cities in very brittle environments are also subject to the adverse effects of rest. When the catchment areas surrounding a town are rested, as inevitably happens when larger parcels of land (5 to 20 acres; 2 to 8 hectares) are set aside from intensive development, the effect is entirely good as long as those towns are in a nonbrittle or less brittle environment. On the land surrounding London, Washington, D.C., Paris, or Sydney rest generally leads to an increase in soil cover and biodiversity. But towns and cities in the more brittle environments cannot afford to rest their catchment areas, particularly when rainfall is also low. Cities such as Albuquerque, Los Angeles, and Perth are surrounded by minimally developed parcels of land that are being rested to death, as shown in photo 20-7. The resulting amount of bare ground produces an enormous amount of runoff that commonly inundates these cities with floods any time they

Photo 20-6 *Fifty years of total rest in a very brittle, low-rainfall environment. Most grass is already dead, bare ground and soil erosion are extensive, and many shrubs are dying. The main plants left are algae and lichens. Chaco Canyon National Park, New Mexico.*

Photo 20-7 *Large residential plots surrounding Santa Fe, New Mexico, a very brittle, low-rainfall environment, are being rested to death. As bare ground increases, so do erosion and gully formation.*

get more than a fraction of an inch of rain over a short time. Their dams and rivers are dangerously full of silt as well. The bed of the Rio Grande, which flows through Albuquerque, is now significantly higher than the original town center.

Few city or county planners in more brittle environments consider these consequences when they allow catchment areas surrounding towns to be divided into the small ranchettes or summer homes so popular with well-off retirees. Even if the owners keep horses and other animals, the tools they will be applying daily will be partial rest and overgrazing. Urban residents will have to live with the destructive consequences and bear the costs for years to come.

Effects of Rest in Less Brittle Environments

The effects of rest are more difficult to decipher in environments that lie in the middle range of the brittleness scale (around 4 to 7 on the 1 to 10 scale). You cannot be sure at which point the effects of rest change over from enhancing soil cover, energy flow, and the health of perennial grass plants to damaging them—just as you cannot be sure, when standing atop a watershed, which way a drop of rain will flow. In these less brittle environments, the effects also take longer to show up. If rest does have adverse tendencies, it may become apparent only after a good many years.

The evidence is easier to show photographically in grassland than forest. Photo 20-8, from the Crescent Lake Wildlife Refuge in Nebraska, shows land that appears to lie in the middle range of the brittleness scale and has been totally rested for twelve years. Although there appears to be no great damage, a high proportion of these grasses are now gray and dead. Closer inspection reveals weakened grasses and an invasion of tap-rooted plants (herbaceous rather than woody) into what once was healthier grassland. All four ecosystem processes show early signs of adverse change.

Photo 20-9 shows nearby land on the same refuge totally rested fifty years. By this stage the water cycle, mineral cycle, community dynamics, and energy flow have all visibly declined. Grasses that earlier provided ground cover are clearly dying and many are dead. All new plants are small herbaceous ones that many would consider weeds. A large proportion of the ground has become bare, and once the dead grass litter breaks down this area will expand.

This environment obviously lies to the right of the midpoint in the scale. It is too brittle to sustain grassland without repeated disturbance, and it receives too little rainfall for the successional process to move it to soil-covering woodland. Thus, when totally rested, bare soil is the eventual

Photo 20-8 *Land lying in the middle range of the brittleness scale that has been rested for twelve years. A high proportion of these grasses are gray and dead or dying. Crescent Lake Wildlife Refuge, Nebraska.*

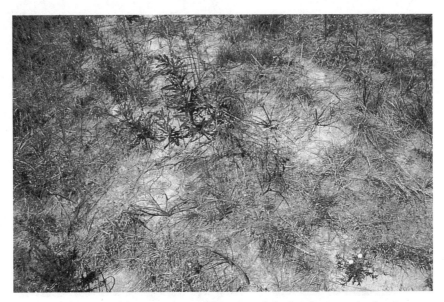

Photo 20-9 *Land lying in the middle range of the brittleness scale that has been rested for fifty years. By this stage a great many plants have died and bare ground has increased significantly. The few new plants are forbs, not grasses. Water and mineral cycles are seriously impaired and energy flow is greatly reduced. Crescent Lake Wildlife Refuge, Nebraska.*

result. If this land had only been partially rested under low numbers of game or livestock, that would only have slowed the rate of deterioration.

Because about two-thirds of the earth's land surface is brittle to varying degrees, and since the dawn of agriculture it has carried livestock under management that paradoxically produces *both* partial rest and overgrazing, the remorseless growth of deserts is no mystery.

As mentioned in Chapter 19 some savanna-woodlands and grasslands in high-, but seasonal-, rainfall areas show clear signs of brittleness in that old grass parts oxidize rather than decay, dead grass and trees break down by weathering from tips rather than rotting near the base first. Yet, if rested long enough, these communities commonly pass on to forest and assume the characteristics of a less brittle environment. The tree canopy keeps humidity at ground level fairly constant, even through dry periods, and thus microorganism populations also remain constant. The *Brachystegia* woodlands that abound in central Africa in high-, but very seasonal-, rainfall areas are a good example.

I have also seen places where the rainfall was much lower, but tap-rooted woody plants provided soil cover and achieved the same stability because subterranean moisture allowed a dense enough stand of brush or

Photo 20-10 *Nature preserve alongside the Rio Grande. This very brittle riparian area, rested for more than thirty years, has in many places deteriorated to bare, eroding ground. Almost all plants have died. (Metal structures were built some years ago to minimize flood damage.) Albuquerque, New Mexico.*

trees. This situation is common along riparian (streamside) strips. If rested for prolonged periods, such environments tend to pass on to stable woodlands. But do not be fooled into believing all riparian areas remain healthy when rested. Some riparian areas lack sufficient subterranean moisture everywhere to maintain dense, woody cover and will deteriorate seriously when rested, as shown in photo 20-10. Unfortunately, in the United States many government agencies have made it standard policy to fence off and protect, that is, rest, riparian areas in brittle environments under their jurisdiction.

Even when the area adjacent to the stream or river is less brittle, it may be surrounded by very brittle catchments. Because the health of the stream entirely depends on its catchments, or watersheds, management has to cater to this larger whole.

Delayed Effect of Rest in Brittle Environments

Most governments dealing with desertification have long been advised that the deterioration was largely due to overgrazing, which in turn was caused by the presence of too many animals. The obvious solution was to drastically reduce animal numbers so the land could heal. However, most politicians lacked the willpower to actually force such a measure. To demonstrate the advantages of total destocking (rest) the U.S. government in the 1930s fenced off demonstration plots of land throughout the western states. The same was also done in parts of Africa and elsewhere.

Once protected from overgrazing and unimpeded by old growth, the plots indeed grew lush and became the justification for often draconian campaigns to reduce stock. Photo 20-11 shows an example in New Mexico taken from the Council on Environmental Quality's report on *Desertification of the United States*, published in 1981.[1] Although the photograph lacks detail within the plot, we can see a good stand of vigorous grass, freed from the overgrazing evident on the other side of the fence. Outside the fence we see a tightly spaced community of overgrazed grasses typical of land under continuous grazing and high levels of disturbance. The caption that accompanied this photo in the report reads: "Range improvement in the Rio Puerco Valley, Sandoval County, New Mexico. Grass on the left is protected from overgrazing (Soil Conservation Service)."

This is a typical situation where the officials were misled by two things, one being the power of paradigms, and the other being the time delay before the effects of rest became apparent. Although the report was written in 1981, a 1930s photograph was used—one that illustrated the imme-

Photo 20-11 *Government demonstration plot established in the 1930s to prove rested land would recover. Grass on the left was fenced off from grazing animals, and within three years was more lush than on the right where livestock were present and overgrazing many plants. Note Cabezon Peak, which appears in the background. Rio Puerco Valley, New Mexico.*

diate benefits of plant recovery from overgrazing in a community still benefiting from the residual effect of the animal impact. In fact, the remaining
demonstration plots in the Rio Puerco in 1981 all looked like what you
see in photo 20-12. The report writers *knew* that land recovers when
destocked and rested and felt no need to check on the current status of the
plots; they merely used the 1930s photograph already on file. Had a 1980s
photograph of any of the demonstration plots been used instead of a 1930s
one, a very different conclusion might have been reached. Because of total
rest these plots are desertifying as badly as any land I have seen in Africa,
Australia, or the Middle East. The authors were not being dishonest, just
human. Why question what we already *know*?

The critical distinction between rest as a long-term tool and rest as the
time it takes a damaged plant to rebuild a root system has thrown our
understanding of desertification off for several thousand years. We correctly observed that animals in certain circumstances overgraze and damage
plants. If we run high animal numbers and overgraze most plants, as many
did in the western United States at the turn of the century, and we then
remove the animals, the land appears to recover quickly and dramatically,
as those early research plots showed. In fact we had stopped two animal-
produced effects, one negative, and one positive. The result was that the
positive and immediate effect of allowing overgrazed plants to recover col-

Photo 20-12 *View of one of the remaining demonstration plots in the Rio Puerco
Valley. Fifty years later (1987), the continued resting of this land has resulted in serious
deterioration. Cabezon Peak again appears in the background. New Mexico.*

"Now here's a pasture that's plainly overstocked, but danged if I know what to do about it. I ain't had a hoof on it in ten years!"

Photo 20-13 *Without realizing he had stumbled onto something vital, cartoonist Ace Reid noted the effect of rest in brittle environments (courtesy Ace Reid).*

ored our ability to determine and even see the eventual damage we created by eliminating beneficial animal impact.

With fewer animals on the land, partial rest increases, but overgrazing still continues. Rangelands become dominated by bare ground, rest-tolerant perennial grasses of the types mentioned earlier, brush, and so-called weeds. Seeing this decline, we have for generations advocated cutting animal numbers even further, and in effect, resting the land even more, while wasting millions of dollars in futile spraying of the resulting noxious plants. Cartoonist Ace Reid summed up this paradox some years ago without realizing he had stumbled onto something vital (photo 20-13).

Partial and Total Rest Have Nearly the Same Effect

By fencing off so many plots of land in the 1930s, the U.S. government also provided excellent evidence for another important point—that partial rest can be nearly as destructive as total rest in the more brittle environments. The government research plots excluded all livestock, but on the land outside them livestock numbers were low and declining, wild grazers were few in number, and pack-hunting wolves and Indians had long since vanished.

It is not surprising that the government at the time wanted to reduce livestock numbers, given that the nation's attention was riveted on the dustbowl that in the 1930s covered a large part of the country. Over the next decades, livestock numbers would continually be reduced in an effort to restore the land to its former productivity. The reductions have continued through the present but without any real recovery of land. Now when you examine the totally rested land inside the old exclosure plots and the land outside them where partial rest and overgrazing have continued, there is very little difference.

Photo 20-14 shows the boundaries of three experimental plots, each of which is in an environment successively less brittle than the first. In each case, the four ecosystem processes have seriously malfunctioned inside the plots after forty to sixty-five years of rest.

Outside the plots the land is no better. Roughly the same amount of ground is bare. The fact that some plants outside the plots were overgrazed has had little impact on the total picture. The level of rest and position on the brittleness scale were a much greater influence. Inside the first plot, no living perennial grasses remain; outside it at least some perennial grasses have been kept alive by grazing, even though they are overgrazed. In the other two plots, two or three species of rest-tolerant perennial grasses have managed to survive both inside and outside the plots.

Unfortunately, researchers who take it for granted that rest is natural, have compared the surrounding land to the rested sites and, because there is so little difference between the two, have pronounced management outside the plots successful. The land, they say, has reached the highest level of development of which it is capable because it matches the totally rested land inside the plots. *They were unaware of or ignored the awkward fact that the plots at first got better and only subsequently declined.*

Rest and Crisis Management

Misunderstanding of what partial rest does to brittle environments often leads to crisis management on land people intend to preserve in pristine condition. I have seen more than one environmental organization acquire badly damaged brittle land and slowly change their management of it from a dogmatic hands-off, leave-it-to-Nature approach to application of the most drastic techniques available. It happens in a predictable sequence.

Following years of overgrazing by livestock, the plants respond vigorously to rest and all looks good. The increase in volume and cover benefits

Land at approximately 9 or 10 on the brittleness scale. Following more than forty years of total rest inside the plot (right side of fence) and partial rest and overgrazing/overresting of plants outside it (left side of fence), no perrenial grasses remain inside the plot and only a few have survived outside it. Central California.

Land at approximately 7 or 8 on the brittleness scale. Following more than forty years of total rest inside the plot (right) and partial rest and overgrazing/overresting of plants outside it (left), only three species of rest-tolerant perennial grasses remain on both sides. Western Arizona.

Land at approximately 4 to 6 on the brittleness scale. Following sixty-five years of total rest inside the plot (right) and partial rest and overgrazing/ overresting of plants outside it (left), plant spacing is much closer both inside and outside, but the few species of perennial grasses that remain on both sides are those that can withstand high levels of rest. Southeastern Arizona.

Photo 20-14 *Research plots established by the U.S. government in the western states over the last fifty or so years demonstrate the effects of total rest (inside the plots) and partial rest (outside the plots) on land ranging from very brittle to less brittle.*

many creatures and complexity builds up. Progress under nature appears on target and no one dissents. Sometimes official transects and measurements record the advance, as has happened on the Audubon Society's Appleton-Whittel Biological Research Station in southeastern Arizona. Lists of small mammals, birds, and insects become impressive as more species reap the new bounty. Gradually, however, the measurements note the first signs of adverse change. Moribund grasses turn up in the log books, various weedy plants increase in number, and bare spots begin to open up. None of this is expected, and for a year or so it proceeds while people hope the problem will go away.

Inevitably when the problem does not go away, the managers conclude that fire should be used as "fire is natural and it maintained grassland in the past." The first unnatural means of returning the land to nature, rest, has led to another. (As mentioned earlier, human-made fires are unnatural.) In a brittle environment, fire invigorates mature grasses, but threatens all four ecosystem processes by exposing soil. Given that rest also tends to expose soil and that the cause of the old vegetation accumulating has not been removed, the situation predictably worsens as fire use becomes too frequent. Technology often comes next in the form of seedings, plowings, plantings, check dams, ditching, and the like. However, the problem remains insoluble until the managers understand the implications of rest in brittle environments.

When confronted by the argument for reintroducing animal impact as a natural influence managers in such situations typically respond, "but no bison ever roamed here." Or "cattle are not native to this environment." This ignores the fact that many animals maintained grasslands, not just bison and that there were many more species of animals, including ancestors of cattle, as recently as 10,000 years ago in North America. Even in the last few centuries, species other than bison, such as deer, elk, pronghorn, bighorn sheep, could break a period of rest, but so little is known about the actual number and distribution of these animals, even a century ago, that debates about them tend to be academic. In some parts of the American Southwest where people insist that large herds never occurred, we now have evidence that hunting peoples thrived even relatively recently (within the last two hundred years). In fact, aerial inspections have revealed a remarkable density of not so ancient pronghorn traps. Although many, including myself, far prefer wildlife to livestock, today we have to employ the tools at hand or accept the dreadful consequences of desertification.

If a pocket of brittle environment land now isolated by ranches, roads, and international borders once supported a teeming grassland, then with very few exceptions animal impact of some sort *by definition* helped to maintain it. Even if no wild population exists that could conceivably do that now, to rule out domestic stock as a less natural tool than human fires and bulldozers for producing pristine habitat seems counterproductive.

Photo 20-2 showed one more case of a brittle area returned to nature through unnatural rest. Fifteen years prior the Sevilleta Refuge was willed to The Nature Conservancy and put under management of the U.S. Fish and Wildlife Service. Unfortunately New Mexico no longer has wolf packs or sabre tooth lions that chase large, free-roaming herds, and small groups of undisturbed deer and pronghorn do not mitigate the regime of rest imposed on the refuge. All the symptoms of desertification that the donor of the land sought to reverse have only worsened.

What Is "Natural"?

Invariably some people at this point close their minds because grassland does exist in parts of America, Australia, and Argentina, for instance, without any evidence of help from herding animals in the recent past. In my experience a grassland will always reflect the degree of its brittleness and the net result of the amount of rest or disturbance it has received. This will show in its complexity, plant spacings, and overall energy flow. If plant spacings are close and age structure good in the absence of disturbance by fire or animals, then that grassland lies lower on the brittleness scale. If plant spacings are wide, age structure poor, and reproduction predominantly asexual, in the absence of disturbance, then that grassland lies higher on the brittleness scale. If we were in fact to discover a grassland that, based on the climate, should be high on the brittleness scale and that had developed great complexity, stability, and closely spaced plants with no disturbance, we would have discovered a distinct new environment with rules of its own and the concept of brittleness would have to be revised.

Brittle grasslands that do persist under prolonged rest are generally unproductive in that very little sunlight is converted to useful energy. Close inspection of the plants shows them to be highly unstable and typified by sparse form, low stature, branching stems, wide spaces between plants, and asexual reproduction from above- and below-ground runners that establish new plants without genetic diversity. Especially where freezing and thawing create puffy soil, such grassland almost never develops on the steeper slopes of canyon and gully walls.

Such cases raise again and again the philosophical question, What is natural? Eons ago, before humankind controlled fire, livestock, and technology, there was an Eden to which we alas can no longer return. Logic tells us that all plant and animal life developed together in wholes including microenvironment, community, and climate. The brittleness scale, although we did not recognize it, existed for millions of years. The extraordinary expansion of deserts in what were grasslands and savanna-woodlands a few thousand years ago can only be the work of humans.

We go to great lengths to avoid this conclusion. The archaeologists delving the secrets of ancient ruins in New Mexico conjecture that the climate changed, that overpopulation led to a collapse of agriculture in fragile bottom land, that war destroyed the social fabric, that their civilization grew too large to administer without the power of the written word, that they really did not live in the large ruins but only came to pray there, and so on, endlessly. They point to ancient tree rings that indicate prolonged drought. They do not consider that even a primitive population, by hunting, by driving game with fire, by setting accidental fires, might have upset the water cycle enough to affect tree growth more than any drought could.

To regain any part of Eden now means reproducing as closely as possible the conditions under which various biological communities, microenvironments, and climates developed. Wherever we manage to do that, the life that flourishes will be natural whether or not it represents what existed in that place at any given moment during the history of "unnatural" human influence.

The high desert of Oregon provided a perfect background when a group of environmentalists discussed that idea with me at a conference near the small town of Brothers. The area is often cited as an example of stability under conditions of rest, for even the earliest records note the scarcity of large game. Near the town, where cattle have run for fifty years, conferees had difficulty stepping without touching some living plant. Although many plants showed signs of overgrazing, many did not, and new seedlings had sprouted everywhere. Not far away, however, where lack of water and a federal jurisdiction thwarted the presence of grazing animals, the people easily found enough bare ground between grass plants to sit on. They found no overgrazed plants, but many weak and dead ones and very few new sprouts, with erosion proceeding apace.

The second area may well have been natural in the light of known history. It had definitely had time to reach its full potential under rest-is-better management, and indeed many a range scientist, citing its history of rest, would use it as a standard for judging the condition of surrounding land.

Yet the same land, the same climate, and the same plants obviously will develop into a richer, more complex, and more stable environment without rest, and that, too, would be natural in terms of natural potential, if not written history. Today humans have so changed the environments they inhabit that we are forced to make choices in managing them. Even to do nothing in the more brittle environments is to choose to use the tool of rest. Thus, for any piece of land, even a wilderness area or national park, we need to decide what it is we really want.

Canyonlands National Park in Utah contains a site called Virginia Park surrounded on all sides by perpendicular cliffs that have excluded large animals for a long tick of geological time. The grass cover is unstable and very fragile. It needs the tool of rest because the American people quite rightly have chosen to preserve a landscape created some eons ago. But Virginia Park does not represent what more accessible places once were or might become in such brittle environments. The visitor's center at the nearby Arches National Monument passes out literature that describes the grassland that existed at the time the monument was set aside for preservation. The rest that has been imposed since then has resulted in a dying grassland where widening bare patches are obvious. Even if you are unobservant, your attention is drawn to areas where nylon mesh holds mulch to the ground (mentioned in Chapter 13) in an attempt to get grasses growing again. Personally, although I once detested herds of cattle, like so many environmentalists, I find them a more natural tool to use to restore grassland health than nylon netting.

Conclusion

In summary, the effects of rest at either extreme of the brittleness scale are as follows.

Nonbrittle Environments

- *Community dynamics.* Biological communities develop to levels of great diversity and stability.
- *Water and mineral cycles* build and maintain high levels of effectiveness.
- *Energy flow* reaches a high level.

Obviously, rest is the most powerful tool we have to restore or maintain biodiversity and soil cover in nonbrittle environments.

Very Brittle Environments

- *Community dynamics.* Biological communities decline and greater simplicity and instability ensue. The lower the rainfall, the greater the adverse effect.
- *Water and mineral cycles* become less effective.
- *Energy flow* declines significantly.

In very brittle environments, rest in either form is extremely damaging to biodiversity and soil cover. At the midpoint on the 1-to-10 scale partial or total rest shifts from being increasingly positive to being increasingly negative in terms of maintaining soil cover, energy flow, and healthy perennial grasses. Because rest has such clearly different tendencies at the extremes, the condition of rested land generally indicates the underlying brittleness of any area.

21

Grazing: The Most Abused Tool

I n Chapter 6 we explored some of the old beliefs about overgrazing—what it is and what causes it—and why those old beliefs were confounding our efforts to reverse the desertification process. Now it is time to look at grazing in more detail so we can begin to apply this tool to beneficial effect.

Grazing ranks as a tool alongside fire and rest because management can manipulate the intensity and timing of it and the animal–plant relationships that govern it. But, like the other tools, it has natural aspects in that humans did not design the mouths of livestock or wild grazers and teach them how and what to eat or how to behave. And as the ways in which they do these things are crucial to the results of management, we need to understand them better.

In this chapter we consider grazing as if animals floated over the ground without dunging, urinating, salivating, or trampling as they fed. Although grazing never occurs apart from these activities, separating the act of grazing from the other simultaneous influences of the animals on the land (animal impact) helps one better to understand the influence of each and thus the use of each as a tool. This is particularly important in the more brittle environments where the large herding animals evolved and where most desertification is occurring. In the less brittle environments, where plant spacing is naturally close, with or without large animals, and where soil cover is harder to destroy, the separation of the two tools is not as vital, although it is still helpful.

Several examples from environments that lie closer to the very brittle end of the scale show how widely the effects of either tool can vary:

216

- Grazing might be maintaining the health of individual plants, while low animal impact (partial rest) is simultaneously exposing the soil between the plants as fewer new plants can establish.

- Grazing applied as overgrazing may be weakening or killing some plants in the community, while at the same time high animal impact tends to increase the number of plants, the amount of soil cover, and the effectiveness of the rainfall.

- Grazing, together with adequate animal impact, can maintain soil cover, keep grass plants healthy and more productive, and in general enhance the functioning of all four ecosystem processes. But overgrazing combined with low animal impact (partial rest) produces the opposite effect. In fact this latter combination is the most commonly applied, and it is the one with the greatest tendency, in the more brittle environments, to lead to desertification. Tragically, it is also the combination most often recommended by extension workers and supported by environmental groups when they are not pushing for total rest.

The ability to analyze the influence of animal impact and grazing as separate tools allows us to better interpret what we are seeing on the land. It also enables us to more easily unravel such questions as how modern ranchers and farmers damaged parts of Africa and the Americas more in 300 years than nomads and their flocks managed to do in more than 5,000 years in other parts of the world.

A thorough discussion of grazing requires a working definition of the term. Strictly speaking, grazing refers only to the eating of grasses, not other types of vegetation, such as brush, trees, and forbs, which are technically *browsed*. The tool of grazing encompasses both. Browsing is covered in more detail later on.

Before we can meaningfully define grazing and overgrazing, however, we need to note the differences between perennial and annual plants, between grass and nongrass plants, and in the types of grazing animals.

Annual plant populations usually fluctuate widely in numbers from season to season. In some seasons they may fail to establish altogether, leaving the soil exposed. They are difficult to overgraze as they do not live long enough; they generally begin to die once they have produced seed. Perennial plant populations, be they grasses, forbs, shrubs, or trees, however, fluctuate far less in numbers, helping to hold soil in place year round, and keeping more of it covered throughout the year. The lower the rainfall and the more brittle the environment, the greater the role played by perennial grasses in keeping soil covered. Their presence and health determine whether deserts advance or retreat. They are easily overgrazed, however, as you will see.

Perennial grasses mainly grow in two forms: upright, or prone, with lateral running shoots. The more brittle the environment, the more likely the upright perennial grasses will appear as distinct bunches. The less brittle the environment, the more likely they will appear as a sward or mat in which individual plants are hard to see. This variation in the upright grasses can occur even within a species. *Themeda triandra*, a common grass in Africa, grows in a matted form in less brittle environments, but in a bunched form in more brittle environments. The runner grasses do not change form at different points on the brittleness scale, and they may become dominant where many plants are overgrazed and animal impact is high. They are often planted as pasture grasses, especially in the tropics, partly because most of them are fairly resilient to overgrazing, as will be explained.

The buds from which new growth takes place on perennial grasses of either form occur either very close to the ground near the plant base or well above ground, along or at the ends of the plant stems. The position of these growth points probably indicates the evolutionary development of the species. Those with growth points close to the ground probably evolved in close association with severe grazing animals that kept the plant clear of old stems so that light could reach the growth points. If they remain ungrazed, these plants eventually die. Those plants with growth points well above ground probably evolved under little or no pressure from severe grazers because they can be set back by severe grazing, but thrive when rested.

Overgrazing

To grasp the difference between grazing and overgrazing, picture a healthy perennial bunch grass plant with ground-level growth points in a fairly brittle environment, and imagine that a large animal bites all stem and leaf down to an inch or two above the soil. That is severe grazing, but not unusual or bad in that most herding animals evolved to graze in such a manner in harmony with such grasses over millions of years. In the growing season, the plant receives a short-term setback while it uses energy from its crown, stem bases, or roots to reestablish growing leaf, but a long-term boost because the plant tends to end the season better off and less encumbered with old leaf and stem than its ungrazed neighbors. The growth points at the base remain intact and no old growth of the previous year stands in the way of regeneration. This defoliation is important in the more brittle environments to maintain the health and longevity of the plants, but even in the less brittle environments, removal of old material promotes grass health.

If the bite comes in the dormant season when the plant *has no further use for the leaves and stems of the past season*, which have become a potential liability, it loses nothing and gains the advantage of unimpeded growth at the start of the new season. Severe grazing thus benefits the grazed plant. Plants surrounding it that were not grazed are hampered by old material when the next growing season starts. This is why so many people use fire. It removes all the dead matter and allows the ungrazed plants to grow freely once again.

Overgrazing occurs when a plant bitten severely *in the growing season* gets bitten severely again while using energy it has taken from its crown, stem bases, or roots to reestablish leaf—something perennial grasses routinely do. This can happen at three different times:

1. when the plant is exposed to the animals for too many days and they are around to regraze it as it tries to regrow;

2. when animals move away but return too soon and graze the plant again while it is still using stored energy to reform leaf; or

3. immediately following dormancy when the plant is growing new leaf from stored energy.

Any time a plant is severely defoliated, root growth ceases as energy is shunted from root growing to regrowing leaves. This movement of energy between leaves and roots and vice versa is important, not only to maintain the plant's ancient relationship with severe grazing animals, but also to sustain the plant over dormant nongrowing periods. At the end of the growing season, most perennial grasses transfer energy and protein from leaves and stems to stem bases, crowns, and/or roots. This reserve carries the plant through the dormant period and supports the next year's first growth.

If bitten during the growing season, however, when such reserves have already been tapped to provide the initial growth of the season, grasses then have to utilize what little energy remains and will severely deplete roots to provide that energy. If subsequent bites are taken before roots have reestablished, roots will die. Some scientists argue that energy for new growth is taken from what leaves and stems remain on the grazed plant and in the process some roots die to maintain root-to-leaf balance. Where the energy for new growth comes from, however, is not as important as what happens to the roots. No matter which theory you subscribe to, it is fairly evident that severe defoliation, repeated too frequently, causes root mass to decrease until eventually the plant dies.

Thus, a simple definition of overgrazing is any grazing that takes place on leaves growing from stored energy, *at the expense of roots*, rather than directly from sunlight. In other words, overgrazing is "grazing of the roots."

If the grass plant is of the runner type, rather than erect or bunched, there is less danger of overgrazing, even where animals linger or return too soon. As figure 21-1 shows, when individual plants are severely grazed, a

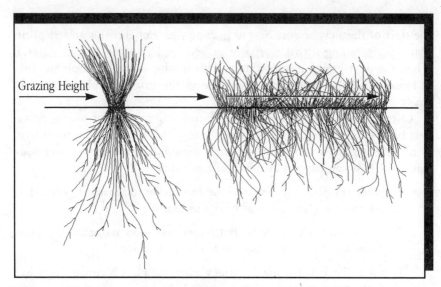

Figure 21-1 *Because of its horizontal spread, less leaf is removed from an individual runner-grass plant when it is grazed severely, than is the case with a bunched grass plant.*

lesser percentage of leaf is removed than is the case with an upright plant, because of the plant's horizontal spread. So much leaf, as well as stems with growing points, remains below the grazing height of most animals that fewer roots are affected. This helps to explain why, as upright grasses are killed by overgrazing, there is a tendency for the space to be filled with a runner grass as long as there is sufficient moisture to sustain it, hence the runner grass mats so common close to water points and areas of very high animal concentration.

Although many perennial grasses can withstand high levels of overgrazing without actually dying, it is still damaging because it reduces the yield of the plant and reduces its root volume. If the above ground part of the plant grows less, it provides less material to feed the animals and less leaf and stem subsequently to cover soil as litter and mulch. Most soil cover comes from litter rather than the bases of living plants in the more brittle environments. If the root mass of the plant is reduced, less energy and organic material are available for soil life. As root mass decreases, soil compacts and loses the air spaces and structure so vital to an effective water cycle and to the well-being of microorganisms living in the soil.

Types of Grazers

Grazing animals fall into three very rough categories depending on how they graze:

1. Nibblers, endowed with narrow mouths, nip a leaf here and there off a plant, seldom overgrazing it because so little total leaf area is taken that the plant's growth, and particularly its roots, are hardly affected. Most of the grazers in this category are solitary, nonherding small animals, such as the stembuck, duiker, and oribi of Africa. They have what we call self-regulating populations and thus never occur in high numbers. None have domestic relatives.

2. A second, broad-mouthed group, feeds by the mouthful. Buffalo, bison, zebra, horses, cattle, and hippo do this. Most are gregarious members of non-self-regulating populations and tend to defoliate grass plants severely. Elephants, which pull up grasses by the trunkful also belong in this group.

3. Somewhere between these two extremes come animals capable of nipping an isolated leaf but habitually given to taking several at a time and concentrating on the same plant to such a degree that they have to be managed as severe grazers. Among them would be sheep, goats, deer, pronghorn, impala, and other herding antelope, as well as perhaps some kangaroos. Again they are gregarious and non-self-regulating and thus capable of building up to high numbers. They are also represented among domestic stock.

The distinction between self-regulating and non-self-regulating populations is an important one that we will return to in Chapter 42. We suspect that the solitary, self-regulating nibblers, which generally do not overgraze, control their population by some form of breeding inhibition allied to social stress above certain densities. The non-self-regulating severe grazers, which can and do overgraze, are heavily dependent for their survival on a high rate of annual loss to accidents, predation, and eventually parasitism, disease, or starvation if predation is inadequate. All of the predator-dependent species appear to herd as the main form of protection.

The presence of a wide diversity of animals on a piece of land often means more thorough utilization of available feed, as becomes evident in studies of complex wildlife situations in Africa or where combinations of sheep, cattle, pigs, goats, and horses run together. It does not, however, change the basic dynamics of overgrazing, and the grazing aspects of planning for most kinds of domestic stock are remarkably similar.

Nonetheless many range scientists persist in trying to prevent overgrazing by limiting utilization. They will specify various levels of utilization for individual species—35 percent for blue-bunch wheat grass, for example—as though it really were possible for a manager to regulate how much an animal will take from plants of one species amidst many. Utilization levels are also specified for different types of communities (e.g., riparian areas 25 percent, and uplands 55 percent). But overgrazing continues no matter what the level of utilization.

Grazing and the Brittleness Scale

A look at the impact of grazing and overgrazing on the four ecosystem processes at the extreme ends of the brittleness scale gives a rough indication of the implications for management.

NONBRITTLE ENVIRONMENTS

Community Dynamics. In such environments where plant spacing is naturally close and soil cover hard to damage, grazing tends to maintain grass root vigor, soil life, and structure. However, it is doubtful it would ever do so to the same depth as occurred under forest vegetation, which pastures in such environments have often replaced. If grassland would normally progress toward woodland in that environment, grazing tends to impede this shift or to halt it at a grassland level.

Overgrazing will reduce root mass but still not expose soil due to the close plant spacing in these environments. Thus overgrazing tends to lead to a solid mat of grass even in upright species. Some species sensitive to overgrazing can disappear, leading to a potentially more unstable community should disease strike remaining plants. Overgrazing may also produce a shift toward woody plant communities, as the reduction in grass roots allows easy establishment of tap-rooted species.

Water and mineral cycles. Grazing will not expose soil but rather will cause even denser cover and thus probably enhance these cycles in grassland. Where human intervention has reduced a natural forest or jungle to grassland and maintained it at that level by grazing, water and mineral cycles probably will never reach the level of effectiveness made possible by the deeper-rooted woody community.

In either natural or planted pastures, grassroot reduction and compaction stemming from overgrazing adversely affect the cycling of both water and minerals. If continual overgrazing allows progression to stable woody communities, as it will given enough rainfall, water and mineral cycles benefit accordingly as pasture gives way to forest.

Energy flow. Grazing increases energy flow both above and below ground in natural grassland or pastures. Where rest would produce woods or jungle, grazing, which holds the community at the grassland level, keeps energy flow down but available for our purposes.

Overgrazing reduces energy flow in grassland or pasture. Only where it produces a shift to woody communities that the climate can sustain does it do otherwise.

VERY BRITTLE ENVIRONMENTS

Community dynamics. Grazing tends to maintain grassland communities, increase their diversity and cover soil, and retard shifts toward woody or herbaceous species. It tends to increase organic content, structure, aeration, and biological activity in the soil because more leaf and more root are produced. In forests, grazing can be used to prevent the buildup of massive amounts of material that become a fire hazard, while maintaining soil cover and promoting the buildup of organic material, thus preventing the death of the forest.

Overgrazing, by reducing litter and soil cover even as it damages roots, fosters shifts away from grassland and woody communities toward herbaceous forbs (or weeds*). It also leads to soil compaction and promotes monocultures with reduced numbers of grass species.

Water and mineral cycles. Grazing enhances both of these through maintaining healthier and more stable root mass, increasing microorganism activity and aeration, and producing plants with more shoots and leaves that later provide more litter.

Overgrazing reduces water and mineral cycling by exposing soil and limiting the production of potential litter. By damaging and reducing roots, it also decreases soil structure, which increases compaction and reduces porosity, organic content, and soil life.

Energy flow. Grazing increases energy flow by preventing old oxidizing blockages of material and promoting vigorous root and leaf growth. Healthier, more massive root systems also support millions of microorganisms and other life underground.

Overgrazing cuts energy flow because it reduces plant roots and exposes the soil surface. When combined with partial rest, it often leads to a change from perennial to annual grassland—as has occurred over much of California, southern Australia, and many parts of Africa—which reduces energy flow enormously. When perennial grasses dominated, grasslands in these areas converted energy over many months of each year. Now annuals convert a fraction of that amount over very short periods.

These are the straightforward tendencies that guide us in management. In practice they proceed in concert with so many other forces that one cannot always predict how significantly they will influence a given case. The feedback loops we establish in Holistic Management, based on the constant assumption that decisions affecting the environment are wrong, enable us to overcome this dilemma to a large extent. Nevertheless, a deep-

---

*I prefer to use the term *forbs* when referring to the smaller tap-rooted, or dicotyledenous, plants. The term *weeds* is almost always used in a negative sense and can apply to a tap-rooted or fibrous-rooted (grass) plant.

er understanding of the adaptations that allow severe grazers and grass to coexist and the situations that lead to overgrazing makes the job easier.

The Relationship between Grass and Severe Grazers

Most perennial grass plants and severe grazing animals developed a mutually advantageous relationship over the eons of the past. They never required human intervention or opinion as to whether it was good or bad. Prior to human interference, the accumulation of old growth on plants in the more brittle environments was largely addressed by the grazing and social behavior of herding animals. But a prejudice against livestock has existed ever since because only recently have we considered regulating the timing of an animal's bite or tried to link the known behavior of animals in the wild to the problem of maintaining the vitality of grasslands.

The severe grazer, let's assume it is a cow, takes a mouthful from a particular plant, then moves on a step or two leaving other plants of the same or different species untouched. The grazed plant should benefit from the bite, but frequently does not because its regrowth, offering more protein and energy and less fiber, is very palatable and will attract a second bite some days later if the cow remains in the area. Thus, one plant gets overgrazed while its neighbors rest ungrazed, and one cow may actually kill a few plants while a great many are rested far too long for their health. Increasing the number of animals increases the proportion of plants damaged from overgrazing and decreases the proportion damaged from over-resting.

This process accounts for the apparent paradox that animals grazing continuously under the management most commonly practiced in the United States usually produce both overgrazed and overrested plants in the same area. Sometimes this may manifest itself as a startling mosaic of ungrazed and overgrazed patches. More often the overgrazed plants are dispersed among a whole population of plants and escape detection until some years later when a particular species disappears altogether.

Photo 21-1 gives an aerial view of a "conventionally well-run ranch" with a so-called correct (light) stocking rate. Over large areas nearly all plants have been overgrazed, as the ground-level closeup (photo 21-2) makes painfully clear. The other areas contain a great quantity of overrested and dying grass plants. The massive death of perennial grasses occurring on this ranch were illustrated in Chapter 20 (photo 20-3). Changing the animal numbers will only alter the proportions of overrested and overgrazed plants.

Very often the overrested sites will shift from grassland to herbaceous or woody plant communities, along with a considerable amount of bare

Photo 21-1 *Aerial view of a conventionally well-managed ranch, stocked lightly to avoid overgrazing. Light patches are severely overgrazed and darker patches overrested. Coahuila, Mexico.*

Photo 21-2 *Ground view on the same ranch as in photo 21-1, showing close-up of overrested and overgrazed patches. Coahuila, Mexico.*

ground. This underlies the invasion of problem woody species into millions of acres of grassland. Vast sums have gone for research, chemicals, machinery, and publicity in the attempt to eradicate plants that never were a problem until our misunderstanding of plant–animal relationships allowed them to become one.

In any case, as stated before, stocking rate has little bearing on what happens to any individual plant, and one should discuss overgrazing only in regard to individual plants. Applying the word to a whole area is irrelevant, as the following example illustrates:

Near Albuquerque, New Mexico, the Sandia Indians have run livestock on a piece of land for over three hundred years, one of the oldest examples of continuous grazing of domestic stock in the New World. In recent decades they have run a low number of cattle scattered thinly over the range in the common American way, and all the while the U.S. Bureau of Indian Affairs has complained bitterly of catchment damage from "overgrazing and overstocking."

A cursory examination certainly bore out the validity of such allegations, but a closer inspection revealed many plants matted with old oxidizing leaves and stems and dying prematurely from overrest. Other plants, however, thrived, as cattle had removed the obstructing matter. Others were weak from overgrazing. Some new plants grew where physical trampling had created the right conditions. Elsewhere rain impact had recapped old disturbance, and many areas had seen no disturbance for so long that little grew there at all. Generally litter and ground cover were scarce due to both the overgrazing of plants and the simultaneous partial rest of the whole. Amid such a variety of symptoms, the blanket label "overgrazed range" means nothing and offers no guide to a solution. The presence of so many overrested plants belies the description "overstocked" altogether.

On rangelands in Africa, the Americas, Australia, and the Middle East, I have seen and heard the same things. Almost all sites commonly called overstocked do contain a high number of overgrazed plants, but almost always a very significant quantity of overrested ones along with much bare ground due to partial rest. Even in those extreme cases where 100 percent of the plants are overgrazed, it still does not represent overstocking as by simply planning the grazing to prevent overgrazing, the animal numbers can, and often must, be increased for the good of the land. As the last chapter explained, partial rest leads to the same, or a greater increase in bare ground as can be produced by overgrazing. The two influences compound each other, but the blame always falls on overgrazing, which is treated as synonymous with overstocking.

Because time, not the number of animals, controls overgrazing and because preventing overgrazing is so critical for maintaining the productivity of the environments in which animals graze, this book pays considerable attention in Chapter 38 to managing the time that plants are exposed and reexposed to the animals, but wild animals don't wear watches. How then does nature maintain the harmonious rhythm of growth and grazing?

Before domestication no doubt cattle behaved like American bison or African buffalo in the wild. Even when feeding, those animals remained fairly close together for fear of predation, and they moved frequently off to new feeding grounds as the old had become fouled. As mentioned in an earlier chapter, grazing animals do not like to feed over ground they have fouled. They keep moving to fresh ground and don't normally return until the dung has decomposed, usually long enough in the growing season for plants to regrow, thus avoiding overgrazing. Horses and cattle, especially in less brittle environments, often avoid dung sites long after the dung has decomposed, but this probably indicates that the extended recovery time given the plants has caused them to grow rank and fibrous. The fouling effect of the dung probably wore off much earlier.

When bison, pronghorn, springbok, kangaroos, wildebeest, or buffalo and other wild herding animals sense no danger from predators, including humans, their behavior changes and overgrazing of plants and overresting of soil and other plants increase. The herd remains spread for longer and longer, and even females with young will graze and lie well away from others. Then their dung and urine are scattered so widely it no longer inhibits feeding or induces movement and the same animals remain on the same ground day after day, overgrazing a great many plants.

Adaptations to Overgrazing

Although wild herds, at least under threat of predation, follow rather constructive patterns of grazing, they often do still overgraze plants. If they did not, plants would not have developed such ingenious defenses against it, and our ignorance would have done more damage than it has.

On my own game reserve and research station in Zimbabwe it was a common experience to see a buffalo herd concentrate for two or three days on a site and then move off the fouled ground. Not uncommonly a herd of zebra, wildebeest, eland, tsessebe, gemsbok, sable, roan, or some other species would follow them, apparently not bothered by the droppings of another species. Although in complex wildlife populations, different animals may favor different plants and feed at different levels, from the rooting wart hog to the tree-nibbling giraffe, overlap is considerable. Plants severely grazed by one herd often get grazed, or rather overgrazed, by another following close behind. The overgrazing of some plants appears to do little damage as long as animal impact is sufficient enough to ensure plants get replaced.

Some grass species cannot stand much overgrazing, and after a certain level of root reduction die out except where protected by thorny bushes and cracks in rocks. Others take evasive or defensive action. Some sacrifice the center of the clump but continue to hang on to life around the edges. Some distort their leaf and stem growth flat along the ground below the grazing height of the animals. Photo 21-3 provides an example of both these adaptations. Normally this plant would grow two to three feet high. Other species develop a tight, round, spiny ball like a rolled-up hedgehog. The prickly aspect comes from old stem remains, among which small leaves persist (photo 21-4).

Where a great many plants are overgrazed in a site that also receives high animal impact, whole communities may shift toward a solid mat of runner-type grasses that more easily maintain leaf growth below the grazing height of animals. One such community I know of continued to thrive under heavy daily cattle pressure but perished quickly under an onslaught of geese that, grazing at a much lower level, demolished growth points.

In all countries I have observed, perennial grasses appear remarkably resilient to overgrazing with one notable exception. For some reason not yet fully understood or explained by anyone, they seem particularly vulnerable in Mediterranean climates, such as predominate in southern Australia, the southern tip of Africa, and along the California coast. These places contain vast areas that have lost almost every perennial grass after years of overgrazing and partial rest. Fortunately, although we do not yet understand their extreme sensitivity, they do return when both overgrazing and partial rest are stopped.

Photo 21-3 *Dying center and severe distortion of growing stems on an overgrazed plant. Normally this plant would be about three feet tall and erect. The knife indicates how close and flat the leaves are to the ground. Zimbabwe.*

Photo 21-4 *Overgrazed for many years, this normally matted perennial grass plant is surviving by forming a hedged ball. Baluchistan Province, Pakistan.*

Browsing

So far we have considered grazing and grazing animals, but what of browsing and browsers? Among wild species, and among our domestic animals, many browse woody plants and forbs more than they graze grasses, some purely browse, some browse forbs in open grasslands, and some subsist entirely on trees and shrubs. Do the same principles apply? In general, yes.

Although not nearly as much research has concentrated on browsing as on grazing, all results seem to point in the same direction. Woody plants can withstand heavy browsing that removes all of the green leaf as long as the plants get adequate time in which to recover afterward. They can also withstand continuous severe browsing as long as sufficient foliage remains out of reach of the animals. A few very sensitive species lacking an effective defense mechanism become conspicuous by their absence when under continuous browsing pressure.

Adaptations to Overbrowsing

The most common response to overbrowsing by resilient plants is called *hedging*. Plants develop the look of a clipped garden hedge in which short, tightly spaced stems protect leaves crowded in amongst them. Photo 21-5 shows a heavily hedged plant growing in the biblical lands where heavy browsing goes back at least 2,000 years. There is no knowing how old this plant is. Plants that do hedge can withstand overbrowsing for such prolonged periods that they may well live a normal lifespan, although I have

Photo 21-5 *Overbrowsed and hedged perennial shrub of great age. Yemen.*

seen elephants reach through the defenses and browse to death trees that had successfully hedged against lesser animals for years.

Other plants do not hedge, but larger individuals develop a browseline below which the animals take everything while the plant continues to grow as higher leaves trap sunlight. Photo 21-6 shows a browseline on the underside of a tree, but you can also see normal growth resuming, once the overbrowsing was eliminated through planning. In this case, animal numbers were actually increased, but the amount of time plants were exposed to the animals was controlled.

Some species, when overbrowsed, develop very heavy root systems and straggly above-ground parts. This, however can also result from frequent fire or in the tropics regular frosting, both of which remove leaf and damage stems routinely. A few species subjected to continuous browsing grow small, matted leaves along the main stems as seen in photo 21-7.

Unfortunately, these survival techniques are of no use to seedlings too small to hedge or to develop browselines, and overbrowsing will eliminate them. Adult plants may hold on for centuries, but without replacements, the population gradually declines. This gradual decline is apparent along many riparian areas in the western United States where livestock are encouraged to wander in low numbers in the belief that the low numbers will prevent such damage.

Browsing enhances the productivity of many forbs and woody plants, and thus, like the perennial grasses, they share an interdependence with the animals that feed on them that we do not understand very well at this point. Some woody plants also have elaborate chemical and physical defenses that provide protection against browsing. But even so, they still

Photo 21-6 *New stems growing below the old browseline once the overbrowsing has stopped, even though animal numbers have increased. Namibia.*

Photo 21-7 *Close-cropped, tightly matted leaves along the trunk of a tree suffering from many years of overbrowsing. Cape Province, South Africa.*

appear to share an essential relationship with the animals that promotes the spread and germination of their seed.

As in the case of grasses, overbrowsing bears no relationship to the number of animals, only to the proportion of leaf removed and the time that a plant has to regenerate. Photo 21-8 shows a browseline on trees in the Navajo-Hopi Joint Use Area in Arizona. A 90 percent reduction in livestock has not affected the overbrowsing at all as the trees and their seedlings are continually exposed to the remaining few animals.

Photo 21-8 *Browseline persisting on all trees following a 90 percent stock reduction. The few animals remaining have continued to overbrowse and no seedlings can establish. Arizona.*

On the other hand, Photos 21-9 and 21-10 show what can happen even when the animal numbers are doubled, but concentrated, and their grazing and browsing times planned. Photo 21-9 shows a highly nutritious, but severely overbrowsed, plant in Arizona called *winterfat*. Every single plant we found on this particular ranch had suffered to the extent of having no observable seed or seedling production.

Photo 21-10 shows these same plants in the same area of the ranch after two years of planned grazing with greatly increased and concentrated livestock. Far more leaf and many more stems have grown on the plants and seeds were produced. A year after, seedlings had established as well.

The role of the concentrated herd will become clearer in the following chapter on animal impact. Suffice it to say that good management can have the same positive impact on browse plants as on grasses, and the number of animals is not as crucial as the time the plants are exposed and then reexposed to the animals.

Where fouled ground induces movement in concentrated grazers it also does so with those browsers that feed on forbs at ground level. Those animals that do their browsing at higher levels of course are not to the same degree feeding on fouled ground as their noses and mouths are well above it. We may never know, now that we have lost natural populations to research in most parts of the world, but I strongly suspect that these species were heavily dependent on certain predators to induce movement. These predators would typically have hunted in bands or packs, such as humans once did and wolves, wild dogs, and hyenas still do in some places.

Photo 21-9 *Heavily overbrowsed stub of a winterfat bush exposed to a few cattle over prolonged time. Arizona.*

Photo 21-10 *Typical winterfat bush, on the same ranch as shown in Photo 21-9, growing out well and seeding with grazing/browsing planned and livestock numbers doubled. Arizona.*

Wildlife and Overgrazing/Overbrowsing

My personal feelings about all of these issues are haunted by the fate of the land mentioned in Chapter 3 that we made into a national park in Zimbabwe. Here I was responsible for compounding one error with another. Once we had removed the people (our first mistake), the game, particularly elephants whose main predators were human, now remained in the Zambezi Valley near the river for prolonged periods. The destruction of vegetation and river banks quickly grew serious. I was the research officer charged with making a plan to deal with it. My research proved that there were simply too many animals, and my recommendation was to drastically cull the elephants, buffalo, and some other species. It was heresy to recommend such a thing in a national park in the early 1960s, and so the government had other scientists visit the area to check on my work and recommendations. They concurred with me and the heavy culling of large game eventually became policy.

When I returned to the area in 1985, elephant, buffalo, and other species had been heavily culled on a regular basis for nearly twenty years, but the damage to vegetation and river bank was as bad as ever. The large old trees were still producing seed each year, and many seeds were germinating, but none survived past the seedling stage to fill the thinning ranks

Photo 21-11 *Heavy overbrowsing of trees persists even though elephant numbers have been greatly reduced because elephants remain in the same area day after day. The majority of trees have had all leaves and stems stripped off to the height an adult elephant can reach. Mana Pools National Park, 1985. Zimbabwe.*

of the species that had once been so abundant. The few elephants that remained continued to overbrowse the trees, now ripping the bark off them as well and speeding their demise.

Photo 21-11 is a view of the general area in 1985 following years of heavy culling designed to prevent such damage. I, like so many others, had missed the full significance of the role of humans as a predator in keeping game wild and moving. The remaining elephants in the park no longer fear humans. Although they are being culled at a high rate, they do not know that humans are doing it, as whole families are gunned down so that none lives to tell the tale. This deception is considered necessary as it is a national park and tourists require tame elephants. And they have become remarkably tame; their response to human scent is very different from what it was in the late 1950s when they were much wilder. Unfortunately tame elephants, or any other game interdependent with predators, are not natural and therefore lose their natural relationship with the plants in their community. Basically they linger too often and too long in the most favored areas and thus overbrowse or overgraze.

Conclusion

The answers to the questions raised in this chapter are not simple, certainly not as simple as just deciding to regulate or not regulate the number of animals. The proper stocking rate is important, particularly to leave enough forage to carry animals through the nongrowing season. But other factors enter the equation.

Wildlife management in particular poses many questions. Since we cannot stop overgrazing by controlling numbers, how do we control time? How do we determine what the land may carry? We must consider what else the animals do on the land—dunging trampling, picking up litter, and so on. We must look at the relationship of different animals to one another. If herds are to move, where will they move to? What territories and home ranges and migration routes do they require? What will induce and maintain the necessary movement? How does population size regulate territory and this in turn regulate the time plants are exposed to them?

In national parks, which we know have limits, we cannot establish stocking rates by simply keeping numbers low enough to avoid a heavy die-off in dry years. In average and good years this phenomenon leads to overrest and shifts in succession to woody plants, which in turn encourages too frequent use of fire and technology in what becomes a form of crisis management. Some of the answers lie in the planning of time, others in the grazing planning, described in Chapter 46, where livestock are used as a tool to assist in the overall management of wildlife populations. Much can also be done with the tool of animal impact, discussed in the next chapter.

22

Animal Impact:
The Least Used Tool

Animal impact refers to all the things grazing animals do besides eat. Instinctively we have considered the dunging, urinating, salivating, rubbing, and trampling of large animals as generally inconvenient conditions of their presence. Especially since fertilizer has become an item sprayed from tanks or poured out of sacks, few people even think of the more pungent aspects of livestock except when downwind of them.

Fortunately nature has not been so shortsighted, and we have recently discovered in the lumbering, smelly, but powerful, behavior of grazing animals, a tool of enormous significance for reversing desertification and for better management of water catchments, croplands, forests, and wildlife.

The Holistic Management framework arose from the discovery of the four key insights described in earlier chapters. Two of them, the fundamental differences between brittle and nonbrittle environments, and the role of herding animals and their predators in maintaining biological communities in the more brittle ones, led to a recognition of animal impact as a tool. The following examples give an idea of the power and versatility of this tool. Although critical to the maintenance of the more brittle environments and most often called for in those conditions, it is useful in less brittle environments as well:

- In a fairly brittle, high-rainfall environment, overrest has allowed plants to accumulate several years of old material. Roots have suffered severe damage, and the community has started the shift to forbs, shrubs, and trees, thwarting our desire to maintain open grassland. Fire would pollute the atmosphere while exposing soil and invigorating many of the woody plants. Chemicals or machinery might clear the ground but could not guarantee that grass would establish or persist if the soil was insufficiently disturbed and compacted. Periodic high animal impact, together with grazing, but not over-grazing, could remove old material, invigorate existing plants without exposing soil, create conditions for new plants to establish, and move the biological community away from noxious weeds or woody plants. Low animal impact for prolonged time, or partial rest, as much observation and research data have shown, does not do so but rather causes such situations.

- In a less brittle environment a farmer is faced with trying to maintain soil structure and cover while having to dispose of crop residues in time to plant his next crop. Where he once used machinery or fire, he now finds he can use very high animal impact by concentrating livestock on small portions of his field for a few hours or a day at a time until the whole field has been treated. Now, the crop residues are used to feed the animals, nutrients are returned to the surface in the form of dung and urine, and the uneaten portions are thoroughly broken up and laid down. Nowhere have the animals been long enough on the soil to cause excessive compaction or damage to the soil surface.

- We need a firebreak through grassland or a strip of brush and scrub. A fine spray of very dilute molasses or saline (salt) solution will attract and bunch a herd of cattle enough to make a firebreak through almost any kind of country at minimal expense without exposing soil or creating an erosion hazard.

- Leafy spurge, knapweed, snakeweed, or some other noxious plant has invaded a piece of ground and thousands of dollars have already been spent in futile eradication efforts. Now we can use continual doses of very high animal impact followed by well-planned recovery periods that cause the offending plants to diminish by moving succession beyond the stage that suits them.

- Bare eroding ground that we once might have fenced off and seeded at great expense can now be subjected to periodic heavy impact by giving a large herd a few bales of hay, which excites and concentrates them on the area. New plants then establish on the broken, litter-strewn ground at no cost or lost production.

- Erosion gullies whose steep banks grant no foothold to plants, spread across the land. Why pay for a bulldozer to slope the banks and chew up more land while consuming diesel and polluting, when a herd of livestock or large game animals attracted to the gully can break down the sharp, cutting edges and create the conditions for plant growth to heal them. This high animal impact, while curing the gully, if also used in the catchment of the gully also tends to correct the noneffective water cycle that caused the damage in the first place.

- We have millions of dollars tied up in legally mandated deposits until land we have stripped for coal mining is reclaimed and returned to productive use. Millions have already been wasted on reseeding and mechanical treatments that have failed. Now we can use hay and other supplementary feeds to attract and greatly concentrate cattle on these sites and reclaim and maintain them for a fraction of the cost.

- Impenetrable brush clogs potential grassland. Although low densities of calm cattle will not touch it, a large herd attracted by the smell of molasses blocks, thrown deep into the thickets, will penetrate and break down the brush. As the thick-skinned, jostling animals open the thicket, sunlight penetrates and grass can again flourish. As grass flourishes with healthy roots, new woody plants establish with difficulty.

- Fish management often requires steep, vegetated banks rather than steep, eroding ones, as shown in figure 22-1. Very high animal impact for very short periods can promote this as the well-vegetated river bank in photo 22-1 shows.

- Stock trails to water or down a hillside threaten to wash out. Although it may seem strange that damage caused by trampling can be cured by trampling, the treatment works because of the vast difference between the effect of prolonged, one-way trailing and the milling of bunched animals for very short periods.

- Coarse, fibrous grass has come to dominate a bottomland where low stocking rates and partial rest have prevailed. Traditionally fire has been used to "keep the grass palatable." But this pollutes while exposing soil and, combined with low animal impact, leads to wider plant spacing and ever-more fibrous plants. A dose of high animal impact removes plant tops and covers the soil, thus favoring more lateral growth, closer plant spacing, and less fibrous plants. Once again this tool removes the cause while curing the problem.

- Desert soils have remained hard capped from lack of disturbance for over 3,000 years. Nomads periodically shepherd their cattle and sheep over the land, overgrazing the few remaining plants while perpetuating the partial rest resulting in such capped soil. Occasionally a new grass plant establishes where a cow, donkey, sheep, or goat has broken the hard surface. However, once a herd is concentrated and bunched for a brief moment the desert starts to make its recovery at last.

All these examples are common situations where animal impact is the most practical tool available. Animal impact is indeed such a versatile tool

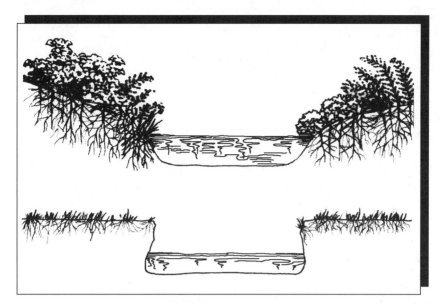

Figure 22-1 *Most stream banks ideally should be well vegetated not only to stabilize them, but also to provide shade and cover for fish, as shown in the upper drawing. The bare stream banks shown in the lower drawing are unstable. Their steep edges are more prone to erosion and will keep cutting back, widening the stream and making it more shallow.*

Photo 22-1 *Well-vegetated river bank produced by using high animal impact with planned grazing to prevent overgrazing or overbrowsing. Zimbabwe. (courtesy R. H. Vaughan-Evans).*

that we run the danger of prescribing it as reflexively as some now pre-scribe knee-jerk technology fixes. The testing guidelines covered in upcoming chapters help to prevent that.

The discovery that brittle environments need periodic disturbance to maintain stable soil cover nevertheless leads us to recognize animal impact as the *only* practical tool that can realistically halt the advance of deserts over billions of acres of rough country. Here and there other tools can help, but what other way exists to treat millions of square miles of often rugged country each year without consuming fossil fuel, without pollution, and by a means millions of even illiterate people can employ even while it feeds them?

The Role of Livestock

No other aspect of Holistic Management has caused such controversy as the suggested use of this tool has. That trampling by livestock damages both plants and soils is a deeply held belief throughout the world, as mentioned in Chapter 5. By some tragic irony, some of our most serious academics have for years rejected the one idea that has more promise of solving the riddle of desertification than any other. Meanwhile machines of extra-ordinary size and cost have been developed to break soil crusts and disturb vegetation through mechanical impact toward the same end. Because we have now lost most of the large herding wildlife species and the pre-dators that induced their movement, we are left only with livestock in most instances to simulate that role. There is no other tool that can both restore *and* sustain healthy grasslands and savannas in the more brittle environments.

Unfortunately, livestock—cattle and goats in particular—are generally seen as an enemy of the land, rather than its savior. Recent concern over the methane released by ruminating cows has reinforced this view. Yet, as far as we know, all ruminants—buffalo, bison, antelope, sheep, goats, prong-horn, deer, giraffe, etc.—produce methane as a byproduct of rumination. As there were previously a great many more grazing ruminants on Earth prior to the emergence of modern humans, something other than the pres-ence of cattle is responsible for the high levels of methane in today's atmos-phere.

The unnatural way most cattle are now fattened for slaughter—in crowded and unhealthy feedlots, where they are fed grains and other rations they are not genetically adapted to eat, is another strike against cattle. Now, not only do cattle destroy riparian areas, damage wildlife habitat, and cre-ate deserts, they also produce fatty and chemically tainted meat and tons of manure and urine that are a liability in the feedlot, but would otherwise be an asset out on the land. Is it the fault of the animal that we have taken a grazing creature, which developed a productive and mutually beneficial relationship with plants and soils over millions of years and turned it into a meat factory? Rather than condemn the animal, we should be condemning ourselves for what *we* have done.

To date, most of our experience with animal impact as a tool has involved domestic stock. On the game reserve I once owned, I frequently noted its benefits when produced by wildlife, but had little reason to create animal impact artificially as the big game enjoyed extremely natural circumstances that included a good level of predation by lions, leopards, hyena, cheetah, and wild dogs. I also hunted periodically myself and made no attempt to tame animals. The same species behaved quite differently on ranches where predators, including humans, had been eliminated. The animals had become more localized and calm. Where baboons in my game reserve thrived in the community but ran at sight of people, in the nearby national parks they sat on cars or got into them and trashed everything and had to be destroyed as a nuisance. Where elephants drank but never hung around water or showed alarm and bunched together on scenting humans in my reserve, in nearby national parks they ignored humans and lingered for hours and days on river banks.

We are in our infancy in understanding the control of time and the relationship of herds, home ranges, territories, and predation in wild populations, but we need to open our minds to such ideas if our national parks are not to deteriorate as they are doing in so many instances today.

What Animal Impact Does

Objectively speaking, few would question the salient aspects of animal impact—there are only three things it does and for which we use it as a tool.

1. Hoofed animals tend to compact the soil, as at every step they concentrate a big weight on a small foot. The "sheep's foot rollers" of modern civil engineering memorialize the herds used to compact road beds and earthworks not even a century ago.

2. When animals are excited or closely bunched, their trampling causes breaks and irregularities on the surface, as anyone who has tracked game, a cow, or a horse knows.

3. Such animals tend to speed the breakdown and reduce the volume of plant material returned to the soil surface through their dung and urine. They also speed the return of uneaten old plant material to the soil surface through the litter they trample down.

Whether any of these tendencies works for good or ill on the land depends entirely on management, particularly of the time factor, not on their intrinsic nature.

I myself did not overcome my old biases without considerable effort, doubt, and false beginnings. Early on I entertained the hypothesis that animal impact had some important function, but I could not articulate it well until I saw the distinction between brittle and nonbrittle environments and understood the importance of time.

The following example illustrates once again how timing may fundamentally change the quality of an event. Suppose you have a small house on a hill and you and your donkey fetch water daily from the stream below. After one year of trampling the same path day after day a substantial gully forms and the stream bank where you load the water cans becomes a trampled-out bog. In this instance you could say that we had had 365 donkey-days of trampling. For thousands of years we observed such damage and in essence said that we had too many donkeys.

Now, suppose you took a herd of 365 donkeys down the hill and hauled a year's worth of water in one morning. In this instance you would again have 365 donkey-days of trampling. Though a passersby that afternoon would remark on severe trailing and trampling of the stream bank, those "wounds" would have 364 days of plant growth and root development to heal before you had to come back. When you did, you could expect to find both the trail and the loading place completely overrun by new growth. In fact both might well be greener and healthier than before with the old grass removed and the dung and urine deposited, though they had still borne 365 donkey-days of traffic per year. Thus, *time*, rather than animal numbers, was the critical factor in trampling.

For thousands of years we simply overlooked the fact that timing, rather than animal numbers, governs whether animal impact acts favorably or adversely on land, and we did not distinguish between the brittle environments that required it and the nonbrittle environments that did not.

Stock Density and Herd Effect

One other observation has escaped many scholars of this subject and poor appreciation of it continues to bias research at many levels. The herding animals that contribute most to the maintenance of the more brittle environments behave in a variety of ways that produce different effects. Normally we use two management guidelines, covered in Chapter 39, in applying animal impact to land: stock density and herd effect. While stocking rate describes the number of animals continuously supported by a given unit of land, stock density reflects the concentration of animals on any subunit of that land at a given moment. Neither describes whether the animals are feeding placidly in a spread manner or bunched, and it is this behavior that makes a critical difference to the land.

We apply the term *herd effect* to the results produced by a herd that is trampling because they are excited or bunched. This trampling, which pushes down dead plant material and chips and breaks hard soil surfaces, is a result of their *behavior* and is different from the effect produced by animals calmly walking. Bunching naturally takes place when the animals are under threat by predators, when in full migration, or when being driven or jostling each other as bison, elk, deer, or livestock do when turned on to hay or supplements. It also occurs when livestock are run at ultra-high densities—1,000 to 2,000 per acre (2,000 to 5,000 per hectare) or more—*and moved every few hours or so* (see photo 22-2). Such ultra-high densities produce enough of a behavior change to ensure high herd effect throughout most of the day and over most of the land. Even when animals are herded at such densities and become so accustomed to it that they do not mill around much, the animal impact remains high because of the sheer density of animals.

Herd effect is difficult to quantify but easy to identify. Normally, grazing or walking animals place their hooves carefully, avoiding coarse plants, barely breaking the soil surface, but still compacting the soil to a degree, all the more so when the soil is wet or where for any reason underground root structure and organic matter are damaged or reduced. When herd effect occurs, the same animals trample coarse plants, lay down litter, raise dust, chip soil surfaces, open them to aeration, and compact them enough to provide seed-to-soil contact.

My observations of how these different modes of behavior affect plants

Photo 22-2 *Cattle being grazed at ultra-high stock density (3,000 per hectare/ 1,200 per acre) to produce and sustain healthy grassland. Cattle moves are planned so that plants are not overgrazed. Zimbabwe.*

and soils led eventually to the definition of partial rest, mentioned in Chapter 20. Land sustains partial rest when animals, either domestic or wild, are present, but never have cause to produce herd effect. They may slightly disturb a recently capped soil or a soil so long capped that it has become covered with algae, lichens, or mosses, but seldom can stimulate a successional shift to more complex communities and stability. The millions of acres of America's more brittle environments that are deteriorating under the combination of partial rest and overgrazing in the presence of livestock, bison, or wildlife, support this conclusion.

Traditional American range management favors protecting long-capped soils and their algal crust because it does inhibit erosion to a degree. Standard doctrine therefore disparages any kind of trampling because breaking the crust obviously increases erosion in the short run. It takes a much deeper, long-term observation to see that a really heavy trampling over a short period leads to the establishment of plants and litter that protect the soil much better than algae ever can.

Photo 22-3 shows a fairly dramatic response, on the right of the fence, to animal impact on land that was deteriorating badly under partial rest and a little overgrazing. This ranch, in a very brittle 9-inch (225-mm) rainfall area of Namibia, once supported a commercial dairy operation, so nutritious and abundant was the forage. It had now become real desert.

Some plants were obviously overgrazed, but there was more bare

Photo 22-3 *Land on the right of fence was treated with high animal impact from five massed flocks of sheep and is showing an immediate response in plant growth. Land on the left continues to desertify under partial rest. Namibia.*

ground than anything else. As you can see on the left side of the fence, the low and continuous level of animal trampling had destroyed algal communities, but not stimulated the successional process enough to maintain grassland. Long-rested sites in the area had an algal crust hard enough that it rang like a drum head when tapped.

The first year we greatly concentrated the sheep, the only type of domestic stock available in large numbers and still profitable, and planned the grazing to minimize overgrazing. The area to the right of the fence, which received high animal impact, shows how the biological community clearly started to move forward again without any other assistance or reseeding. Forbs dominated the first successional advance, but grasses soon took over on this ranch in a pattern that has become familiar to those using animal impact to reclaim bare ground.

Overtrampling

Trampling, carried out for too long always causes damage to soil and plants. Trampling carried to extremes but over a very short time, can cause temporary damage to the ecosystem processes, but most environments have astounding resilience. Some 2,000 cattle concentrating at a fence corner during a heavy downpour of rain created the scene in photo 22-4. The first time a rancher called me out to inspect the damage my advice had caused

Photo 22-4 *Extreme trampling, which occurred during an overnight thunderstorm when 2,000 head of cattle crowded against a fence for too long. Chaco, Paraguay.*

when his large herd concentrated during a violent storm, we photographed and discussed the resulting quagmire at great length. Finally, we decided to ignore it and keep on with the concentration and movement as planned. About eighteen months later we recalled the incident but could no longer determine exactly where it had happened as all paddocks looked much the same. In many cases, the temporarily overtrampled area looks much better after a season.

The continuous trampling we see so often around gates, water points, and feed troughs does not allow recovery to take place, but such examples often figure in arguments against trampling in general. Even sophisticated time management may not eliminate all such cases totally, but usually the area involved right at the water trough is insignificant and can be treated as a sacrificial area.

On Croplands

We have much to learn about how animal impact might serve in cropland management. But it could easily be viewed as a primary, or *biological*, form of tillage that can be used periodically. It also has additional benefits in that it saves the farmer having to haul manure or fertilizer.

The concept of brittle and nonbrittle environments has not yet entered the thinking of most farmers, and although we suspect that cropland in brittle areas deteriorates fastest under our conventional row cropping practices, they are deteriorating almost everywhere.

The American Dust Bowl of the 1930s became a legendary monument to the discovery of the rate of cropland destruction in the more brittle environments. Perhaps the problems in this case were related to those arising on brittle rangeland from the difficulty of maintaining organic soil components and adequate ground cover in the absence of naturally functioning animal populations.

In this context, work under way in the United States at the Land Institute in Kansas and at the Rodale Institute in Pennsylvania on developing perennial grain crops could open up enormous possibilities for us to get away from the known destructive effects of annual shallow-rooted crops. Success in these efforts would go a long way to solving two major problems in agriculture, high production costs and soil destruction, brought about by our vast commitment to annual grain monocultures. However, developing perennial grain crops will not be the simple solution many believe it to be in the more brittle environments of the world, including most of the prairies.

Like rangeland, perennial grain crops, if successfully developed, will require the removal and recycling of the old material that does not decay fast in the more brittle environments. Animal impact may well provide the

answer where machinery and fire never have. Where surface crumb structure and porosity are vital on croplands, livestock can be introduced in high
concentrations for very short periods to speed cycling and decay of crop
residues.

Forests

The management of forests that lie in the more brittle environments is a
major challenge in Australia, Africa, and the United States in particular,
where lightning or human fires burn vegetation readily. In many instances
forests dependent on numerous small fires lit by humans have developed
both in response to the burning and the protection such burning afforded
from major conflagrations. In Australia and the United States such practices
over thousands of years have favored tree species that require an occasional fire to reproduce and thrive. This is increasingly the case in Africa,
although the change from fire-sensitive to more fire-dependent tree
species appeared to begin only after European settlement when the frequency of burning greatly increased.

Management in either case tends to alternate between using controlled
fires to burn the understory that, left in place, can fuel larger, more damaging fires, and doing nothing at all—leaving things to Nature. The pendulum generally swings from the latter to the former when doing nothing
results in a dangerous and costly conflagration. As pointed out in Chapter
19, neither approach will maintain the few remaining forests populated by
fire-sensitive tree species. But the well-planned use of animal impact and
grazing, with no overgrazing, can. Animals used in this manner can clear
the understory as effectively as fire, and can do so without damaging the
soil surface or decreasing soil organic matter.

The African teak forests mentioned in Chapter 19 did, in all probability, develop with a large animal component. It is difficult to imagine how
else sand dunes eventually developed into mature teak forests that are so
fire-sensitive. Today cattle, goats, and donkeys are allowed to graze in these
forests but they are few in number, rarely if ever concentrate, and remain
in the same areas for prolonged time. In effect the tools being applied are
overgrazing and partial rest, as well as fire, and this is as destructive as one
would expect such tools to be in a very brittle environment.

Forests that now contain mostly fire-dependent species may survive
several millennia under conventional management, but because of the
atmospheric pollution stemming from the burning, we cannot afford to
continue this practice. Animal impact can and probably should replace fire,
but because the use of animal impact will eventually lead to a reduction of
fire-dependent tree species, we must be clear on what we do want, and that
clarity can come only through a holistic goal.

Conclusion

One of the greatest immediate benefits from animal impact can be seen in the restoration and maintenance of brittle environment water catchments. Partial or total rest can sustain soil cover in nonbrittle environments, but no technology could replace animal impact on all the ranches, farms, tribal lands, national parks, and forests that cover the bulk of most brittle environments where either form of rest is so damaging to soil cover. The effects of animal impact at either end of the brittleness scale follow.

Very Brittle Environments

Community dynamics. Periodic high animal impact promotes the advancement of biological communities on bare, gullied, and eroding ground. In dense grassland, high impact tends to maintain the biological community at the grassland level, preventing a shift to woody communities.

Low animal impact, or partial rest, tends to produce bare ground as it disturbs algal communities but does not stimulate the establishment of more complex communities. It allows plant spacings to increase and on a vast scale generally has effects remarkably similar to those of total rest. Under low impact, dense grassland with close plant spacings may proceed toward woody communities and forbs, but these will give way to a landscape of scattered shrubs or trees and much bare or algae-covered ground unless rainfall is sufficient to sustain a full woody cover.

Water and mineral cycles. Periodic high animal impact generally improves water and mineral cycles. Fire and/or machinery have been used traditionally, but fail to achieve anything like the results that animal impact achieves.

Low animal impact reduces mineral and water cycles below the land's potential. Where significant overgrazing of plants accompanies this, the adverse effects are compounded.

Energy flow. Periodic high impact tends to build community complexity and to improve water and mineral cycles, and as a direct consequence energy flow also tends to improve. A possible exception would be certain tropical areas, which, although quite brittle, have enough rainfall to support a solid woodland canopy. Even then, periodic high impact could keep the land in grass with scattered trees, which might make more energy available for human use through livestock and game.

Low impact generally reduces energy flow below its potential. The shortfall often becomes severe if compounded by the overgrazing of plants, and unfortunately this is the most pervasive situation worldwide. It is endemic in the management of many national parks in Africa, the United States, and elsewhere. In the more brittle environments the effects animal impact tends to produce can, in many respects, be viewed as the opposite of those produced by partial and total rest.

Nonbrittle Environments

Community dynamics. Periodic high impact, by maintaining grass root vigor while discouraging the establishment of new woody plants, slows shifts to woody communities. In cases of grassland in potential forest this alone may not, however, entirely halt the movement back to forest. If grassland is intended, other measures, such as the periodic application of technology, have to be considered as well.

Nonbrittle grassland, which cannot advance to forest because of shallow soil, elevation, or annual frosting, increases in complexity under periodic high animal impact. Amazing shifts in plant composition, even in less brittle grasslands, can take place depending on when the impact is applied relative to prevailing weather conditions. This makes it very important to plan where the animals will be at any given time (see Chapter 46).

Low animal impact, or partial rest, has little effect on these grasslands. Woodland will develop if the climate allows. Wherever the community cannot develop to woodland, low impact does not cause the deterioration seen in brittle environments. Even combined with the overgrazing of a great many plants, low animal impact will not produce bare ground in a nonbrittle environment.

Water and mineral cycles. High animal impact tends to improve both water and mineral cycles. However it also tends to sustain grassland, and the mineral and water cycling in the grassland will usually not be as effective as they would be if the community advanced to forest. Low animal impact has little effect.

Energy flow. Periodic high animal impact tends to increase energy flow, although again, when used to maintain grassland in lieu of forest, energy flow will never reach the full potential of the land. Low animal impact has little effect.

Like rest and grazing, animal impact is a natural phenomenon that we choose to call a tool because we can manipulate it to serve our ends. That distinction becomes less obvious in regard to the next tool, *living organisms*, although they can be our most vital allies in achieving a holistic goal.

23
Living Organisms: The Most Complex Tool

The phrase *living organisms* may seem an ambitiously broad way to define a tool, and it is. *Plants and animals* sounds earthier, but does not force us to consider the utility of bacilli and viruses in the same breath as corn and sheep, and we must. All living things share the power to change their microenvironment by their mere presence, and that must concern everyone, but particularly those whose holistic goal is directly tied to the management of land.

The two previously discussed tools, grazing and animal impact, of course involve the use of living creatures in the service of management. Technically this tool encompasses those also.

But *living organisms* stands apart for two practical reasons. A separate heading encourages us to weigh possible biological solutions to a problem against technological ones: community complexity against pesticide and herbicide; crop polycultures and intercropping rotations against monocultures; garden composting against chemical fertilizers; healthy water catchments against silt traps and other mechanical measures built to protect dams or cities from devastation. Also, it makes us treat the whole complex of life in an environment as a whole rather than a menu of pesky or beneficial creatures that we may kill or husband at will.

Failure to think along these lines accounts for much of the environmental damage humans have wrought. Only recently has the human race even considered that the current rate of extinction of other species might have highly dangerous consequences, aside from the sheer horror of our destruction of other life. Yet people in less developed cultures than our own, living closer to the land and using simpler levels of technology, have instinctively used living organisms as tools for a long time. Thus, much of the information in this chapter will be more easily embraced by them than by those working in mainstream agribusinesses or even by urban professionals tending home gardens.

Living Organisms and Community Dynamics

The living organisms tool, because it involves all life, will play a role in the forms of production and/or the future resource base described in any holistic goal, no matter the type of business or other situation being managed. Some might try to argue that mining does not concern itself with living organisms, but even there a person could argue that biological activity accounts for all hydrocarbons and even for the precipitation of uranium, iron, and some other minerals into ore. The question is however unarguable because no matter who you are or what your business, you could not even read or comprehend these words without the plants that provide the energy and oxygen you require to read and think. Living organisms provide the bulk of the biological capital without which no civilization can be sustained. Economists, particularly agricultural economists, hunched over their financial models as they tally capital and operating costs against commodity prices, characteristically ignore this foundation that supports all their reckoning.

In the Holistic Management model, a broken line surrounds both the ecosystem process of community dynamics and the living organisms tool because they merely represent two aspects of the same thing. The dynamics of any biological community is manifested in living organisms.

The relationship of this tool to the others in the tools row looks a bit clearer from the viewpoint of the earliest cave dwellers. Assuming they could have analyzed their situation and made decisions holistically, they would have seen that they required a certain landscape from which they could produce the food, cover, and water necessary to sustain the quality of life they desired. They would have recognized that all this depended on the same four ecosystem processes that sustain us. But their tools row was nearly empty. They had no fire, no livestock, and no technology. They knew implicitly that the dynamics of the community they inhabited controlled them absolutely and defined what they could do in their environment.

When they harnessed fire and made their first spears they may have thought they had escaped that relationship, but the widespread use of these tools initiated many of today's deserts, and that line of reasoning revealed itself as faulty. With increasingly sophisticated technology we continue to think we can escape the influence of the biological communities we inhabit, but we cannot any more than our earliest ancestors could. Yet, to the extent that we understand this, we can use living organisms to our advantage, as a tool, and the breadth of our options is remarkable as the following examples illustrate.

Practical Applications

In 1978 the Chinese, noting that the Gobi desert annexed to itself over 600 square miles annually, began planting green belts of trees, an overt case of enlisting living organisms as tools in their struggle against the advancing sand. Seven years later, they had hand-planted some 14.8 million acres (5.9 million hectares). The success or failure of this stupendous effort to establish a more complex plant community by main force depends on many factors. Later discussion of the testing guidelines (Chapters 23–32) explains in detail how to estimate the odds on the trees' survival and success in halting the desert's advance.

In simple terms, however, trees planted in the desert, effective as they may be as wind breaks, cannot grow and reproduce independent of the level of development of the biological community as a whole. Even if trees once did flourish on the edge of the Gobi, whatever human disruption of the community killed them will, if still active, prevent the new plantings from establishing young, sustaining themselves, and reclaiming the desert.

By contrast, the Japanese scientist Masanobu Fukuoka undertook to use the principles of biological succession and the organisms associated with

Photo 23-1 *Concrete ramp into cattle watering trough that provides access to water for small animals and birds and prevents their drowning. Coahuila, Mexico.*

particular successional levels to produce high yields of small grain crops without synthetic fertilizers, compost, pesticides, soil disturbance, or weeding. He succeeded because his understanding of community dynamics allowed him to enlist a great number of plants, insects, birds, small animals, and microorganisms as tools in creating an environment where his grain thrived in the protection of such complexity.[1]

I once saw a less complex, but equally dramatic, example on a Mexican ranch where the owner had built a small concrete ramp up the outside and down into a water tank, as shown in photo 23-1. One night, while camped nearby a terrific noise aroused us, and we took flashlights to investigate and discovered a massive mating of toads in the tank. By dawn they had dispersed to resume their pursuit of bugs and flies around the ranch. The simple ramp to water in fact enabled a great variety of insects, birds, and rodents, to survive and contribute to the complexity and stability of the whole area. This is what the rancher needed for the recreational and aesthetic portions of his family's holistic goal, which also included big game, such as black bear, deer, turkey, and javelina. By contrast, photo 23-2 shows a poorly constructed watering point provided to increase game populations in a national forest. The intention was good, but these young warthogs were finally able to water only because a pipe nearby leaked.

Photo 23-3 shows a leaking water pipe on a Namibian ranch. Water pipes run along the fences to frustrate the local porcupines' appetite for

Photo 23-2 *Two young warthogs trying unsuccessfully to drink from a poorly constructed water trough provided for wild game in a national forest. Zimbabwe.*

Photo 23-3 *Water pipeline strung along a fence to avoid damage by porcupines. A leak has developed and been turned to advantage as a watering point for birds and small animal life. Namibia (courtesy Argo Rust).*

plastic, but many leaks are created by baboons finding it easy to bite through the plastic when they want a drink. For years the rancher struggled to control minor leaks. Then, when he articulated a holistic goal involving complex living communities to sustain his family, he saw opportunity in the leaks. Half drums below them created additional watering points for thousands of birds, insects, and small mammals. Previously this rancher had thought such creatures had no connection to his family's wealth or to cattle ranching. Now he jokingly talks about his enormous unpaid force of millions of "little people" all busily working for his family.

When we nurture crops and domestic animals, and even when we produce wild animals on game ranches or cultivate fish, we tend to proceed as if Earth were more a machine than a living thing. Whatever we produce in this way does represent the use of living organisms as a tool to manipulate our environment and sustain ourselves, but we typically fail to see them in the context of a dynamic community of living organisms. Rather we assume that the communities they inhabit will adapt and sustain themselves, which of course they do not. The hope that technology will enable us to completely protect our harvests from predators, competitors, and diseases, and thus reap a bounty independent of the communities they inhabit, has always proven false and will undoubtedly continue to do so.

The so-called Green Revolution of extravagantly productive hybrid crops has foundered, and will continue to founder, on this fact. The high-yielding strains owed their productivity to extreme uniformity and an engineered ability to make good use of fertilizer, but they required lavish protection from insects and disease. The combination of chemicals damaged the living soil, polluted both soil and water, increased insect damage and generated resistant pests, and resulted in such escalating costs that thousands of American farmers are leaving their land and homes of generations. Some countries are already starting to ban chemical farming because of pollution or increased insect damage.

The arrogant assumption that technology can supplant natural laws has embedded itself deeply enough in our culture to distort scientific reasoning. A booklet, *New Mexico Range Plants*, issued in 1980 by the Cooperative Extension Service of New Mexico State University, and still in use, makes the following statement about Hall's panic grass (*Panicum hallii* Vasey): "Growing Hall's panic grass is highly palatable for all livestock. It retains this quality after curing, because some leaves remain green most of the year. Palatability causes the grass to decrease quickly under grazing, even when associated grasses are properly utilized. *Therefore, this species can be maintained only on areas reseeded as pure stands*" (emphasis added).[2]

Here we have a valuable indigenous plant that has maintained itself for perhaps millions of years as part of a complex community, while countless billions of once-plentiful large animal species prized it as much as today's few domestic animals. Yet, the booklet tells us it needs the technology of modern wheat farming to survive at all. We have failed to sustain pure stands or monocultures of any plant without massive injections of capital in fertilizers, herbicides, and pesticides. I doubt that it ever occurred to the authors that one might reap the benefits of Hall's panic grass by respecting its place in the community, something that naturally functioning grazers accomplished without conscious thought.

The use of biological controls in lieu of chemicals represents a generally more positive marriage of modern science and our knowledge of how communities function. Clear examples are the breeding of lady bugs to prey on aphids and the nurturing of certain bugs that eat problem plants. Parasites that attack fly larvae can decimate the fly population in feed yards and other mass breeding sites. Of course we can also do this by just getting the animals out of feedyards on to the land where they belong. Screw worms have so far been controlled through the use of sterile males. When they mate, the female dies without reproducing.

When prickly pears were introduced to Australia in the early 1920s they thrived, so much so that vast acres were so heavily infested the land was considered useless. The cost of removing the cacti mechanically or poisoning them with chemicals was more than the land itself was worth, so entomologists ransacked their American homeland to find an insect that might help to control the pest. They found it in the larvae of a small moth that proved to be voracious eaters of the cacti. Within five years of its being released in Australia the moth had done a spectacular job of destroying the vast majority of the cacti.[3] However, the prickly pear would probably not have spread and become a problem had the land been managed so as not to produce conditions ideal for its establishment. Though not without risk, biological controls have usually proven less damaging to the ecosystem processes than direct use of chemical poisons.

Genetic Engineering

Modern breakthroughs in genetic engineering open the door to tremendous possibilities, but also equal temptations and dangers. Civilization might have spared itself some grief if it had gained more wisdom about the four ecosystem processes before acquiring this new power to intervene on an even bigger scale than previously. The new genes have escaped the test tube, however, so we must do the best we can to avoid embarking on a new Green Revolution as faulty as the last. A fundamental understanding of the reasons for our massive agricultural failures and the decision making that caused the bedeviling spread of deserts should temper the creation of new forms of life.

The problems are not altogether unfamiliar. Traditional breeding techniques have produced species such as corn, or maize, that have departed so far from their wild ancestry that we can no longer trace the link with certainty. They now depend totally on human cultivation. Genetic engineering merely shortens this process by several thousand years, but the new forms do not escape the successional principles of community dynamics any more than corn, sheep, or white leghorn chickens. Every organism, including humans, has its place in the community and a functional role.

The current attempts to escape natural laws by creating crop plants that survive ever more powerful herbicides used to kill all other plant forms represent the wrong kind of thinking, in my opinion, and will not solve any of the world's problems. Such thinking considers soil as simply a medium for holding plants upright, while humans feed and nurture them in an artificial, hydroponics-type situation. Geneticists who have lost their connection with the land may dream that success lies in that direction, but reality dictates that living soil must do far more than physically support plants if humans are to survive in intelligent form.

Genetic engineering can become a powerful tool for good if handled with wisdom, and I hope that holistic decision making will play a role in assisting us to that wisdom. Up until now we have been enamored of the technology, and we have ignored the importance of the web of relationships that define any biological community. The neglect and destruction of genetic material, even in the few principal plants sustaining civilization today is in my mind criminal. Yet we continue to spend billions to genetically engineer ever more specialized plants for artificial environments. Much of this ill-advised work is being conducted on the basis of legal and economic decisions that are seriously flawed. I do not believe we are going to see any successful quick-fix solutions from such genetic work, marvelous as it can be, and if the way we make decisions about its continued development does not change, I foresee disaster on an enormous scale.

Looking to the future of science and resource management, it is clear that we must turn far more to studying ecological processes and how they function so we can better understand the relationships that exist among the living organisms, including ourselves, that populate any biological community. This will enable us to concentrate more on preventing the problems our ignorance has led to, and less on developing cures that, in damaging ecosystem processes, only create more problems.

Isolated people and organizations have thought more about our connection to the communities of living organisms that sustain us, but for several thousand years the mainstream of human interest has flowed in other channels, with the result that civilizations have come and gone and now all civilization is endangered. Avoiding the inevitable outcome of such a threat will require more humility than past generations have shown and a greater acceptance that the unknowns in nature and science still far outweigh the knowns. In addition, it will demand clarity in human goals and the will to plan, assume any decisions affecting the environment are wrong, monitor them, and replan if necessary—all of which is more likely to flow if people are committed to a holistic goal.

24

Technology: The Most Used Tool

How many times have we heard it said that technology, the hallmark of modern humans, holds the key to the future? No doubt this belief has been reflected for thousands of years, first around campfires and later in boardrooms and cabinet meetings. Technology will feed us better. It will provide lightning-fast transportation and communications. It will heal our wounds and cure our diseases. As a tool for modifying and controlling an environment, we have not seen the beginning of its potential.

The twentieth century provided a constant stream of wonders that strengthened this faith, but only recently have we had to entertain the possibility that technology does more than simply produce better and better appliances, artificial organs, weapons, and entertainment. It now forces humanity to make choices not imagined since the beginning of time.

Two events, the atom bomb and the landing of men on the moon, symbolize our dilemma. The bomb dramatically demonstrated that humanity does have the power to destroy itself, while the moon landing, which far surpassed the legendary tower of Babel in its vision, dares us to set no limits to our endeavors. Over fifty years after Hiroshima, however, we are beginning to understand that atomic power is not the *only* invention that can destroy us. We now realize that our pursuit of technological triumph can have dire consequences, particularly for the ecosystem that sustains us all.

Our current use of technology often expresses a pre-bomb state of mind that considers only the problem at hand without thought of larger implications. Many of the products of technology that we use daily—

detergents, dyes, automobiles, pesticides, and so on—can affect the environment in ways we never anticipated. The effects can be delayed by days, months, or years and may express themselves far from the site of application where an innocent public cannot connect them to their source. The principle known as the "tragedy of the commons" compounds this syndrome.[1]

Most societies long ago encountered the paradox of common land. If people freely graze livestock on common ground, then individual operators reap all the profit from an extra animal, and the cost, divided among all the users, appears minimal and will not be noticeable for a long time. Thus, everyone has a strong incentive to run more stock until the land is so damaged it can no longer feed a single animal. Technology tempts us into the commons tragedy on a far grander scale, and the debate of recent years over acid rain, global climate change, water and air pollution, and toxic waste shows that we still haven't developed a sense of collective responsibility. As you wash your hair in the morning with the latest scientifically formulated shampoo, think of the other 100 million people doing the same, 365 days of the year. Each of you has placed one animal each day on that common field. Can it carry 36.5 billion animals this year, and even more the next?

Most of our most hazardous inventions have existed for less than one hundred years. Humankind did remarkably well for many thousands of years using simpler technology for many of the same tasks, but such is the nature of human advancement that in many areas there is no going back. We cannot return to rudimentary living where a smaller human population exists on subsistence agriculture, nor can we abandon our cities. Yet recognition that going forward will demand wisdom and humility is a breakthrough in thinking more significant in its way than the notion of space travel.

Technology and the Quick Fix

Much technology subconsciously stems from our desire to dominate nature, a desire that goes back a long way and that has generated its own philosophical justifications and patterns of thought. In resource management, agriculture, health care, and many other fields, all but a few professionals define their work entirely in terms of their technological tools. Their education and professional traditions do not even consider the broader principles that govern our ecosystem. Such people naturally devote their best energy to quick, unnatural answers and often achieve immediate, dramatic, popular, and profitable results. Yet such quick fixes can prove very costly in the long term. Nowhere is this more apparent than when we use technology to bolster production on deteriorating land or to drastically modify an environment to better suit our purposes. Consider the following examples:

- Suppose we want to change the successional level of a community. On unproductive rangeland machines or herbicides will clear the brush and scrub, and we can drill in seed. Where a mixed forest makes logging inconvenient, we can remove the native trees and plant uniform stands of faster growing species that permit mass processing. When our chosen plants falter, we can kill their enemies and fertilize their soil. Some even predict total control in the form of plants genetically engineered to thrive in an artificially fertilized environment, chemically rendered lethal to *everything* else. All these actions conflict with how nature functions. Successful as they appear, in the end they generally fail, often generating new, more severe problems.

- When water cycles become less effective, we can use machines to scour out contour and drainage ditches, deep rippers to reverse the compaction caused by heavy wheels, and irrigation pumps to put water back where it came from. Again, we show little understanding of how water cycles function, and our immediate successes often result in long-term failure.

- When mineral cycling is poor, we might turn to the local agrichemical dealer who can supply anything our land lacks and change the soil pH to suit any crop, and with the help of some diesel fuel, the old John Deere can plow it in. In implementing these measures we so damage soils, through loss of crumb structure and soil organisms, that the mineral cycle only becomes poorer. The treatments need repeating in ever-stronger doses.

- We want more energy flowing into cash crops, so we look to jungles, marshes, and forests, believing that we can cut, burn, drain, irrigate, spray, or bulldoze them into any form we imagine suits that end. As the face of the earth changes, so, too, do its atmospheric gases. Thus in implementing these measures we ultimately risk damaging all life.

Agriculture's Addiction to Technology

Such thinking overlooks two important attributes of nature. First, our ecosystem is not a machine but a living thing that energetically moves and reproduces itself according to its own principles. Second, the life that we artificially suppress or take to extinction may have contributed to our own survival. To ignore these attributes triggers the same mechanisms of dependency familiar from cases of drug and alcohol abuse.

The parallel is striking. The clinical stages of alcohol or heroin addiction—becoming hooked, denial, degradation, skid row, death—occur routinely now in mainstream agriculture in every nation. Farmers get pulled in by sales pitches on the wonders of fertilizers and pesticides. The pushers themselves get hooked on profits or research grants and everybody feels great. However, rapidly breeding microorganisms and insects adapt far faster to new conditions than do humans or many of the predators that once provided natural control. Once the array of chemicals we use show signs of failure, we simply increase the strength and quantity of our attack or attempt to isolate new compounds.

We now have somewhere over 21,500 chemical pesticide remedies on the world market, most of them inadequately tested for human safety, and virtually none for their impact on our ecosystem as a whole.[2] Crop damage continues to increase, even as evidence mounts that we are now poisoning ourselves and other slow-breeding creatures while strengthening the pests we set out to kill. Statistics on condemned water sources and sales of bottled water alone are powerful indicators of this.

Right now Zimbabwe justifies the use of DDT (banned in the United States) against tsetse fly over a wide area with the argument that "only low dosages are being applied in specific sites." Such pronouncements have calmed public doubt, yet in the same country excessive levels of DDT have already turned up in human milk. Entomologists contend that the slow-breeding tsetse fly will not likely develop DDT tolerance. However, malaria mosquitoes and myriad agricultural pests present a far greater threat to Africa then the tsetse fly, and low dosage spraying is a doctor's prescription for enhancing their resistance. We cannot apply any pesticide to just one target organism; thousands are affected.

We now have reached the denial stage. Government and industry point fingers every which way but at the real problem. Sympathetic people and organizations offer stress counseling for farmers and ease relocation from countryside to city.

No one wants to talk about a debilitating dependency because we can no longer conceive of life without it. Perpetual monocultures, inadequate rotations of monocultures, chemical treatments, and heavy machinery have become standard practice, but have so simplified soil communities and structure that, like a junky's worn-out body, the land demands even harsher stimulation to produce the same high. The habit quickly becomes expensive: the money received for 53.3 kg of corn could buy 100 kg of manufactured nitrogen in 1973, but within a decade it took 527 kg of corn to buy it, and many cornfields now demand a bigger injection than before.[3] Not surprisingly, many corn growers become desperate raising money for that fix, but their cash flow can't stand a cold turkey withdrawal either, because the dying soil won't grow enough to pay last year's debt.

Developing a Collective Conscience

Having been a farmer and householder myself I understand the frustrations, pressures, and urge for quick fixes. "They are eating my crops! What else can I do?" "Last night I went to the kitchen, and you should have seen all the cockroaches when I turned on the light!" "If my house is on fire, you surely don't expect me to just watch it burn!" No, of course not, but mind you don't throw kerosene on it instead of water. The flames will gutter only an instant before they explode.

That happens sometimes. A decade ago over a million Ethiopians died mainly because misguided technology had damaged the four ecosystem processes and crippled the capacity of their country to support its population through a dry period. To prevent just such a tragedy from occurring, a number of well-meaning countries had helped finance much of that technology: irrigation schemes; hybrid seeds, synthetic fertilizers, pesticides, and other Green Revolution technology; dams and boreholes (wells) to help to scatter stock on the rangelands; and so on. *Homo sapiens*, thanks to a flair for technology, appears to be the only creature that occasionally starves itself before its population reaches the potential carrying capacity of its territory.

On the other hand, we can never hope to feed future generations without sophisticated technology, and we certainly can apply it in ways that don't become pathological. Even the most ardent campaigners against drug abuse seldom forgo a bit of Novocain when their dentist unlimbers her drill. Research into biological pest control and genetic engineering, machinery for handling intersown crops, cultivation techniques that do not excessively compact soil, and even better mouse traps in place of stronger poisons represent a healthier direction for development.

A change in attitude can lead to simple ways to supplant destructive practices. Householders, builders, and appliance manufacturers can significantly dent the stocking rate of kitchen vermin by sealing cracks behind refrigerators and stoves to deny them a sanctuary. Physical traps for cockroaches and mice cut populations without cumulative damage. The state of California alone spends millions of dollars annually poisoning Californians unlucky enough to share their environment with roaches. As the bugs have survived from the age of the trilobites, smart money says this will give them an even greater long-term edge over humans than they enjoyed before.

Given a holistic goal and a way to test decisions for their economic, social, and environmental soundness, both short and long term, we can expose nonsolutions among technological remedies. Sometimes we might choose to solve a short-term problem, out of urgent necessity, with a form of technology that has adverse long-term effects. But where the wrong thing has to be done today to survive until tomorrow, we now know we have to quickly work on ways to prevent a recurrence of the situation. In many other cases, merely having a holistic goal that people are committed to encourages them to forgo technologies that provide immediate gratification in favor of those that provide lasting gain.

At present we have no traditional land ethic or collective sense of conscience and responsibility, either to our fellow humans or to other life, and our governments reflect this only because our governments reflect us— they make decisions the same way most of us do. The testing guidelines covered in the following chapters offer a way to assess technology and foresee where it is likely to lead to crisis. It is my hope that they will also contribute to a new political attitude toward technology that embraces everyone, from the householder who shampoos his hair and poisons roaches, to multinational cartels that dam rivers and chainsaw jungles. I would like to know for certain, for example, that the pages of this book do not reflect profiteering on bad forestry, destruction of land, air and water pollution, and exploitation of people. They could as easily represent solar wealth and a stable community in an ever vital landscape where the hunting is good now and will be better. Technology can achieve that, but only a public will and holistic decision making, in some form or another, can ensure it.

Part VI

Testing Your Decisions

25

Making Economically, Environmentally, and Socially Sound Decisions

Up until now this book has concentrated on the framework that guides holistic decision making: definition of the whole to be managed; formation of the holistic goal; the four ecosystem processes that serve as the foundation on which the holistic goal rests; the tools for managing ecosystem processes, and the different effects some of those tools produce in brittle and nonbrittle environments. Now you are ready to put holistic decision making into practice.

Each of the next seven chapters describes a simple test in the form of one or two questions you ask yourself prior to implementing any decision. Some tests will not apply to certain decisions and can be skipped. Some tests will raise points you will again consider in other tests. The testing should take you minutes, rather than hours. Once you are familiar with the tests and have internalized the questions, the testing will be accomplished in seconds and will be something you begin to do subconsciously.

When asked and answered in quick succession, the testing questions enable you to see the likely effect of any decision on the whole you manage. You do not want to dwell on any one test to the point that you lose sight of the picture formed by scanning them all. With this picture in sight, you can be fairly sure that any decision tested is not only economically sound but *simultaneously* environmentally and socially sound, both short and long term.

This is the critical factor missing in conventional decision making, where few decisions prove sound in all these respects. Some decisions may appear to be economically sound, but will be implemented at the expense of the environment or the well-being of people, or be environmentally sound, but hopelessly uneconomic or damaging to human welfare. Many of these decisions will have undesirable consequences in the long term.

As you will recall from earlier chapters, the testing questions are more or less a final check. You have in effect already made your decision, in the same way you have always made decisions. You will already have gathered whatever information you needed to make the decision—what it will cost, what the research shows, what the experts say, what you've learned from past experience, and so on. In addition, you may have consulted the management guidelines, covered in Chapters 34 through 42, before deciding how best to apply a tool or carry out an action. Simple decisions that require little planning to implement will probably have been based on little more than past experience, or intuition. Your purpose in now testing a decision is to ensure that it is simultaneously economically, environmentally, and socially sound and will take you toward your holistic goal. If the decision passes most or all of the tests that apply, you should feel fairly confident in implementing it. If it fails one or more tests, you may want to modify the decision, abandon it altogether, or, in some cases, go ahead anyway—a subject we will return to.

Each of the seven tests, and the questions asked, is summarized in figure 25-1. There are no rules on the order in which to ask these questions,

---

1. **Cause and Effect.** Does this action address the root cause of the problem?
2. **Weak Link**
   - *Social.* Could this action, due to prevailing attitudes or beliefs, create a weak link in the chain of actions leading toward your holistic goal?
   - *Biological.* Does this action address the weakest point in the life cycle of this organism?
   - *Financial.* Does this action strengthen the weakest link in the chain of production?
3. **Marginal Reaction.** Which action provides the greatest return, in terms of your holistic goal, for the time and money spent?
4. **Gross Profit Analysis.** Which enterprises contribute the most to covering the overheads of the business?
5. **Energy/Money Source and Use.** Is the energy or money to be used in this action derived from the most appropriate source in terms of your holistic goal? Will the way in which the energy or money is to be used lead toward your holistic goal?
6. **Sustainability.** If you take this action, will it lead toward or away from the future resource base described in your holistic goal?
7. **Society and Culture.** How do you feel about this action now? Will it lead to the quality of life you desire? Will it adversely affect the lives of others?

Figure 25-1 *The seven tests.*

except one: the Society and Culture test should always be last. Your answers to the questions asked in this test should reflect the impression gained after passing through all the others.

As you become more familiar with the contents of each test, you will automatically tend to order the tests according to the nature of the decision being tested. If the decision addresses a problem, for instance, you will tend to go to the cause-and-effect test first. If you fail this test, it is often pointless to continue. If the decision involves an organism whose numbers you want to increase or decrease, you might go to the weak link test first. Again, if you fail this test, it may be pointless to continue. Before long, you will instinctively know which tests apply to any decision and which ones you can skip. Likewise, there will be times when your common sense tells you that, in light of your holistic goal, a certain decision is going to fail most of the tests, and you will probably modify the decision before actually testing it.

As mentioned at the outset, speed is essential to the testing process. If you cannot quickly answer "yes" or "no" to a question, simply bypass the test and move on to the next. If you cannot reach a conclusion after passing through all the others, then come back to the one or two you bypassed so you can give them more consideration. In most cases, you have bypassed a test because you don't have enough information to know whether the decision passed or failed the test. You may, for example, need to take time to diagnose the cause of a problem before you can answer the question asked in the cause-and-effect test. Or you may need to gather actual figures, rather than estimates, for a gross profit analysis before you can pass this test with confidence. Once you have the needed information, test the decision once again and make a final judgment.

Don't worry that the speed of the testing will lead to an unsatisfactory result. You will be monitoring your decisions to ensure they in fact lead toward your holistic goal, and will replan—and retest—any time you veer off track. When a decision you test involves an attempt to alter the ecosystem processes in any way, you will assume at the outset that because it is impossible to account for nature's inherent complexity, the decision, *even though it was tested,* could be wrong. On the assumption you are wrong, you will determine the criteria you should monitor to give you the earliest possible warning of a need to replan.

One of the quickest ways to get familiar with the seven tests is to practice testing some of the decisions you routinely make in your own home. Not only will it build your confidence in the process, but also it will show you how even small decisions can affect progress toward your holistic goal. Question the detergents you use and the paper towels and light bulbs; how you dispose of waste products, such as garbage, batteries, computer parts, oil, paint thinners; how you deal with termites or cockroaches; your dietary habits, a new exercise routine, and so on. Two or more tests will apply to any one of these sorts of decisions. If your holistic goal is similar to my family's, you may find that in the first year a lot of the things you are currently doing may fail a lot of the tests. By the next year not nearly so many will fail as you begin to modify your actions to bring them in line with how you want to live and what you want to accomplish. It won't be long before the tests become so familiar that you subconsciously test most decisions.

Testing decisions as a group also speeds learning, simply because some people will be more familiar with certain tests and can point out aspects others might have overlooked. You are more likely to be confident in your judgment on whether a decision passes or fails a test, when others come to the same conclusion.

Naturally, the person or group making a decision should be responsible for testing it. However, there may be times when an individual or a smaller group working within a larger one might have made and tested a decision that others have doubts about. If such a situation arises, then by all means formally retest the decision as a group. This situation is more likely to occur in the early stages when the holistic goal is still very temporary and lacking in specifics. There will be varying levels of commitment to the holistic goal at this stage and hidden agendas and unconscious biases are bound to influence the testing of some decisions. Retesting the decision as a group will help to bring these things to light and may well lead to revisions in the holistic goal, a subject we will return to.

Ideally, all decisions you make should be tested, but in the early stages this is unlikely to happen. Where the testing is likely to make the biggest difference, especially in the beginning, is with any decisions that involve significant expenditures of money, for routine or emergency purchases, new business enterprises or products, and so on. Most of these sorts of decisions will be made when developing a financial plan for the year. Chapter 44, Holistic Financial Planning, shows how to create such a plan, using the testing to finalize all expenditures. Among other things, you are likely to find that decisions you may never have questioned in the past, because the expenditures involved were so routine, will now have to be revised.

The testing will also make an enormous difference when you attempt to deal with a crisis or unexpected problems that suddenly arise. The testing will help to ensure that whatever decisions you take to resolve the crisis or problem are in line with your holistic goal, and not merely quick fixes undertaken in a panic.

As you become increasingly familiar with the seven tests through practice and begin to appreciate their value, you will automatically start to test every decision you make. In fact the process will become so familiar that it will begin to shape your decisions before you make them. In deciding what to do about a problem, for instance, you won't even contemplate what to do about it until you have identified its cause.

Be assured that the testing will not lead you into doing things you do not want to do. Often, in the beginning especially, the testing will show that some of the decisions you have already implemented are unsound. This does not mean you suddenly have to stop doing whatever it is you are doing. The testing merely warns you of the dangers you face over the long haul. Now you can plan what to do about it before it is too late.

For example, the decision a farmer makes this year to grow monocultures of corn and soybeans, may pass the gross profit analysis test because the revenue they bring in is greater than the costs associated with their production, but they are likely to fail most of the remaining six tests. Rather than go out of business or leave the land, the farmer wisely decides to make no change for now. But he does know that finding more sustainable ways to grow his crops—ways that cater to many of the hidden, but real, costs—has become a high priority and that the testing will help him to decide when and how best to incorporate them.

Like the farmer, you may well find that you have to do something you know is damaging because, when viewed holistically, it is the correct thing to do *at the time*. In such situations, few of us, whether we are running a mining, manufacturing, or service-related business, or even a government, can change what we are doing overnight. But all of us can begin to plan for change. How to regulate the pace of that change is itself a decision we will need to test toward the holistic goals we form.

The Power Lies in the Holistic Goal

On first exposure to the testing guidelines, some people become so paralyzed by a fear they won't "do it right," they avoid testing any decisions at all. However, it is no big deal if they don't get it right. Initially, *everyone* is a little fuzzy in asking the questions. Some people will accidentally skip an important test. Others will attempt to run decisions through tests that don't really apply. In the end, however, they will still arrive at the right decision *for them,* as long as they have a holistic goal and are committed to achieving it.

Your holistic goal is more important to decision making than an infinite understanding of each of the tests will ever be. And as you increasingly gain commitment to achieving your holistic goal, most of the decisions you make, even if you do not consciously test them, will automatically tend to take you toward it. If half the readers of this book were to learn the testing guidelines to perfection and could run through them with 100 percent accuracy, but had a holistic goal to which they only paid lip service, they would fare no better than before. If the other half were committed to a holistic goal in which they had a great deal of ownership, but could only perform the testing with 10 percent accuracy, I would back their decisions every time.

Think of the testing process as the needle on a compass, and the holistic goal as the magnetic north that, no matter how much you twist and turn, the needle always points to. The testing will ensure that even though the needle deviates as you deal with changes in markets, technology, weather, family, staff, political upheavals, or even war, it will always be pointing you in the general direction you want to go.

If you do not have a holistic goal, the testing becomes pointless, for obvious reasons. More subtle are the consequences that stem from having a holistic goal to which people only pay lip service. Humans will always bias any decisions they make—even in rigorously controlled experiments—in favor of what they really want. *So what you really want must be in your holistic goal.* That is why forming and developing ownership in your holistic goal are even greater challenges than testing decisions. Unless you and all those forming the holistic goal with you feel free or comfortable enough to speak up, all that you and they want to accomplish in the particular whole you are managing is not likely to be expressed. As a result, the testing of some decisions, as mentioned, will be skewed in favor of hidden agendas and unexpressed biases.

I cannot overstate the critical difference that ownership in a holistic goal makes to the whole process. Yet, I also realize that ownership takes time to develop. That should not stop you from beginning to test decisions immediately after forming a holistic goal. The testing itself will start to show you where your holistic goal needs more clarity of expression. As you work to gain it, ownership will develop. Even the unconscious biases and hidden agendas that are bound to influence the testing in the early stages will eventually be sorted out as long as you continue to strive for clarity in what you really desire and want to accomplish. Before long the testing will increasingly become a subconscious exercise, which is what you should aim for. At that point you will begin to appreciate that the testing guidelines are only a mental crutch that helps you to see the big picture from many angles simultaneously.

Almost all the problems that beset humankind stem not from acts of Nature but from the way we make decisions. I would stake my life on the premise that if millions of humans in all walks of life would merely start making decisions holistically, toward holistic goals they are genuinely committed to achieving, most of the problems we face would evaporate.

26

Cause and Effect: Stop the Blows to Your Head Before You Take the Aspirin

The cause and effect test is one that carries considerable weight when a decision is taken to address a problem. It enables you to winnow out tools, actions, and policies that suppress symptoms only when you need to correct the cause. The question you ask is: *Does this action address the root cause of the problem?*

The logic of going to the root cause of a problem presents no difficulty to the simplest mind, yet political and economic expediency so often subvert that course that we have developed a culturally programmed habit of doing just the opposite. I don't apologize therefore for using the most simple-minded metaphor to illustrate my point.

If I followed you around and periodically bashed your head with a hammer, you would develop a headache sooner or later. You could say the headache is a problem, but it is in fact a symptom produced by my hitting you on the head. You might take some aspirin to ease the symptom, and then even more powerful pain killers, adding yet more treatments for the side effects, or new symptoms, produced by the medicine. Or you might try to stop my hammering and address the cause. Common sense dictates the latter, but in practice we usually do the former.

Real life presents situations of more deviously related cause and effect. Symptoms, or effects, can appear to result from multiple causes. Cause and effect is seldom a simple chain but a mesh extending infinitely in all directions (figure 26-1). Nevertheless, the lesson of the aspirin and the hammer still holds, and as a practical matter we can usually see how cause A leads to B without necessarily knowing why A happened or what will follow B. In other words, *why* I am hitting you on the head should not blind you to

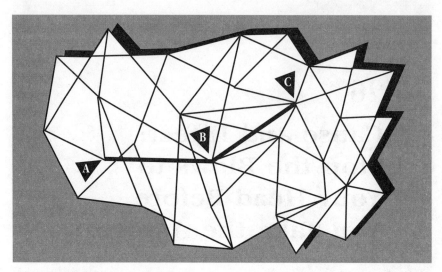

Figure 26-1 *Cause and effect is never a simple chain of events leading from A to B to C, but a mesh extending infinitely in all directions.*

the fact that the blows are causing your headache. We can act effectively on that insight—to stop the blows rather than take the aspirin—without necessarily untangling the infinite ramifications that stem from it.

That we often don't act this way is probably allied to human nature. We generally tend to favor a quick fix over more permanent solutions because by nature we seek to avoid discomfort, which a quick fix alleviates right away. Since most of our quick fixes involve the use of some form of technology, it is tempting to believe that technology is responsible for this quick fix mentality, but it is more likely the other way around: to evade discomfort we developed technology. Whichever it is, the fact remains that we are naturally inclined to resort to any one of the quick fixes modern science so often conjures up at the drop of a hat, rather than seek to address the underlying cause of the problem. Once the fix alleviates the symptoms, however, we tend to forget we even had a problem—until it recurs, as it surely will if the underlying cause is not rectified.

The seduction of the quick fix has weakened humanity's endeavors in all areas, from economics, to human and veterinary medicine, to the conduct of war and diplomacy, education, governance, and of course the management of natural resources. Instead of fixing what's really broken or finding a fundamentally different path, we print more money, invent a new drug, make a bigger bomb, suppress or buy off dissent, or build a dam. This test seeks to avoid nonsolutions by first asking you to think carefully about what might be causing your problem. If the decision under consideration addresses that cause, then it passes this test.

Identifying the Cause

Identifying the cause of a problem can be fairly easy, but it can also require considerable probing. In most situations, this is a relatively unstructured exercise. You merely pose and answer the same questions over and over again: "What is the cause of this?" and when you have your answer, "Well, what is the cause of that?" You may have to ask this question three or four or more times, peeling away layers of symptoms, before you find the cause you should address. An incident from my farming days illustrates the principle.

I was developing my farm from raw bush and the cost of maintaining my three tractors was very high, enough to cause me considerable alarm. My men insisted that the reason for this was the age of the tractors, all of which had seen use for twenty years or more by the time I bought them. My accountant sided with my staff and tried to convince me that I would be on firmer financial ground if I took out a loan and bought new tractors, which had all kinds of tax advantages.

But I wasn't so sure. Was the age of my tractors really responsible for the high cost of maintaining them? My neighbors had all bought new tractors but their maintenance costs were high too, even though they only used their tractors for light work. Mine were clearing virgin bush fourteen hours a day.

As I did all the repairs myself, I thought about the chain of events leading to each of my breakdowns and ultimately traced nearly every one back to dry bearings, dust in the oil, infrequent oil changes, cracked hoses, or some other neglect. Poor maintenance, rather than the age of the machinery, it appeared, was the cause of the problem. But why was maintenance so poor?

My initial response was to assume that my drivers, who were responsible for maintenance, were lazy and careless, and that I should think up ways I could penalize them for these faults. I found, however, that they often had a good explanation for a breakdown. They worked into the dark or started so early in the morning that they could not see the stump that cut the tire, for instance. So I continued to probe until I hit on yet another underlying possibility: perhaps maintenance was poor because my drivers had no incentive to make it otherwise.

There was no need to push this line of questioning further. If they lacked incentive, then it was because I had not provided it. Accordingly, I did provide it by changing the nature of their employment. Each driver would become a private contractor who agreed to provide his services for a very small daily amount and a large daily bonus if the tractor he drove was maintained according to a specific list of criteria. However, one or more days of bonus could be lost if the oil level in the engine or gearbox was low, sludge appeared in the air filters, grease fittings were blocked, a fanbelt was cracked, a screw or bolt was loose, and so on.

Everyone received their bonuses for the first month while I made random inspections to ensure that each driver understood the criteria spelled out in his contract and what would constitute an infraction. I did have to deduct several days' bonus for a couple of drivers shortly afterward, but never again. My drivers earned far more than they had as salaried workers and developed a sense of pride in being independent contract drivers; it became a game to see if I could ever catch them out. And my maintenance costs dropped to 50 percent of what my neighbors' averaged, despite my running three tractors to their one. Had we been managing holistically in those days, the diagnosis of this problem might have led to a slightly different remedy. But the story does illustrate why it pays to keep probing for an answer until you can go no further.

Some Japanese companies are noted for insisting their people ask "why" at least five times to get to the root cause of a problem. A few years ago, one such company found that the water consumption in its office building was much higher than it should be. They were advised to install low-flow toilets and water-saving faucets, but before spending any money, the company wanted to determine the cause of the high water consumption. By asking a series of "why" questions, they eventually discovered that when people used the toilets, they flushed twice: once to cover up the sound of urinating; and again when they were done. Having identified the cause, the company simply installed a small tape recorder inside each washroom cubicle with a button the person using the cubicle could push to produce the sound of a flush. The company's water bill plummeted.

There will be some instances, perhaps many, when you think you've got to the bottom of a problem and later find you have not. If you have probed as deeply as you can and still not found the root cause, then you may need to look wider, rather than deeper. Sometimes outsiders, not necessarily experts, can readily diagnose the cause of a problem when the answer has eluded you, simply because they can view the situation more objectively. A number of apparent problems will fall into one of two categories: (1) those related to resource management; and (2) those related to human behavior. The approach you take in diagnosing the cause in either category is slightly different.

Resource Management Problems

If the problem concerns land or resource management (e.g., soil erosion, a plague of grasshoppers, a decrease in the number of snow geese) look first to the four ecosystem processes for an answer, particularly community dynamics. Then consider the tools (covered in the last section) that may have been used in the past. How they have been applied will affect how the ecosystem processes are functioning now.

For example, if you have brush encroaching into a fairly brittle grassland, but your holistic goal describes a landscape where brush is limited to fringe areas, you have a problem. In fact, when I first visited the United States on a lecture tour of eight western states in the late 1970s, everyone mentioned brush encroachment as the big problem of the hour. I saw where literally millions of dollars had gone toward both eradication research and actual control to no avail. Nobody, however, seriously discussed the cause, and when I asked the question a chorus answered in unison, "Overgrazing. And livestock spread the seeds." Yet most of those present should have recognized that brush *also* invades areas that have no livestock, and moves *less* rapidly into areas where nearly all plants are heavily overgrazed.

Under pressure to do something about the brush and unable to really explain why the brush has come, most people just stop asking the question and look around for the best ways to kill the brush. John Deere, Caterpillar, Dow Chemical, and Monsanto accept the challenge. A whole new industry arises out of the ensuing competition, complete with research grants predicated on *not* asking the main question, and advertising to make it appear irrelevant in the light of apparent technological success.

Brush encroachment is in fact a symptom of an underlying problem resulting from prior management decisions. As Chapter 13 on community dynamics explained, a species can only establish in a place when conditions are favorable to its survival. So, one or more decisions you or your predecessors made in the past helped to create conditions that favored the establishment of brush. As Chapter 20 explained, partial rest applied in the more brittle environments tends to promote the establishment of brush. All grasses have fibrous roots, but all brush species are tap-rooted. For a shift from fibrous-rooted grassland to tap-rooted brush to occur, two factors must coincide: good germinating conditions, and porous or easily penetrated soil, which happens to be typical of rested areas where dead fibrous roots remain in the soil. These old and dying root systems assist the tap-rooted invader.

Let's say you know that for years the land in question has been partially rested. Animals have been present but scattered and unexcited and thus have hardly disturbed the soil or plants. If partial rest has been the main tool applied to the land—either deliberately or accidentally—and you know it produces conditions ideal for tap-rooted brush plants, then it is reasonable to suppose that partial rest is likely to be the cause of your brush encroachment. That's what you should begin to rectify before killing any plants.

If instead you decide to attack the symptom (or *effect*) and poison, chain, or root out the brush, it won't be long before you have to repeat the treatment. The brush will keep coming back until you have remedied the cause. Clearing the brush with aspirin, or more potent remedies, is a costly nonsolution as long as the hammering from partial rest continues. Paradoxically, the likely solution, ending the partial rest, will probably make money rather than cost it.

Photo 26-1 shows from the air an area that demonstrates the point. On the left of the fence we ignored the dense acacia encroachment and doubled the livestock numbers while stopping the partial rest that was occurring, and the overgrazing as well. The brush still dotting the landscape, which developed into grassland within a few years, became a definite asset because it provided shade and habitat diversity. On the right, the government concerned still recommended stock reduction, reseeding, and brush clearing—three costly forms of aspirin doomed to fail.

Going straight to the basic question of what is causing the problem demands no little courage, perseverance, and willingness to entertain new ideas, as everyone rapidly discovers who applies this test to the host of situations that arise in everyday land management. When you can actually hear the army worms stripping a crop field, can you stop and say to your-

Photo 26-1 *By planning the grazing (and doubling livestock numbers) on the left side of the fence we greatly reduced the bare ground that had caused the brush encroachment. Grassland improved despite the brush, which was not the cause of the bare ground. On the right, the government continued to tackle symptoms by destocking and clearing woody vegetation, but the brush continued to thrive. Lebowa, South Africa.*

self, "I'm not going to spray until I know what I can do to cut the chance of army worms becoming so thick again?" In an emergency such as this you may well go ahead, but only in full knowledge of the dangers and only to buy time to rectify the cause. To knowingly repeat the application of a faulty tool is never wise.

The repeated spraying of grasshoppers on American rangelands represents a similar case of continually attacking the symptom at ever-increasing cost without thought for the cause. The cost not only extends to the amount and price of the poison and many ecological side effects, but also shows up in the price we pay for water to drink. Pesticides, together with other agricultural and industrial pollutants account for much of the $2.8 billion Americans pay for bottled drinking water each year.[1] A gallon in many places now costs more than a gallon of gasoline. Homeowners, too, are part of the problem if they use pesticides routinely to rid their homes, gardens, and lawns of weeds and insects.

Massive monocultures in farming have spawned a whole cluster of spiraling problems characterized by public unwillingness to question the root cause. Rather than admit the inherent instability of monocultures, we try to keep them viable through chemistry, machinery, genetic engineering, and ultimately cash subsidy. More often than not, however, the side effects of these fixes exacerbate the problems. Although few farmers in the world enjoy higher product prices or cheaper input costs in machinery, vehicles, fuel, and fertilizers than we do in the United States; we still have broke farmers blaming overproduction, low prices, and high costs. If those really are the causes, one might wonder why the Amish and many other farmers who approach agriculture with different assumptions remain highly profitable in the same markets.

Politicians, more than those in any other profession, have most difficulty in overcoming the temptation to ignore cause and effect. Pork barrel legislation is only the most mundane example. The worldwide response to desertification shows how people may fall into the same trap without the slightest trace of cynicism. We've fed starving people, reduced livestock herds, settled nomads, imposed grazing systems, installed mighty irrigation works, and done a host of other things time and again. Ancient Hebrew texts apparently mention many of the same measures, including settling the nomads, yet the deserts grow because none of these actions tackles the cause.

In this sad tradition, a plan presented for signing at the 1992 Earth Summit held in Rio de Janeiro called for an annual expenditure of $6 billion on quick fixes for the symptoms of desertification.[2] To point out that none of the proposals made has ever reversed the decline of any land anywhere offends certain diplomatic and political sensibilities, however honest the intent.

Problems Related to Human Behavior

When the problem is related to human behavior you should generally look first to how your organization is structured, how management functions, and how it is led. Very seldom, perhaps 10 to 20 percent of the time, does it turn out that something is wrong with the people involved and that *they* are the cause of the problem.

If you had a furniture factory, for instance, where productivity had been declining for some months and eating into your profit, you might assume, based on talks with your floor managers, that the cause of your problem is a lack of skills and motivation. The cabinetmakers, for instance, grumble a lot about minor matters and cannot wait to get out the door once they have finished their shift. New employees take much too long to learn the ropes. To rectify the problem, you are considering a couple of actions: a workshop on motivation and team building, and a training program for supervisors that teaches them how to better train those they supervise. You have read about how effective these types of programs can be in sorting out your problem, and you know a consulting firm that can provide both the workshop and the training program for a reasonable fee. Before you go ahead and spend money on the workshop and training program, you want to test the decision to do so.

Because your decision attempts to address a problem, declining productivity, you go to cause and effect first. Now you have to ask yourself whether the apparent lack of motivation and skills is the cause of your problem or only a symptom stemming from an underlying cause. In considering this question, you begin to have some doubts. After all, your diagnosis of the cause was based on a fairly informal survey of floor managers, and not all of them had agreed.

It could be that bureaucracy and red tape has built up to such an extent that it is stifling worker creativity and their ability to get the job done. Perhaps the lines of communication between the various departments have become tangled. If the company is new to Holistic Management, it may be that there are still one or two individuals in supervisory positions who do not buy into the idea and are hampering the efforts of others. Perhaps the top decision makers dominated the discussion when forming the holistic goal and those on the shopfloor had had little say, and thus had no commitment to achieving it.

Enough doubts have been raised that you cannot answer with any certainty that you are in fact addressing the cause of your declining productivity. Therefore, the proposed action, the workshop and training program, would likely fail the cause-and-effect test. When this happens, you generally need go no further with the testing.

Once you think you have found the cause of the problem you can then determine the appropriate actions to take to rectify it. If they address the cause, they will pass this test. You will know your diagnosis was correct if the problem begins to resolve itself—productivity will increase. Because you are dealing with human nature, however, which is more complex than we may ever understand, your diagnosis may also prove faulty. If the problem does not begin to resolve itself, you will have to dig deeper to find the cause. But find the cause you must.

Dealing with Short-Term and Long-Term Effects

Bear in mind that occasionally things may get worse before they get better, no matter what sort of problem you are dealing with. Sometimes this will affect your decision about the actions you plan to take. A farmer who suddenly stops fertilizing his crops with chemicals because of the groundwater pollution they create may have addressed the cause of the pollution, but may also reduce his crop yields so significantly that he does not survive financially. It makes more sense for him to *begin* to address the cause by weaning himself off the chemicals gradually. If the factory were to revamp its bureaucratic structure overnight, the resulting confusion could cause productivity to decrease even further. It makes more sense to begin addressing the cause by dismantling the bureaucracy gradually.

Sometimes, decisions that pass the cause and effect test result in short-term "problems." A rancher who uses animal impact to overcome the partial rest that has created a lot of bare ground and a moribund stand of a few rest-tolerant grass species may find that all he produces in the first year or two is a healthy crop of weeds. This was not what he had in mind when he described a future resource base that included dense perennial grassland. Rather than consider the weeds as yet another problem to be tackled, he should view them as an intervening stage of succession that he is likely to move beyond. *Any* new plant is progress when you start with bare ground and dead or dying plants. The influx of weeds is just as likely to be an indication that progress is being made. Dense perennial grassland will not appear overnight, but given time—and planning that ensures little or no overgrazing occurs and that animal impact is provided where needed—perennial grasses will appear and flourish.

To get out of monoculture cropping, which was responsible for a lot of the insect damage in his fields, one farmer switched to planting several crops (corn, beans, and oats) in narrow strips he rotated each year. This successfully reduced the insect damage and also the number of weeds and the incidence of disease. But it led to an outbreak of ground squirrels who found the changed environment ideal and quickly became pests when they dug up newly planted corn seeds. Because the farmer was now a certified organic farmer, conventional options for dealing with rodents were out of the question. But he did gather information on the squirrel's habits. For one thing, he learned they ate a lot of insects and wire worms, which made him think it might be a good idea to keep them around. Once the corn plants emerged, the squirrels were no longer a problem anyway. He solved his dilemma creatively by spilling inexpensive waste seed into the middle of the rows as his planter was burying the rest of the seed. The squirrels then busied themselves gathering waste seed off the soil surface and left the planted corn alone.[3]

In the furniture factory you may have found that the cause of your declining productivity was a lack of ownership in the holistic goal. The workers on the shopfloor had not felt free to speak up about what they really wanted and were only paying lip service to it. One of the actions you take to rectify the problem is to open up weekly departmental planning meetings, which had previously included only those in supervisory positions, to all departmental employees. Shopfloor workers are encouraged to share their ideas and speak of their desires. And they do. But they also begin to air grievances that previously they would have feared to express in the presence of supervisors. This causes considerable discomfort among the supervisors and among some of the shopfloor workers and worries upper-level management staff. This could be seen as yet another problem that has to be dealt with, or again it could be considered progress because supervisors and management staff are getting information they need to have and shopfloor workers are learning that they have no retribution to fear in speaking up, that their views, both good and bad, count. When they all next come together to refine their holistic goal, the results should be very different.

Unleashing Problems Down the Road

Sometimes decisions you make can unleash future problems, even when the original decision had nothing to do with solving a problem. One or more of the remaining six tests is likely to cover this possibility, but an early warning here—by asking, Could this action unleash problems later?—will keep you on the lookout. The furniture factory, for example, may use varnishes and other finishing products that, although they are disposed of safely while in the factory, become a problem when the furniture is eventually discarded because these products will not break down in the landfill. This concern is addressed in the sustainability test (Chapter 31). Sometimes you may have to let a situation deteriorate because the action you plan to take to rectify it would be blocked by human attitudes and beliefs. The weak link test (Chapter 27) and the society and culture test (Chapter 32) address these possibilities.

Summary

In general, the cause and effect test dictates that you not implement a decision unless you feel sure that it addresses the cause of the problem, rather than a symptom. In an emergency you may proceed, but only in full knowledge of the dangers and only to buy time to rectify the cause.

It can be argued that it is sensible at times to remove a cause and treat the symptom simultaneously. Be wary, though, because in practice this often results in draining resources from the most efficient action, and represents not effective policy, but a response to advertising or to peer or political pressure. From years of practice I have found it wisest to remove the cause first and see what happens. Most often the symptom disappears at no additional cost.

When performing the cause and effect test, also bear these points in mind:

- Go to this test first, when you are dealing with a problem.

- When dealing with a resource management problem, look first to the four ecosystem processes for answers. How management tools have been applied in the past will be reflected in the condition of the ecosystem processes and give clues to the cause of your current problem.

- If a problem is related to human behavior, first search for the cause in organization, management, and leadership style.

- If the problem persists or returns, you have not addressed the cause.

Remember that Holistic Management takes a totally different approach to decision making. In conventional management, "getting rid of the weeds" would be the goal. In Holistic Management, "producing prosperous people on healthy land that is so rich in its diversity of plant and animal life that the weeds cease to be a problem" would be the comparable, but holistic, goal.

Once you realize that the weeds are an "effect," that is, they are symptomatic of a deeper problem, you change your plans. Rather than looking for other ways to destroy the weeds, you now look for ways to increase complexity and diversity in the community so the weeds become minor players. Remember that the cause and effect test is only one in a series of seven and that the testing itself is only one aspect of a process that eventually gets you beyond your problems.

27

Weak Link: The Strength of a Chain Is That of Its Weakest Link

A chain stretched to breaking will, by definition, fail at the weakest link. At any moment in time every chain has one, and only one, weakest link that alone accounts for the strength of the entire chain, regardless how strong other links might be. To strengthen a chain when resources are limited, one must always attend first to the weakest link. Other links, no matter how frail they appear, are nonproblems until the weakest link is first fixed. If $100 would correct the weakest link, and we spent $200 to make sure, we would have theoretically squandered $100, because after the first $100 repair, the chain had a different weakest link on which the second $100 should have been spent.

The undetected weak link can cause mighty undertakings to fail outright or to suffer continual setbacks. Thus, we have a test that compels us to check our actions to ensure they address the link that is weakest at any moment. The test applies in three different contexts: social, biological, and financial. The questions you ask are:

- *Social:* Could this action, because of prevailing attitudes or beliefs, create a weak link in the chain of actions leading toward our holistic goal?

- *Biological:* Does this action address the weakest link in the life-cycle of this organism?

- *Financial:* Does this action strengthen the weakest link in the chain of production?

The Social Weak Link

Consider the question: *Could this action, because of prevailing attitudes or beliefs, create a weak link in the chain of actions leading toward our holistic goal?*

You, and the future you envision in your holistic goal, are linked by a chain made up of all the actions you will take to get there. What you are asking in this test is whether the decision you are making now is likely to offend or confuse people whose support you will need, in the near or distant future, to achieve your holistic goal. Any action that runs counter to prevailing attitudes and beliefs is likely to meet with resistance, creating a blockage that, if not addressed, will at some point become the weakest link standing between you and the achievement of your holistic goal.

The Center for Holistic Management struck just such a situation on a piece of land we own and manage as a learning site in Zimbabwe. When we took it over, the land was deteriorating because for many years it had been overrested and frequently burned. Thorn bush had invaded open grassland and much of the ground was bare. The once perennially flowing river that rose on the property had now become an intermittent stream, and the populations of elephant, buffalo, sable, zebra, lion, cheetah, waterbuck, and so on, had gradually declined. To produce the future landscape described in our holistic goal, we realized we would need to use animal impact and grazing to begin healing the land and that we would need to use cattle to provide it. The wildlife populations were not sufficiently large to do so, nor functioning naturally.

However, we also knew that a decision to bring cattle into an area recently designated for wildlife would anger some members of the public and likely be condemned by government wildlifers because of prevailing beliefs. Thus, in realizing that the only way forward would create a weak link (hostile attitudes) we took the holistically correct decision to let the land continue to deteriorate and the wildlife continue to decline while we worked to overcome ignorance and prejudice. Had we done otherwise, our efforts would have been set back many years by lawsuits and bureaucratic wrangling.

When you suspect that the implementation of a decision is likely to result in a reaction that blocks further progress, you will fail the weak link test *if* your decision does not also include a plan for dealing with the blockage. An ounce of prevention is more than worth the pounds of cure it would take to undo the problems associated with the ensuing conflict. If there are no foreseeable obstacles in implementing the action, you of course pass this test.

The Biological Weak Link

Consider the question: *Does this action address the weakest link in the life-cycle of this organism?*

In the biological context the weak link test applies when you are dealing with populations of plant or animal organisms that have become a problem, either because they are too many or too few in number: the parasites infesting the farmer's sheep, the loco weed that invades the range, the water hyacinths that choke the hydroelectric plant, the cockroaches that infest the kitchen, the rare aloe that needs protection, or the tortoise or owl threatened by extinction. Whether we see these organisms as friend or foe, the same question is asked and the same logic used. Before any action is taken to increase or decrease their numbers, we need first to ensure that it addresses the weakest link in the organism's life cycle. In doing so, we are likely to maximize the effectiveness of the treatment and to ensure the results will be lasting.

Every organism in its life cycle has a point of greatest vulnerability, a weakest link. Recognize this, and you have a good chance of inexpensively and effectively increasing or decreasing the ability of that species to recruit new members to its population. When the tool or action addresses that weak link, it passes this test.

Finding the weak link in the life cycle of any organism can be a challenge. Sometimes the answer is fairly obvious, other times it will require some research. Nature often provides clues that can help because all plants and animals have developed ways to reduce their vulnerability. Most plants, for instance, are most vulnerable during their initial establishment when the seed has germinated and root and leaf must find sustaining conditions in a limited time. If seeds, once sprouted, do not encounter the right soil, moisture, temperature, and sunlight for long enough to establish, they will not survive. Plants are able to overcome this vulnerability to some extent by the sheer number of seeds they produce and the ability of those seeds to survive in the soil for many years awaiting the right conditions.

Insects and amphibians that produce a mass of eggs, would appear to be most vulnerable while still in the egg or larval stages. Mammals, such as lions or dogs, that produce several young at once would appear to be most vulnerable between birth and young adulthood. Mammals that produce only one or two young at a time, such as humans, but remain fertile and sexually active throughout the year, would appear to be most vulnerable from conception through infancy.

With some animal populations, careful observation should tell you fairly quickly at what stage they are most vulnerable. If you have a population of antelope, for instance, whose numbers you want to increase, you might observe that many fawns are being born, but that very few are surviving to adulthood. Thus, if the decision you planned to take was to purchase more adults and to release them on your property, it would not pass this test. You first need to address why so few fawns are surviving, because that is the weakest link in their life cycle—from fawning to young adulthood. Any action that enhanced fawn survival, such as the provision of more cover, if cover was lacking, *would* pass this test.

Far too often we make the mistake of concentrating on the adult members of the species when the adult stage of the life cycle is rarely the point of greatest vulnerability. Thus, while we bulldoze mature brush or poison well-established weeds we are creating favorable conditions for millions of their seeds to germinate and establish. Sometimes we use expensive and dangerous poisons to attack mature insect pests and unwittingly select for new, unscathed, and poison-resistant replacements. It is more sensible and more economical to address the invading brush, weeds, or insect pests by changing the environment that has become so favorable to their establishment. How will the tools available—rest, fire, grazing, animal impact, living organisms, and technology—affect the four ecosystem processes relative to that organism's needs at its most vulnerable stage?

As mentioned in Chapter 26, brush establishes easily where seedling tap roots can take hold—on grasslands that have been overrested. Many forbs establish under the same conditions, although they tend to occur more among grasses whose fibrous roots have been weakened by overgrazing. Animal impact and grazing, carefully planned to avoid overgrazing, will help to invigorate grass roots, while creating conditions more favorable for higher successional grass seedlings, and will gradually decrease the success rate for both types of tap-rooted invaders.

Many insects flourish in sites where eggs are guaranteed a high rate of survival—on bare ground or on specific plants (made all the more attractive when a great number of the same plants are present, as in a monoculture). Animal impact can be used to help to cover bare ground through trampling down old-standing plant material, breaking the capping, and compacting the soil to provide seed-to-soil contact, so new plants can grow. Living organisms can be enlisted—increased variety of crops, hedgerows, tree-belts—to increase the diversity of plants on croplands.

Understanding this concept enables us at minimal cost to manage and control undesirable species and often leads to surprisingly simple ways to supplant destructive practices. My family once had to draw water from an irrigation canal infested with parasites that cause bilharzia, a major scourge of Africa that leads to paralysis and even death in humans. Naturally, I did not want my family or my farmhands and their families to become infested. The government researchers recommended adding copper sulphate to the water, but I rejected that idea because I was not sure at which stage the parasite was most vulnerable. While doing some research to find the weak link, a solution offered itself. I found that the parasite had to find a human host within twenty-four hours after leaving the host snail that carried it. So all I had to do was to ensure that the delay in finding a human host was longer than the parasite could survive. By keeping our water in a holding tank for forty-eight hours before letting it into our main cistern, we imbibed only parasites that had suffered a natural death, and no chemicals.

If you have not identified the weak link in the organism's life cycle by the time you are ready to test a decision, this test will alert you to the need to do so. You will have to take the time to find out where that weak link is, either through your own observations, reading up on the basic biology of the organism, or seeking the help of a local extension agent or other advisor. Once you have your answer, you should know whether or not the proposed action treats the organism at its most vulnerable stage. If it does not, your research may suggest an alternative action, as my research did, that is likely to pass.

The Financial Weak Link

Consider the question: *Does this action strengthen the weakest link in the chain of production?*

Each year in conjunction with Holistic Financial Planning (Chapter 44) you need to identify the weak link in the chain of production that stretches from the raw resources you work with to the money you receive for the products produced. This chain has three links to which human creativity is applied: resource conversion; product conversion; and marketing (or money conversion), as shown in figure 27-1. The first link, *resource conversation,* involves the use of human creativity and money to convert resources that differ slightly depending on the type of business or enterprise, of which there are two broad categories:

1. *Sunlight harvesters.* This first category includes those businesses whose primary production is based on the conversion of sunlight energy (through plants) to a salable or consumable product, such as food, fiber, lumber, or wildlife. The money their efforts reap represents solar dollars, as long as soils are not damaged in the process, and is the only form of wealth that can feed people. Thus, what they do is fundamental to our civilization's long-term survival.

2. *Resource enhancers.* The second category includes businesses that are one step removed from the sunlight-conversion business, such as a shoe store, bakery, or accounting firm. (This would include, incidentally, pig and poultry producers or any others who buy, rather than grow, their own feed.) Their primary production is based on the conversion of raw materials and energy to a salable product (goods or

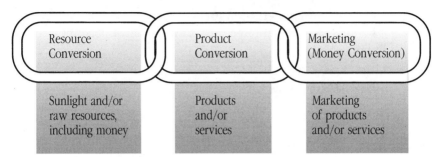

Figure 27-1 *The chain of production. Human creativity first needs to utilize money and raw resources (including sunlight) to create a product or service. Then the product or service needs to be perfected and finally marketed to produce money. The chain is only as strong as its weakest link.*

services). The money their efforts reap represents mineral or paper dollars. What they produce enhances human civilization and improves the quality of life, but cannot sustain a civilization.

In the *product conversion link,* the sunlight harvesters turn the plants grown in the first link into a marketable form, such as crops for humans, and fodder for livestock, wildlife, or fish. The resource enhancers convert the resources in their first link into a plethora of goods, services, or marketable skills. In the *marketing* (or *money conversion*) link the products or services of the second link are marketed and money is finally derived from the sunlight captured, or the raw materials and energy utilized, in the first link.

Obviously, whenever strengthening the chain of production requires money, and profit is included in your holistic goal, the proposed investments should pass the weak link test. No amount of money invested in advertising (marketing link), for example, will profit a business that turns out a poor product (product conversion link). Only investment in the weak link will result in more profit at the end.

In practice, we normally determine the weak link for each enterprise or line of goods or services for sale immediately prior to financial planning. Some businesses will have only one enterprise, such as the rancher who runs a yearling operation or the professional income tax preparer, but many businesses will have several. In this case, each enterprise will have one link in its chain of production that is weakest at any moment. And that enterprise will be only as strong as that weakest link.

The aim of Holistic Financial Planning is to keep constantly strengthening the chain of production. Obviously, the entire year's budget cannot be spent on the one link that is weakest in any given year, but until money has been allocated to actions that do strengthen this link, other actions will fail this test. Let's look at the three links in more detail, according to the type of business.

The Sunlight Harvesters

The aim of these businesses should be to produce the maximum they can in solar dollars. Because soil and water are used to grow plants, some of the money they receive in the end will represent mineral dollars. Solar energy is an unlimited resource, but soil and water are finite. Thus, to reflect a true profit, one that is socially, environmentally, and economically sound, both soil and water must be enhanced or used in a nonconsumptive manner to produce solar dollars. If soil is destroyed rather than enhanced or water polluted or depleted in the process, the results would not be genuinely profitable. Nor would they be if you expended vast amounts of petrochemical energy (solar energy stored in the past), tied up in fuel, fertilizers, and pesticides, to capture less solar energy today.

The plants, from algae to trees, that convert solar energy in the first link can themselves become potentially marketable products (vegetables, cotton fiber, logs) without undergoing further conversion. Hay sold from the field, for example, will hardly undergo much product conversion compared to frozen orange juice. Plants can also be converted to meat, wool, and hides when consumed by livestock and wildlife. And in some cases the plants or the animals dependent on the plants can be marketed in a nonconsumptive manner (scenery for tourists, hikers, and others; hours of fly fishing or birdwatching, and so on). In the marketing link, we consider everything involved in selling the product and getting it to the customer, such as pricing, promotion, and transportation.

It is generally not difficult to determine which of the three links is weakest in each enterprise. If you are a farmer, you would not put money into growing a bigger crop of potatoes, either by increasing acreage or nutrients, if you could not market the potatoes you already produce or if you could increase the price through better marketing. You would not invest in a bigger and better harvester if your average yield does not justify it, and so on. Much of this is common sense, and a cautious, sensible farmer makes these judgments without even thinking in terms of the chain.

In a ranching context weakness in the resource conversion link shows up as a shortage of forage for livestock and/or wildlife. In farming poor crop yields naturally indicate poor solar energy conversion, but in this era of mechanized, chemical agriculture, exorbitant input costs are a more common, but less obvious, symptom. Once the farmer sees resource conversion as the weak link, he can begin to decrease the amount of hard-earned solar dollars he invests in fossil energy inputs that do what a healthy soil community does for free.

Weakness in the product conversion link becomes evident to the rancher when his animals are too few and unable to utilize a good share of the available forage. The farmer detects it when he produces a solar energy crop, one that requires minimal fossil energy inputs, but cannot market his crop well because of an inability to harvest it completely.

The Resource Enhancers

The aim of resource-enhancing businesses should be to produce mineral or paper dollars as efficiently as possible. The raw materials in their resource conversion link include any number of things: lumber for furniture; minerals, mined or refined; crude oil, for production of plastics and other products; foodstuffs, for production of baked goods; fibers, for cotton clothing; and so on. In most businesses the raw materials have to be combined with human creativity, energy, and capital to develop a product with sales potential. In some companies, human skills and money are the only resources available, as in companies that sell services, such as accounting or legal advice, ideas, entertainment, and so on, rather than tangible goods.

In the product conversion link, businesses that produce a tangible product, such as manufactured goods, are considering everything related to its production, from choosing a product and its design, to the manufacturing process involved in making the product. This, of course, impinges closely on the resource conversion link where creativity is used to come up with product ideas. In the marketing link, these businesses would market those products to finally derive money from the resources utilized in the first link.

Businesses that provide a service rather than a product would be using their human creativity to convert the knowledge and skills in their resource conversion link into the services they provide—their product link. Then they, too, would market those services to derive money from the resources utilized in the first link.

Here again, finding the weak link is often fairly easy to do. You would not put money into producing more goods if you cannot sell what you already produce or if you could increase the price of the goods through better marketing. In some businesses the resource conversion link shows a weakness when a new enterprise lacks sufficient capital to get up and running, or lacks people with the skills needed to design the product envisioned. When product sales drop off, the product conversion link would need attention if the product was faulty or needed an upgrade. The marketing link would need attention if the problem was poor promotion or unreliable transport.

At the Personal Level

This thinking would also apply on a personal level. Individuals working for a salary, for example, would be using their human creativity, time, and money to gain knowledge and skills to improve themselves (their product link) and marketing their abilities to derive money from the resources utilized in their first link. They might need to address the resource conversion link if they lacked skills, or the product link if, despite high skills, their attitude made them unemployable. They would have to market themselves better to get a raise or move to a new job.

In All Businesses

In virtually every kind of business, the product conversion and marketing links are closely related. Marketing is usually the weak link when the producer fails to meet the needs of his or her market, such as the manufacturer who continues to build chrome and horsepower into automobiles when consumers want durability and fuel economy or the cattle rancher who raises fatty, chemically tainted beef when buyers want it lean and clean.

Marketing is also the weak link whenever available markets remain untapped because they are not researched, because the product is poorly presented or badly promoted, or because the supply is erratic or out of synch with peak demand. One farmer I knew did exceptionally well year after year in a market where other onion farmers continually failed. He merely perfected his storage system and released his crop whenever supplies ran low in the local market.

There will always be gray areas where you are not quite sure which link applies. Is the bruised fruit you are trying to market a production problem (product conversion link) or a transport problem (marketing link)? In the end it really does not matter as long as you detect it and address it. The power in this test is that it asks you to focus on the chain of production as a whole, and only then to determine where your money is needed most in any one year. *The products you finally sell are not responsible for your profit: how you reinvest your money in the chain of production each year is.*

In an earlier example I talked of misspending exactly $100, but real life never allows that kind of accuracy. Being consistently right with the vast majority of your dollars is what matters. Remember, however, that once the weak link has been discovered, it *has* to be dealt with. It is not merely desirable or important to do so.

Once you have identified the weak link, you look at all the possible actions you could take that would strengthen that particular weak link right away. When allocating funds for expenses, these actions will receive priority if they have also passed the remaining tests, because they will generate the most revenue. However, funds are often limited, so you will not be able to allocate dollars to every action that addresses the weak link, but will have to choose among them. The marginal reaction test, covered in the next chapter, helps you to select the action (or actions) that provide the greatest return in terms of your holistic goal for the money and effort spent.

28

Marginal Reaction: Getting the Biggest Bang for Your Buck

The marginal reaction test ensures that your commitment of time, effort, and money provides the maximum possible thrust toward your holistic goal at any moment. It thus parallels and works in close conjunction with the weak link and cause and effect tests, but also differs in significant ways. The question you ask is: *Which action provides the greatest return, in terms of our holistic goal, for the time and money spent?*

Many people summarize the marginal reaction test with the phrase "getting the biggest bang for your buck," and the example generally used to illustrate the principle involves just that. This test, however, should become one that we apply continually in many less tangible situations, including the mundane dilemmas of everyday life that consume so much of our time.

I do not know of any management situation right down to the family budget or the planning of your personal time, where the marginal reaction test would not be of great benefit. Governments are notorious for their lack of use of such a principle, which reflects in unbalanced budgets and wasted effort.

In applying the test you are essentially asking yourself which of two or more actions will result in *each additional dollar or hour of labor* being invested where it provides the highest return in terms of your holistic goal. No two actions can possibly give you the same return for each unit of effort (money or time) invested at that moment. Thus, when resources are limited you want to select the one from which you gain the most. In doing so you will end up spending less time or money and achieve what you want more quickly. The following hypothetical example illustrates this principle in dollars and cents.

Suppose you have $20,000 and must invest it in two banks under a peculiar set of rules. You may only open one account in each bank, and the interest earned on each additional deposit declines. Bank A pays 5 percent on the first $5,000 but on each additional $1,000 they give you 1 percent less (i.e., extra deposits up to $6,000 pay only 4 percent, the next $1,000 brings only 3 percent).

Bank B pays 4.5 percent on the first $7,000, but the rate declines 0.75 percent on each additional $1,000. In practice such rules would discourage saving, but you can get the best possible yield from your capital only by following the marginal reaction test. Think about it and then look at figure 28-1 to see how the investment would take place.

As you discover, you wind up investing $9,000 in Bank A and $11,000 in Bank B. No other combination except opening four accounts in Bank A—a violation of the rules—will yield more interest. Figure 28-1 was worked out by taking each dollar and asking where it would earn the highest interest. The first 5,000 dollars earned 5 percent in Bank A, but Bank A would pay only 4 percent on the very next dollar instead of the 4.5 percent offered by Bank B. The next $7,000 would thus go to Bank B, but the $1,000 after that would go to Bank A because its 4 percent now beats Bank

Bank A	Bank B	Interest %	Balance	Interest Earned
5,000	–	5.00	15,000	250.00
–	7,000	4.50	8,000	315.00
1,000	–	4.00	7,000	40.00
–	1,000	3.75	6,000	37.50
1,000	1,000	3.00	4,000	60.00
–	1,000	2.25	3,000	22.50
1,000	–	2.00	2,000	20.00
–	1,000	1.25	1,000	12.50
1,000	–	1.00	0	10.00
9,000	11,000	–	20,000	542.50

Figure 28-1 *The investment of $20,000 in Bank A and Bank B illustrates the principle of marginal reaction per dollar invested. If you took each dollar and asked where it would earn the highest interest, the first $5,000 would go to Bank A, but the very next dollar, in fact the next $7,000 would go to Bank B. The next $1,000 would go to Bank A, and so on.*

B's 3.75 percent. Similar thinking for each of the remaining $1,000 deposits determines the final outcome. Such neat examples rarely occur in management, but the real-life situations that we cannot quantify are no less real.

Marginal Reaction per Dollar Invested

This test should be used any time expenditures are to be made and there are alternatives to choose from. In practice, this will most often occur in conjunction with holistic financial planning. But emergencies do arise and money may have to be allocated to address them. If your one and only delivery van throws a rod through the engine block, for instance, you have to take action right away. There are three alternatives you might consider: rebuild the engine, buy a second-hand, low-mileage van, or buy a new van. Assuming each of the alternatives passes most of the other tests, the marginal reaction test is likely to clinch your decision. Several factors would influence your comparison: the actual costs associated with each alternative, the lifespan of the rebuilt engine, or the used or new van, the time each alternative will take to implement, and how that will affect your ability to get the deliveries made, and so on. Whichever alternative provides the greatest return, in terms of your holistic goal, is the one you should select.

In Holistic Financial Planning this test is used in two ways. Initially it will help you to prioritize the actions to be taken that address the weak link in your chain of production, as mentioned in Chapter 27. Each action will provide a different marginal reaction. Those that provide the highest will get the most money allocated to them. Some may be dropped altogether because funds are limited and they cannot earn, dollar for dollar, what other actions would.

Once you have allocated money to those actions that address your weak link this year and provide the highest marginal reaction, you allocate what is left to the many items that require money to keep the business going—your maintenance expenses. Here, you use the marginal reaction test again to see if money can be shaved from each of your maintenance items and added to those priority actions. Every dollar you can pull off a maintenance expense, as long as you do not get to the point where management is impaired, will earn you more spent on the priority expenses because these expenses actually generate income, while maintenance expenses never do.

Let me use a few examples to illustrate these points. Before I do, I should remind you that this test, in most instances, never does boil down to the simplicity of the Bank A/Bank B case. Many times you cannot produce quantifiable figures, and your judgment will be highly subjective. That being the case, your answer to this test question will be only as good as your knowledge, common sense, and determination to achieve your holistic goal. Yet again, another reason to have a clearly defined holistic goal.

Prioritizing Actions

Suppose you were creating a financial plan for the bakery you manage as a family business. A month or so before, you had determined that marketing was your weak link this year. Sales had fallen off in the previous six months while, to the best of your knowledge, the quality of your products had been maintained. In discussing the various actions you could take to address the marketing link, two appear most promising, enhancing your advertising program and engaging a student from the local business college to conduct a customer survey. Redesigning and enlarging the ad you run in the local paper and running it more frequently will cost $3,000. The survey will cost somewhere between $500 and $1,000.

Either action is likely to address the falloff in sales, but you now use the marginal reaction test to see which one should receive priority in the allocation of funds. You find it difficult indeed to quantify the return from each alternative but after some discussion you realize that knowing why customers have deserted you might enable you to bring them back and attract new customers as well and that it could also influence the content of your advertising. This discussion and your own intuition convince you that you will gain more per dollar from the survey. Increasing your advertising budget does not make much sense now, and for the time being you won't allocate additional dollars to it. If the survey indicates a need, you might adjust your plan later and add this expense. Let's say that the survey is done, and you learn that the falloff in sales was largely due to the temporary assistant you hired while some family members were away on vacation. At the counter, he had been rude and unhelpful to a number of customers and he had also neglected to fill several home delivery orders. Customers complained among themselves, rather than to you, so you were not aware of the problem.

This example illustrates the parallels between this test and the weak link and cause and effect tests. Had this family noted the drop in sales earlier on, they could have diagnosed the cause of their problem then and addressed it sooner. Even so, they would still have used the marginal reaction test to help them to choose among the alternative actions they could take to address the cause.

Shaving Maintenance Expenses

You are part of a team managing a garden furniture store that is shortly to open for business. There are similar stores in town, but none offers the range, quality, and durability of merchandise you do. Marketing is very definitely your weak link this year and needs all the attention you can give it. You have already done considerable market research and prioritized all the actions you plan to take using the marginal reaction test. In your financial plan you have allocated $50,000 to a promotional campaign that includes television advertising (40 percent), newspaper and garden club magazine advertising (30 percent), press releases (5 percent), and two special events in the spring and summer where customers tour garden furniture show rooms and get free advice on designing outdoor living space (25 percent). The rest of the money available from your start-up capital, plus the earnings you project from furniture sales, has been allocated to maintenance expenses (salaries, travel, telephone, office and legal expenses, insurance, and so on). All of these expenses are vital, and your business could not run without them, but they do not actually generate income. That can be generated only through the chain of production. So now you look at each of these maintenance expense categories and determine how many dollars you can shave off each one of them without impairing your ability to get the job done and put toward the marketing program. Every one of those dollars will be giving you a higher marginal reaction applied to the marketing program until you reach the point that the next dollar taken starts to impair the running of the business. In doing this exercise you find you can shave dollars off your phone bill by using a different telephone service; reduce your travel budget by scheduling fewer trips; save on vehicle running costs by making some refinements to your delivery system that ensures fewer trips; and so on. You are challenging all maintenance expenses here and nothing is sacred. You do not assume that because an expense is routine and has had money allocated to it in the past it should automatically continue. When you have finished this exercise, you find you have a lean and clean plan, and $15,000 additional dollars you can put toward your marketing program.

When Your Business Is Sunlight Harvesting

In sunlight-harvesting businesses, where money is being generated directly from the sun's energy, the effects of the marginal reaction test are profound indeed. The test also shows in many cases that, of the actions being compared, only one will survive because no other comes close to yielding the return it does this year. This can also be the case in other businesses, but is less common.

Suppose you and your family manage a cattle ranch and have determined that this year resource conversion is your weak link: you need more grass to feed your animals. There are a number of actions you could take, but you are leaning in favor of clearing the brush that still covers large portions of the ranch. Your holistic goal describes dense grassland in which only a few patches of brush are included to provide cover for wildlife and livestock and diversity in the vegetation. You have removed the cause of the brush encroachment and have halted its spread, but now you want to remove some of what's left to provide room for more grass to grow. So, why not buy a used bulldozer at auction and root out the brush?

Before you do that, you need to use the marginal reaction test to compare the brush clearing to the other possible alternatives for increasing solar energy conversion to make sure you are getting the highest return possible on the dollars invested. Again, this comparison will not be quantifiable like the Bank A/Bank B example, so it demands careful thought. Other actions that could grow more grass are:

- Subdividing grazing areas or paddocks through fencing. This would increase animal impact, and it would improve the ratio between grazing/trampling and recovery periods as animals would spend less time on each unit of land.

- Improving your skills in holistic grazing planning.

- Improving drainage and/or aeration through increased animal impact (herd effect) in selected areas.

- Buying or leasing more land.

These are but a few of the more obvious measures that could increase the volume of solar energy converted through plants, but for simplicity's sake and also because many situations in fact boil down to this choice, we will compare brush clearing to the case for more fencing.

What does brush clearing offer on the land compared with more fencing this year? If you clear the brush it will allow more grass to grow by letting in more light, and the disturbance created by the tractors and chains may increase soil respiration and water penetration much as animal impact would do. Dead roots left underground will provide a mass of organic matter that will eventually enhance water retention, mineral cycling, and soil structure for some years. More forage in the cleared paddock may allow you to hold animals there a day or two longer and that means more recovery time elsewhere and thus more grass growth over a wider area. (Chapter 38 on time management explains this in more detail.)

The cost of brush clearing will be $30,000. On the other hand at $300 a mile, you could build 10 miles of electric fence and split four large paddocks into eight for a cost of $3,000. From this you could anticipate the following benefits:

- Halving the size of the four paddocks would double the animal impact in the divided areas during each use. This will improve the distribution of dung and urine in the eight new paddocks. Forage production will consequently improve steadily in these paddocks for many years to come.

- With four additional paddocks the grazing periods can now be decreased on average in every paddock on the ranch in every growing season over the fifty-year life of the fences. Thus, this single investment will increase the amount of grass that grows in all paddocks over the next fifty years.

- Disease risks are reduced because animals receive a higher plane of nutrition and spend shorter times on fouled ground.

- Grazing planning becomes easier, thanks to the versatility of having more paddocks to use. In addition, increasing paddocks now brings the possibility of cutting supplements by more efficient use of forage in dormant seasons.

Although you cannot quantify perfectly the comparison of brush clearing and fence building as ways to increase energy conversion, clearly the fence beats the bulldozer in terms of what you gain. Not only do you grow more grass year after year, you have also cleared another $27,000 to be added to the profit planned this year. But you are not finished with this test yet. You next have to decide which paddocks should be split, again using the marginal reaction test. You will achieve a higher marginal reaction by splitting the most productive paddocks, if there is no overriding need to split others, because that's where you will get the highest return per dollar invested. This subject is covered more fully in the *Holistic Land Planning Handbook*.

Marginal Reaction per Hour of Effort

Nowhere does the marginal reaction test apply more than in our allocation of time. We have only a fixed amount, and it ticks by day and night. Constant awareness of the marginal reaction when it comes to investments of time frees time to do things we love, and the emergencies and crisis management we thereby avoid saves the money to pay for them.

Some years ago I visited a tobacco farm where near-panic reigned, as reaping was to start in ten days and the curing barns still had no roofs. Somewhere in the prior year, the owner had spent time in the coffee house or fixing a tractor when he might have worked out a construction schedule. Now he was paying heavily in extra labor, rushed transport, and high blood pressure, not to mention the probability of getting shoddy work and losing part of his crop anyway.

Naturally the marginal reaction per hour of effort figures in Holistic Financial Planning. The cost of most actions contemplated will naturally be influenced by the amount of labor or hours of effort involved in implementing them. So will your judgments about how much each maintenance expense can be trimmed. If, for instance, you decided to save money by cleaning your offices yourself, rather than pay someone else to do it, you may be going too far if your time could reap higher gains when devoted elsewhere. Or imagine spending a day of your time, at your salary, in the laundry business you own and manage, trying to fix one of your new computerized machines. How does that compare to bringing in a specialist who immediately knows what to do, has the right tools, and guarantees the repair?

In Chapter 26 I mentioned how, as a struggling young sugar cane farmer, I managed to cut my machinery maintenance costs to a fraction of what they had been simply by spending my time where it would provide the highest return at that moment, thinking through the chain of events leading to each breakage and then planning what to do about it. When my neighbors and I compared our costs, I realized that I had cut mine to half of theirs. Had we compared the number of hours each of us spent thinking and planning with paper and pencil, I estimate I probably spent 10 hours to their one. The marginal reaction achieved per hour of my time was so high, it saved my family and our farm at a time when the bottom had fallen out of the sugar market and our country's products had been sanctioned by the rest of the world.

Conclusion

I have stressed that the marginal reaction test is always in the end a subjective one. It has to be because you are not just comparing actions to reap the greatest return in terms of profit, but also in terms of everything else included in your holistic goal. There will be times when profit is secondary to other needs and desires, particularly those relating to quality of life, and this will be reflected in your judgment of where the highest marginal reaction is to be found.

The next test is far less subjective and is focused entirely on generating profit. Having the potential to convert sunlight or raw materials into a marketable product is of little help if you cannot be sure which of many possible enterprises enable you to do that most effectively. The gross profit analysis will enable you to find out.

29

Gross Profit Analysis: Bringing in the Most Money for the Least Additional Cost

The gross profit analysis test is used to select those enterprises (products or services from which you derive income) that, after associated costs and risks have been factored in, produce the most income. The income from these enterprises has to cover your overhead costs *and* generate some excess for there to be any profit. The question you ask is: *Which enterprises contribute the most to covering the overheads of the business?*

This is one of the few tests that requires a pencil and paper, and I suspect that this may keep those with an allergy to paperwork from doing it. Yet the marginal reaction per hour of effort is hard to beat, especially if you plug along for a year putting hundreds of hours into an enterprise that, although it provides massive income, produces a low gross profit, and thus a lower net profit for the business as a whole at year's end.

In most businesses a great deal of money is tied up in overheads, or fixed costs—land, buildings, machinery, equipment, salaries, and so on. While essential to the business, most fixed costs do not generate income, and thus the wherewithal to keep the business going. That is only done by the various activities that actually lead to the sale of a product or service. To be most profitable we need to find that enterprise or combination of enterprises that brings in the most income for the least additional nonoverhead costs each year. The greater the spread between income per year and additional nonoverhead costs, the greater the contribution of that enterprise or combination of enterprises to covering overheads and producing the surplus that becomes profit.

Various techniques exist to help you to do this, but I find most too complex, confusing, and impractical for widespread use. Computer programs are also available for this purpose, but they generally do away with the need to *think through* the variables involved. It is this thinking that is so essential to the success of this analysis, particularly when it involves potential new enterprises.

The gross profit analysis test, derived from the work of a Cambridge University agricultural economist named David Wallace, has flaws when performed in isolation in that it does not take into account the social or environmental costs associated with an enterprise. But when used along with the remaining six testing guidelines this drawback is overcome, and the test provides a clear and simple way to determine which enterprises are likely to generate the most profit.

In the gross profit analysis you simply look at the income likely to be derived from each enterprise and deduct the additional money you will have to spend to bring in that income. *The difference between money in and money out is the gross profit.* The additional money to be spent is that money you would not spend *unless* you undertook the enterprise. Through the analysis and comparison of many possible enterprises with this test, you are selecting the best enterprise, or combination of enterprises, to create profit and minimize risk.

Wallace originally used the term *gross profit* in describing his analysis, but was later persuaded to change it to *gross margin,* a term that has no intrinsic meaning. Although Wallace realized that net profit, which factors in overhead costs, is quite a different animal from gross profit, struggling British farmers found it confusing to compute positive profits of any kind when their actual bottom line was bright red.[1] For many years I went along with Wallace's change, but encountered a number of problems. First of all, I found that American businesses had "improved upon" the gross margin analysis, in ways I will cover shortly, but in doing so largely had destroyed its value. Second, I found that many people confused gross margin analysis with marginal reaction because both contained the word "margin." To avoid both problems, I decided to revert back to Wallace's original name, gross profit analysis.

The key to Wallace's gross profit analysis, particularly when researching possible new enterprises, is the careful distinction of fixed (overhead) and variable (direct or running) costs *at a given moment in time.* Wallace divided all business costs into these two categories. Fixed costs exist no matter what or how much is produced. Variable costs are a function of volume of production—the more you produce the more these costs increase. However, when performing a gross profit analysis, the definition of what is fixed and what is variable changes depending on the current situation.

When you plan wheat production, for example, seed and gasoline for the machinery during sowing and harvesting are variable costs. You incur them only if you grow wheat, and you compute the amount from the acreage you intend to plant. Payments on the harvesting combine you already own, however, are fixed costs because *even though you use it exclusively for wheat,* you must make the payments whether or not you actually grow wheat. No matter how much wheat you grow, these fixed costs remain unchanged.

Many of the techniques used for analyzing enterprises, including the "improved" gross margin analysis, try to apportion the fixed costs among various enterprises. In the case above, for example, all combine expenses would be charged against the wheat. Perhaps half of the tractor costs would be charged to wheat and half to something else. Labor costs might wind up apportioned under many headings. This practice, however, only clouds the picture and makes for a much poorer analysis, as figures 29-1 and 29-2 illustrate.

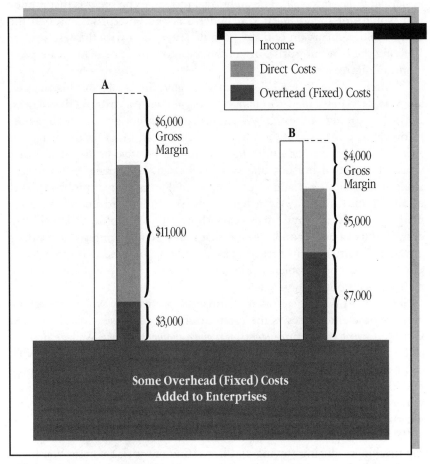

Figure 29-1 *In a conventional gross margin analysis, fixed costs are apportioned. In this case enterprise A looks slightly better than B.*

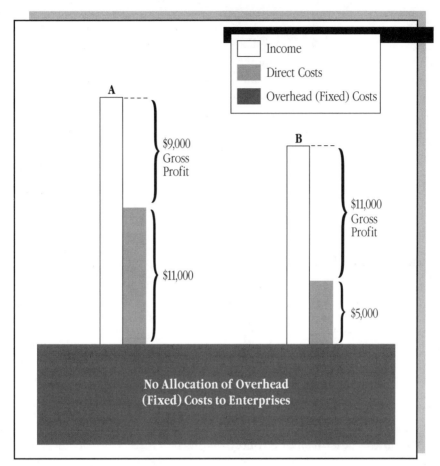

Figure 29-2 *In a gross profit analysis, fixed costs are not apportioned and the outcome is often different. In this case enterprise B looks far better than enterprise A.*

Figure 29-1 compares income and expense projections for two enterprises in a conventional gross margin analysis where fixed costs are apportioned. I have used A and B to represent any two alternatives. The gross margin for A is only slightly better, but if all other factors were equal you would, based on this analysis, probably favor enterprise A over B as it shows the highest gross margin.

In figure 29-2, using a gross profit analysis, fixed costs are not apportioned and the story is very different. Because most of the expense allocated to enterprise B would have to be paid anyway, clearly enterprise B contributes far more toward covering the overhead expenses of the business than enterprise A. And if you needed an operating loan to cover variable costs, obviously B would take far less than A.

Many find the matter of sorting out fixed and variable costs rather confusing, particularly when considering a new enterprise. No formula or list
can assist you in this because whether an item is fixed or variable depends
on the situation and the time frame under consideration—hence my
apprehension concerning computer programs used for analyzing potential
new enterprises. When contemplating the addition of a new enterprise, it
helps to remember that *in the very long term all costs are variable* (you could
sell the business) and *in the very short term all costs are fixed* (the new enterprise could be started by utilizing materials on hand and already paid for).
To determine the fixed costs to be ignored in the *new enterprise* and the
variable costs to include, picture yourself standing on a bridge looking
upstream. Any water (cost) that has passed under your feet is fixed and
should be ignored, while any water (cost) upstream is still variable and
should be included.

If I were thinking of adding a new line of products to those I already
manufacture, for instance, the factory I own, but am still paying for, would
be a fixed cost and not included in calculating the gross profit for this new
enterprise. The expense involved in the purchase of the new machinery
required would be a variable cost, and that would have to be offset against
the income I could expect to receive. However, because I would not use
up the machinery in one year, this variable cost would have to be spread
out over the estimated life span of the new machinery and the average
yearly cost used in my calculations. The actual payment for the machinery
and how that will affect cash flow are planned later (see Chapter 44 on
Holistic Financial Planning) if the new enterprise passes the gross profit
analysis test and any others that apply.

If, on the other hand, I did not need to purchase new machinery, but
could utilize some old, but out-of-date, machinery on hand, the machinery would be considered a fixed cost. However, it would take money to
renovate and modernize the machinery, and this cost, annualized, as it was
in the case of the new machinery, would be variable. It would be offset
against the annual income anticipated to provide the gross profit.

Used in conjunction with Holistic Financial Planning, the gross profit
analysis test will enable you to weed out any enterprises that drain the
business in that they contribute little or nothing to covering overheads.
Surprisingly, it is not uncommon, at least in agricultural businesses, to find
that the main line of business fails this test, and that it is the subsidiary
enterprises that have kept the business afloat—something more complicated analysis techniques often conceal.

The gross profit analysis test is used at three different times in holistic
financial planning. Initially, when you have brainstormed a list of possible
income sources, you use this test to narrow down the list. Very rough estimates of anticipated income and variable costs are all that is needed and
the exercise can be done in your head, as you are only looking for major

differences in enterprises at this point. A quick run through the rest of the tests will narrow your list down further. Then you use this test a second time, but more formally. You will need to gather fairly accurate figures before you can pass the final list of enterprises through this test, and you will need to use pencil, paper, and calculator to get your answers. Those enterprises, both old and new, that pass this test by contributing the most to covering overheads, *and* pass the remaining tests, will be the ones you engage in. Finally, you analyze each enterprise again at the end of the year to determine how well it actually performed. You then take this information into account in planning for the next year.

Refining Your Analysis

There are several refinements that can, and often should, be made in calculating gross profits that will further clarify the picture.

Common Units of Measure

In agricultural businesses in particular there will be occasions when you have to compare very dissimilar enterprises. How, for instance, does putting land into crops stand up against using the same land to graze livestock or for various forms of recreational, income-bearing activities? You can compare various crops, mixtures of crops, livestock, and recreation or other enterprises to find the best strategy for covering those fixed overheads and making a profit at minimum risk. To do so effectively you will have to find a common denominator on which to base your gross profit calculations. That common denominator in turn should be based on the factor that most limits production, generally the amount of land available, capital (in cash or assets), or labor. When land area is the most limiting factor, as it commonly is in agricultural businesses, gross profit *per acre or hectare* per year shows best how to put the land to use. In other cases, gross profit per dollar of capital or per human-hour of labor makes more sense. The *Holistic Financial Planning Handbook* explains in more detail how to calculate these figures.

When Enterprises Do Not Overlap

There will be occasions when one or two enterprises do not overlap with others because they use only a portion of the production base (land, capital, or labor) and can stand on their own. An example would be a ranch that was considering the establishment of a bed and breakfast enterprise on one small corner of the property near a highway. The amount of land involved would be so insignificant it would not be a factor. The capital used to build the establishment could be provided by a couple in town who wished to retire and run the enterprise. The only variable costs associated with the enterprise might be the money required to pay the lawyer for drawing up the agreement. That would be offset against the income received for the lease of the land to provide a gross profit that could be fairly high. If the remaining tests showed the decision to be sound, you would go ahead with it. A similar scenario would unfold if you wanted to lease out unused office space.

An increasingly common example that fits this case, but is generally missed, is when your business is game ranching and you are operating in a more brittle environment, as most of these businesses do. You are likely to need to bring in livestock to keep the land vital and capable of producing adequate forage if the game cannot do this on their own. In this case, the livestock are not competing with the main enterprise (game), *but are an essential tool for sustaining it.* The livestock could in fact be considered a variable cost, but because they generate income in their own right, they should be considered a separate enterprise, in this case, one that should stand on its own.

Break Enterprises into Segments

Some enterprises will yield to analysis best if broken into subunits or segments. For example, cattle production could be broken out into raising the calf, growing the calf, or finishing the animal for market. When you analyze each segment as though it were a separate enterprise, and you know what each segment's gross profit is, you can, if you choose, limit your effort to those segments that contribute the highest gross profit. Thus, a cow–calf operator may find it more profitable and less risky to reduce the cow herd and thus free up land to carry the progeny longer before marketing them. The same thinking would apply in many other production businesses. Most manufacturing firms have already found that it does not pay to undertake all facets of production within their own factories. By contracting (outsourcing) certain segments of production, as the automotive and aerospace industries do, they are able to achieve a higher gross profit overall.

Assessment of Risk

While doing a gross profit analysis and calculating the anticipated income and the variable costs involved in any possible new enterprise, you could be far off the mark in your estimates because of a number of variables outside your control. To assess the risks involved, you should project the worst, average, and best scenarios. When doing so, keep most income or expense figures average, and in each scenario vary the figures for whatever is least under your control. For example, for a dryland farmer of pinto beans in the

American Southwest, weather might be the most critical factor. For a clothing manufacturer, input costs (mainly the cost of fabric) might be. The dryland farmer would therefore pick an average price and compute his gross profit for low, average, and high yields. For the clothing manufacturer, a comparison of low, average, and high fabric costs would mean more. Obviously, one could add infinite levels of sophistication to this process, given a computer and a bit of time. Your focus, however, should be on major differences, not minor ones. If in comparing new enterprises you find that the risks associated with any one of them are far higher, because the spread between the low, average, and high gross profits is very great, this may influence your decision on which ones to adopt.

Conclusion: Generating a Net Profit

Having selected an enterprise or a combination of enterprises based on the gross profit analysis, you still don't know if you can make a *net* profit, the Holistic Financial Planning process, which Chapter 44 and the *Holistic Financial Planning Handbook* describe in some detail, will show whether your strategy does or does not add up to black ink.

In spite of all its benefits, gross profit analysis has some serious shortcomings, some of which show up in the context of other testing guidelines and some in the light of common sense. In the theoretical case portrayed in figure 29-2, enterprise B turns out so far ahead of enterprise A that you could easily argue for committing the entire business to it. In practice, however, that could be very unwise. First of all, the advantages of B derived from being able to use assets already on hand and accounted for as fixed costs. If, however, doubling enterprise B meant paying for more equipment or labor, those would become variable costs and might lead to a very different conclusion.

More important, gross profit analysis takes no account of ecosystem processes or many less tangible considerations. In farming it quite frequently shows a complete and chemically enhanced monoculture as the most profitable strategy, and yet we know that this damages soils and the life in them and leads to spiraling chemical dependency and rising costs. The chemical companies that manufacture the pesticides and fertilizers no doubt find that these enterprises yield a fairly high gross profit as well, which, when social and environmental costs are *not* considered, appears very attractive.

Despite these problems, however, the technique still throws fresh light on many situations, and other testing guidelines usually compensate for its limitations. The ideal is to find the best enterprise or combination in which all the technology and other tools pass all tests. At that point to the best of our knowledge, you have enterprises that are economically, socially, and environmentally sound.

30

Energy and Money: Using the Most Appropriate Forms in the Most Constructive Way

C hapter 29 explained how gross profit analysis helps to determine the most profitable enterprises, but it ended on a note of warning. The means to profit may not be holistically sound. Not only the enterprise itself, but also the secondary inputs that support it, should pass all the other tests that apply.

Will profit depend on suppressing symptoms rather than addressing causes? Do some inputs pass most tests, but then fail to represent the best marginal reaction per dollar or hour invested? Rather late in the development of Holistic Management, it became evident that we had to press the testing one level deeper and examine both the sources and the patterns of use of the energy and money involved in production. We lump money and energy together because any action contemplated usually requires one or the other, and often both. The questions you ask are: *Is the energy or money to be used in this action derived from the most appropriate source in terms of our holistic goal?* and *Will the way in which the energy or money is to be used lead toward our holistic goal?*

Sources of Energy

In terms of availability energy sources fall into two categories: sources that are abundant or unlimited, and sources that are limited in supply. The sunlight energy used to grow the farmer's crops is unlimited in that supplies are inexhaustible until our sun burns out; but the petroleum he uses to fuel his tractor is limited because it took millions of years to produce, and we will eventually run out of secure and affordable supplies. In terms of their effects on the environment, energy sources also fall into two categories: sources that are benign or sources that are potentially damaging. This depends on the rate at which they are consumed and the methods used to harness and distribute them. Obviously, we stand a better chance of long-term success by favoring the energy sources in unlimited supply, but only if we can ensure that their effects on the environment are benign.

Most energy is derived either directly or indirectly from sunlight. When green plants convert sunlight directly through photosynthesis to a useable or edible form, they do no damage in the process. When those same plants are burned as a fuel, they can produce polluting byproducts; but if allowed to decompose first, to produce biogas, their effect on the environment is, as far as we know, benign. Solar panels or collectors can also be used to convert sunlight directly to a useful and benign form of energy.

Geothermal energy and energy derived indirectly from sunlight (wind, the falling action of water, the rising and falling action of ocean tides) is abundant or unlimited and generally considered benign, although the manner in which it is harnessed, such as a hydroelectric dam, may not be. Nuclear energy, the only nonsolar form of energy we use, is virtually unlimited in supply, but its production, through nuclear fission, is potentially damaging, and its radioactive by-products can be lethal.

Modern society is powered by energy sources derived from sunlight trapped by ancient plants and converted to coal, oil, and natural gas. Because they are also the fuels of choice of electric utilities, they also provide very convenient power. But all fossil fuels are finite, and we are consuming them at such a rapid rate that our ecosystem cannot reincorporate the residues of their consumption quickly enough to maintain a stable climate. Although you as an individual are often limited in your ability to select the source of energy you use in your home or business, you always have the option of using that energy sparingly and of gradually converting to benign alternatives.

You are choosing a benign source of energy over a potentially damaging source of energy any time you decide to walk or ride your bicycle rather than drive a car. So is the farmer who uses livestock to break down the stubble on his corn field rather than a tractor. What should concern you in this test is whether or not the source of energy you plan to use in implementing any action is appropriate in your situation at the present time in light of your holistic goal.

Ideally, governments should consider the long-term health of nations when forming energy policies, but their track record is poor for reasons that sooner or later (and hopefully the former) most societies will have to question. Although we understand the danger now, our social and economic structure, based on high consumption rates of firewood, fossil, and now nuclear energy, still runs on tracks laid down long ago when a much less numerous humanity could more easily ignore its impact on nature. The Industrial Revolution that set us on this course did not occur painlessly, and neither perhaps will the changes that put us on a new path.

Sources of Money

The money used to implement any action can be derived from either internal or external sources. The source is internal if the money is taken from your own earnings, what the business or land generates. Any time you can rely on an internal source, you are likely to be better off, but there will be many occasions when money will have to come from outside the business for you to move forward. Economists sometimes argue that when you finance a venture with your own internal money, you should also consider the "opportunity cost," the interest you lose on your money by not investing it elsewhere. In managing holistically, that is rarely a concern because the marginal reaction test helps to determine where, among various alternatives, your money gives the highest return in terms of your holistic goal, which is the more important consideration.

If you are in a sunlight-harvesting business, then you want most of the internal money you invest in an action or enterprise to come from solar dollars, and not mineral dollars gained through using soil in a nonrenewable manner.

When the money to be invested is derived from an external source, you need to be wary of the strings attached to it. If the outside source is a bank or other lending institution, interest will always be included, and in most cases interest is compounded, which means you will be using a much greater sum of money to repay the loan. Americans are made aware of just how astronomical this sum can be when they purchase a home mortgage. In many states the law requires the borrower to sign a document indicating he or she has been shown the full amount and is aware of the cost of borrowing the money. It is unfortunate lenders are not obliged to do the same for any type of loan that carries compound interest.

External money can also be derived from the government in some form of cost-sharing or subsidy. This is a source of money that commonly becomes addictive, and its sudden withdrawal can spell financial ruin. There are strings attached, as well, generally in the form of regulations that may lead you away from, rather than toward, your holistic goal. It is also important to realize that governments have no money to give, unless they first take it from you and your fellow citizens. Bear this in mind if you are considering an action purely because the government is giving you half the money. If the action fails most of the tests and you go ahead anyway, it means that not only the half supplied by you, but also the half supplied by the taxpayers, is wasted. We'll return to ethical and moral considerations such as these in Chapter 32 on the society and culture test.

Philanthropic organizations are another source of external money, and a common one for nonprofit organizations. Only in relatively few instances are philanthropic grants or gifts made without strings attached, often in the form of influence or bureaucratic red tape or, on occasion, outright interference in management. Foreign aid programs are notorious for making money available to a developing country, then insisting the money be used to buy technology and expertise from the donor nation. If the influence or interference that comes with the money in such situations will cause you to deviate from your holistic goal, you will likely fail this test unless you can negotiate more favorable terms.

Energy and Money Patterns of Use

In the second part of this test you look at the specific way in which the energy or money will be used and whether it will take you toward your holistic goal. There are no rules that tell you what is right or wrong, but there are some questions that will help you decide:

- *Is the proposed use providing infrastructure that will assist in reaching your holistic goal?*

Infrastructure refers to the sort of things that are essential to running your business more effectively: knowledge, skills, trained staff, buildings, roads, equipment, machinery, transport. In the case of the farmer mentioned in Chapter 27 whose marketing strategy demanded a storage shed so his onions could hit the local market when other farmers had sold out their crop, the storage shed was essential infrastructure. He would earn money if he built it. Building a luxurious home on his farm would not be. I am not saying he shouldn't build one when he can afford it, if that figures in his quality of life. He just should not fool himself into believing that the luxurious home is essential infrastructure.

If energy or money are used to create infrastructure and all the materials or other aspects involved pass the other tests, you would tend to say that the proposed infrastructure passes. If you are creating infrastructure that is not needed this year, and it does not pass the other tests, you would likely fail this test, too. You might think this is so obvious it hardly needs stating, but you would be surprised. A number of ranchers have put money into fencing when it fails other tests, particularly the weak link test, which would indicate the money would yield far more if spent elsewhere. In this case, although the money would be building infrastructure, that infrastructure is not needed now.

- *Is the proposed use merely consumptive, with no lasting effect?*

A use of money or energy is consumptive if it is consumed in a one-time use. If the same action were to be undertaken again, it would require new money and/or new energy. Many of the running costs involved in a business are consumptive uses, such as the fuel required for your vehicles, accounting fees, or salaries. So are many of the services you might purchase relating to a particular action, such as legal fees or consulting advice. If the source of the money or energy used is in line with your holistic goal, and the action passes most of the other tests, a consumptive use automatically tends to pass this one as long as it moves you toward your holistic goal.

> • *Is the proposed use cyclical in that once initiated, it would not require more money, or the purchase of more energy?*

A good example of cyclical use would be the single expenditure of money to install a hydraulic ram for pumping water. Since falling water provides the energy that drives the pump, all water is thereafter pumped at no cost, assuming you ignore the minimal maintenance it takes to operate the ram, which has few moving parts.

Using animal impact to break down crop residues is another. This might require an initial expenditure of money for the temporary polywire fencing that confines the animals in any one place. But each year thereafter, it would merely require planning, implementation, and reuse of the moveable fences to have the animals do the job using only solar energy.

A cyclical use of money can be achieved in a number of ways. When money is used for a community revolving loan, for instance, it is cycling constantly, and, if employed wisely, it is growing, too. So is the money you invest to purchase equity in a growing business.

Generally, a cyclical use that makes your money grow or enables you to forgo further purchases of energy is highly desirable, but again, the answer will depend on what you have specified in your holistic goal.

> • *Is the proposed use addictive in that once initiated, you risk an undesirable dependence on further inputs of energy or money?*

It is usually wise to avoid an addictive use of money or energy. An addictive use is one that obliges you to take the same action again and again, possibly with increasing frequency and/or increasing cost. Addictive uses are commonly associated with agricultural businesses, particularly when they involve a cause and effect situation in which the cause is not addressed. An example of an addictive use of money and energy would be a parasite control program where the animals were dipped in a chemical (derived from the energy contained in fossil fuels) that not only killed the parasites but also their predators and thus generated a greater parasite problem needing more chemicals and more money. Mainstream agriculture is full of similar examples.

In other businesses, addictive uses of money will more often be due to human behavior patterns, and thus the action or tool tested would not likely be addictive, but your behavior in using it could be. Credit card purchases are a good example. Your decisions to purchase the items may well pass the testing, but your behavior would need watching. The millions of Americans using credit cards probably feel each purchase is needed, but the average credit card debt has climbed to over $7,000, on which compound interest at 18 percent or more must be paid.[1]

The most obvious example of energy used in an addictive fashion is the fossil fuel–based economy we live in today. Our dependence on these finite energy sources is frightening and possibly lethal. We are consuming ever greater amounts of fossil fuels and spending more and more money to do so. As communities or individuals with holistic goals that specify a different scenario, we can begin weaning ourselves away from the addiction. I am not suggesting we stop consuming fossil fuels entirely. It is not their consumption, but the high *rate* of consumption that endangers life on our planet.

Conclusion

As I mentioned, most individuals have only limited power to control the source of energy they use, although citizens can speak out for better governance, policies, planning, and regulation. You can also let conscience enter your own decisions to flip a switch, design a building, or raise a crop. In the decade that spanned the 1980s, the millions of little things Americans did to weatherize their homes and plug up leaks, plus the purchase of more fuel efficient cars, yielded over seven times as many additional BTUs as the net increase in supply from all the new oil and gas wells, coal mines, and power plants built in the same period.[2]

Remember that your final decision will seldom be based on any one of the tests. You will be building a mental picture based on your answers to each of the testing questions. Only at the end of the testing, when the picture is fully formed, will you decide whether or not to implement the decision.

31

Sustainability: Generating Lasting Wealth

The sustainability test asks you to consider the long-term environmental and social consequences of your decisions relative to your future resource base. The question you ask is: *If we take this action, will it lead toward or away from the future resource base described in our holistic goal?*

In every case there will be *people* who influence or are influenced by your decisions and *biological communities* on land and in the air or water that will be affected either directly or indirectly by your decisions. In many cases, the *human community* you live in or work in will greatly affect your success, and the *services available* in that community may be critical to your future.

This is one of the few tests that asks you to focus on a specific aspect of your holistic goal, the future resource base. The quality of life you seek and the forms of production that will support it are things you need to have as soon as possible. The future resource base is something you may want just as much and can begin moving toward, but achieving it in the short term is not essential. In the long term, it does become essential for sustaining a way of life and all that it takes to produce it. Thus the sustainability test ensures that all the decisions you make to meet short-term needs also provide lasting gain—that they are socially, environmentally, and economically sound in terms of both the future and the present.

Far too many decisions that prove correct in the short term have disastrous consequences in the long term. This test seeks to avoid that. In earlier chapters, I wrote of past civilizations that had been destroyed along with their environment as a direct result of decisions people made to meet their immediate needs. The millions of environmental refugees caught in the mire of increasing civil unrest and violence, disease, and starvation today are a product of circumstances produced by short-term decisions their parents, grandparents, and past governments made. Their desperate plight will be shared by us all if we do not begin to consider how every significant decision affects our future resource base.

Social Considerations

For ease of expression, I have divided the elements of the future resource base into two categories—social and environmental. The people affected by your decisions, the community you live in, and the services available in your community, if applicable, involve similar considerations, while the environmental category requires a different focus.

The People Affected by Your Decisions

No matter what type of business you are in, you need to consider how the perceptions of the people included in your future resource base (clients/customers and suppliers, extended family, advisors, and so on) are affected by the decisions you make. If you have described yourselves as honest, reliable, and professional, you want to make sure that the actions you take reflect this behavior.

In a workshop I ran some years ago, one of the participants had a small engineering firm that designed and manufactured spare parts. He asked if we could help him to decide whether or not to buy an expensive piece of new machinery that would enable the firm to do some jobs they currently subcontracted to others. As a class, we developed a temporary holistic goal with him, where he expressed the need for his customers to see the firm as reliable, timely, and quality conscious.

As we began to test the decision of whether or not to buy the new machine, he told us that the subcontractors he had worked with up to this point did not pay as much attention to quality as his firm would have liked. Also, they rarely got the job done when they said it would be done.

Buying a new piece of expensive machinery for a small start-up company, as his was, would require a relatively large investment of money, most of which would have to be borrowed. But the new machine would enable the company to greatly improve the quality of their products and would enable them to get those products to the customer on time. Thus, they would begin to meet the conditions they had stipulated in their future resource base, and buying the new machine passed this test. It also passed all the others that applied.

Although the purchase of the machine would require the diversion of money to interest payments, the profit specified in the holistic goal was still enhanced. This decision happened to be one that would result in a certain amount of growth for the firm. But the need to compete or grow was not part of the decision. Making a better product and being able to deliver it to customers on time *was*. The firm already had plenty of business. This decision would help to ensure they kept it.

The Community You Live In

If the success of your efforts depends on the community you live in, you need to be sure that the actions you take promote what your holistic goal envisions and espouses, or at least do not adversely affect it. Suppose, for instance, that you purchased a timber lease in a national forest, a resource you shared with multiple users. In describing your future resource base, you would have included references as to how those people would have to perceive you, but you would also likely have expressed the desire to work in a community where relationships were harmonious and peaceful. In planning how you will extract the timber, you see the highest profit in grading roads capable of handling heavy equipment. However, this method of extraction fails several tests toward your holistic goal (sustainability, and energy, money source and use, in particular). Your road grading would wash into the trout streams, and your equipment and the recreational vehicles and poachers that followed it would upset the wildlife, livestock, and aesthetics of the area in general.

Do you lobby for special treatment and risk creating discord in the community or fold up your business? Such dilemmas can be agonizing, but rarely do we face only two choices, given a little human creativity. In this case skidding logs with mule teams or elephants (depending on the continent) might satisfy all parties, including your banker.

Community Services

If the future resource base in your holistic goal includes a description of the sort of services that will need to be available in your community to provide the kind of life you aspire to, you want to ensure that your decisions gradually lead to those services being available. In this case your decisions are likely to play only an indirect role, but then again your holistic goal might compel you to reshape certain decisions that could lead directly to the desired result.

One of the small rural communities I have worked with in Zimbabwe has listed in its holistic goal a number of services they hope to have in their community one day. One of these is a dental clinic, which at this point is only a dream and is unlikely to be provided by the cash-strapped government.

The community has recently been invited to participate in the hunting safari business. In return for making their land available to hunters, they receive a sizeable fee that, in theory at least, is shared all around. However, in similar schemes in other parts of the country, middlemen have taken their share of the fees and left little for distributing in the communities. Although they have made no decision yet, I know the people in this particular community are hesitant to accept the offer because they are aware of the problems others have experienced. Instead, perhaps they could develop an alternative that would also enable them to get the desired dental clinic. Suppose they made their land available specifically to groups of European or American dentists who relished the chance to hunt or view game in exchange for their periodic services and donated equipment. This could rather quickly and inexpensively produce a desired service they might not otherwise see for decades.

Environmental Considerations

It is impossible to have a properly formulated holistic goal without some reference to the environment. There is not a citizen among us who does not eat, drink, produce bodily wastes that must be disposed of, or consume products that affect our environment either in their manner of production or in their final resting place (usually the landfill).

Those specifically engaged in land or resource management will have described a future landscape in terms of how each of the four ecosystem processes (community dynamics, water cycle, mineral cycle, and energy flow) should function.

Others may have only a fairly general reference to the environment in their future resource base that refers to the landscape surrounding their business or community. However, the civil engineer and the land use planner should attempt to find out how the layout and design of a new road or plans for a residential development, or for disposing of water runoff from roads and roofs, are going to affect the four ecosystem processes, relative to the future resource base described by the community and the level of brittleness that exists in that environment. As more urban communities begin to manage holistically and describe their resource base of the future, they will begin to appreciate the value of this test.

Most people and many businesses, particularly those that provide services rather than manufactured products, may find it difficult to see how their actions affect land they are not directly responsible for. As mentioned in Chapter 9, all of them at some point, through consumption of raw materials manufactured into a product and their use of technology, have a tie back to the land and affect the functioning of the four ecosystem processes. Thus, any actions they take should pass through this test if they involve the consumption of products or the use of technology. I single out sunlight-harvesting and manufacturing businesses below because in both cases they involve fairly detailed considerations and demonstrate the considerable power of this test.

Sunlight Harvesting Businesses

If you are in a sunlight-harvesting business (farming, ranching, wildlife, or forest management) most of the decisions you make will be related to land management. The actions you test often deal with one or more of the tools covered in Chapters 16 to 24. In this test you want to determine how the proposed action or tool is likely to affect the four ecosystem processes relative to the brittleness of your environment. Is the likely result going to take you toward or away from the future resource base described in your holistic goal?

If your future landscape describes open grassland, and certain areas are moving toward dense brushland, you might consider applying the tool of fire, but before taking this action you would first review the effects of fire on the four ecosystem processes:

- *Community dynamics:* Will fire actually kill the brush in question or merely damage the above-ground parts temporarily and cause the brush to resprout more thickly? What fire-sensitive species are present that you do not want to kill? How will other species and their young fare in the microenvironment that fire creates at the surface? What species will find opportunity in the bare soil exposed by the flame? How often will fire be necessary? What about the atmospheric pollution created and its effects far from the site?

- *Water cycle:* Fire will damage it some. How much damage can the land stand? What loss in soil structure and aeration quality can the land afford?

- *Mineral cycle:* How well is this functioning now? When the fire exposes the surface and reduces its population of microorganisms, how long will it take to build them back to levels that cycle minerals effectively? Do you have ways to cope without burning again before that?

- *Energy flow:* How much of the present energy flow enhances production? Would this be increased or reduced by fire?

Your answers to each of these questions will vary depending on how brittle your environment is. If many of these answers turn up negative, you should consider another tool to stop the brush. Ideally it would be one that would maintain grass root vigor without exposing the soil between plants or aggravating the brush problem. You might well decide in this particular case to use herd effect (animal impact) and to apply limited doses of herbicide (technology) in the worst places, but again only if these decisions passed all the same tests.

Any time you are dealing with organisms that become a problem because they are either too few or too many in number, focus first on community dynamics. As mentioned in Chapter 13, when you manage for the health of the whole community, various species tend to take care of themselves and thrive within their community without becoming so numerous as to be classified as pests or so few that we classify them as rare and endangered. Any actions that address a particular species in isolation, *with little regard for the whole,* can meet only with short-term success and will generally fail this test for long-term sustainability.

Many people dedicated to saving a particular species find this thinking surprisingly difficult to translate into action, as numerous laws and programs for saving the ferret, the owl, the tortoise, the gorilla, or the local trout show. How many commit enormous resources into protection, often to the detriment of the protected species as well as other species and little into regenerating the environment as a whole? No amount of captive breeding, plantings, culling of predators, poisoning of competitors, or other narrowly focused actions will bring back a creature that has lost its niche entirely or even a critical element, such as cover or water, in its habitat.

The world abounds in examples of failures stemming from failure to consider the community as a whole. I think back to Zimbabwe where early in this century vast ranches in the southern part of the country had high populations of sable and roan antelope alongside significant herds of wildebeest and zebra. As the ranchers regarded the latter as serious competitors, they shot them on sight by the thousands, while the majestic sable and roan, valued as "royal game," enjoyed complete protection from hunting.

Nevertheless, within about thirty years the roan and sable disappeared completely, and the shooting of zebra and wildebeest continues, now for the commercial market. During this time the four ecosystem processes have changed profoundly in this area. Biological communities have simplified as many species have disappeared, water and mineral cycles are badly damaged, and energy flow has declined to a fraction of its potential as the land desertifies. It is this, not hunting policy, that explains what happened to the game. Had the government's extension service and legislators focused on the health of the four ecosystem processes and how they had to be to sustain the sable and roan populations and ultimately people, the outcome would have been very different.

Zebra and wildebeest survive over a wide range of successional communities, whereas the sable and roan thrive only in a much narrower range that is higher in succession. Figure 31-1 shows what happened. European colonists found wonderfully productive cattle country in condition A, but by the 1950s they had reduced it to condition B through the way they

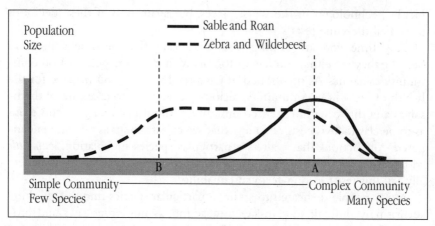

Figure 31-1 *Sable and roan populations declined because the environment had deteriorated to such an extent that it could no longer support them. In the 1920s the environment was at condition A, but within 30 years had been reduced to condition B. The zebra and wildebeest could survive over a wider range of environmental conditions than the roan and sable populations and therefore continued to thrive.*

decided to apply the management tools. Overgrazing of plants, partial rest of the soil, fencing that impeded game movement, killing the predators that had promoted game concentration and movement, and increased use of fire caused succession to slip below the level that supports roan and sable.

Typical policies toward predators present another example of deeply ingrained blindness that attention to community dynamics in particular might enlighten. We need much more research into the role of predators, but we at least are beginning to sense how the relationship between predators and herding animals kept brittle environments from desertifying over millions of years. We can only guess at the number of other situations where our uninformed destruction of predators has cost us dearly. Chapter 42, on population management, discusses possible ways to deal with predators that become a problem.

The sustainability test also is particularly important in assessing the policies that predominated during the so-called Green Revolution, that era when we had supreme confidence that modern high-tech agriculture could feed the world without any problem. As a result, we still rarely question the fertilizers, pesticides, extraordinary machines, and other tools emerging under the heading of technology. These have encouraged monoculture plantings of annual crops, and the engineering of new plants and new pesticides to which these plants and no others are immune. However, abundant evidence now indicates the resultant damage to all four of the ecosystem processes.

When phasing farms from Green Revolution agriculture to more scientifically, and holistically, sound practices, we often have to use measures initially that fail the sustainability test, just to stay solvent. However, this is not done in ignorance. Knowing that a measure is unsound allows you to start shifting your management, in the time bought by its use, and to find a way back to sustainable agricultural practices.

Manufacturing Businesses

The majority of actions taken in a manufacturing business will involve the tool of technology, which, although it may not be used directly on the land, will impact the environment at various stages: when the raw materials to be used in manufacturing are extracted or produced, during the manufacturing process itself (and the wastes it generates), and in the final disposal of the manufactured products. In this test, you are considering how actions relating to any one of those three stages will affect the ecosystem processes relative to the future resource base you have described. Few manufacturing businesses include a detailed description of the ecosystem processes in their future resource base, but some knowledge of them becomes necessary to weigh the effects of any decision on the environment. Those effects are most obvious when you look at community dynamics. The waste produced in the manufacturing process and many of the materials used in the products themselves may not break down.

Very few products manufactured today are biodegradable, meaning that organisms of one form or another can consume them rapidly and completely. Even wooden furniture is often varnished with products that can persist in the soil, water, and air for years. The cumulative effects of these nonbiodegradable and unnatural substances affect the web of interrelationships that exist in all biological communities, their health, and stability. Being "unnatural" the substances are frequently toxic to many organisms, adversely affecting their ability to function, impairing their ability to produce healthy offspring, and occasionally killing them and the organisms that feed on them. Because water and mineral cycles and energy flow all depend on living organisms, these are adversely affected as well.

Almost certainly, the future resource base of any manufacturing business will include customers, clients, and employee families who will be concerned with the business's impact on the environment. So there is no situation when these considerations and this test would not apply. In Chapter 3, I noted the many successes and the genuine comfort that technology have afforded us. Each example, however, could be considered successful only if we ignored the effects on our environment stemming from its manufacture or disposal. This test is a reminder of that, and should encourage manufacturers to find ways to create products that from their conception to the end of their useful lives, are environmentally benign, if not enhancing.

Sometimes developing environmentally benign products can be as easy as making a switch from raw materials suppliers who use environmentally damaging methods of extraction or refinement to those who have minimized the damage or eliminated it altogether. Sometimes with considerably more creativity and effort you can modify the manufacturing process itself to eliminate dangerous wastes by converting them to nontoxic by-products that can be safely consumed by living organisms or recycled for other uses. Eliminating the environmental damage that occurs when a product is finally disposed of has its own challenges. Ultimately, product disposal will require a different relationship than currently exists between the manufacturer and the product consumer. Manufacturers can do everything in their power to reduce or eliminate nonbiodegradable materials in the products they manufacture, but are unlikely to be able to eliminate them all. Thus, if the manufacturer is to ensure that the product is not to be environmentally damaging when finally discarded, it is likely that the manufacturer will have to take the product back from the consumer and recycle the materials that do not break down.

This is not as far-fetched as it sounds. At least one German auto manufacturer, BMW, has built a pilot *disassembly* plant to recycle its older cars, and newer models are being designed with disassembly in mind. The number of different types of plastic and other materials have been reduced to enhance reusability. With these and other modifications, the designers hope to create a car whose components are 100 percent reusable.[1]

Once mining companies come to see themselves as primarily in the business of providing minerals, rather than limiting themselves to mining minerals from diminishing deposits, they can expand their business opportunities enormously by extracting minerals from manufactured products and making them available for reuse. Many mining companies already have the technology and most of the skills to do this.

The International Organization for Standardization (ISO) on Environmentally Responsible Management, headquartered in Geneva and representing over a hundred countries, has produced a series of environmental management standards known as ISO 14000. These standards are a major step forward, and a number of manufacturers are already attempting to comply with them. The Natural Step, a program developed in Sweden and recently introduced in the United States, also aims to encourage environmentally responsible management. The program is based on four principles or system conditions that serve as a standard for environmental and social responsibility.[2] This program emphasizes internal motivation and creativity over compliance with more specific standards and although less well known has attracted the attention of a number of large manufacturers.

Service Providers, Households, and Consumers

Not only does the company manufacturing products need to concern itself with the pollution it creates, but so do the people who purchase, use, and then discard the products. If an action you plan to take involves the purchase or use of a product that, once discarded, will not be consumed by living organisms, you may want to substitute it for another or find ways to recycle it. In some cases your options will be severely limited because most of what is manufactured and available today is not environmentally benign. But you will know that if the future resource base you have described in your holistic goal includes healthy land and healthy people on it, you will have to do something—and fortunately, you will not be alone in your dilemma.

All of us face the same future, and if we wait much longer to tackle this fundamental problem it will ultimately destroy us. You can make a start by decreasing your consumption of nonbiodegradable products, supporting with your purchasing power manufacturers who work to create products that do not damage the environment and participating in recycling efforts in your own community.

Conclusion

None of what is described in your future resource base will be attained quickly and with only a few actions. Yet every action, however small, that takes you in the direction you want to go is progress, and cumulatively small actions add up to a big difference.

All of this may seem a lot to concern yourself with. But until you do, until we all do, we cannot hope to create a community, nation, or even a civilization that is viable or sustainable.

32

Society and Culture: Personal Values and Social Responsibility

How do the actions we take affect the quality of our lives? In our pursuit of progress no consideration deserves more reflection, and typically none gets less. Corporations concentrate on shareholder response to the next quarterly report; politicians on the next election; ranchers concentrate on production of livestock; farmers on production per acre; environmentalists on growing trees; loggers on cutting trees. Generals fixate on counting bodies and missionaries on counting souls. Few of us stop long enough to notice that in our pursuit of progress, we shoot down our own dreams and those of others. Where the other tests have only touched on quality of life concerns, this one addresses them directly. The questions you ask in this test are: *How do we feel about this action now? Will it lead to the quality of life we desire? Will it adversely affect the lives of others?*

The society and culture test is normally performed last because it should take into account the mental picture that has formed after passing through all the others. In each of the previous tests you have in effect been looking at one of the small squares in the hologram of Lincoln's face. Now you are asked to blur them together to see the face as a whole, and, based on that picture, make your decision. But where each of the other tests asked what you think, this one asks how you *feel*.

How you feel is in large part going to be based on the values reflected in your quality of life statement. And these, in many respects, are a reflection of the traditions, customs, and culture shared by those who have formed the holistic goal. Occasionally, this test may cause you to question the value of certain customs or traditions. Are they really worth preserving? Have circumstances changed to such an extent that they have become counterproductive? If you did not ask these questions when forming your holistic goal, they may have to be addressed here.

The answers may well cause you to revise your view of how you want your life, in this particular whole, to be. As mentioned in Chapter 10, the testing process often leads to refinements in your holistic goal, and this example is a case in point. On the other hand, this test should also be used to ensure that customs and traditions you value are not lost.

Last, this test asks you to consider how an action could affect the lives of those outside your immediate whole, from the society you live in, to the greater society that comprises all humans. Pleasing everybody may seem impossible, but you can go a long way by embracing the holistic principle that the health of your particular interest is not distinct from the health of the greater whole. This is, in effect, a test for social consciousness, and more than any other, it helps to ensure that a decision is socially sound.

The lack of attention to the quality of our lives in our national decision making has resulted in numerous tragedies, one of the most obvious being the state of American agriculture. The American government, with the acquiescence of many in the industry, undertook to increase production solely in terms of quantity. From government and universities and industry leaders the message was put over powerfully: get big or get out. No one paid enough attention to the families that would be displaced as big farms swallowed smaller ones and more powerful machinery and larger monoculture fields displaced labor.

Production boomed, but at the cost of a polluted environment, massive soil erosion, and enormous social dislocation. Hundreds of thousands of family farms vanished, dissipating generations of practical knowledge. The dispossessed drifted to urban centers and struggled to adjust to an alien culture. The churches, small businesses, and cultural centers in the small towns that served those people have withered away. Suicide has now overtaken accidents as the chief cause of death among the farmers that remain.

Hindsight gives us perfect vision. What if we had formed a national holistic goal and used the society and culture test before so optimistically turning agriculture into a mechanized, chemically addicted, capital-intense industry? With its once vast and fertile prairie soils, the likes of which no nation had ever enjoyed, the United States would still most likely have become the world's greatest agricultural producer, while maintaining its healthy rural populations, the villages and towns that served them, and vast, diversified markets. Some people, such as the Amish, did not ignore the quality of life factor in making their decisions. Quality of life was and still remains paramount. Yet while more so-called progressive, production-oriented farmers flounder, the Amish continue to flourish.

Most of the decisions you consider will not be of this magnitude. Yet it is just as important that your holistic goal spell out quality of life desires as clearly as possible. Individuals or families managing their own lives have no less need to do this than others. The difference that clarity in the quality of life statement makes in considering the society and culture test can be startling, as one couple discovered when they tested a decision almost as an afterthought.

Chris Knippenberg's mother had offered to give her a horse that her two children could ride. All Chris and her husband Phil (Hobbie) had to do was pay the cost of having the horse shipped from her parents' ranch in Colorado to their farm in Vermont. Chris immediately started pricing transportation, which turned out to be expensive, but the horse was after all a *gift,* and the horse itself would be free.

"I was a phone call away from hiring the shippers," says Chris, "when Phil suggested we test taking the horse against not taking it. Well, the gift horse started failing all the tests, particularly the financial ones. This horse wasn't going to earn us any income on the farm; it would require feed and possibly new fencing and even a shelter. And we knew almost nothing about taking care of horses."

But the society and culture test clinched their decision. "We want to have a close, caring family where we do things *together.* With one horse and four people, we would not be able to enjoy it as a family. The horse would be yet another solitary pursuit for one of us. It would take time and resources away from us, rather than bring us together."

In figuring out how to break the news to Chris's mother, they noted that their quality of life included strengthening ties with their *extended* family. "It dawned on us that for the price of shipping the horse out here to Vermont, we could instead afford to fly the whole family out to my parents' ranch for a week, and spend time with them. They have lots of horses, and all the facilities and expertise, and we could spend a week riding horses together as a family. I was amazed at how clearly the testing enabled us to see what was so obviously the right decision for us."[1]

If you have been slightly overwhelmed by all the factors considered in each of the seven tests, I hope the above example demonstrates how easily and quickly most day-to-day decisions can be made. This is just as often the case when you are running a business and planning your profit. One example Washington farmer Bruce Gregory likes to cite involved a decision he and his wife, Colleen, made between upgrading some old fencing, as part of a long-term program, and building a new solar-powered pumping station. Both actions had much in their favor, but there was money enough to implement only one of them. According to Bruce,

> Both actions ultimately dealt with the harvesting of solar energy and addressed the weak link in our chain of production. Neither would lead to an addictive use of energy or money

(energy, wealth source and use), and both would lead us toward the future resource base described in our holistic goal (sustainability).

Marginal reaction, however, really showed up the differences and helped us to make the decision. Our filbert orchard had suffered over each of the last twelve years during the dry months due to lack of water, which the new pumping station could provide at little cost. The primitive watering technology we were using was inefficient and was dragging us down with extra human labor. It provided a poor marginal reaction per hour of effort. New fencing, on the other hand would do little in terms of marginal reaction per hour of effort, nor would it give as high a return in terms of the additional dollars invested in it.

How did we feel now? The solar-powered pumping station was the obvious way to go that year; it would enhance the quality of our lives and it wouldn't adversely affect anyone else. Our fencing program would be set back a year, but the existing fence could easily last another grazing season. Our backs and the tractor used for hauling tankfuls of water could not. We really didn't have to talk about this decision for more than ten minutes, the differences between the two actions were pretty evident.[2]

Because your final decision is based on the mental picture that forms as you pass through the other six tests, the society and culture test may be one that those unfamiliar with the process fail to understand. These people may in fact exert considerable pressure, often out of genuine concern, to dissuade you from taking a particular action. That's only one more reason why ownership in your holistic goal is so essential.

Several years ago, I spent a day in a workshop with a number of business executives, one of whom attracted my attention because he was running a profitable business based on an ambitious social mission: to encourage all mothers to breastfeed their babies. His firm manufactured all-cotton clothing for women that was designed to make breastfeeding in public easy and discreet, and therefore, more desirable. The firm was profitable enough that each year they could make generous contributions to social programs that supported the company's mission. Recently the executive had commissioned an outside firm to conduct a "green audit" that scrutinized every aspect of the operation to assess the impact of his business on the environment. The results had been very positive.

When I asked him about the source of the cotton fabric he purchased, he named a local supplier who in turn purchased it from mills located in the United States and overseas. I suggested that where he bought his fabric was a decision he might want to test. Cotton grown in the conventional manner generally requires large doses of pesticides and damages soil structure and microorganisms, which in turn causes soil to erode and silt to clog lakes, rivers, and dams and ultimately leads to social problems associated with land degradation. In a number of developing countries, DDT, a pesticide commonly applied to cotton, is now present in human breast milk. Obviously this is *not* something a socially responsible firm would want to contribute to.

So I asked the executive to roughly define a holistic goal that he and his employees would aspire to so we could compare two sources of cotton fabric—the supplier he was already using and another who specialized in organic cotton fabric. Many of the tests did not apply in helping us to decide which source was better. We weren't dealing with a problem (cause and effect), comparing enterprises (gross profit analysis), assessing the weak link in the chain of production, or concerned at this stage with the source or use of the energy and money. But the other tests gave us plenty to consider. The sustainability test favored the organic cotton over the conventional, but the marginal reaction test favored the conventional cotton over the organic in terms of the dollars invested. The final decision would be based on the society and culture test, which I left to him to consider on his own.

This final test, more than any other, can be done only by those who formed the holistic goal. Outsiders can often help with advice or expertise on many of the others, but it is counterproductive in this test. You are considering decisions in this case based on your own cultural and social values, and it would be close to impossible for anyone else to understand them as well as you do.

I can only guess what this man decided to do. Because his company had a well-deserved reputation as a socially conscious business, I am sure he and his co-workers decided to do *something,* although they would not be able to make radical changes overnight.

Testing Guidelines Summary

We have now covered all of the testing guidelines developed to date. If you have considered each of these tests in evaluating any action you plan to take, you will have gone far in preventing costly and unsound decisions. Ideally, all actions should pass all tests that apply, and those that do almost certainly will give economically, ecologically, and socially sound results. Any actions that fail this year may pass later as your management takes effect and the whole situation changes.

Remember that speed is essential to the process. It is the speed that gives you the big-picture clarity you need. If you cannot quickly answer "yes" or "no" to a question, bypass the test. Most of the time you will come back to that test only if you are unable to reach a conclusion after passing through all the others. However, if you have to bypass the cause and effect or weak link tests, it may be pointless to continue the testing until you have answers for these two.

Given time and practice, the concepts underlying the seven tests will become so familiar that you will automatically take them into account before you come close to making a decision. You will start to look for the underlying cause of a problem before you even begin to consider potential remedies. Before you contemplate what to do about the borers eating your corn, you will look for the weak link in the borer's life cycle. Going into a preliminary financial planning session, you will already have calculated the gross profit on that enterprise you are so keen to develop.

When you have reached this stage, the testing really does go quickly and genuinely becomes nothing more than a final check to ensure the decision is sound and in line with your holistic goal. In the meantime, bear in mind the following points:

- All actions must be tested toward a holistic goal, otherwise the tests become meaningless. The tendency to slip back into conventional decision making will always be with you, especially in emergencies. Take actions to deal with the emergency by all means, but test each of them toward your holistic goal, not toward the problem.

- When you are dealing with a problem, go to the cause and effect test first. If an action does not address the underlying cause of the problem, you will not solve it.

- The gross profit analysis test applies only when two or more enterprises are being compared, the marginal reaction test applies only when two or more actions are being compared.

- The weak link test applies in three different contexts: financial, biological, and social. Look for the financial weak link (in the chain of production) when engaged in Holistic Financial Planning; consider a biological weak link only when an action is taken to increase or decrease a population of organisms; look for a social weak link any time an action is contemplated that will affect people whose support you will need.

- The society and culture test is based on the picture that emerges after passing through all the other tests that apply and should be done last.

Remember that there is no tyranny in the testing. You may decide to implement a decision that fails one or more tests simply because you have little option at present to do otherwise. You at least know that the decision is not in line with what you hope to achieve in the long run, and that you have to do something about it, which brings us to the subject of the next chapter. Even when a decision passes all the tests, it could still prove wrong. You cannot be sure unless you monitor what you have planned.

Part VII

Completing the Feedback Loop

33

Monitoring Your Plans and Keeping on Track

O nce a plan is made, monitoring becomes essential because even though the decisions involved have been tested, events rarely unfold exactly as planned. Monitoring can mean many different things, but in Holistic Management it means looking for deviations from the plan for the purpose of correcting them. Although most quality-conscious corporations would define monitoring in the same way as would any number of engineers, in far too many situations we merely monitor "to see what happens."

Nowhere is this more apparent than in agriculture. The tendency there, over the last fifty years or so, has been to seek and apply the best grazing system or the best cropping system or the best of various management practices, and not worry about the outcome until things go wrong. When things do go wrong, another system or another practice is tried until things go wrong again. In the long run, things never do go right because there never can be one system or practice that applies everywhere and gives uniform results. There are always too many variables operating in any situation. That is why plans have to be specific to each situation and monitored relative to the environmental conditions that exist and to the needs and aspirations of the people involved.

In *any* situation we manage, we should be monitoring in order to make happen what we want to happen, to bring about desired changes in line with a holistic goal. The word *plan* becomes a twenty-four-letter word: *plan-monitor-control-replan,* with positive action following each step. All hope of reaching any goal or objective without great deviation or waste depends on this process: Once a *plan* is made, it is then *monitored*. If results begin to deviate from what was planned, then *control* is instituted and the deviation is brought back to plan. Sometimes events go beyond our control, and there is a need to *replan*.

A simple analogy illustrates the process. Let's say my objective is to visit a friend who lives in a house at the top of a hill at the end of a winding road. My *plan* is to use my car to get there. I start the car and move off, but clearly I have no hope of achieving my objective unless I do something more than just drive. I am going to leave the road at the first bend unless I *monitor* the road well ahead of me. Then I am going to have to *control* by turning the steering wheel to stay on the road. Now if all goes well and there are no earthquakes or flash floods, or my car does not break down and my monitoring and control are adequate, I will get to the house.

In real life, however, things seldom go so smoothly. I may not monitor well because I am watching the scenery and my mind wanders. I may not control well because when I stop my daydreaming and with a sudden fright realize I'm going off the road, I turn back too sharply and go off the other side. If anything does cause me to break down, hit the ditch at the roadside, or whatever, I have to *replan* to ensure that I still reach my objective. In replanning I will always be working with a changed set of resources—my car has broken down and I am now on foot, for example. I now plan to walk to the house on the hill, but I still have to monitor the road ahead and turn to keep on it, and so on.

In the Holistic Management model, we depict this process as a circle or loop because it is a continuous effort. Throughout the process you should be seeking indicators of change and responding to the feedback you receive, constantly adjusting your actions to stay on track. When you fail to respond to the feedback, you fail to complete the feedback loop, and you will not achieve what you set out to achieve.

Completing the feedback loop is the final step in the holistic decision-making process, and it is what makes management proactive rather than reactive. On several occasions I have been asked, "What will happen to the deer, or the weeds, or the people, or whatever, on my place if I manage holistically?" My routine reply is: "I don't know. What do you want to happen?" What you want to happen should be incorporated into your holistic goal. Then it becomes *your* responsibility to achieve it. When your monitoring shows that no change has occurred where change was planned, or if any change occurs that is adverse to plan, and thus your holistic goal, *take action immediately*. If control is quick, a simple adjustment may be all you need to get back on track.

Most quality-conscious companies routinely monitor using the feedback loop principle. The concept helped to revolutionize Japanese manufacturing and has made an enormous difference to the success of thousands of businesses in the United States and elsewhere. The main difference in how we use the concept is that monitoring is done not just to ensure you reach the objective for which a plan was created and a feedback loop established, but that you also move closer to your holistic goal. We have also developed a specific monitoring process allied to Holistic Financial Planning (see Chapter 44) and guidelines for monitoring the effects of any plan made to alter ecosystem processes.

In many cases, your biggest challenge initially is in identifying which indicators to monitor. If you have made a plan for dealing with a problem, for instance, monitoring should tell you whether or not you have found the root cause of the problem. If the problem remains or worsens, you obviously have not. What can you monitor that will indicate that the cause has in fact been removed? Let's say your problem concerns poor quality in a line of goods you produce, and that you have identified inadequate training of workers on the assembly line as the cause. To address the cause and rectify the problem you have initiated a formal training program, a decision that passed through all the testing guidelines that applied and will take you toward your holistic goal. One of the most obvious indicators to monitor would be the number of defects per so many items produced. If there is a marked decrease in the number of defects following the training program, then you will know that the program has been effective and that you have probably identified the root cause of your problem.

This example is admittedly simple, and one that has probably been experienced by countless companies. The only real difference in this case is that the decision to initiate the training program was first tested to ensure that it was in line with the holistic goal and only then implemented and monitored.

The same sort of reasoning would apply in most situations. If you are clear on what you are trying to achieve, you will have little difficulty identifying the indicators that will give you the feedback you need. In some cases, you will also need to consider how to gather the feedback. A plan for improving client satisfaction, for instance, may require the use of questionnaires, telephone surveys, and so on.

The majority of the decisions you make and test will not involve a formal plan, such as a decision to buy office supplies from a certain vendor, or any of the many smaller decisions you make on a day-to-day basis. The actions involved will be implemented and the results achieved immediately. Nothing you could monitor would affect the outcome. Most decisions involving an expenditure of money will be monitored in a larger context—how they affect the overall financial plan.

Monitoring a Holistic Financial Plan

Those managing any well-run business will appreciate the importance of monitoring a financial plan. The job of keeping the plan on track should be a priority. In Holistic Financial Planning (Chapter 44) income, expense, and inventory figures are monitored monthly to ensure that actual figures match with what was planned. This should be done *within the first ten days of the following month*. No excuses accepted.

If your business utilizes the services of an outside accountant, you can't afford to wait for her to supply these figures, and you don't usually have to. You know how much money you have spent and how much you have received and can record the amounts as the money comes in or as you commit to each expense. You need to have actual figures quickly so you can respond quickly if some figures are not on target. You don't need to nail down every cent. Monitoring quickly and on time matters more than perfect accuracy. If survival prospects look critical, then monitor actual figures *daily*, and project them to month's end daily to see where they stand relative to your plan.

In developing a sugar farm from virgin bush in Africa, I came to the point of daily monitoring, and the ability to see expenses mounting toward the planned monthly limit saved me more than once. Short of capital and heavily in debt, I was pushed to the edge of desperation by a rapid fall in prices. Planning a way out took ages. My main crop, sugar cane, would not return any income until 18 months from the date it was planted, and the price trend and interest rate destroyed any chance of borrowing more against the crop.

Eventually I managed to plan survival around a series of crops that would mature at different stages and sustain cash flow, but all aspects of the plan simply *had* to work. Even one month of over-budget expenses on any crop would have put me out of business. Only daily monitoring and projecting trends ahead allowed me to take corrective action in time.

In Holistic Financial Planning whenever any expense item is greater than planned, actions are taken to bring *that item* back into line. The out-of-line expense is not balanced against other expenses that may have come in less than planned. You cannot allow yourself the luxury of saying, "Well, I used too much fuel this month, but we're okay because the meeting in Cincinnati was canceled, so we're ahead on travel." Just be grateful for every item that is better than planned. Balancing against other expenses will lead to sloppy management and erode profits; every surplus you can retain will soften the shock of emergencies you do not foresee.

An income item that falls short of plan creates a more complicated situation. You can seldom control it against itself as there may be no further income from that source in that year. You can respond only by finding new sources of income, which is generally difficult to do, particularly later in the year, or by reducing expenses, which offers more possibilities. You will have to rework as many expense items as it takes to find the money while figuring how to prevent the same problem in the future.

Such control is vital to success and warrants a formal process, recorded in writing, of recognizing a problem, analyzing it, deciding on corrective action, and naming the individuals responsible for seeing that through. The *Holistic Financial Planning Handbook* describes this process in more detail.

Control is the hardest part of financial planning, but it is essential for completing the feedback loop. Although you might have spent months creating the best possible plan, when your monitoring turns up a few adverse figures you have no option but to do better than your best. You cannot afford to simply ignore the signs and grind on in hopes that fate will err in your favor somewhere down the road. If you are serious about making a profit, knuckle down and do that seemingly impossible control.

Monitoring may of course show drastic problems, as will happen when income slumps because of some internal or external crisis. Then mere control makes little sense. Immediately get everyone concerned together, and spend the necessary time to replan entirely.

Biological Monitoring

With our rising comprehension of the holistic nature of our ecosystem, we are gaining some idea of its truly incredible complexity. Thus, we must take the attitude that much of what we do as land managers may lead to unanticipated effects. Anytime you plan to alter ecosystem processes in any way, you must *always assume you could be wrong,* even though the decision, or decisions, involved have passed all the relevant tests.

As you apply any one of the management tools (technology, animal impact, fire, grazing, rest, or living organisms) you will need to determine what criteria you can monitor that will give the earliest warnings of adverse change. Make sure you are clear on what you are trying to achieve, and then ask yourself, "If this does not happen, where is the very earliest point at which I could detect it?" That is the point you need to monitor in the simplest way you can devise. Remember, you are not trying to *record* change, you are trying to steer all changes in the direction of your holistic goal.

Monitoring changes in plant or animal species, a common practice, is a measurement that comes too late, indicating that considerable change has already occurred that may not have been in line with your holistic goal. You want to detect changes well before that. *The earliest changes are most likely to occur at or near the soil surface.* They could show up in plant spacings, soil litter cover, soil density, soil aeration or organic content, insect activity, seedling success, quality of water runoff, and a host of other things.

Depending on what your monitoring indicates, you will either continue to apply the tools as you have been or you will need to make adjustments. Obviously, if all is going as anticipated when the particular tool was selected, no adjustment is necessary. If not, you will have to diagnose what went wrong (see Chapter 48) and develop alternatives you can use as you replan.

Ideally the monitoring should be done by the people managing the land, who usually lack the time to do a full-dress academic study. In the *Handbook for Early-Warning Biological Monitoring* the simple technique we have developed over many years for monitoring rangelands and pastures, and more recently croplands is covered in more detail. We are constantly improving this technique and working on others for monitoring wetlands, forests, and so on, in a never-ending attempt to incorporate ever simpler and more practical methods for measuring precursors to major change.

The main thing to remember is that you are looking for basic information you can measure and understand that indicates *to you* what changes are taking place, rather than a mass of data that is of little practical use. Soil surface changes are the most important because they precede most changes in populations that make up the communities under your responsibility. Observing these allows you to preempt many future problems.

Obviously, you do not start monitoring a week or a month or a year down the road. Start now, *before* implementing your plans. You need a good idea of the health of all four ecosystem processes right at the outset. From that baseline, you can build toward the future landscape described in your holistic goal.

Any time your monitoring throws up a serious deviation from a plan that cannot be controlled with minor adjustments and you are forced to re-plan, again assume your plans are wrong, determine the early warning criteria you will monitor, and continue working your way around the loop.

When the feedback loop is not completed, progress can be seriously affected. Some years ago the U.S. Forest Service initiated a pilot project in Arizona in which Holistic Management was to be practiced on land leased by a local rancher. A holistic goal was formed, and animal impact and grazing were the main management tools that would be used to move toward the future landscape described.

Over the next eight years, the rancher operated more or less according to plan, and the Forest Service methodically monitored the results, ably assisted by the local university. They rightly focused on soil capping, soil erosion, and plant spacing, all of which would provide early warnings of any adverse changes. Each year the monitoring showed that, as planned, soil capping was decreasing. But it also showed that soil erosion was increasing when it should have been decreasing and that plant spacing was widening when it should have been narrowing. Something was clearly wrong, *yet no control was implemented*. Everyone involved was waiting to "see if it (Holistic Management) worked," instead of responding to such a serious deviation from the holistic goal. A simple and timely adjustment in animal numbers and behavior in the second or third years would have changed everything. Nothing was done, however, and when the project wound up at the end of the eight-year period, it was considered a failure.

Monitoring Technology in the Environment

New technologies are continually being developed that have the potential to affect the environment profoundly. While these technologies are often monitored for their effects on site or in specific applications, their effects elsewhere and much later seldom are, although awareness of the need to do so is increasing. The CFCs used in refrigeration systems, fire extinguishers, and cleaning solvents and their effects on stratospheric ozone are one of the better examples that have alerted the public to just how much later and just how far from the site of application the effects can become manifest.

In the case of substances, such as CFCs, that can persist in the environment, the problem of deciding what, where, and when to monitor is enormous. Not only can the time delays run to many years, but the adverse effects may show up in places we would never think to look. To compound the problem, although a substance may on its own be proven safe, in combination with other substances in the environment it can become lethal.

How do you determine which criteria to monitor for the earliest warning that the cummulative effects of any new technology are damaging, when we have so little understanding of nature's complexity? I do not have answers, but I do know that most of us now see the need for answers.

When humans see a need and put their minds to it amazing things can happen. Prior to introducing new products, I envision us thinking out the path the products (or their by-products) will take from the earliest stages of production to their ultimate resting place, presumably the scrap heap. How a product affects *any* life forms encountered along that path could provide the earliest warning of changes that would adversely affect the four ecosystem processes.

This sort of monitoring will require considerable expertise and very sophisticated technology, both of which are potentially within our reach. However, in the case of unnatural substances that persist for many years once released in the environment, we may have little alternative but to ban their production altogether if containment cannot be guaranteed.

Conclusion

A plan, no matter how sound, serves little purpose unless its implementation is monitored and deviations are controlled. Otherwise, even assuming no lapses at all in management, unpredictable events sooner or later render the best plan irrelevant or even destructive. Some will ask, "Then why plan in the first place?" We must plan, monitor, control, and replan simply because it is the only way we can make happen what we have said in our holistic goal we want to see happen.

Part VIII

Some Practical Guidelines for Management

34

Lessons Learned
in Practice

The management guidelines covered in the next eight chapters have crystalized out of a struggle to connect what is possible in theory with what is practical in real life. They reflect years of experience in a variety of situations and the contributions and criticisms of many people, but these guidelines are chiefly the result of what we have learned through continually making mistakes. They represent the cutting edge of Holistic Management, the area of greatest change so much so that within a very short time, some of what I have written here is likely to be out of date.

The management guidelines will influence any number of decisions you test because they in fact help to shape those decisions, providing definition and detail that might otherwise be lacking. This is certainly the case for the oldest of the guidelines, those which arose when we discovered the significance of herding animals to the health of brittle environments. Before we could utilize livestock to restore deteriorating land, we had to develop guidelines for managing their grazing and trampling to ensure that the animals, the land, and the people involved all benefited.

Other guidelines emerged as a result of the holistic decision-making process itself, which forced us to look anew at conventional approaches to learning, leadership, and running a business. Some of the guidelines that developed as a result were gradually transformed into fairly methodical planning and monitoring procedures, which are introduced later in Part IX of this book.

General Guidelines

The next three chapters cover the guidelines that apply most generally. Much of the material covered will be familiar to some readers, particularly those who have expertise in adult learning, organizational development, and marketing. But for many others these three chapters will provide a basic understanding of subjects they need to know about, particularly in the context of Holistic Management.

Chapter 35 deals with the challenges people face in learning to practice Holistic Management. A number of guidelines are given to assist you in moving beyond the obstacles that inevitably arise and to better prepare you for introducing the ideas to those whose support you will need.

Your ability as an organization to make happen what you want to happen will depend largely on how free people are to think and be creative and how the organization is led. Chapter 36 discusses ways to structure and lead a business or organization that will enhance creativity and holistic decision making.

The approach you take to marketing may change substantially in the context of Holistic Management because each of the steps involved, from developing the product or service to reaping a profit, will require decisions that should be tested toward your holistic goal. Chapter 37 provides guidelines for developing a marketing strategy in line with your holistic goal and thus your values.

Land Management Guidelines

The guidelines covered in the last five chapters apply more commonly in land management situations. If you are managing land, study these chapters thoroughly. If you are not, a lighter reading will suffice. Anyone making or supporting decisions that will affect the land in any way should find these chapters relevant.

Any time we attempt to alter ecosystem processes we do so through the use of a particular tool. The last five chapters include specific guidelines for the use of four of those tools—fire, grazing, animal impact, and living organisms—in a variety of situations. In each case, the guidelines attempt to work with Nature rather than against her to ensure that when you use a particular tool it will achieve what you want it to achieve.

When achieving your holistic goal involves grazing animals for any reason, you need to make sure that their presence enhances all four ecosystem processes. Timing the exposure and reexposure of the plants and soils to the animals will be critical to ensuring plants are not overgrazed or soils overtrampled. Chapter 38 gives guidelines for managing grazing and trampling time depending on the climate, the season, the types of plants, and the needs of the animals.

The stock density and herd effect guidelines, covered in Chapter 39, apply when you are using the tool of animal impact to alter soil conditions or vegetation. The guidelines for managing stock density mainly seek to avoid low-density grazing, which almost always causes problems on the land and can impair animal performance. The biggest challenge in inducing herd effect, which requires that you produce a behavior change in the animals, is inducing it often enough and over a large enough area, particularly in the more brittle environments. Chapter 39 summarizes the techniques developed to date.

If we are to sustain our present civilization and its enormous population, we must strive to create an agriculture that more closely mimics nature, one that enhances rather than diminishes water and mineral cycles, energy flow, and community dynamics. Toward that end Chapter 40 gives some fundamental guidelines that apply in any cropping situation.

While fire is a tool that has a definite and useful role to play in land management, we always need to question its use. Chapter 41 reminds us of the dangers associated with burning, while providing appropriate safeguards. Guidelines are given for when and how to burn and which tools to apply following a burn.

The population management guideline, covered in Chapter 42, bears on the tool of living organisms, but more generally on the management of community dynamics. It applies any time we want to encourage or discourage the success of a species. Guidelines are given for assessing the health of a species' population, for determining the environmental factors that will enhance or limit that population's success, and for dealing with predators that become a problem.

The management guidelines are merely a set of principles that help you to determine a course of action. These chapters include only the most obvious principles and the relevant guidelines developed to date. As Holistic Management expands into new realms and as new challenges are created, further guidelines will surely be added.

35

Learning and Practice: Shifting Your Paradigms

L earning to manage holistically is very much a *practical* exercise. You won't really come to understand Holistic Management until you *do* it. It is no different from learning how to fly. How far would a student pilot fly, if his training consisted only of reading books on flying, watching videos, or using flight-simulation computer programs, but no actual practice time in a plane? Of course, the new pilot will benefit from the books, videos, and so on, but only when their use accompanies practice sessions. In the student pilot's case, practice time in the plane requires the presence of a qualified instructor. In learning to practice Holistic Management, that is not always necessary, but it helps to have someone available who has more experience than you do and, in the early stages in particular, training and experience in teaching others.

The advantage of working with an instructor is that you have the opportunity to ask questions in the presence of someone with more experience who can coach you in answering them. That is also the advantage of training with a group of people, rather than going it alone. In any case, training is a lifelong process, not a one-time event. To be effective, it should occur in small doses over time to avoid information overload and to provide opportunities between sessions to practice what you have learned.

Whether the whole you are managing encompasses your personal life, a small family business, or a large corporation, you will face a number of challenges, particularly in the early stages, that a little training and support from others will enable you to meet more effectively.

Early Challenges

In the early 1980s I was paid rather handsomely to provide training to hundreds of government agency and land grant college people. I saw this as a wonderful opportunity to broaden the practice of Holistic Management, but found I had taken on more than I had bargained for. I had not realized how difficult it was for people vested in old paradigms to adopt new ones, nor was I even aware of the phenomenon of paradigms. As it turned out, many of the ranchers, farmers, and others I was training at the same time found it just as difficult to shift to the new, although they fought it less.

Shifting Paradigms

A major part of a continuing education in Holistic Management is about shifting paradigms, learning to operate under a new set of guidelines. Your ability to do this will depend to a large extent on how deeply vested you are in some of your old paradigms, particularly those brought into question by the four new insights (Chapters 3 through 6). This comes as a surprise to some people. If you think a rancher would be eager to concentrate his animals and keep them moving because in doing so he could run many more of them, you would be wrong. Even though intellectually he grasps the reasoning in the new ideas related to grazing and animal impact, the rancher's subconscious fears often prevent him from putting the ideas into practice. The environmentalist who can see with her own eyes that rest is killing the plants in a brittle environment and thus the habitat of a wildlife species her group is trying to save, will go to great lengths to deny it if the only practical way of reversing the damage requires the use of livestock. For most of us, thinking in terms of wholes will fall by the wayside when a quick fix appears to solve problems we don't otherwise have the time and energy to tackle.

In each of these cases, a little practice can help the shift to occur. The rancher can conduct an experiment on a small area of his own land that simulates what would happen all over if he bunched animals together in one place for a very short time. The environmentalist could do the same if she was comfortable enlisting the help of a rancher. Any of us who have chosen the quick fix route often enough generally know what happens: the problem we fixed only returns or leads to new ones. A little practice using the testing guidelines soon convinces most people that holistic alternatives to the quick fix require far less time and energy, particularly over the long run, than they originally thought.

Holistic decision making is itself a new paradigm that, like all new paradigms, requires a fundamental shift in thinking. *You cannot adopt parts of it and hope to succeed.* You could not, for instance, test decisions without having a holistic goal to test decisions toward. Yet a number of people shy away from writing out a holistic goal because they fear the responsibility they take on for achieving it. That is why such large segments of our population just want to be told what to do and why we so often prefer the answers prescribed by experts to thinking out solutions for ourselves. Taking back that responsibility can be an enormous leap for some people.

The biggest stumbling block for many is the idea of the feedback loop. If a decision has been thought out carefully and tested, how could it be wrong? Why should you monitor? This is particularly difficult to accept for people in positions of authority who are expected to make the "right" decisions. I'm not just talking of bureaucrats or academics, but also of corporate CEOs, symphony conductors, teachers, and many others, especially parents. Once they do realize they don't always have to be right, they heave a collective sigh of relief. But only through practice will they make this discovery. Most will find that confidence in their abilities does not depend so much on making the right decisions as in knowing quickly when those decisions prove wrong or need modification.

Fear of Making Mistakes

In the early stages of practicing Holistic Management, you are likely to feel that you do not know enough to really manage holistically. More than likely you *do* know enough, but are afraid of making mistakes. Rest assured that even when you do know enough you will make mistakes. What you really want to avoid are the big ones you do not discover until too late. That is one reason for establishing a feedback loop that enables you to correct mistakes before they cause much damage.

To avoid making mistakes, the natural human tendency is to attempt to change gradually—fewer changes mean fewer mistakes. However, when you decide merely to adopt "some of the Holistic Management principles" or take a "holistic approach," you are not actually shifting any paradigms—decision making remains fundamentally unchanged.

Gradual change, when fundamental change is required, ultimately leads to confusion and a lack of progress. In Sweden some years ago the government decided to change from driving on the left of the road to driving on the right. They set a date and changed on that day. What do you think would have happened if they had tried to change gradually?

Once you have a basic understanding of Holistic Management and have formed a holistic goal, set a date for change and change your decision making on that day. You have nothing to fear in doing so; you risk far more by not changing. However, any time you make a fundamental change there is bound to be some confusion, and you will be tempted to revert back to what is more familiar. Resist this temptation, and keep practicing. Sooner, rather than later, there *will* come a day when the new decision-making process beats the old one every time.

Anyone who has attempted to learn to play a musical instrument knows that proficiency only comes through practice—and lots of it. Progress may seem to be minimal, or even to backslide, if judged at the end of each practice session, particularly in sessions where you try harder and make more mistakes. Over time, however, the improvement is measurable. You are unlikely to achieve perfection, but you do not need to become proficient or even accomplished. On the other hand, if you decide to forgo the practice sessions, no amount of thinking about it, or wishing it, would result in your being able to play the instrument. Learning to practice Holistic Management is no different.

Those who have become proficient most quickly in practicing Holistic Management have often been those who had the most to lose. They overcame their fear of the new, of making mistakes, and of taking responsibility simply because their situation was desperate. They had no greater confidence than the rest of us and no time to prove anything to themselves. They simply began to practice, operating more on faith than knowledge, which taught them what they needed to know and pulled them through.

Peer Pressure

Until practice enhances your confidence, it is easy to succumb to peer pressure—perhaps the biggest deterrent there is to acceptance of new knowledge in any human community. Anytime you make a change, you open yourself up to ridicule and misunderstanding. The banana that leaves the bunch gets skinned. That is why, for us, training individuals in isolation from their families, coworkers, or community proved singularly unsuccessful. When these people returned to their homes or offices and attempted to explain, perhaps a little too enthusiastically, what they had learned, they were regarded as somewhat deranged. This unexpected response, generally proved too much for them to bear—humans are social creatures, after all—and they quickly fell back into line.

Peer pressure is only slightly less bearable when it comes from outsiders looking in on what you are doing. Neighbors and colleagues will question decisions you make because they have no knowledge of the context in which they were made. If well meaning, these people will try to convince you to change your mind; if not, they may simply ridicule your efforts. The cowboys on one ranch I worked with some years ago were ostracized by other cowboys in the community because of their commitment to this "nutty fad from Africa." Attitudes later changed as the ranch staff worked to educate others in the community, but the sting planted in those early days was quite painful.

Maintaining Momentum

In *The Path of Least Resistance,* human development consultant Robert Fritz traces the creative process from the moment of inspiration through to the work or product that finally results. He identifies three stages in the process that I believe apply equally when learning something new and putting it into practice. In the *germination* stage, you feel the special energy that comes as you are introduced to the new idea and begin to put it into practice. The next stage, *assimilation* is the period during which you incorporate skills in such a way that they become a natural part of yourself. In practicing Holistic Management, this is where you make most of your mistakes as you work to solidify your understanding. The last stage, *completion,* is reached when you have internalized concepts you may previously only have grasped intellectually and become reasonably confident in practice. You will still make mistakes, of course, but they will no longer threaten your confidence in the process.

The assimilation stage is the most difficult to pass through because sometimes, even for long periods, it seems as if nothing of significance is happening or being learned. The momentum that has propelled you forward until now may stall. This is when most people who enter fitness programs give up or when many adults who want to learn a foreign language lose interest or become "too busy to continue." And it is when those attempting to practice Holistic Management begin to question whether it is worth the effort.

People often feel discomfort, frustration, and disappointment at this stage and may seek to ease these feelings by lowering their expectations. This is something you must resist, because it will curtail your forward momentum. In any creative endeavor, says Robert Fritz, the process has to start with a vision of what you really want, followed by an assessment of what you currently have. The discrepancy between the two creates a tension you can use to help to propel you toward the vision. As long as you hold to the vision of what you want to create, enormous energy and power are generated because the path of least resistance to resolve this discrepancy between what you currently have and what you really want favors the latter. So, when you lower your expectations, you weaken the creative tension because you are no longer aspiring to what you truly want.

Something similar is at work when in practicing Holistic Management, you outgrow a temporary holistic goal. In the months since you formed it, people have gained many insights through practice, and these now need to be reflected in the holistic goal. This will increase buy-in and make the goal better reflect what people truly want for themselves and for the organization as a whole. If you can keep the focus on what you really desire and want to accomplish, as clearly expressed in your holistic goal, the outcome of the assimilation stage is that it teaches you what you need to learn to create what you want.

Introducing Holistic Management to Others

You cannot, after reading this book, merely rush home or into the office bent on forming a holistic goal with the others in your whole. People will naturally resist anything that is thrust on them, no matter how enthusiastic you are, if they do not know much about it. Generally, a brief outline of the decision-making process will serve as an initial introduction, followed by the quick formation of a very temporary holistic goal and the testing of one or two decisions. Don't try to explain the testing guidelines in detail. Your understanding of them is likely to be fuzzy anyway, and your aim should merely be to show how the process works. This exercise usually generates enough interest that at least some people will want to learn more. How you address that desire will depend on several factors relating to the position you hold in the whole being managed and on the nature of that whole.

Within an Organization

If you are a recognized leader, it can be relatively easy to introduce Holistic Management to an organization, although not necessarily smooth. If you are not, your task can become extraordinarily difficult, depending on the type of organization. Bureaucracies are notoriously slow in adopting new ideas, or even being open to them, but even in a small family business a younger member may risk reprimand from a parent if the parent perceives Holistic Management as a threat to his or her authority. There are no sure-fire methods for overcoming this dilemma, but suggestions are offered later in this chapter.

In either case, to move past the initial introduction into practice and some sort of training program, you either need to engage someone to work with you or to struggle through as a team, using this book as your guide and any other written material available and developing a network of outsiders who are further along and can provide some coaching. Learning groups and networks are helpful in many situations, as you will see.

If you are responsible for leading the organization, then it is important that you have some training yourself, even if that means training alongside those you are leading. It will be your responsibility to facilitate the change to holistic decision making by providing an example others can follow as you learn together. People should be allowed to make mistakes, but it is important that you help them to recognize what they have learned from them. It is also your responsibility to keep people focused on the holistic goal and to ward off the natural human tendency to slide back into conventional decision making. The fact that you are in a position to do this is what generally ensures success.

If you are not in a position where you can openly introduce new ideas and facilitate further training, you will need far more patience and skill. It will be essential that you engage the leaders of the organization in the process at some point, or you will end up in conflict. In a typical hierarchy superiors may feel threatened if you move forward without them, and they can make life very unpleasant. Some individuals in government bureaucracies have received career-threatening reprimands or have been transferred to insignificant positions elsewhere in the bureaucracy. Occasionally, a superior has given the go-ahead to others to begin practicing Holistic Management, but refused any personal involvement. This only puts the others on the spot to "prove it works," but without the superior's participation it never will.

What can you do in such circumstances? You have several options. The first one is to establish or join a learning network outside the organization that will at least provide some support as you learn to practice in your personal life. This is something you should be doing anyway because it enables you to speak to others with greater conviction. Second, you can gradually build a learning network within the organization made up of those who have expressed an interest in learning more. If the group creates enough momentum, the leaders may well follow. Finally, you can merely form a temporary holistic goal for the organization that you keep to yourself and use for testing decisions. When you are asked to express your opinion in meetings or discussions, your views on decisions under consideration are bound to differ from the others, but the logic and common sense of your ideas are likely to appeal to many. You can judge when the time is right to let the others know what you are doing and have them try doing it with you.

Within a Community

Moving from a general introduction to Holistic Management to practice within a community is sometimes much easier than it is within a rigidly structured organization, although the challenges can be equally great.

As a center we have had experience working both directly and indirectly through our certified educators with communities that range from a fairly remote island community off the Washington coast to sprawling counties in Colorado and Wyoming, a handful of villages in southern and western Africa, the inhabitants of a critical watershed in Australia, and a group of Indian tribes in the American Northwest. We have not worked with any of these communities long enough (none more than four years at this point) to know what works with any certainty. But we can provide guidelines based on what we have learned so far, much of which is applicable to introducing Holistic Management in an organizational setting as well.

In most of these communities, someone living or working within the community was responsible for generating an initial interest in Holistic Management. In at least two communities, we as a center sparked the initial interest, in one of them only after spending two years getting to know the people first.

What is important in moving beyond initial interest into practice is to identify one or two local leaders who grasp the importance of Holistic Management and are willing to assume responsibility for coordinating the effort. In some cases these people also provide training. They generally do not hold official leadership positions, but rather serve informally as opinion shapers whose advice is sought out. They tend to be well-known, trusted, and involved in community activities, and they have their hand on the pulse of community relationships. They also tend, in many cultures, to be women.

Ideally, those who provide training should come from within the community and, if applicable, should do so in the local language, or languages if more than one is spoken. Otherwise members of the community might see the new ideas as something being imposed from the outside and will take longer to make them their own. Depending on the circumstances, it may be necessary for outsiders to initiate the process by first training a smaller group of individuals, including the local leaders, who can then facilitate the training of others. In every case leadership skills are essential for the facilitators, as are skills in consensus building. If these skills are lacking, efforts should be made to acquire them.

Fairly early on the local leaders need to identify a group of people who share their commitment to bringing Holistic Management into the community and will support their efforts. In larger communities (200 or more individuals) these people have proven invaluable in helping to gather support, keeping everyone in touch, and facilitating some training themselves. Without them, the local leaders find their job much more difficult.

It is often just as important for community leaders to network with each other, exchanging what each has learned that could be of help to the others. In the African villages, in particular, this sharing of information has played a critical role in communities just getting started. The experience shared by others has helped them to avoid common mistakes and has increased their confidence in the process.

In most communities there will be some individuals or groups who prefer to sit on the sidelines, waiting to see what happens before they join in. Sometimes they stay out of sight, and sometimes they make an appearance only to criticize what they perceive is going on. These people may negatively affect your efforts, usually unintentionally, and cannot be ignored. Develop a plan for engaging them, and continue to provide opportunities for their involvement.

Learning Groups or Networks

People generally find that learning in groups enhances their understanding of Holistic Management and promotes collaboration in other areas. That is why I so strongly support the idea of learning networks, support groups, management clubs, or whatever one prefers to call them. The idea of structured learning groups is certainly not new. In the late nineteenth century Scandinavians developed what they called study circles to enable their largely uneducated populations to better understand current issues and to acquire new skills. Then, as now, the study circles met in participants' homes, without formally trained teachers, to appraise their knowledge, compare notes, and achieve new insights. Study circles have proven so valuable a method for involving the public in discussion of a wide variety of issues that the governments of both Sweden and Denmark today subsidize them and almost a third of all Swedish adults participate in them.

Ranchers and farmers living in geographically isolated communities have used what many call management clubs for years to sharpen their understanding of Holistic Management and to keep up-to-date. But the same sort of group-learning effort is useful even within a corporation or among unrelated businesses or families, if you follow these simple guidelines:

- *Don't try to force participation.* Put the invitation out, perhaps several times, but don't pressure people to get involved. When the readiness is there people will come, and not before. It is better to start with two people who are committed than with twenty who are not.

- *Meet regularly.* Set regular meeting times (once a month seems to work well for most) and stick to them so they become routine and the learning is continuous. One of the most successful groups I am aware of has met monthly for over six years and postponed a meeting only once.

- *Clarify your expectations.* Find out what each person hopes to gain by the meetings. Then decide how often you will meet and where, who will set the agenda, if there is one, what rules you want to put into effect (e.g., Should some or all discussions be kept confidential? Should outsiders be allowed to join in from time to time?), and so on.

- *Keep numbers small and fairly constant.* The smaller the group, the better individuals tend to know one another and the better able they are to provide meaningful feedback. However, you need to balance the need for intimacy with the need for diversity, which greater numbers will provide. A dozen or so people, about the number that would fit into an average-size living room, seems to work well. With more than twenty you may need a microphone to make yourselves heard, and fewer people will have the opportunity to express themselves in a given time. If numbers remain constant, but people continually leave and join, you do not have the opportunity to develop the trusting relationships or the continuity and momentum that are crucial to successful learning.

- *Keep the focus on learning.* Your purpose in meeting as a group is to enhance your learning. Socializing is a natural by-product of getting together, but if the focus shifts too much in that direction, motivation will wane and the group will eventually break apart. If you find this happening you may need to structure the learning to some extent. Determine topics for discussion beforehand, and make someone responsible for leading these discussions or using their own experiences as case studies. Pool funds together and arrange for an outsider to come in to provide training in areas where everyone feels weak. Better still, teach each other. There is no better way to increase your understanding of Holistic Management than to teach it. If one member of the group has recently attended a training session, have that person teach the rest of you what he or she learned. Or select one or two people from the group who have more experience in Holistic Financial Planning, or any other subject, to run training sessions for the whole group.

- *Be patient.* It takes time for a group to mature to the point that their meetings truly become an effective learning tool. Relationships within the group will fluctuate, depending on the circumstances each individual faces—people will at times be confused and angry and at others engaged and exuberant. As one learning group member put it, "We have had boring meetings, painful meetings, exciting meetings, and we have had a lot of fun together. It is all part of building a learning community. And it is a rich, stimulating highlight of my life."[1]

I am aware of at least one learning group that, because of the geographical distance between them (three countries were involved) has had to forgo face-to-face meetings in favor of electronic ones via the Internet. They have found that most of the guidelines apply—they have had to limit their numbers, agree on their expectations and some rules at the outset, and so forth. Their meetings may lack the warmth and nuance that comes from physical contact, but they have made some headway nonetheless. And they are benefiting from support they otherwise would not have had. If you are isolated as these people are, this is an option you might consider.

Role of the Center for Holistic Management

Holistic Management has developed far beyond what it was ten years ago, when the first edition of this book was published. It will continue to develop as the number and diversity of practitioners grow. The primary role of the Center for Holistic Management is to ensure that this knowledge is not lost. We are continually collecting, synthesizing, and disseminating information based on the lessons we and others have learned through practice, and hope always to remain a place anyone wishing to be kept abreast of developments can approach. (We publish a bimonthly journal that includes regular updates and we also maintain an information-exchange conference on the Internet.) Our own training efforts are focused mainly on training and continually updating trainers. These people, as Certified Educators, then work with groups of individuals or businesses in their own or neighboring communities. For more information on how to contact these people, see About the Center for Holistic Management on page 617 of this book.

Without some point of focus and coordination there is always a danger that knowledge will dissipate or become unintelligible, as some languages have become when introduced into new countries that lost contact with the old. As a center, however, we are also aware that coordination can be perceived as a form of control that stifles, rather than encourages, creativity. Maintaining a balance between the two tendencies is likely to remain a challenge.

As mentioned, training should not be considered an event, but a continual process. What you learn today will be enriched by what you learn tomorrow and throughout the rest of your life. Holistic Management is not a subject any of us, including me, can ever say we have mastered, merely something we can continually get better at practicing.

36

Organization and Leadership: Creating an Environment That Nurtures Creativity

Organizing is an instinctive habit. All higher forms of animal life and a good many rather primitive ones do it in ways ranging from the simple pecking order of the chickens in the backyard, to the territorial patterns established by many predators, to the highly complex divisions of labor in the termite colony. Organization in a flying wedge of geese, colony of beavers, hive of bees, or pride of lions defines the species as much as feather, fur, stinger, or claw do.

Leadership is an integral aspect of organization in all higher life forms, and realization of the need for it is also instinctive; without leadership, the organization dissolves into chaos. Thus, the two, organization and leadership, are inseparable, and survival depends on them.

Humanity is no different from other species in this respect. No creature whose offspring spend so long in helpless infancy could persist for long without the caring family structure from which in time grew the myriad clan, tribal, and national structures that still define us today. However, unlike other creatures, *we have also organized around the need for management.*

Over the millennia we have elaborated ever more complex organizations and leadership structures to cater to increasing population, growing economies, warfare, and especially technological innovation. The flood of information occurring today as the result of enhanced communication technologies has only accelerated the pace of change and the need to find organizational structures and leadership styles that can deal with it. To a large extent this search is for structures and leadership styles that enhance creativity—humanity's unique and most potent attribute and the only one that enables us to adapt to ever-changing circumstances.

As Chapter 18 explained, because all wholes are unique, and uniquely different every year, no formula or management system can work other than short term. Different persons in different situations have to be able to think creatively for themselves and their situation. Creativity is key to using money, labor, and the other tools of management successfully, and it is the *only* tool that can produce a holistic goal and plan its achievement.

We use the organization and leadership guideline to help us to enhance creativity through organizational structure and function, seeking those that foster the most open, fearless, and genuine communication, without which creativity shrivels.

Hierarchies and Bureaucracies

One of the simplest forms of human organization, and therefore perhaps the most primitive, is the hierarchy, the chain of command down which orders travel from the head person to successive layers of subordinates. The argument for organizing in this way rests on the assumption that the person or people at the top have greater wisdom or can see the bigger picture because of access to more information. Therefore, lower levels must obey for the good of the whole and for the sake of efficiency.

Formal structure, however, does not always determine how well an organization functions. In the case of hierarchies, that generally depends on how much wisdom or access to information the commanding layer actually has. Wise commands depend on good communication of intelligence, but commanding and communicating differ so fundamentally that in the functioning of many hierarchies they become mutually exclusive.

Commands are messages that go in one direction only and accept no reply but, "mission completed." Although that has a definite place, an environment built only on commands is unlikely to foster the open and fearless two-way communication between people necessary for informed actions at any level of the organization. Nor is it likely to encourage individual creativity; in most cases such an environment actually stifles it.

Although the leader at the top may have the big picture in mind, he cannot see the detail familiar to the worker at the bottom. When the latter sees a way to do a job better, he has to ask permission to implement the change, and that goes up the chain of command from supervisor to supervisor, each of whom distorts the message to some extent because of their state of mind, their reaction to the message, or their relationship to the messenger. An old army joke tells of how the urgent request "Send reinforcements. We're going to advance." got rendered by this process into "Send refreshments. We're going to a dance." When that kind of thing happens, the message understandably comes back down the chain to reprimand the hapless individual who started the wave. Thus, a low-ranking person risks reprimand with every open and honest communication he or she makes, and creativity withers.

Bureaucracy was a natural outgrowth of the hierarchical structure. Fairly early on it became obvious the head person could not make *every* decision, but regulations and procedures could be devised that those at each descending level of authority could follow to ensure they made the right decisions. This practice only widened the communication chasm and discouraged creativity even further. As regulations and procedures were open to interpretation, and as the punishment for, or the humiliation of, not interpreting them correctly could be severe, decisions were postponed, sometimes forever.

Most of us have been part of, or have dealt with, bureaucracies long enough to know that this form of organization produces efficiency only occasionally, is often immune to new knowledge and rapid change, and routinely creates spectacular blunders. All of this is encapsulated for me in one example: the 200 years it took Britain's Royal Navy to abolish scurvy, a disease that commonly killed the majority of sailors if they remained at sea for long.

In 1601 Captain James Lancaster discovered that scurvy could be prevented if sailors drank lemon juice. He fed a few teaspoons of it each day to the sailors on one navy ship and none to the sailors on three other ships traveling in the same fleet. Close to fifty percent of the sailors on the other three ships died of scurvy, but none on the ship where sailors had consumed lemon juice. Yet the Royal Navy, led by highly intelligent officers, argued and discussed the issue for the next 150 years while tens of thousands of sailors died of scurvy. When a naval surgeon, James Lind, repeated Lancaster's experiment, using oranges and lemons, he achieved the same results, showing furthermore that the fruit not only prevented scurvy, but also could cure it even when the disease was well advanced. Still, it took the Royal Navy another forty-eight years to provide citrus rations to sailors and finally banish the disease. Britain's Merchant Navy, although in frequent and regular contact with the Royal Navy, suffered huge losses in men due to scurvy for another seventy years before they, too, adopted the practice.[1]

Even universities, which originated as an attempt by wandering scholars to sidestep the control on learning exerted by church and state bureaucracies, have generally succumbed to the power of their own bureaucracies. Many an independent scholar is now working outside the university system in order to pursue creative ideas. Although many academics recognize this problem and do promote independent scholarship, creative people in a university all too often must risk losing tenure and security. That universities themselves have done some of the best work on ways to improve organizations does not contradict the fact that they also are among the best laboratories for that effort.

When the emphasis in an organization is on obedience to commands or adherence to regulations and procedures, people tend to become noncollaborative, manipulative, and competitive in carrying them out. Even in the more benevolent hierarchies or simpler bureaucracies, people at all levels come to fear rejection, fear what others may think, fear going against the mainstream. None of this leads to the openness required for good communication, creativity, and informed decision making, all of which are essential in the practice of Holistic Management.

However, in an organization that operates with fewer layers and less stringent dependence on regulations and procedures, communication should vastly improve, creativity flourish, and decision making be enhanced. Whether or not these things do occur depends on how the organization is led, a subject we will return to. I call such a working environment *collaborative* simply because it enables people to work together more effectively.

The Collaborative Organization

A collaborative organization first and foremost treats people as human beings rather than as "machines of production." In structure it may resemble other organizations, but it functions quite differently. The autocratic boss has disappeared, but there is still a leader who bears ultimate responsibility for getting the job done. Now, however, that job includes encouraging leadership skills in those who work alongside him or her so they can share some of that responsibility.

Leadership style distinguishes a collaborative organization. To create and maintain a collaborative environment requires different beliefs, skills, and practices from those traditionally emphasized. The leader must become less of a manager and more of a coach. His or her chief responsibility is to empower and support people, giving them more leeway to utilize their creativity and to manage for themselves.

The rest of this chapter examines the qualities needed in the leader of a collaborative organization. Much of what I write is based on personal experience working in a number of organizations—from a traditional university, to the vast bureaucracy of the British Colonial Office, and the slightly smaller one of a national army; from a farm and a ranch with numerous employees, to several large corporations, and a national government (as a member of parliament and president of a political party); and finally in a nonprofit corporation, the Center for Holistic Management, struggling to manage itself holistically. Along the way, I have benefited a great deal from others who have thought more deeply on the subject and have shared their results in numerous books, referenced at the end of this one.

Leadership Beliefs

What leaders believe about their people greatly influences what those people and thus the organization can achieve. The following four beliefs appear to be widespread among leaders who have managed to create collaborative organizations that not only function effectively, but also consistently perform well:

- Most people have a need and desire to exercise and display personal competence. When they are allowed to come up with their own solutions, they will work harder to implement them. A good leader seeks to empower people by continually seeking to better understand what it takes to bring out the best in them.

- People can do what needs to be done *if* they are competent in their areas of responsibility. No matter how committed or well meaning, a person lacking the basic skills or knowledge required of them will undermine the overall effort. A good leader can spot the difference between knowledge or skills that merely need sharpening and those that are fundamentally deficient, and will act quickly to rectify the situation in either case.

- To the extent people feel recognized, appreciated, cared about, and supported, they will go to extremes to help those who help them. The leader's primary role is to support the efforts of others. A good leader will go out of his or her way to help people to discover their own answers. A good leader appreciates each individual's strengths and makes sure they are utilized.

- Most people perform at their highest level when they find meaning and challenge in their work. When they derive a sense of personal identity and self-esteem from doing a task well, they give more to the job and get more from it. A good leader helps people to stay focused on what they want (the holistic goal), rather than what they don't want (the obstacles that stand in the way of its achievement).[2]

A leader whose behavior does not reflect these beliefs will find it difficult indeed to create an environment in which creativity can flourish. In my own case, one major experience colored my leadership beliefs ever after. Qualified only by a pristine undergraduate degree in botany and zoology and instructions on filling out a government purchase order for ammunition and fuel, I entered the workaday world as a lowly game ranger. Then at age 21, after less than a year in the bush, I was suddenly promoted to Provincial Game Officer in charge of two provinces containing 8,000 square miles of some of the world's richest game reserves and 200 widely scattered employees. I arrived in heavy rain in my mud-spattered Land Rover, had a brief handover from my superior, and did not see another superior, in the provinces for nearly two years.

In the course of the transfer formalities, I learned that a game ranger was being transferred to my headquarters to deal with elephants that were causing trouble in the surrounding villages. When I questioned the need for that in the light of other priorities, my superior added in confidence that the man in question was a dishonest, lazy, drunken thief. If he worked from my headquarters, perhaps I could catch him out and fire him.

Soon the fellow arrived in a three-ton truck loaded down to the blocks with furniture and family, and we had a candid talk. I couldn't imagine how in my need to learn the ropes of my new post I could waste energy spying on one ranger, so I told him the true agenda.

The news shattered him, and he wondered aloud why I had told him. In fact, however justified his reputation, I said I couldn't afford to believe it. I had no time to watch someone day and night. We had a tremendous task to accomplish and too few good men to help. One more could really make a difference. I told him he had a clean slate and the chance to prove himself by starting a lechwe antelope control unit in the Banguelo swamps.

The Game Department had for years argued lack of funds while the fine lechwe antelope of the swamps were slaughtered by the thousands. I had at the moment no house for him and no staff and no money. He would have to find a suitable place to camp with his family and start from there and trust that I would start sending him men, equipment, and money as soon as I could.

He never let me down, doing a superb job on very little. He caught more poachers than all the rest of my staff put together. Despite the lack of any support initially, he succeeded in establishing a control unit nonetheless. No doubt under my superior his sins did match the accusations, but because I had no time to give to following that suspicion, I learned a greater truth about human nature.

Leadership Skills and Practices

The skills and practices that accompany the leader's beliefs are equally important in creating a collaborative environment. Creativity tends to be greatest when the leader's actions display trust and confidence in his or her people, when work is seen to be meaningful, when all feel free to express ideas, and when all feel valued.

Trust and Confidence

As I learned in my game department days, a leader who displays trust in people from the outset, can bring out the best in them. People may jeopardize that trust if they betray a confidence, break a commitment, or consistently underperform, but there is less likelihood of this if the leader's trust is given at the outset.

A leader displays confidence in people by giving them opportunities to develop their own solutions to management challenges. If the leader truly believes people are capable of this and asks to hear about potential solutions, the creativity can really begin to flow. If the leader does not believe this, people will sense it and may feel that the whole exercise is a setup that will not benefit them in any way. In *Enlightened Leadership* Ed Oakley and Doug Krug stress that the way in which leaders ask questions is also important. Among other things, they say, *effective* questions emphasize *what* and *how* rather than *why* (e.g., "What should we do?" and "How do we go about doing it" rather than "Why did this happen?"). *Why* questions often put people on the defensive—they may assume they are being blamed for the problem in some way. *What* and *how* questions force people to think and to be creative in identifying solutions, which in turn builds *their* confidence.

Meaningful Work

People want to feel they are contributing to a vision that is greater than themselves. In Holistic Management the holistic goal should provide that vision, but it will not be very helpful if everyday practices do not reinforce it. The leader needs to ensure that the organization's focus is kept on the vision, rather than on any obstacles that stand in the way. When our attention is focused on something we don't want, we tend to be drawn closer to it. It makes more sense to focus on what we *do* want, so we keep moving toward the desired outcome. People always have this choice, but many are unable to exercise it without some reinforcement, which the leader should be ready to provide.

For work to be meaningful, people must also understand where their own tasks fit within the overall effort. They cannot contribute meaningfully if they do not have access to the big-picture information, including financial figures. Nor can they contribute meaningfully if communication isn't constantly flowing and everyone informed of progress. Meetings will be necessary, and it is the leader's responsibility to make sure not only that they occur, but also that discussions are informative and focused.

Freedom of Expression

You, as leader, must create an emotional climate where people really are free to speak, not only of what they think, but more importantly of what they feel. Often feelings precede clear understanding of crucial issues. Together you may plan a project that no one criticizes, although many may feel antagonistic or doubtful. Normally such a project would go ahead, sometimes to disaster, as those who feel doubts they cannot articulate keep silent.

When people feel free to speak up, and do, you often find a common pattern in their response to new ideas. Oakley and Krug, who specialize in change implementation, have made a study of this phenomenon which they discuss in *Enlightened Leadership*. About 20 percent of the people in a group, they say, are continually open to new ideas and will look for ways to make them work; the other 80 percent are more likely to resist new ideas to some degree, no matter how much sense they make and may unconsciously sabotage their implementation. You cannot address the concerns of the latter unless you know what they are. In some cases, however, these concerns will be tied to self-esteem, as a suggestion for doing something differently is seen as an indication people have done something wrong. If the leader is aware of this possibility, he or she can work with these individuals to build their confidence.

People must also feel free to argue amongst themselves when trying to hash out a new project or in deciding how they will reach an objective. Good argument leads to good questions and eventually new insights. But arguments can get a bit rowdy, especially when those engaged in them sacrifice politeness for the sake of clarity.

In *No More Teams,* Michael Schrage writes at length on what he calls "constructive disagreement." To make a point about the candor needed for good argument, he quotes from the memoirs of the well-known musical collaborators Rogers and Hart: "The noise [from our arguments] could be heard all over the city. Our fights over words were furious, blasphemous, and frequent, but even in their hottest moments we both knew that we were arguing academically and *not personally*" (emphasis added).

The latter point is critical. Argument serves little purpose, and can even be destructive, when it becomes personal. I learned this lesson myself some years ago while serving as a member of parliament at the height of the bitter civil war in what was then Rhodesia; I was at the time a one-man opposition against forty-nine members of the ruling party. In our debates over the war, racism, and resource management, I was repeatedly ruled out of order by the Speaker—to the extent that I felt justified in publicly accusing him of bias in favor of the ruling party and thus incompetent in his role as Speaker. In private, however, he explained that he was forced to rule me out of order because I was attributing bad motives to those I was debating and thus attacking them personally, rather than attacking their proposals. I took his advice and found I was able to speak far more effectively, even winning the debate on one major issue despite overwhelming opposition.

FEELING VALUED

People feel valued when their contributions are acknowledged and genuinely appreciated. Annual awards and the public recognition that accompanies them, have long been used to acknowledge a good effort, but spontaneous expressions of praise may have more power. In my own case, private acknowledgment from leaders I admired and respected has meant far more than public praise, especially when the acknowledgments were followed up with more responsibility. I was ready to move mountains for these people.

This brings me to some final thoughts on the role of a leader in a collaborative organization. Although that role differs in many ways from the role of the leader in a conventional organization, some aspects are the same. Leaders still need to balance the energy they put into taking care of people with the need for creating results through those people. Good leaders readily accept *who* people are, but cannot afford to tolerate unacceptable behavior. And leaders still need to inspire people. This is not something a leader can do in a series of pep talks, but rather something people derive from the example the leader sets. Leaders must be open and honest for their associates to become so. Leaders must demonstrate the behaviors they would like to see from others, such as trust, appreciation and caring, a willingness to admit mistakes quickly, and the ability to say, "I don't know." Leaders can talk about collaboration all day long, but if their behavior doesn't match their words, people will not trust them. As Gandhi said, "You have to *be* the change you expect."

Conclusion

Holistic Management is a proactive process in which you are attempting to make happen what you want to happen. Your ability as an organization to do this will depend largely on how free people are to think and be creative. The way an organization is structured and the way it functions can enhance or diminish creativity. What I have called a collaborative organization is one that tends to enhance it.

Leadership is critical in a collaborative organization, because it fills the vacuum left when the command-and-control structure of the hierarchy is gone and the regulations and procedures of the bureaucracy no longer govern function. Most collaborative organizations will retain elements of the hierarchy in their structure and will utilize regulations and procedures to guide some activities. In the end, the people within the organization will need to define for themselves what they mean by a collaborative environment. Most important, though, is that however it is defined or named, the right environment is one that is capable of unleashing the creativity inherent in us all.

37

Marketing: Developing a Strategy in Line with Your Holistic Goal

The words *marketing* and *selling* are often used interchangeably, and although they both deal with getting a product into the hands of a paying customer, they are far from synonymous. Marketing has to do with strategy: how to develop a product that meets your customers' needs, and then get it to the customer at a profit to you. Selling is only one aspect of a marketing strategy.

The following guidelines for developing a marketing strategy include information that might be found in any basic marketing text, but are based mainly on lessons gleaned from the experiences of a variety of Holistic Management practitioners. Because the marketing challenges for agricultural producers are often greater than for any other commercial sector, however, I want to digress somewhat and discuss them first.

These challenges go back a long way, to the development of the first cities, which only became possible when farmers were able to produce more than was required to feed their own families. But ways also had to be found to transport the products from small farms scattered over a large area to the cities, which were often a fair distance away. The farmer, who generally lacked commercial knowledge, adequate transport, or the means to finance it, was obliged to sell soon after harvesting. The transporter, or "dealer," he sold to became indispensable.

Because the products were perishable, outlets for their distribution had to be set up in advance by the dealer so the products could be resold or further processed before spoiling. Thus, fairly early on the dealer took on the responsibility of marketing and enjoyed a much stronger economic position than the farmer. Once the dealer perfected some form of storage, he could respond better to fluctuations in market prices because he had an ability to build up stocks when prices were low and release them when demand was high. However, such buying and selling often turned into speculation, which tended to exacerbate price fluctuations. The farmer, on the other hand, had little control over the volume of his business because his output was subject to natural variations, weather conditions, pests, and so on. In good years he fared well, but in bad years he might have little for sale.

As urban economies became more industrialized, they could not afford to lose the farmers that supplied them with food and other raw materials, so governments began to shelter farmers from price fluctuations with regulations of various types, price supports (subsidies), and tariff protection in the event imports flooded the market at prices below local production costs.

Meanwhile, the dealers became ever better at marketing and grew more powerful, integrating transport, delivery, and processing until their businesses eventually became huge manufacturing concerns that dominated the food market and linked it to many other markets. In the United States, for example, excess oil production was diverted into the manufacture of fertilizers and pesticides for grain farming. When excessive amounts of grain were produced as a result, food industry marketers convinced Americans that grain-fed cattle were superior in taste and redefined the cattle business.

Given that history, it is probably not surprising that so few agricultural producers have become skilled marketers and that so many have remained passive sellers. Whenever I have the chance to talk to groups of farmers or ranchers, I often ask for a show of hands from those who like marketing. No matter what country I'm in, very few hold up their hands (I would guess less than 3 percent). But times are changing, particularly in the industrialized nations, where many farmers and ranchers have access to education, information, and technology and are not encumbered by the bureaucracy that exists in most food manufacturing corporations. These producers can avoid competing directly with the corporations by carving out their own niche in the food market, which is exactly what the most successful producers are doing.

The niche marketers have a distinct advantage over the food corporations in this regard because they have the opportunity to develop face-to-face relationships with their customers. Likewise, they can guarantee the quality of the finished or value-added products they produce, because they also raise or grow the raw materials that go into them. This additional amount of control over product quality enables them to tailor their product to the needs of their customers, and this added value is something customers are prepared to pay for. Thus, niche marketers are able to set their own prices—they become price makers.

Producers who only raise or grow commodities for the generic mass market, however, are far less concerned with quality, and they have no idea who the ultimate consumers of their products are. Their anonymity and the lack of any reward for a higher quality product only tempts them to cut corners, with both environmental and social consequences, and to produce products that are less perfect than they could or should be. Nothing discourages integrity more than anonymity. These producers remain hostage to prices they have no part in setting. They continue to be price takers.

Niche marketing is used in every commercial sector for similar reasons and generally with impressive results, but agricultural producers have only just begun to explore the limitless opportunities it affords them.

Developing a Marketing Strategy

Farmers and ranchers aren't the only ones who have a tendency to dislike marketing. Any number of people from a variety of businesses find it onerous. I believe much of this is due to a misunderstanding of what marketing entails. Far too many assume that marketing must include sophisticated research into the attitudes, preferences, habits, and purchasing power of the consumer, or that it entails poring over mountains of statistics on price trends, distribution channels, and so forth. Although some research is necessary, it does not have to be this sophisticated. Those who specialize in market research admit that it is not a very exact science anyway. Market research has not eliminated important areas of uncertainty and probably never will. It only indicates the conditions that exist, not what to do about them. Market research may also be expensive, and its value must be measured against its cost. Finally, the information provided soon becomes out of date.

Although there is hardly a form of commercial activity that does not require some market research, it is most widely used in manufacturing where the product is furthest removed from the consumer. The service provider, the retailer, and even the wholesaler all have opportunities to meet face-to-face with consumers and to ascertain their needs and preferences firsthand.

The approach anyone takes to marketing may change substantially in the context of Holistic Management, because each of the steps involved (developing the product, finding the customer, distributing the product, and turning a profit) will require decisions that should be tested toward your holistic goal. As you will see, the products you develop will be influenced by the quality of life you aspire to. (I am using the word *product* in the broadest sense. *Services,* such as accounting or consultation for instance, are a form of product.) Relations with customers will be largely governed by how you have described your behavior as it affects those relations in your future resource base. Both the creation and distribution of products will affect the natural environment needed to sustain your efforts in the long run. Thus, marketing, in effect, begins with the formation of your holistic goal. With these points in mind, let me go through the steps that should be included in any marketing strategy.

Developing a Product

Marketing is not really about products, it is about people. If you design a product without knowing something about the people who will buy it, you will only be gambling with success. At the outset, however, what you mainly need to consider is the kind of product, or line of products, you will produce. What do you already have in the way of raw materials, skills, or equipment that could potentially be turned into a product people will want to buy? What are you good at? What do you want to be known for?

In Holistic Financial Planning, these are the sorts of questions you ask yourself prior to creating a plan for the year. Then you brainstorm a list of all the product possibilities, from the most practical to the ridiculous. You do not necessarily have to come up with something entirely new. You might choose to alter an existing product or develop new uses for it.

People generally brainstorm more than one hundred ideas and then whittle those down to a handful that appear realistic when tested toward their holistic goal. Any ideas that obviously conflict with the quality of life statement (society and culture test) are dropped, as are those that would fail to contribute anything toward covering the overheads of the business (gross profit analysis). The products or enterprises that remain are then passed through the other five tests, which usually pares the list down to three or four products with real potential.

Even though these final possible products emerged because you felt they could meet a demand someone was not already filling and that you could meet that demand better than anyone else, you still need to find and talk to the potential consumers of a product before you finalize its design.

Identifying Your Customers and Meeting Their Needs

If you are a manufacturer attempting to reach a mass market, you will probably need to engage the services of a market researcher to help you to identify potential customers and their needs. But there is much you can do on your own, particularly if you aim to serve a niche, or specialty, market, whose clientele is already somewhat defined. Ideally, you should talk directly to the customers themselves, but this is not always practical or possible. You can, however, talk to people that you know are likely to be in direct contact with them, namely, retailers who promote and/or sell products similar to yours.

One rancher who sought to learn more about the market for "lean, clean, and natural" beef first talked to a fitness club director who assured her there was a demand for her product, but that his clients didn't know where to get it. The rancher then visited restaurants and grocery stores that catered to health-conscious consumers and found they had special requirements that, if met, would pave the way for the sale of her product. These special requirements necessitated visits to meat packers and distributors to find one or two who could help her to get her product to the retailers in the form they needed it, when they needed it. Each one of these needs influenced the development of her product line.

This rancher's case illustrates another point. You have to know not only who your customers are, but also where they can be found. In her case, she figured correctly that the ultimate consumers of her product would be health-conscious and likely to frequent stores and restaurants that catered to the health conscious. Since none of these retail outlets were found in her own neighborhood, but only in college towns and larger metropolitan areas, she had to figure out how she was going to get her products to the retailer. And that brings us to the next step, which is one that will also influence the development of your product.

Getting the Product to the Customer

This really means *distribution,* and there are a number of different ways to accomplish it. Any time you include a middleman for any reason in your distribution network, you risk distancing yourself from the consumer and decreasing your profit. Nevertheless, there are often good, if not essential, reasons for including middlemen in some cases, as you will see. Here are some simplified descriptions of the various distribution structures to consider.

DIRECT TO THE CONSUMER

This is the oldest and simplest form of distribution in which the link between producer and consumer is shortest. It has the big advantage of putting you in direct contact with the consumers of your product and affords the opportunity to build the kind of personal relationships that lead to loyal customers.* In this structure you are basically assuming the role of retailer and can affect distribution in three ways: (1) the customer comes to your production site; (2) you go to the customer (delivery); or (3) you send your product through the mail. There are varying legal requirements and restrictions involved from state to state and country to country that may limit your ability to distribute directly to the consumer (particularly if agricultural products are involved), but many people have found creative ways to work around stifling regulations, while remaining well within the law.

The retail business is not for everyone. Some people have a knack for it, others do not. It's important to be realistic here about who you are as people, what you are seeking in terms of quality of life, and whether this is right for you. In addition, you have to realize that while you are cutting out the middleman, you may be adding to your overhead expenses—someone still has to promote the product(s), and someone has to do the paperwork involved in any sales transaction, even when the customers come to your production site. If you are delivering a product, vehicles may need to be purchased. If direct mail is used, someone must be responsible for processing and sending orders. In a very small business, where a handful of people can handle both production and distribution, overhead expenses may not increase immediately, but if the business is allowed to grow, they surely will. At some point you may decide that including at least one middleman spares you a lot of stress and that what you lose in revenue to this person or firm is more than made up for in the overhead you do not have to take on. This is the sort of decision you will want to test toward your holistic goal.

WHOLESALE

Wholesale usually means distributing your product to someone else who then gets it to the consumer, either directly or through yet another middleman. If you manufacture furniture, for example, you might sell directly to one or more furniture stores or to a furniture distributor who then sells your product to a variety of retailers. By the time your product reaches its ultimate consumer, it may have risen in price as much as 200 percent or more, depending on the number of middlemen in between. Each of these middlemen has taken over *some* of the responsibility for delivering your product and for maintaining relationships with the customer, leaving you

---

*Some people prefer to use the term "client" rather than "customer" to distinguish between a person who may or may not be a continuous buyer of your product, and one who has a more lasting connection to you as the producer. I appreciate this difference, but I have held to the conventional definition of client (one for whom professional services are rendered) throughout this book.

somewhat freer to concentrate on making furniture. I stress the word *some* here, because a necessary part of your marketing strategy is to maintain relationships with the middlemen who serve as valuable conduits for feedback on the reception of your product. They are generally the first to hear of problems with quality or why demand for your product is decreasing.

The number of middlemen you choose to use generally depends on the volume of your business, the amount of work you are willing to do yourself, and the particular market. When you sell directly to a retailer, you have to work hard to build a mutually beneficial relationship. You want to be able to meet her needs so she can meet yours. She is now the one selling directly to the consumer, and she often has any number of other products to sell as well. You want to make sure that selling your product is easy for her.

Working through a wholesale distributor, who then sells to various retailers, requires even more effort at relationship building, as you are now several steps removed from the consumer. The wholesaler is generally not the person you want to work with as you begin to market a new product. It is wiser to work directly with the retailer or consumer. However, if the product fares well and you choose to allow the business to grow, a wholesale distributor will probably become necessary. You need to think carefully about just how large you want your business to grow, and be sure to test any decisions associated with growth. There are a number of reasons why you may want to limit growth—quality of life being a major one. As your business grows, so do the pressures.

The rancher I spoke of earlier who was working out a marketing strategy for lean, clean, natural beef, started working first with retailers, but quickly added a wholesale distributor who could then handle deliveries to several restaurants. She did, however, work to maintain relationships with the restaurant owners so she could continue to get firsthand feedback on ways to improve her product.

COOPERATIVES

Co-ops are another structure worth considering if you just plain do not like marketing, find buyers difficult to deal with in general, and, in some cases, are willing to give up a degree of control over your business. Long used by farmers as a structure in which they could pool their products together, market them as a batch, and thus compete with larger distributors, cooperatives have long since expanded into other industries. However, they vary considerably in aim and structure. In addition to taking on the responsibility of marketing for their members, who generally have a say in the approach taken, some cooperatives purchase supplies, obtain loans, encourage research, and offer a host of services, including further product processing, all of which need to be paid for. Membership in most cooperatives is limited to producers, but some also include consumers who purchase shares in the co-op through memberships, providing needed capital in exchange for products they receive later on. Before forming or joining a cooperative, make sure you understand the costs involved and that the group holds values similar to your own.

Promoting Your Product

Based on your research so far, you should have gathered a fair amount of information to use to finalize the design of your product. Before you go into production, however, you still have some decisions to make, an important one being how you will promote your product. I will not deal here with the vehicles for promotion (advertising through various media, publicity, cross-promotion, etc.) because they are constantly changing, as is the technology (videos, the Internet, and so on) for utilizing them. Whatever ones you choose, however, will entail some costs and these have to be considered in pricing your product. Any number of books and trade magazines are available to help you to determine the most effective media for promoting your product.

Packaging is another aspect of promotion that I will not dwell on. Originally used as a means for protecting a product from damage or spoilage, packaging has become a major promotional tool in itself, particularly for manufacturers serving a mass market who depend on flashy labels and fancy wrappers, rather than relationships, to win customers. If you are manufacturing on a smaller scale and/or producing for a niche market, you don't necessarily have to compete with big-name producers because you can build relationships with the consumer, either directly or indirectly, with the help of a retailer. Nevertheless, in most cases you will require packaging in some form, and even if a distributor or retailer is doing the packaging for you, you want to have a hand in its design, and certainly in the creation of your product label.

What I want to address specifically in this step is your promotional message. Some businesses have earned a deservedly bad reputation over the years for engaging in promotional campaigns that attempt to psychologically manipulate consumers into buying products they don't really need or that may not be good for them. This is easy to do when you view your customers as nameless, faceless beings with money to spend, and your products solely as vehicles for raking in that money. If you are attempting to manage your business holistically, however, it is not likely you hold these views. The inclusion in your holistic goal of the many things besides money that are important to you and the specific mention of how you want to relate to customers would discourage such thinking. Generally, you will want to feel good about your products and what they can provide for people. Any products you do not feel good about are not likely to pass the testing toward your holistic goal.

In your promotional message you should share your reasons for choosing to produce the product and let the customer know how it was produced. If you are managing holistically you have to the best of your ability ensured that the decisions that led to the development of your product(s) as well as your methods of production were economically, socially, and environmentally sound. This is something that should become mandatory for *any* business. As it is, a growing number of market surveys indicate that consumers are increasingly concerned about the social and environmental consequences associated with products they buy. Any number of companies have attempted to address this concern in their promotional messages, but can't always supply evidence to back up their claims. Bear this in mind when developing your promotional message. If you cannot provide meaningful evidence, you will not convince anyone that what you are saying matches what you are doing.

In promoting the product itself, emphasize its benefits over its features—in other words, what the product *does,* rather than what it *is.* For example, in promoting a copier you would emphasize the number of copies it can produce per minute, the excellent quality of the copies, and so on, over the size of its motor, the dimensions of its paper trays, or the materials used in its frame. When your product competes with others, you need to convey what yours *does well* that the competition's does not. Yet, avoid focusing too much on the competition, or you may lose sight of what makes your product special.

This is a lot to consider in promoting a product, but it is essential if your message is to be effective. Try to capture the essence of your message in a phrase that you can then back up with further explanation in pamphlets or other promotional materials you might produce. Be careful, however, that you don't try to convey too much or give the impression that your message is constantly changing, or you will only confuse the customer. Keep your message simple, honest, and consistent and you cannot lose.

Establishing a Price for Your Product

By now, you should have a fairly good idea of what it is going to cost to produce your product and get it to the consumer. Thus, you are ready to determine what price to charge for it. Ideally, you want the product to produce a healthy gross profit (income minus direct costs), but you also want to be sure that, no matter what your volume, your return is emotionally rewarding as well. If you are not making a satisfying living from what you are doing, it is only a matter of time before you either quit doing it or are forced to quit. Obviously, any market has limitations, and if you price yourself too high, you will price yourself out of the market. But it is surprisingly common for people to err in the other direction. Don't be afraid to ask a fair price for what you produce. There are a lot of people who will pay for quality and who want to do business with someone they like and trust.

Keeping Your Customers

No marketing strategy is complete if it does not include a plan for monitoring customer satisfaction. The greater the satisfaction with your product and the way you conduct your business, the higher the likelihood of repeat customers—the cornerstone of any business, and key to creating the future resource base that will sustain it. Keeping customers is far more lucrative than finding new ones. So when you do lose a customer, do as much research as you can to find out why, and respond to their reasons accordingly.

When you build relationships with customers—whether they be consumers, retailers, or wholesale distributors—that are based on meeting their needs, you have a built-in feedback mechanism. If the relationship is a close one, they will tell you when you *aren't* meeting their needs without having to be asked. They will want your products to succeed because they want *you* to succeed.

Conclusion

Follow all these steps and your marketing strategy should be fairly complete. At some point along the way, you will have gathered enough information and tested enough decisions to know whether or not the product under consideration is the right one for you. If it is, then your challenge is to remain committed to marketing it. Commitment is what makes marketing work. A less than perfect marketing strategy to which everyone is committed will work far better than a brilliant marketing strategy without that commitment.

Now, let's move on to the guidelines that specifically address the management of land, livestock, wildlife, crops, and populations of living organisms.

38

Time: When to Expose and Reexpose Plants and Soils to Animals

M ost holistic goals that involve grazing animals for any reason require maximum functioning of all four ecosystem processes. To meet this requirement, overgrazing and overbrowsing need to be avoided or minimized. Earlier chapters have mentioned the finding of André Voisin that overgrazing is linked to the time plants are exposed to animals rather than to the number of animals, but how in practice do we time the exposure and reexposure of plants to animals?

Should we monitor "key indicator" plants, set arbitrary grazing or recovery periods, or follow some aspect of animal performance? Should timing in planning reflect the growth rates of plants, and if so which of the millions in the community? Do we choose individuals of a particular species or a random selection? What about the time animals are exposed to poisonous plants? What about the wildlife grazing the same land? Should animals be allowed to select their diets, or should they be forced to eat everything in a nonselective manner over a short time?

Voisin's outstanding work in pastures in nonbrittle environments answered only a few of these questions for me when, back in the 1960s, I first began to see that timing mattered on the savannas of Africa and began to look for ways to successfully manipulate it. Healthy savannas include a mind-boggling diversity of plant species, from the simplest algae-like forms to a variety of trees. Animal life ranges from billions of microorganisms to a vast complexity of birds and animals, small and large. The greater mass of both flora and fauna is hidden amongst the plants or underground, and even if one could see it all, activity differs greatly from day to night. In such a whole, any change produced by management in one area inevitably changes everything to some degree. So when we decide that a particular plant species can be sacrificed to overgrazing, as some range scientists do, we unleash consequences beyond human ability to even understand, let alone manage. Other species depend on species that depend on species that depend on those we have sacrificed, and on and on.

We cannot play God and in good conscience eliminate anything. If your holistic goal involves rebuilding and sustaining biological communities, you need to minimize overgrazing on every plant you possibly can. To achieve this you base the time of exposure on the most severely grazed plants, wherever they are and whatever species they are.

Adverse consequences of trampling are also a function of the time soil and plants are exposed to animals rather than the absolute number of animals. Prolonged trampling has largely adverse effects, such as pulverization of the soil surface, excessive underground compaction, and injury to plants. Chapter 22, on animal impact, gave the example of 365 successive donkey-days of traffic producing a beaten-out track between a house and a water hole. However, the same traffic produced by 365 donkeys on a single day, followed by 364 days of recovery time, would produce a far different result. The plants and the whole soil community could recover from any damage due to trampling and benefit from the intense deposition of dung and urine. Time, rather than numbers, governs the ultimate impact.

In the donkey analogy every animal would tramp on exactly the same piece of ground, thus maximizing the damage on the day it occurred. In reality that seldom happens—even on trails, as animals follow multiple routes—but the principle remains the same. Maximum impact *over minimum time* followed by a sufficient recovery period makes trampling an extremely effective tool for maintaining brittle savannas and water catchments as well as cropland soils. Specific guidelines for trampling are given in Chapter 39.

As I eventually came to learn, a number of factors affect one's ability to plan the moves of animals to minimize overgrazing. Because of the many variables involved, a systematic accounting of time is nearly impossible. Grazing animals select different plants and different parts of plants in different seasons. Different plants recover at different rates. And plants on different parts of the land are experiencing very different growth conditions daily. At the beginning of my wrestling with this problem, I had to make a practical compromise, pursue it, monitor the results, and modify as necessary. I chose to watch the perennial grass plants as the group most vital to the stability of the whole community.

Monitor the Perennial Grasses

We did not then recognize the distinction between brittle and nonbrittle environments, but experience has borne out the hypothesis that, particularly in low-rainfall, brittle environments, perennial grass stability in fact contributes to the health and stability of the whole biological community more than any other factor. Perennial grass provides the main source of soil cover required for the stability of everything else. Since well over half the world's land surface leans to the more brittle end of the scale and little of that enjoys enough rainfall to support a full tree cover, the health of perennial grass acquires enormous significance.

In less brittle environments where the future landscape includes the maintenance of grassland, perennial grasses are naturally dominant over annuals, and their health will affect your ability to prevent or slow the community from moving to woodland or forest. The overgrazing of perennial grasses in these environments causes little or no soil exposure. Some pastures in England have been overgrazed for centuries and still remain completely covered. However, forage volume and thus energy flow are greatly decreased when plants are overgrazed.

In choosing to consider perennial grass first, we risk overlooking two important factors. A tree or shrub species might suffer severe defoliation before animals start on the grass. Also, time allowed for recovery of a severely bitten grass plant might not suffice for a severely browsed shrub or tree. This potential problem had to be worked out, and I will return to it further on in a way that still justifies the practical guideline: *to reach the richest level of biological diversity in any predominantly grassland environment, time grazings according to the needs of perennial grasses.*

Monitor Plant Growth Rates

Overgrazing, remember, occurs when a severely bitten plant is bitten severely again while using energy it has taken from its stem bases, crowns, or roots to reestablish leaf. This can happen in the *grazing period,* when the plant is exposed to the animals for too many days and they are around to regraze it as it tries to regrow. It can also occur following a *recovery period,* when animals have moved away but returned too soon and grazed the plant again while it is still reforming leaf using previously stored energy. The plant can be safely regrazed when all its roots have reestablished.

So how long is too long a grazing period, and how short is too short a recovery period? No matter what the perennial grass species, this depends on two things: the proportion of leaf removed by the grazing and the daily growth rate of the plant. The less leaf removed, the quicker the subsequent regrowth and the faster the recovery.

To be safe, we assume that the grazing has been severe because some plants are always grazed severely, and thus we focus on plant growth rate. If growing conditions are favorable, and a severely grazed plant can thus grow half an inch (one centimeter) or more per day, you can expect plants

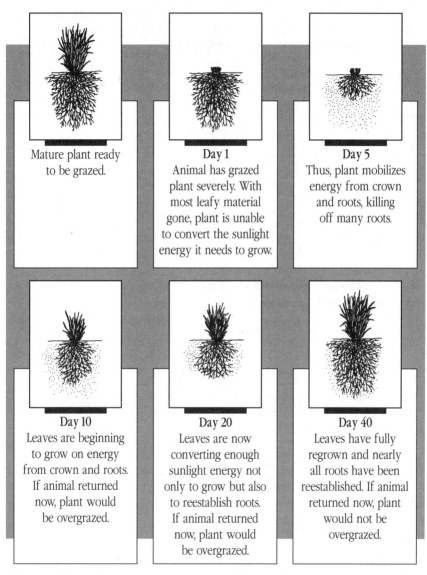

Figure 38-1 *To avoid overgrazing, monitor daily growth rates.*

to be overgrazed after about three days' exposure to animals. If growing conditions are poor and a severely grazed plant can only grow half an inch (one centimeter) every four or five days, overgrazing will occur after about ten days. *Thus, the faster the growth rate, the shorter the grazing period needs to be.* The slower the growth rate, the longer the grazing period can be.

When it comes to the recovery time needed for plants to restore root growth, the situation is similar. When the daily growth rate is fast, because growing conditions are good, the plant restores its roots quickly. Thus, the faster the growth rate, the shorter the recovery time needed. With runner-type grasses, where a smaller proportion of leaf is always removed, the recovery time needed can be as short as 12 to 15 days. With bunched grasses, where a higher proportion of leaf is usually removed, recovery time can be as short as 25 to 30 days. When the daily growth rate is slow, the plants need longer to restore their roots following a severe grazing. Recovery times for runner grasses can stretch to 30 to 50 days, for bunch grasses 60 to 120 days or even a year or more. Figure 38-1 illustrates the principle using a bunch grass as an example.

Grazing and Recovery Periods Are Always Linked

As long as a herd of livestock remains on the same property and moves through a series of subdivisions or paddocks, the grazing periods will be inextricably linked to the recovery periods. The dynamics of this relationship are simple, but easy to overlook. Assume that the top diagram (A) in figure 38-2 represents a piece of land divided into 6 areas that animals will graze for 4 days each. From the time they leave an area until they return to it will then take 20 days (4 days in each of 5 areas [6 grazing areas minus the one they are in]). Plants in each area will get 4 days of exposure to grazing and 20 days to recover.

If, on leaving area 1 you decided it will require 40 days for a severely grazed plant to recover, you will have to add 20 more days somewhere in the other 5 areas, as the middle diagram (B) shows. Therein lies the rub. Any change in recovery time in one area will change the grazing times in the remaining areas to be grazed. In the bottom diagram (C), the operator planned a 40-day recovery period for the plants in each area and thus 8-day grazing periods. But after 5 days of grazing, area 3 looked a bit sparse, so he moved on. He thereby cut the recovery time in all areas back to 37 days. Each area that is grazed for fewer days than planned *reduces recovery times in all areas.* Conversely each day that stock are held longer in an area adds a day of recovery to all remaining areas.

To maintain adequate recovery periods you have to plan them well ahead (as covered in Chapter 46 on Holistic Grazing Planning), because it

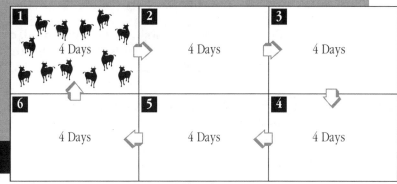

If animals are to spend 4 days in each of 6 grazing areas, then from the time they leave an area until they return to it will take 20 days—4 days in each of 5 areas (6 grazing areas minus the one they are in). The plants in each area thus have 20 days to recover.

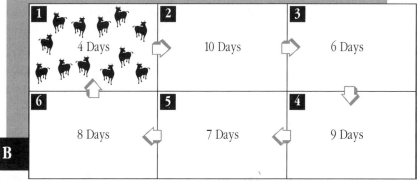

If, on leaving area 1 you decided it would require 40 days for a severely grazed plant to recover, you would have to add 20 more days somewhere in the other five areas (10 + 6 + 9 + 7 + 8 = 40 days).

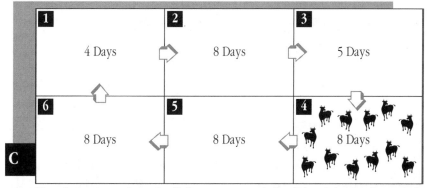

Here the manager planned a 40-day recovery period and thus 8-day grazing periods. But after 5 days of grazing, area 3 looked a bit sparse, so he moved on. He thereby cut the recovery time in all areas back to 37 days (8 + 8 + 8 + 8 + 5 = 37).

Figure 38-2 *Grazing periods and recovery periods are linked. Any change in grazing time in one area will change the recovery times in all the remaining areas.*

takes time to build them up. Grazing periods, on the other hand, can be changed on impulse by simply moving the animals, *but* remember that any time you do this, it will have a cumulative effect on recovery periods.

Base Grazing Periods on a Preselected Recovery Period

Land managed as a unit for grazing, I call a *grazing cell.* The timing of herd moves within the cell naturally depends on the number of subdivisions, or *paddocks.* Domestic stock, being severe grazers (as are most of their wild cousins), will predictably defoliate some plants severely, soon after entering a paddock, regardless of how few animals there are. Photo 38-1 shows what one horse did in one hour to one plant among hundreds of thousands of plants.

Perennial grass plants in the Rio Grande Valley of New Mexico, where this photograph was taken, might need a recovery period of 60 days in slow growth. If, in our simple case, the grazing cell contains nine equal paddocks, then a 60-day recovery period will require a 7.5-day grazing period in each paddock. The reasoning goes thus: After leaving any one of the nine paddocks, the horse can pass through the eight others before coming back. A 60-day recovery period divided by eight paddocks yields 7.5 days of grazing in each paddock.

Photo 38-1 *One of a few severely grazed perennial grass plants amongst millions of plants after one horse had grazed for one hour in a paddock. New Mexico.*

In contrast to this method, seat-of-the-pants management would tend to eyeball each paddock after stock had been in it awhile and then decide when they should move. It might work, but it more likely would not, because it leaves to chance the really crucial time, the recovery period. As the number of paddocks increases, naturally the length of the grazing period decreases, because the same recovery period gets divided by a larger number. As it turns out, there are a number of other advantages that flow from having many paddocks in a cell.

The Advantages of Many Paddocks

Increasing paddock numbers, by subdividing a cell further, either by fencing, or by strip grazing within a paddock using herders and/or temporary fencing, decreases the time in each paddock (or strip) and thus increases your ability to minimize overgrazing. What is more, as paddock size decreases stock density increases, causing better distribution of dung, urine, and trampling and a number of the following benefits:

More Even Grazing

As paddock size decreases, given a constant herd size and constant recovery period, the *proportion* of plants grazed increases. This does not, however, mean that animals are any less able to select and balance their diets. Because the time they spend in the paddock also decreases, the same volume of forage essentially is taken. In general, *only a change in the number of animals or in the time they spend in the cell as a whole will change the amount of forage they will harvest.*

What we do tend to find is that, as the animals select a diet balanced for levels of protein, energy, fiber, and other nutrients, they tend to feed over a higher proportion of the plants available. This has the marked tendency to keep a higher proportion of the leaf and stems on more of the plants fresh and young. When grazing at lower densities, animals generally feed off a smaller proportion of the available plants and thus allow a higher proportion to become cluttered with old stems and leaves of low nutritive value. I have also found that the longer we hold any number of animals in any paddock, the higher becomes the proportion of plants that get severely grazed.

Increased Energy Flow

Much research in several countries has shown that during the growing season the amount of green leaf removed greatly affects the rate at which plants regrow after being grazed. Figure 38-3 shows two equal perennial

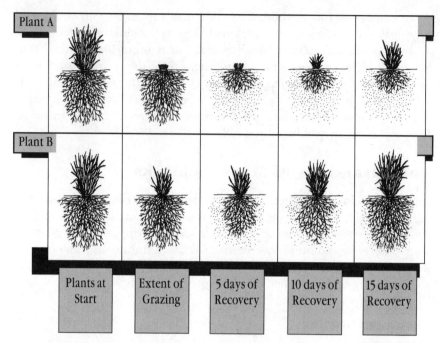

Figure 38-3 *The amount of leaf removed in a grazing affects the rate at which the plant regrows. Plant B loses far less leaf than plant A and thus draws less energy from roots, stem bases, and crowns. Less root is killed and it begins to regrow almost immediately.*

grass plants. Both had almost all their old leaf and stem material removed in the previous year and began growth as equals in this season. Early on some animal severely defoliates A, removing 90 percent of the leaf, but takes only about 40 percent of the leaf on B. The two plants then recover at very different rates. B draws less stored energy and loses less root and starts regrowth almost immediately. Over the next two weeks, it produces much more volume of leaf and stem than A. At some point, however, B slows down and A will catch up. Plant A, on the other hand, suffers a severe setback to root growth following the severe grazing because so much leaf has been lost. It will be a while before enough new leaf has grown to concentrate sufficient energy to regrow the lost roots. The higher the proportion of less severely grazed plants to severely grazed plants, the more total forage produced in a given recovery period.

Thus, in practice the more paddocks per cell, the better the distribution of the grazing on the plants, the fewer severely grazed plants, and the greater the proportion of plants able to recover quickly from grazing, all of which results in increased energy flow.[1] Unfortunately, many people in such situations try to prevent animals from selecting their diets by forcing them to eat everything. This is hardly necessary and generally unwise.

For a time in the early days, I reasoned that we could capitalize further on the increase in energy flow stemming from fewer severely grazed plants by shortening recovery periods. This would in turn shorten grazing periods (remember, they are linked) and produce a snowball effect. But, where the theory appeared sound, in reality some animals always did graze some plants severely. As the recovery periods shortened, these plants did not recover and were overgrazed. As they weakened and vanished, the same fate befell others.

In Africa I noticed this first around ant hills (termite mounds) where cattle are attracted to more nutritious plants. When I shortened grazing and recovery periods, plants in these areas began to show visible signs of overgrazing when all should have been well. We had to go back to basing recovery periods on the assumption that some plants would be grazed severely, and on the first day.

Improved Animal Nutrition

The fact that animals move more frequently onto fresh, unfouled ground, means they receive a better plane of nutrition and reduced danger of parasite infection and buildup. Animals moving into a fresh paddock are free to graze almost everywhere, as they encounter no fouling of past dung and urine. They easily take in a good volume of a well-balanced diet. Most often, they select for high protein and energy and for low fiber. One can watch them take mouthfuls of the most leafy material available on first entering a paddock and within a few hours see the paddock transformed from dark to light green in color, even though forage volume appears to have hardly changed.

During the first day in a paddock, the animals tend to select what is readily available, while at the same time dunging, trampling, and urinating over much of the paddock. They do the same the following day, but do not find it quite so easy, because less of the most desirable leafy material remains and they try to avoid grazing on their own fouling of the previous day. Consequently, the second day the animals may experience a lower quality diet. Quality drops again the third day, and so on. The pattern of declining quality and/or volume of diet continues until the animals go to a new paddock. If they ever stay in a paddock until all forage is depleted, the consequent severe drop in nutrition inevitably results in poor performance.

The next chapter will further explain how to manage the generally beneficial aspects of smaller paddocks. Nevertheless, reducing paddock size has one other effect that falls under the heading of time management.

Because animals are grazing at higher density, if they are left in a paddock long enough to overgraze plants, they will overgraze many more plants than they would if grazing at a lower density. Even a twenty-four-hour mistake in timing could mean extreme depletion of forage in a given paddock, loss of selectivity, and a drop in animal performance, so time management and planning becomes more critical as paddock sizes decrease.

Some, on considering this possibility, have decided that more paddocks mean more *risk*. This word implies chance beyond management control. I would rather say that more paddocks decrease risk from weather problems but increase the *penalty for poor management*—poor planning, poor monitoring, or leaving crucial stock moves to untrained people. Some ranchers are now working with what amounts to well over five hundred paddocks in a cell by using a combination of moveable electric fencing and herding. They have almost eliminated risk of weeds, droughts, disease, but would pay dearly in animal performance for negligence and poor planning.

Time and Overbrowsing

Earlier I promised to return to the question of possible discrimination against woody plants when grazing is timed to the needs of perennial grasses. A couple of real-life examples illustrate how this apparent dilemma generally works out in practice. The Karroo area of South Africa has seen some three hundred years of overgrazing of plants and partial rest of soils over a vast expanse of low-rainfall, very brittle environment. Some of the ranches where I worked had once been grassland under herding wildlife populations, but had long ago declined to bare soil and a few scattered desert bushes. In the absence of any alternative, these desert bushes had become the main feed for all livestock and were consequently highly prized by ranchers and range management professionals alike.

Given a holistic goal requiring the reestablishment of perennial grassland, I advised the use of recovery periods that would promote perennial grass plants. To many academics this seemed illogical, as for all practical purposes perennial grasses no longer existed. They claimed, as did many ranchers, that severely defoliated desert brush could not recover in the short recovery periods my recommendation suggested. Available research showed that the desert shrubs in question required anything from a year to 18 months to recover after severe browsing. Pressure grew to make recovery periods reflect this finding.

The ranchers generally had between 5 and 16 paddocks available. To plan on an 18-month recovery period in a 9-paddock cell means grazing periods of about 67 days. Even in a 16-paddock cell, 18-month recovery periods would require average grazing periods of 36 days. Such grazing periods would guarantee overgrazing of any perennial grass plant that might try to establish. In addition, such grazing pressure at the increased stock density of the smaller paddocks would severely defoliate the desert shrubs, thus probably causing them to require the very long recovery period. At the same time, it would put extraordinary nutritional stress on the livestock and could lead to damage from overtrampling in some areas. It would, in other words, make the reestablishment of perennial grassland extremely difficult, if not impossible. Also it would make it difficult to achieve good animal performance without heavy and costly supplementation.

With nine paddocks, 60-day recovery periods would result in 7.5-day average grazing periods. Sixteen paddocks lowers this to 4 days. Such a regime reduces stress on animals, cuts trampling time, and ensures a good chance of achieving a grassland landscape. Also, it does not in fact expose bushes to the kind of heavy and prolonged browsing that necessitates long recovery. Bushes do not regrow from energy in crowns or roots, as do grasses, but rather from remaining leaf. Thus, the species that had survived under the conditions described were not likely to die out from a little overbrowsing. Even their seedlings, once complexity returned, would have more chance of survival.

In this case, perennial grass and many other plants, vestiges of which had in fact persisted, did increase, lowering the pressure on the shrubs still further. As the grass began to provide soil cover, better water and mineral cycles and energy flow supported increasingly rapid change back to a predominently perennial grass community.

In Chapter 21, I gave the example of the very desirable winterfat plants that greatly increased production on an Arizona ranch under higher animal numbers but with the grazing properly planned. Within three years, we began to find young seedlings of this valued plant, which had not occurred in the community for years. In this case, planning recovery periods that advanced perennial grasses lessened severe browsing and allowed a critical amount of regrowth. Furthermore, it provided a healthier grass community that probably lessened the tendency of animals to select winterfat, and it obviously improved the microenvironment at the soil surface through increased animal impact, permitting seeds to establish where they could not before.

The argument that woody plants can also thrive when the length of recovery periods is designed for the benefit of perennial grass may seem paradoxical in light of my statements about shifting the composition of the biological community away from woody plants and toward grassland. The length of recovery periods, and thus grazing periods, and the degree and nature of animal impact, however, can be manipulated to move the composition of biological communities in either direction. By having animals graze grasses without overgrazing them and by using high animal impact, for instance, most grasslands remain grassland without excessive weeds or shrubs.

Grazing in the Dormant Season

So far we have looked at managing time to minimize overgrazing, over-browsing, and trampling during the growing season. What about manipulating recovery periods and grazing periods while perennial grasses are dormant, and thus not as susceptible to overgrazing? Even then of course animals eat and have a physical impact on soil and plants, so many of the same considerations govern the situation as before. Stock will avoid ground fouled by dung and urine, and parasites and infection will usually increase when herds linger in the same area. Hooves will continue to trample. The timing must still ensure that these factors contribute to the health of the soil surface microenvironment and good performance of animals, both wild and domestic.

Dormant periods are the most critical times of year for most wildlife, and their food and cover requirements are heavily influenced by the grazing plan for the livestock. If livestock are merely rotated through the paddocks on an arbitrary schedule, as is tragically so common, it can devastate wildlife. In addition, such rotational grazing commonly results in very high supplemental feed costs because domestic animals will suffer from the same decreasing plane of nutrition inflicted on the wild ones.

Limit the Number of Selections

From what we currently know, animals select their diet in the same way, regardless of season. Each time stock enter a fresh paddock, they balance their diets as best they can. If they enter the same paddock a second time during dormancy, plants will not have regrown any new leaf. However, the effect on animal nutrition will not be the same as a single prolonged stay. An intervening recovery period will have allowed fouling to wear off and the mere act of moving onto fresh forage, even when depleted, seems to stimulate livestock in ways we do not properly understand. Yet undoubtedly the selection from the forage remaining the second, third, and fourth time around will certainly contain less protein and energy and more fiber than before, because no regrowth has occurred between each of these grazings.

In the dormant season, your aim therefore is to limit the number of times the animals have to select forage from the same paddock *and* to move the animals as frequently as possible. The more paddocks you have, the greater your ability to meet both requirements. For example, given a 200-day dormant period, 100 paddocks would enable you to plan one selection from each paddock and grazing periods of 2 days on average in each paddock. If you had only 10 paddocks, stock would have to select over the same forage more than once, probably several times, and moves would be far from frequent. Toward the end of each grazing period, stock would require supplementation to maintain the rumenal microbe populations essential to their digestion. (The rumens, or stomachs, of cud-chewing animals, such as cattle, sheep, goats, deer, and antelope, cannot achieve digestion without these microorganisms.)

In contrast, with 100 paddocks, the stock will constantly move to fresh ground throughout the dormant season, and even on the last day will still enjoy a reasonable plane of nutrition and a quick move to fresh ground. Both cover and forage conditions for wildlife will improve considerably as we have found. But the high amount of fencing that inhibits free wildlife movement counters this to some extent. If herding or strip-grazing can be substituted for massive fencing, not only does the wildlife benefit, but the landscape is far more pleasing to the eye.

Plan a Drought Reserve

It used to be that ranchers would plan for drought by withholding certain areas from grazing during the growing months so they could accumulate forage to be kept in reserve if the following dormant season lasted longer than expected. This practice, however, always decreased the productivity of both forage and animals. Now, we plan for drought by *reserving time*. There are any number of reasons why this method is superior and far less risky, which the *Holistic Grazing Planning Handbook* covers in detail.

Suffice it to say here, that all the land available is used in the growing season because with more paddocks, the better your control of grazing time and thus the greater your forage production. If the dormant season is expected to last 200 days, you add an additional 30 to 90 days or more to that figure, depending on the reliability of your rainfall. The number of selections and the frequency of moves through the dormant season will be based on this higher figure. To ensure that you do not run out of forage, you calculate the number of *animal days* of forage (the amount of forage an animal harvests in a day) available from every paddock and ration them out carefully. This reflects the fact that we also measure drought in days—days until the rain comes, days until growth starts. Your banker doesn't ask, "How many acres do you have in reserve?" but simply, "How long can you hold out?"

Time and the Management of Wild Grazers and Browsers

Exactly the same principles that apply to livestock govern wild grazing and herding animals. Trampled litter and soil do not distinguish between buffalo and cow. The health of the community in the more brittle environments demands some trampling, but any number of animal species can provide it either in a beneficial way or in a detrimental way if they stay too long or come back too often.

In the case of livestock we can easily distinguish between time and numbers as, no matter what the numbers are, we can control the time through fencing or herding. Wild animals do not submit to the same kind of control, and the distinction blurs, especially *because in their case, numbers can influence time*. The social behavior of large unrestricted herds on home ranges bears little resemblance to that of small bands moving randomly in a limited area. In addition, predators, including humans, have a decided effect on the time their prey spends in the proximity of any plant.

Where heavy predation, accident, and disease control numbers, the size of a herd's territory or home range tends to regulate the frequency of return to feeding areas. The concentrated fouling of animals bunched for self-protection will ensure short periods of grazing on the same ground. If lack of predation or of other causes of death allow numbers to rise, home ranges and territories appear to become smaller as more herds occupy the same area and herds return to past feeding grounds sooner. This starts a snowballing breakdown of the ecosystem processes, including the loss of many nonherding wildlife species.

I thought through the logic of all this years ago when doing my early work in the Luangwa and Zambezi Valleys of Zambia and Zimbabwe. However, one bit of evidence did not fit and appeared to disprove the theory. Both the areas in question had very heavy natural predation, which should have provided both population control and reinforced herding instincts. The Luangwa in particular had the highest known concentrations of lions in the world. Why were the ecosystem processes breaking down so badly after we formed game reserves?

One thing both areas had in common was the removal of humans as a predator. Did Man the Hunter have a niche that nothing else could fill? Nearby areas where human hunters and game still coexisted were also breaking down, so perhaps humans were not a vital predator.

A closer look at hunted and protected areas however revealed another difference. *Where humans still held rank among natural predators, the deterioration could clearly be linked to soil exposure through frequent fire.* In the protected areas, soil exposure clearly came more from overgrazing and the consequent destruction of vegetation. The evidence was striking in the 1950s and early 1960s, when the Zambian side of the Zambezi had predation from humans and the Zimbabwean side did not.

Chapter 21 described the destruction of vegetation and soil communities on the Zimbabwean side despite years of heavy elephant culling, initiated as a result of my own faulty research. To keep the elephants tame for tourists, park managers shot them well away from the river, and the elephants soon learned that the river was the safer place to be. As more elephants crowded into the riparian areas, park managers increased their culling efforts, but again, they shot them well away from the river. As a result, the vegetation along the river was badly overgrazed and overbrowsed. Yet much of the vegetation away from the river remained ungrazed and grew rank and old. To make it more palatable, park managers burned it. The more they burned, the more fibrous and less palatable the vegetation gradually became as species changed. More elephants congregated along the river. The cull-burn–cull-burn cycle has continued without letup, even though elephant numbers are a fraction of what they once were and the deterioration of the riparian areas has only worsened.

Where we once, as principal predator, ensured constant movement of the herds we preyed upon and had limited ability to light fires, we have now taken the part of protector and friend, stopping movement and reducing other predators while increasing the frequency of fire worldwide. Successional communities that evolved over millions of years could compensate no better if wolves and lions donned business suits, moved to the suburbs, and sent their agents out to burn the forage and expose soil.

Our concept of national parks set aside for large game needs to change, and fortunately circumstances are compelling scientists in many disciplines to rethink old concepts. In Africa in particular, home of most of the large-game national parks, the sense of urgency to increase understanding has grown dramatically as the decline of the parks is so obvious.

Much new work will be needed to find ways of inducing movement again in wild herding populations and to maintain concentrations in brittle environments. Management schemes now commonly call for cutting off water periodically to force herds to move to other sources. To an extent, this causes movement. However, it does not cause concentration. It does not cause frequent enough movement. It may let nonmobile species die of thirst, thus hindering the buildup of complex communities. I have seen attempts to use this technique, but never seen it work as a realistic means of managing the crucial time factor.

Attractants such as we use with livestock (about which more in Chapter 39) need more research. I started some work in my own game reserve, with encouraging signs, but when the land was expropriated to form a national park, the work was not continued.

In the 1950s a man by the name of Vesey-Fitzgerald, working in the Rukwa valley of Tanzania observed what he called "grazing succession," which might give a clue to the use of livestock herds to induce movement in other species. In each wet season, most big game moved out of the valley and vegetation became very rank. At the onset of the dry months, the game returned in a definite pattern. Those, like elephants, that could handle and digest very coarse, tall, fibrous grass returned first. Next came others that could handle coarse forage opened up to some extent by the elephants. This group included zebra (which have front teeth on both jaws), and buffalo. Finally smaller species requiring more opened forage came in.

It is common in Africa to travel miles looking for game and see nothing. Then one type of animal is seen and immediately several others come into view. Different species of grazing animals do associate to varying degrees, including game and domestic stock. We first detected this on a Zimbabwean ranch that ran 60,000 cattle and a game ranching operation on one and a quarter million acres. We had a test project on 4,000 acres in which we used for the first time a central watering point and a radial layout of 30 paddocks divided by simple fences that, while restraining cattle, allowed game to move freely.

We trebled the stocking rate of the cattle and ran them as one large herd to test the new design under very rapid increases in livestock numbers, all of which attracted condemnation from range and wildlife experts. Hunters in the test area soon discovered that the game, mainly zebra, kudu, wildebeest, giraffe, and impala, routinely turned up in paddocks two moves behind the large herd of cattle. Depending on plant growth rate and speed of cattle move, they thus chose to feed two to four days later on the resprouting plants.

Investigation on other ranches confirmed a similar link between livestock moving in concentration and game. Sometimes the game followed cattle or sheep, and at other times moved with them in what amounted to a mixed herd, although the game might stay slightly off to one side or else mingle at night when human disturbance was absent. Such assocations open up real management possibilities for better control of time when both wild and domestic grazers are present.

In the case of our test project in Zimbabwe, the coming of the game only a few days after the stock lengthened the grazing period. Even when the cattle moved every day, plants were exposed for three days (a single intervening day between the cattle and the game was not enough time for grazed plants to recover). In the same way, the recovery period was shortened from the time the game left until the cattle returned. In this case, I took the decision to leave the timings as they were to see if high animal impact would overcome a slight degree of overgrazing periodically, and it did. The land recovered dramatically.

At this stage, you may feel that even a superhuman time manager could not simultaneously restore the most severely bitten plant and think about game tagging along behind his cattle. Fortunately time factors do not stand alone, and perfection is not necessary. Other influences, such as animal impact, go on simultaneously in the community, and you will not have to reach your holistic goal solely through time management and grazing.

You should do your best, through careful planning of time, to minimize overgrazing, but between the livestock and the wild grazers some will occur nonetheless. Yet, even as overgrazing tends to push biological succession backward, at the same time high animal impact can overwhelm that tendency and keep it moving forward. Today's alarming degree of overgrazing in the more brittle environments came about under low animal impact, which in turn provided less than ideal conditions for the establishment of young plants. If seeds and sprouts can establish, losses to overgrazing matter far less, as eons of evolutionary history show.

Conclusion

Because it is so new to us, it has been necessary to devote considerable space to the concept of time as it relates to our management of plants, soils, livestock, and wildlife. Experience in many contexts in many countries is now showing clearly that planning grazings to manage time will be important in maintaining the health of savannas and water catchments and in halting the advance of deserts throughout the world. I am sure we have by no means yet seen the full implications. Let's now proceed to those management guidelines that cover animal impact, the other aspect of livestock grazing that has to be understood and planned for.

39

Stock Density and Herd Effect: Using Animals to Shape the Landscape

Stock density and herd effect are the two management guidelines that apply when the tools of grazing and animal impact are used to alter soil conditions or vegetation.

Stock density refers to the number of animals at a given moment in time in a given confined area of land. Thus, if 100 animals are in a 100-acre paddock today, the stock density is 1 to 1 (one animal to one acre). If tomorrow these 100 animals are moved to a 200-acre paddock, the stock density would then be 1 to 2 (one animal to two acres).

Herd effect, on the other hand, cannot be quantified. It is merely the effect on soils and plants that a large number of animals have if they bunch so closely that *their behavior changes.* When the animals are spread out, their hooves leave few signs of disturbance on the soil surface, apart from when it is wet. When they are bunched and milling around on the land or are excited, they tread down old coarse plant material, raising dust at times, and chipping the soil surface. The larger the herd, the greater the effect.

Stock Density

As Chapter 38 made clear, stock density has a strong relationship to the management of grazing, browsing, and trampling time, but it deserves some discussion in its own right. Because of the prejudice that hooves in any context damage soils and plants, low stock density has usually characterized management of livestock on croplands, grasslands, and water catchments. Unfortunately, grazing at low stock density almost universally causes problems on the land—chief among them partial rest of soils and plants—and, in the long term, for the animals. Our traditional bias, however, made us attribute the many damaging side effects of grazing at low stock density to other causes.

Low stock density and the partial rest allied with it, not overgrazing or overstocking, should bear the blame for many serious range and production problems, including severe trailing, successional shifts toward brush and weeds, grasshopper outbreaks, poor animal performance and high supplemental feed costs, excessive use of fire to even out grazing and to suppress brush, the development of mosaics of grazed-out patches, decreased water cycle effectiveness, and thus an increase in both drought and flood problems.

A high degree of patchiness and trailing is a hallmark of low density, the grazed patches commonly ending sharply where ungrazed plants, often of the same species, begin, as if a gardener had laid them out. Some people seeing this talk of patch grazing or spot grazing. When I first recognized it, I called it hippo grazing because hippos move over grassland like a lawn mower, their wide flat mouths taking everything and leaving a sharp edge where they stop. The term *low-density grazing* serves better than any of these names because it describes the process and suggests a solution.

Photo 39-1 is an aerial view of a ranch that has seen many years of low-density grazing. A mosaic of heavily overgrazed and seriously overrested

Photo 39-1 *Low density grazing pattern seen from the air with two different stocking rates. The land in the foreground, grazed at very low density (and a lower stocking rate), shows less of the light-colored patches where grasses are heavily overgrazed and more of the darker-colored patches where grass plants have overrested and a shift is occurring to woody vegetation, mainly mesquite. Coahuila, Mexico.*

patches shows clearly. This situation developed at the old so-called correct stocking rate and under continuous grazing. When I have shown similar pictures before, some viewers have insisted that the pattern of dark and light patches was due to soil differences and not grazing at low densities. So I took this picture along a fence between two paddocks on the same ranch that were grazed at different densities. The land in the foreground, grazed at very low density, shows less of the light-colored patches where plants are heavily overgrazed, and thus shows clearly that the mosaic seen is due to grazing patterns and not soil differences.

Chapter 38 made an ample case for developing many paddocks or strip grazing within paddocks and described how, as this proceeds, certain things follow automatically. Time in paddocks, or on the land within a paddock, gets shorter, while stock densities get higher, dung and urine are more evenly distributed, and animals move faster to fresh ground. However, aside from these effects, there are good reasons for increasing stock density for its own sake. Animal performance commonly ranks first among them.

Stock Density and Animal Performance

Poor animal performance plagued my early work with ranchers. Although careful monitoring clearly documented the improvement of plant communities and soils when we started managing grazing time, no class of livestock performed as well as the same animals continuously grazing a deteriorating control area. On stable irrigated pastures, André Voisin's work guided us to success, but large concentrated herds on rangelands did not thrive until I grasped the full significance of stock density.

For eight years, I carried the albatross of almost continuous poor animal performance while my many critics rubbed their hands and snickered. As it turned out, a major part of the problem was my failure to question the conventional wisdom that patchy grazing was due to animals selecting certain species of more palatable grasses and rejecting others less palatable. Academic papers and textbooks had belabored the subject ad nauseam and allayed any doubt.

One day, while discussing the problem of poor performance with a ranch manager in Swaziland as we walked over his land, a pair of grass plants of the same species caught my eye, and the pieces of the puzzle began to fall in place. Range scientists considered this species undesirable, believing that its strong aroma made it unpalatable, and indeed one plant stood untouched in a rank clump, but another, right next to it, had been eaten right down. I had noticed such things before but had never paid them much attention, so I just sat down and thought for a long time.

I asked myself, "Why would two plants of the same kind, enjoying the same weather, soil, moisture, and exposure to cattle, come to such different ends?" After a while, I startled the already bewildered manager by blurting out the observation that "cattle don't select species, they don't even know the Latin name of this plant." What they were selecting was the freshest and leafiest forage on *any species.*

It had taken me years to register that although cattle carefully and intelligently select their diet, they do it by what they actually sense in front of them, not by choosing from a Linnean menu of desirable and undesirable species. They will eat fresh tender leaves of undesirable brand X and leave old, stale leaves of desirable brand Y.

I immediately determined to approach my old dilemma from a new tack. I had already noted that in smaller paddocks, where animals grazed at higher density, the plant community tended to have more leaf and less fiber. If we increased stock density all over, by subdividing large paddocks and combining several herds into one or two larger ones, we should be able to improve animal performance generally. To convince the ranchers I was then working with to try it, I used the following analogy.

Assume I asked you to visit for a year. As a good host, I ask you for a list of your favorite foods (your most desired species), and on your arrival you find a smorgasbord of every one of your selections, from which you choose a substantial meal but of course leave many items untouched or only nibbled. While you rest, I replace exactly what you ate, leaving everything else as before. At the next meal you choose again, and I replace only what you actually ate.

After a few months, you will only dare eat things I replaced in the last day or so, despite the fact that everything on the table started out as a "desirable species." Some of the most delectable dishes now reek from mold and decay. If I suddenly stopped replacing your daily selection, your performance would take a nasty drop as you spent eating time picking through that old garbage. The problem was, of course, low-density feeding! Had I invited enough people to sit around the table and replaced everything in the same way, every meal would have been as good as the last.

As soon as the ranchers increased stock density, animal performance did in fact improve, but the degree of improvement varied on the different properties and with different managers. By this time I had several hundred clients in five countries and ample evidence led to a diagnosis that helped to clarify the spotty results. All of these ranchers had started out with a fairly high percentage of overrested or stale plants because of low-density grazing in the past, and this was a factor in every case. However, rainfall and soil type and the manager's ability to plan and monitor the grazings were largely responsible for the variation in animal performance once stock density was increased.

Rainfall and Soil Type Make a Difference

Animal performance improved the most in low-rainfall areas with highly mineralized and more alkaline soils. These areas supported forage that had less fiber, shorter height, and better curing properties. Higher mineralization in the plants from these soils, I surmised, kept rumenal microbe populations high in the animals, thus maximizing digestive efficiency and leading to better performance, *even on old forage*. Higher-rainfall areas, however, characterized by leached and more acidic soils, produced generally taller, tougher forage of much higher fiber content. Older perennial grass plants had little or no feed value compared to plants of similar age in low-rainfall, highly mineralized soils. Without heavy mineral, protein, and energy supplementation rumenal microbes most likely decreased and livestock performance fell badly.

It was apparent that we could increase stock density immediately in the low-rainfall/highly mineralized soil situation and experience little or no initial drop in performance. From there on, the situation would only get better. In the high-rainfall/leached soil situation, however, we had to make some decisions about how to deal with the old forage and the inevitable drop in performance: we could burn the forage or perhaps mow it, at considerable expense; we could provide a high level of supplementary feed to the animals, or we could bite the bullet and accept the performance loss during the first few times through the paddocks, recognizing it as a legacy of the past. The latter could be mitigated somewhat if one tried to graze and to trample down the old stale forage at a time when the animals could drop in condition without the rancher suffering a financial loss.

Rainfall and soil type also affected the *amount* of stock density needed. In low-rainfall areas with highly mineralized soils, you could get by with less density and could afford to increase it gradually. In these areas, grazing cells with as few as eight paddocks typically showed the patchiness of low-density grazing at least part of the year. Although stock density had more than doubled in these cases, it still was not sufficient to even out the forage before the end of the growing season. Many plants would be left ungrazed, simply because in the growing season you are basing recovery periods on how long it takes a severely grazed plant to recover. During periods of rapid growth, when grazing periods were shorter, many plants would remain ungrazed. During slow growth, animals would start to graze some of the ungrazed plants that, because they were still fairly nutritious caused no drop in performance. Most of the time, however, you would end the growing season with a degree of patchiness. Once growth ceased and you began to ration out the remaining forage, the ungrazed patches would generally be cleaned up, with the animals dropping in performance only slightly.

In areas of high rainfall and leached soils, animal performance almost always suffered when paddocks were this few and stock density relatively low, even though stocking rates had been doubled. In the growing season, animals would start to drop in performance when growth slowed and grazing periods lengthened, because much of the forage available had not been grazed previously and had lost its nutritional value. The patchiness that developed in these areas was even greater because of the volume of forage produced as a result of the high rainfall. By the end of the growing season, a large proportion of the forage was rank and of little use in sustaining animals through the dormant season, unless missing nutrients were provided in a supplement.

In the days before I understood the full implications of stock density and time, I cost my long-suffering clients in high-rainfall areas many thousands of dollars in poor animal performance by recommending they start off with as few as eight to ten paddocks. Now, in order to attain good animal performance in that situation, I would try to get to one hundred paddocks or strip-graze within paddocks as quickly as possible. That would allow enough density to ensure that animals would graze or trample a much higher proportion of plants in each paddock during the growing season, keeping them fresh and nutritious in fast or slow growth and more capable of sustaining animals through the dormant season.

Grazing Planning Makes a Difference

Once we had sorted out the variations occurring because of rainfall and soil types, we still had to contend with the differences that appeared to be attributable to management. The poorest results occurred among managers who failed to monitor plant growth rates and thus to properly adjust the grazing and recovery periods they had planned. The problems generally arose when fast growth slowed down, but grazing and recovery periods were not changed to reflect this. Rapid moves, and thus shorter grazing periods generally led to a short-term benefit to the animals as they moved onto new ground. However, the quicker moves meant that recovery times were shortened as well, and in slow growth periods that meant the animals would return before plants had had time to recover from a previous grazing. Those plants grazed severely in the previous grazing period would now be overgrazed. Those plants not grazed at all or only lightly would tend to be left and to grow somewhat more stale.

Using the smorgasbord analogy once more, it is as though people have suddenly found they don't have time to eat all they actually can because their meal time has been shortened. The butler moves them on half way through the main course. That food eaten gets replaced according to standard practice, but the rest grows a little more stale. When again the next day they have only ten minutes to eat, the stale gets staler. Once again, matters progress until they have to eat stale food, and performance drops. Technically we have enough people (density) at the table to keep the food fresh, but without enough time to clean their plates, much of the food grows stale anyway.

In this case, the animals are forced to eat the stale food almost immediately because the plants they overgrazed the last time have been unable to produce enough fresh forage to feed them all. In a low-rainfall area with highly mineralized soils, performance in this case may drop too little to draw immediate attention. In high-rainfall areas, the old grass will have so little nutritional value that serious stock stress and hunger appear almost at once.

By moving the animals according to plant growth rates, both overgrazing and overresting are thus minimized and the plants are more evenly used. Whenever livestock moves have to be slowed down with slower daily growth rates, individual animal performance is likely to be less than it would have been on continued fast moves. However, as we have just learned, where continued fast moves benefit the animals in the short term, they damage both land and animals in the long term if recovery periods are too short. Even at high stock densities, grazing planning is abandoned at great peril.

In speaking of stock density I have not made much distinction between brittle and nonbrittle environments because stock density seems to be required at either extreme of the brittleness scale *if you are attempting to manage and maintain grasslands*. Rainfall and soil leached by high rainfall play a bigger role than position on the brittleness scale in determining how much density you need or how little you can get away with.

The brittleness scale very much influences the need for herd effect, however, for the simple reason that herding ungulates and pack-hunting predators evolved with the soils and vegetation in the more brittle, lower-rainfall environments, which herd effect helped to shape.

Herd Effect

Herd effect is the main management guideline we use to achieve high animal impact wherever needed, be it on croplands, rangelands, or critical water catchments surrounding towns and cities in brittle environments. As mentioned, herd effect is produced by a change in animal behavior. Although this bunching, milling, excited behavior strongly affects the entire biological community, and wild herds in truly wild conditions exhibit it frequently, herding either wildlife or livestock do not produce much herd effect without outside stimulus. Inducing herd effect thus constitutes one of the biggest challenges in the management of brittle environment grasslands and forests, and the difficulty of inducing enough of it is equally taxing.

It is clear from the study of herding animals (and some fish and birds), that large numbers and bunched, milling behavior were the most effective protection developed against predators until the advent of modern humanity. Many excellent television documentaries show how hard predators must work to beat that defense to isolate the weak calf or the aging bull and to bring it down. While the carnivores do their job, the ungulates in the milling herd, concentrated for protection, do not respect the grass and brush beneath their hooves as they do when grazing unmolested. Free from fear of fang, claw, or the spear of pack-hunting humans, even instinctively timid wild animals soon lose the habit of vigilance, scatter widely when grazing, and avoid stepping on anything as uncomfortable as a tussock of old grass or a spiny shrub.

Starting in my game department days, I gradually built on the observation that wherever predators caused bunching and the formation of large herds, the concentrated dung and urine of the herd also induced movement, and this in turn regulated the overgrazing of plants by governing their time of exposure and reexposure to animals. Wherever the pack-hunting predators and their large prey were reduced or absent altogether over prolonged periods, the grassland became much more fragile, plant spacing widened, and more algae flourished on ground that became bare between plants. Rhizomes, runners, and stolons, rather than seeds, often became the main agents of grass propagation.

For several years I lived close to large buffalo herds, as well as elephants and many other game animals, followed by a varied host of predators in high numbers. Buffalo gathered into herds running to thousands, and even elephants on good grassland gathered in loose herds that I estimated at six hundred or more. At times, I would pick up tracks several days old and follow them to find a herd. In places, even an inexperienced tracker could follow the spoor at a trot. Elsewhere the trail would dissipate almost entirely, although the country did not change. That happened whenever the animals spread to feed. At such times, their hooves avoided coarse plants and did not break soil surfaces or trample old plant material as much as they did when they were bunched or excited.

Since then I have observed the same differences among all herding animals and even humans. When tracking men, as I did often during Zimbabwe's long civil war, one learns much about the mental and physical state of the quarry by noting the way he places his feet. Individuals in an excited group, walking and talking, leave a very different trail from an individual walking quietly alone. A starving, thirsty, or panicking person will not place his feet the way a calmer man would.

Without pack-hunting predators, most herding animals break into smaller herds and remain spread out most of the time. For several million years, predator-induced herd effect was a feature of evolving grasslands. But in the last instant of the last million years, human activity changed that, initially by eliminating many of the large herding populations, and later their predators when they turned on domestic stock. In environments that are brittle to any degree, we have generally failed to grasp what this massive change in animal behavior means to a piece of ground and the biological community living within and on it.

The vast scale of desertification in the world today attests to the enormous impact of these human-induced changes. We would instinctively understand the devastation caused by withholding rain showers that had occurred for eons, but *the damage to water cycles, in particular, caused by eliminating herd effect and replacing it with fire, has in reality done that very thing.*

Earlier, we defined stock density as a function of paddock size and number of animals. Herd effect, however, results from animal numbers and behavior, regardless of paddock size. Long ago the world's most productive brittle grasslands, such as those in North America and Africa, had extremely low stock density, as the paddock was a whole continent. However, as herds were so vast and wolves, lions, cheetahs, hyenas, wild dogs, and hunting tribes so prevalent, herd effect was great and occurring somewhere most of the time.

Chapter 22 explained that the tool of animal impact is applied through the guidelines of stock density and herd effect. A situation may call for one or the other or both for maximum effect. A number of researchers have published papers concluding that animal impact does not produce the sort of changes in the biological community, water and mineral cycles, and energy flow that I describe in my work. In fact, they designed their projects without any understanding of the totally new concept of herd effect and made no effort to apply it. Thus, they have effectively proved that *low stock density* does not do what I claim *high herd effect* does. In two of the research projects that I have in mind, stock density was applied to brittle environment communities that really needed herd effect. The herds, in fact, were minute, in one case consisting of two steers that could not have done much even if the researchers had excited or bunched them.[1] Two steers enclosed in a one-acre paddock will not have anywhere near the same effect as two hundred steers bunched for a time within a 100-acre paddock, although the stock density is the same.

Why researchers studying animal impact have consistently ignored herd effect is not easy to understand. A great deal of money and effort has been wasted over the years studying low animal impact over prolonged time instead of studying high animal impact over brief periods. Although it cannot easily be isolated for research, herd effect can readily be observed and monitored in the field. Grazing, too, cannot be easily isolated for study, but many researchers have still studied it and given us many insights. Perhaps our belief that heavy trampling is damaging is so deep that we cannot bring ourselves to investigate a *known* fact.

Practical Demonstrations of Herd Effect

To help researchers and stockmen alike to overcome their fear of trampling, and therefore of herd effect, we now encourage them to conduct

Photo 39-2 *The response to herd effect. Nearly every plant was grazed or trampled down (top photo) when four hundred cattle were crowded into this five-acre test enclosure for the better part of a day. One year later (bottom photo) the growth inside the enclosure was more lush than any outside it. Arizona (courtesy Dan Daggett).*

simple experiments for their own benefit. These usually take the form of placing hundreds of animals very briefly—a few hours at most—into small enclosures to see what happens to the land over time. Photo 39-2 includes before and after photos of one of these experimental plots. In this case both the ranch manager and his staff, as well as local environmentalists, wanted to see for themselves if what I was saying about herd effect applied in their case. The day before 400 cattle were to be enclosed on about 5 acres of land, it rained heavily and they phoned me to see if they should wait until the soil dried out. I saw no need as wet soils have been trampled billions of times over the eons. They went ahead, and as you can see in the top photo, nearly every plant was grazed or trampled down. But one year later, the bottom photo shows that the growth inside the enclosure was more lush than any outside it. Although the demonstration was convincing, its greater value was the confidence it built in those who participated in the exercise.

Commonly, these enclosures are made fairly small, such as one acre (half a hectare) or less in size. The number of cattle (or other stock) used has ranged from 300 to 1,000. In all cases, the aim is to achieve maximum density for minimum time—anything from an hour to a few hours, depending on the number of animals and the amount of trampling and dunging they are able to produce within the space allowed them. Bear in mind that a herd of 5,000 wild grazers would normally have given any particular piece of ground only a *few minutes* of concentrated impact in many months or even years.

Inducing Herd Effect Routinely

When our ancestors first domesticated livestock and protected them from predators by herding them, we removed much of the tendency to produce herd effect. This holds true for the American rancher as well as the Andalusian shepherd or African nomad today. Fencing and grazing systems designed to spread livestock evenly over the land in a totally unnatural manner have exacerbated the problem, severely disrupting the evolutionary interdependence of animals, plants, and soils.

Unfortunately, even though we now see the need to produce herd effect over large areas, generating it routinely remains a problem. Obviously, wolves and lions enlisted in the management of domestic sheep and cattle might eat into profit. Many people, however, do not see that the same problem arises in managing wild animals even in our national parks. In many parks predators are few, and typically subsistence hunting by indigenous human populations is rarely permitted. Frequently the land base is so limited that it does not allow herd sizes large enough to provide adequate trampling, or sufficient to sustain enough predators.

Now, we must learn how to simulate the predator-induced behavior, and we have learned much over the past thirty years. The most successful methods so far involve training and attracting animals to an edible reward that induces excitement and is consumed quickly or using a combination of herding and temporary electric fencing to push stock density so high that animal behavior changes. More on both these techniques will come later.

The Type of Livestock Matters

While herd effect provided by any type of animal is better than none, the type of animal may make a difference. Almost any livestock—sheep, goats, cattle, or horses—can produce adequate impact on sandy soil. However, on tropical clay soils that produce a hard surface cap, sheep and goats have limited effect. Only cattle or horses are capable of breaking it enough for soil respiration to improve. On some soils, horses have a much more effective impact than cattle, but unfortunately we seldom have very large horse herds, so cattle must suffice.

The vegetation also should influence the type of animal you select. Although sheep and goats in animated herds can trample short vegetation, they simply avoid very tall old grass clumps. For such situations and for opening up very dense brush to let in light and increase grass growth, larger animals, such as cattle, are necessary.

Herd Size Matters

Deeply rooted emotion and myth surround the question of herd sizes, especially among cattle producers. Prominent cattlemen heavily condemned me for even suggesting that herds of 200 cows could be run and still breed well. Beyond 140 cows lay the edge of the world and a long fall to disaster. Nevertheless, we have gradually increased herd sizes without encountering any problems. To date, we have not yet had one scrap of evidence that conception rate or weaning weight in breeding herds depends on anything outside quality of handling, health, and nutrition. We have no evidence yet of any drop in performance in any large herd, given good handling facilities, calm handling, and well-planned grazing.

Having worked with vast buffalo herds, as well as cattle herds of up to 5,000, I have no doubt in my own mind that, to manage brittle-environment water catchments in particular, the larger the herd the better. Herds of 2,000 to 5,000 head followed by longer recovery produce far better results than small ones of 200 to 500 followed by shorter recovery periods. Unfortunately land is now so divided and attitudes so entrenched that we often have to make do with small herds and accept the painfully slow land recovery that results.

Using Attractants to Induce Herd Effect

Two methods for inducing herd effect have so far proven effective. The use of attractants to bunch and excite the animals for short periods is the technique we have used the longest, and it is the simplest to apply.

Supplemental feed cubes, a bale of hay, or a few handfuls of granular salt, for animals purposely deprived of salt, will work as attractants. Long-lasting blocks of supplement, molasses/urea liquid licks or salt blocks do not because they generally do not excite the animals, which come for the blocks a few at a time and linger too long in the vicinity, pulverizing the surface and excessively compacting the soil. Occasionally situations arise that allow use of herd effect without a concern for keeping the time short. Say, for example, you needed a firebreak through very dense brush. In this case attractants can be used that hold animals for longer periods, such as a dilute molasses or saline spray over the vegetation, or supplement blocks.

You can easily train animals to come to a piece of ground on which you have scattered an attractant if you blow a whistle each time you do. The animals soon associate the sound of the whistle with a reward and will generally come to you anywhere. If you have a constantly changing herd, as ranchers running yearlings often do, it helps to hold back a few trained animals so the new group learns faster. Once they learn to respond, a herd can be drawn in an excited bunch to any spot on the land where herd effect is needed to build toward a future landscape.

Photo 39-3 shows a herd of 2,000 animals on a Texas ranch. The herd

Photo 39-3 *Part of a herd of 2,000 cattle. Not fearing predation, the animals are widely dispersed; even very young calves lie far from their mothers. Texas.*

has no fear of predators and is spread out in the fashion typical today on most ranges. Even young animals lie in the grass away from others, fearless and safe. Photo 39-4 is a close-up view of the ground itself under the influence of this large, but thinly spread, herd. The soil is barely impacted, and a slick of algae covers the surface despite three years of relatively high stock density. New plants have difficulty establishing, and soil respiration is badly impeded.

In photo 39-5, the herd has been attracted to the area shown in the previous illustration. The animals are bunched, milling and excited to the extent that they are kicking up dust. Photo 39-6 shows the same piece of ground about three minutes later. The contrast is great indeed. Any gardener wanting to grow seeds on that soil would appreciate the difference immediately. Soil respiration is improved, water can penetrate faster, and new plants can germinate and establish more quickly.

This technique has one major drawback: very little ground is impacted over time. Two thousand head will seriously affect an area only about 50 yards across each time they are attracted, although somewhat lesser impact grades out from there. Very few managers are able, nor is it practical, to induce herd effect with attractants more frequently than once a day.

The herds of the past were of many different species and vulnerable to predation day and night, year round. Each herd might have remained bunched for about sixteen hours a day while not feeding. Now, we typically have one species, usually cattle or sheep, feeding or resting unbunched

Photo 39-4 *Close-up view of the soil surface between grass plants in the foreground of photo 39-3. The soil is hard-capped, covered with algae, and barely able to breathe, making it difficult for new plants to establish.*

Photo 39-5 *To induce herd effect, the herd of 2,000 has been attracted to the spot shown in Photo 39-4 with supplementary feed. The bunched and excited animals place their hooves carelessly, breaking the soil cap and raising dust.*

Photo 39-6 *Close-up view of the same spot three minutes later. The soil looks as if a gardener had hoed it and can now breathe. Water can also penetrate faster, and new plants can germinate and establish more quickly.*

for over twenty-three hours a day. When we supply attractants we might concentrate them on a smidgeon of land for only five or ten minutes.

Using Ultra-high Densities to Induce Herd Effect

At this writing, three ranchers in Zimbabwe, Johann and Wessel Zietzman and Hendrik O'Neill, are pioneering the use of ultra-high densities of cattle to produce herd effect similar in extent to what may have occurred in the past. Using a combination of herding and portable electric fencing to strip-graze very small areas of land within a few paddocks during the day, they have achieved unimaginable stock densities—ranging from 1,000 to 2,000 animals to the acre (3,000 to 5,000 per hectare)—and nearly continual herd effect. Remember that as paddock size decreases, so do grazing periods, and thus on these ranches grazing periods are measured in hours rather than days. Recovery times, on the other hand, run as long as 200 days or more, depending on the grazing plan and the needs of the land, cattle, and wildlife.

The behavior of the animals clearly changes at such densities—their hooves break up capped soils and knock down old plants. Though we cannot say for sure why it does, we do know it is related to the large animal numbers and the limited grazing space that each animal appears eager to call its own. Although one might expect otherwise, animal performance appears not to suffer unduly, even, as in the case of these three ranchers, when running breeding herds that include small calves.

As you can see in photo 39-7, a photo taken on the O'Neill ranch, there is no shortage of forage. It is the dormant season and the cattle are being used to clean up what remains of the old forage, which is now less rank than it was in earlier years. The cattle are in reasonably good condition, even though this is a fairly high-rainfall (30-inch/750-mm) area. They

Photo 39-7
Cattle grazing at ultra-high density. The herdsman is removing the single electric wire that contains the herd so the animals can move onto the next small area, which they will graze for about an hour. Zimbabwe.

Photo 39-8 *Healthy stream vegetation following planned grazing and periodic ultra-high cattle densities. Zimbabwe.*

are about to move into the area to the left of the fence, which was last grazed many months before. Photo 39-8 is a view of a riparian area on the same ranch that has healed nicely after several doses of herd effect produced by animals grazing at ultra-high density.

Obviously, herd effect is greatest when the animals are new to grazing at such high densities and decreases as they grow accustomed to the practice. However, herd effect is still greater and more continual on these ranches than we have ever managed to achieve before. This, for me, is the most exciting development in years, because it offers a practical (and profitable) way to attain increased herd effect over millions of acres of rangeland that have suffered from several centuries of low-density grazing and partial rest. The *Holistic Grazing Planning Handbook* covers this subject in more detail.

Conclusion

The guidelines for stock density and herd effect concern a tool new to us of great power—animal impact. I hope readers other than livestock operators have stuck with me thus far, as an understanding of herd effect in particular is essential in making informed decisions regarding the water catchments that sustain towns and cities in brittle environments. In the future, as knowledge increases and attitudes change, I believe that fewer, larger herds will become the principal tool in watershed management on the public lands of America and in desertification reclamation work all over the world.

40

Cropping: Practices That More Closely Mimic Nature

G rowing crops always involves the creation of artificial conditions and the loss of the natural balances and inherent stability of the original biological community. Instead of a variety of plants and perennial ground cover, a small number of crops make only part-time use of the space available. The soil is exposed to wind and rain to a far greater extent than before, particularly where fields are left bare for part of the year, leading to much higher rates of soil erosion and a less effective water cycle than under natural conditions. Mineral cycling is also disrupted and extra inputs in the form of manures or fertilizers are required to keep soils productive.

The history of agriculture is, in effect, the story of how various societies have attempted to deal with the inevitable problems linked with its development: soil erosion, loss of fertility, loss of biodiversity, and the instability associated with simplicity. More than twenty civilizations, starting with those in Mesopotamia, the Indus Valley, China, and later the Americas, have collapsed, largely because these problems overwhelmed them.

The advantage of growing crops, as opposed to gathering them in the wild, is that more food can be produced from a smaller area of land, generating a surplus over the needs of the farmer. This surplus is what made civilization possible because, as mentioned elsewhere, it freed some people to pursue other activities. However, reliance on a small number of crops grown in a specialized environment increased vulnerability to crop failure and initiated the decline of increasingly vast areas of land. Continuous cultivation of the same area lowered soil fertility, crop production became more difficult, yields fell and with them the surplus available for distribution within society.

Human population growth compounded the problem. Productivity would rise as more land was brought under cultivation to feed growing numbers; as new crops, such as those discovered in the Americas, were added; as crop rotations improved; or when better equipment was developed. But population would also rise. As most people tended to be malnourished even in the best of times, crop failures that occurred when a population was at its peak frequently led to famine. Historical accounts catalog an unrelenting series of famines on every continent on which agriculture had been adopted right up to the nineteenth century. Until that time, most of the world's human inhabitants lived on the edge of starvation.

A number of innovations gradually helped to even out fluctuations in the food supply. Improved transportation, beginning with railways, enabled crops to reach areas where they were in demand before the crops perished; chilling and refrigeration made it possible to ship produce over even greater distances. But the most notable innovation was the use of fertilizers. Until the nineteenth century farms depended almost entirely on manures and composts produced on the farm itself to maintain soil fertility. Then European countries, and later the United States, began to import guano and phosphates mined from territories under their control, which increased production in these countries markedly. With the creation of the first artificial fertilizers (superphosphates) in the 1840s and nitrogenous fertilizers in the 1920s the focus of agriculture in the industrialized countries began to change from one based on a relationship between soils, plants, and animals, to one based on inputs and outputs. Agriculture became an industry.

Mechanization of agriculture had an equally dramatic impact because it led to a shift from small, mixed fields to large ones devoted to a single crop that machines could harvest more efficiently. Since monocrops are more susceptible to diseases and pests, this resulted in the increasing use of chemically engineered herbicides and insecticides, a further decrease in biodiversity, and ever rising input costs.

Productivity soared under high-input mechanized cropping practices, but the social and environmental costs were staggering. Millions of small farmers have since been displaced, more land is now lost to cultivation (through deterioration) than is brought into production annually, and we have rendered many environments toxic or sterile to varying degrees.

There can be little doubt that a change in direction is needed for agriculture if we are to sustain our present civilization and its enormous population. In the last fifty years we have tended to treat our soils merely as a medium in which to hold crops upright while we pour chemicals over them. In reality, soil is a living organism, one that respires and reproduces itself, as most living organisms do, and it has to be nurtured. To do so we must strive to create an agriculture that more closely mimics nature, one that enhances, rather than diminishes, water and mineral cycles, energy flow, and community dynamics. In my own experience and that of others seeking to find better ways, this focus leads to some fundamental guidelines.

Keep Soil Covered Throughout the Year

All living organisms have a skin or protective covering of some sort. If a significant proportion of it is removed, the organism dies whether the organism be living soil or human burn victim. A soil's skin is made up primarily of plant material—some of it living, but most of it dead or decaying at the soil surface. This covering insulates the life in the soil from temperature and moisture extremes over short periods and protects the soil crumb structure so essential to water penetration and aeration from destruction by raindrops. It also provides a hospitable environment for billions of organisms that break nutrients down so they can return underground for recycling. An exposed soil is at the mercy of wind and rain, which will erode it ruthlessly. The World Resources Institute estimates that worldwide farms are losing about 24 billion tons of topsoil a year because of soil exposure.

On conventionally managed croplands, the majority of the soil surface between the plants is exposed. After harvest, even more soil is exposed. Many croplands remain bare over winter. Others are deliberately kept bare and harrowed over a fallow year to grow a crop on two years' rainfall. Yet, there are any number of ways to keep cropland soils covered *throughout the year* including the use of conservation tillage; the planting of cover crops over winter; intercropping low-growing, shade-tolerant crops among taller ones; using animals rather than fire, plow, or harrow to remove crop residues (while leaving enough material to provide soil cover). If the American researchers mentioned in Chapter 22 are able to develop perennial grain crops that can replace the annual grains we cultivate today, this will enable us to keep many millions of acres of soil covered year round.

Do Not Turn Soil Over

To mimic nature, soil should be worked from the surface just as for millions of years the hooves of herding animals have done, or the claws of turkeys, guineafowl, other birds, and many small creatures have done. Yet, dating from the invention of the first plow, we have generally done just the opposite. In the 1940s Edward Faulkner, in his book, *Plowman's Folly,* alerted farmers to the damage done by deep plowing in which top soil is turned right under and subsoil brought to the surface en masse. In turning over the protective surface mulch, he explained, plowing not only exposes soil to the elements, it also compresses the turned-under "trash" into a narrow layer deeper down that is unable to decay and thus hampers the growth of plant roots.

When you think of soil in terms of the complex biological community that it is, Faulkner's argument makes sense. If a mass of plant material grows and only a small proportion of it is harvested (corn for instance) what happens to all that residue? Generally it is plowed under "so the organic matter can be returned to the soil." But this is *raw* organic matter, not the mature humus that develops gradually with the help of plant roots and billions of microorganisms. Raw organic matter, together with the mass aeration caused by the plowing, leads to problems, including an increase in bacteria that consume the much-needed humus.

Any time you turn soil over, organisms that have established in a certain microenvironment, either deeper underground or close to the surface, are suddenly placed in a different one. The result is not unlike what would occur if you dumped all the residents of a European city into the middle of the Sahara and the Sahara's few inhabitants into the city overnight. Although we can imagine the chaos, suffering, and death caused by such an action, we fail to see its parallel in the billions of soil organisms that are displaced any time we turn soil over. Unlike the plow, the surface disturbance provided by herding or rooting animals, or even human gardeners, is generally beneficial as they do not actually turn deeper soil layers over.

After a field is plowed, soil communities will start to rebuild, but they are immediately set back once the field is plowed again. In the 1960s French pasture specialist André Voisin recorded the "years of depression" that followed the plowing of a field. Production steadily dropped to a low in about the seventh year. If the field was not plowed again, it would steadily improve, eventually surpassing its initial productivity.[1]

A few years ago I took a handful of pristine soil from an uncleared forest in Pennsylvania that bordered an organic farming research station. The forest soil was dark and alive and smelled like soil should. Placed on the organically farmed fields nearby, which had been plowed for many years, the contrast was stark indeed, although management on that farm far surpassed most in the country. So much of the fragrance, life, and organic content had left the pale soil in the cropped field.

Fortunately, there are alternatives to plowing. Crop residues can be dealt with by animals, livestock in most cases, wildlife in some, that reduce them to dung, urine, and mulch, leaving dead roots in the soil to further enhance fertility. Conservation tillage can be used in preparing fields. In fact, roughly a third of all U.S. cropland is now under some form of conservation tillage. In most cases, however, it is linked with heavy herbicide usage that tends to counteract the benefits. The solution to the problem of unwanted plants, which often increase when tillage is minimized, lies again in approaches that try to mimic nature. In this case, the answer may lie in combatting diversity (which weeds represent) with even more diversity.

Endeavor to Maintain Diversity and Complexity in the Community

What we call weeds should not be blamed for stealing water and nutrients from our crops, but valued for the diversity they contribute, including the insects and microorganisms they attract. This added complexity offers protection against the few insects or microorganisms that actually damage crops or cause disease.

All too often we reduce this complexity in our croplands for no good reason. Photo 40-1 portrays just such an example. The apple trees in this organically farmed orchard are being irrigated and thus are not short of water. They are tap-rooted trees with extensive, well-established root systems. Thus, the surrounding grasses and weeds cannot deprive them of water; in fact they help to create a more effective water cycle and to protect against soil erosion. The grasses and weeds also provide ideal habitat for a multitude of insects and microorganisms that help to control apple pests and thus could do nothing but good in this orchard. Despite this, and at some expense in nonrenewable resources, the orchard has been mown and a host of habitat niches removed. Similar practices are common throughout the world.

Photo 40-1 *Organic apple orchard that is regularly mowed to keep it looking neat, but the mowing has removed ideal habitat for a host of insects and microorganisms that help to control apple pests. Pennsylvania.*

Avoid Monocultures

You should avoid planting monocultures, particularly over large areas, as much as possible, if for no other reason than to avoid large-scale damage from insects and plant diseases. Unfortunately, the majority of farms in the United States and many other countries today are monoculture deserts. The recently planted bean field in photo 40-2 is a typical example. Such large fields of one crop are very attractive to insects that only feed or lay eggs on that one crop, and they will congregate in great numbers. Unless some form of pesticide is used, the farmer will reap little from this field. If he continues to plant beans in it year after year, even insects that have never fed on bean plants might soon find them to their liking, given the ability of their populations, through rapid breeding cycles, to adapt so quickly. When a farmer plants a monoculture, he invites insect damage apart from all the other adverse effects brought about by so much bare soil.

Farmers in some of the most heavily insect-infested areas of the world—tropical rain forest environments—have for thousands of years grown crops in complex polycultures without using pesticides. Although cultivated on a smaller scale, these polyculture fields yield far more per acre than high-input monocultures. However, many farmers in developing nations are being persuaded to abandon polyculture fields in favor of

Photo 40-2 *View of a recently planted monoculture of beans. If you were an insect living in this field, what would you eat? Iowa.*

machinery and chemical-dependent monocultures of cash crops, with unfortunate results for both the land and the people.

Monoculture fields cannot be converted to polyculture fields overnight. Although that might be desirable, it would be highly impractical and financially risky. It makes more sense to move progressively away from monocultures, or rotations of monocultures, to strip cropping, intercropping, alley cropping, and, ultimately, more complex polycultures. Strip cropping involves the use of three or four (or more) crops planted in strips within a field that can generally be harvested with conventional equipment. Intercropping involves the planting of low-growing or early maturing crops (which may or may not be harvested), among taller, later maturing crops. In alley cropping, mixed crops are grown between rows of trees. In some cases, tree branches are lopped off to provide green manure and added sunlight for the crops below. As the crops mature and no longer require full sun, the trees regrow the limbs and leaves they sacrificed.

By moving progressively toward a more complex community, you can learn as you go, minimizing the risk of financial setbacks, and steadily moving toward your holistic goal. *There will be much to learn.* Insect damage may continue until the right combination of crops is worked out or until small or large stock are brought in, either to feed on insects or to render the environment less conducive to their reproduction. The role of livestock in cropping programs is discussed later.

Create Edges

One of the quickest ways to increase the diversity of species in any environment, whether you are managing a garden, a ranch or farm, a stream or ocean inlet, is to increase the amount of *edge*—where two or more habitats join.

Aldo Leopold, the father of modern game management, was the first to note the phenomenon of *edge effect,* particularly as it related to wildlife populations. Most wildlife occurs, he said, where the types of food and cover they need come together, that is, where their edges meet. "Every grouse hunter knows this when he selects the edge of a wood, with its grape tangles, haw-bushes, and little grassy bays, as the likely place to look for birds. The quail hunter follows the common edge between the brushy draw and the weedy corn, the snipe hunter the edge between the marsh and the pasture."[2] The reason for all these *edge effects,* according to Leopold, is probably related to the greater variety of border vegetation and the simultaneous access the wildlife has to more than one environment. Where forest meets meadow, animals find cover in the wood, visibility across the open land, and feed from two types of environment.

It is, of course, possible to have too much edge, as can be seen in forests where timber harvesting has produced a patchwork of trees and clearcut areas, and thus eliminated plant and animal species that required a larger expanse of forest to thrive. In the artificial environment of the cropfield, however, too much edge is rarely a problem; creating enough edge more commonly is.

In figure 40-1, one very large field provides minimum edge. Two different crops provide two different habitats and the one water point provides a third. The greatest diversity of species of all types will be along the edge where the three habitats meet, followed by the edges where the two crops meet. Assume that a certain species of insect-eating bird required cover from its predators, feed, and proximity to water. If one of the habitat types provided cover and the other feed, but no water, there would be no birds of this species. Even with intercropping in this field there is little diversity.

In figure 40-2, hedge rows and trees have been used to divide the large field into six smaller ones and water has been dispersed. What a difference! The trees and hedge rows add another dimension of complexity, and the proportion of edge is many times greater. Many creatures can obtain food, cover, and water. Where an insect-eating bird was restricted to the cover at the edge of the field in figure 40-1, it can now range over the entire crop area.

Once upon a time most farmers planted hedge rows and trees around their fields, which were much smaller than they generally are today, creating edge and habitat for numerous species, including insects (90 percent of which are beneficial to crops), insect predators, such as birds and bats, and larger animals as well. If the crops within these smaller, bordered fields were of mixed species, even more edge was created. When machinery forced the use of crop rows, a good deal of mixing could still be attained by alternating the crops in each row.

Modern-day farmers, of course, have the option of returning to smaller fields bordered with natural or planted vegetation. They benefit even more if a planted border produces a harvestable crop and additional income, or fodder for livestock, or serves other functions, such as willows or eucalypts that help to drain boggy areas.

In designing your fields also give thought to the needs of nocturnal creatures. You might add nesting boxes for birds but what about bats? The tonnage of insects eaten by bats each night is staggering. A single little brown bat can catch 600 or more mosquitos in an hour, a colony of 30 could easily catch more than 30,000 insects in an evening's feeding. Unfortunately, many bat populations have been seriously decimated or destroyed altogether by poisons used in our struggle to sustain monocultures. You can encourage their return by providing habitat for them. Most

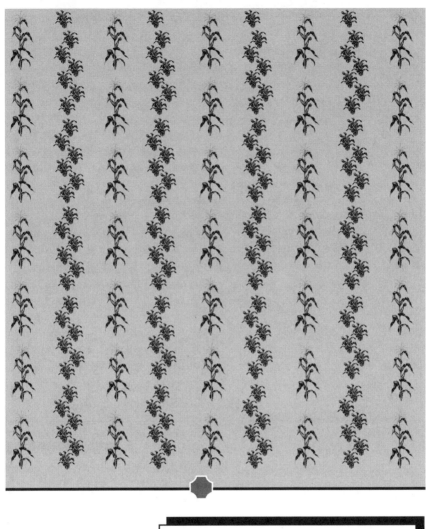

Figure 40-1 *Crop field with limited edge—two different crops provide two different habitats and the one water point provides a third.*

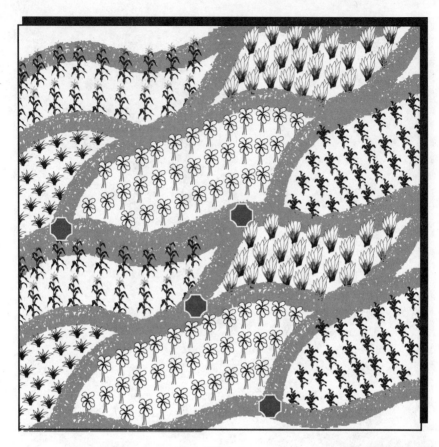

Water

Figure 40-2 *In this crop field, the proportion of edge is many times greater.*

colonies of bats choose roosts within a quarter mile of water in areas of diverse habitat, especially where there is a mix of croplands and natural vegetation.

Creating edges of course also affects the species you cannot see, and they will number in the millions or billions. All animal species are in one way or another struggling for the best assortment of places to feed, hide, rest, sleep, play, and breed. By creating edges, you can assist them all in their quest.

Preserve Genetic Diversity

Maintaining diversity refers not only to species diversity but also to the genetic diversity within each species. Genetic diversity is just as important in domesticated plants as it is in wild ones. We only have to remember what a lack of it did to the potato crops in nineteenth-century Ireland.

It used to be that the farmer's most valued possession was her seed, which reflected generations of selection for adaptation to a particular environment. However, in many countries today, most crops are grown from hybrid seed that must be purchased each year because seeds from the resulting crop are infertile or do not breed true. Because most farmers no longer raise their own seed, they are increasingly at the mercy of the giant corporations that patent and market hybrid seed and control both their price and supply. Any farmer who works toward a holistic goal that includes security and self-sufficiency should begin to question the use of hybrid seeds and perhaps consider growing at least some of her own seed to lessen the dependency.

The genetic material we have lost as a result of the move to manufactured hybrids has led to the development of seed banks to preserve what remains. But this is little different from placing endangered animals in zoos in an effort to preserve their species. Our chances of sustaining them are slim if they aren't at some point returned to the environment that originally helped to breed and shape them.

Incorporate Livestock

Up until fifty years ago livestock played an essential role in maintaining cropland fertility, and no farm was without them. Only in the earliest forms of agriculture, known as slash and burn, or swidden, were crops grown in the absence of domestic stock. Forests were cleared and burned and crops planted in soil that was rich in nutrients and organic matter. But within five or so years, much of the organic matter was lost and nutrients leached by rainfall down to layers shallow-rooted crops could not reach and the people would be forced to move on. When the forest had regrown and the soil rejuvenated, twenty years or more later, the land could be cultivated once more.

When rising populations made swidden agriculture impossible, people were forced to settle and continually crop the same land. Fertility could then be maintained only through the use of animal manures, but the number of animals that could be fed throughout the year was often quite small because of the lack of fodder crops. Manure was removed from pastures to fertilize cropfields, and this, combined with overgrazing, which even then was believed to be associated with animal numbers rather than time, reduced hay and grass yields on the pastures. In colder climates, many animals had to be slaughtered in the autumn because of a shortage of winter feed. When food was short, more land would be put under crops as a short-term measure to try to increase food production, thus setting up a vicious cycle. When more land was put into crops animal numbers had to be reduced. Less manure was produced and crop yields decreased.

Today, with improved forages and better grazing planning we can grow much more forage on less land and can better integrate livestock into cropping plans as well. Forages, such as alfalfa, that are built into crop rotations feed not only livestock but soil organisms too. Forages grown on terraces and in grassed waterways, or interseeded as cover crops, also provide stock feed while stabilizing eroding soil. Livestock can also utilize many so-called wastes, such as damaged grains, a drought-failed corn crop, food processing by-products, grain screenings, and especially weeds. The combination of crops and livestock makes the waste of one enterprise a valuable resource for another.

One of the most practical and important uses of livestock (cattle, sheep, goats, pigs, or poultry) is for breaking down after-harvest crop residues. As mentioned, plowing raw organic matter into the soil does more damage than good. Burning residues is equally destructive because of the soil exposure and atmospheric pollution it causes. Animals, on the other hand, will reduce the residues to dung and urine and still leave a mulch to cover the soil. Poultry also consume insects and help to keep their numbers in check. However, the time the animals spend on any unit of land must be carefully planned. Concentrating the animals on small areas for very short periods usually achieves the best results and can easily be done using portable electric fencing, tight herding, or for poultry, mobile, bottomless cages. When they are allowed to spread over the whole field for an extended time, the animals are likely to consume too much material and may leave some areas exposed. And hoofed animals will almost certainly pulverize the soil, destroying its structure and making it highly susceptible to erosion.

On land that is marginal because it contains steep slopes or highly erodible soil you may be better off growing sod-forming forages that livestock can graze, rather than annual crops. As long as the grazing is well planned, you are likely to achieve a better financial return while improving the land. In fact, some farmers have used animal impact to help to establish grass on steeper slopes and saved the time and cost of reseeding them.

When livestock—be they cattle, sheep, goats, horses, pigs, chickens, ducks, geese, or rabbits—are incorporated into a cropping plan, you want to keep them on the land and out of buildings as much as possible. A number of farmers have already demonstrated that even small stock, such as chickens, turkeys, and rabbits, can spend a good portion of the year out on the land, given adequate protection from predators and frequent moves. However, the trend on most farms has long been in the other direction. Confining animals to pens, stalls, or barns not only promotes ill health, but also requires extra work in moving manure out onto fields. The nutrients contained in urine may be lost altogether. The beneficial trampling, digging, and scratching that helps to loosen mulch and aerate soils is certainly lost.

Some farmers who would otherwise keep their animals out on the land find it necessary to confine them during the winter months. They have developed ingenious ways to overcome the pollution hazard created by the wastes that accumulate over the months of confinement, but still have the job of transporting manure back onto fields. They may yet overcome this obstacle by developing portable buildings that can be moved with minimal effort to new sites each winter. Some Canadian farmers have managed to keep cattle on the land all winter by piling dried forage in large rows that animals can easily find under the snow.

Minimize Irrigation

Irrigation renders the cropland environment even more artificial than dryland farming, which relies on rainfall only. To date we have been unable to sustain any irrigation-based civilization over time. Overwatering, through the most common form of irrigation, flood irrigation, is largely the reason why. In a sandy soil, overwatering causes nutrients to leach down below the crop root zone. Although the excess water still produces crops, yields are reduced and food value is diminished through plants picking up fewer nutrients. In a poorly drained soil (one that is mostly clay or contains an impervious clay layer) overwatering leads to waterlogging, which prevents plants from absorbing needed nutrients. It also alters the mineral content of the soil and may eventually, especially in hot areas with high evaporation rates, produce a thick layer of salt on the surface that makes further cropping difficult, if not impossible.

Thus, overwatering should be avoided. The use of drip irrigation, or porous piping, or any other technology that enables water to be rationed, currently offers the most promise for sustaining land under irrigation. That these alternatives are not used more widely is largely due to the higher outlay of capital required to purchase the materials and, in some cases, the energy for pumping the water. Unlike most flood irrigation systems, which rely on gravity to carry water to fields, water in a drip irrigation system usually has to be delivered under pressure, and energy is required for pumps that can do this.

Manage the Water Catchments

Up to this point our focus has been on the health of the soil on the croplands themselves, but no crop field can be sustained for long if the land surrounding it is exposed and losing biodiversity. As mentioned, livestock have been used on some farms to help establish soil-stabilizing perennial grasses on hillsides and other marginal areas that are unsuitable for cropping. But such individual efforts, necessary as they are, will prove futile in the long run if land anywhere above the farm is also bare and eroding.

Unable to soak in where it falls, rainwater moves downward, gathering silt as it goes, more often than not creating a flood at some point. Floods can destroy crops, of course, but the silt they carry also fills irrigation canals and drainage channels. The loss of the first great civilization based on irrigated agriculture in Mesopotamia was largely due to the silt from eroding catchments that filled canals and dams. The demise of the Mayan civilization in the jungles of Central America was largely due to silt from deforested catchments that filled the channels draining the marshes in which their raised-bed crops were grown.

The only civilization we know of that did manage to survive and sustain its agriculture, despite massive erosion higher up the catchment, was the Egyptians of the lower Nile Valley. Deforestation and soil erosion occurring *2,000 miles away* in the highlands of Ethiopia and Uganda provided nutrient-rich silt that annual floods deposited in the narrow valley through natural overflow channels. The flooding occurred at just the right time and land remained moist long enough afterward to grow a plentiful supply of crops. The sandy soil ensured good drainage and thus waterlogging, and a buildup of salts did not become a problem. By exploiting a natural process, *and someone else's environmental problems,* the people of lower Egypt managed to sustain their fields over 7,000 years. This security ended when the Aswan dam was built in the 1960s and the silt that had kept the fields fertile was trapped behind it.

Obviously, if we are to create a sustainable agriculture, which depends on healthy water catchments, we cannot put all the responsibility on individual farmers. They can do their best to stabilize the catchments on the land under their care, but even if every farmer managed to stabilize the catchments on every farm, we could not guarantee future food supplies unless the remaining catchments (the mountains, forests, prairies, savanna-woodlands, and rangelands) that cover a far more extensive area, are stabilized. This will require a much larger effort than I can even begin to describe in this book. Nonetheless, it is one that must be undertaken. In the meantime, you as an individual farmer can make a start by working to ensure that the rain you receive, anywhere on your farm, soaks in where it falls.

Minimize Energy Consumption

Most so-called primitive agricultural systems are highly energy efficient, producing about twenty times as much energy as they use. Paddy fields in China and southeast Asia produce 50 percent more energy than they use. Modern industrialized grain farming, on the other hand, produces only about twice as much energy as it consumes in the form of synthetic fertilizers, pesticides, and machinery, and it is becoming steadily less energy efficient. When processing and distribution are taken into account, then all food production in the industrialized nations uses more energy than it creates.[3]

Even farmers who feel no moral obligation to curtail energy inputs will be forced to do so because of the mounting costs associated with the use of synthetic, fossil-fuel-based fertilizers, pesticides, and machinery. Although fossil fuel supplies may last another century or more, they will become increasingly costly.

Feed Soil Rather Than Plants

We can reduce the need for pesticides simply by increasing diversity in our croplands, as mentioned. But reducing the need for fertilizer is a slightly different matter. With the development of synthetic fertilizers, we changed our focus from feeding the soil to feeding the plants, with catastrophic consequences. We need to shift our focus back to where it belongs—on the soil. Soil fertility involves much more than mere nutrients. As I found on my own farm, you can have all the necessary nutrients, but many may be unavailable to plants because the soil is poorly aerated. Poor drainage, excessive acidity, and exposed soil all affect fertility. It is just as important to identify and to correct these limiting factors as it is to supply the appropriate nutrients.

When you do supply nutrients, you should attempt to supplement only what is lacking. Sometimes an otherwise healthy soil will produce poor yields merely because a minor element or micronutrient is deficient. Long ago some farmers found they could correct a copper deficiency merely by dragging a piece of copper wire behind a plow. All too often, when we base fertilizer applications on the needs of plants rather than the needs of the soil, we overfertilize, creating a chemical imbalance in the soil that damages organic material, soil structure, and soil life. Groundwater also becomes polluted by excess chemicals.

Because most of the crops we grow are annual grains that concentrate nutrients taken from the soil into the plant's seedhead, when we harvest these seedheads, we are removing a significant amount of nutrients that would otherwise be returned to the soil. In most cases we will have to replace what we have taken away. At present, however, *nutrient losses due to harvested grain are insignificant in comparison to the nutrients being lost through eroding soil.* Fortunately, there are a number of alternatives to synthetic fertilizers.

By including legumes in crop rotations, for instance, we can replace some of the nitrogen lost with the removal of a corn crop. The legume's deeper roots will also draw up nutrients that may have leached down to lower soil layers.

Animal manures and composts can provide most of what the synthetic fertilizers do and, as long as they are not applied in excess, without killing microorganisms. However, they do not replace all that is lacking or has been lost, a challenge that still requires research, into both what may be lacking and benign methods for providing it.

Biodynamic agriculture uses minute amounts of various preparations that enhance soil microorganisms and thus soil structure, with impressive results that warrant further research. As a general rule, *any* nutrients added to a soil should enhance the life within it. Otherwise, we cannot keep soil alive nor benefit from the "interest" such biological capital could provide.

Human Labor versus Machines

Humans provided the main energy input into farming in every society until the mechanization of agriculture. For thousands of years the foundation of every civilization rested on vast amounts of human toil and effort, often provided unwillingly and under insufferable conditions. Animals were always a secondary source of power in agriculture because although oxen, donkeys, and horses produced a higher energy output they ate more than humans and were generally considered less economic.

Modern, mechanized farming has produced its own forms of cruelty and human suffering, even though machinery has replaced a good deal of human labor. I don't believe the answer is a return to an agriculture that is fueled predominantly by human labor but it certainly could be one that incorporates more human labor, that is neither degrading, nor inhumane, and perhaps more animal labor as well. It *should* be one that features smaller, more energy-efficient machinery that can harvest small fields of mixed crops effectively and at low cost. Fortunately, this is within the realm of our technological capabilities.

Conclusion

Throughout this chapter I have referred often to the agriculture of the past in an attempt to show that, good as much of it was, it is not something we can emulate altogether to solve today's problems. Slash-and-burn agriculture managed to maintain small human populations, but quickly broke down when those populations increased. Settled populations managed to prolong the useful life of continuously cropped fields by adding animal manures and composts and later crop rotations and soil-building cover crops—more or less farming organically. But soils continued to deteriorate in what is likely to always remain an artificial environment as long as we cultivate crops within it.

The agriculture of the future, I believe, will have to include greater complexity still in the crops we plant and the animals we manage with them. It will also require the use of new technologies that, unlike those used in the past, are first tested toward a holistic goal for their ecological, social, and economic soundness.

Perhaps one day even genetic engineering will be put to good use, producing crops that enhance, rather than attempt to overwhelm, ecological processes. And maybe new, more benign forms of energy will be developed. What we do know is that a number of changes will have to be made if we are to continue modifying our environment without destroying it and ourselves.

Now let's proceed to the guidelines developed for the use of that powerful and ancient tool, fire.

41

Burning: When and How to Burn, and What to Do Before and After

F ire is at times the only tool for the job, but as we learned in Chapter 19, there are dangers when it is used excessively, as it undoubtedly is today. Most people have no idea of the amount of burning that takes place each year on croplands, grasslands, and savanna woodlands, or of its consequences, and would not be aware of the amount occurring in wet tropical forests if the media had not exposed it. Although fire is a tool that has a definite and useful role to play in land management, we need to question its use more rigorously. The burning guideline serves to remind us of the dangers while providing appropriate safeguards.

Use fire only when the testing guidelines show it to be the most appropriate tool at the time for taking you toward your holistic goal. Particularly avoid burning purely for the sake of tradition, accepted practice, or what other people say. Because results may vary considerably even in the best of circumstances, you must, as with any decision that attempts to modify an environment, monitor closely after a burn on the assumption your decision was wrong.

If the future landscape described in your holistic goal includes great diversity, then maintaining species that depend on periodic burns will require it. Nevertheless, many who advocate burning to invigorate grassland in brittle environments fail to understand that the benefit comes from disturbance in any form, not just fire. Animal impact, for instance, can often be used to achieve the same end, but without the adverse effects of fire. However, any uniform type of disturbance applied continually, including animal impact, will tend to produce a more uniform, less diverse, community, so even an animal-maintained grassland may require occasional burning in part or overall to sustain fire-dependent species.

When you are managing holistically, the most common justifications for burning include:

- to invigorate and freshen mature or senescent perennial grass plants if, for some reason, animals cannot be used, or in cases where you want to sustain fire-dependent vegetation

- to invigorate and thicken up brush as cover or feed for wildlife

- to expose soil in patches to create a mosaic of different communities that can support a greater diversity of plant and animal species

- to reduce selected woody species that are fire-sensitive at certain stages of their lives

- to provide intense disturbance to a community in which many dead plants are hindering growth

Before You Burn

To burn or not to burn is a decision that must always be tested toward a holistic goal. Some of the concerns the testing should address follow.

Cause and Effect

If you intend to burn to overcome a problem produced by past management decisions, you must at least ensure that you simultaneously act to rectify the problem's cause. Not doing this commonly results in people using fire to fight the effects produced by past fires. Burning very rank, fibrous grass to make it more palatable is a good example seen in the management of many ranches and national parks. The fire will freshen individual plants by clearing the old growth, but because it exposes the soil between plants, it tends to increase the spacing between plants. This results in fewer, larger plants that in turn become coarser and more fibrous, thus requiring further burning to be edible at all.

Burning forbs considered weeds that spring from the cracks in bare, exposed soil is equally self-defeating. Such tap-rooted plants, which take hold easily in the cracks left by a previous fire, are the beginning of an advance in biological succession. The material of their stems, leaves, and so on, will provide the soil cover for other species as the community becomes more diverse, dynamic, and stable. Burning them sets the process back to square one, lengthening the time it will take to reach the landscape you require in the future.

Elsewhere I mentioned my belief that the tsetse fly population in

Africa, *Glossina morsitans* in particular, increased when we burned frequently, because burning exposed soil and increased breeding sites. We burned as policy to make it easier to hunt the game providing the blood needed to feed the flies. These efforts proved useless in the end, because enough small host animals remained to supply blood anyway, and our frequent burning increased the fly's egg-laying sites a thousandfold.

Weak Link (Social)

Because the prevailing belief is that fire is natural and therefore an acceptable management practice, it is not likely that your burning will offend or confuse the people whose support you will need in achieving your holistic goal. However, this belief might well change in the future.

Weak Link (Biological)

If you were attempting to reduce the population of a fire-sensitive woody species by burning, you would need to be aware of the weakest point in the species' life cycle. If it was a species that established best in cracked bare soil you might, by burning, kill adult plants, but you would also be likely to enhance the success of the next generation. If it were a species that established best in long-rested clumps of perennial grass with weakened root systems, you would then be likely to kill the adult plants and reduce the ability of their seedlings to establish.

Weak Link (Financial)

The weak link in the chain of production that stretches from raw resources to money should always be considered before you burn. Burning to reduce a fire-sensitive woody species becomes most tempting in years of low forage production because the brush stands out amid the poor grass. But low forage production often indicates that energy conversion is the current weak link, in a livestock or wildlife management situation, and if that is the case, it could be a mistake to burn. You need all the forage you've got this year, and you do not want to risk losing any to fire. Burning would best be left to a year in which forage is abundant and energy conversion is not the weak link.

Marginal Reaction

We often view the tool of fire as cheap because the only investment involved is a box of matches. However, when burning either forage or crop residues, factoring in lost forage and grazing time and the reduced effectiveness of rainfall shows the true cost to be high in relation to the minimal financial investment. With the contribution of biomass burning to atmospheric pollution factored in, the cost becomes higher still.

Gross Profit Analysis, Energy/Money Source and Use

As burning is seldom an enterprise that can be marketed, gross profit analysis would not normally apply. The Energy/Money test probably will not affect most decisions on burning either, but that does not mean you can forget either test. Like the pilot who keeps "landing gear" on his check list, even though he flies a fixed-wheel plane, by keeping all the tests on yours, you too will avoid the chance of someday coming in wheels up.

Sustainability

In this test, you look specifically at the future resource base described in your holistic goal. In terms of the land and the four ecosystem processes, you need to consider a number of questions: What degree of soil exposure do you have now? What litter will you lose? What might fire do to the mineral and water cycles envisioned in your holistic goal? What will happen to the microenvironment at the soil surface, and how will that influence the biological community you are attempting to create?

In considering these questions, remember to think about the entire future community and the age structure of its populations, not just adult plants and animals that will be present only for the short term. In Chapter 19 I cited the example of the annual burning of teak forests early in the dry season to save the trees from more damaging fires later. The practice doomed the forest because teak seedlings could not establish on the bare, inorganic sand left by the frequent, low-intensity fires set to save the forest.

Burning to eradicate brush, a common reason given by extension services, almost always fails to pass the sustainability test. Fire, rather than killing, invigorates many woody species, causing them to thicken up and send out multiple stems. Because it exposes soil, it also tends to produce long-term damage to the grassland you might hope to enhance.

In terms of the people in your future resource base, you will at least have to consider how a burn might affect your neighbors and what the ramifications will be should the fire get out of control and spread to their properties. Are there people nearby who might be adversely affected by the smoke, such as asthma sufferers? Are there regulations or common courtesies you should respect that, if ignored, would affect your standing in the community?

Society and Culture

After passing through all these tests, how do you feel about burning now? If you, or any others making this decision with you, have had a strong disposition toward burning in the past, based on long-held beliefs or custom, I hope the other six tests have helped you to question that stance. You want to be sure that the decision to burn is in this instance economically, environmentally, and socially sound. You should bear in mind that any time you burn you are releasing carbon and other pollutants into the atmosphere that are beginning to adversely affect all of humanity. You will contribute to this worsening situation if you use fire reflexively when alternative treatments are available or when you burn large areas when much smaller ones will suffice.

Planning Considerations

Several factors involved in planning for a burn will affect the outcome of your testing. *How* you plan to burn is just as important as *why* in making your decision. So let me go through each of these factors.

Prior to Burning

Apart from the legalities that may apply in any particular area regarding warnings to neighbors, you will probably need to create firebreaks. To avoid the eroding eyesores often created by burning or mechanically creating firebreaks, you can use animal impact to create them instead. As mentioned in Chapter 39, you can spray a fine molasses–water or salt–water solution (when animals have been deprived of salt) in a strip where you want the firebreak in order to attract stock to the area. They will remove enough flammable material to create a break from which to backburn, but without exposing the soil.

Types of Burn

Burns may be either hot or cool, depending on the amount of fuel, its moisture content, and atmospheric humidity. Hot burns occur when large amounts of combustible material and dry conditions produce large flames that persist for a long time and can seriously damage the above-ground parts of woody plants. In the tropics where the year divides into wet and dry seasons, the best time for hot burns comes toward the end of the dry season. In temperate zones, opportunities may depend on several factors.

Cool burns are done when forage is still partially green or damp and difficult to ignite. In this case, the fire trickles along, barely scorching the woody plants. When cool burns come at the beginning of a dry season, as they often do in the tropics, where they are also called early burns, the soil will remain exposed longer than it would be with a hot burn that comes later in the season. This consideration also varies considerably according to local conditions. Where hot fires, being fierce, tend to burn uniformly, cool burns are generally patchy and broken, as not all the material burns equally well.

If you decide your situation calls for a hot burn for high heat, more uniform burning, and shorter soil exposure, you must ensure the presence of sufficient fuel by not grazing it down just before you need it. The Holistic Grazing Planning procedure covered in Chapter 46 deals with this in more detail. If you intend the hot burn to kill a fire-sensitive plant, then the burn date should be when it is at its most vulnerable stage, be it during fast growth, dormancy, or just before dormancy. The stage of life of the plant, whether seedling or more mature, may also be crucial. A cool burn requires less fuel, which may mean taking some grazing out before the burn. Again, the grazing plan should assure this well before the event.

For some years I tried to perfect another form of burn in the high-rainfall areas of Zimbabwe and Paraguay that I called a singe burn. It was supposed to consume only the old oxidizing grass during the early rains when wet ground would keep litter from burning and thus not expose soil. Although attractive in theory, it was nearly impossible to achieve in practice. For fire to run over litter without burning it, perfect wind, temperature, and moisture conditions must coincide, and that may happen for only a few hours on one or two days. Without a mammoth labor force standing by to seize the moment, you cannot cover much ground.

For our experiments, we would start early in the morning after an inch of rain during the night and spend the morning battling to get the fire to run. If we decided to wait a few hours until the tops dried a bit more, the wretched fire often as not caught too well, dried out whole plants, and burned the litter anyway. To cover more ground we had lines of men on horseback dragging burning tires, but nothing proved workable over wide areas. Although the idea failed as a substitute for grazing to rejuvenate grassland, it is worth mentioning because it did succeed in isolated patches, and that sometimes has value in itself.

Tools to Associate with Burning

When using fire, you need to remind yourself that the decision to do so is not complete until one other tool is selected to be applied following the burn. Fire on its own, by default, becomes fire followed by rest. If the environment happens to be a brittle one, and most are where burning is done, then fire and rest mean you are choosing to use two tools in concert, both of which have the tendency to produce bare ground. Unfortunately, fire followed by rest is standard practice in most parts of the world where government extension services advocate prescribed burning. On public lands in the United States regulations generally require it.

Animal impact will of course offset the rest and is the tool you would most often want to employ in conjunction with fire. Wild grazers often concentrate on burned areas, which provide good visibility, and soon flush green, among other reasons. In Africa they will move on to a burn even before the ground cools off. However, in most cases, we depend on livestock to provide the animal impact. We can induce them to provide it by creating herd effect on the burned area using an attractant or using a single-strand temporary electric fence to greatly increase stock density over the area. If the area is fairly large, the fence can be moved until all areas have been treated. When neither of these ideas are feasible, you can at least achieve some degree of impact if animals have access to unburned areas for grazing while in a paddock. In most cases they will tend to wander over the burned areas and lie up on them.

If you are ranching on public lands and are prohibited from using animal impact following a burn, you might consider establishing some test plots for the benefit of the government agency people who may in fact be persuaded to help change the regulations. You will need two small enclosures. One which you burn and then rest, and one which you burn and then subject to animal impact (animals at ultra high density to create herd effect). Within the next year or two, this should allow everyone interested to observe the differences for themselves.

Burning to Enhance Wildlife Habitat or Reinvigorate Biological Communities

As so many plants and animals are to varying degrees fire-dependent, it can be a mistake in some environments to suppress fire altogether if your holistic goal requires increased biological diversity. A community depressed by excessive old, oxidizing plant material will commonly require a hot burn if animal impact cannot be used to reinvigorate it. However, the patchiness that characterizes cool burns often produces the most varied wildlife habitat.

Patchy burning increases edge effect, which, as mentioned in the previous chapter, can enhance your ability to support large and diverse populations of game animals, birds, and other creatures. If with firebreaks and control you can make a hot fire burn in patches, all the better. By eliminating more woody vegetation, at risk of more erosion, it will increase the contrast with unburned areas. Repeated cool burns, although initially providing patchiness, eventually lead to greatly increased woody communities of somewhat fire-tolerant species and loss of patchiness. This may significantly reduce the contrast in habitat type.

Monitoring

Once the decision has been made to burn, you need to assume that despite all the testing you could still be wrong. Determine what criteria you can monitor from the outset that will give the earliest possible information on the direction your decision is taking you. Because the key to management of all four ecosystem processes is the soil surface, which fire can expose so ruthlessly, you generally start there. Another common indicator of early change is the type or species of plants that establish following a burn.

Apart from helping to avoid potential crises, your monitoring will help you to gain a better working knowledge of the effects of fire on the land. Where fire itself does little damage in many situations and advances the landscape toward the holistic goal, frequent use of fire, as mentioned, can become very detrimental. Had we monitored the effects of fire on the soil surface and the incoming generation of plants during my game department days, we would surely never have set fires with such cheerful abandon. We never even considered the ecosystem processes or realized their importance. Thinking only of adult trees, grasses, and animals, we managed for species, not process or population structure, a topic covered in more detail in the next chapter.

But one must manage for the whole, not for select species and therefore must monitor constantly the factors that reflect the health of all four ecosystem processes, such as litter cover, soil exposure, and plant spacings. Changes in these give the earliest warning of change in the water cycle through increased runoff and surface evaporation and decreased penetration. Changes in the age structure of plant populations, in particular, show what is happening to community dynamics. Which plants show the greatest influx of young that survive through the seedling stage? When they mature, will that be the community you want?

You must particularly watch for any early signs indicating a need for another burn within a few years. If such develop, try to find an alternative tool to do the task, especially in more arid areas. The drier the climate, the more dramatic the effects of fire and the less frequent its use should be. But what is frequent?

For many years in Zimbabwe, the four-paddock–three-herd grazing system was common practice. One paddock was burned each year and the animals rotated through the other three; thus each paddock was burned once every four years. In the early days of my search for better ways, I visited numerous ranches as well as the research stations promoting this practice to see if it offered any hope. This took me to a variety of areas that included both sandy and clay soils and rainfall averages that ranged from 8 to 70 inches (200 to 1750 mm). Nowhere, including on the research stations, did I find land on which the water cycle was not deteriorating. Many published papers had attested to the healthy grassland produced by burning every four years, but all were based on the plant species present, rather than what was happening to the soil surface and reflected in the ecosystem processes.

Conclusion

Monitoring the soil surface for change will help you determine how frequent a burn should be. Where a periodic fire every twenty to fifty years can do good, a burn every two to five years, by exposing soil, can lead to tragedy.

Now let's move on to the last of the management guidelines, population management, which relates in some respects to many of the others.

42

Population Management: Look to Age Structure Rather Than Numbers, Diversity Rather Than Single Species

The population management guideline bears on the tool of living organisms, but more generally on the management of community dynamics. It applies any time we want to encourage or discourage the success of a species. Commonly, when we say we want more corn or cattle, or fewer fruit flies and mosquitoes, or more of our team, and less of theirs, we tend to consider only the raw numbers of whatever interests us at the moment. The rancher asks, "What is your stocking rate?" Game enthusiasts ask, "What is the deer count?" Farmers ask, "How many bushels?" Economic development specialists talk about people per square mile, consumption per capita, and growth of GNP. All of these questions are important, but in addition, or even ahead of them, this guideline raises other considerations that clarify the management of populations in the context of whole communities.

One example shows both how much this broader approach can contribute to the solution of some of our most urgent problems and how easily the best of minds fall into the old rut. Some years ago, a consulting assignment from the United Nations Food and Agriculture Organization took me to Pakistan's Baluchistan province. Having been charged with reporting on the overall status of resource management in this province, I had read numerous reports previously prepared by other consultants to Pakistan and the United Nations, as well as government officials. These all cited one problem that overshadowed most others: the overharvesting of desert bushes for fuel. People were scavenging an ever-expanding area surrounding their villages for desert bushes, the only fuel remaining, and did not just lop off branches, but took roots and all. An ever-widening circle

439

of bare ground extended around most settlements. All the reports stressed what this was doing to expand the desert, but how else could the villagers cook their food?

Most of the reports concluded that alternative stoves and fuel had to be found, but no one had an idea the villagers could afford. The report writers, however, looked only at the number of bushes available and the rate of harvesting, ignoring all other aspects of population dynamics and the maintenance of healthy biological communities. No reporting scientist apparently noticed the fact that there were no young bushes, even though new growth, lacking fuel value, did not interest wood gatherers and billions of seeds had been produced over the life of the plants. It was like worrying about a disease killing very old people while failing to notice the people hadn't raised any children successfully in eighty years.

Without any harvesting at all, a population that does not reproduce will disappear. Bushes that reseed themselves will provide a source of fuel that satisfies a good share of the village demand forever. The rate of consumption of mature bushes was not the problem that needed to be addressed at all. The challenge lay in determining why none of the billions of seeds produced over a great many years by the mature bushes survived.

We will return to this case later. The point I wish to make now, which this case highlights so well, is that there is a need for two kinds of knowledge in managing a living population. First, one must be able to assess its health and stability. Then one must pinpoint the cause of its condition. The population management guideline addresses these questions on the basis of some rather obvious principles that modern production systems have increasingly obscured.

In crop farming particularly, we have come to think in terms of annual or short-term monocultures where we plant an entire population, nurture it artificially, then harvest it completely. The same logic extends to the clear cutting and reseeding of timber. We even rip up fruit orchards at a certain age and replant them because it suits our mechanized handling techniques to have everything the same age and on the same schedule. All of that, however, does violence to the natural dynamics of populations in whole communities and inevitably leads to instability and failure at some point.

Self-Regulating and Non-Self-Regulating Populations

Among animal populations there are two fundamental types, which I referred to briefly in Chapter 20: those that regulate their own numbers and those that do not. We don't yet understand how some of the self-regulating populations manage to limit their numbers, but they do, even though they have very high breeding rates and thus a potential for rapid expansion. Some of the small antelope of Africa, such as the duiker or stembuck, are good examples. If we protect them for years, they do not increase. If we try to shoot them out, as various tsetse fly eradication schemes attempted, they breed about as fast as they are shot.

Such antelope, which are solitary creatures, appear to have small, but strict, territories that may be threatened when numbers reach a certain threshold. Quite possibly this threat stresses the animals in some way that inhibits breeding. No matter how abundant the food, cover, and other requirements, the population appears to somehow remain limited.

Self-regulating populations present little known difficulty in management. Non-self-regulating populations, on the other hand, present a very different picture, unless the communities they inhabit are intact and complex. Some non-self-regulating populations do not appear as such, as long as they exist in complex biological communities that remain relatively stable. Predation and other forms of attrition limit population growth. Among mammals, birds, and insects, most of the herding, flocking, or gregarious species seem to fall in this category. Their populations often remain limited in a complex community, but can break out in problem numbers should the integrity of the community as a whole be damaged. Once predators, in particular, are removed or reduced, such populations can explode and face periodic heavy die-off or become severe pests. This danger from non-self-regulating species threatens whenever we simplify any biological community.

A few species are notorious for their unrestricted growth potential, such as prickly pear and rabbits in Australia and quelea finches and locusts in Africa. The bison of North America and the springbok of South Africa are some of the best known. No matter how much predation they encountered from indigenous hunters and other predators, bison and springbok numbers grew so high that *their survival depended on die-offs and high accident rates*. Early travelers told of incredible numbers of bison that annually broke through the ice on rivers like the Yellowstone and drowned in whole herds. Apparently millions of springbok marched to their deaths on the seashore.

Excellent films on the migration of the wildebeest and zebra herds in the Serengeti plains of East Africa show something of the culling that occurs as they cross steep-banked rivers leaving many individuals crushed or drowned. One should not view this as bad, as such populations have gone beyond predation's capacity to control them.

Humanity, to its sorrow, belongs to the same category. For millions of years as hunter-gatherers, our populations remained small and in balance with the communities that sustained us. No longer! We historically overcame so many limiting factors that our numbers exploded and continue to do so. Yet even today, some cultures, such as the Bushmen of Africa, depend on heavy infant mortality, slow breeding, and short lives for their very survival, because their world will not sustain greater numbers. Does one pity them and thus provide the basic hygiene and medicine that may eventually destroy them as a culture, or does one create a vast reservation for them and allow them to exist for many more centuries in harmony with their biological community, but as museum pieces in the modern world?

Since *Homo sapiens* cannot escape nature's principles we have but two options: become self-regulating through birth control and family planning; or continue as a non-self-regulating population and allow massive death losses from war, accident, disease, and starvation to regulate our numbers. To date, we have most often chosen the second, which holds no promise of a bright future, as we know all too well from our past. The series of famines that occurred in Europe throughout the Middle Ages were preceded by a steady growth in population that dropped precipitously following two or three years of poor weather in which many crops failed. Many people died of starvation, and many more of diseases, such as Bubonic plague, that they could not survive in their weakened condition. Cannibalism was rampant. Bodies were dug up from graves to provide food and executed criminals were eaten.[1]

Age Structure and Population Health

Figure 42-1 shows what is known as the sigmoid, or S-shaped, curve that describes the growth of virtually all populations. Starting at point A with very few individuals, the population of a species increases gradually. By point B, growth accelerates as the population expands geometrically. At about point C, further growth in numbers encounters difficulties of some kind and the rate falls off as numbers approach the biological community's capacity to sustain them. Although individuals may breed as fast as ever, the pressure for food, cover, space, and so on becomes so extreme that accident, disease, malnutrition, increased success of predation, and the like impose heavy losses on the population. In the case of a self-regulating population, it appears that breeding is somehow reduced.

The importance of the individual changes as the population grows. At point A, the survival of each individual has a great influence on progress along the curve. Without that first plant there can be no others; without that first breeding pair, there will be no further animals. The old anecdote about a penny that doubles every day illustrates this point. If I agree to give you a penny today and then double it every day for a month you would have over $10 million by month's end. However, if I didn't happen to have a penny that first day and waited until the second, by the thirty-first you would have only $5 million. By contrast, if I came up one penny short on

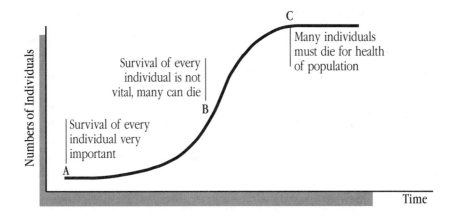

Figure 42-1 *Virtually all populations grow according to a sigmoid, or S-shaped, curve. Numbers increase gradually between point A and B, but then accelerate geometrically until point C when the biological community begins to lose its capacity to sustain them.*

the sixteenth day you would lose only about $16. Obviously each penny, seedling, or breeding pair has tremendous impact at the outset, but less as the geometric progression advances. By point B, the loss of one individual hardly matters to the health of the whole community.

In practice, this concept is frequently overlooked. The rancher who wants to advance his annual cheat grass range to perennial species may allow, for instance, a couple of horses free rein of the place throughout the year, thinking it unnecessary, and even inconvenient, to put them with the main cattle herd. When this happens, the first perennial grasses that try to establish are exposed to 2 x 365 = 730 horse-days of grazing, most of them when the cheat grass has dried off and the horses have every incentive to scavenge remorselessly for every blade of green. Rare indeed is the perennial grass that can withstand such overgrazing. The same 730 horse-days of grazing done by 365 horses over 2 days of the year would of course lead to the establishment of many perennial grasses.

By point C, the very survival of the population depends on the death of many individuals. Sometimes this occurs in ways that allow the population to remain high and relatively stable. This would be the case if the high numbers have not, in and of themselves, damaged the biological community sustaining them. When it is otherwise, a number of limiting pressures will produce a catastrophic die-off that returns the whole process to point A.

Environmental Resistance

The father of game management, Aldo Leopold, called the limiting pressures on a population at point C *environmental resistance,* because they come from the entire biological community. Unfortunately, when we upset the built-in checks and balances, as we do, for instance, by removing predators, some populations, commonly of herbivores or omnivores such as pigs, monkeys, or baboons, explode to higher numbers that in turn exert great pressure on yet other populations and thus destabilize the whole. Predators, remember, consist of more than lions and coyotes. Spraying pesticide on insect pests also kills millions of their predators, most of which are themselves insects.

At each point on the sigmoid growth curve, the population has a characteristic age structure. Figure 42-2 shows in sketch 1 how at point A (from figure 42-1), the proportion of young is high, although numbers are low. At point B, the age structure looks more like sketch 2. The young remain numerous and numbers decline regularly through all age classes.

Sketch 2 represents a very healthy population within a biological community. It will remain healthy if kept at that level by human management or by predation that takes off individuals in a way that maintains the age structure.

Sketch 3 shows the age structure at point C, where broader environmental resistance becomes important. Because disease, starvation, and accidents affect the very young and the very old more than they do adults in their prime, the numbers dip sharply at point A. This low reflects the high proportion of last year's young that did not survive. A herd of deer that bear young once a year, for example, might have relatively few two-year-olds. The age classes at point B are relatively abundant, however, because they represent individuals in their prime that can better withstand disease, or starvation. By point C the numbers drop off again as fewer individuals reach really old age under the stress of environmental resistance. These diagrams of population age structure cover almost all situations where individuals in a population have any sort of prolonged life. Annual plant and insect populations, of course, would not follow this pattern.

Most living organisms acquire the age structure in sketch 3 when they reach the limit of their biological community to support them. Humankind, however can get there prematurely. We are perhaps the only creature that can so damage its environment that it starts to die off before reaching its full potential. Every decade or so, in Africa in particular, millions of people starve, not because of overpopulation, but because human decision making and management have led to deterioration of water and mineral cycles, energy flow, and loss of biological diversity. Well managed, I believe Africa could sustain its present population.

Likewise in New Mexico, the four ecosystem processes have suffered as

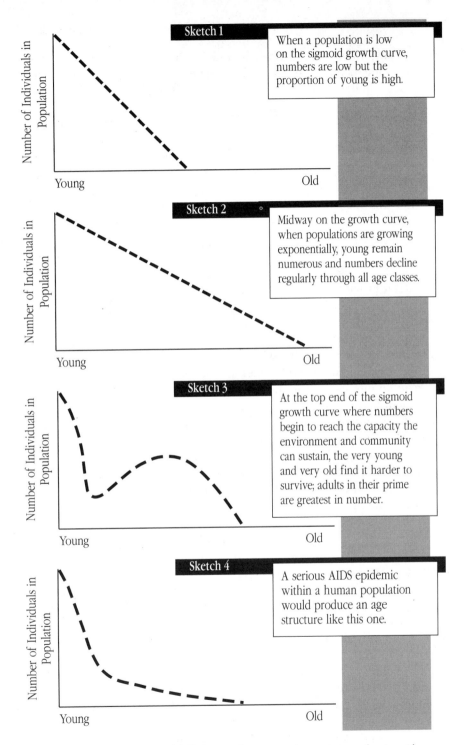

Figure 42-2 *Proportion of different age classes at various points on the sigmoid growth curve of a population.*

dramatically as I have seen anywhere, and the rural population is in fact low and declining. If New Mexico had to support the sort of population that many developing countries must on a similar area of land, its chief export would also be gruesome photographs from relief agencies.

Humans also occasionally kill off the prime age classes of their populations first. Warfare does this when the brunt falls on the actual soldiers, as opposed to civilian populations. Now the AIDS epidemic threatens the adults of the population more than the very young or the very old. A serious AIDS epidemic would produce a human population as shown in sketch 4, as some African villages now demonstrate.

Age Structure versus Numbers

Because age structure reflects so precisely where on the S-curve a population lies, it provides much more useful information for management purposes than numbers of individuals generally do. Knowing the size of a population seldom helps to decide what to do about it, whereas the age structure often does. Accurate counts, especially of wild and mobile populations, are nearly impossible with currently available techniques, whereas a simple random sample will tell a lot about age structure.

Field counts, even of immobile plants, frequently fail to meet acceptable scientific standards. In Pakistan, for instance, I had no way to count those desert bushes. Even if I could have counted every one, how would it have helped in management? After sampling several sites, however, I can argue for the high degree of accuracy in the age structure shown by the solid line in figure 42-3. The dotted line represents what a healthy desert bush population in this biological community should be, as people do not pull out seedlings or young plants.

If the Pakistani villagers formed a holistic goal it would likely describe a future landscape of great diversity and health with many millions of desert bushes. Given such a holistic goal, I believe the villagers would find that the correct decision would be to continue to harvest desert bushes for home cooking. Total protection of these plants is not needed. The population is nowhere near point A in figure 42-1, where every plant is terribly important to the health of the population. In Chapter 48 I will discuss this case in more detail showing what management tools the people could use to save the brush.

The failure of people to notice and act on such readily apparent information extends far beyond the developing world. When I first visited California in 1978 I traveled through miles of oak woodlands without seeing a single seedling or young tree, but no one voiced the slightest concern. Deer and cattle populations had produced a browse line as high as adults could reach on nearly every tree so early in the season that few fawns could possibly survive after weaning. Hunting, confined mainly to mature

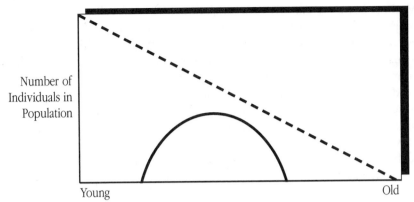

Figure 42-3 *The solid line shows the age structure I found in the desert bush population. The dotted line shows what a healthy desert bush population would look like.*

males, was clearly not helping to reduce pressure on the fawns. As local ranchers killed coyotes on sight, little besides annual starvation of the fawn crop, accidents, or disease was keeping the deer numbers in check.

When major tree populations as well as game show no significant survival of young, bad trends already afflict all four ecosystem processes, and of course human prospects as well, but a numerical count of deer or oak trees does not reveal this, whereas an age structure sample does.

On rangelands, plant age structure tells us much more about the health of the biological community than numbers within key species. Photo 42-1 is a close-up view of an important piece of range in New

Photo 42-1 *Relic site used by government agencies as the yardstick against which to measure similar sites as it reflects the potential they could reach if "left to nature," that is, rested. "Desirable" species are present, but if looked at in terms of age structure, the situation is not healthy. All the desirable plants are either dead or senile and dying. Even though millions of seeds have been produced, new plants have been unable to establish for many years. New Mexico.*

Mexico. Long rested, this relic, or pristine, site was believed to be at its optimum development when the photo was taken and was being used by government agencies in the state as the standard against which to measure management on similar sites as it reflects the potential they could reach. It contains the key, or desirable, species all right, but every plant is already dead or senile after sixteen years of total rest. Despite the fact that millions of seeds were produced in those sixteen years, there is not a single young plant. All four of the ecosystem's fundamental processes are functioning at very low levels and the desertification process is well established. When such sites are used as the standard for management, it renders most government statistics on success with range management suspect at best.

The Limitations of Game Counts

The management of game provides many dramatic examples of the limitations of counting, and yet we persist in doing it. Whenever a game management program is initiated, people usually sink a large part of the initial budget into a census and base further decisions on that. However, the numbers counted in the census seldom come close to the numbers actually present.

When construction began on one of the world's first megadams, the Kariba Dam on the Zambezi River between Zimbabwe and Zambia, I was working with the Game Department, which was responsible for rescuing game from the islands that formed as the lake filled. The large number of islands and the logistics involved required a high level of planning and good estimates of game numbers. The perfect hindsight possible, as we took the last animals off the dwindling bits of land, consistently revealed the utter inaccuracy of our best techniques.

I recall one island with a large, flat, 35-acre (14-hectare) top that was grassy and easy to move over. It had large trees scattered about that made good viewing platforms, and the game had browsed off all leaves below about six feet, making visibility excellent. Our highly experienced crew, amounting to more than a man per acre, counted 60 kudu, 150 impala, and numerous other animals. But there were in fact 120 kudu and over 300 impala when all were finally captured. Our experience was by no means exceptional. How many people rely for management on the counting done by one or two people over a few days over thousands of acres of heavily vegetated land?

The mystique of aerial counting has also proven hollow in my experience. I used to allow tourist planes to fly over my own game reserve regularly when the public game reserves and national parks forbade them. If I was flying myself and happened to spot a herd of elephant or buffalo, I would radio the tour pilots and tell them where they could find the animals for their clients, but often they could not see the animals until I flew close overhead and dipped a wing. At other times, they would see herds and report to me, but I could not find them.

Few animals stand out better from the air than elephant and buffalo. With less conspicuous animals the situation was hopeless. Once I circled four times at very low altitude over a herd of sable antelope in open woodland while four observers in the plane classified them as to sex and age. Only after the fourth turn did any of us notice the herd contained more zebra than sable. Four times we had circled without noticing a single zebra. The moment one was seen, many were seen. Such is the nature of aerial surveys.

Large masses of game can render themselves practically invisible. I remember one 20,000-acre tract in Zimbabwe where I was assisting the owner to start game ranching. There were many species, but the most numerous were impala. We had been using the plane to count hippo because it enabled us to look down on them in the river pools. The reedbeds were too thick to even get near them on the ground. While airborne, we decided to fly over the rest of the ranch so the owner could see his approximately 5,000 impala. We flew the area at various altitudes searching all the places we knew them to spend the day, without seeing a single one. The owner, in despair, concluded that since they obviously migrated on such days to neighboring land, he could not count on a commercial harvest. Then, driving back from the air strip along the river, we saw hundreds standing there as usual.

Ultimately, I came to mistrust aerial counting more than any other technique. We have learned the same lesson when trying to spot humans from the air. During Algeria's war for independence, the Algerians marched large bodies of men over open country right under French spotter planes. They had only to walk in ragged fashion, rather than in formation, and not look up at the planes. We have to use spotter pigeons to find people lost in boats at sea because humans cannot see them, even when the boats are day-glo orange and the water a calm dark blue.

If aerial counting is hopeless, what about estimates by people who live among the game and "know the place like the back of their hand." Surely after many years in the field, a rancher or park ranger knows roughly how many deer, elk, impala, or kangaroos he has.

I once spent a full week strip-counting game on an African game ranch in the company of the owner. In this procedure, one covers roads and tracks morning and evening with several observers recording the distance traveled and the distance from the center of the track to the nearest animal sighted in each herd. Using the distance traveled and the average width of the sample strip one assumes a constant density over the whole area and computes total population figures, which, though better than most estimates, usually turn out low.

After spending a week at this, the rancher declared that in all his years on the place he had never actually seen so much of it. When we worked out the size of the sample, however, we had covered only two percent of his land. What did either of us really know?

On many ranch inspections, I have recorded every cow and deer or impala sighted as we traveled the roads. The rancher might tell me he had about 300 impala, deer, or whatever. On questioning, he would agree that they lay up in cover most of the day and hid from the sound of vehicles, while the cattle hung around the roads and gates. The rancher would always be dumbfounded when I later pointed out we had seen over 60 percent of his wild animals, based on his estimate of their numbers, and less than 30 percent of his cattle.

In order of importance, probably twenty other questions deserve more attention than numbers in the management of game. Besides age structure, other factors such as the sex ratio in adults; the feed, cover, and water requirements; home ranges; levels of use of feed plants; the age structure of those feed plants; and so on, deserve far more attention than game counts.

Monitoring a Culling Program Through Age-Class Sampling

Years ago an American wildlifer, Archie Mossman, and I assisted the Forestry Commission in Zimbabwe to start game ranching in their forests. The project called for culling and marketing sable antelope and eland, our largest antelope. The forest was dense and large, and eland in particular avoid people. I personally did the first survey and found them impossible to even sample by sighting them. Even though their tracks and dung indicated a large population, I saw only six after traveling the tracks for days and lying in wait countless hours at waterholes.

In this case, we said "let there be X number of eland that we assume from evidence to be large enough to allow culling of 200 animals." Although we had seen few from our vehicles or at water holes, professional hunters had no trouble tracking and shooting that number. Then, of course, we had a random sample, as the animals were shot on sight without regard to age, condition, or sex, as long as they appeared adult.

The age structure of such a sample can be worked out by weighing the eye lenses, which get heavier with age or by noting tooth wear and replacement. Ranking the jaws of all 200 eland on a scale of 1 to 10 produced the age structure shown in sketch 1 of Figure 42-4. This, plus the

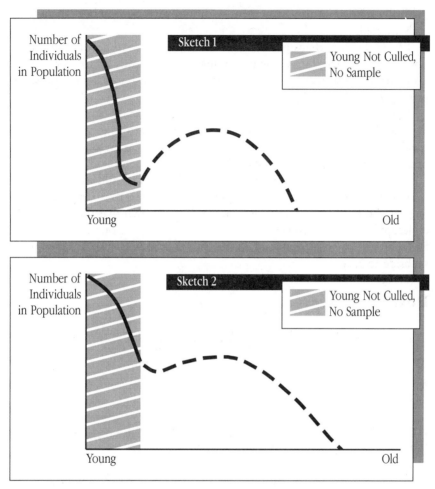

Figure 42-4 *Age structure of a land population before (Sketch 1) and after (Sketch 2) well-planned culling operations.*

signs of browsing on vegetation confirmed that the X number of eland had arrived at point C in figure 42-1.

After three years of culling at this level, the curve changed to that shown in sketch 2 of figure 42-4. This indicated that the culling had begun to reduce the number of young animals dying each year and to increase the number becoming breeding adults. By steadily watching this age structure and sampling the density of tracks and the response of vegetation, we gradually refined herd management without ever knowing how many animals we had.

I have dwelt perhaps overlong on this matter of numbers because it so obsesses many people. My own examples come mostly from game management, because natural cases give the purest illustrations, but the same principle applies to all plant and animal populations.

One vital consideration worth mentioning is that the amount of habitat available may ultimately determine whether any one population of species thrives or declines to extinction. This finding grew out of the work of island biologists who first noted that the smaller the island and the more remote the mainland, the fewer the species the island could sustain and the more extinctions it suffered. Subsequent research into the "islands of habitat" created by developments on mainlands has shown that the same principle applies. Thus, without some alterations many of our national parks and reserves may not be able to ensure the survival of the species they were set aside to save.

Bottlenecks

To survive, all creatures must be able to satisfy basic needs for food, cover, and water *throughout the year*. If there is even a short period when any one of these needs cannot be met in full for high numbers of a particular species, its population will be limited. We refer to this phenomenon as a bottleneck, or limiting factor.

The Mexican rancher, mentioned in Chapter 12, who acquired a large population of toads by constructing ramps in his water troughs, illustrates the bottleneck principle. By making water accessible to his resident toad population at a time when they might not obtain it any other way, he eliminated a bottleneck that had probably been keeping toad numbers low.

When attempting to increase the numbers of a certain species you should make sure that the actions taken first address the weakest link in the species' life cycle, as the weak link test reminds you. If you then find that numbers still don't increase, look for a bottleneck that could be limiting the population.

Water for crucial short periods often constitutes the bottleneck for populations that must drink routinely. They may have feed, cover, and water enough for enormous numbers, but if water lacks for several days at one point in the year, the entire population, if nonmobile, dies.

Having water present is often not enough, as it has to actually be available to the species. I had many sand grouse in my game reserve in Zimbabwe. They not only needed water, but also had to be able to walk into it each evening to thoroughly wet their breast feathers. In this manner, they carried water miles out into the dry country for their chicks, which could not survive without it. A simple ramp providing drinking access, then was not enough. I had to ensure the birds could walk into water that was deep enough to wet their chests, but shallow enough to prevent drowning.

Many a rancher has told of placing waterpoints out on the land that can be used by birds, small animals, and game, but failed to understand that steep-sided stock troughs in sites of maximum disturbance and no cover do not serve those species and may even kill them. At low water levels, birds and other creatures frequently can clear the sides, but drown when they cannot get back out. I like to ask such ranchers how they would fare if they crossed a hot desert toward the scent of water to find a 10,000-gallon reservoir six inches out of reach.

Many bottlenecks, however, require more diligent observation than that. I have a falconer friend in Scotland with whom I have enjoyed some good days of sport on his grouse moor. Once, after many hours of trudging through the heather behind the pointers, he commented that the grouse population should be higher given the quantity of food, cover, and water—the most common bottlenecks. After mulling the evidence, we hit on the fact that a more productive moor nearby had graveled roadsides that might offer more grit for a bird's crop and digestion of heather.

Soon afterward he put out mounds of broken shells at several sites, but later reported that the grouse ignored them, so he abandoned the idea. Close inspection a few years later when I returned, nevertheless showed that although the piles had not visibly diminished, some creature, presumably grouse, had methodically removed the tiniest bits of shell, leaving only larger, unusable pieces.

The bottleneck principle applies equally to plants. A good example are the potentially very productive vleis (grassy valleys) in much of southern Africa. Moisture, soil depth, and all other conditions for a highly complex biological community exist. However, in the dry season, the low-lying vlei can experience a frost or two that limits development to communities dominated by grasses and forbs. Beyond the frost line, the biological community can develop to woodland.

Absence of a particular trace mineral is another common bottleneck in plant growth. I once worked with a rancher in Africa in open, grassy country that, for no obvious reason, lacked a good mixture of woody, deeper-rooted plants. One day while surveying the bleak countryside from the ranch house veranda, I noticed that the scraggly hedge his wife had tried to establish round the house was noticeably healthier at one point. Neither the rancher nor his wife could explain this, so we dug up the earth for evidence and discovered the copper ground of their lightning rod. As a consequence, I recommended the addition of copper to the supplementary feed given the cattle so they could begin to spread it on the land.

Unfortunately, as the war heated up in Zimbabwe, I was unable to get back to the ranch and never knew the outcome.

Dealing with Predators That Become a Problem

Typical policies toward predators reveal a deeply ingrained blindness that an understanding of community dynamics and population management might enlighten. We need much more research into the role of predators, but we at last sense how the relationship between predators and herding animals keeps entire communities in brittle environments vital. We can only guess at the number of other situations where our uninformed destruction of predators has cost us dearly.

Livestock owners the world over have tended to regard all predators as enemies. Nowhere has this aversion led to further extremes than the United States, where ranchers and government agencies go to incredible lengths to kill predators while making little genuine effort to live with them or to protect livestock by other simple means.

I have worked with ranchers who went out of business killing predators, while not making the slightest effort to protect their stock. In one case, the rancher had access to at least half a dozen well-known and tested methods to eliminate losses to coyotes without killing a single one, yet he kept killing coyotes until he went broke. That his war on the coyote did not save him was not surprising. Typically the predators that take on man and his livestock are particular individuals that learn to be increasingly cunning as attempts to kill them fail.

Killing coyotes does little good, particularly if you fail to get the one that is killing your stock. No matter how many you kill that have not acquired the habit, the killer remains and becomes ever more clever and will in time educate others. If you doubt that animals do learn destructive habits from each other, consider how quickly a cow that breaks through fences can pass on the trick.

With man-eating lions, tigers, and leopards, as well as problem hippos, elephants, and bears, we have long known that one must deal with the particular animal, not the whole population. We have recognized the same principle when one of our own kind becomes a murderer. Killing people at random is no response. We have to try, no matter how hard, to catch the murderer.

Some years ago in Zimbabwe, a nasty-tempered elephant had brought railroad maintenance to a virtual halt on an important section of a much-used line to the seaports. Each night, he harassed the workers as they slept and so terrified them that they refused to turn out the next day. Several bulls were shot in the vicinity, but each time the section camp turned in in peace, it woke in terror. By the time I arrived the rogue had acquired a definite style. I waited on the edge of the camp at night, and when an elephant singled me out for attack I knew I had the culprit. After that, despite many elephants in the area, the camp slept in peace.

Chapter 5 mentioned a research study in which only one species of predator was removed from a community. With no other disturbance, as we saw, within one year the number of species in the community had been drastically reduced. Few simple studies have so clearly illustrated the vital stabilizing role of predators in communities. Unfortunately in many areas, particularly those now set aside as national parks in brittle environments, humans were for thousands of years a major predator, keeping animals healthy and wild, but today's sightseeing crowds want tame animals.

Many years ago Charles Elton, one of the earliest animal ecologists, as they were then called, described the Eltonian pyramid of numbers. In concept, it resembles the energy pyramid shown in Chapter 15 (figure 15-1). Although we normally see the relationship in terms of the number of lower animals it takes to support one predator, if predation plays the crucial role we suspect it does, the pyramid also shows how many prey animals depend on a single species of predator.

Having been a rancher, I understand the frustration when a wild hunter turns on domestic stock, but it does not excuse the wholesale slaughter of predators that were innocent and play a vital part in balancing populations, including many that are agricultural pests. Certainly as I think back on the many years that I have worked with croplands, rangelands, livestock, and game populations, the healthiest situations contained high levels of predators. The only exception was where a population of omnivores, such as baboons, monkeys, pigs, or humans, turned predatory. Because omnivores are not solely dependent on predation for their subsistence, they can kill out the species they prey on and continue to thrive. To prevent this outcome, omnivore populations may have to be reduced through direct intervention.

Conversely, the most unhealthy situations for the land, crops, wildlife, and stock have always had a history of predator persecution. I don't believe this is coincidence. Clearly, we have much to learn and many attitudes to change before we will see intelligent and wise management of predator populations and of our ecosystem as a whole.

Conclusion

In summary, humanity depends entirely on living organisms, which are indivisible components of communities of complexity beyond our comprehension. We must, however, manage populations within those communities. The fundamental importance of the whole community can too easily be overlooked when we focus on rare, endangered, or preferred species.

But in reality, the members of any one species cannot exist outside their relationship with millions of other organisms of different species. In the short term, a species might have to be favored to be saved, but in the long run truly saving it can only rest on sustaining the biological community in which it thrives.

Part IX

Planning Procedures Unique to Holistic Management

43

Departing from
the Conventional

The next chapters introduce planning techniques used in three areas where Holistic Management has enabled us to depart substantially from conventional practice: the annual planning of any business finances; the layout of facilities and infrastructure on extensive land areas; and the management of grazing animals. Each chapter is an overview of a particular procedure that is addressed fully in separate handbooks: *Holistic Financial Planning, Holistic Land Planning,* and *Holistic Grazing Planning,* all of which are currently in preparation.*

Chapter 44, Holistic Financial Planning, applies most generally to people in a variety of situations, although for reasons of focus it is written for those who are running a business of some sort. Unless you are actually managing grazing animals and large tracts of land, such as a farm, ranch, national park, or forest, you may want to skip Chapters 45 and 46, although if you have a particular interest in these subjects, a light reading of these chapters could prove enlightening.

Holistic Financial Planning

The Holistic Financial Planning procedure is so closely allied to holistic decision making, that its development over the last thirty or so years has

---

*Contact the Center for Holistic Management (see page 617) for more information on these handbooks or on the interim planning and monitoring guides available from the center.

followed a similar convoluted path. Chapter 3 described my frustration as a consultant in watching a number of my ranching clients go bankrupt even though we were healing the land and improving livestock production. In the main, this was occurring because of other ventures these people had been lured into by attractive government programs and soft loans, particularly those relating to the building of dams to irrigate cash crops.

Their financial situation improved rather quickly once we brought in a couple of consultants who worked with these clients to develop a sound financial plan that went well beyond the "cigarette box" calculations most of them had operated on for years. But this success was short lived. Income increased, but within no time at all expenses rose to match it, and by year's end they might be worse off than ever. This was especially the case when they planned expenses based on the income they *anticipated* receiving and that income did not come in on time, or came in short. But even more worrisome was that the planning did not account for any "externalities"— the social and environmental consequences stemming from their plans.

Holistic Financial Planning grew out of these challenges. My clients' tendency to let costs rise to the anticipated income appeared to be a trait most humans share, including myself. In an attempt to thwart this tendency, we now plan the profit before planning expenses. Then when planning expenses we give priority to those that will generate the most new income this year over those that merely keep the business ticking along. With the development of the holistic goal and the seven testing guidelines in the early 1980s, we finally had a way to account for all the externalities normally absent from conventional planning approaches.

Years of trial and error and many mistakes have finally given us a planning procedure in which we have confidence and that produces lasting results. Although it was originally developed for use by those engaged in sunlight-harvesting businesses, particularly farming and ranching, the planning procedure has since been modified for use in other businesses.

Holistic Grazing Planning and Holistic Land Planning

The procedures for grazing and land planning were developed in tandem. Once we understood the role of time in grazing and trampling, we knew that animals would have to move continually, but to do that required new thinking in the way fencing, water points, and handling facilities were laid out.

When we took on this challenge in the 1960s, we were pressed by war and international trade sanctions following Rhodesia's unilateral declaration of independence from Britain. Most farmers had to diversify from what had become a traditional crop rotation of one year of tobacco and five years of grass. To make ends meet, the continuous grass fallows had to yield to other crops interspersed between the years of tobacco and grass. In addition, serious livestock raising entered the picture for the first time on many tobacco farms as a way to produce extra income off the remaining range, grass fallows, and crop residues.

Prevailing wisdom required fencing off range sites of different types to prevent overgrazing or overtrampling of favored areas. Stock were to feed in certain paddocks at certain times according to a systematic pattern. However, this never succeeded in practice because most of the farms were in broken, hilly country where arable land lay in small pockets among a matrix of roads, tracks, rivers, grassy valleys, and woodland remnants. We had to find a new approach that would handle such complexity on the ground amid ever-changing circumstances.

After several years of trying out all sorts of fencing designs and planning techniques, we finally developed a combination of the land planning approach summarized in Chapter 45 and the grazing planning covered in Chapter 46. The two go hand in glove where livestock run on any land. The land planning procedure should be used whenever large tracts of land requiring a considerable investment in infrastructure, such as roads, water development, or working and storage facilities, are involved. The old rules no longer apply when planning new developments or when modifying old ones. As you will see, the opportunities for improvement are immense and only limited by the creativity of the planners.

Smaller tracts of land, such as those surrounding a homesite, rarely require a long-term land plan as the amount of infrastructure needed is minimal and can usually be developed within a few years at relatively low cost. The infrastructure required might include technology that enables one to recycle household wastes or a cistern for storing rainwater collected on rooftops, small stock pens, or a web of foot paths. But the emphasis in such cases is on planning for different vegetation patterns—the siting of trees, shrubs, vegetable gardens, and so on, rather than major physical developments. This sort of planning is something that those familiar with the principles of permaculture design have addressed very well. For further information on permaculture design refer to the references pertaining to this chapter at the end of the book.

Currently we, as a center, have no experience in planning any town or city holistically, but there would obviously be benefits to doing so. Towns and cities demand a great deal of infrastructure, the development of which should be guided far more than it is now by social needs and, despite the artificiality of the urban environment, by ecological principles. An earlier chapter suggested that the least we might do in the latter case is improve the water cycle by encouraging rainfall to soak in rather than run off. In brittle environments, we should pay particular attention to the water cycle on the catchments surrounding urban areas. If these catchments are not managed in a way that enhances the effectiveness of the water cycle, the town or city is ultimately doomed.

Holistic Financial Planning is tactical in scope. You plan once a year and implement the plan within that year. Holistic Grazing Planning is also a tactical exercise, although the planning is usually done twice a year. In both financial and grazing planning, monitoring what you plan is critical and almost certainly will lead to modifications of the plan throughout the year, sometimes even daily in the case of the grazing plan. Holistic Land Planning, on the other hand, is strategic in scope and only needs to be done once. Implementing your plan is an ongoing process that is likely to take many years.

The biological monitoring process, referred to in Chapter 33 as essential for ensuring the production of the future landscape described in your holistic goal, is not strictly a planning procedure and is not covered in this section. It is explained at length, however, in the *Handbook for Early-Warning Biological Monitoring* (currently in preparation), which is essential reading for anyone engaged in land management.

Other areas of endeavor that require developing a specific planning procedure to facilitate Holistic Management have not yet come to light. There is the likelihood, however, that this could change as practitioners in many more fields of endeavor shift away from planning that focuses on short- or long-term objectives to planning that focuses on achieving a holistic goal.

44

Holistic Financial Planning: Creating the Financial Roadmap to Your Holistic Goal

Holistic Financial Planning is the single most important activity undertaken each year to ensure that all the money earned and spent is in line with your holistic goal. If prosperity and financial security are included in your holistic goal, then few activities during the year count more than this planning. It takes precedence over vacations, interruptions, or excuses of any kind.

In Holistic Financial Planning you plan according to attitudes, priorities, and considerations not normally included in preparing an annual budget. Although the completed physical layout of the holistic financial plan, either on paper or on computer spreadsheet, looks like a conventional budget or cash flow plan, the resemblance ends there.

Conventional financial planning generally has three stages. First, comes an estimate of income from enterprises determined most profitable. Then, expenses are budgeted in columns for capital investment, overhead and variable costs, loan repayments, and so on. You try to keep costs below the anticipated gross income by using past records and information from experts and other sources and by adjusting for inflation and cost trends. Finally, you calculate the cost of borrowed money, and out comes a bottom line in red or black. If this is not satisfactory, you redo this and that and juggle the figures till the results are acceptable. As long as all endeavors appear cost-effective and the plan "cash flows" well in that it predicts no cash shortages the bank will not cover, all should go well.

For many years I did such financial planning in great detail with economists and accountants and also taught it to clients. With the development of the holistic decision-making process, however, I realized how far short this approach fell from what was attainable through Holistic Management. Holistic Financial Planning departs from conventional methods in two significant ways: (1) it is guided by a holistic goal and decisions that take you toward it; and (2) it accounts for human nature and requires an attitude bent on success, especially when your holistic goal includes profit. But even when it does not, as may be the case in some government agencies and nonprofit organizations providing a service, this same positive attitude will result in less waste and the provision of better services at less cost.

Psychology of the Planning

After years of consulting in many countries for clients of great variety in sophistication and enterprise, I came to the conclusion that the attitudes held by the people involved in financial planning caused far too many of them to actually plan nonprofitability and then complain loudly when they achieved it.

How could this be? Thorough research, rigorous computation of cost-effectiveness, and sophisticated accounting techniques seemed to make little difference. People of every description finished the year in the same nail-biting suspense over their bottom line. No matter what state, country, or currency, no matter what size of business, what market or price conditions, I always found the same picture. Planned income, $200,000; expenses $195,000. Planned income $1,350,000; expenses, $1,340,000. Like the unanimous elections in totalitarian countries, this defied logic. Profit margins simply could not be so uniform and proportionately small across so many situations.

Eventually it dawned on me that the problem must lie in the only common factor, human nature. Like most people, my clients were allowing their expenses to rise to meet the income they anticipated receiving. I suffered from the same weakness.

Point A in figure 44-1 shows my condition on graduating from university. The left-hand bar of the graph shows my income from which I buy the essentials of life at a cost represented by the right-hand bar. The minuscule surplus surprises me as I had thought that earning real money after years of scrounging through university would put me in clover, so I looked forward to getting a raise.

Point B shows my situation after getting the raise. I still don't have any extra money and wouldn't even say I am living better. On the other hand, I traded my motorbike and some cash for a car so I could get around more comfortably, and I really did need that new rifle, that pair of binoculars, and so many other things.

Points C and D represent further raises, but each time the expected savings account never materializes. Most people manage life in this way until

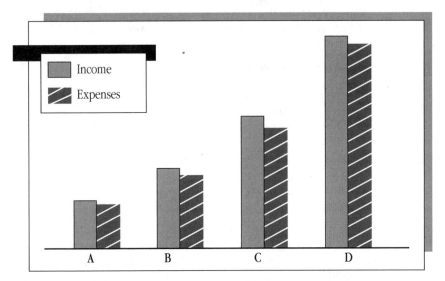

Figure 44-1 *My personal expenses always rose to match the income I anticipated receiving.*

they have to make do on a pension. If you look back over the years at what you earned and what you saved, they probably bear little relationship. Far more important than savings were the things you bought because of peer pressure, advertising, or simply because the material culture around you made them seem necessary.

The Debt Trap

Businesses tend to operate in the same way, automatically allowing their expenses to rise toward the anticipated income. When the income comes only once or twice a year, however, as it does for those engaged in seasonal businesses or producing agricultural commodities, the tendency to let expenses rise to anticipated income often leads to trouble because the money to cover expenses is commonly borrowed. The retailer whose business is open only over a three-month tourist season, can easily calculate the income she expects to receive once the tourists arrive, and then borrow on the strength of that future income. The farmer can do the same for the crops or livestock he will have ready for sale in the fall. In either case, almost always the expenses will come close to anticipated income. However, in the retailer's case, the tourists, for a variety of reasons, may not materialize in the numbers expected. In the farmer's case, wheat or lamb prices could suddenly tumble. Neither of them would be able to repay what they borrowed when the bill came due. Servicing that debt now becomes a major expense, most of which is interest, and all of which is unproductive in that it will not generate any additional income.

Plan Profit Before You Plan Expenses

Crudely expressed, profit is the difference between the money received for products or services sold and the money spent on producing those products or services. No matter how you look at it, every aspect on either side of this simple equation lies within the control of the people running the business. Production costs are certainly within your control, and because controlling them is so vital to profitability, we will return to this subject again. The price you receive for your products is also within your control. Even when your products are sold as raw goods (calves, wheat, copper ore) and their price is set by the commodities market, you can elect to add value to the raw goods or in some cases produce something else entirely. If you have made up your mind that you are powerless to plan a profit, and therefore not responsible for the outcome of your planning, you cannot expect anything but the most mediocre results.

To counter the tendency to let the costs of production rise to the anticipated income level, in Holistic Financial Planning you plan the profit *before* allocating any money to expenses. Once you have figures for the total income you expect to receive, cut that figure by up to one half and set that

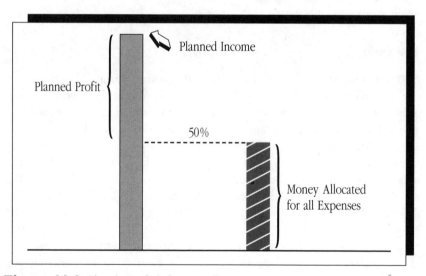

Figure 44-2 *Plan the profit before you allocate any money to expenses. Once you have calculated the total income you expect to receive, cut that figure by up to half and set that amount aside as your profit.*

amount aside as your profit. You have now set a limit on the amount of money available for expenses and to which costs can rise. The principle is illustrated simply in figure 44-2.

If you are planning for a government agency or nonprofit organization you use the same principle and plan a "profit." However, this profit, which by law (usually) must be used within the organization to meet the purpose for which it was formed, can now be used to enhance the services provided, as will become clear later.

The profit planned needs to be substantial so that severe restraints are placed on the funds left for running the business. If the amount of profit set aside is too great, however, people will be demoralized as there is so little left to run the business. If the profit planned is too low, plenty of money is left and there is little challenge in keeping costs of production down.

This mental exercise is vital, yet most people at first blush consider it impossible to do. Nevertheless, collective creativity and concentrated effort can produce amazing results when you plan your profit first.

The Planning Process

The Holistic Financial Planning procedure includes two phases. The preliminary phase is devoted to information-gathering and decision testing. It takes place in several sessions held periodically over several months. In the second phase, which generally requires a day or two (or more in a large or fairly complex business), you create the actual plan—set aside the profit, finalize income and expense figures, and make any adjustments needed to ensure an even cash flow over the year. It is important that you schedule this final session well in advance and that you find a quiet, well-ordered workspace in which to hold it. As your mental state governs the quality of your planning, you should pick the time and place carefully. You cannot afford to have this session disrupted by key people who leave to attend to phone calls or to other chores. If there are daily tasks that are essential to the business, spread the planning session over several uninterrupted half days. Some people, particularly those engaged in a family business that is run out of the home, find it easiest to schedule their planning session at a hotel or retreat center away from home.

Start the preliminary phase well before the end of your financial year, anywhere from three to six or more months prior to your final planning session. It will take this amount of time to gather the information you need, discuss it, test it, and to arrive at a number of decisions. Be assured that the sessions involved in this phase need not be long and that the information gathering is generally divided among various teams of people. Decisions will be made at each preliminary session that will prompt further research, the results of which will influence the outcome of the following session. We will look at the content of each of these preliminary sessions in more detail shortly. First, however, we need to consider *who* does the planning.

Determine Who Should Be Involved and to What Extent

Far too many businesses turn their financial planning over to the firm's in-house accountant or accounting department because these individuals deal with figures all the time and have a record of previous business transactions they can consult. The skills and knowledge required of an accountant, however, are not the same as those needed for Holistic Financial Planning. There will be times when it is appropriate to utilize their expertise, but accountants should never lead the planning process. That role should go instead to a person with a good grasp of the business and skills in facilitation and coordination.

In larger organizations, it will be necessary to divide responsibilities among teams. Generally each enterprise (a specific product or service, or line of products or services, from which you derive income) will have a team of people associated with it. Those people will be responsible for much of the information gathering required in the preliminary phase, as well as for testing a number of decisions related to their enterprise. Expenses that are not linked directly to one enterprise, but affect the business as a whole, also need to be assigned to one or more people or teams who will assume the same responsibility. In smaller organizations, each team member also serves on the main planning team, which is ultimately responsible for producing the plan. In larger organizations, the main planning team includes representatives from each of the management teams.

The people responsible for earning and spending the money, that is, those creating the products, dealing with the clients, purchasing supplies and consuming them, need to come up with the figures that are directly under their control. If someone else does this for them, the figures are likely to be inaccurate. More important, the people who earn and spend the money and consume the supplies have no ownership in the figures someone else plans, and thus no incentive to make sure that once the plan is implemented the figures stay on target. When you do not involve everyone to at least this extent, the results you obtain will be far from ideal. People will be at all different levels of understanding and sophistication, and you will have to make judgments and decisions on how much each individual can handle, but err on the side of giving people responsibility rather than not doing so out of fear.

You also need to remember that everyone in the business or organization is working toward the same holistic goal and needs to feel assured that the plan as a whole is taking them toward it. The main planning team needs to be limited in size, simply because with more than a dozen or so people doing the actual planning on spreadsheets, the process will bog down. In most small businesses this is not an issue because nearly everyone is included in the main planning team. In larger businesses it becomes an issue only when communication is poor or access to information is denied. Everyone involved in the business needs to have a hand in developing the figures for which their team is directly responsible, but must also understand the figures developed, including the decision testing that led to them, for the business as a whole. Otherwise they may not see how their work relates to the work of the whole and the achievement of the holistic goal.

Preliminary Planning Sessions

Each of the planning sessions in the preliminary phase requires some preparation if it is to be productive and brief. In large businesses, only the main planning team needs to be present at these sessions, but each of its members must be able to reflect accurately the views of the management teams they represent. In some cases, the preparation involved is merely to ask each individual to reflect on the content so that discussions are more meaningful. In other cases, facts and figures have to be researched in advance, or the session will be fruitless. The preliminary sessions outlined are those we as a center have found necessary. Other businesses and organizations may find that combining sessions or rearranging the content serves them better. Treat the following as a guide that you can adapt to your own situation.

First Session: Annual Review

An annual review is an essential first step in Holistic Financial Planning. It is a time for you to reflect on where you have been and what might be standing in the way of where you want to go. There are three basic questions to answer in the annual review, each of which is likely to influence your financial plan for the coming year:

Is There a Logjam? Each year, it is essential that you mentally scan through your whole operation to see if a logjam exists that is preventing you from making genuine progress toward your holistic goal. If you have been managing holistically for a couple of years and you have yet to see a dramatic turnaround in your situation, you need to find the blockage and identify its cause. As Chapter 48 will explain, the first place to look is within your own organization, particularly at the degree of commitment people have to the holistic goal. Commitment may be lacking because of any number of reasons: the holistic goal may need to be more clearly defined, knowledge or skills may be lacking, communication may be poor, and so on. Market factors are seldom responsible for impeding rapid progress toward your holistic goal. Insufficient capital occasionally is. You will find the answer more quickly if everyone takes time to reflect prior to the session. If a logjam is found and it takes money to help to remove it, then that expenditure will have priority when you begin to allocate money to covering expenses. The reason for this is obvious. If that one expenditure helps to remove the blockage, the whole business can move forward.

Are There Any Other Factors Adversely Affecting the Business As a Whole? There may be administrative shortcomings that although not directly connected to a specific enterprise could adversely affect all enterprises if not rectified. Your accountant might need an assistant, for instance, because the volume of work has increased to such an extent that she can no longer support each enterprise adequately. You may require a new copy machine in the coming year because the one you currently have is constantly in need of repair and the frequent breakdowns waste everyone's time and cause unneeded stress. Or you may be running a business out of your home and now find you need to build an office or rent space nearby, because your ability to work is seriously impaired by constant interruptions from family and friends and by the lack of a place where you can keep all business-related items within easy reach.

In each of these cases the expenses involved—to hire an assistant, to buy or lease a new copier, or to build or rent office space—would rank high on your list of priorities as long as you are sure they are genuinely needed. In relieving everyone of a fair amount of stress, they would help to increase productivity in each enterprise and thus benefit the business as a whole. Don't worry too much at this stage about the number of items needing attention. Later sessions will help you to sort out the ones that will benefit you most in the coming year.

Are the Gross Profits on Current Enterprises As Good As Planned? Although you are not at the end of your current financial year, you will know how each enterprise is faring because you are monitoring figures monthly. Will the gross profits planned be achieved this year? Are the gross profits likely to remain the same, increase, or decrease next year? If the planned gross profits are not likely to be achieved by the end of the current year, you need to know why. Unless you are dealing with a new enterprise that involves a learning curve, which can easily throw your calculations off, you may need to enhance or modify the product or service involved, or perhaps drop the enterprise altogether. The latter consideration will be addressed more thoroughly in later sessions.

If your answers to any one of these questions require further research before you can incorporate the expenses involved into your financial plan, make sure that individuals are assigned to do that work in preparation for the following sessions.

Optional Session: Brainstorming New Sources of Income

No matter what enterprises you are engaged in, you need to challenge them as you start to manage holistically and periodically thereafter. All too often businesses add or drop enterprises only when faced with hardship or crisis. Why wait until circumstances force a change? You are generally better off and more secure if you take a proactive attitude. Many businesses today view growth solely in terms of sales volume, but in the future may well seek to grow in terms of quality—in their products and in the lives of those producing and consuming the products. The idea that enables you to move in this direction could well emerge from brainstorming.

Periodically brainstorming new ideas will help to keep you ahead of the game. But don't overdo it. Few businesses survive by chopping and changing enterprises every year. Any new enterprise always involves a learning curve and will take a year or more to prove out. Brainstorming sessions held every three to five years are usually sufficient.

The formal brainstorming process we use is described in detail in the *Holistic Financial Planning Handbook*. Briefly, it should involve everyone who works with you, as well as some outsiders who do not know your business well and thus are not already convinced of what can't be done. It pays to even include children, when appropriate, because their creativity and imagination are boundless. Within a very short time the group you have gathered should be able to brainstorm a list of one hunded or more possibilities for new enterprises, or modifications to old ones, ranging from the patently ridiculous to the eminently practical.

This brainstorming session can be held any time prior to the actual planning session, but the earlier the better because it will take time to narrow down the list, to estimate the income and expenses for enterprises that make the final cut, and to run these enterprises through the testing guidelines.

Before engaging in new enterprises consider the following:

- It takes time to develop skills and perfection in any enterprise. There is always a learning curve, which can be costly. As you change to the new, plan a solid overlap with the old where possible.

- Your managerial effectiveness is diluted by the number of enterprises for which you are responsible. This is especially applicable to small businesses with few staff. In taking on new enterprises, the staff are often stretched too thin, which tends to destabilize all enterprises and the business as a whole. This problem can be overcome if the management of the new enterprise is contracted out to someone else.

- There is a direct relationship between management effectiveness and the proximity to what is being managed. This is the reasoning behind the old cliché that the finest fertilizer in the world is a farmer's foot-steps or behind the more current notion of "managing by walking around." Obviously, the more frequent the contact with the enter-prise, the greater your chances of spotting trouble early, and the more opportunities you have for finding ways to improve the enterprise. I experienced a similar phenomenon as a schoolboy. At my school we had four boarding houses and we competed as houses in all sports. The tennis courts for the house I resided in were only five paces from the back door. The boys in the other three houses had to walk several hundred yards to get to their courts. Even though we were allocated to our houses at random, my house won the tennis cup twenty-six years in a row. I believe our winnings were directly re-lated to our distance from the tennis courts. We played or watched tennis constantly, even while waiting to go for our meals. Our rivals spent far less time playing or watching tennis because, for them, it took some forethought and effort.

- It is often easier to alter an existing product, or develop new uses for it, than to create something entirely new. Bear this in mind as you brainstorm new sources of income. There may well be a variety of uses your current products could be put to that you are not promot-ing. The first artificial kidney (dialysis machine) was created from a slightly modified Maytag washing machine. Countless other inven-tions have been developed by finding new uses for old products.

SELECTING THE APPROPRIATE ENTERPRISES

Bearing these points in mind, you now need to narrow down the list of possibilities you have brainstormed to find the ones that suit you best. Add your present enterprises to the list to see how they compare to the new possibilities. We use the following process to weed out inappropriate enterprises.

- In the first cut, drop any ideas that conflict with how you have said you want your lives in this particular whole to be (society and cul-ture test). There are likely to be many, if the brainstorming was free flowing, fun, and irreverent.

- In the second cut, drop the ideas that are patently ridiculous, such as raising purple mice or engaging in the flea circus business. *But be care-ful.* The best ideas are initially often ridiculed by people who are the most knowledgeable. The first person to propose the post office use small pieces of gummed paper with a financial value printed on the reverse—the postage stamp—was ridiculed by the Post Master General of Britain. The first copy machine, which few offices are without today, was rejected by every manufacturer it was originally presented to. The world is riddled with such examples. So look twice at ridiculous ideas. Even though you may reject them outright, they could spark ideas that are not so ridiculous.

- The third cut involves the rather informal use of the gross profit analysis test, as you will not have actual figures to use. Look at the remaining possibilities and, thinking broadly, ask what each might bring in as income over and above what it might cost to engage in that enterprise. You want to keep for later consideration those enterprises that bring in the most income for the least cost. These will result in the most gross profit, which, after covering all costs, will finally lead to a greater net profit. Some enterprises may bring in a lot of income but will not necessarily lead to a large gross profit, because the costs associated with running them would be so high. In this step you are purely trying to single out for more detailed work those enterprises that clearly offer far more return than others. You are not looking for minor differences, but major ones.

- In the fourth cut, use the rest of the testing guidelines to help you to assess whether the likely actions and inputs involved in each possible enterprise will move you closer to your holistic goal. Would the enterprise use significant energy? Where from and what type? Where would the money come from? Would it use substances in its manufacture that do not break down? Would it result in products ultimately damaging to the environment, or could all components be returned for reuse? Would there be social consequences not in line with your holistic goal? If any of the tools or actions used in the enterprise would obviously not take you toward your holistic goal, but lead you away from it, eliminate the enterprise for now.

- By the time you have reached the fifth cut, you are likely to have only three or four of your original hundred ideas left, plus, in all likelihood, your current enterprises. Now you are ready to do a detailed gross profit analysis with actual figures, comparing each enterprise to the others to see which ones are most profitable. You cannot do this in the current session as it will take time to gather the information needed, which includes reasonably accurate income and expense figures. Assign those responsible for each enterprise to get that information and bring it to the next session.

Second Session: Determine the Enterprises You Will Engage in This Year

The main task of this session is to perform a *detailed gross profit analysis* of all the enterprises you might engage in over the coming year. These enterprises will include the ones you are currently engaged in and any new enterprises you may have brainstormed or that your market research shows have promise. In the case of the latter, make sure that any actions associated with these enterprises pass the testing, much as you did for enterprises you brainstormed.

Remember that in determining the gross profit on each possible enterprise (the income it generates minus the expenses directly linked to it) you are merely figuring what each is likely to contribute to covering the overheads of the business each year. If you are considering a new enterprise that involves the expenditure of substantial capital you don't now have, you first need to know that its gross profit is satisfactory and how it compares to the other enterprises being analyzed. If it still looks promising, then following this session you will need to determine how that capital will be raised and the terms and conditions for repayment. This information will be needed in planning the cash flow during the second phase of planning.

If you are not considering adding any new enterprises, this session is likely to be brief, but it is still essential because the gross profits on current enterprises are likely to change as a result of price increases or decreases, product modifications you make as part of your marketing strategy, and so on. All of these factors and more will have to be considered prior to this session so you can be reasonably sure that your income and expense figures for current enterprises are accurate. These same figures will be used in determining total income and expenses in the second phase of planning.

If you are considering additional enterprises, the gross profit analysis will give you a very good idea of which ones should be added in the coming year. If your original product lines or services were sound, you will likely continue with them. But if one of the new enterprises offers far more promise, you should devote the remainder of this session to discussing how to accomplish the changeover from the old to the new without loss or disruption.

Third Session: Determine the Weak Link in Each Enterprise and How to Address It

In preparation for this session, the teams responsible for each existing enterprise need to consider which link in the enterprise's chain of production is weakest—and there will always be one. As Chapter 27 explained, the chain of production has three links (resource conversion, product conversion, and marketing), the first of which varies depending on the type of enterprise. When you allocate money to cover expenses, actions taken to address the weak link will have priority because they generate additional money over and above what you are currently able to generate.

Once each team has determined the current weak link in their particular enterprise, they need to consider the actions that will address it, some of which may have already been considered in gathering figures for the gross profit analysis. An in-depth discussion among team members may turn up other possibilities, each of which should be run through the following tests, any of which could apply: cause and effect, weak link (social or biological), energy/money—source and use, sustainability, and society and culture.

Each team now reports on the results of their work on each enterprise to the main planning team, the reason for this third session. The main planning team needs to be aware of the weak link in each enterprise, how each management team plans to address it, and how the team arrived at these decisions. Although this is largely an information-sharing session, it can also lead to changes in some decisions, as people not directly engaged in a specific enterprise often contribute insights gained from their perspective as outsiders. Some actions may need to be tested again with the participation of the whole group, which could lead to some modifications. Only rarely, however, would the main planning team determine that another link was weakest because they seldom know the enterprise as well as those directly responsible for and working with it daily.

Fourth Session: Make a Preliminary Allocation of Expenses

When you conducted your annual review, and later when you determined the weak link in each enterprise, you were beginning to determine the expenses that would have priority as you allocated funds. Many other expenses of course will have to be considered, and this becomes easier if you lump them into categories:

- *Wealth-generating expenses* are those that will increase your income over and above what you are currently earning. In the case of a government or nonprofit organization these expenses would be those that would enhance the services provided. Wealth-generating expenses include, but are not limited to, any expenditures that would address the weak link in each individual enterprise, clear a logjam, or rectify administrative shortcomings adversely affecting all enterprises. Occasionally, what starts out as the weakest link in a particular enterprise might be addressed quickly and with minimal expense early in the year, and another link could then take over as the weakest. Go ahead and also include the expenses that would address the upcoming weak link in the wealth-generating category. You will later test the various wealth-generating, or service-enhancing, expenses against each other, and some could be dropped in favor of those that generate the most new income or provide the greatest enhancement of services.

- *Inescapable expenses* are those that are absolutely inescapable: they cannot be adjusted, delayed, or changed in any way, *and you are morally obligated to pay them.* Very few expenses are assigned to this category and many businesses will have none. An example might include payments on a contract you have with your parents or a partner to buy them out of the business on fixed terms, or a land tax that cannot be delayed or negotiated. If you have any doubt whether an expense falls in this category, assign it to the next one, maintenance expenses. The inescapable category is a minor one. It merely gives you a place to park expenses you are morally obligated to pay in the coming year, so you can concentrate on the remaining expenses, which you will have to think a great deal about.

- *Maintenance expenses,* are those that are essential to running the business and maintaining present income levels, but will not in themselves generate additional income by strengthening the weak link in any of your enterprises, clearing a logjam, and so on. Most expenses fall into this category: the running costs associated with any enterprise, salaries (with the exception of new staff that will generate additional income in the coming year), taxes, professional services, machinery maintenance, fuel, travel, parts and supplies, utilities, telephone, postage, insurance, and so on. An expense we often suggest be included in this category as well is a depreciation fund to which you contribute annually so that when an asset has lived out its lifespan you have the money to replace it without having to borrow.

Placing an expense in the maintenance category does not imply that it is unimportant. It only means that although it is vital to maintaining present income levels it will not generate *additional income* in the coming year. If marketing is your weak link and you have identified a number of wealth-generating expenses to address it, you still have to cover the routine maintenance expenses associated with your marketing plan or risk a drop in income.

In preparing for this session, you will need to obtain fairly accurate figures for all the expenses considered to date—those associated with each enterprise and those that support the business as a whole—the overhead expenses. The teams responsible for each enterprise should be responsible for gathering the figures relevant to their particular enterprise and for separating the wealth-generating expenses from the maintenance expenses. (Inescapable expenses generally fall into the maintenance category.) The team responsible for overhead expenses should gather the rest of the figures and assign them to a category. The only wealth-generating expenses they will be responsible for are those that address a logjam or a shortcoming affecting the whole business; most of the expenses they deal with will be maintenance expenses.

The wealth-generating expenses should have money allocated to them first. But, since you can never allocate all the money you would like to them without coming up short in trying to cover inescapable and maintenance expenses, each team needs to decide which wealth-generating expenses will be funded in the coming year and how much they will get. Here's how you do this:

First, divide the wealth-generating expenses in each enterprise into two groups: those that must have a specific amount allocated to them or nothing will happen; and those that need every dollar they can get, but can still generate additional income with whatever you can allocate to them. An expense belonging in the first group would be the $3,000 it costs to buy a computer and the lessons in how to use it. It would be pointless allocating only $1,500 to this expense. If you were developing a new marketing program that included advertising in several publications, you could spend anywhere from $1,000 to $10,000 on advertising, depending on the funds available. This advertising expense would fall into the second group, because you could get the program off the ground even if you were able to allocate only $1,000, although obviously you would want to allocate more. Relatively few expenses fall into the first group and the amounts involved are usually small; those that help to rectify an administrative shortcoming, for example, often require an all-or-nothing allocation. Sometimes a wealth-generating expense in the first group might be the first installment on payments that will continue for several years. In those subsequent years they become a maintenance expense because they are not generating additional income, but merely help to ensure that present income levels are maintained.

Second, use the marginal reaction test to compare the wealth-generating expenses within each enterprise. What you are attempting to do in passing through this test is to eliminate any expenses that provide a relatively small marginal return toward your holistic goal compared to the others. Remember, the marginal reaction test is always a subjective one. You will not be able to quantify the dollar figures precisely in most cases, and you do not need to in order to get your answer.

If the expenses in the first group, which require an all-or-nothing allocation, look fairly good, then allocate money to them right away so you can turn your attention to the wealth-generating expenses in the second group. The expenses in the second group, remember, can generate additional income with a minimal investment, but will generate even more with a larger investment. In livestock enterprises in particular, one of these income generating expenses may produce such a high rate of return that it is senseless to invest in *any* of the others. The example I used in Chapter 27 of the rancher choosing between two alternative wealth-generating expenses that would address his resource conversion weak link, is a case in point. When he compared brush clearing to fence building the return on his investment was thousands of times greater for the fencing. Thus, he would spend the $3,000 required for the fencing, but allocate nothing to clearing the brush in the coming year. Any additional money he was able to find would be used to build more fence rather than to clear brush this year.

In other cases, you will more commonly need to allocate a minimal amount of money to several wealth-generating expenses in the second category because the return they provide is spread fairly evenly between them. Suppose you were managing a wildlife park and that one of the enterprises from which you derived income was drive-through tourists, several thousand of which visited each day. This year you have identified product—specifically, the experience of the visitors once they arrive—as your weak link. To address the weak link you have proposed a number of actions, one of which is to acquire a new phone system that requires an all-or-nothing allocation. Your old system cannot handle all the incoming calls and frequently cuts off the callers who do get through—thus giving a bad impression before visitors even arrive at the gate. The problem is fairly serious, so you allocate money to a new phone system and turn now to the other proposed actions that require a minimum investment but need all the money they can get:

- Improve the internal roads. There are bad potholes that are unsightly and potentially damaging to visitors' cars and distract them from their viewing of the park.

- Improve the signs along the drive. The original signs were constructed hastily of poor-quality materials and the paint has faded, making them hard to read. New signs could also provide more educational information.

- Some of the shelters at rest stops along the drive are looking shabby and losing their plaster, and the paths leading from the shelters to the lavatories have large cracks and irregularities in them, making it difficult for the elderly and handicapped to get around.

- You are short of internal communication radios. Sometimes key staff cannot communicate in a visitor-related emergency.

- You are short of vehicles. Sometimes staff have to use their personal vehicles to reach visitors who need assistance.

All but the last two actions indicate that in the past inadequate funds were allocated to maintaining the business's infrastructure, a not uncommon plight for businesses struggling to survive. Such expenses have become wealth generators now because if these actions are taken, they are certain to lead to greater customer satisfaction, an increase in visitors, and thus an increase in revenue. All of these actions probably require money allocated to them. Allocate only the minimum each expense requires. Later on, in the final planning session you will seek ways to increase these amounts.

Remember that the wealth-generating expenses are producing additional income over and above what you planned last year. Occasionally, this additional income might be delayed until the following year, merely because some actions will take more than a year to produce the desired effect. If you do not allocate money to them now, you will further delay the potential increase in income.

Important as wealth-generating expenses are, you still have to have money available to cover all those maintenance expenses to ensure you sustain present income levels, and any expenses that are inescapable. Any wealth-generating expenses that are questionable or, as in the livestock enterprise example, yield very little when compared to another, should be dropped, at least for this year.

Each of the teams responsible for planning the expenses for their various enterprises, as well as the team responsible for planning overhead expenses, will need to summarize the results of their work for the main planning team in this fourth session. The purpose of this session, as for the third session, is to share the information gathered and the decisions made. It also provides an opportunity for discovering where efforts might be overlapping and possibly where some expenses might be shared. Those planning the overhead expenses will have made some preliminary decisions that will affect everyone if they allocated money to expenses that addressed a logjam or a shortcoming affecting all enterprises. Their results, in particular, are likely to engender some discussion before everyone understands and supports them (salaries, remember, are considered an overhead expense) and could engender a fair amount of discussion at this point.

Now having looked at all the expenses in detail, you are ready to move on to the last session of the preliminary phase.

Fifth Session: Brainstorm Ways to Cut Expenses

Until now, the focus has been mainly on the various enterprises of the business. In this session the focus turns to the routine costs involved in running those enterprises as well as the business as a whole. Every dollar you can cut from a maintenance expense, as all of these are, can in the final planning session be added to those wealth-generating expenses that needed every dollar they could get to produce new income—and thus more profit—in the coming year. This session should include everyone, not just the main planning team members, and could also benefit from the creativity of a few outsiders—a very large group is no disadvantage. The session will be fairly brief and should include nothing else on the agenda.

At the start, list your current expense headings on a chart or board everyone can see and make sure that each person understands what each heading entails. In brainstorming ways to cut these expenses you have the option of considering the whole list in one go, or better, considering various categories of expenses, such as fuel, machinery, labor, or office supplies, in several rounds of about ten minutes each. To be effective, brainstorming must be done quickly.

The resulting list of eighty to one hundred or more cost-cutting ideas will require some sifting, testing, and in many cases additional information that will have to be gathered in order to implement them. Generally, these tasks can be assigned to the various teams whose enterprises would benefit and to the team responsible for planning and monitoring the various categories of overhead expenses. In considering the ideas, those completing these tasks should be careful that in cutting expenses they don't also cut corners and sacrifice quality—something the testing should ensure.

Creating Your Plan

Once you have completed the steps in the preliminary planning phase, you should have gathered all of the figures needed for creating the actual plan. These should be recorded on simple worksheets that list each income or expense item and the months in which the money will be received or spent. Each enterprise generally requires one worksheet for income figures and one or more for expenses. Separate worksheets are usually needed to plan the rate of consumption for any supplies purchased in bulk. Once the rate of consumption is known, you will know the amount that has to be purchased and when. When you later implement the plan, you will monitor the rate of consumption planned to avoid the unpleasant surprise of having to order, and thus spend money, ahead of plan.

Each overhead expense category usually has its own worksheet (e.g., office expenses, salaries). Agricultural businesses often have livestock enterprises that require a more sophisticated worksheet because they must track animals that breed, die, change age classification, are culled, or have their wool or hair sheared, and so on within the year. When the figures from all these worksheets are finalized, they will be transferred to a general spreadsheet with columns that correspond to each supporting worksheet.

The main planning team—which, in a small business, remember, includes everyone, but in a larger business (more than a dozen staff) includes representatives from the various teams—is responsible for finalizing the figures and completing the spreadsheet. Once completed, it will provide a big-picture view of the final plan and will later be used for monitoring cash flow and to ensure that the income and expenses planned remain on target. (Computer software is available from the Center for

Holistic Management that greatly eases the task of creating a holistic financial plan and monitoring and controlling it.)

Creating your plan involves four basic steps: plan the income; plan the profit; plan the expenses; and assess the plan before implementing it. The bulk of the planning session, however, is devoted to planning expenses, and for good reason: they are the key to profit.

Plan the Income

This can be done fairly quickly if the teams responsible for each enterprise have completed income worksheets. Although each team estimated income figures much earlier, when determining the gross profit for their enterprise, these figures may have changed by the end of the preliminary planning phase. *Any actions taken to address the weak link will most likely increase income estimates* and this increase should be taken into account when estimating the figures recorded on the worksheets. Once you have transferred all these income figures to the spreadsheet, which covers the entire year, you can immediately see the months in which income from all enterprises will peak and when it could be dangerously low. Add together the income totals for each month to get the total planned income for the year.

Plan the Profit

Now determine how much of your total planned income to set aside as profit. The amount remaining, remember, will have to cover all your expenses. Having made a preliminary allocation of money to these expenses in earlier sessions, you should know the approximate total amount needed. In the happy event that the gap between total income and preliminary total expenses is very wide, and thus the profit margin very high, you will only have minor adjustments to make when it comes to finalizing your expenses. More likely, the gap will be too narrow for comfort and you have some hard replanning to do if you are serious about making a profit.

Deciding how much to set aside as profit is once again a subjective exercise. Remember, your sole purpose in taking this step is to place a ceiling on how high your expenses can rise. For some people, setting aside 50 percent of total income as profit provides a doable challenge; for others, 50 percent would be demoralizing—20 to 30 percent would provide enough challenge. If you are deeply in debt and a large portion of your income must go to servicing that debt, a smaller percentage still may be all you can afford to set aside. If you allocated too much to profit, the money left to run the business, after subtracting debt service payments, would depress rather than challenge everyone. In these cases, it is sometimes better psychology to first subtract annual debt servicing payments from the total income figure and then determine how much of the remaining amount to set aside as profit. The profit you are planning, remember, is mainly to ensure that you place a firm ceiling on how high you will allow expenses to rise. Once that profit is achieved, you will of course do whatever suits you, such as reinvest it in the business, pay off your debt, or take a vacation.

Plan the Expenses

If you have to reduce expense allocations made in the preliminary session to stay within the limits you have set, start with the maintenance expenses. Cut out any that are not absolutely essential to running the business or that can be put off for another year without damaging the business. Here you are challenging all maintenance expenses and nothing is sacred—even routine expenses don't necessarily have to continue. If you cannot trim enough off the maintenance expenses to guarantee your planned profit, then the profit planned is probably too high. Before decreasing the amount set aside as profit, however, consider reducing some of the wealth-generating expenses. In doing so, however, be aware that you will lose the additional income they would have generated. In the end you may well decide that, in lieu of decreasing your wealth-generating expenses, you accept a lower profit. You have in effect taken the decision to forgo profit in favor of investing more money in the business which is fine *as long as you are doing this intentionally* and not just letting the expenses rise to your total anticipated income.

Now you need to look at those maintenance expenses once again to see if you can shave them a little closer (without impairing your ability to function and produce income) and apply what you gain to those wealth-generating expenses that needed every dollar they could get. As mentioned in Chapter 28, you could shave dollars off your phone bill by using a different telephone service; reduce your travel budget by scheduling fewer trips, and so on. Plenty of ideas should have emerged when you brainstormed ways to cut expenses in the preliminary planning phase. If you do your job well, the dollars shaved will add up to a tidy sum. Your decision on which wealth-generating expenses in which enterprises should get those dollars will depend on where they give you the highest return in terms of your holistic goal.

Assess the Plan Before Implementing It

Once the expenses are finalized on the worksheets, you should record their totals on the main spreadsheet. It is a good idea also to add a separate expense column on the spreadsheet for the profit you plan to set aside, marking in predetermined amounts each month, that could be paid into an interest-bearing account.

In assessing the plan, check to see that the total income planned for each month offsets total monthly expenses. You may have to do some juggling to make sure that the cash flows smoothly month by month. If the business is currently running on borrowed money or an overdraft arrangement with the bank, each month's interest should be calculated and given a separate column at the end of the sheet. Add the interest to the accumulating or decreasing debt each month in a column next to it. From this you can see the total cost of borrowing, spot peaks of indebtedness months ahead, and compute that final bottom line figure. The *Holistic Financial Planning Handbook* shows the details. Finally, check to make sure that the total income is equal to or slightly greater than the total expenses. Since the profit has been set aside or included as an expense, these total figures are almost always close.

Have your accountant review the plan, which should provide all the information she needs to assess its tax consequences and advise on how best to address them. She will, of course, calculate depreciation based on standard depreciation tables rather than any figures you may have used in setting aside amounts to cover the replacement of assets. She will also have to calculate any "non-cash income" or increase in your net worth, on which you may be taxed.

Monitoring the Plan

Be prepared to modify the plan as you progress through the year. Events will rarely transpire exactly as planned, which is why you must plan in the first place; if you knew what was going to happen beforehand, there would be no need to plan. Chapter 33 described in some detail the approach we take to monitoring and controlling the financial plan. The *Holistic Financial Planning Handbook* elaborates further.

Rewarding People

An environment that produces motivated people is one in which their ideas and efforts are recognized and where they are genuinely involved in planning and management decisions, which Holistic Management routinely promotes. When recognition is accompanied by any sort of financial reward, however, you can easily get into trouble. Establishing a financial reward program that is fair to everyone and does not in any way destroy trust is a perennial challenge in most businesses. Conventional bonus programs generally fail on both accounts. For instance, when people are given a bonus for increased production, you may well find that input costs have increased right along with the output and thus no greater profit has been realized. Even though the business may be running at a loss, you are obliged to pay the bonuses, which people feel they have earned. All too easily bonuses become a right and are no longer associated with extraordinary performance.

Alternatively, you can base rewards on net managerial income (NMI), which provides a direct and immediate measure of management success in keeping income up and costs down. NMI is derived by subtracting all the expenses under the control of those running the business or enterprise from all the income they are responsible for producing. If there are absentee owners who occasionally inject money into the business, that income would not be considered, nor would income provided by investors or in the form of a loan from the bank. If an absentee owner incurs expenses over which the management team has no control, a common occurrence on absentee-owned farms and ranches, these would not be considered in figuring the NMI. However, you do need to factor in a return on the capital invested by absentee owners, investors, or shareholders, if applicable, before deciding the percent of NMI to share among staff because these are real expenses that have to be met before any sharing takes place.

In allocating a percentage of NMI among all staff, I would encourage you to divide the amounts equally. In a traditional bonus program, a higher percentage is paid to the people "at the top," even though it is the effort of everyone, not just the top few, that is responsible for your success. Those lower down are often in the best position to find ways to reduce costs and are often closest to the clients. They are also generally younger, raising families, and in greater need of income. Higher-level managers are often quick to tell people in mundane jobs how vital their performance is to the success of the whole, but slower to show just how vital when it comes to sharing the rewards. Higher-level managers are paid higher salaries, for good reason; the sharing of success, however, should, in my opinion, reflect everyone's efforts equally.

Conclusion

When profit is included in your holistic goal, the Holistic Financial Planning process will help to ensure that you achieve it in the most socially, economically, and environmentally sound way. All of us have been guilty in the past of contributing to social, economic, and environmental problems by the lifestyles we have adopted and the purchases we have made, and can begin to make changes to rectify this. Those engaged in sunlight-harvesting businesses, such as ranching, farming, fishing, timber, or wildlife production, carry a much bigger burden than the rest of us, however, because in making a profit they have the ability to enhance or diminish the biological capital that sustains us all. That ability has now become a responsibility that people who make a living directly from the soil or the seas have no choice but to accept.

The bill for decades of treating their businesses as industries independent of nature has come due in the form of lost or lifeless soil and water. To reflect a true profit, a successful business must also enhance the soil and water and the life within them that fuels their production. If soil is destroyed rather than enhanced, or water polluted or depleted of life, the profits gained will not be genuine because biological capital is being consumed. However, when you enhance biological capital, you benefit not only the land, but also yourself; biological capital is the one form of capital gain no government can tax, even though it is the most productive.

45

Holistic Land Planning: Developing Infrastructure on Large Tracts of Land

I f the whole you have defined includes land directly under your management and that land is extensive enough to require a fair amount
of infrastructure, you want to ensure that this infrastructure truly serves
your holistic goal—and this takes some planning. Many question this need
to replan when, on most properties, roads, fences, water delivery systems,
cropfields, working and storage facilities, timber extraction routes, and so
on have been in place for years, sometimes hundreds of years, and considerable expense has already gone into developing them. But you have to
remember that the people laying out that infrastructure did so based on
conventional decision making. They had no knowledge of such concepts
as brittle and nonbrittle environments or of the essential role of large
animals in managing certain lands, and they generally focused on immediate needs rather than long-term social, economic, and environmental
soundness.

Up until now we have rarely planned the developments on farms
and ranches, public forests, national parks, or tribal lands with any
long-term vision in mind. Forests were planned for easy extraction, and
national parks for the needs of tourists. Farms were planned around the
original home site, and fields were often dictated by roads and tracks or
hedgerows and more recently by the machinery used to work them.
Ranches were planned around home sites and handling facilities as well.
Fencing went in according to where the water was and, more recently,
where "range sites" differed, the belief being that certain soils and plant
communities needed different grazing regimens to limit damage from

overgrazing or overtrampling. National parks often developed from the first access track and administrative settlement. As tourist growth and demand expanded, tracks, campsites, water points, and other developments were added, but almost always without any long-term vision (or holistic goal) in mind.

If you are not to be tied forever to an inferior infrastructure layout, which can have many hidden costs associated with it, it pays to start afresh and to plan now according to the needs and desires expressed in your holistic goal. The plan you create will be for the long term (one hundred years or more) and will be implemented in steps and stages, guided largely by your annual holistic financial plan. As you will later see, the changeover from old to new need not be costly; in fact it can usually be accomplished in ways that earn money.

After going through the planning procedure described in this chapter you may find that your existing layout is the best that can be devised. In most instances, however, even minor revisions will make a big difference in efficiency and profitability and in achieving your holistic goal. My own experience bears this out.

When I took over the last ranch I owned, I inherited a fence and water layout that greatly decreased my efficiency as manager and was very expensive to maintain. There were eighteen water points for cattle and only two that were available to wildlife, whose presence was one of the main reasons I bought the place. Along with all those water points was a complex of roads and tracks that had to be maintained as well as water pipelines, troughs, and float valves. Once I had completed the planning process described, the ranch only had three water points serving cattle, five serving wildlife, and far less pipeline, road, and track to maintain. You don't need to be exceptionally bright to work out the annual savings in time and dollars created by the new plan.

But I did not go out and borrow money to make the changeover. I moved toward the new plan gradually, generating the capital from the land to do so and adding a new feature only when my financial plan indicated it would make money.

Holistic Land Planning involves four distinct phases. The first phase is devoted to gathering information and the preparing of planning maps and can take up to a year or more to complete. In the second phase, which lasts only a day or so, you brainstorm many possible layouts for the planned developments. In the third phase, which lasts a year or more, you create the ideal plan based on the work entailed in the first two phases. In the fourth and final phase, which can take decades to complete, you gradually implement the plan using the Holistic Financial Planning process to determine the order of implementation.

Phase 1: Gather the Information

This phase can take several months to a year or more to complete and includes the following series of steps, not all of which will apply in every case. Before you start, you will need the best contour maps available and of a scale suitable to work on in some detail. In the United States, for example, U.S. Geological Survey 1-in-24,000 maps are generally adequate for planning most ranches and other extensive properties. In the case of smaller properties or farms, you will need a larger-scale map that shows more detail. These can generally be made by using a copy machine to enlarge existing maps. Avoid using aerial photographic strips and stereo viewers, because these are generally too small in scale and contours tend to be exaggerated in the three-dimensional view.

Map the Future Landscape Described in Your Holistic Goal

If the land you are managing covers an extensive area, measured in hundreds or thousands rather than tens of acres, and/or varied terrain, you will need to record on a map the broad landscape features described in your holistic goal. If you described a variety of environments, such as a tree-lined riparian community, wetlands, open woodland, cropping areas, dense brush, or open grassland communities, you need to indicate *generally* where you intend to produce these. They are likely to differ considerably from the features of your present landscape, as shown in figure 45-1. Thus, if you do not map the different communities and features you want to produce, you can easily lose sight of them.

The most useful way to record these features is on a transparent or clear plastic sheet overlaying the contour map of the property. You will refer to this overlay when brainstorming many possible layouts and later when selecting the best of them. On a crop farm, you may want to pencil in areas where you plan to produce or maintain a woodlot, or riparian areas where you might want trees to establish. Cropping areas will be marked in, but individual fields and their hedgerows would be considered infrastructure and will be planned later.

On a livestock ranch you would also mark in riparian, woodland, brushy, or open areas because, unless they are mapped, there is nothing to remind you that they have to be produced through the grazing planning procedure discussed in the next chapter. In a national park or forest, your holistic goal may have described many different successional levels to maximize the diversity of the wildlife or the age structure of the trees. But these levels generally cannot be maintained on the same site forever; they may need to shift within the park or forest over time. Do not attempt to map these shifts as part of your holistic goal; a written description indicat-

Figure 45-1 *The features recorded on the map of your future landscape are likely to differ considerably from the features of your present landscape.*

ing the desire to facilitate the necessary shifts over a very long time frame (usually several hundred years) is generally sufficient. Shortly, in considering all the management factors affecting your plan, you will map the different communities you want to produce through successional shifts over time.

Remember that your holistic goal should never include items within it, such as infrastructure or any developments requiring a financial investment, that will need to be tested. This is why the mapped features of your future landscape are so general in nature.

Identify and Map the Natural and Social Factors Affecting Your Plan

These factors will vary, depending on the entity being managed. In most cases they will include things you cannot change, such as weather patterns, or that are not directly under your control, such as public roads.

Natural factors to consider include those related to weather, such as the direction of prevailing winds and areas likely to be covered in deep snow or prone to flooding; geographic features such as water sources and riparian areas, if not already indicated on your base map, eroding catchment areas that lead onto your property, major differences in soil types (because they could determine the placement of crop fields); areas of major fire threat; wildlife concerns such as the need for roosting, mating, and nesting sites, and seasonal movement routes; areas of heavy predation; and areas in which endangered species are present.

Social factors to be considered include present ownership boundaries (some properties may be divided among different owners or portions may be leased) and future boundaries (an estate plan might require that the land be divided later among several family members), areas where mineral rights are leased or could be, any future developments planned on the land surrounding the property, recreational access areas for hunters or hikers, areas prone to vandalism, archaeological sites needing protection, and so on.

All of these factors can affect your plan in one way or another. The prevailing winds might influence the placement of roads that can serve a dual purpose as firebreaks. You would not want to place a home or a road in a flood-prone area and be forced to engage in costly repair work year after year. Locating a fence where it would inhibit the movement of the public in an area they have access to could invite vandalism.

Record these factors on clear plastic or transparent paper sheets superimposed on your contour map. Several factors can be put on one transparent sheet as long as the sheet does not become cluttered. The more complex the situation, the greater the number of overlays likely to be required. These overlays will be used later on in helping you select the best of many possible plans.

Identify Management Factors Affecting Your Plan

Review your holistic goal in its entirety as you work through this step. Make sure that all the relevant forms of production are addressed in considering management factors—not just those related to producing profit. Quality of life and aesthetic concerns are also major considerations.

List all the management factors you can think of. Many of them will require further research before you embark on the actual planning phase. Unlike the previous steps, most of this information will not need to be recorded on maps or overlays, but notes should be kept of all these factors because they will determine the infrastructure needed and where you place it.

Following are examples of some of the management factors that would need to be considered in planning the infrastructure on a ranch where livestock graze primarily on rangelands; on a farm where crops are the main enterprises; on stock farms or dairies where planted pasture is the main crop, and meat, milk or breeding/growing stock the main products; and finally in national parks and forests.

ON A RANCH

To control livestock movements, fencing in some form is usually necessary, as are handling facilities, water points, and a minimum of roads or tracks. Before you can determine the extent of these "improvements," you must consider the following:

- *Possible future stocking rates.* These will influence the size and number of grazing cells, or grazing areas, and handling facilities.

- *Herd sizes.* These will enable you to determine how much water needs to be available in any one place.

In the future, you are likely to require many more divisions of land (fenced paddocks or unfenced areas in which livestock moves are planned) than you now have (from as few as twenty or thirty divisions to as many as three hundred or more. *Also bear the following in mind:*

- Access by livestock to water and other points, such as overnight hold-ing areas, should   allow nonrepetitive movement to avoid damage from trampling. For every day of trampling, you need many days of recovery time for soil and plants.

- Less brittle environments tend to need high stock density (meaning small paddocks) and frequent livestock moves to ensure good animal performance.

- More brittle environments tend to need higher herd effect, as opposed to stock density. Paddocks can thus be large if a behavior change is brought about by attractants, which cause animals to briefly bunch, mill around, chip the soil surface, and lay down litter over a small area. Animals grazing at very high densities can produce the same effect almost continually over a much larger area. To reach these densities, a great many *very* small paddocks are required. Fortunately, these paddocks can be created with portable electric fencing or by tight herding within larger paddocks. The ranchers who are pioneer-ing this concept (mentioned in Chapter 39) have removed most of their existing internal fencing, but they still find some is required and that its placement is critical.

Even if future technological innovations enable us to bunch and move animals without any form of fencing, we still need to plan roads, handling facilities, and grazing distances from water and to demarcate larger grazing areas for grazing planning purposes.

Other factors you could consider are potential dam sites, if additional water is going to be needed; storage facilities; and areas from which hay could be harvested if necessary. In addition, you should think seriously about running more than one species of livestock if the environment allows it. If you are now running cattle only, you might want to consider adding sheep and/or goats, hogs, pastured poultry, and so on, all of which could affect the amount and type of fencing needed (as would resident game populations) and water availability and handling facilities. Though you may not run additional species for years to come, planning for the possibility now saves having to modify your plan later when it would be more costly to do so.

ON A CROP FARM

Where farms include row crops, orchards, pastures, and perhaps timber, soil types and their distribution may partially determine the layout of your infrastructure. If the land is flood irrigated and you have no plans to change to a less wasteful form of irrigation, the layout of crop fields will be determined largely by the canals you irrigate from.

There are a number of factors that are entirely within your control and should be considered:

- Small fields are more manageable ecologically than large ones.

- The greater the proportion of "edge," both in and around fields, the greater the diversity and numbers of insects, birds, and other wildlife.

- Use surroundings (i.e., hedgerows, tree belts, and naturally vegetated waterways) as well as the fields for attaining overall complexity.

- Consider utilizing grazing animals in your crop rotations. This is especially important in the more brittle environments, where livestock play a critical role in nutrient and carbon cycling. We may not, in fact, be able to keep soils alive in such environments without the help of grazing animals that speed decay by passing crop residues through their gut. In nonbrittle environments, small organisms alone can perform this role, but livestock, small or large, are often desired as a source of manure, and may in the end prove necessary to keep soils vital.

If you plan to add either small or large stock in the future, what facilities or developments will be needed? Would the animals remain on the farm throughout the year, or only seasonally? How would you move them to and from fields without trailing? If you want to attract birds, bats, and other wildlife, what are their habitat requirements? If you plan to develop a pond or dam, what general siting requirements do you need to be aware of? Do you need to research different techniques for including more diversity in fields, such as strip cropping, alley cropping, and so on? What machinery will be needed in the future? As mentioned in Chapter 40, the smaller, more intelligent machinery that can plant and harvest polyculture crops does not exist yet, apart from the odd inventions some creative farmers have produced in their own workshops, but it is likely to become available at some point as demand increases. If you are growing crops under irrigation, is the form of delivery likely to change in the future (i.e., from flood or overhead irrigation to drip irrigation)?

STOCK AND DAIRY FARMS

The management factors to consider in planning stock or dairy farms would in many instances parallel those considered on a livestock ranch or crop farm. Fencing layouts for a dairy herd need to take into account the frequency of animal handling (two or three times per day) to make these times as unstressful as possible for the animals and people. You will want to avoid repetitive movement over the same ground and site corridors and any other sacrificial areas carefully to minimize soil erosion and pollution problems.

Remember that pastures are severely damaged when they are plowed up and replanted, as mentioned in Chapter 40. Thus, you might want to develop pastures that are "managed" almost entirely by your animals.

NATIONAL PARKS AND FORESTS

In national forests and national parks, far more attention must be paid to planning for the specific biological communities we hope to produce or sustain within these confined areas, none of which are natural, as boundaries are a human invention. Within them we are attempting to manage wildlife populations whose home ranges and territories have been restricted by physical barriers and to utilize vegetation within forest interiors that are now too small to sustain many species. Immense amounts of research are needed if we are to attempt to mimic what once occurred naturally and restore some of what we have lost.

In addition to these challenges, management of national parks and forests must often cater to a variety of users, all of whose needs will affect the developments included in a land plan. The users who specifically need to be included in the land planning team would be those who helped to form the holistic goal with the government agency, foresters, or park rangers responsible for overall management. These users would primarily include managers of hunting, timber, grazing, or tourist-related concessions within the park or forest, all of whom make day-to-day decisions that can affect overall management.

All too many national parks were formed at a time when the best management was believed to be management by benign neglect, with the exception of concerted efforts to eliminate poaching of the resident wildlife. It is highly unlikely that the communities within any of today's national parks, in brittle environments in particular, have ever been static, although they can appear so in the very short term. The biological communities found in Yellowstone National Park when the first Europeans "discovered" the area were probably very different from the communities that attracted the first Americans to the area thousands of years earlier, although we often use the former as the benchmark in trying to restore communities to a so-called pristine state.

Deciding which communities to favor or modify within a national park should depend entirely on the holistic goal. Achieving that goal, however, will require very long-term considerations and planning. In many cases, the planning team will need to map the various changes to be produced over a hundred or more years. They may seek to have certain areas shift from grassland to savanna-woodland, brush or forest, or vice versa, over time using the tools at their disposal: rest, fire, technology, living organisms, and the grazing and animal impact provided by either wildlife or domestic stock.

A series of map overlays will help to illustrate where the planning team wants to develop various communities and how they want them to change over time. While considerable thought will have to go into such a long-term plan, what the planning team finally draws on the overlays will only be an approximation of where the shift from one community to another will occur and when. Research in the future, as well as lessons learned over time, will almost certainly result in continuous refinements.

Much the same approach is required in mapping vegetation shifts in a national forest, where the planning team is attempting to move a community from meadow to brushland to new forest and eventually old-growth forest, or to rotate small areas of clearcut within larger areas of mature forest, and so on. This sort of mapping, however, is done over the very long term (500 years or more). Such planning is of course far removed from most of today's efforts, where thinking twenty years ahead would be considered long term.

In some national forests, planning must also cater to human inhabitants, and their representatives should be included on the planning team. Some wet tropical forests have to sustain human populations practicing swidden (slash and burn) agriculture. As mentioned in Chapter 40, swidden agriculture can remain remarkably productive, as long as the human population is low enough. It quickly breaks down when populations rise and people must return to a previously cultivated site before soils have fully recovered and the forest reestablished. We can conceivably learn how to meet the needs of a larger human population without damaging the forest if, through better cropping practices and the use of soil amendments, we can prolong the period of cultivation in each site. In most instances, land can be cultivated only for a period of three to five years before nutrients are lost through leaching. If we are able to stretch that period to thirty or fifty years, the fallow period could likewise be lengthened to ensure full soil and forest recovery. The planning team would need to map the shifting cultivation sites carefully and over prolonged time.

Timber harvesting methods will also influence vegetation mapping, particularly if they include clearcutting. Though the days are, I hope, numbered for those who continue to clearcut extensive areas of forest, clearcutting smaller areas can make sense when you want to create different successional levels within the forest or increase the amount of edge. However, you risk doing damage if these smaller clearcuts become too extensive and break up too much of an intact forest at any given time. *Selective* harvesting, in which the best trees are taken from the forest as a whole, and the more sustainable *selection* harvesting, in which the best trees are left to produce seed for future generations, will have little influence on vegetation mapping, although the use of these methods will later affect the layout of infrastructure.

A number of other management considerations will influence the layout of infrastructure in a national forest or park. In forests you should strive to minimize the number of roads and the use of heavy machinery. Many existing roads could be eliminated with a change in logging methods. Damage done to soils by heavy machinery can be reduced if logging is planned to coincide with a time of year when the risk of damage is lower. In the northern United States, for instance, little or no damage is done to the forest floor when logging takes place in winter on frozen ground. Machinery is now under development that is less damaging to the soil than the large, heavy equipment used today. In Norway, for example, a timber extractor that simulates an elephant walking into the forest and picking up a felled tree is being tested. However, such a machine would still have to be transported to the worksite and the collected logs also moved to wherever they will be processed, so the new machine has not eliminated the need for roads entirely.

America's national forests contain more miles of road than the country's freeways, which are the most extensive in the world. Inevitably such a great expanse of unpaved road amounts to many billions of gallons of water runoff and tons of pollution, erosion, and silt. Clearly this is not in the interests of any forest intended to last and serve human needs for centuries to come.

Maintaining biodiversity in managed forests, while we extract timber, inevitably means we have to determine a sustainable rate of cut, which might require a reduced cut in some old-growth forests, but an increased cut in young forests where dense stands of young trees can retard development to healthy, mature forest. A decrease or increase in the rate of cut in the future will obviously influence the infrastructure to be planned.

One of the important management factors to consider in a national park is how best to handle the hundreds or thousands of visitors that usually spend time in the park each year. Can they be transported through the park without having to rely on personal vehicles that not only add to congestion but also diminish the aesthetic values for which the park was formed? How is the whole experience to be designed to be educating and satisfying for the visitors? These two questions may affect the future infrastructure needed as much as the natural factors related to the management of the land and wildlife.

National parks and forests that lie in environments that are brittle to any degree may benefit from the use of livestock in accomplishing a variety of objectives: to clear flammable understory and so reduce the risk of forest fires; to return from fire-dependent forests to the fire-sensitive forests that may have preceded them; to prevent meadows from returning to scrub or forest; and so on. Obviously, the use of livestock would affect the planning of infrastructure considerably.

Make a List of the Infrastructure Needed

Based on all the management factors you have considered and the management plans you have undoubtedly developed as a result, you should have a good idea of the infrastructure required to achieve your holistic goal. Draw up a list of the basic facilities you will need and keep the list handy for the next phase, when you will share it with those who will assist in creating a number of possible plans.

Preparation is now complete. If you have done your job well you will greatly enhance the results of the next phase.

Phase 2: Brainstorm a Series of Plans

In this phase, which generally lasts no more than a day or two, the aim is to create as many plans as possible, with the help of as large a group of people as practical. The people who know the land well and how it is presently managed are the worst people to do the creative planning that is now required. You want people who do not have your prejudices and do not know what is impossible. Each planning group should include three to six people working on a single map. Although they can come from any walk of life, it is important that at least one member of a team understands the significance of the management factors that must be taken into account as they work to create their plans. You and the people knowing the land and business well will ultimately select the best plan, as you are most qualified to do so.

Prepare Maps for Planning

You will need to duplicate the basic contour map you used when creating the overlays (ten or more copies will be needed for each planning team). Ideally these maps should have nothing on them but geographic features (contours, rivers, lakes, etc.) and any constructed features, such as public roads, railway tracks, or homes, that it would be illegal or impractical to change. Do not draw any other inherited developments on these maps because you do not want them to influence the planning.

Then, if you don't already have one, prepare a map with all existing developments (water points, buildings, fences, croplands, roads, working facilities, etc.) marked on it. Make one copy for each planning team and set it aside. Each team will be given an opportunity to create a final plan using this map after they have exhausted all possibilities with the basic maps.

Where livestock will be run over large tracts of land, there is one more thing to prepare. These are what we refer to as planning circles, circular disks cut from transparent or clear plastic overlay that are scaled to your basic contour map. Each disk represents the acreage you want to include in grazing cells or around a given distance to water. If, for example, you want to ensure that livestock have to walk no further than two miles to water at any time, you would size the circles so that the radius equals two miles on your map. (More detailed instructions are included in the *Holistic Land Planning Handbook.*)

Brief the Planners

Once you have divided the group into planning teams, you need to make sure they are clear on their task. Share those aspects of your holistic goal with them that will influence the planning, and display a copy of your future landscape if you have mapped it. Give a general overview of the management factors you listed in the first phase of planning and how those relate to the developments being planned. Display or pass out a list of all the infrastructure needed, so the planners can refer to it throughout the session.

Where livestock are involved, make sure that you indicate whether herding or fencing will be emphasized. Ask for a specific number of paddocks or divisions because high paddock numbers in particular affect the siting of water and approaches to it within grazing cells. Do this to force the planning teams to look very hard at the topography and complications in transportation, moving, handling, and watering stock. If you have a vision of 500 unfenced "paddocks" in which cattle are grazed to manage a national forest, have the planners figure out how to create them so that animals are seldom moved over the same ground within a given year, especially as they move to and from water.

Create Many Possible Plans

Each of the planning teams should now be asked to create as many possible layouts as they can for the infrastructure needed, bearing in mind all the factors mentioned. Provide each team with ten or more copies of the basic contour map and give them three to four hours to accomplish their task. In creating each plan, they should be concerned only with the layout of major features, such as grazing areas (not the actual subdivisions within), access to water for livestock, cropfields, working and storage facilities, and landings, or staging areas, where timber is being extracted. More detailed planning, such as the siting of individual fences or minor roads, will be done later.

For now you want the participants to avoid concentrating too much on any one possible layout because it may close their minds to further possibilities. As soon as any team has captured an idea on one of the maps, set it aside and have them start on a new one. Although this is a serious exercise in many respects, it is important that each team brings a playful attitude to it and has fun in the process. The more you can encourage this, the more creative and promising the results.

Make One Last Plan Based on Existing Structures

Finally, at the end of the day, give each team a copy of the map on which all existing physical structures are shown. Have them see if they can creatively develop a layout for the infrastructure of the future from the present situation. *Make sure you do this exercise last because an awareness of the existing structures earlier on will reduce the planners' creativity.*

Phase 3: Design and Select the Ideal Plan

In this third phase you will take considerable time to select the best plan or to create the best one by combining ideas from several. People who know the land and business well should select or create the ideal plan from the many possibilities already proposed. Use the map overlays you made earlier—the one illustrating your future landscape and those recording natural and social factors affecting the plan—to help you in your selection. If you are planning the infrastructure for a national park or forest, you will probably have a number of additional landscape overlays, representing changes over time, to consider as well.

Before coming to any conclusions, you should also take into account the detail that was not considered when the planning teams created their layouts. For example, if many paddocks are required, certain grazing cell, or grazing area, layouts will facilitate this while others may not. If you have planned many small cropfields that will be harvested mechanically, bulk handling from centralized crop collection points, and the routine use of livestock in the management of the cropfields, certain layouts will enhance management efficiency while others might decrease it. In either case you are specifically looking for layouts that enable you to move livestock and/or machinery to almost any point without constantly moving over the same ground.

As you place the overlays over each possible plan, you will begin to see both good and bad features from the point of view of each consideration on the overlay. Quite commonly at this point, you will begin to draw up new plans that combine the best features of the others. But don't rush to any final decisions yet.

In considering all the possibilities, think both short and long term. For example, a capital-intensive layout may lead to higher short-term cost but much lower long-term operating costs, and vice versa. Careful thought at this stage may also prevent the loss of valuable future sites to development. In Zimbabwe, for instance, villagers who initiated a wildlife tourism enterprise discovered that the campsite from which they could earn the most revenue was already occupied by the facilities of the government agency assisting them. Had they identified potential campsites before committing to the development of any infrastructure, this could have been avoided.

One set of plans you should consider after assessing all other possibilities are those derived from the maps that included currently existing developments. If the current layout is indeed the best, you will now confirm it. If not, you now know that there is a better layout to which you should gradually convert.

Phase 4: Implement Your Plan

Once you have settled on the ideal plan for the future, you can begin the gradual process of changing over from the old to the new. Commonly the cost of the changeover is a major limiting factor in the rate of change. However if adequate money is available, the rate of change need not be slow, but it should be sound and in line with your holistic goal in every respect. In creating your annual financial plan you will be allocating money toward the desired developments in a way that differs from the conventional. Normally you would regard most of the physical structures to be developed as capital expenditures—the capital coming from your previous earnings or more commonly from an outside source that involves repayment with compound interest or high dividends. Eventually capital expenditures yield a return on the investment, although there can be some delay before this return is seen. Provided a profit can be penciled in, the capital is usually invested. This approach can be very costly.

Fortunately, in many land management businesses, having a lot of capital available upfront is no more necessary than it is in a small start-up company run out of a home. No development should cost you outside money unless you choose to apply it. Over the years, the land itself should be able to generate most, if not all, of the funds you will need.

To implement your plan in such a way, you will have to break it down into the smallest plausible steps and compute the cost of each, then determine the sequence in which the developments need to come on line. Each year thereafter, when creating your holistic financial plan, you will decide how much you can allocate toward the land plan. Ideally, no costs should be incurred on any development until that development becomes a wealth-generating expense (as discussed in the last chapter). This will ensure that each dollar spent on new developments or on moving old ones will earn more money than was spent.

Implementing your plan in this gradual way, and generating the capital to do it from the land, means that you can continue to operate at a profit year after year, and that each year the other needs expressed in your holistic goal continue to be met.

Conclusion

Many people try to avoid any long-term planning of this sort, especially when the land involved has a considerable amount of infrastructure in place. These people automatically assume that any changes will be very costly. I hope, after reading through this overview of the Holistic Land Planning process, that you now understand that the cost of the planning is very low indeed—mainly a few pencils, paper, transparencies, and maps. The cost of *not* planning, however, can easily amount to hundreds of thousands, or even millions, of dollars over the years. Likewise, as you gradually implement your ideal plan, its greater efficiency and soundness will cause income to rise and running costs to fall. Few can afford not to plan afresh.

46

Holistic Grazing Planning: Getting Animals to the Right Place, at the Right Time, and for the Right Reasons

When livestock are included in the whole you are managing, their movements must be planned. If left in any one place too long, or if returned to it too soon, they will overgraze plants and compact and pulverize soils. But more than this is at stake. The whole you are managing includes much more than livestock, although they will be critical to achieving the holistic goal you have formed. The traditional goal of "producing meat, milk, or fiber" generally becomes a by-product of more primary purposes—creating a landscape and harvesting sunlight.

In the process of creating a landscape, you must also plan for the needs of wildlife, crops, and other uses, as well as the potential fire or drought. To harvest the maximum amount of sunlight, you have to decrease the amount of bare ground and increase the mass of plants. You must time livestock production cycles to the cycles of nature, market demands, and your own abilities. If profit from livestock is specified in your holistic goal, you will need to factor that in too. At times you must favor the needs of the livestock, at times the needs of wildlife or the needs of plants.

Because so many factors are involved, and because they are always changing, most people throw up their hands at the idea of planning for them. One can easily be swayed by those who say you can ignore all the variables—you'll do all right if you just watch the animals and the grass or if you just keep your animals rotating through the pastures. What a relief! You hate planning anyway. But choosing to ignore the whole, and the many variables that influence it, is not the answer. In this case what you don't know *can* hurt you. And hurt you plenty.

The Holistic Grazing Planning procedure described in this chapter is an adaptation of a formal military planning procedure developed over hundreds of years to enable the human mind to handle many variables in a constantly changing, and often stressful, environment. The technique reduces incredible complexity step-by-step to absolute simplicity. It allows you to focus on the necessary details, one at a time, without losing sight of the whole or of what you hope to achieve in your holistic goal.

Each of the factors influencing your plan—when you expect to breed and wean, when and where areas will be covered in snow or threatened by fire, when and where antelope are dropping their young, when and where ground-nesting birds are laying, when and where you will need to create herd effect, or graze or trample a cropfield, etc.—are recorded on a chart. This provides a clear picture of where livestock need to be and when, and this determines how you plan their moves.

A good plan can deploy livestock to reduce or cure excessive growth of problem plants, reduce brush and remove its causes, heal a gully, maintain wildlife habitat, or decrease grasshopper breeding sites, and at the same time produce a high volume of forage and quality animal products. As most livestock owners list profitability in their holistic goals, their stock must enjoy the best possible plane of nutrition and the least possible need for supplementary feed. Planning must also routinely handle unexpected fires, flash floods, droughts, poisonous plant infestations, and other catastrophes. In low- and erratic rainfall environments, droughts are not an unknown; they are predictable more than half the years and thus can be planned for.

The list continues almost without end, but Holistic Grazing Planning requires consideration of all factors simultaneously. Jokes aside about not being able to walk and chew gum at the same time, the human brain has difficulty working on two thoughts at once, and large numbers of animals, extensive tracts of land, and long periods of time are particularly hard to conceptualize, even singly. Clearly, a methodical planning process, *on paper,* offers the only hope in most situations. However, because many parts of the world are under the influence of illiterate livestock operators, there is a greatly simplified version of this procedure that requires no paper, but a great deal of knowledge of the land and livestock. I will touch on this briefly later.

In this chapter I have limited the discussion to the principles involved in Holistic Grazing Planning, rather than the details. Study these principles first, and then refer to *The Holistic Grazing Planning Handbook* for the step-by-step instructions on developing your own plan.

The Planning Approach

A large percentage of the farmers and ranchers who have heard my case for planning have volunteered vigorous arguments why their own situation makes it impossible for them to do it. "Too many things change all the time," goes the excuse, or "I'm a practical person and have to be able to make decisions one day, and change them the next." What they do not understand is that planning is not an event and that no plan can be rigid. Planning must become a *process* that incorporates modifications based on continuous feedback. If we knew how everything would turn out, we would not need to plan at all. The only reason we need to plan is because we *can't* be sure what will happen next.

When I encountered such remarks as a consultant in Africa, and perhaps because so much of my life was tied up in war at the time, I could not help making comparisons with armies. What would a general think of a brigade commander in the field who gave the same reasons for not planning? "What do you mean plan, sir? I don't know what the hell the enemy's going to do next. I'm a practical soldier. I just deal with whatever comes when it gets here."

War had its own ways of eliminating such attitudes if the general didn't, and economic reality, like war, culls farmers and ranchers who do not plan. Slowly but surely they fall by the wayside, blaming droughts, prices, and everything but themselves. A really professional soldier understands that the worse and more unpredictable events become, the more he must plan.

After researching the procedures of many professions, the parallels between agriculture and the military still impress me. Like farmers, generals must know not only how to plan thoroughly but also how to replan instantly if all should fail. In addition, they have had to face the problem of large civilian call-ups and the need to train people rapidly in planning techniques. Whole nations have over centuries employed some of their best brains to perfect such techniques.

My academic specialty, biology, had no history of forward planning. Much of the business planning that is taught in schools has become very academic and requires considerable training before it can be mastered. Consequently I have taken the simple planning procedure developed at the Royal Military Academy at Sandhurst, England, and adapted it to biological use. It thus represents several hundred years of experience in fields of battle, and several decades of use in agriculture have shown the same approach to be just as effective in managing complex land, wildlife, and livestock situations.

The Aide Memoire

Because so many factors influence any plan, you cannot tackle them all at once, but as anyone who has reassembled a complicated machine knows, putting things in a sequence that is not carefully planned has risks too.

Toward the end of the job you discover a piece that won't fit without the disassembly of half the day's work, or worse, a piece that appears important but remains in the parts bucket when you're ready to clean up and go home.

The expression used at Sandhurst for a guide that prevents those problems is aide memoire, which is derived from the French for "memory aid." This is much more than a simple checklist because it gives a sequence for making decisions that takes into account the effect of one decision on another. The questions raised in the aide memoire are generally quite broad and demand a good deal of creative, detailed thought, and they are arranged in a specific order so that the answers build upon one another.

The specific aide memoire used for Holistic Grazing Planning has undergone over thirty years of adjustment and development by ranchers, farmers, foresters, wildlifers, tribal people, and others using livestock to sustain themselves and/or achieve holistic goals. Every situation and problem experienced by thousands of people on several continents has influenced the development of the aide. Even now, if a practitioner encounters a problem not anticipated by it, we (the Center for Holistic Management) modify it at once, adding a footnote or changing a sequence to cover that case.

A main benefit of planning according to such a tested procedure is peace of mind. Using the aide you can truly relax in the most alarming situations, have confidence in the process, and concentrate fully on one step at a time without worrying about something that might come first or get left out. At each step you record your work on a grazing planning chart, wipe that from your mind and move on to the next. *Because your mind can handle only one thing at a time, you concentrate only on what is asked. Once you have completed the step, you forget about it completely and concentrate in turn on the next.* In doing so, you will find that the overall plan that emerges has covered every imaginable detail in a logical fashion and represents the best plan possible for the present. This ability to concentrate completely and confidently on one point at a time bears fruit, particularly in emergencies when a tendency to panic and to lose focus can destroy you.

This point came home forcefully to me when I got a call one night from a client in Zimbabwe after a fire had raged through about half of his very fine ranch. It had struck worst in the areas where he had water for stock but spared some areas where water points had already dried up. He needed advice on whether to lease land to get him through the season or destock, and, if the latter, by how much.

When he met me at the local airstrip he was eager to take me off to see the burned area and the cattle as soon as possible, but I asked to see his grazing plan. "No," he said. How could that help, if I had not seen the fire damage or his livestock? He got extremely hot at the suggestion that one more look at blackened ground and idle cattle would waste my time and his money, so perhaps he had rather muddle through by himself.

He did not of course have a plan. The various charts we had developed together had disappeared, but by luck his wife retrieved the aide memoire, reeking of tomcat, from the bottom of her son's toy chest. I got out some fresh charts and insisted, against vigorous protest, that we now plan step by step. Gradually, however, his protests weakened as a picture of his ranch began to emerge on the planning chart he had been taught how to use but had not thought important. His enthusiasm really began to mount after we laid out all the problems and began to plot actual cattle moves.

It was a very sheepish man who finally accompanied me to the burned areas to confirm some final judgments. Without any input from me, other than the knowledge that the longer he put off planning, the more hours I would add to my bill, he had proved to himself on paper (followed by a couple of final field checks), that he could carry his whole herd through without risk or leased pasture. In a couple of hours of planning, he had saved many thousands of dollars.

In ranching, sad to say, losses due to lack of planning are the rule, not the exception. That stems only in part from ignorance of the planning tools available. In the main, it stems from a life-threatening allergy to paper that unfortunately afflicts many people besides ranchers. It is an allergy they will fail to overcome unless they develop some real ownership in their holistic goal.

Obviously, Holistic Grazing Planning ties in closely to the long-term land planning discussed in Chapter 45. For instance, a common concern for stream banks damaged by years of livestock presence can be addressed through a combination of a fencing or herding pattern developed especially for riparian management and the grazing planning just described.

The Planning Chart

As you cover each step in the aide memoire, you record the details on the planning chart, the principles of which are shown in figure 46-1 (details are included in the *Holistic Grazing Planning Handbook*).

The body of the chart is divided into seven-month sections for the sake of size but across the chart smaller divisions account for time down to the day. The rows represent areas of land, paddocks in a fenced cell, or major grazing areas where portable fencing or herding is used. In this main planning portion covering both days and areas of land, all problems and needs can be shown by color-coded marks. Orange shading in paddock 3 in May might show poisonous plant danger. Brown in paddock 4 in August might show lack of water. Red in November might show prime hunting sites. Then, within the context of all these factors, you plan the livestock moves

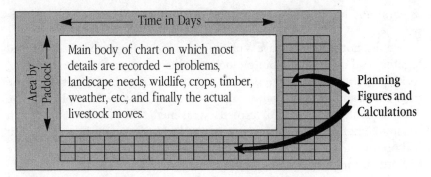

Figure 46-1 *The layout, in principle, of the grazing planning chart.*

in a rational way, using the slowest moves that the stock are likely to make in periods of slow daily plant growth.

Where grazing "rotations" are normally planned on *grazing* periods and planned forward in the sense that from a certain paddock the animals will go to another and then another, most commonly in a clockwise rotation, this planning is very different. First of all, the emphasis is on the planning of *recovery* periods, rather than *grazing* periods. This is one reason a chart is required: recovery periods show up only when plotted on a chart. Second, and especially over critical months for the animals, *moves are plotted backwards*. You first reserve certain areas for the animals at crucial times, and then indicate on the chart where the animals would have to come from to get there, and so on, backwards.

At the base of the chart and on the left- and right-hand sides are space and format for various planning figures and calculations. The latter include procedures for shortening grazing periods during times when rapid plant growth is indicated by the daily monitoring that is required when paddock numbers are few and thus grazing periods long.

Figures showing planned and actual animal days per acre/hectare (ADA/H) of forage harvested during each grazing period accompany entries for each paddock on the main body of the chart, showing at a glance how much on average every acre/hectare of ground is required to contribute to total forage consumed. That allows for fine-tuning future plans and provides increasingly accurate assessments of forage availability.

When Do You Plan?

Holistic Grazing Planning by definition requires that you plan, monitor progress continuously, control deviations as soon as possible, and replan whenever necessary. Nevertheless, although this plan-monitor-control-replan sequence proceeds without gaps and covers emergency situations, normal practice in livestock operations calls for major planning twice a year in most climates.

Make the first plan at least a month before the onset of the main growing season. In this plan, you are trying to grow as much forage as possible and you do not have to plan to a specific date. The plan remains open, because you do not know when growth will slow or end or exactly how much forage will grow before that date.

Make the second plan toward the end of the growing season, when forage reserves available for the nongrowth period become known. In this plan, you ration out the forage over the months ahead to a theoretical end point, which should be a month or more after your most pessimistic estimate of when new growth could occur. This additional "month or more" becomes your *drought reserve*.

Figure 46-2 illustrates the open- and closed-ended plan principle, showing how the time reserve for drought fits in. In some regions where rainfall is very low and unreliable, there may be a major overlap of the

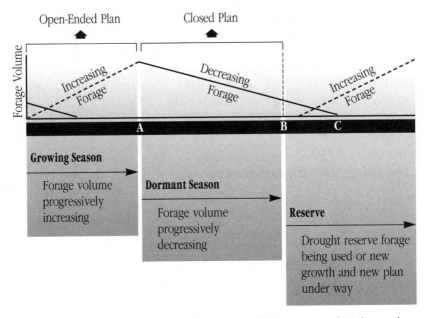

Figure 46-2 *The growing season plan is open-ended because you don't know when growth will end or exactly how much forage will grow before that date. The dormant (nongrowing) season plan goes into effect once growth stops (point A). It is a closed plan in that you are rationing out a known amount of forage over a specific period of time (from A to B), which should extend a month or more later than your most pessimistic estimate of when new growth could occur. This additional time (from B to C) is the drought reserve.*

drought reserve in the closed plan and the start of the next open plan due to the necessity of making drought reserves extend to as long as a year or more.

Record Keeping

The record of actual grazing times and animal days per acre/hectare (ADA/H) harvested plus the weather and growth rate information set down on the chart should provide all the information needed for future planning and will give an excellent picture of the strengths and weaknesses of each part of the land.

That benefit notwithstanding, professional grazing advisors following my work frequently fall into the mistake of turning the planning chart into nothing but a record of the past, dropping the aide memoire and all forward planning. This is fatal. In fact most recordkeeping that I have come across on farms and ranches yields little profit for the time and effort given to it. Not infrequently the least profitable ranches had the most complete records to satisfy their advisors. Thus, the grazing chart without the aide memoire is just a waste of paper.

I cannot make this point strongly enough. Planning is like looking forward through the windshield of your car to see where you want to go, monitoring for curves that may put you in the ditch, and controlling speed, gears, and steering to keep you on the road until you reach your destination. Obviously, you cannot do this efficiently facing backwards. Excessive record keeping is like gazing out the rear window to savor where you have been, when all you really need is a periodic glance in the rearview mirror.

Assessing Stocking Rates

Many critics have charged that Holistic Grazing Planning ignores the fact that a given piece of land can feed only a limited number of creatures. This misunderstanding arises because we do not base stocking rates on the conventional criteria. Based on the old belief that linked overgrazing to high animal numbers, scientists developed a variety of methods for determining stocking rates. These methods commonly linked animal numbers to the physiology of important grasses in ways that required a good deal of expertise and subjective judgment.

The discovery that overgrazing reflects timing, not numbers, means that we now determine stocking rate by much more straightforward criteria, chiefly the volume of forage, the time it must last, and the holistic goal. Almost by accident I hit on a way to make this assessment under normal working conditions in the field.

In the midst of a drought in Africa I got an emergency call to assist a ranch owner and two managers in deciding how much to destock. All the way to the assignment I puzzled over ways to add anything to the considerable knowledge these three must already have of their land and local climate. As an outside advisor, I could only fall back on the theoretical assumptions used in planning, but to everyone's relief they proved perfectly sound in practice. If one can compute how many ADA/H of forage a herd will require for a whole season, then one can also figure out how many animals a single acre/hectare must feed for one day.

In this case the 15,000-acre ranch had 950 head of cattle, and from the beginning of the dry season they faced at least 180 days of no growth and conceivably 40 more in a hard luck situation. No one, no matter how experienced, can visualize that many acres, cattle, and days simultaneously. However, a quick calculation shows that, including the drought reserve time, forage demand works out to 13.9 ADA.

We went out on the land and began to pace off a random sampling of one-acre plots and asked ourselves, "Could this acre feed 14 cows for a day on the forage here now?" Consistently we agreed it could. Next we sampled known poorer areas and came to the same happy conclusion. In the end, the evidence pointed against any reduction at all. None was made and all went well.

Following this experience, which prevented the loss of thousands of dollars through unnecessary reduction, we refined the technique so that we only had to assess the area required to feed one animal for one day. Figure 46-3 shows the calculations (using both American and metric figures). If one acre (or 4,048 square yards) must feed 13.9 cows for a day, then 348.2 square yards must feed 1 cow for one day. The square root of this (fortunately most calculators have a square root button) is 18.6. You only have to pace off a square about 19 yards on a side and judge whether it would feed a cow for a day.

The weaknesses in this technique are almost entirely due to a human tendency to fudge, first in selecting samples and then in judging them. A truly random sample will include every kind of area—roads, hillsides, and brush. If your way of selecting samples does not allow for that, then before you start, reduce the total acreage by the amount of land tied up in roads and rough country that you don't intend to measure.

Likewise, in judging each sample, set yourself up to err on the conservative side. First, "estimate like a cow." Imagine yourself with a large bag around your neck and the job of filling it in eight hours using only one hand by picking leafy material a whole handful at a time. A cow, having teeth only in the lower jaw, cannot pick individual leaves and will avoid taking old oxidizing stems among the leaves.

If you imagine any difficulty in this task, then a cow would probably

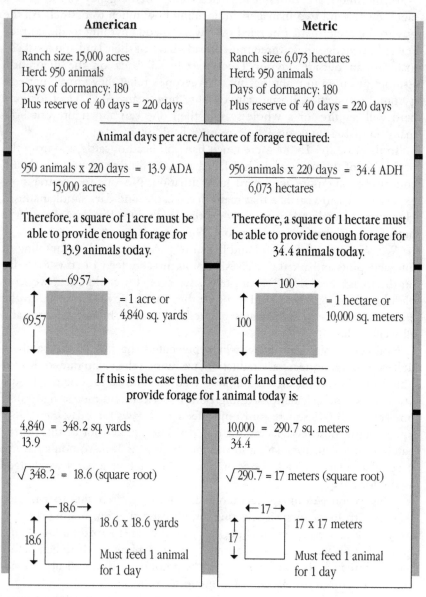

Figure 46-3 *Assessing the forage required to feed one animal for one day.*

have trouble, too. Again, to keep all errors on the safe side, fail the sample if you hesitate even a moment. In other words, if you cannot instantly see that full bag when you look at the sample, record it as deficient. If it is sheep, horses, pigs, or any other animal you are running, you can make a similar judgment. You would have to make allowances for the fact that horses have teeth on both jaws and can bite plants right to ground level; and the narrow mouths of sheep or goats can nibble the leaves and get down into clumps of old material that a cow cannot, and so on.

André Voisin first used this idea of filling the bag in evaluating nonbrittle pastures, but I have found it to be of even greater value in evaluating the more brittle rangelands. For all its apparent crudity, it yields very good results. At training sessions, we inevitably have academics who suggest that the grass be clipped, weighed, and recorded, but we do not encourage that for several reasons:

- Cattle and other livestock do not clip grass. Their grazing far more resembles a human's harvesting by the handful and avoiding old stems.

- Ranchers will not, and often cannot, clip, dry, and weigh grass, but they can make good estimates by eye "like a cow."

- Clipping and weighing, though perhaps less subjective in terms of one sample, takes time, and thus reduces the number of samples. More sample judgments by eye, even if less precise, yield a more accurate overall picture.

In addition, you will find with experience that you can vary the question to suit your own needs. Given lactating cows it might go, "Would this sample feed one cow very well?" In another case it might go, "Will it keep a steer alive?" or "What could a pronghorn find tomorrow, after the cow has gone?"

The *Holistic Grazing Planning Handbook* adds embellishments to this general method for assessing stocking rates given a prolonged dormant period. The same techniques, however, will work during the growing season, even though regrowth occurs between grazings. Regrowth makes the problem tricky, however, because one cannot predict tomorrow's weather.

During the growing season when a herd depletes the forage in a given paddock before you plan to move them, this signals a warning that the stocking rate may be too high or the grazing period too long for the size of the paddock. You could of course ease the situation by cutting grazing days from a poor paddock and adding them to a better one. However, a series of slightly shortened grazing periods add up to a much shorter recovery period; and in slow growth conditions, *that* ensures that many plants will be overgrazed, the most common downfall of rotational grazing schemes.

Knowing that there are only two factors responsible for the amount of forage taken out of a paddock (the number of animals and the amount of time spent in each paddock) helps you to assess whether or not you are overstocked. If you find, for instance, that you will run out of forage before the animals are due to leave a paddock, it means that you have either too many animals or have allotted too many days of grazing to that paddock. If in the latter case you cannot reduce the number of grazing days without overgrazing plants (because recovery periods would become too short and animals would return too soon), then you *may* be overstocked. If the problem occurs only in one paddock then you probably misjudged the paddock, and may not be carrying too many animals overall. But if it shows up in several paddocks, then you are almost certainly overstocked. By minimizing time, you leave only one variable to judge, animal numbers.

In this way stocking rates can be checked at any time of year on the basis of forage available at the time. Suppose for example that you made this check midway through a very dry summer and found that the next few paddocks your herd was due to enter did not have enough forage for even the shortest foreseeable grazing period. That would indicate overstocking *even if ideal conditions return tomorrow.* So you would immediately replan considering all your alternatives to find the one that would advance you toward your holistic goal.

Basing Stocking Rates on Annual Rainfall

Some ranchers and grazing consultants have tried to use running averages of actual precipitation to determine stocking rates. The figure includes the rainfall received over several of the past years and as each new year's rainfall total is added, the last is dropped. This is an appealing strategy, but it breaks down for the simple reason that running averages of actual rainfall do not reflect the *effectiveness* of that rainfall, which depends on many factors.

Some years ago, I had a chance to demonstrate this point in the field to a group of World Bank officials on a tour of a Texas ranch. The night before their arrival, a soaking rain fell over the entire area. We first visited three sites where we had used high animal impact with a large herd and many paddocks for one, two, and three years, respectively. Then we looked at an area protected from livestock for many years.

I claimed that grass in the last area had poor color due to the low effectiveness of the previous night's rain, but the visitors did not believe it. To settle the question, and so I wouldn't bias the result, I had them pick clumps of green growing grass themselves from all four areas and arrange them in order along the roadside. They did in fact range from pale to quite a rich green according to the treatment on the place where they grew, although all were the same species and had received the same rain.

Had stocking rate been based on volume of rain, it would have been meaningless, as the resultant growth was so different in four close areas receiving the same rain but different management. Had we based our judgment on effectiveness of rain, we would have recommended a stock reduction in the area that had no stock. The only realistic means of assessing stocking rates is on the actual forage grown in every season, which will be determined in large part by the effectiveness of the water cycle.

Conflicts with Wildlife

Holistic Grazing Planning also helps to overcome the age-old conflict between wildlife and livestock, that widespread destruction of wildlife habitat by commercial grazing interests has made a political issue.

The planned grazing of concentrated herds gives positive control over where the livestock go on any given day and takes into account all of the known wildlife needs (nesting, cover, habitat, breeding privacy, etc.) so that livestock will not disturb crucial areas at critical times. The concentration of herds means that most sites have no livestock present up to 90 percent of the time and even then, where they are has been carefully planned considering all factors. Fitting in wildlife considerations seldom presents as much difficulty as many people fear.

The one weakness remains the problem of assessing the numbers of wild grazers or browsers reliably enough to use in planning, as Chapter 42 explained. Sex and age structures provide some handle for management, but in terms of actual numbers and stocking rates, we can only make educated guesses on the basis of the animals' condition, vegetation bulk, and evidence of browsing throughout the year. Unfortunately, although people can easily learn to observe signs of overbrowsing by wildlife, it is not as easy to detect overgrazing by them. Also, although the former quickly leads to high mortality among juvenile browsers that cannot reach as high as adults, overgrazing does not have this effect because even the youngest can reach the ground. This area requires research on better management techniques, but when that bears fruit, the grazing planning process outlined here can put the new knowledge to work.

Planning without Paper

Millions of hectares of land are today occupied by people attempting to subsist, to varying degrees, on grazing stock. With few exceptions these lands are under communal ownership or tenure, rather than privately held, are located in brittle environments, and are rapidly turning to desert. Many of the people involved are unlikely to have the ability or the inclination to plan on paper. Fortunately, there is a way to plan that does not require the use of paper or even much arithmetic, but it does require that the operators of the plan have extremely good memories, are highly observant, have a deep knowledge of both their animals and the land, and are able to herd their livestock—abilities and skills these people generally have.

This simpler planning process is covered in more detail in The *Holistic Grazing Planning Handbook;* here again, I only cover the basic principles it entails. Chief among them is the need to achieve maximum density (of animals) for minimum time, followed by a prolonged recovery period. When this guideline is followed, plants are favored throughout the year because overgrazing will be minimized in the growing season, and most of the old growth cleared by the end of the dormant season. No matter what the class or type of livestock, the animals tend to receive the highest plane of nutrition and suffer the least amount of disease and the least danger of parasite infestation if they are constantly moving and thus offered fresh, unfouled forage to feed on—as long as the animals are moved without stress. The soil, no matter what type, also benefits from the same treatment because more plants grow, root systems are healthier, soil-covering litter is abundant, plants grow more closely together and hold more litter in place, and the soil surface is periodically broken and aerated and compacted sufficiently to provide seed-to-soil contact.

Using the principle of maximum density for minimum time in combination with the people's skills, knowledge, and talents makes it relatively easy to create a grazing plan. When herding stock, you have the ability to create very high "paddock" numbers immediately. However, in most cases, water points are limited and animals must return to the same one each day, no matter which area they might be grazing. Therefore, planning the grazing also requires planning the routes to water in such a way that these routes are not damaged by overgrazing and overtrampling.

For example, let's say we have divided our grazing lands into 365 paddocks, but that we have only two water points to serve them. How can we water all our animals each day and not trample over the same plants and soil day after day? One possibility is to use stones, or a short length of fencing, to demarcate thirty approaches radiating out from each water point, giving us a total of sixty ways to approach the water without trampling over the same ground. Then we can use one of these narrow approaches as the route for moving the animals out to the small area they will graze each day and back to water for a period of 3 to 10 days (an average of 6 days) before utilizing the next approach route. There is very little chance any plants will be overgrazed within an approach route over this amount of time, or that damage will ensue from overtrampling, because the approach route will have almost a year (359 days on average) in which to recover.

If we were in an area where rainfall tended to be more reliable and the growing season extended through six months or more, we could base our plan on half the number of grazing areas (182) and approximately six-month recovery periods, which would give us two grazings per year on average.

In practice there may be more than two water points, and there will be additional factors to consider, such as integrating livestock with crop rotations, creating firebreaks, improving wildlife habitat, healing gullies, and all the other things a rancher or farmer would plan on a grazing chart. Simple maps may be required in some cases, but maps drawn on the ground are often quite adequate to clarify any points over which there might be confusion. In my own experience of working with people in such situations, their knowledge of the land and their common sense generally make them capable of working out the detail of the plan with minimal help. A clearly thought-out holistic goal, in which they have ownership, is essential in every case. Without it, the motivation for creating the plan and seeing it through will not be there.

Monitoring and Controlling

A plan, no matter how sound, serves little purpose unless its application is monitored and deviations controlled. Otherwise, even assuming no lapses at all in administration, unpredictable events sooner or later render the best plan irrelevant or even destructive.

Once again, some will ask, "Then why plan in the first place?" We must plan simply because it is the only way to produce desired results in complex situations. If the situation is simple enough, a rough plan in our heads with commonsense adjustments as we go is adequate. Unfortunately such simplicity is almost nonexistent in the management of biological resources, including livestock.

In creating your grazing plan you will be using your livestock to produce, among other things, the landscape of the future described in your holistic goal. Progress toward that future landscape must be monitored annually through the biological monitoring process described briefly in Chapter 33 and more fully in the *Handbook for Early-Warning Biological Monitoring*. The monitoring to which I refer now is the monitoring of progress with the grazing plan itself.

Monitoring Daily Growth Rates of Plants

Monitoring daily growth rates is less critical if your plan involves a hundred or more paddocks or grazing areas. This would make grazing periods no longer than three days and recovery periods more than adequate for roots to recover, no matter what the growing conditions. However, you may want to monitor daily growth rates anyway to benefit from the knowledge gained. If your grazing plan involves few paddocks or grazing areas (i.e., less than a hundred) and thus grazing periods run from three to fifteen or more days, you will need to monitor daily growth rates throughout the growing season. You always plan for slow growth, as mentioned, but when you find rapid growth occurring, you need to shorten grazing and recovery periods or plants will be overgrazed. As soon as growth slows, once again you have to lengthen both grazing and recovery periods.

You will recall from earlier chapters that plants can be overgrazed in three situations:

1. When the plant is exposed to the animals for too many days and they are around to regraze it as it tries to regrow.

2. When animals move away but return too soon and graze the plant again while it is still using stored energy to reform leaf.

3. Immediately following dormancy when the plant is growing new leaf from stored energy.

Experience has shown us that the greatest damage is usually done when shortened grazing and recovery periods have not been lengthened once again after growth has slowed down. Remember that the grazing and recovery periods are always linked. When you shorten the grazing period, you also shorten the recovery period. This is what catches off-guard those who stop planning and merely rotate their livestock based on short grazing periods. They fail to see that recovery periods have also shortened and thus that animals are returning to paddocks in which plants have not recovered from their first grazing and many plants are overgrazed as a result.

On the bunch grass ranges that typify the more brittle grazing lands, we judge growth rates on the basis of severely grazed individual plants and not on the general view of the plants on the range as a whole. To do this, we find and mark severely grazed plants alongside ungrazed plants of the same species just as livestock leave a paddock. A two- or three-foot wire carrying a fluorescent flag, such as surveyors use, makes finding the severely grazed sample plant days or weeks later a simple matter, and a kink in the wire can record the grazed-down height. Such flags of course need to be removed before animals return to prevent them from eating the plastic.

As the livestock graze in the manner planned, we periodically return to the marked plants and assess their recovery rate using the nearby ungrazed plants as a yardstick. If the plants have barely grown weeks later and the livestock are due back in that paddock any day, then we know the movements are too fast for the prevailing slow growth and overgrazing will occur as the livestock return to the unrecovered plants. The livestock, however, will undoubtedly perform well on the fast move, which is why rotational grazers keep moving the animals too fast.

If our inspection shows that the plants are growing so fast that they are already barely distinguishable from the ungrazed plants, and the plan shows that the livestock are not due back for a month or more, overgrazing is probably occurring in each of the paddocks grazed since you marked plants, unless you have very high paddock numbers and consequently always short grazing periods. If this is occurring in cases where you have few paddocks and long grazing periods, then livestock performance will be poorer than it need be, as the animals are being held longer than necessary on fouled ground that has already been well selected over.

People commonly ask *when* a plant has recovered; the answer is we don't really know. Much research confirms overgrazing as a function of the time plants are exposed or reexposed to animals, but few have investigated the point at which a plant has fully recovered from a severe defoliation. In practice, however, this matters little on rangelands because so many other factors obscure the question. A healthy range contains myriad species that all have different growth rates. Slope, soil variations, shade, aeration, and other things all affect the growth rate within species and within areas of the paddock. You only can observe the most severely grazed plants of whatever species and consider them recovered when they resemble ungrazed plants alongside them under virtually identical conditions and health. This apparently rough method has produced excellent results for over thirty years.

In planted pastures or natural grasslands in less brittle environments, individual plants are not always distinguishable, and you have to use less precise methods. It is still important to monitor the daily growth rate, but you do so by examining the color of the grass and checking the height of forage both behind and ahead of the livestock. When grass is growing fast the color is normally a darker or richer shade of green. Also you will notice this when you find yourself having to cut your lawn frequently. As growth slows down, so the color becomes paler. By going behind the livestock to paddocks they grazed one to three days or more before, you can judge the speed of regrowth by checking the height in the areas where grazing was heavy. By checking paddocks ahead into which the livestock will soon be going, you can see if they have recovered enough for their next grazing by again checking the height of the forage and how well grown out it appears. If paddocks due to be grazed soon are visibly not ready for grazing, then clearly your moves have been too fast for the prevailing growth rate. You will need to slow the moves by lengthening your grazing and recovery periods.

A common question that arises in any number of situations runs, "When the general rule is fast growth fast move–slow growth slow move, what happens when some grasses grow slowly and some fast?" Fortunately, this question is not as difficult to answer as it first appears.

Figure 46-4 shows how you would pencil out such a situation, and then make a decision. In this case, you have only a few paddocks for your herd. As you see, with 5 paddocks you have grazing periods that are long, whatever the growth rate of the plants (7 to 22 days if you use recovery periods of 30 to 90 days). Let's assume that you are monitoring in the period toward the end of April (Point A) and you detect slow growth on some severely grazed warm-season grasses and fast growth on severely grazed cool-season grasses.

Ask yourself these questions and work out the answers. What if I move fast? Clearly with the 7-day grazing period, you are doing the best you can with five paddocks in the grazing period for either type of grass. What of the recovery period? Looking at the diagram you can see that the cool-season grasses are likely to be in dormancy on your return in 30 days (Point B), but that the warm-season grasses could be growing fast. If the warm-season grasses have continued to grow at a slow rate, then you are likely to overgraze those plants that were bitten severely. Your alternative was to go to the slow move, but then you would have increased the chances of overgrazing some of the cool-season plants that were growing fast.

Now what of the animals? Holistic Management strives to consider all factors. A look at the livestock management year (top row) shows lactating cows in late April and bulls joining them on May first. This might justify faster moves to gain higher animal performance at this short, but crucial time of year, even though it means accepting the chance of overgrazing the warm-season plants, if growth continues slow into June.

How serious will that be? Not very, if you are applying high animal impact and your planning is good. This is not even near the degree of overgrazing that we accept daily under conventional grazing management or rotational grazing systems. It will affect one period only enough to set back the vigor of those plants that get bitten twice before recovery. We are not talking about repeated overgrazing to the point of plant distortion or death.

This situation would look somewhat different with 35 or more paddocks per herd. Recovery periods of 30 to 90 days would mean grazing periods of only 1 to 3 days. Even the fastest growing plant will not suffer overgrazing during the longest grazing period of 3 days, so slow moves might work. Again, however, livestock factors could qualify that decision. The 35 paddocks mean much higher stock density and faster consumption of ADA/H in each paddock. Holding stock in paddocks too long at a crucial time could cause a drop in conception rates. Moving faster, to gain on conception rates and calf/lamb/kid weights, might result in coming back onto plants after 30 days but at high stock density, thus overgrazing many

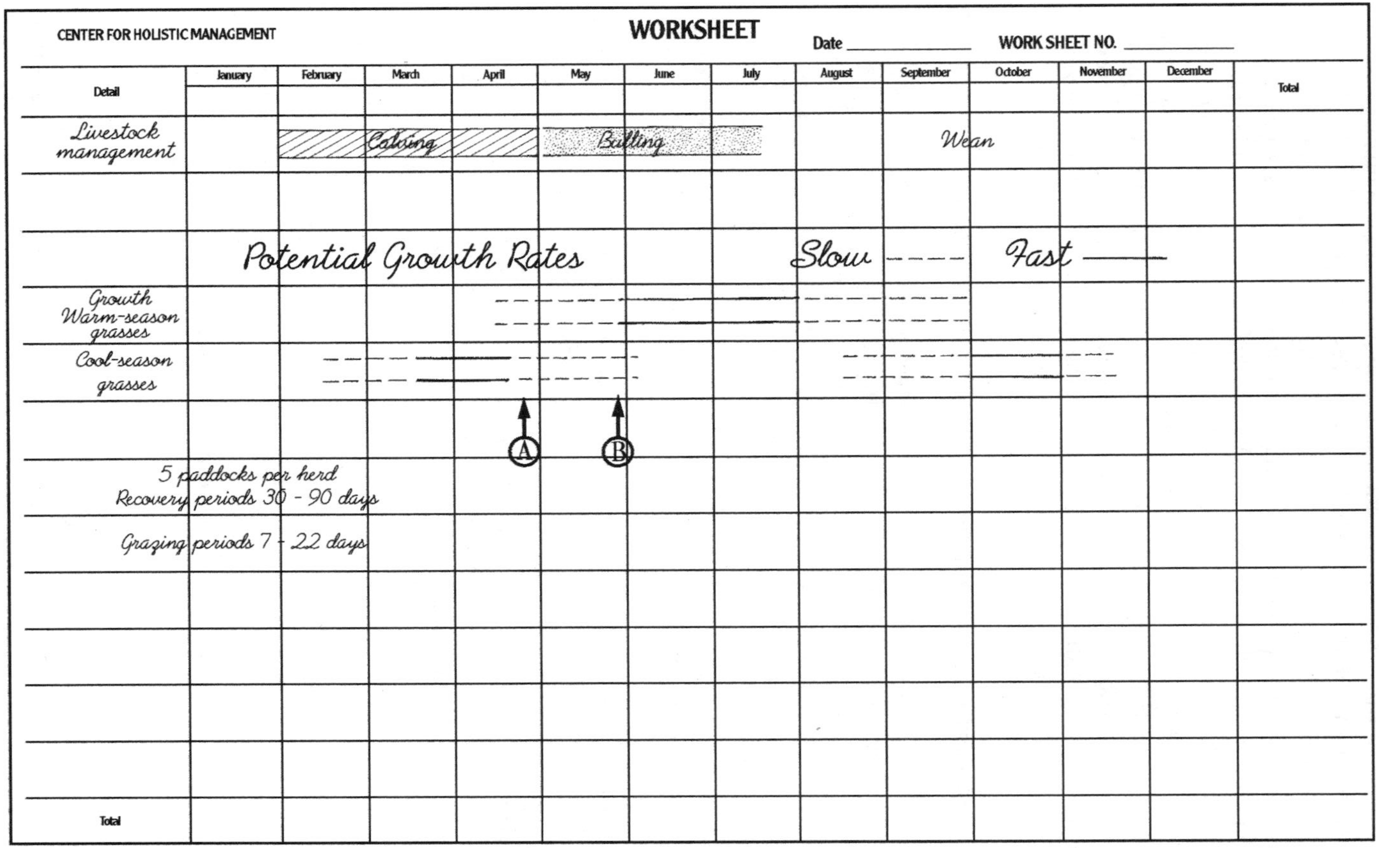

WORKSHEET

Date _____ WORK SHEET NO. _____

Detail	January	February	March	April	May	June	July	August	September	October	November	December	Total
Livestock management			Calving		Bulling				Wean				
		Potential Growth Rates					Slow – – – – –		Fast ———			
Growth Warm-season grasses				– – –	– – –								
Cool-season grasses		– – –		– – –	– – –				– – –	– – –			

Ⓐ → Ⓑ →

5 paddocks per herd
Recovery periods 30 – 90 days
Grazing periods 7 – 22 days

| Total | | | | | | | | | | | | | |

Figure 46-4 *How to determine speed of moves when you have few paddocks and are dealing simultaneously with different growth rates among warm- and cool-season plants.*

warm-season plants if growth rates continue to be slow. A management decision has to be made and the consequences accepted.

In either of these cases, and generally in most cases, the land will forgive a reasonable compromise as long as you have a good grazing plan and keep applying high animal impact. You truly overcome the dilemma of how to deal with simultaneous fast and slow growth when you reach high paddock (or grazing area) numbers (i.e., 100 or more). At high paddock numbers, remember, stock density is also high, and exposure of the plants and animals to one another very short. This tends to keep the proportion of leaf-to-fiber in the plants high, and this, together with the short grazing periods, allows better animal performance on longer rested grass.

The Importance of Monitoring Actual Growth Rates

Do not make assumptions about growth rates just because rain has fallen or the temperature seems right. Remember the story of the World Bank team in Texas that found four shades of green in grass plants that had all received the same rain the night before but had been under different management. The darker color represented faster growth that stemmed from a better water cycle.

Some years ago on a New Mexico ranch, I saw a good demonstration of why it is a mistake to assume that rain always translates into rapid growth. Under pressure from lengthening drought, this rancher had combined four 8-paddock cells into one 32-paddock plan and combined his herds into one. Three-day moves gave each paddock over 90 days' recovery time.

Both his thinking and his planning were sound, but when 2 inches of rain fell and the view from his pickup looked a bit greener, he assumed immediate fast growth and cut back to daily moves and a 30-day recovery period to enhance animal performance. Nine days after the rain I visited, and we got out of the truck and actually checked the plants. We found no evidence of fast growth. Out in the paddocks, the general level of soil capping and consequent poor aeration had suppressed the growth rate. Only the roadsides, which had better aeration, were showing fast daily growth and darker green color. The wrong assumption had led to a plan that would soon put cattle at quadruple normal density on paddocks that had had a third the required recovery time—the most rapid path to disaster he could have chosen in a drought.

New Zealand sheep farmers have a great awareness of the attention one must pay to plant growth rates, and in some districts the radio announces daily growth rates as a service to them. There and elsewhere the daily evaporation rate is also broadcast, so farmers can compute transpiration rates for crops and alter irrigation schedules accordingly.

Personally, I worry about such approaches because soils, slopes, and plants vary too much to fit a general formula. In New Zealand, where generous and predictable rainfall and heavy fertilization make a fairly homogeneous environment, perhaps it pays. In more brittle areas, I believe it wise to judge from actual plant growth rates made by on-site managers.

When your monitoring of growth rates tells you plants are growing rapidly then you need to complete the next step in the planning process and that is to control. In the case of a few paddocks, where the planning produced two alternative grazing periods, one for rapid and one for slow growth, you switch to the shorter grazing periods. You then keep monitoring, and as growth rates slow down the livestock moves begin to lengthen toward the longer grazing periods planned. As you go through the season, monitoring and adjusting to the prevailing growth rate, you will need to keep an eye on the recovery periods, which show up clearly on the grazing chart.

What you should never do, and which unfortunately some people have done, is to say, "Well the growth rate will be somewhere between fast and slow, so I'll plan and graze on an average." When you do this you quickly find yourself in trouble because growth rates are seldom average. They tend to swing widely between fast and slow through a growing season, especially in environments with erratic precipitation and noneffective water cycles.

Replanning

Replanning, the final step in the planning process, becomes necessary only in a few instances. Occasionally you could experience a prolonged period of rapid growth and will keep to shorter grazing periods for so long that the plan, which is based on longer grazing periods, will get skewed, and animals that were supposed to be in a certain place at a crucial time will get there much sooner. In such cases, all that is needed is to erase the plotted grazings over the next few months ahead and to replot them. The only other situations that would call for major replanning would be any that involved a major catastrophe, such as a fire that sweeps across most of the land, or a major breakdown in the water supply to some areas. Droughts, which people think constitute a need for replanning, seldom require it, as they should have been planned for in the beginning.

Conclusion

From the very first series of lectures I gave in the United States, I have stressed that the Holistic Grazing Planning procedure underpins all my work in grazing situations and all my claims for success. None of the academics and researchers who have since then criticized my work seems to have been willing or able to grasp this point. The vast majority of research projects conducted in America, allegedly to study my methods, ignored the heart of the matter—this planning process and the continual monitoring allied to it. Instead they set up countless short duration grazing rotations with radial fence layouts, paying no attention at all to the planning procedure.

What planning was done was usually in the project manager's head, although he or she often recorded the date a paddock was grazed in a notebook or computer. Moves were generally planned forward, rather than backward and were based on short grazing periods, rather than adequate recovery periods.

There are any number of rotational grazing systems that involve dividing large pastures into smaller ones and rotating livestock through them. They are commonly referred to as "management-intensive" because they involve much more than turning animals out in the spring and gathering them in the fall. Grazing rotations can work fairly well in less brittle environments, where livestock are mainly run on planted and fertilized pastures and the variables are fewer. Animal performance and forage production are generally not as high as they could be, and very dry or very wet years can cause real problems (which managers feel they can do nothing about). In the more brittle environments, where livestock are mainly run on rangelands, grazing rotations break down quickly because there are so many variables, and very few, if any, are addressed.

Many of the rotational grazing systems were derived from the work of André Voisin, who first discovered the link between overgrazing and time. He developed *rational* (meaning well-thought-out) *grazing* in response to this discovery and would probably turn in his grave to see what has become of it. He spoke out vehemently on the dangers of rotational grazing. In less brittle environments, rational grazing can be very successful and for a prolonged time. But it, too, breaks down quickly in the more brittle environments for which it was not designed.

Figure 46-5 attempts to show where rotational grazing, rational grazing, and Holistic Grazing Planning differ. Bear in mind that I have generalized the information under each column for simplicity. In practice, the columns are probably not quite so distinct.

The Holistic Grazing Planning procedure was developed over thirty years ago. Since that time, it has undergone continuous refinement based on the experiences of thousands of people on several continents, an effort that continues to be coordinated by the Center for Holistic Management. This procedure offers the simplest way we have found for managing the complexity of any ranch, farm, water catchment, forest, or any other area

	Rotational Grazing	Rational Grazing (Voisin)	Holistic Grazing Planning
Grazing periods are based on:	Number of paddocks and desired rest period	Recovery periods needed during fast and slow growth	Recovery periods needed during fast and slow growth
Adjustments to grazing periods based on:	Height of grazed plants in paddock	Daily growth rate of plants	Daily growth rate of plants, livestock performance, and/or wildlife needs
Stocking rate based on:	Estimated dry matter intake and/or rainfall received	Animal days per acre/hectare (ADA/ADH)	ADA/ADH available for the dormant season, plus a "time reserve" for drought, and *effectiveness of water cycle* rather than rainfall received
Animal nutritional needs addressed by:	Estimated dry matter intake and daily monitoring of animals	ADA/ADH estimates and daily monitoring of animals	ADA/ADH estimates, daily monitoring of animals and allocating best paddocks for critical times, then planning backward from those critical periods
Use of herd effect for land restoration	Not planned	Not planned	Incorporated into plan— essential in brittle environments
Wildlife and other users/uses	Not planned for	Not planned for	Incorporated into plan so livestock can be used to enhance
Drought planned for by:	Reserving grazing areas	Reserving time (days of grazing) spread over all paddocks	Reserving time in all paddocks, and ADA/ADH estimates at end of growing season in a closed plan
Performance in brittle environments (most of the world)	Breaks down in brittle environments	Breaks down in brittle environments	Does not break down in any environment
Performance in less brittle environments	Good short term, but likely to break down long term	Good short and long term	Does not break down in any environment
Fire prevention	Not planned	Not planned	Routinely planned
Management decisions based on:	Multiple goals involving either forage, animals, or finances at any one time	Multiple goals involving either forage, animals, or finances at any one time	A single holistic goal that addresses social, environmental, and economic factors simultaneously

Figure 46-5 *Rotational, rational, and Holistic Grazing Planning—how they differ.*

shared by livestock and other users. It will lead to the best possible plan in the most difficult and seemingly hopeless situations. Even when the rains have failed to come at all, and even through times of crisis, including war, this planning procedure has never failed me. Nor do I believe it will ever fail you.

Part X

New Perspectives

47

Expanding the Uses of the Holistic Management Model

W hen many years ago I set out to find a solution to the environmental degradation occurring in Africa, I had no idea where the quest would lead. Obviously haphazard remedies did not work, but neither did prescribed systems of management that did not account for actual conditions. What we needed was a methodical way to think through real cases and make plans that led to specific improvements. The various planning procedures entailed in Holistic Management arose from that insight, but they were hopelessly inadequate for solving the larger problems we faced, mainly because the decision-making that created the problems had not yet changed. The new framework for decision making, reflected in the Holistic Management model, developed only gradually in response to each of the obstacles we struck as we tried to find a solution that truly worked, could apply anywhere, and would give sustained results.

My early aim had been merely to understand what was causing much of the environmental deterioration I had witnessed and successfully tailor a response, but as the Holistic Management model evolved into an ever better tool for doing this, the breadth of its power became evident. In at least three areas of endeavor, the new framework greatly enhanced our perspective: diagnosing the underlying cause of problems related to the functioning of the four ecosystem processes, or to a general lack of progress toward the holistic goal; orienting research to better meet management needs; and analyzing policies of many kinds to predict the likelihood of their success.

Key to holistic decision making are the holistic goal and the planning, monitoring, controlling, and replanning it takes to move steadily toward it.

As this process was increasingly put into practice on the land, we found a need to diagnose what was going wrong when monitoring showed we were deviating from our intended result. Later still, we realized that obstacles sometimes existed that could block overall progress toward the holistic goal. These had to be identified and their cause diagnosed. Chapter 48 describes how the Holistic Management model can be used to assist in both tasks.

In any number of management situations we found instances where we lacked knowledge of certain finer points, such as the establishment conditions for certain plants, that pinpointed areas for further investigation. But how could we be sure, once the information was available, that it was relevant to our particular situation? As Chapter 49 explains, the Holistic Management model can be used to help you find out. The model can also serve as an organizing framework in designing new approaches to projects undertaken by multidisciplinary research teams.

Finally, we began to realize that if we understood the intent of a policy and knew or could deduce a holistic goal for those affected by it, we could use the Holistic Management model to help us analyze such a policy. We did not need to wait for the result to learn that yet another effort to fight crime, halt deserts, save a community, or whatever, had failed. We could determine before application whether or not a policy was likely to succeed, and, if not, why. If we could do that, we could then work out how to modify the policy to increase its chances for success, as covered in Chapter 50.

The enhanced perspective the Holistic Management model provides for diagnosing causes, orienting research, and analyzing policies has greatly changed the way we view and approach these challenges. In years to come we will undoubtedly find that the same applies in many more areas of endeavor.

48

Diagnosing the Cause of Problems

Very early on we realized that the Holistic Management model could be used to help diagnose what had gone wrong when land we were managing failed to respond in the way we had anticipated. It could also be used to help find the cause of distortions in the functioning of the four ecosystem processes generally (e.g., outbreaks of problem plants and insects, or disease; the disappearance of species; increased floods or droughts). In either instance, diagnosing what had gone wrong rested on knowing how brittle the environment was, and knowing the effects the six categories of tools (Chapters 19–24) tend to have on water and mineral cycles, energy flow, and community dynamics. Much later, we found we could also diagnose problems of a very different nature by using the model to help identify obstacles, or *logjams,* that might be holding up overall progress toward a holistic goal. In each of these instances, the approach to diagnosis is fairly straightforward.

Land Management Monitoring

In any land management situation, your holistic goal will need to include a description of the four ecosystem processes in terms of how they will have to function if they are to sustain your efforts. Each year, you will be monitoring your progress toward that end, looking for the earliest signs that you could be straying off track. (The *Handbook for Early-Warning Biological Monitoring* describes the process we use.)

The earliest signs generally appear first at the soil surface. Conditions there in large part determine the effectiveness of the water and mineral cycles, the amount of sunlight energy captured, and the health and diversity of the biological communities that occupy a site. If the soil is bare, for instance, the functioning of all four ecosystem processes is diminished; if it is covered, all four are generally enhanced.

If your monitoring shows you are moving away from, rather than toward, the description included in your holistic goal, you need to take action (*control*) and adjust what you have been doing. Before you can act, however, you have to find the cause of the deviation.

Consider a ranch in a very brittle environment where monitoring shows that *capped soil has decreased, but bare ground has increased.* Plant spacing has not changed, but there is less litter covering the soil. The rancher, however, had intended just the opposite. To find the cause of the problem, which will indicate the management changes he needs to make to get back on track, he now considers each of the tools he might have used:

- *Rest.* Although rest does increase bare ground in a very brittle environment, it also causes increased soil capping. Capping decreased, however, and deliberate efforts had been made not to rest the land (he had increased the number of animals and bunched them often).

- *Fire.* No fire was used.

- *Grazing.* Monitoring does not show overgrazed plants, and the grazing plan appears sound on this point. Grazing, as opposed to overgrazing, has the tendency to increase grass vigor and thus to produce more material that can be trampled down to serve as soil-covering litter, but clearly something offset this.

- *Animal impact.* This was applied well with plenty of herd effect induced on selected sites. The decrease in capping reflects this, as does the fact that plant spacing is no wider. Such good animal impact, particularly allied to well-planned grazing, should have *increased* litter because more old plant material would have been trampled down. Yet declining litter cover appears to have created the bare ground problem.

- *Living organisms.* Aside from the livestock, none were used as a management tool. Did the livestock change significantly in any way? Yes, livestock numbers were increased, as mentioned.

- *Technology.* Apart from fencing, none was used. Practices remained unchanged from prior years and would be unlikely to produce the symptoms in question.

This first review of the tools does not throw an answer into high relief, but the heart of the problem seems to lie in the reduction of litter. As no major catastrophe such as unusual weather or an outbreak of harvester ants would explain the loss of litter, a closer look at the tools should.

Fire played no part in this case. Rest, partial or otherwise, did not occur, as supported by the decrease in capping. Animal impact light enough to cause decreasing litter would be likely to increase capping.

Grazing was not applied as overgrazing, but how did it measure up in other respects? Also, did the change in stocking rate noted in the review of rest and living organisms have any significant effect? In fact, a look at the grazing plan shows that livestock ran short of forage in late winter and grazings were shortened to maintain animal condition until spring growth started. This did not result in overgrazing, as the grass was dormant, but it did leave less plant material behind for litter and might have caused stock to actually eat litter already on the ground. Thus, overstocking appears to explain the situation best.

Control would then involve adjusting livestock numbers and improving the accuracy of forage estimates in the next grazing plan. Future monitoring should soon show an increase in litter, reduced bare ground, and more insect activity if the diagnosis was correct.

The same sort of analysis will also diagnose problems on cropland or forest, the only difference being a more thorough monitoring of soil conditions both above and below ground on croplands and, in forests, age structure in the trees and the diversity of other organisms. Surface cover and litter breakdown, soil movement due to wind or water, compaction, organic content, and biological activity in response to various tools need monitoring in almost all cases.

Problems that occur in aquatic environments will often be associated with how tools have been applied in the catchment areas drained by the lake, river, or stream. Partial or total rest applied in a more brittle environment tends to increase runoff, flash flooding, turbidity, and silt loads within waterways. The overgrazing of a large number of plants and continual trampling by livestock or wildlife would do the same in environments that range from less brittle to very brittle. Of course, many cropping and forestry practices produce considerable silt, flooding, and pollution.

Keep reminding yourself that most changes, barring those brought about by a major natural catastrophe, result from the application of one or more tools by people over time. Avoid snap judgments, and reason through the six tool categories one by one.

Diagnosing Ecological Problems Generally

In diagnosing the cause of problems revealed through regular biological monitoring your focus is almost entirely on the tools *you* have applied in the last year or two to manage the situation. In diagnosing the cause of a malfunction in any one of the four ecosystem processes more generally, such as a widespread infestation of an undesirable plant or animal, you have to consider how the tools have been applied by others over large areas and for many years. The following questions can help to focus your attention and speed the diagnosis.

1. Which ecosystem process is the most appropriate to focus on to help you reason out what is happening? If the problem involves an increase or decrease in a particular organism, for example, look to community dynamics; if it involves a gain or loss of water (e.g., a falling water table or increased flooding) look to water cycle, and so on. How would you describe the condition of the ecosystem process under consideration in relation to how it potentially could be?

2. Has any natural disaster occurred that could have contributed to the problem?

3. How brittle is the environment?

4. Which tools have been applied generally, for a prolonged period of time, and how?

5. How does each tool applied tend to affect the ecosystem process under consideration at that level on the brittleness scale?

6. Based on your answers, what is the probable cause of the problem?

7. What should be done to remedy the cause? Is this something you can test on a sample area to confirm that the diagnosis is correct?

8. What criteria could you monitor to ensure your diagnosis and the proposed remedy are on target?

The case cited in Chapter 42 of the desert bushes in Pakistan that did not regenerate illustrates the approach. As the problem deals with an organism that is decreasing (the desert bushes) the ecosystem process to focus on is community dynamics. A healthy population should have had many young, fewer adults, and even fewer adults of very old age. This population had no young plants whatever. Government advisors were seeking to redress the situation by forbidding bush harvesting and seeking an alternative fuel, when the real problem to be tackled was the lack of regeneration, which had little to do with harvesting of the adult bushes.

There had been no change in the weather, such as a run of very wet, dry, or cold years, and no natural disasters had occurred that might have contributed to the lack of regeneration. So, in diagnosing this problem, we look to the tools that have been applied most commonly to large areas over time and the effects they would tend to produce in this very brittle environment—particularly at the soil surface.

- *Rest.* Total rest was applied in isolated areas under government protection. Partial rest was applied on the bulk of the land, although it was grazed by many small flocks. Because it was a low-rainfall, very brittle environment in which the community could move only beyond algae and lichens with difficulty, rest in both forms had resulted in a mature cap of algae and lichens on the ground between bushes that was utterly inhospitable to new seedlings.

   Near market places where concentrated livestock periodically provided considerable disturbance, there were plenty of seedlings, but few were able to survive because of the very high level of overbrowsing. The mere presence of the seedlings, however, confirmed my suspicion that the smooth, capped surfaces everywhere else were not suitable sites on which desert bushes could establish.

- *Fire.* Fire had not been used for a very long time.

- *Grazing.* This tool had been applied mainly in the form of overgrazing/overbrowsing which would tend to reduce the number of plant species and kill the seedlings of any favored plant. Although animals were herded, herders had inadequate knowledge to herd in such a manner as to minimize overgrazing and overbrowsing.

- *Animal impact.* Apart from those areas near market places, animal impact was always applied at a low level. Although animals were herded, *herd effect* was never induced. Lack of animal impact over most of the land tends to produce bare ground, which again, if hard-capped, is not suited to the establishment of desert bush seedlings.

- *Living organisms.* Apart from the livestock, no other living organisms were used in management.

- *Technology.* None was used, other than the primitive digging implements for harvesting bushes.

In sum, the evidence clearly showed that the problem stemmed from a combination of low animal impact and overbrowsing, either of which alone could account for the failure of the bushes to establish new generations. Any remedy that did not address both overbrowsing and low animal impact would surely fail, most decisively if the remedy also involved fire or increased rest. Animal impact would need to be increased to break up capped soil surfaces so new plants could establish, and animal movements would have to be planned so plants would not be overbrowsed or over-grazed.

Identifying Logjams

Periodically, it pays to stand back and look at your business, or entity, as a whole and ask whether anything could be blocking overall progress toward your holistic goal. If you find something is, then you will need to determine what has caused it before you can clear the blockage.

It helps to view such a blockage as a logger would. If you were floating hundreds of logs down a river and one or two got stuck, they would gradually snare others until you had a major logjam. A skilled logger will climb a tree or hill where he can view the jumble from above and identify the logs that initiated the blockage. Once he removes them, all the others are freed to continue their downstream float. And so it is with Holistic Management. If the logs causing the jam are not identified and dealt with, progress could halt altogether.

In practice, at least once a year you should determine whether or not a logjam exists, and prior to creating your annual holistic financial plan is a good time to do so. Funds may be needed to remove the cause of the blockage and such an expense will have high priority, as mentioned in Chapter 44.

Especially in your early years of practicing Holistic Management, the logjam may be related to an inadequate understanding of the process, which in turn leads to a lack of commitment to the holistic goal and the process itself. Once you change to holistic decision making, you should begin to improve the quality of your life, lessen any conflicts that were present, become more profitable, and so on. It is inconceivable that a change for the better would not occur if the decision makers in your whole formed a holistic goal to which they were all committed, tested the decisions they made to ensure their plans would take them toward it, monitored their plans once implemented, and responded immediately if the results began to deviate from the outcome envisioned.

If you have been practicing Holistic Management for a year or more and not much has changed, you have a logjam somewhere. To find it, start at the top of the Holistic Management model and work your way down.

- *The whole under management.* Have you defined a manageable whole (decision makers, resource base, and money)? Are all the right people included and in the right places, either as decision makers or as resources to you in achieving your holistic goal? Is the whole too large to be managed effectively as a single entity? Should smaller wholes be formed within it?

- *The holistic goal.* Does it lack clarity? Are you able to test all your decisions toward it, or do you need to revise and update it? Are people committed to achieving it? Are you still working toward a temporary holistic goal formed in some haste and without the involvement of all the decision makers?

- *The tools.* Pay particular attention to the tools of Human Creativity, Money, and Labor. There are times when undercapitalization prevents you from applying the tool of money effectively, but experience has taught us that most logjams are related to human creativity and labor. A lack of knowledge, specific skills, poor communication, or any other human behavior could be affecting your ability to use either tool effectively.

- *The management guidelines.* Are these guidelines being heeded, particularly Organization and Leadership and Learning and Practice? As you will recall from Chapter 26, in determining the cause of problems related to human behavior, look first to how your organization is structured, how management functions, and how it is led. The Organization and Leadership guideline addresses these issues specifically. A lack of knowledge of Holistic Management, or a lack of skill in practicing it is just as likely to be the cause of the problem, which the Learning and Practice guideline addresses. Both these guidelines were developed in tandem with the holistic decision-making process. The struggles that resulted in the development of these guidelines forced us to look anew at conventional approaches to organization, leadership, and learning in the new context of Holistic Management.

- *The Planning Procedures.* Have you put into practice those that apply, particularly Holistic Financial Planning?

- *The feedback loop.* When results begin to deviate from what you have planned, are you taking action immediately to correct the situation, or are you merely waiting in the hope the situation will resolve itself? Holistic Management, remember, is a proactive process in which you are constantly responding to the feedback gained from monitoring the results of your decisions.

We as a center took several years to identify and address one logjam. Together our board and staff had formed, and gradually refined, a holistic goal. Yet two years later, we had failed to make much progress toward its achievement. We identified poor communication between board and staff as the logjam, and its cause as the failure of the staff to keep board members adequately informed between quarterly meetings. Accordingly, the staff made a concerted effort to rectify this by keeping in touch with board members more regularly through phone calls, faxes, e-mail, more frequent reports, and so on. But this made little difference.

Several clues eventually led us to a diagnosis. First of all, we realized, the commitment to achieving our holistic goal varied greatly among the members of our board and staff team. The staff members, whose very livelihoods depended on achieving our holistic goal, were deeply committed. The board members, who lacked this inducement, as well as daily exposure to the rewards and challenges faced by the staff, had less of a sense of ownership in the holistic goal. This was not surprising, but we had failed as a team to even discuss it. It was important, though, because it influenced the results of the decisions we tested together.

Second, we realized that although we considered ourselves one team, we were still legally separated into two teams. Our bylaws required that the board meet separately to vote on policy and financial decisions that could profoundly affect the staff. Yet staff were prevented by our corporate bylaws from voting. Staff could provide input before a vote was taken, and almost always did, but on occasion were unable to provide enough information in the time allotted to truly clarify a situation. Some of the problems this resulted in could have been prevented if we had ensured at the outset that all members of our board–staff team had a reasonably good understanding of the holistic decision-making process.

We came to the conclusion that we could begin to clear our communications logjam by changing the bylaws that dictated not only our structure but also, to some extent, how we had to function. With the help of a legal advisor, we redrafted the bylaws to allow for up to three staff members to serve (and vote) on our board of directors, all of whom had to have experience in the practice of Holistic Management, and reduced the total number of directors from fifteen to a maximum of seven. To a large extent, these changes helped us to overcome the communication problems that had existed. The varying levels of commitment to the holistic goal, which is to be expected when some members of a team are only occasionally present and their livelihood is not directly connected to the goal's achievement, remains but it has ceased to be the problem it was.

In making these changes, we were aware that we would lose the perspective contributed previously by the large number of talented and concerned individuals who had served on our board at any one time. To make up for that loss, we created a board of advisors whom we could consult, and many of whom also proved willing to critique our efforts without our having to ask. We also worked at strengthening relationships with the clients we served in the expectation that because they would want to see us succeed they would tell us what we needed to know.

There could be any number of obstacles standing between you and your holistic goal that an orderly review of the Holistic Management model may throw no light on. The cause of a logjam could prove to be an unsuitable location for your business, for instance. Or, in managing your personal life, you may find you have fallen into a rut and need to change jobs or careers. Sometimes, a logjam becomes apparent only when a series of unrelated problems begin to form a pattern. If, when creating a holistic financial plan, you discover that each enterprise shares the same weak link, which is not uncommon, a logjam probably exists that has not yet been identified. If, for instance, marketing was the weak link in every enterprise, it could be that your business has a public image problem, the cause of which is an inappropriate name for your business or an inability to express what your business is about in terms the public, and thus your potential clients, can understand.

In attempting to identify a logjam and diagnose its cause, the most important thing to remember is the need to step back from the concerns of day-to-day management or daily living so you can see the bigger picture—much as the logger who climbs the hill or tree so he can spot the one or two logs that are key to releasing the flow of all the others.

49

Making Research Relevant

O ccasionally when testing a decision we discover a gap in our knowledge that research could help to bridge. If such research exists, we have to ensure that it is relevant to our own situation and in line with what we hope to achieve in our holistic goal. That, too, we can assess through the seven testing guidelines, but only by monitoring our application of that information can we ensure that the expected results do materialize.

Most scientific research tends to be reductionist in that it seeks to reduce phenomena to a simple form for study by controlling most variables. It does this to show that one factor and not another contributes to a given result. Management, on the other hand, deals with innumerable variables and cannot ignore any of them without adverse consequences. Although this fundamental difference exists between the two types of endeavor, they can still complement each other, and in fact need to, a subject we will return to.

Closing Knowledge Gaps

In seeking to address the cause of a problem, we often make use of information derived from reductionist research. In diagnosing the cause of an insect outbreak, for instance, we often rely on such research to help us determine the weakest point in the insect's life cycle so we can deal with the insect at its most vulnerable stage. Similarly, basic biological research has provided information on the establishment conditions for various plants and thus made it possible for management to increase populations of desired plants and to decrease populations of undesirable ones.

However, there are also instances when conventional research has misled us. Many scientists, for instance, have sought to disprove the positive effects of animal impact, specifically trampling, yet their attempts to do so have been largely inappropriate; commonly, some form of metal artifact was used to simulate the animal hoof. Isolated from the whole in the simplified context of a laboratory experiment, simulated hoof action compacted barren soil in just the same manner as a sheep's foot roller compacts an earthen dam. Based on these experiments, the researchers concluded that if we used the tool of animal impact it would only cause damage, not help to reverse it.

In practice, however, trampling by real animals never occurs in isolation. The hoof action itself varies according to the behavior of the animals, which may reflect territorial restrictions, fences, predators, avoidance of fouled ground, and other factors. It never occurs independently of dung and urine and other organisms, litter, root action, and climate. And of course, timing is everything. Livestock that move according to a holistic grazing plan rarely linger long enough to severely compact soil, and assuming that the plan minimizes overgrazing, the root growth of vigorous plants will loosen what compaction does occur. Even when soils are of a type that compacts severely when wet and trampled, experience shows that healthy plant roots soon loosen the compaction.

Knowing that a certain research finding comes from reductionist methodology simply warns us to observe and to monitor carefully as we apply it in the whole we are managing. Because all wholes are unique, the results of any research findings may not follow predictions or even be replicable, as we know from the disappointing lack of success of the many prepackaged management systems or "best management practices" promoted for widespread application.

In determining whether research is relevant to your own management situation, you also have to know something about the circumstances in which it was conducted. In the United States, for instance, a fair amount of data have been collected on species and their interrelationships in areas set aside as bioreserves. The Sevilleta Wildlife Refuge in New Mexico, mentioned in Chapter 20, is one of these. In this case, the environment is very brittle and thus requires some form of disturbance of vegetation and soil surfaces to maintain plant vigor, complexity of species, and healthy soils, but instead the land has been rested for many years. The aim of the research is to provide guidelines for better management, but how useful will this research be to managers when it is based on such an unnatural and deteriorating situation?

In any number of situations, you may be in a position to conduct your own research or to collaborate with others to address a knowledge gap. For example, there is a growing movement of farmer-initiated, on-farm research in many U.S. states in which farmers, university researchers, and extension agents all collaborate. These research efforts become far more meaningful when the farmer can explain how the knowledge he needs will be used and for what purpose—to enable him to move toward his holistic goal. Together, he and the researchers can test the research plan they develop to make sure it delivers the needed information and that it can be used.

At other times you might need to contract others to do research for you. A small manufacturing company, for instance, may have decided to find a profitable and environmentally responsible way to utilize some of the residues left from its manufacturing processes. Some of the research could be conducted in-house, but much of the technical information may have to be gathered by outside specialists. The company would have to ensure that these researchers are aware of the desires expressed in the company's holistic goal and that the information gained from their research will have to pass each of the seven tests that apply to be useful.

Product Development

Product development generally falls in the realm of marketing, a subject covered in Chapter 37. It is relevant here as well because the research behind so many products that have proven to have adverse social and environmental consequences was driven by narrow goals or objectives related to a company's bottom line. Given the challenge of producing products that will pass testing toward a holistic goal they have helped to form, I believe the same researchers would be capable of creating products that are socially and environmentally sound—and just as profitable.

One of the greatest challenges manufacturers will face is in developing products that do not in their manufacture, use, or final disposal, release substances that will not break down. No early warning methods have yet been developed for monitoring the effects of persistent substances within our ecosystem. We do know that the effects are likely to be adverse, that they may not be apparent until many years later, and that we cannot predict where they will manifest themselves. Detecting them only when animals produce deformed offspring or fail to breed, or when stratospheric ozone is depleted, is far too late. Research that is oriented to the development of products composed of biodegradable substances or products in which non-biodegradable substances can easily be extracted for recycling would have high priority when tested toward the holistic goals formed by most manufacturers. As mentioned in Chapter 31, companies attempting to comply with the ISO 14000 standards or to follow the principles of The Natural Step program, are beginning to respond to this challenge.

Beyond Reductionist Research

Where once any but the most reductionist research was frowned upon or even ridiculed, we are becoming increasingly wary of relying on it totally. Although some research is conducted out of pure curiosity, most research efforts are driven by a desire to better human life in some way. All research deals with the world around us, and if the world is organized in wholes, as we are increasingly beginning to acknowledge, then much of that research would benefit from a holistic perspective.

Often in diagnosing a problem we can expect to find that we just do not know enough about the problem to address it effectively, particularly in the case of heretofore unknown or recently introduced fungi, bacteria, and viruses, and these are areas for urgent research. To date, management as well as research on such problems has tended to be reductionist, as isolated calls for a broader approach generally went unheeded.

It is highly unlikely that such simple organisms live outside the successional process and ecosystem functioning generally. Where we create ideal survival conditions for an organism, or where we introduce one without the predators and diseases that restrained it, an invading organism can flourish to problem levels, as rabbits and prickly pear did in Australia, or as syphilis did in renaissance Europe, and measles and smallpox in North America. It is highly likely that present-day epidemics, such as Dutch elm disease or even AIDS, exist *because an environment exists that supports them.* Our task is to find what we have done to produce that environment. In our passion to cure with technological nonsolutions rather than prevent these diseases, we often overlook this basic question. Let me cite three instances that would support this approach.

The Great Plague

Today we know that the bubonic plague that devastated Europe's population in medieval times, was derived from bacteria that were spread by fleas living on rats. The plague reached epidemic proportions when overcrowded urban slums produced the right conditions for a massive increase in the rat population, which in turn provided the right environment for a massive increase in fleas. Attempts to tackle the disease head-on by seeking a cure for the individuals afflicted by the plague were unsuccessful. It wasn't until the slum conditions were rectified, and thus the environment made less conducive to rat and flea, that the disease was contained.

Foot and Mouth Disease

This viral disease, which mainly affects cattle, is indirectly responsible for the destruction of game in Africa on a massive scale. American and European importers of African beef insist that the meat come from disease-free areas, which is a reasonable demand as the virus apparently takes on a particularly virulent form when it reaches northern climes. Veterinarians believe the virus is carried by wildlife, buffalo in particular, and spread to cattle through close contact. To prevent any contact, they fence livestock areas to exclude game, sometimes shoot out the game, and vaccinate the livestock as well. In tackling the problem head-on, today's veterinarians have failed to address the larger questions, the most obvious one being what kind of environment is conducive to the virus?

In India during the 1930s, British researcher Sir Albert Howard demonstrated repeatedly that cattle running on healthy soils and maintaining a healthy diet could actually rub noses with infected animals and not contract the disease. My own experience backs this up. The outbreaks that occurred in Zimbabwe up until 1964, when I left the Game Department, always showed a far greater correlation with nutritionally stressed livestock, certain soil types, and a deteriorating environment than they ever did with game populations. In fact in our areas of greatest buffalo-to-cattle contact, outbreaks were almost unknown. When one did occur in a small cattle herd in the middle of a large game reserve, the veterinarians jumped on it as proof that buffalo were spreading the virus. When we investigated further, we found that immediately before the outbreak the area had been visited by a veterinary officer, who had come from a foot-and-mouth area in nearby Zambia.

Whenever an outbreak occurred, a cordon was placed around the area, which meant that all roads leading out of it had check points where shoes and tires were sprayed. This control of human movement effectively controlled the spread of the disease. Many species of game, including buffalo and vultures, still moved freely back and forth, which indicated that game were not the main agent in spreading the disease. In fact, it would be hard to imagine a better experiment to clear game of the accusation that they spread the disease. Despite this, fences continue to be built and game shot to keep them away from livestock.

Clearly we need to research the relationship between health and infection—the health not only of the cattle but also of the soil and plant communities. Much like the urban slums of medieval times contributed to outbreaks of plague, I believe livestock living in "slum conditions" are more susceptible to foot-and-mouth and many other diseases. In the meantime, hundreds of thousands of game animals are dying of thirst because fences deny them access to water, and whole buffalo herds are shot when fences do not contain them.

The Irish Potato Famine

Over a million people starved as a result of the blight that struck Ireland's staple crop in the nineteenth century. Although the situation was exacerbated by the ineptitude of the British bureaucracy, we now understand why the blight's spread was so extensive: we had created an environment that was ideal for that particular fungus to flourish. Not only were the potatoes grown as near monocultures, they were also virtually all derived from the same seedstock and thus lacked genetic diversity. Therefore, the blight encountered little or no resistance in that environment and spread readily. The same principle is at work today wherever monoculture cropping is practiced, but we put large-scale blights off to a later day by poisoning the offending fungus, virus, or bacteria. Developing poisons that can kill the offending organisms, while not taking steps to reduce them through environmental management, carry the real danger that the organisms mutate and become even more lethal. Tragically most research efforts still concentrate on these instant cures rather than the longer-term prevention brought about by greater diversity in the environment.

In the future we must concentrate on whole communities rather than on the offending organism in our endeavors both to understand and to prevent major disease outbreaks. Once the cause is determined and rectified, we commonly find we need do nothing further to contain the disease to proportions we can live with.

Multidisciplinary Research

As we enter a new era in research, multidisciplinary research teams will play an increasing role. But they will first have to overcome the major shortcoming mentioned in Chapter 3: their tendency to favor the perspective of their individual disciplines at the expense of the "whole," which has qualities not present within the individual or even the combined disciplines. This is easier said than done, but the experience of one researcher is promising.

Dr. Cliff Montagne, a soil scientist at Montana State University, is part of a multidisciplinary team researching ways for rural communities to enhance their sustainability. The experience, he says, has shown him how valuable the Holistic Management model can be as an organizing framework in designing research projects. It did not start out that way, however.

> The project began as a brainstorming session, by a group of academics sitting in their ivory tower, on how to conduct the research. What information would be needed? Who would collect it? and How would it be measured? We would need to know this in order to validate particular hypotheses. This of course was something we were all trained to do.

Suddenly it dawned on me that we couldn't do anything relevant without defining a minimum whole, which would have to include the members of the community we planned to use as a case study. Somewhat reluctantly, the others agreed. The community members would have to be included intimately in the planning and in the conduct of the research.

Through a series of evening dinner meetings, the values and aspirations of a spectrum of community members have since been shared and used to drive the research hypotheses for the project. This inclusivity has been a major key to the success of the project so far. However, we are currently battling (myself included) to truly internalize and utilize the model in taking things further. I am convinced that it will be necessary for both the team members and the community to "buy in" to holistic decision-making for this research to produce results that will make a difference.

The consumer-centered approach is currently gaining popularity in research. The U.S. Department of Agriculture's Fund for Rural America and the Sustainable Agriculture Research and Education (SARE) programs, for instance, call specifically for involvement of the farmers as integral participants in the research process. Our experience so far suggests that if research dealing with humans is to be relevant, it must be centered around identification of a management whole that includes the people who will be affected by the research, as well as the researchers themselves. I believe that the Holistic Management model is one of the best tools available to do this effectively, and I suspect other researchers may well come to the same conclusion."[1]

Researchers have long resisted a close involvement with those who would benefit from their research for fear that such involvement would compromise the researchers' objectivity. One could also ask why the same fear does not appear to exist when research is funded by corporations with a vested interest in the results. Nonetheless, the researchers' lack of involvement in the practical realities of management has often resulted in conclusions that are out of touch with reality and thus of little use to those who could otherwise benefit from them. The trend toward consumer-centered research is well worth cultivating if research is truly to benefit management. In a larger sense, one could just as easily conclude that if reality is structured and functions in wholes, *that* is what researchers should primarily study.

50

Creating Sound
Policies

M ost policies are created either to solve a problem or to prevent a problem from occurring. In the case of the former, the policy will prescribe a course of action; in the latter, a set of rules or guidelines to be followed. However, in either case a policy formed within the context of a holistic goal is likely to fare better than one oriented toward objectives to solve or prevent problems. Formed within the context of a holistic goal, the policy would then reflect, and lead to, what you do want that the problem or potential problem is preventing (or would prevent) you from having.

Policies designed to prevent problems are by far the most common and are used in a variety of situations. In your home you might have a policy that limits the number of hours your children watch television (to prevent them from watching too much of it). In the workplace, you might have a policy for handling customer complaints (to avoid confusion), a policy covering safety precautions when working in a dangerous area (to avoid accidents), and so on. Because these sorts of policies are fairly straightforward and easy to form, I do not dwell on them in this chapter. I mention them only because they often change in detail, when the rules or guidelines they prescribe are assessed in terms of what you want, as described in your holistic goal.

Policies designed to solve problems are more common than they should be, because all too often they fail to tackle the underlying cause of the problem and merely work to suppress symptoms. When enforced, they may in fact alleviate some of these symptoms, but because the cause has not been addressed, the symptoms (and the problem) persist. Another policy may then be developed, but it too fares no better for the same reason. The many policies created to combat crime are an example. When more and better equipped police officers do not solve the crime problem, we build more prisons, and when that does not solve it, we enforce stiffer penalties on repeat offenders, and so on. Each of these policies might help to reduce crime, but because none of them address the underlying cause, the problem never goes away.

When policies aim to solve a problem, the holistic goal will help to put the problem in perspective, but a thorough analysis of the policy using the Holistic Management model is also required. This should start with a diagnosis of the problem's cause. Then, each of the actions prescribed in the policy needs to be passed through the seven testing guidelines. If none of those actions address the root cause of the problem (cause and effect test), the policy may require fairly drastic revision. If an action fails any of the remaining tests, slight modifications may be all that are required to make the policy economically, socially, and environmentally sound and in line with the holistic goal.

Nowhere is such an analysis needed more than when forming policies that attempt to solve resource management problems—the focus of this chapter. It appears that nothing remotely resembling the Holistic Management model directs resource management policy currently, at any level nationally or internationally. In policy analysis courses the Center for Holistic Management has run for university educators and researchers, government officials, and advisors—those who most often provide technical advice to politicians—we asked the participants to comment on the following policies actually implemented in the United States:

1. With the aim of rescuing a vanishing breed of trout in a wilderness area, a predatory trout is being poisoned.

2. To stave off the day when a large and vital dam inevitably fills with silt, its wall is being raised. There is some controversy on whether to raise it a few feet at a time so as not to immediately destroy eagle nesting sites, or all at once (the cheaper course).

3. To help to rid rangelands of noxious plants, livestock numbers are being reduced and the plants poisoned. At the same time ranchers are being encouraged, with cost-sharing programs, to invest in more fencing and water points.

4. To destroy grasshoppers that threaten crop and forage yields, an aerial spraying program is being implemented.

5. To reduce brush encroachment (mesquite trees), a liquid herbicide is being applied.

6. To heal the land after a severe drought, extension agents are advising a prolonged rest period.

Every policy except the last prescribes actions involving the tool of technology, and in nearly all situations the testing toward even the most rudimentary holistic goal would show it to be counterproductive. All the proposed solutions address a symptom and fail the cause and effect test. None passes the sustainability test either. Where profitability and ecosystem stability are factors, the weak link and marginal reaction tests would eliminate most, if not all, of them.

After the brief exposure to holistic policy analysis given in the courses, all the participants—numbering well over a thousand, and including some of the very people who had masterminded these policies—came to similar conclusions. All agreed that public funds had been wasted on these policies because none of them could succeed in the long run. All agreed that the sample was not biased. Such policies were typical, they said, both in the United States, and in countries the United States was assisting. One class of thirty-five, after some discussion, actually stated as a group that *they could now see that unsound resource management was universal in the United States.*

The only point on which they were not unanimously agreed was in determining who actually produced the policies. Some laid the responsibility on the politicians, and others on the public, or professional advisors and consultants from private or public institutions, the media, or industrial firms with vested financial interests. When asked to think about where we might start to rectify such a situation, discussion ranged widely, but most participants arrived at a similar breakdown. About 75 percent believed the policies ultimately emanate from our educational system and the professional advisors and consultants it produces. About 25 percent felt that though this accounts for most cases, vested interests (financial, professional, lobbyist groups) also influence a certain proportion of policies. Even assuming that some participants might have publicly accepted the majority opinion while not entirely agreeing, the consensus indicates a real need to rethink our approach to forming resource management policies.

Also significant is the conclusion that procedures presently enforced in America to screen out bad policies apparently don't work. In the United States neither public nor private undertakings affecting the land can proceed without an Environmental Impact Statement that presents an interdisciplinary study of the policy according to strict guidelines. Yet unsound and damaging projects routinely slip through this filter. The Environmental Impact Statement usually consists of a compendium of various viewpoints, unconnected by anything even remotely resembling a holistic goal as a point of reference for relating one view to another. The interpretation of the document remains a matter of negotiation between forces in which vested power, academic seniority, and political expediency often count more than logic or common sense.

Analyzing an Existing Policy

I could take any one of the policies mentioned to illustrate the process in detail, but I will use the grasshopper spraying policy because it is large in scope and representative of many others. Emergency appropriations in the millions of dollars to spray malathion or some other pesticide on offending grasshoppers are not unusual. In this case $35 million was appropriated to address the grasshopper problem in the state of Wyoming.

The Cause of the Problem

As Chapter 48 explained, when diagnosing a problem involving an increase or decrease in the numbers of a particular organism, focus your attention on community dynamics. As you will remember (from Chapter 13), populations cannot build in numbers unless an environment has been created that enables them to flourish. To figure out what that ideal environment is, you need to know something of the basic biology of the species. What stage in the grasshopper's life cycle is its weakest, and what conditions does it require to survive at that point? In grasshoppers, the weakest point is at the egg or nymph stage, so we look for the conditions that would promote survival of the eggs and nymphs. It turns out that the grasshopper species that tend to become pests prefer to lay their eggs in bare ground, which must remain warm and dry for the nymphs to hatch. Bare ground has steadily increased in Wyoming, as it has in most western states, and thus so have egg-laying sites.

In most years the majority of eggs laid in the bare ground or the nymphs that emerge from them will not survive because temperatures and rainfall are too high or too low. But when the right temperature coincides with the right amount of rain, millions of eggs will hatch and grow into nymphs, and eventually grasshoppers. The cause of the problem is most likely to be the production of vast areas of bare soil between plants providing ideal breeding sites.

The Whole

In this case, all of the people in the state of Wyoming are affected, but most directly the farmers, ranchers, and others whose livelihood has been damaged by the loss of forage and crops. The land within the state and the biological communities it encompasses serve as the resource base. The money available for implementing this policy is $35 million, gleaned from state and federal treasuries.

The Holistic Goal

We can probably surmise that the people in the state of Wyoming would like to have stable families, prosperity, good health, physical and financial security, and so on. To sustain the forms of production that will produce all this, they are bound to require a healthy land base in which water and mineral cycles are effective, energy flow high, and communities rich in biological diversity—all of which would reduce the likelihood of grasshopper outbreaks. Even such a simple statement as this is enough to enable us to use the testing guidelines to discover if the course of action outlined in the policy is likely to produce desirable results.

The Actions Proposed

The policy prescribes only one action—the use of a poisonous spray (the tool of technology) that kills grasshoppers.

The Testing

The spraying clearly fails the cause and effect test because it does nothing to treat the bare ground—the underlying cause of the outbreak. We might also predict a negative verdict on the sustainability test, particularly when we gauge the likely effects of spraying on community dynamics. This is because we have already established that the weak link in the grasshopper's life cycle is at the egg and nymph stage, but the spraying mainly affects adult grasshoppers. Research shows that once nymphs assume the adult form, they require about fourteen days before they can reproduce and most probably have done so before any sprayers can mobilize. The bulk of the adult population will die at the end of the growing season, and thus the spraying program will be killing grasshoppers doomed to die shortly anyway. Poisoning the adults will at best save some crops and forage, but the poison never kills all individuals. Some survive to breed a more chemically tolerant strain, even if timely spraying catches the bulk before they get a chance.

Wyoming probably hosts more than two hundred organisms that prey on grasshoppers in their various stages and help to limit outbreaks, but spraying does not in the least benefit any of these predators. It is likely to kill off high proportions of many and thus to promote the hatching and survival of more grasshoppers. Research from the U.S. Department of Agriculture documents the importance of these predators. Working in

Montana, Dr. J. A. Onsager has shown that natural populations of grasshoppers in a reasonably healthy environment suffer 2 to 13 percent daily
mortality at the nymph stage, which at the low end translates to a 50 percent reduction of adults. At the high end, less than 1 percent survive to
maturity.[1]

Chapter 42 discussed the characteristic S-shaped growth curve of populations and explained the extreme significance of early mortality. Spraying
that also decimates a broad range of predators unleashes the full power of
the principle in the wrong direction, however, because prey populations
always recover before the predators. The next time ideal conditions prevail,
an abundant egg supply and reduced predators will guarantee another outbreak. Clearly this policy fails the sustainability test.

Even without further testing, we can definitely call this policy unsound.
The spraying program, apart from not addressing the cause of the problem,
adversely affects community dynamics by reducing the diversity within
biological communities. People face increased pollution danger. And a
country struggling to balance its budget wastes $35 million. Obviously we
should seek other solutions.

Unfortunately, today most people still look for further remedies in
other forms of technology, such as more specific pesticides or genetic engineering, when living organisms could be harnessed to perform the same
task without damaging the four ecosystem processes. However, neither
technology nor living organisms will help to prevent future grasshopper
outbreaks in Wyoming if the underlying cause is not addressed. That would
figure largely in the revised policy we would create using the Holistic
Management model to guide us.

Revising the Policy

Given the generic holistic goal described, consider how you as a politician
might approach the grasshopper problem. As a primary rule, you would try
to center on the holistic goal and avoid confusing that by debate over
chemical poisons, biological controls, or any other tools. Then, given the
possibility of a $35 million appropriation, you might propose allocating it
in the following way.

1. To soften the immediate impact of the grasshoppers you might use
    some of the money to directly compensate people who truly suffered
    damage to their livelihood. If biological pest control, or any other
    method of controlling adult populations could pass the testing, funds
    might go to that as well. Suppose this cost $20 million.

2. Of the remaining $15 million, $5 million could go to training farm-
    ers, ranchers, refuge, and park managers, and so on, in management

practices that would promote the generic holistic goal and address the cause of the outbreak. Increased ground cover would reduce egg-laying sites. Increased ground cover would enhance the water cycle as well, which in turn would enhance the population of fungi and microorganisms that destroy grasshopper eggs. Increased biodiversity would help to keep predation levels high. All of this would move us in the direction of the holistic goal and provide a long-term solution. More species of grasshopper might inhabit the increasingly complex communities that develop, but in lower numbers characterized by smaller, if any, outbreaks.

3. You could return $10 million to the treasury to help to balance the budget and reduce taxation. If such a commonsense solution proved hard to sell, $1 million might go toward a public awareness campaign.

From my own political experience, I believe it possible sell such a program to voters far more easily than the poisoning that will add to taxation, endanger human health, and ultimately lead to more grasshoppers. In an extreme case, where spraying just had to employ all of the money to prevent excessive crop damage, it would not make sense to do this without simultaneously taking measures to prevent a recurrence. Any policy that concentrates on cure rather than prevention and that at the same time *exacerbates the cause* ultimately contributes to ever-mounting crisis management.

Grasshoppers represent only one of thousands of problems throughout the world consistently exacerbated by management that remains focused on problems rather than on what lies beyond them. Altogether, many nations annually spend hundreds of millions of dollars on futile policies attempting to combat soil erosion, the spread of deserts, noxious plants, and so on through actions that are either socially, economically, or environmentally unsound.

Analysis Prior to Forming a Policy

When a problem has been identified and various recommendations made to address it, you can analyze these recommendations prior to forming a policy and save considerable time in the process. The analysis follows the same basic steps as those listed earlier, although it is usually less detailed. Take for example, the recommendations made a few years ago by a group of scientists allied in their concern for the biomass burning occurring throughout much of Africa, mainly in the grasslands. The smoke from these fires has become a major source of the greenhouse gas emissions affecting global climate change, which is the main concern of these scientists. They have addressed their recommendations to policymakers in the hope that through policy, the burning might be greatly curtailed. Once more, the focus is on the problem rather than on what the problem is preventing people from achieving. These recommendations include removing livestock altogether from grasslands and feeding them in pens; where possible, converting grasslands into plantations (orchards and energy crops mainly), that could feed both people and livestock; burning strategic areas to limit the extent of any natural fires that occur; incorporating wild grazers into game ranching schemes; and where nomadic or seminomadic cultures exist, settling the people in permanent villages where they could cultivate crops and would require fewer livestock.[2]

The Cause of the Problem

Africa's grasslands are most commonly burned in order to produce more nutritious forage for livestock or wildlife, and to prevent a shift to woody vegetation. The burning is most frequent where animal numbers are too low to fully utilize the forage produced each year, which results in the accumulation of old material. Where forage is so sparse that few animals can survive, there is not enough material to burn. As described in earlier chapters, old, unused grass stems and leaves choke out new growth, and tap-rooted shrubs can more easily establish among the weakened roots of the dying grass plants. Given enough animals and enough *herd effect*, the plants would not grow stale and moribund. Too few animals scattered too thinly on the land appears to be the cause of the problem, which should come as no surprise to anyone who has read the preceding chapters of this book. Government destocking programs throughout most of Africa have reduced livestock numbers substantially over the decades. Droughts have further reduced the numbers of both livestock and wildlife, and wildlife culling programs in national parks and tsetse fly-infested areas have also taken their toll.

The Whole and Holistic Goal

Africa's grasslands support millions of people, most of whom depend to varying degrees on livestock for their living and to maintain their culture. Many of these livestock-dependent cultures are nomadic or seminomadic. We can envision the basic desires that would be expressed in a holistic goal on the reasonable assumption that the people living in Africa's grasslands would have similar needs, such as prosperity and self-sufficiency, freedom to follow their own religions and to preserve what they value in their cultures, and so on. To sustain this they would need to produce healthy grasslands with covered soil, biological diversity, effective mineral and water cycles, and high energy flow.

The Testing

Obviously, none of the actions proposed by the scientists would pass the cause and effect test because none of them address the problem: too few animals (scattered too thinly). In fact, most of the actions exacerbate the problem by reducing animal numbers in one way or another. Other tests would be failed as well, most notably the sustainability and society and culture tests.

Removing livestock altogether would disrupt people's lives and destroy nomadic cultures. It would also affect the land dramatically since most of these grasslands tend to be very brittle. Resting the land in a low-rainfall brittle environment causes it to desertify. Where rainfall is high enough, the grassland would shift to forest, which would sustain fewer people. Placing livestock in feed pens would lead to pollution and an increase in disease. Growing the feed to support the animals could mean that people had less land available for feeding themselves.

Converting grasslands to orchards would require high rainfall or irrigation, and again would lead to a drastic change in the way people live their lives. It would also require a capital investment that probably is not available locally.

Burning strategic areas to lessen the chance of natural fires occurring would expose soil and create pollution.

Incorporating remnant wild animals into game ranching schemes would continue the partial resting of the land, disrupt the lives of those in livestock-based cultures, and increase the need to burn the grasslands. (Some of Africa's national parks have to be burned as frequently as every two to three years.)

Settling millions of nomadic or seminomadic people in permanent villages where they could cultivate crops and would require fewer livestock would only add to the overpopulation that already exists on lands suitable for cropping. Conflict would inevitably result.

Even this quick assessment of the various actions proposed is enough to call them unsound in the context of the generic holistic goal described. Most would only aggravate an already serious situation. Had this assessment shown any of these recommendations had serious merit, then a more detailed analysis would have followed to see if any minor modifications needed to be made.

Any policy that eventually is formed to promote the healthy grasslands that would sustain these people and their way of life would need to deal with the issue of biomass burning by addressing the cause of the problem: too few animals, domestic or wild, are present to keep grasses and soils healthy. Livestock and wildlife, properly managed, are the obvious tools of choice for dealing with the problem on millions of acres. However, any policy formed would also have to address the widespread ignorance that attributes overgrazing to too many animals—when we now know it is the result of how long they remain in any one place—and that fails to recognize the importance of *herd effect* in maintaining healthy grasslands in a brittle environment.

Conclusion

Any policy that aims to solve a problem should be analyzed, ideally in the planning stages. Seven basic steps are involved in analyzing a policy holistically:

1. *Identify the cause of the problem the policy seeks to address.* First make sure you understand what the problem is, then identify its cause. (See Chapter 25, on cause and effect, for ways to approach this, and Chapter 48 if the problem is related to resource management.)

2. *Loosely define the whole the policy encompasses*—the people involved, the resources affected, and the money available. You do not need to be as specific as you would in defining a whole for management purposes.

3. *Depending on the policy, form a holistic goal or identify the conditions that would exist if the problem did not.* Don't worry about making assumptions on behalf of people you may not know. You can assume that for most people quality of life involves meeting basic needs, such as food and shelter, and basic desires for security, health, comfort, love, and companionship, one or more of which may be threatened by the problem the policy addresses. What the people have to produce to meet these needs or desires can be left vague in most cases. The future resource base required to sustain them should be fairly obvious and can be described in very general terms. You need not be any more specific than this. All you are attempting to do here is to enlarge the perspective so that the focus is not on the problem but on what the problem is preventing you from achieving. This will enable you to better see the ramifications of any actions taken, something that is not visible when the focus remains fixed on the problem.

4. *Identify the actions proposed in the policy.* Policies that attempt to resolve a problem will always prescribe one or more actions and how they are to be carried out. However, the language used in some policies often obscures this information. You may have to read through a document several times before you understand what actions are being proposed (which you must do to test the actions). Occasionally, you may find some policies totally incomprehensible. I have often wondered in such cases if even the policymakers or their advisors understand what they are proposing.

5. *Test each of the actions identified to see if they would lead to achieving the holistic goal.* The cause and effect test is particularly important in analyzing any policy. If none of the actions prescribed address the underlying cause of the problem, the problem will remain and probably spawn new symptoms. If even a few of the actions prescribed address the root cause of the problem, success is more likely. More often than not, a policy will need to address symptoms to alleviate interim suffering or damage. This is not an issue as long as the root cause of the problem is being addressed simultaneously.

   The remaining tests can be just as powerful in helping to ensure a policy succeeds. The marginal reaction test, for example, may show that the return on time or money spent is far greater for one action than another and that more resources should be allocated to it. A weak link that is not addressed will thwart the best of intentions, as will any actions that adversely affect the lives of the people involved.

6. *Modify the policy if necessary.* By the time you have finished testing the actions prescribed in the policy, you will undoubtedly find that the policy could be improved. Any test that points out a weakness automatically forces you to consider alternatives, and these will help to shape the necessary revisions. In some cases the policy may need to be rewritten entirely. In a few the policy might not be needed at all if the underlying cause of the problem it addresses could be dealt with more effectively without a policy.

   In finalizing your revisions, give some thought to how the revised policy might be received. No policy is workable in the long run if people do not understand and accept it. However, it is important that you not worry about how to sell the policy before you have clarity on the revisions that need to be made. Once you have that clarity, you can determine what actions might need to be included in the policy that would address this issue. For example, some of the funds used in implementing the policy might have to be allocated for education.

7. *Determine what criteria to monitor to ensure that the revised policy, once implemented, will be successful.* If the policy is sound, then obviously the problem will be resolved or will never materialize. But can you afford to wait to find out? What if you were slightly off the mark in identifying the cause of the problem, or what if you missed the mark altogether? And what if the modifications you have made fall short in achieving what they are supposed to achieve? Identify *what* you can monitor for the earliest sign that you might be wrong.

These steps can serve as a guide in analyzing or *forming* any policy that aims to solve a problem, no matter how large or small in scope or importance. Although this chapter has focused on resource management policies,

I hope you can see that policies of many kinds would benefit just as much from holistic analysis.

Although Holistic Management is still in its infancy, it is developing exponentially, particularly as its practice expands into new realms of endeavor. This, combined with an equally rapid increase in our scientific knowledge in general and a worldwide awareness that humanity faces extraordinary challenges in the new millennium, has made me more curious than ever about what the future might hold, the subject of the next chapter.

Part XI

Conclusion

51

Changing Course: Creating the Future We Want

Our lovely planet now staggers under massive human impact and fast-rising populations that if unchecked can only lead to poverty, war, disease, and starvation. Some people remain optimistic that technology in one form or another will alleviate the damage we have done and enable us to continue on our present course. Others are deeply pessimistic that anything can save us, and it is easy to see why. As figure 51-1 shows, human populations are growing exponentially even as the health of our environment declines precipitously. If we do not act, the two curves will collide in a catastrophe for humanity, and all higher life forms, too terrible to contemplate.

That we are accelerating toward catastrophe means that minor improvements that only slow the rate of acceleration are ultimately meaningless. Slowing down will not prevent you from driving your car over a cliff, only delay the time of the crash; *you have to change direction altogether.* That is what we must do now to avoid a future none of us wants. Doing so will not be easy on a world scale, but I believe it is more possible now than ever before because four developments have coincided that will enable a significant turnaround to occur:

1. *A new framework for decision making.* Until recently not a single scientist, including myself, whether he or she commanded the wealth of Texas or the poverty of sub-Saharan Africa, understood why agriculture and resource management were running into crisis everywhere. On the other hand, for 10,000 years humankind dreamed of flying and not a single person knew how, although other creatures had done it for millions of years. Then, within seventy years of the first

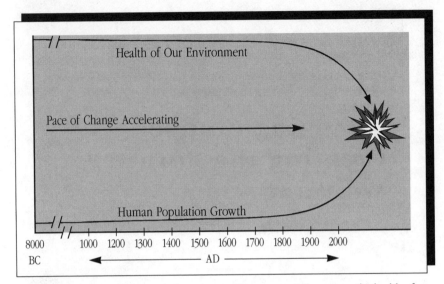

Figure 51-1 *Human populations are growing exponentially even as the health of our environment has declined precipitously. If we do not act soon, the two curves will collide with catastrophic consequences.*

successful flight, humans walked on the moon. Holistic decision making and management promise the same kind of phenomenal advance. Although we have unintentionally advanced the destruction of life on our planet over many millennia, given what we now know and what we will learn as we go, we can begin to restore much of what we have lost, and at ever-increasing speed. The simple but successful framework for management and decision making outlined in this book will surely be improved and extended by thousands of people. As long as it remains simple enough for ordinary people to use, the power of the ideas behind it will encounter few limits.

2. *A common enemy.* Historically, people have seldom been united in outlook or actions unless faced with tragedy or a threat from some external force. The rest of the time we have generally fallen to squabbling among ourselves over any number of divisive issues. If we have failed to learn to live with each other and our environment harmoniously on a global scale, it is perhaps because we have lacked a common enemy of similar magnitude. This we now have in the phenomenon of global climate change, which is a direct result of our inability to gauge the effects of human actions on the greater ecosystem that sustains us all.

We now know that the amounts of carbon and other substances released into the atmosphere due to the burning of fossil fuels and forest and grassland vegetation is more than our atmosphere can absorb. And we are becoming increasingly aware that a deteriorating Earth can no longer absorb them either. The majority of the planet's land surface is now bare and capped, or sealed, reducing the soil's ability to breathe and the ability of new plants to establish. Both plants and living soils play a critical role in maintaining the balance of atmospheric gases essential to sustaining all higher life forms.

Although the majority of people may not recognize the enemy yet, they surely will within the coming decade.

3. *Advances in technology.* The development of sophisticated instruments has enabled us to discover that ozone holes exist and that chemicals produced on Earth have contributed to their expansion. These instruments have also enabled us to discover just how long certain human-made substances can persist in an environment. People can no longer argue that the deterioration occurring on Earth or in its atmosphere is due entirely to natural causes. Technology is also enabling us to reduce our consumption of fossil fuels and to develop alternative energy sources that are environmentally benign. In many areas of endeavor it is enabling us to do much more with far less. Although the use of technology has led to many of our problems, we can now see that it will also be critical to solving them.

4. *Advances in communications.* With the help of modern technology, we have, for the first time in history, the ability to pass information to millions of people simultaneously and on every continent. Ideas that have been ignored by the mainstream media or censored by others, or that risk being lost in a maze of bureaucracy, now have an outlet on the Internet. This uncontrolled exchange of views may yet prove to be the greatest benefit computers bring to humanity.

Without these four developments in place I do not believe we could have changed course. Had you and I lived in the days of the Roman Empire when North Africa was moving from productive grasslands to desert, what could we have done about it? We knew nothing about the brittleness scale then, or about the role played by grazing and trampling herds and their predators in preventing such devastation in brittle environments. Even if we had known, how could we have communicated what we knew to Aborigines in Australia or the Indians in North America? How could either of those cultures have evaluated the enormous impact their burning would have on the landscapes that would have to sustain future generations?

How could we have known anywhere that healthy soil, plant, and animal communities were responsible for maintaining a balance of gases in our atmosphere conducive to human and other life forms? How could we have known of the existence of ozone, let alone upper-level ozone, and its importance in protecting the immune systems of all living organisms? Only now, as we enter a new millennium do we have answers, and only now are we able to take meaningful action. Thus, I am not pessimistic about our future. In fact, I am more optimistic than I could have been at any time in history.

I believe we will inhabit a future where the world's deserts are healing, where life is once again diverse and abundant in our soils, rivers, and seas and able to absorb the far smaller amounts of carbon and other substances released into the atmosphere. Key to creating such a future will be to address the underlying cause that has prevented us from creating it up until now: the way we make decisions.

Some years ago I attended a conference at which Norway's Prime Minister Gro Harlem Brundtland in a keynote speech suggested that the environmental problems besetting the governments and development agencies in every country were in fact interlinked. Figure 51-2 illustrates the interlinking problems she touched on. More progress could be made, she said, and at lower cost, if our policies and programs took this into account. Most of those present nodded their heads in agreement, and many have since acted on her suggestion. But based on what we now know—that all these problems ultimately have the same root cause, as depicted in figure 51-3—we can progress much further and more rapidly by first addressing that cause. Instead of spending billions of dollars on each problem, or cluster of problems, as many governments do today, a few million spent on addressing the common cause would enable people to solve most of these problems on their own.

Alongside the deterioration of land, water, and our atmosphere, the explosion of the human population that has paralleled the degradation of our resources will also have to be tackled. We cannot manage resources holistically according to the natural laws of our ecosystem if we continue to act as if those laws did not apply to humanity as well.

Various cultures and religions favor large families for reasons deeply rooted in historical conditions in which security in old age or survival of a race depended on many children. Now, however, uncontrolled population growth threatens our survival, and we have other means to provide old age security.

The institutionalized religions in modern society that encourage high numbers of children do not reflect the present state of the world. The sages who founded them spoke out of the conditions of the times in which they lived, but in all cases their universal message was compassion. I find it difficult to believe that, were they preaching today, they would suggest that we continue to produce high numbers of children knowing that by doing

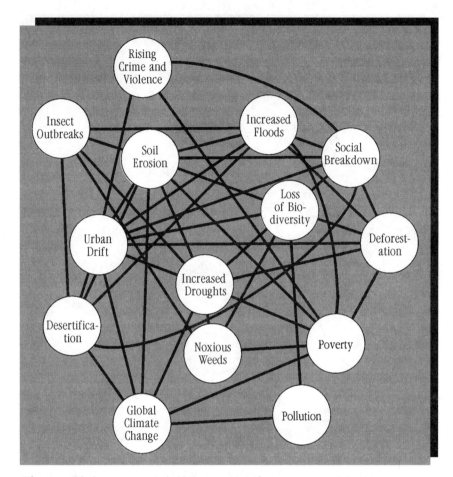

Figure 51-2 *Some people hold the view that if governments and development agencies saw most of the environmental problems they seek to address as interlinked, they could solve these problems more quickly and at lower cost.*

so we ensure poverty, violence, social breakdown, even genocide, and ultimately threaten our survival as a species.

I myself am not a conventionally religious man. I do however feel infinitely small and powerless in the presence of the wonders of Nature and our universe. Such marvelous creation did not occur by chance. There is a power that is greater than all humankind, and out of deference to it we should respect each other and the ecosystem that sustains us all. This means controlling our population and respecting the diversity of cultures, tribes, nations, and spiritual beliefs as a great gift to all humankind, and the same duty includes the companion task of halting the deterioration of life on Earth.

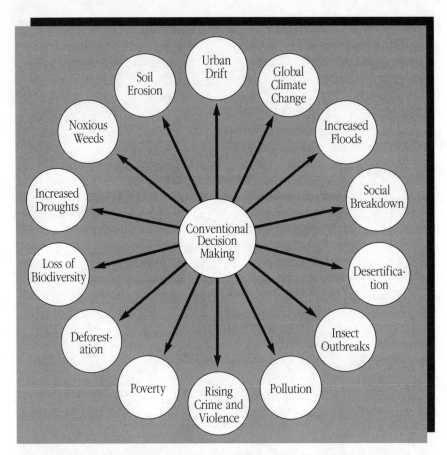

Figure 51-3 *Based on what we now know—that all these problems ultimately have the same root cause—we can progress much further and more rapidly by first addressing that cause. A few million dollars directed toward the cause, compared to the billions now spent addressing each problem, or cluster of problems, would enable people to develop their own solutions at low cost.*

Fortunately we do not have to wait for an era of world peace and collaboration to make a start because holistic decision making leads to conflict resolution and the Holistic Management model will function for any people in any place, regardless of religion, system of government, economic base, or climate.

A great many of our conflicts arise directly out of the deterioration of resources and out of ignorance about the tools we have to manage them, but even such a materialistic explanation has a philosophical aspect. I once heard of a Navajo medicine man who, in mediating a grazing dispute between two families said, "You are neighbors whether you want to be or not, because the land itself unites you. It links you both as you walk on it today, and you will both lie in it together when you die. Then the plants that grow in the soil you become will infect your children with either your hatred or affection as you can choose now. If you bless your land, it will return the blessing and your present argument will become insignificant."

To the prayers, songs, and practical gestures the medicine man had in mind I would add holistic decision making. In case after case we have already witnessed what it can contribute to conflict resolution, and this role will surely become ever greater. The conflict often begins to resolve itself as antagonists brought together to form a holistic goal discover that what they have in common is far greater than their differences. Several years following the civil war in Zimbabwe, for instance, I ran a workshop that included participants who had fought on opposing sides. We were attempting to analyze a national policy, and in advance I had prepared a holistic goal I felt most Zimbabweans would aspire to. When I read it aloud, there was a long silence, followed by some discussion among the participants. One of them spoke for all when he said, "My god, if we had only known we all wanted the same things, we would never have fought the war."

Holistic Management starts with a holistic goal because it establishes at the outset what people want. Because people always act in their own self-interest it is important that they express what *is* in their own interest. In the same breath, however, they must also express what they will have to produce to sustain what they need and want for themselves and for future generations. When they then test decisions toward *that*, they begin to see that keeping the land vital is in their own self-interest, and that building human relationships, rather than destroying them, is in their own self-interest. Their actions begin to reflect this understanding. Self-interest becomes enlightened self-interest.

Selfish national interest in a world inextricably linked by geography, economics, and communications has subverted more enlightened management of the world's resources as much as any other force. Few things indicate this more clearly than our willingness to let pollutants that we would not tolerate drift downwind or downstream to bedevil foreigners. Or when we ban the production of harmful substances, such as DDT or CFCs by manufacturers in our own country, but allow them to continue to produce these substances in other countries. Similarly, the American appetite for hamburger or the Japanese demand for lumber is somehow allowed to justify the destruction of tropical forests that the world as a whole cannot afford to lose. Such actions would become a thing of the past if governments worked toward a national holistic goal and began testing decisions toward it. Selfish national interest would give way to enlightened national interest.

However, no government is currently structured to manage its own resources holistically, let alone control its international impact. Most government structures divide every aspect of our lives into portfolios, or departments, and nowhere can you discuss the whole as one. As I found in my own parliamentary experience, if you try to discuss a broad field under any one minister's portfolio you are ruled out of order. If you try to discuss a broad field under the prime minister's portfolio you are again ruled out of order as that should be discussed under each appropriate minister's portfolio.

When we cannot even debate the whole and the interconnectedness of all that governments take upon themselves to do, how can we ever transcend the problems that are created by compartmentalized thinking and actions. Too often governments perform like a team of blinkered horses all pulling in different directions, but you are forbidden by the system to remove the blinkers and get them pulling together. Only in their mechanisms for control of finances and budgets do most governments even come close to some form of coordination.

In the thousands of years of struggle to find ways to govern ourselves, we have acted in terms of power, wealth, defense, religion, tribe, or race but never out of concern for living within the confines of our life support system. Only in the twentieth century did we encounter the harsh necessity to even think about that. An axiom of politics that impressed me early in my own political career says that unless all feel secure and well governed none are. As long as we continue to undermine our resource base, few, if any, governments can truly govern their citizens well.

Then again, any government that is able to make decisions and formulate policies that are in line with a national holistic goal and consistently socially, environmentally, and economically sound, will provide good governance. Governments would have to restructure their bureaucracies to govern along holistic lines, but this is not an impossible task. Although long noted for their ability to resist change, some bureaucracies are already beginning to build a different reputation. In *Banishing Bureaucracy*, David Osborne and Peter Plastrik cite a number of cases in which elected leaders and bureaucrats have worked together to make fairly radical changes in bureaucratic structures, and have documented the essential steps taken so that others might follow.

As much as governments will have to change, they cannot lead a change to holistic decision making. By definition, democratically elected leaders cannot lead, other than in crisis or war, but must always follow the will of the majority. That means the change to holistic decision making has to start at the grass roots.

The magnitude of world desertification alone, taking but one of the factors responsible for global climate change, has already grown beyond the power of any human organization to handle. So great is the challenge now of re-creating a planet that is rich in biological diversity and where deserts are healing, that only ordinary people can do it—you and I—teachers, farmers, foresters, range managers, mothers, fathers, businesspeople, or whatever we are outside our institutional or social identities. Until each of us individually begins to change the way we make decisions there will not be a sufficient groundswell of opinion to make it safe for elected leaders to change the way they make decisions. Fortunately, that groundswell is beginning to build.

Earlier in my life the magnitude of problems without solutions depressed me utterly. Now, at last, I see the possibility of wonderful times ahead as we both enjoy the fruits of technology and learn to live within our ecosystem's rules. Had I another stock of years to replace those I've spent already, I could not imagine a more exciting time to live them than now.

Glossary

A number of new words and phrases are associated with Holistic Management, particularly for aspects related to the use of grazing animals in restoring degraded landscapes. This glossary defines many of those new terms, along with a few others that involve new ways of looking at the land in order to judge its condition.

Animal days per acre (ADA) or hectare (ADH). A term used simply to express the volume of forage taken from an area in a specified time. It can relate to one grazing in a paddock or several, in that more grazings than one can be added to give a total ADA or ADH figure. The figure is arrived at by a simple calculation as follows:

$$\frac{\text{Animal Numbers} \times \text{Days of Grazing}}{\text{Area of Land in Acres or Hectares}} = \text{ADA or ADH}$$

Animal impact. The sum total of the direct physical influences animals have on the land—trampling, digging, dunging, urinating, salivating, rubbing, etc. Most commonly achieved with herding animals in high concentration.

Biodiversity. The diversity of plant and animal species—and of their genetic material and the age structure of their populations—within a given community.

Biomass. The mass, or volume, of life—plants, animals, and microorganisms.

Brittleness scale. All terrestrial environments, regardless of total rainfall, lie somewhere along a continuum from nonbrittle to very brittle. For simplicity, we refer to this continuum as a 10-point scale—1 being nonbrittle and 10 being very brittle. Completely nonbrittle environments are characterized by: (1) reliable precipitation regardless of volume; (2) good distribution of humidity throughout the year as a whole; (3) a high rate of biological decay in dead plant material, which is most rapid close to the soil surface (thus, dead trees rot at their bases and topple over relatively quickly); (4) speedy development of new communities on any bare surface; and (5) the development of complex and stable communities even where they are not physically disturbed for many years. In such environments it is virtually impossible to produce or maintain millions of acres where the ground between plants is bare, other than on croplands that are continually exposed by machinery.

Very brittle environments, on the other hand, are characterized by: (1) unreliable precipitation, regardless of volume; (2) poor distribution of humidity through the year as a whole; (3) chemical (oxidation) and physical (weathering) breakdown of dead plant material, generally slow and from the upper parts of plants downward (thus, dead trees remain standing for many years); (4) very slow development of communities from bare soil surfaces unless physically disturbed; and (5) soil surfaces that can be covered with algae and lichens for centuries unless adequately disturbed. In such environments it is very easy to produce millions of acres where the ground between plants is bare or capped by algae or lichen by merely by resting the land excessively, burning it frequently, or overgrazing many grass plants. Such areas tend to maintain biodiversity and stability only when adequately disturbed.

Capping, immature. A soil surface that has sealed with the last rainfall and on which there is no visible sign yet of successional movement. Capping is initiated by raindrop action on an exposed soil. The energy from the raindrop breaks crumb structure and frees fine soil particles; and these in turn seal the surface so the soil cannot respire easily. Some people use the term *crusting* instead of *capping*.

Capping, mature. An exposed soil surface on which succession has proceeded to the level of an algae-, lichen-, and/or moss-dominated community and has stalled at that level. If not adequately disturbed, such communities can remain in this state for centuries provided the soil is level enough to inhibit erosion by water.

Community dynamics. The development of communities of living organisms. This process is ongoing because of the constant interplay of species, changing composition, and changing microenvironment. However, the greater the biodiversity within a community, the more complex, and thus the more stable, it tends to be.

Crumb structure. A soil that has good crumb structure is made up largely of aggregates or crumbs of soil particles held together when wet or dry with "glue" provided by decomposing organic matter. The space around each crumb provides room for water and air, and this in turn promotes plant growth.

Desertification. A process characterized by a loss of biodiversity, plant mass, and soil cover. Symptoms include increased incidence of flood and drought, declining levels of soil organic matter, increased soil surface exposure, and erosion.

Forbs. Tap-rooted herbaceous plants, often referred to as *weeds*.

Grazing cell. An area of land planned for grazing management purposes, normally as one unit to ensure adequate timing of grazing/trampling and recovery periods. It is generally divided into smaller units of land (paddocks) by fencing in some form or marks on the ground or vegetation that herders can observe. A grazing cell will normally contain livestock year round or at least for a prolonged period.

Grazing, frequent. Grazing that takes place with short intervals between the actual grazings on the plant. With most plants, frequent grazing is not harmful as long as the defoliation is light.

Grazing, severe. Grazing that removes a high proportion of the plant's leaf in either the growing or nongrowing season. In the growing season this causes a temporary setback in the plant's growth. In the more brittle environments severe grazing at some time during the year is generally beneficial to most bunched perennial grass plants, and especially those with growth points, or buds, at their bases.

Herd effect. The impact on soils and vegetation produced by a large herd of animals in high concentration or in an excited state. Herd effect is not to be confused with stock density, as they are different, although often linked. You can have high herd effect with very low stock density (e.g., the bison of old that ran in very large herds at very low stock density, as the whole of North America was the paddock.) You can have high stock density with no herd effect, such as when two or three animals are placed in a one-acre paddock. At ultra-high densities, the behavior of livestock will change adequately to provide herd effect. *Note:* Herd effect is the result of a change in animal behavior and usually has to be brought about by some actual management action—stimulating the behavior change with the use of an attractant, or crowding animals to ultra-high density. Herd effect is generally used to break up a capped soil surface, to compact soil enough to get good seed-to-soil contact, and to trample dead plant material to the ground where it provides soil cover and slows water movement and erosion. Applied too long or too frequently it tends to pulverize most soils and cause excessive compaction.

Low-density grazing (sometimes referred to as *patch* or *selective grazing*). This refers to the grazing of certain areas while others nearby are left ungrazed and on which plants become old, stale, and moribund. Normally it is caused by stock grazing at too low a stock density, too small a herd, or a combination of these, with too short a time in a paddock. Once it has started, even by only one grazing, it tends to get progressively worse, as the nutritional contrast between regrowth on grazed areas and old material on ungrazed areas increases with time. The common remedy calls for holding stock longer to force them to graze everything equally (nonselectively), but this is a bad mistake and results in stock stress and poor performance. It is low-density grazing and is corrected by increasing density and *generally* shortening time to avoid stock stress.

Overgrazing. When a plant bitten severely in the growing season gets bitten severely again while using energy it has taken from its crown, stem bases, or roots to reestablish leaf. Generally, this results in the eventual death of the plant. In intermediate stages it results in reduced production from the plant. Overgrazing occurs at three different times: (1) When the plant is exposed to the animals for too many days and they are around to regraze it as it tries to regrow; (2) when animals move away but return too soon and graze the plant again while it is still using stored energy to reform leaf; or (3) immediately following dormancy when the plant is growing new leaf from stored energy.

Overrested plant. A bunched perennial grass plant that has been rested so long that accumulating dead material prevents light from reaching growth points at the plant's base, hampering new growth and eventually killing the plant. Overrest occurs mainly in the more brittle environments where, in the absence of large herbivores, most old material breaks down through oxidation and weathering rather than decay.

Paddock. A small division of land within a grazing cell in which stock are grazed for short periods—hours to days. Paddocks can be fenced or merely marked for herders to observe.

Planned grazing. (A common abbreviation for Holistic Grazing Planning.) The planning of livestock grazing that caters simultaneously to many variables: animal behavior, breeding, performance, wildlife needs, other land uses, weather, plant growth rates, poisonous plants, dormant periods, droughts, etc. The purpose of such planning is to utilize livestock to bring about the future landscape described in a holistic goal.

Rest, partial. Takes place when grazing animals are on the land but without a full complement of pack-hunting predators to excite them and cause them to bunch. In walking around the grazing animals barely disturb soil surfaces and trample very little material onto the ground.

Rest-tolerant grasses. Perennial grasses able to thrive under rest in very brittle environments. Commonly, such plants have some growth points, or buds, well above ground along their stems where unfiltered sunlight can reach them; or they are short in stature or sparse-leafed, enabling unfiltered light to reach their ground-level growth points. In the past, such grasses tended to be found in steep gorges and other sites large grazing animals did not frequent, but today where overgrazing is believed to be linked to animal numbers and thus numbers have been reduced, these grasses can be found all over.

Rest, total. Prolonged nondisturbance of soils and plant or animal communities. A lack of any physical disturbance and/or fire.

Rotational grazing. Grazing in which animals are rotated through a series of paddocks, generally on some flexible basis, but without any planning that caters for the many variables inherent in the situation.

Strip grazing. The grazing of animals in narrow strips of land generally behind a frequently moved electric fence. In some cases, different areas are strip-grazed within a paddock.

Stock density. The number of animals run on a subunit (paddock) of land at a given moment of time. This could be from a few minutes to several days. Usually expressed as the number of animals (of any size or age) run on one acre or hectare.

Stocking rate. The number of animals run on a unit of land expressed usually in the number of acres or hectares required to run one full-grown animal through-out the year or part thereof.

Succession. An important aspect of community dynamics, succession describes the stages through which biological communities develop. As simple communities become ever more diverse and complex, succession is said to be advancing. When complex communities are reduced to greater simplicity and less diversity, succession is set back. If the factors that set it back are removed, succession will advance once again.

Ultra-high-density grazing. The grazing of livestock in such a manner that they are at extremely high stock densities throughout the day. Generally, these densities are achieved either by herding the stock, by enclosing them in a small area with the use of moveable fencing, or by utilizing a combination of both. The aim is to induce herd effect, and thus high animal impact, over most of the land most of the time.

References

In addition to the works cited within the text of this book, a number of other resources were utilized in preparing the manuscript, many of which are listed here for the reader who wishes to pursue the various subjects in greater depth. Additional background information is also provided on some of the topics raised.

CHAPTER 1. CHANGING THE WAY WE MAKE DECISIONS

In the last few decades advanced radiocarbon dating techniques have begun to show that the majority of the world's large mammal species became extinct relatively recently and that their disappearance strongly coincides with the arrival of skilled human hunters. Though mammals had been the dominant animals in terrestrial environments for over 70 million years, the majority of the larger species—those weighing at least 100 pounds (44 kg)—suddenly became extinct at the very end of the Pleistocene, from 10,000 to 35,000 years ago, depending on the continent.

All continents except Antarctica were affected, the Americas and Australia to a much greater degree than Africa and Asia. In North America 74 percent of the large mammal genera disappeared, possibly within a few centuries. In South America 79 percent of the genera disappeared in an equally short time, and in Australia 86 percent became extinct over a slightly longer period.

Geoscientist Paul Martin (University of Arizona) has developed a theory called the "blitzkrieg hypothesis," the central tenet of which is that the extinctions occurred within a few hundred years of the first arrival of humans in any one place. He and other proponents of the theory suggest that the large mammals, as well as large flightless birds, were easy prey to early humans because they did not recognize humans as predators. To back his claims Martin points out that the extinctions occurred at greater intensity on continents of human invasion than on those of human origin. In Africa, where humans evolved for millions of years with large mammals, the extinctions had been minimal (19 percent), compared with the tremendous losses in the Americas, which were colonized by highly advanced hunting societies at the peak of their powers.

The idea that people wiped out the great animals within a few hundred years of arriving on the scene does pose a problem: there is no archaeological evidence, other than in New Zealand—and even that was within the last 1,000 years—that humans systematically slaughtered the biggest animals. Maori butchering sites have been found where between 30,000 and 90,000 moa were killed. Analysis of these sites by modern-day archaeologists suggests that the wastage of meat was enormous. Entire moa legs have been found baked in ovens that were never opened. Whole bodies were frequently left to rot.

In Australia there is no sign of hunting at all, despite the fact that Aborigines were hunters. Indeed, not until the recent excavation of a site near Cuddie Springs was there unequivocal evidence that put people and the large mammals in the same place at the same time.

Some scientists still attribute the mass extinctions in Australia and the Americas to climatic changes, most notably the last ice age. However, in North America the large mammals persisted another 20,000 years after the ice had retreated to the poles; in Australia, almost all the large mammals appear to have vanished 15,000 years before the ice age reached its maximum. Even so, the last ice age was only one of seventeen that had occurred over a 2-million-year period, and none of the others had triggered such a rash of extinctions.

I am inclined to believe that our earlier ancestors of 10,000 or more years ago played a critical role in the late Pleistocene extinctions—both through overkill and through the dramatic changes they produced through their burning. There is considerable evidence that a much greater proportion of the pre-human arrival vegetation was fire sensitive following millions of years of coevolution (of plants, soils, and large mammals). The burning of fire-sensitive vegetation on the scale early humans did alone probably would have produced enough of a change to cause major extinctions, even if over-hunting were not a factor. One simply cannot change a continent from largely fire-sensitive vegetation to fire-dependent vegetation (as the pollen record shows, for instance, in Australia) without causing massive disruption to animal populations. Any prey population stressed by environmental deterioration is more susceptible to predation, which human hunters would have exploited.

Although Africa's extinctions, in terms of the number of genera lost, were low during the Pleistocene Epoch, the continent is enormous and a number of large mammals have become extinct in areas where they were once plentiful, such as in the savannas and marshes now consumed by the Sahara desert and more recently all along its boundaries. In the last century many extinctions have occurred in sub-Saharan Africa as a direct consequence of overhunting.

For further reading on this subject, I recommend:

Flannery, Tim. 1994. *The Future Eaters.* Chatswood NSW, Australia: Reed Books.

Kay, Charles E. 1994. "Aboriginal Overkill: The Role of Native Americans in Structuring Western Ecosystems," *Human Nature,* vol. 5, no. 4: 359–398.

Martin, P. S. 1984. "Prehistoric Overkill: The Global Model." In P. S. Martin and R. G. Klein, eds., *Quaternary Extinctions: A Prehistoric Revolution,* pp. 354–403. Tucson: University of Arizona Press.

Steadman, David W. 1995. "Prehistoric Extinctions of Pacific Island Birds: Biodiversity Meets Zooarcheology," *Science,* vol. 267: 1123–1122. The author states that the loss of birds due to human overkill may exceed 2,000 species, some 20 percent of the world's bird species.

For more on the archaeological sites at Cuddie Springs, Australia, see:

Stephanie Pain, 1997. "Cooking Up a Storm," *New Scientist,* vol. 156, no. 2107: 36–40.

Two books that treat the relationship of humans to their environment more generally are:

Leakey, Richard, and Roger Lewin. 1995. *The Sixth Extinction: Patterns of Life and the Future of Mankind.* New York: Doubleday.

United Nations Environment Programme. 1983. *The Human Environment: Action or Disaster? An Account of the Public Hearing Held in London, June 1982.* Dublin: Tycooly International Publishing Inc.

CHAPTER 2. THE POWER OF PARADIGMS

For more on the paradigm effect, see:

Barker, Joel A. 1993. *Paradigms: The Business of Discovering the Future.* New York: HarperCollins.

Kuhn, Thomas S. 1962. *The Structure of Scientific Revolutions.* Chicago: Harper Collins.

Readers interested in the long history of ideas in science and how humans have consistently reacted to new knowledge should see such books as:

Beveridge, W. I. B. 1957. *The Art of Scientific Investigation.* New York: Random House.

Boorstin, Daniel. 1983. *The Discoverers.* New York: Random House.

Ferguson, Marilyn. 1980. *The Aquarian Conspiracy.* Boston: Houghton Mifflin.

Sobel, Dava. 1995. *Longitude: The True Story of a Lone Genius Who Solved the Greatest Scientific Problem of His Time.* New York: Walker and Co.

CHAPTER 3. THE WHOLE IS GREATER THAN THE SUM OF ITS PARTS

Readers interested in learning more about the origins of holism and about the man who coined the term should read *Holism and Evolution,* by Jan Christian Smuts, reprinted in 1996 by The Gestalt Journal Press (Highland, N.Y.), and the biography written by his son, J. C. Smuts, *Jan Christian Smuts.* London: Cassell & Company, 1952. Useful information is also contained in Piet Beukes's *The Holistic Smuts: A Study in Personality* (Cape Town: Human & Rousseau, 1990).

Understanding the difference between the integrated approach and the holistic approach is crucial and readers are encouraged to read Maurice Berman's *Reenchantment of the World* (Ithaca, N.Y.: Cornell University Press, 1981). Whereas I concluded that the integrated and the holistic approach are opposites from the practical failures in management of my own and other integrated teams, Berman arrived at this conclusion from an academic and philosophical perspective.

Other recommended reading to help one understand the problems inherent in reductionist or linear approaches is Peter Senge's *The Fifth Discipline: The Art and Practice of the Learning Organization* (New York: Doubleday, 1990), and James Gleick's *Chaos: Making a New Science* (New York: Penguin Books, 1987).

Currently I am aware of few references to the shortcomings of the integrated and interdisciplinary approaches. Zev Naveh and Arthur Lieberman refer to these shortcomings in *Landscape Ecology: Theory and Application,* 2nd ed. (New York:

Springer-Verlag, 1994). It is my belief that such approaches still have a vital role to play. While I do not believe that systems thinking alone will provide the success desired of these approaches, were the decision making within them to be changed, I believe most of their shortcomings would be addressed.

CHAPTER 4. VIEWING ENVIRONMENTS A WHOLE NEW WAY

The following sources outline the fate of earlier civilizations:

Bennett, Hugh. 1939. *Soil Conservation.* New York: McGraw-Hill.

Dasmann, Raymond. 1959. *Environmental Conservation.* New York: Wiley & Sons.

Lowdermilk, W. C. 1975. "Conquest of the Land through 7,000 Years," *Agriculture Information Bulletin No. 99,* U.S. Department of Agriculture, Soil Conservation Service, Issued 1953 and slightly revised in 1975.

Ponting, Clive. 1991. *A Green History of the World: The Environment and the Collapse of Great Civilizations.* New York: St. Martin's Press.

Where earlier plant ecologists tended to see plant communities independent of large animal populations and disturbance and viewed such things as essentially "unnatural," a number of researchers now come to the opposite conclusion. See, for example, Andrew H. Williams, 1997. "In Praise of Grazing," *Restoration and Management Notes,* vol. 15, no. 2: 116–118; Jocelyn Kaiser, 1998. "Bison Prime Prairie Biodiversity," *Science,* vol. 280: 677; and Scott L. Collins, Alan K. Knapp, John M. Briggs, John M. Blair, and Ernest M. Steinauer, 1998. "Modulation of Diversity by Grazing and Mowing in Native Tallgrass Prairie," *Science,* vol. 280: 745–747. Also of interest are publications such as S. T. A. Pickett and P. S. White's *The Ecology of Natural Disturbance and Patch Dynamics* (New York: Academic Press, 1985), and "Disturbance, Diversity, and Invasion: Implications for Conservation," *Conservation Biology,* vol. 6, no. 3: 324–337, by Richard J. Hobbs, and Laura F. Huenneke.

David Western, in his autobiography, *In the Dust of Kilimanjaro* (Washington, D.C.: Island Press/Shearwater Books, 1997), engagingly describes his research and eventual understanding that constant change and disturbance are the norm in the brittle environment of East Africa's Amboseli National Park and its surroundings.

Eventually I believe we will look at whole *communities,* rather than plant communities alone, and come to understand that both major climatic and seasonal weather fluctuations, combined with the natural presence of large herding ungulates and their predators, provided the constant change essential to the health of communities in the world's brittle environments. Several of the papers by S. J. McNaughton, listed in the references to Chapter 5, contain remarks about the coevolution of herding animals and grasslands.

Information on the collapse of wildlife populations in the brittle environment of the Tuli Circle area of Zimbabwe is contained in the following reports and papers written by myself: "Range Assessment—Tuli Circle (National Land)," unpublished Report to Game Ranchers Association of Rhodesia (1966); "Game Utilization in Rhodesia," *Zoologica Africana,* vol. 1, no. 2 (1964); "The Utilization of Wildlife on Rhodesian Marginal Lands and Its Relationship to Humans, Domestic Stock and Land Deterioration," *Proceedings of the First Congress of the Associated Scientific Societies of Rhodesia Symposium on Drought and Development,*

Bulawayo (1966); and "Crisis in Rhodesia," *Oryx, Journal of The Fauna Preservation Society,* vol. 10, no. 1 (May 1969).

These papers represent some of my early observations and thinking. The most significant, "Efforts in Rhodesia to Apply an Ecological Philosophy and Practice to the Human Environment to Avert Semidesert Formation," is regrettably not available. Presented at the Symposium on Terrestrial Animal Ecology, Pretoria, South Africa, 1967, it was not published with the proceedings because the findings and views expressed offended the scientific thinking of the day. Attempts shortly afterward to have the work published in America in the *Journal of Range Management* met with the same fate. It was in those years unacceptable that livestock could even be considered as constructive agents in the reversal of desertification.

CHAPTER 5. THE PREDATOR–PREY CONNECTION

Nothing has generated as much controversy in the development of Holistic Management as the use of large herding animals as a tool in land restoration and management, although in recent years the controversy has subsided. Early references to the positive role of animals, at least in pasture management, are contained in André Voisin's, *Grass Productivity,* which was first published in 1959 (and reprinted by Island Press in 1988), and *Better Grassland Sward* (London: Crosby Lockwood & Son, 1960). Other references to the beneficial effects of large herbivores are contained in:

Bell, Richard. 1971. "A Grazing Ecosystem in the Serengeti," *American Scientist,* vol. 225, no. 1: 86–93.

Collins, S. L., A. K. Knapp, J. M. Briggs, and E. M. Steinauer. 1998. "Modulation of Diversity by Grazing and Mowing in Native Tallgrass Prairie," *Science,* vol. 280: 745–747.

Davies, William. 1938. "Vegetation of Grass Verges and Other Excessively Trodden Habitats," *Journal of Ecology,* vol. 26: 38–49.

Geist, Valerius. 1974. "On the Relationship of Social Evolution and Ecology in Ungulates," *American Zoologist,* vol. 14: 205–220.

Gordon, Iain, and Patrick Duncan. 1988. "Pastures New for Conservation," *New Scientist,* vol. 117, no. 1604: 54–59.

McNaughton, S. J. 1979. "Grazing As an Optimization Process: Grass-Ungulate Relationships in the Serengeti," *The American Naturalist,* vol. 113, no. 5: 691–703.

McNaughton, S. J. 1984. "Grazing Lawns: Animals in Herds, Plant Form, and Coevolution," *The American Naturalist,* vol. 124, no. 6: 863–883.

McNaughton, S. J., M. B. Coughenour, and L. L. Wallace. 1982. "Interactive Processes in Grassland Ecosystems." In J. R. Estes, R. J. Tyrl, and J. N. Bunken, eds., *Grasses and Grasslands: Systematics and Ecology,* pp. 167–193. Norman: University of Oklahoma Press.

McNaughton, S. J., F. F. Banyikwa, and M. M. McNaughton. 1997. "Promotion of the Cycling of Diet-Enhancing Nutrients by African Grazers," *Science,* vol. 278: 1798–1800.

Paige, Ken, and Thomas Whitham. 1987. "Overcompensation in Response to

Mammalian Herbivory:The Advantage of Being Eaten," *American Naturalist*, vol. 129: 407–416.

Williams, Andrew H. 1997. "In Praise of Grazing," *Restoration and Management Notes,* vol. 15, no. 2: 116–118.

Bell and McNaughton in particular draw attention to the importance of large herding ungulates on the grasslands of East Africa (mainly brittle environments). In all cases, unfortunately, the role of herd behavior and predation was missed. McNaughton theorizes that the herding ungulates in some manner learned that their concentration produced a more palatable form of the grass plants on which they fed and thus developed the herding/moving pattern. Based on my observations, I believe that predators produce the tendency to concentrate and that concentrated dung and urine deposition produces the tendency for animals feeding close to the ground to move.Where large predators have been removed, their prey remain scattered and become more static. Another reason for my belief concerns the different hoof action and placement under excitement not produced while feeding as a herd—hence the development of animal impact as a new tool in Holistic Management. Just as scientists are beginning to understand the coevolution of herding herbivores and grasslands, I believe they will come to understand that predators were also vital components. The research of Iain Gordon and Patrick Duncan indicates that the impact of large herbivores is greater than we realized, even in less brittle environments.They report the loss of species diversity in European wetlands with the removal of livestock. Andrew Williams reports the same loss of biodiversity in Wisconsin grasslands, as does S. L. Collins et al. in the North American tallgrass prairie. Both papers also report that with the reestablishment of grazing, biodiversity was enhanced.

Chapter 6. Timing Is Everything

Researchers in a number of countries have observed the damage to grass root systems from severe defoliation, but none have related their observations to the time animals were present as opposed to animal numbers more clearly than André Voisin, who reported his findings in *Grass Productivity* (first published in 1959 and reprinted in 1988 by Island Press), *Better Grassland Sward* (1960), and *Rational Grazing: The Meeting of Cow and Grass, a Manual of Grass Productivity* (1962), all published by Crosby Lockwood & Son, London.

American researcher Franklin Crider also discussed the fate of grass roots under severe and frequent grazing in his 1955 paper, "Root Growth Stoppage," which appeared in *Technical Bulletin No. 1102,* published by the U.S. Department of Agriculture. It was from his work that the U.S. Soil Conservation Service (again missing the time element) developed the idea of stocking at a rate that would have the livestock "take half and leave half" of key indicator plants. Also in 1955, in Africa H. Weinmann confirmed the damage to roots following severe defoliation and wrote "The Chemistry and Physiology of Grasses," which was published in D. Meredith, ed., *The Grasses and Pastures of South Africa* (Cape Town: Central News Agency), and which he later followed up with "Effects of Defoliation on Veld Pastures," in *Proceedings of the Veld Management Conference,* Bulawayo, May 1969 (Salisbury, Rhodesia: Department of Conservation and Extension).

The findings of John Acocks are reported in his 1966 paper, "Non-selective

Grazing As a Means of Veld Reclamation," *Proceedings of the Annual Conference of the Grassland Association of South Africa*, vol. 1: 33–39.

Classic range management texts such as Laurence Stoddart and Arthur Smith's *Range Management* (New York: McGraw-Hill, 1955), and Harold Heady's *Rangeland Management* (New York: McGraw Hill, 1975), contain information on the effects of grazing and browsing on plants. However, in the light of prevailing paradigms, the authors interpret the data to mean that when "overuse" occurs, too many animals are the problem.

CHAPTER 8. DEFINING THE WHOLE: WHAT ARE YOU MANAGING?

This chapter refers to two eight-year-long "trials" of Holistic Management conducted by the U.S. Forest Service in cooperation with two ranching families who had permits allowing them to run cattle on two allotments. Two reports published by the U.S. Department of Agriculture Forest Service, Southwestern Region, summarize the results: "Holistic Resource Management (HRM) Dodson Pilot Project Summary, Apache-Sitgreaves National Forest," September 1990; and "Holistic Resource Management (HRM) Bonyback Pilot Project Summary, Tonto National Forest," September 1991, both prepared by myself and Darrol L. Harrison, USDA Forest Service, Southwestern Region.

CHAPTER 9. FORMING A HOLISTIC GOAL: WHAT IS IT YOU REALLY WANT?

CHAPTER 10. DEVELOPING A SENSE OF OWNERSHIP: ARE YOU SURE THAT'S WHAT YOU REALLY WANT?

Many groups have found it helpful, even necessary, to utilize special techniques or processes to set the stage for holistic goal setting. One consensus-building process a number of practitioners have used successfully was developed by Robert Chadwick in the United States. For more information contact Chadwick at Consensus Associates, PO Box 235, Terrebonne, Ore. 97760, tel: (503) 548-7112.

Families attempting to improve communication while forming and later refining their holistic goal would benefit from Virginia Satir's *Peoplemaking* (Palo Alto, Calif.: Science and Behavior Books, 1972), a very readable and informative book on family dynamics that contains exercises to enhance self-awareness and ideas to stimulate family discussion. Steven W. Vannoy's *The Ten Greatest Gifts I Give My Children* (New York: Simon & Schuster, 1994) is also helpful, both for families and for those working in large corporations.

The importance of creating a common vision and developing commitment to it is addressed in Peter Senge's *The Fifth Discipline: The Art and Practice of the Learning Organization* (New York: Doubleday, 1990), and *The Fifth Discipline Fieldbook* (New York: Doubleday, 1994), by Peter Senge, M. Senge, Art Kleiner, Charlotte Roberts, Richard B. Ross, and Bryan J. Smith. The section in the *Fieldbook* on "Building Shared Vision," particularly Chapters 44–47, is helpful in developing a quality of life statement in organizations of any kind, as is Chapter 29, "Corporate Constitutions," in *Principle-Centered Leadership*, by Stephen R. Covey (New York: Simon & Schuster, 1990).

Two books have been helpful to individuals and families attempting to define what quality of life means to them. In *Flow: The Psychology of Optimal Experience*

(New York: Harper, 1991), Mihaly Csikszentmihalyi reviews the research on the importance of having a vision beyond yourself and provides many examples of people who have led fulfilled lives, sometimes after the most debilitating accidents. In *Your Money or Your Life* (New York: Penguin Books, 1992), authors Joe Dominguez and Vicki Robin examine the relationship between money and what we really want in life.

To better understand the challenges one faces in maintaining commitment to the holistic goal, I suggest Robert Fritz's *The Path of Least Resistance: Principles for Creating What You Want to Create* (Walpole, N.H.: Stillpoint Publishing, 1984).

CHAPTER 11. THE FOUR FUNDAMENTAL PROCESSES THAT DRIVE OUR ECOSYSTEM

CHAPTER 12. WATER CYCLE: THE CIRCULATION OF CIVILIZATION'S LIFE BLOOD

CHAPTER 13. COMMUNITY DYNAMICS: THE EVER-CHANGING PATTERNS IN THE DEVELOPMENT OF LIVING COMMUNITIES

CHAPTER 14. MINERAL CYCLE: THE CIRCULATION OF LIFE-SUSTAINING NUTRIENTS

CHAPTER 15. ENERGY FLOW: THE FLOW OF FUEL THAT ANIMATES ALL LIFE

I have yet to find a single publication where the four ecosystem processes covered in these chapters are simply stated and described. Knowledge about them has to be gleaned from many sources, some of which I have listed here. Although these books and papers give a general outline of these four basic concepts, none refer to the different nature of the breakdown of material (decay or physical oxidation and weathering) and early successional processes in brittle and nonbrittle environments, which is a more recent discovery. (*Note:* Many of the books listed below will have newer editions available. I have listed the editions I have personally read, only because newer editions occasionally change in scope or focus and may not include the material that to me was valuable):

Albrecht, William A. 1982. In Charles Walters, ed., *The Albrecht Papers, Vol. I.* Kansas City: Acres USA.

Allee, W. C., Alfred E. Emerson, Orland Park, Thomas Park, and Karl Schmidt. 1955. *Principles of Animal Ecology.* Philadelphia: W. B. Saunders Company.

Branson, Farrel A., Gerald F. Gifford, Kenneth G. Renard, and Richard F. Hadley. 1981. In Elbert H. Reid, ed., *Rangeland Hydrology.* Dubuque, Iowa: Kendall/ Hunt Publishing Company.

Dasmann, Raymond F. 1975. *Environmental Conservation,* 4th ed. New York: Wiley.

Ehrlich, Paul. 1981. *The Machinery of Nature: The Living World around Us and How It Works.* New York: Simon & Schuster.

Odum, Eugene P. 1963. *Fundamentals of Ecology.* Philadelphia: W. B. Saunders Company.

Russell, Sir E. John. 1961. *Soil Conditions and Plant Growth.* London: Longmans.

Satterlund, Donald R. 1972. *Wildland Watershed Management.* New York: Wiley.

In the vast brittle environments of the world it is probable that we could provide far more water for cities, enhance the balance of atmospheric gases, and reverse the desertification process with a greater understanding of how the ecosystem processes function. An interesting paper aligned with this idea is Pimentel, David, James Houser, Erika Preiss, Omar White, Hope Fang, Leslie Mesnick, Troy Barsky, Sephanie Tariche, Jerrod Schreck, and Sharon Alpert. 1997. "Water Resources: Agriculture, the Environment, and Society: An Assessment of the Status of Water Resources," *Bioscience*, vol. 47, no. 2: 97–106. The authors point out that new water supplies are likely to come from conservation, recycling, reuse, and improved water use efficiency rather than from large development projects.

In "Conservation Tillage Impacts on National Soil and Atmospheric Carbon Levels," *Soil Science Society of America Journal*, vol. 57, no. 1: 202–210 (1993), J. S. Kern and M. G. Johnson provide useful information on carbon retention in covered soils.

In "Green Grass, Cool Climate?" *Science*, vol. 274: 1610–1611 (1996), Jocelyn Kaiser provides information on the greater carbon storage in the root systems of healthy grasslands than in unhealthy ones.

In "Influence of Nitrogen Loading and Species Composition on the Carbon Balance of Grasslands," *Science*, vol. 274: 1720–1723 (1996), David A. Wedin and David Tilman report on a twelve-year study indicating greater carbon storage in more natural and healthy grasslands.

In "Environmental and Economic Costs of Soil Erosion and Conservation Benefits," *Science*, vol. 267: 1117–1121 (1995), David Pimentel, C. Harvey, P. Resosudarmo, K. Sinclair, D. Kurz, M. McNair, S. Christ, L. Shpritz, L. Fitton, R. Saffouri, R. Blair, attempt to put an economic cost on priceless soil and provide some useful figures on the scale of soil erosion worldwide.

The following explore some of the topics covered in the chapter on community dynamics in more detail:

Albrecht, William A. 1975. In Charles Walters, ed., *Soil Fertility and Animal Health*, vol. II, Kansas City: Acres USA

Angermeier, Paul L., and James R. Karr. 1994. "Biological Integrity versus Biological Diversity As Policy Directives," *BioScience*, vol. 44, no. 10: 690–697.

Elton, Charles. 1956. *Animal Ecology*. London: Sidgewick & Jackson.

Fukuoka, Masanobu. 1978. *The One Straw Revolution: An Introduction to Natural Farming*. Emmaus, Penn.: Rodale Press.

Fuller, Buckminster R. 1978. *Operating Manual for Spaceship Earth*. New York: E. P. Dutton.

Howard, Sir Albert. 1975. *The Soil and Health*. New York: Schocken Books.

Leopold, Aldo. 1966. *A Sand County Almanac: With Essays on Conservation from Round River*. New York: Ballantine.

Lovelock, James E. 1979. *Gaia: A New Look at Life on Earth*. New York: Oxford University Press.

Lovelock, James E. 1988. *The Ages of Gaia: A Biography of Our Living Earth*. New York: Norton. (Few publications approach these two by Lovelock for giving meaning to the concept of our planet as a living organism, so complex and interdependent is everything on it.)

Maser, Chris. 1988. *The Redesigned Forest.* San Pedro, Calif.: R & E Miles.

Moore, John. 1985. "Science As a Way of Knowing—Human Ecology," *American Zoologist,* vol. 25: 486–637.

Quammen, David. 1996. *The Song of the Dodo: Island Biogeography in an Age of Extinctions.* New York: Simon & Schuster.

Weaver, John E., and Frederic E. Clements. 1938. *Plant Ecology.* New York: McGraw-Hill.

CHAPTER 17. MONEY AND LABOR: ONE OR BOTH OF THESE TOOLS IS ALWAYS REQUIRED

Although a nation's well-being ultimately depends on the sound functioning of our ecosystem, and although we have witnessed civilization after civilization collapse because it destroyed its foundation (soil), I have yet to read any economic text that even mentions the essential processes whereby our ecosystem functions, even though the two words, economy and ecology, share the same Greek root. Books I suggest are:

Drucker, Peter F. 1986. *The Frontiers of Management: Where Tomorrow's Decisions Are Being Made Today.* New York: E.P. Dutton.

Hawken, Paul. 1983. *The Next Economy.* New York: Ballantine.

Hawken, Paul. 1993. *The Ecology of Commerce.* New York: HarperCollins.

Hawken, Paul, Amory Lovins, and Hunter Lovins. 1999. *Natural Capitalism.* New York: Little, Brown.

Hazlitt, Henry. 1979. *Economics in One Lesson.* New York: Arlington House.

Henderson, Hazel. 1996. *Building a Win-Win World: Life Beyond Economic Warfare.* San Francisco: Berret-Koehler Publishers.

Walters, Charles. 1991. *Raw Materials Economics: A Norm Primer.* Kansas City: Acres USA.

In "The Capitalist Threat," *Atlantic Monthly,* vol. 279, no. 2: 45–58 (1997), George Soros makes a convincing case for his view that the free market capitalist system undermines the very values on which open and democratic society depend.

Compounding interest is responsible for much of the enormous increase in the trade of money as a commodity as well as the increase in the money supply, otherwise known as inflation. German author Margrit Kennedy in her book (with Declan Kennedy), *Interest and Inflation Free Money* (Okemos, Mich.: Seva International, 1995), illustrates the effects of compounding interest with this example: One penny invested at the birth of Christ at 4 percent interest would have bought one ball of gold equal to the weight of the earth in 1750. In 1990 it would have bought 8,190 balls of gold. At 5 percent interest it would have bought one ball of gold by the year 1466; by 1990, 2.2 billion balls of gold equal to the weight of the earth.

Clearly that single investment at moderate interest would become impossible to honor at some point. Now think of all of the borrowing that millions of individuals, businesses, and governments engage in every day, at much higher compounding interest rates. Although a lender should be entitled to charge the borrower a fee, when that fee becomes compound interest it creates havoc in most economies. To cover the escalating cost of borrowed money, individuals demand higher salaries, while businesses and governments pass the cost on to the consumers (and taxpayers) of the goods or services they provide. So even those who do not borrow end up paying for those who do. And inflation becomes inevitable, no matter how sophisticated a nation becomes at manipulating its money supply. Any economy in which heavy borrowing is a feature cannot avoid running into severe problems. Where real wealth was once dispersed among many people, money, the token of that wealth, becomes concentrated in ever fewer hands, largely due to compound interest, until revolution or draconian readjustment starts the process all over again.

Some of the latest thinking by ecological economists is currently being published in *Ecological Economics: The Journal of the International Society for Ecological Economics*. In 1991, I attempted to introduce Holistic Management to members of the Society in, "Holistic Resource Management: A Conceptual Framework for Ecologically Sound Economic Modeling," *Ecological Economics*, vol. 3: 181–193.

CHAPTER 18. HUMAN CREATIVITY: KEY TO USING ALL TOOLS EFFECTIVELY

A book that has proven helpful to a number of people attempting to manage their time more effectively is *First Things First,* by Stephen Covey, Roger Merrill, and Rebecca Merrill (New York: Simon & Schuster, 1994). A number of books describe techniques and ideas for releasing the creativity latent in most people, but among the best are Robert Fritz's *The Path of Least Resistance: Principles for Creating What You Want to Create* (Walpole, N.H.: Stillpoint Publishing, 1984) along with his later book *Creating* (New York: Ballantine, 1991).

In *The Mind Map Book* (New York: Penguin, 1996), Tony and Barry Buzan introduce an innovative tool (mind mapping) that enables you to find your way through the confusion that precedes understanding.

CHAPTER 19. FIRE: THE MOST ANCIENT TOOL

Henry A. Wright and Arthur W. Bailey in *Fire Ecology* (New York: Wiley, 1982), cover the role and management of fire in some detail, but not holistically. Despite this it is worth reading for the wealth of detailed information. An important reference book for anyone interested in the effects of fire on our atmosphere is: Joel S. Levine (ed.), 1991, *Global Biomass Burning: Atmospheric, Climatic, and Biospheric Implications*. Cambridge, Mass.: MIT Press. Additional papers on this subject include the following:

Cicerone, Ralph J. 1994. "Fire Atmospheric Chemistry, and the Ozone Layer," *Science*, vol. 263: 1243-1244.

Fishman, J., K. Fakhruzzaman, B. Cros, and D. Hganga. 1991. "Identification of Widespread Pollution in the Southern Hemisphere Deduced from Satellite Analyses," *Science,* vol. 252: 1693–1696.

Mano, Stein, and Meinrat O. Adreae. 1994. "Emission of Methyl Bromide from Biomass Burning," *Science,* vol. 263: 1255–1256.

Alston Chase's *Playing God in Yellowstone: The Destruction of America's First*

National Park (Boston: The Atlantic Monthly Press, 1986); and John Bakeless's *The Journals of Lewis and Clark* (New York: New American Library, 1964), provide information on the early Native American use of fire and list a number of other references. In *The Future Eaters* (Chatswood NSW, Australia: Reed Books, 1994), Tim Flannery provides information on early Aboriginal burning in Australia, which appears to have been even more extensive than in North America. When the first Europeans "discovered" Australia, they described it as "the continent of smoke."

In the references for Chapter 21, I have mentioned the work being done in the Kruger National Park in South Africa. The references cited will be of interest to anyone engaged in national park management and who uses fire to offset the adverse effects of low animal numbers.

A useful study that shows how much more frequent human-lit fires were than lightning-induced fires over a 2,000-year period can be found in Christopher H. Baisan and Thomas W. Swetnam, "Interactions of Fire Regimes and Land Use in the Central Rio Grande Valley," (Research Paper RM-RP-330, Fort Collins, Colo., U.S.D.A. Forest Service, Rocky Mountain Forest and Range Experimental Station, 1997).

CHAPTER 20. REST: THE MOST MISUNDERSTOOD TOOL

So deeply ingrained is our belief that rest is always beneficial to soils and plants that little serious investigation has been done. Where exclosure plots were put in during the 1930s by government agencies and universities to prove a positive response to rest, which they generally did initially, no one bothered to follow up the recordings. Where established in brittle environments, plots that still survive have suffered varying degrees of deterioration. Many of these plots are still intact in a number of western states and are worth visiting.

Several papers are available describing the situation in very brittle long-rested environments in Utah:

Dunne, Jim. 1989. "Cryptogamic Soil Crusts in Arid Ecosystems," *Rangelands,* vol. 11, no. 4: 180–182.

Kleiner, Edgar, F., and K. T. Harper. 1972. "Environment and Community Organization in Grasslands of Canyonlands National Park," *Ecology,* vol. 53, no. 2: 209–309.

Kleiner, Edgar, F., and K. T. Harper. 1977. "Soil Properties in Relation to Cryptogamic Groundcover in Canyonlands National Park," *Journal of Range Management,* vol. 33, no. 3: 202–205.

Kleiner, Edgar, F., and K. T. Harper. 1977. "Occurrence of Four Major Perennial Grasses in Relation to Edaphic Factors in a Pristine Community," *Journal of Range Management,* vol. 30, no. 4: 286–289.

The observations in a brittle environment grassland in Utah never reached by large game animals and livestock (Virginia Park) indicate the development of algae and lichens (cryptogamic communities) as a major part of the soil cover. The authors refer to it several times as a "climax community" because of the absence of large animals. It is my belief that the surrounding rock formations that have accidentally precluded the large animals, which generally coevolved with soils and vegetation in the brittle environments of North America, have made it a less-than-natural community to which the term *climax* cannot be attributed. The implication is that if this is truly climax, then large ungulates were unnatural, which clearly is not the case.

Throughout, Virginia Park is compared with Chesler Park, which has been subjected over the years to overgrazing of plants and partial rest brought about by prolonged light stocking with livestock. We now know that these two influences are detrimental to the health of brittle environment grassland communities and do not approximate the manner in which natural populations of ungulates functioned in such environments. It follows that any comparative conclusions drawn are of limited value since two unnatural situations are, in effect, under comparison. It is important to note the relative flatness of the land in Virginia Park. Where equally brittle areas are not flat (i.e., sloping canyon walls in the immediate area), the community under equal rest has been unable to stabilize at even the algae level.

Two works will be of interest to readers concerned by the rapid deterioration of land in the western United States since the 1890s, which I believe is due mainly to the partial rest that occurred as a result of decreasing animal numbers (though the authors attribute the deterioration to overgrazing):

Cottam, Walter P. 1947. "Is Utah Sahara Bound?" *Bulletin of the University of Utah,* vol. 37, no. 11, 40 pp.

Lockett, H. C. 1940. *Along the Beale Trail* (a publication of the Education Division, U.S. Office of Indian Affairs, Printing Department, Haskell Institute, Lawrence, Kansas). This small booklet contains photographs of actual sites described in his travels by Lieutenant Edward Fitzgerald Beale, who was commissioned by the War Department to survey a wagon road from Fort Defiance, Arizona, to the Colorado River in 1857. Alongside Beale's description of each site is a picture of it as it appeared eighty-one years later. Many of the early photographs used to illustrate changes over the years were taken around permanent mining or army camp sites, which rendered them less useful than general range sites. In this case Beale's descriptions of the open country serve us better for comparison purposes because the land was not yet disturbed by people or their domestic animals. The adverse changes in these brittle environment areas subjected to livestock overgrazing and partial rest over these years are dramatic indeed.

In my observations of the reduced health and premature death of brittle environment bunch grasses that are neither grazed, trampled, or burned, I had assumed it was the lack of total light reaching growth points that mattered. But research conducted in Argentina suggests that it is the *quality* of the light that matters. The researchers report their findings in:

Casal, J. J., V. A. Deregibus, and R. A. Sanchez. 1985. "Variations in Tiller Dynamics and Morphology in *Lolium* multiflorum Lam. Vegetative and Reproductive Plants As Affected by Differences in Red/Far-Red Irradiation," *Annals of Botany,* vol. 56: 553–559.

Deregibus, Victor Alejandro, Rodolfo A. Sanchez, and Jorge Jose Casal. 1983. "Effects of Light Quality on Tiller Production in *Lolium* spp.," *Plant Physiology*, vol. 72: 900–902.

Deregibus, V. A., R. A. Sanchez, J. J. Casal, and M. J. Trlica. 1985. "Tillering in Responses to Enrichment of Red Light Beneath the Canopy in a Humid Natural Grassland," *Journal of Applied Ecology*, vol. 22: 199–206.

CHAPTER 21. GRAZING: THE MOST ABUSED TOOL

The references cited earlier in Chapter 6 are all pertinent to this chapter. In addition, those readers grappling with the severe difficulties of managing game animals now confined to relatively small national parks that often offer inadequate predation and home ranges will find the approach of the biologists in the Kruger National Park of interest. Two good papers both appear in R. Norman Owen-Smith, ed., *Management of Large Mammals in African Conservation Areas* (Pretoria: Haum Educational Publishers, 1983). The first is U de V. Pienaar's, "Management by Intervention: The Pragmatic/Economic Option," pp 23–36, and the second is V de Vos, R. G. Bengis, and H. J. Coetzee's, in "Population Control of Large Mammals in the Kruger National Park," pp. 213–231.

The fact that the Kruger Park is no longer "natural" is accepted along with the realization that it has to be scientifically managed. A policy of holding animal numbers down through culling has been adopted in preference to periodic high die off in dry years. This policy is of course based on the belief that vegetative damage is caused by too many animals rather than time of exposure. This park lies in a moderate-rainfall, very brittle environment, and thus large quantities of forage accumulate (through the slow breakdown involved in oxidation and weathering) when animal numbers are deliberately held at a low level. Consequent vegetative changes lead to excessive brush encroachment and excessive use of fire as the main control mechanism. This in turn leads to desertification and contributes to atmospheric pollution.

CHAPTER 22. ANIMAL IMPACT: THE LEAST USED TOOL

The references cited in Chapters 5 and 6 are also applicable to this chapter. Due to our deep antagonism to livestock trampling over prolonged time we have little in the literature of its possible benefits over short time periods.

One of the few people in the United States to see the importance of livestock trampling was August L. Hormay, who wrote "Principles of Rest Rotation Grazing and Multiple-Use Land Management" (publication of U.S.D.I. Bureau of Land Management, and U.S.D.A. Forest Service, Washington: D.C.: Government Printing Office, 1971).

Harold F. Heady devotes a chapter in *Rangeland Management* (New York: McGraw-Hill, 1975) to the physical effects of grazing animals with a number of references to the observations of others. In all cases, the importance of the time dimension was missed. Trampling is without meaning if its duration and frequency are overlooked. Time and trampling, like time and grazing, are inseparable. Despite this, Heady mentions some beneficial effects of trampling in breaking capped algal soil surfaces and allowing better seed establishment, as well as laying dead material on the surface where decomposition increases and the minerals return to the soil.

CHAPTER 23. LIVING ORGANISMS: THE MOST COMPLEX TOOL

Many of the publications mentioned in connection with Chapters 11–15 concerning the complexity of living communities are applicable to this chapter.

As acceptance of the need to seek solutions other than chemical poisons—with or without genetic engineering—gains ground, there will be much new information emerging on the use of complex crop mixes, beneficial insects, and more. In the meantime the following periodicals often provide good information: *Acres USA: A Voice for Eco-Agriculture* is a monthly publication obtainable from Acres USA, P.O. Box 8800, Metaine, LA 79911-8800; *American Journal of Alternative Agriculture,* published by the Henry A. Wallace Institute for Alternative Agriculture, Inc., 9200 Edmonston Road, Suite 117, Greenbelt, MD 20770-1551; *Biodynamics: Farming and Gardening in the 21st Century,* published by Biodynamic Farming and Gardening Association, Inc., P.O. Box 550, Kimberton, PA 19442; and *The IPM Practitioner: Monitoring the Field of Pest Management,* published by Bio-Integral Resource Center (BIRC) P.O. Box 7414, Berkeley, CA 94707.

The permaculture publications listed in the references to Chapter 43 are excellent sources for ideas and techniques already in use in many parts of the world. Readers may also find Charles Walters, Jr., *Weeds: Control without Poisons* (Kansas City: Acres USA, 1991) helpful.

CHAPTER 24. TECHNOLOGY: THE MOST USED TOOL

A good source of information in the United States on both new and traditional technology is: Appropriate Technology Transfer for Rural Areas (ATTRA) (P.O. Box 3657, Fayetteville, AR 72702).

Increasingly we are becoming aware of the actual or potential damaging effects of persistent substances on biological communities. Good sources of information are: Rachel Carson's *Silent Spring* (Boston: Houghton-Mifflin, 1962); Barry Commoner's *The Closing Circle: Nature Man and Technology* (New York: Alfred A. Knopf, 1971); and *Our Stolen Future,* by Theo Colborn, Dianne Dumanoski, and John Peterson Myers (New York: Penguin, 1997). *Our Stolen Future,* documents the long-term effects of extremely small concentrations of certain substances, often in association with other substances, on humans, and particularly how these substances affect fetal development. Samuel S. Epstein's 1987 paper, "Losing the War against Cancer," in *The Ecologist* (vol. 17, no. 2/3: 91–101), explains the connection between cancer and environmental factors, but in particular discusses carcinogenic pollutants in our air, water, and food. It contains a wealth of additional references.

Two watchdog organizations providing information on possible effects of persistent and/or unnatural substances on a regular basis are: the Northwest Coalition for Alternatives to Pesticides (P.O. Box 1393, Eugene, OR 97440) and the National Wildlife Federation (8925 Leesburg Pike, Vienna, VA 22184).

An interesting study of the effects of our technology on decreasing mineral cycles and the health of American watersheds is G. T. Fincher's paper, "Importation, Colonization, and Release of Dung-Burying Scarabs," in *Biological Control of Muscoid Flies,* Miscellaneous Publication No. 61. USDA Agricultural Research Service. College Station, Texas.: Veterinary Toxicology and Entomology Research Laboratory, 1985.

While high level technology will, I believe, be essential to finding solutions to environmental degradation, there are inherent dangers in the concept of sustaining monocultures through biotechnology that is unbalanced with a broader approach. Views worth noting are expressed in a number of papers and articles, including:

Kloppenburg, Jack, Jr., and Beth Burrows. 1996. "Biotechnology to the Rescue? Twelve Reasons Why Biotechnology Is Incompatible with Sustainable Agriculture," *The Ecologist*, vol. 26, no. 2: 61–67.

Steinbrecher, Ricardia A. 1996. "From Green Revolution to Gene Revolution: The Environmental Risks of Genetically Engineered Crops," *The Ecologist*, vol. 26, no. 6: 273–278. The author warns that genetically engineered plants are likely to increase the use of pesticides and herbicides due to the acceleration of "superweeds" and "superbugs." She states that risk assessments are limited and mainly based on an outdated understanding of gene behavior.

Wuethrich, Bernice. 1994. "Migrating Genes Could Spread Resistance," *New Scientist*, vol. 144, no. 1947: 9.

CHAPTER 26. CAUSE AND EFFECT: STOP THE BLOWS TO YOUR HEAD BEFORE YOU TAKE THE ASPIRIN

We use the term *cause and effect* often and casually, but few realize how much we ignore it in daily life. For further reading, I recommend the works of Henry Hazlitt and Peter Senge. In *Economics in One Lesson* (New York: Arlington House, 1979), Hazlitt goes to great lengths to identify the common smokescreens that cloud the simple connections from an action to its consequences. He points out, with many examples, how missing the simple cause-and-effect relationships leads to increasing depths of crisis management, as we react to the unexpected.

Senge deals particularly well with the complexity of the interconnections in business, cause-and-effect relationships, and the long delay in the effects of our actions in both *The Fifth Discipline: The Art and Practice of the Learning Organization* (New York: Doubleday, 1990), and *The Fifth Discipline Fieldbook* (New York: Doubleday, 1994), written with co-authors M. Senge, Art Kleiner, Charlotte Roberts, Richard B. Ross, and Bryan J. Smith. The latter book provides practical guidelines for corporate managers attempting to track down the causes of their problems.

In *Farming in Nature's Image: An Ecological Approach to Agriculture* (Washington, D.C.: Island Press, 1992), Judith Soule and Jon Piper document the many environmental and social problems whose roots can be traced to modern industrialized agriculture.

CHAPTER 29. GROSS PROFIT ANALYSIS: BRINGING IN THE MOST MONEY FOR THE LEAST ADDITIONAL COST

A good account of the original gross margin analysis, as opposed to the American "improved version," is found in "Planning the Farm," by D. B. Wallace and H. Burr, *Farm Economics Branch Report No. 60*, Farm Economics Branch, School of Agriculture, Cambridge, University, June 1963. Wallace's choice of the original name "gross profit analysis" described in the text is from personal correspondence.

CHAPTER 30. ENERGY AND MONEY: USING THE MOST APPROPRIATE FORMS IN THE MOST CONSTRUCTIVE WAY

Entropy: A New World View, by Jeremy Rifkin (New York: Bantam Books, 1981) is an excellent, thought-provoking book about our current attitude toward energy. The author also provides a wealth of references. The reader interested in energy use in agriculture in the United States will find interesting, "Energy and Agriculture," by Amory B. Lovins, L. Hunter Lovins, and Marty Bender in *Meeting the Expectations of the Land: Essays in Sustainable Agriculture and Stewardship*, edited by Wes Jackson, Wendell Berry, and Bruce Colman (San Francisco: North Point Press, 1984).

The Rocky Mountain Institute produces a number of publications on energy conservation in the home, workplace, and factory. Write for their free Publications Catalog, RMI, 1739 Snowmass Creek Road, Snowmass, CO 81654, (970) 927-3851, (970) 927-3420 (fax), orders@rmi.org (email).

CHAPTER 31. SUSTAINABILITY: GENERATING LASTING WEALTH

For more information on The Natural Step, contact their offices at P.O. Box 29372, San Francisco, CA 94129, (415) 561-3344, tns@naturalstep.org.

Inside ISO 14000: The Competitive Advantage of Environmental Management by Don Sayre (St. Lucie, Fla.: St. Lucie Press, 1996) is an informative guide for corporations wishing to comply with the guidelines established by the International Organization for Standardization on Environmentally Responsible Management. Although needed, well-meant, and a serious start to do the right thing internationally, the guidelines tend to be bureaucratic, regulatory, and in many ways demotivational. There is far more emphasis on regulatory compliance than on sound training or understanding of ecosystem processes and functioning.

CHAPTER 32. SOCIETY AND CULTURE: PERSONAL VALUES AND SOCIAL RESPONSIBILITY

A good introduction to the basic ways in which cultures differ and the importance of understanding how those differences affect communication can be found in Edward T. Hall's *Beyond Culture* (New York: Doubleday, 1976).

CHAPTER 33. MONITORING YOUR PLANS AND KEEPING ON TRACK

In *The Fifth Discipline: The Art and Practice of the Learning Organization* (New York: Doubleday, 1990), Peter Senge discusses at length the importance of feedback loops. He makes a powerful point about learning from experience when he states, "Herein lies the core *learning dilemma* that confronts organizations: We learn best from experience but we never directly experience the consequences of many of our most important decisions." Utilizing feedback loops helps overcome this dilemma.

CHAPTER 36. ORGANIZATION AND LEADERSHIP: CREATING AN ENVIRONMENT THAT NURTURES CREATIVITY

The publications below were useful to me in preparing the manuscript of this book and are highly recommended for those who wish to explore these subjects in greater depth:

Case, John. 1996. *Open-Book Management: The Coming Business Revolution.* New York: HarperCollins.

Covey, Stephen. 1990. *Principle-Centered Leadership.* New York: Simon & Schuster.

Gibb, Jack. 1978. *Trust: A New View of Personal and Organizational Development.* La Jolla, Calif.: Omicron Press.

Hayward, Steven. 1997. *Churchill on Leadership: Executive Success in the Face of Adversity.* Rocklin, Calif.: Prima Publishing Forum.

Herzburg, Frederick. 1982. *The Managerial Choice: To Be Efficient and to Be Human.* Salt Lake City: Olympus Publishing.

Land, George, and Beth Jarman. 1993. *Breakpoint and Beyond: Mastering the Future Today.* New York: HarperCollins.

Lipnack, Jessica, and Jeffrey Stamps. 1993. *The TeamNet Factor.* Essex Junction, Vt.: Oliver Wight Publications.

Oakley, Ed, and Doug Krug, 1991. *Enlightened Leadership: Getting to the Heart of Change.* New York: Simon & Schuster.

Osborne, David, and Ted Gaebler, 1992. *Reinventing Government: How the Entrepreneurial Spirit Is Transforming the Public Sector.* New York: Penguin. (Gives many encouraging case studies, although almost all are fairly small bureaucracies.)

Schrage, Michael. 1995. *No More Teams! Mastering the Dynamics of Creative Collaboration.* New York: Doubleday.

Senge, Peter. 1990. *The Fifth Discipline: The Art and Practice of the Learning Organization.* New York: Doubleday. (Senge stresses the importance of leadership and a shared vision in what he refers to as "learning organizations.")

Wheatley, Margaret J. 1994. *Leadership and the New Science.* San Francisco: Berrett-Koehler Publishers. (Wheatley seeks a simpler way to lead organizations, based on mimicking nature: "Our concept of organizations is moving away from the mechanistic creations in the age of bureaucracy. We have begun to speak in earnest of more fluid, organic structures, even of boundaryless organizations.")

CHAPTER 37. MARKETING: DEVELOPING A STRATEGY IN LINE WITH YOUR HOLISTIC GOAL

Numerous books have become available in recent years that focus on marketing for smaller businesses. Those I would recommend include:

Anderson, Kare. 1994. *Walk Your Talk: Grow Your Business Faster through Successful Cross-Promotional Partnerships.* Berkeley: Spiral Publishing.

Hawken, Paul. 1987. *Growing a Business.* New York: Simon & Schuster.

Levinson, Jay Conrad. 1993. *Guerrilla Marketing: Secrets for Making Big Profits from Your Small Business.* New York: Houghton Mifflin.

Levinson, Jay Conrad, and Seth Godin. 1994. *The Guerrilla Marketing Handbook.* New York: Houghton Mifflin.

Those engaged in agricultural businesses who want to develop a niche market would benefit from the two books written by Joel Salatin, *Pastured Poultry Profits* (1993) and *Salad Bar Beef* (1995) (Swoope, Va.: Polyface). Although neither book is devoted strictly to marketing, both contain valuable information based on Salatin's experience in developing his products and building relationships with his customers.

CHAPTER 38. TIME: WHEN TO EXPOSE AND REEXPOSE PLANTS AND SOILS TO ANIMALS

The references in Chapter 6 are relevant here. In this chapter I mention my observations on the correlation of certain soils with better livestock nutrition. Two authors who have recorded such observations are Sir Albert Howard in *An Agricultural Testament* (New York: Oxford University Press, 1943), and William A. Albrecht in Charles Walters, Jr., ed., *The Albrecht Papers*, vol. II, (Kansas City: Acres USA., 1975).

The first culling of large game in Zimbabwe's game reserves was instigated by my "Report on the Status of Game and Management Needs in the Urungwe Non-hunting Area," unpublished report to the Department of Wildlife Conservation, Southern Rhodesia, 1961. This official report on the extensive damage that was taking place in what is today the Mana Pools National Park of Zimbabwe contained my recommendations to undertake heavy culling of elephant, buffalo, and some other species. Like most scientists, my conclusions were strongly influenced by my training, and thus my paradigms at the time. Vegetative damage equaled too many animals, I believed, and thus did not suspect that the damage could be due to the change in behavior of these animals, brought on by the removal of most of the large predators, including humans, and the increased use of fire.

In the Dust of Kilimanjaro (Washington, D.C.: Island Press/Shearwater Books, 1997) by David Western moves beyond traditional attitudes toward national parks and contains refreshing new thinking about wildlife conservation in Africa.

CHAPTER 39. STOCK DENSITY AND HERD EFFECT: USING ANIMALS TO SHAPE THE LANDSCAPE

Whereas I lived with and experienced some of the vast game herds of Africa, their North American equivalents had vanished from the continent before today's scientists could witness them firsthand. There are, however, some references to the large herds that once existed in North America, even as recently as two centuries ago.

The Journals of Lewis and Clark: A New Selection by John Bakeless (New York: New American Library, 1964) includes several accounts of large numbers of bison breaking through the river ice and drowning. Another good source of material about past numbers is David A. Dary's *The Buffalo Book: The Full Saga of the American Animal* (Chicago: The Swallow Press, 1974), which has a number of references to the enormous herds and their accompanying predators that characterized the vast and productive prairies as found by European settlers.

Unfortunately our obsession with published literature ("If it is not in the literature it is not so") often obliterates common sense and observation in science, which can hinder our learning. A great deal can be "read" in the book of nature. Once you know how grasslands in the very brittle environments function you can then glean a fair amount of information about the land's history from archaeological records. There are areas of Arizona, for instance, that are today characterized by millions of acres of bare ground. Yet relatively recent records show that bountiful grasslands once existed—so we know for certain that herding animals had to have been present. We also know that hunting tribes, such as the Apaches, either headquartered or camped there frequently, which would again indicate the presence of enough animals to feed them. Because the grasslands have disappeared, many environmentalists today maintain that there were no large herds of bison, and that may well be true. But they are ignoring all the other herding species, such as pronghorn, elk, and deer, and the fact that hunting tribes favored such areas. Such arguments are used to exclude large domestic stock, the only tool now left with which to restore the degraded landscapes to healthy grassland.

CHAPTER 40. CROPPING: PRACTICES THAT MORE CLOSELY MIMIC NATURE

For a good history of agriculture and cropping practices, read Clive Ponting's *A Green History of the World: The Environment and the Collapse of Great Civilizations* (New York: St. Martin's Press, 1991). It is often stated that if one does not heed history, one is bound to repeat it. This book is full of many historical lessons, including an account of the agricultural practices that led to the numerous famines that plagued Europe up until fairly recent times. Ponting makes the point that while modern mechanized agriculture and its vast infrastructure—transport, processing, and storage—finally helped end the famines, it is rapidly depleting the underlying biological infrastructure, which, if not checked, is likely to cause the demise of our current civilization. In a related article, "Old England's Bitter Harvest," *New Scientist*, vol. 148, no. 2209/2010: 15 (1995), Philip Cohen cites historical evidence of the serious breakdown of soil nutrients under early organic agriculture in England.

Neal Kinsey's Hands-on Agronomy, by Neal Kinsey and Charles Walters (Kansas City: Acres USA, 1993), is an invaluable book for farmers striving to move beyond conventional crop fertilization to the use of supplemental amendments to help build soil life.

In *The Soul of the Soil: A Guide to Ecological Soil Management*, 2nd ed. (St. Johnsbury, Vt., and Erle, Quebec, Canada: Gaia Services, 1986), Grace Gershuny and Joseph Smillie show great sensitivity to the nature of soil. They have a delightful sentence on page 4: "Find out what soils *live in your area*, how they are classified and described by soil scientists, and how that compares with what you observe about them yourself (emphasis added)." They point out how hard it is to find literature that is helpful to the farmer which is not dominated by technology use and sales interests. For the serious student of soil science, the classic text by Nyle C. Brady and Ray R. Weil, *The Nature and Properties of Soils*, 11th ed. (Englewood Cliffs, N.J.: Prentice-Hall, 1996), contains a wealth of information.

In "Alley Cropping: Trees As Sources of Green Manure and Mulch in the Tropics," *Biological Agriculture and Horticulture*, vol. 3, no. 2/3: 251–268 (1986), G. F. Wilson, B. T. Kang, and K. Mulongoy report on the promising results achieved when mixed crops are grown in rows between trees.

Good management of the timing of various operations, together with his deep understanding of biological succession, has enabled Masanobu Fukuoka to apparently increase yields and decrease insect damage in his crops. He describes his methods in *The One Straw Revolution: An Introduction to Natural Farming* (Emmaus, Penn.: Rodale Press, 1978), and *The Natural Way of Farming: The Theory and Practice of Green Philosophy* (New York: Japan Publications, 1985).

More than fifty years ago in *Plowman's Folly* (Norman: University of Oklahoma Press, 1943; reprinted in 1987 by Island Press, Washington, D.C.), Edward H. Faulkner showed conclusively that soil impoverishment and decreasing crop yields, and many of the adverse effects following droughts or floods, could be traced directly to plowing natural fertilizers deep into the soil. By incorporating green manures into the soil surface with a disk harrow he was able to transform ordinary and even infertile soils into extremely productive, high-yield crop lands.

CHAPTER 42. POPULATION MANAGEMENT: LOOK TO AGE STRUCTURE RATHER THAN NUMBERS, DIVERSITY RATHER THAN SINGLE SPECIES

The case of the desert bushes dying out is contained in my report "Holistic Resource Management in Pakistan" of November 1983 to the United Nations Food and Agricultural Organization TCP/PAK/2305 PROJECT. Assistance to Rangeland and Livestock Development Survey in Baluchistan.

A number of the readings suggested for Chapters 11 to 15 contain valuable information on population dynamics and principles. Aldo Leopold's *Game Management* (Madison: University of Wisconsin Press, 1986) is still one of the best for clarity and simplicity, followed closely by Raymond F. Dasmann's *Wildlife Biology* (New York: Wiley, 1966). David Quammen's *The Song of the Dodo: Island Biogeography in an Age of Extinctions* (New York: Simon & Schuster, 1996) explains in simple and compelling prose how the size of a territory can limit the growth and survival of a population. Anne H. Ehrlich's "The Human Population: Size and Dynamics," in *American Zoologist,* vol. 25: 395–406 (1985) is also good reading.

In my early life as a game ranger having to deal with problem lions, elephants, hippos, and other large game turned killer, I learned that such situations were never resolved until the actual rogue animal was killed. Little has been written on this aspect of predator control in the scientific journals. However, two authors who had to deal with such problems wrote fascinating books. *Man-Eaters of Kumaon,* by Jim Corbett (New York: Oxford University Press, 1946), tells of the author's experiences in having to kill man-eating tigers in India. In *The Man-Eaters of Tsavo* (New York: St. Martin's Press, 1986), Lt. Colonel J. H. Patterson recounts the story of two lions that killed a great number of railway workers in East Africa. Railway construction was brought to a halt until Patterson was able to identify and kill the lions responsible.

CHAPTER 43. DEPARTING FROM THE CONVENTIONAL

Those interested in learning more about permaculture design will find good introductory reading in:

Marrow, Rosemary. 1993. *Earth User's Guide to Permaculture.* Kenthurst NSW, Australia: Kangaroo Press.

Mollison, Bill, and Reny Mia Slay. 1991. *Introduction to Permaculture.* Tyalgum NSW, Australia: Tagari Publications.

Mollison, Bill. 1990. *Permaculture: A Practical Guide for a Sustainable Future.* Washington, D.C.: Island Press.

CHAPTER 44. HOLISTIC FINANCIAL PLANNING: CREATING THE FINANCIAL ROADMAP TO YOUR HOLISTIC GOAL

Some of the references included under Chapter 37 could be of help in creating your financial plan. For a greater understanding of the philosophy behind this planning and the need to account for biological as well as monetary capital, the books mentioned in the references for Chapter 17 will be helpful.

If you have difficulty generating ideas through brainstorming, read Doug Hall's *Jump Start Your Brain* (New York: Warner Books, 1995). Hall's irreverent approach would be helpful to anyone attempting to produce new income-generating ideas, but the book appears to have been written largely for those working within large, tradition-bound, or conservative corporations.

CHAPTER 49. MAKING RESEARCH RELEVANT

With most research today conducted within a reductionist framework, there is not much in the literature that is helpful in understanding how to place research within a holistic framework. Some useful papers are:

Agricultural Research for Resource Poor Farmers: A Parsimonious Paradigm, by Robert Chambers and Janice Jiggins (Brighton, England: Institute of Development Studies, University of Sussex, August 1986) is a refreshing look at research for developing countries from the perspective of a social anthropologist who considers the needs of the people themselves. The authors' ideas approach the findings of the Center for Holistic Management. Management cannot be imposed but must flow from the desires of the people themselves.

Towards Sustainability: A Plan for Collaborative Research on Agriculture and Natural Resource Management (Washington, D.C.: National Academy Press, 1991) was published in response to the call by the U.S. Congress for the U.S. Agency for International Development to create a new Collaborative Research Support Program (CRSP) to focus on the research needs of sustainable agriculture and natural resource management. This publication contains much useful information but is a classic example of the shortcomings of the conventional top-down interdisciplinary approach.

"Biodiversity As an Organizing Principle in Agroecosystem Management: Case Studies of Holistic Resource Management Practitioners in the USA" (*Agriculture, Ecosystems and Environment,* vol. 62: 199–213, 1997), by Deborah H.

Stinner, Benjamin R. Stinner, Edward Martsolf, describes an attempt to move beyond purely reductionist research in order to document what happens when whole situations are managed.

The inordinately long delay between the birth of new innovations and their acceptance is associated both with the paradigm effect and with the research required to confirm the results of the innovation's application. A valuable contribution to the better understanding of this problem is: "Innovation and Evaluation," by Frederick Mosteller (*Science,* vol. 211, no. 4485: 221– 226, 1981).

CHAPTER 50. CREATING SOUND POLICIES

The work that provided some of the information used in the grasshopper spraying policy analysis was done by a group of researchers in Montana and published in the following papers:

Onsager, J. A. 1985. "An Ecological Basis for Prudent Control of Grasshoppers in the Western United States," Proceedings 3rd Triennial Meeting, Pan American Acrididae Society 5–10 July, 1981.

Onsager, Jerome A. 1986. "Current Tactics for Suppression of Grasshoppers on Range," *Symposium Proceedings, Integrated Pest Management on Rangeland: State of the Art in the Sagebrush Ecosystem.* Bozeman, Mont.: Rangeland Insect Laboratory, Agricultural Research Service, USDA. On page 11, the author states, "In summary, it appears that any range management practice that significantly opens up the plant canopy, either temporarily or permanently, will tend to improve the microhabitat, either temporarily or permanently, for important pest species of grasshoppers. Decreased relative humidity, increased temperature, and increased solar radiation all will tend to enhance grasshopper development, and all will tend to debilitate important grasshopper pathogens."

Onsager, J. A., and G. B. Hewitt. 1982. "Rangeland Grasshoppers: Average Longevity and Daily Rate of Mortality among Six Species in Nature," *Environmental Entomology,* vol. 10: 127–133.

Information on the biomass burning policy was obtained from "Policy Options for Managing Biomass Burning to Mitigate Global Climate Change," by Kenneth J. Andrasko, Dilip R. Ahuja, Steven M. Winnett, and Dennis A. Tirpak in Joel S. Levine, ed., *Global Biomass Burning: Atmospheric, Climatic, and Biospheric Implications* (Cambridge, Mass.: MIT Press, 1991).

CHAPTER 51. CHANGING COURSE: CREATING THE FUTURE WE WANT

The obvious fact that the decline in resources leads eventually to serious conflict, genocide and war is slowly gaining acceptance with the publication of such papers as, "Environmental Change and Violent Conflict: Growing Scarcities of Renewable Resources Can Contribute to Social Instability and Civil Strife," by Thomas F. Homer-Dixon, Jeffrey H. Boutwell, and George W. Rathjens, in *Scientific American,* vol. 268: 38–45, 1993.

I am not aware, apart from the Green Movement initiated in Germany, of any concerted effort to bring ecological thinking into government. I entered parliament in Zimbabwe during a very difficult period of civil war but did endeavor to bring about ecological coordination of government policies. Interested readers will find one debate in the Record of Parliamentary Debates, Rhodesia, House of Assembly, First Session, Twelfth Parliament, 1970. Hansard columns 737 to 741.

My idea was to have an Ecological Coordination Council at cabinet level through which all government actions would have to pass. My efforts at the time were overrun by war and by my crossing the floor in parliament to rebuild and lead the opposition, but I believe the idea still has merit. Today, however, I would expand it and would have government make all decisions toward a national holistic goal.

In "Will We Be Able to Sustain Civilization?" *Population and Environment,* vol. 16, no. 2: 139–147 (1994), I outlined my concerns about our ability to sustain civilization under either organic or conventional agriculture. In the main, however, I attempted to focus the debate on sustainable civilization rather than sustainable agriculture, and for good reason. As long as we continue to talk of sustaining agriculture, the mass of people who today live in cities will feel it is the farmer's problem and of little concern to them.

The problems associated with bureaucratic organizations are well documented in *Voltaire's Bastards: The Dictatorship of Reason in the West,* by John Ralston Saul (New York: Random House, 1993). Successful strategies for overcoming many of these problems are suggested in *Banishing Bureaucracy: The Five Strategies for Reinventing Government* (Reading, Mass.: Addison–Wesley, 1997), by David Osborne and Peter Plastrick.

Notes

Chapter 1. Changing the Way We Make Decisions

1. Tim Flannery, 1994. *The Future Eaters* (Chatswood NSW, Australia: Reed Books).

2. P. S. Martin, 1984. "Prehistoric Overkill: The Global Model," pp. 354–403 in P. S. Martin and R. G. Klein, eds., *Quaternary Extinctions: A Prehistoric Revolution* (Tucson: University of Arizona Press).

3. Charles E. Kay, 1994. "Aboriginal Overkill: The Role of Native Americans in Structuring Western Ecosystems," *Human Nature*, vol. 5, no. 4: 359–398.

Chapter 3. The Whole Is Greater Than the Sum of Its Parts

1. J. C. Smuts, 1973. *Holism and Evolution* (Westport, Conn.: Greenwood Press), 336.

2. J. C. Smuts, 1952. *Jan Christian Smuts* (London: Cassell & Company), 290.

3. Robert T. Paine, 1966. "Food Web Complexity and Species Diversity," *American Naturalist,* vol. 100, no. 910: 65–75.

4. Zev Naveh and Arthur Lieberman, 1983. *Landscape Ecology: Theory and Application* (New York: Springer-Verlag), 56.

Chapter 5. The Predator–Prey Connection

1. Researcher S. J. McNaughton (Biological Research Labs, Syracuse University, New York) has conducted a number of field studies in East Africa documenting the relationship between herding grazers and the plants they feed on:

S. J. McNaughton, 1979. "Grazing As an Optimization Process: Grass–Ungulate Relationships in the Serengeti," *The American Naturalist,* vol. 5: 691–703.

———, 1984. "Grazing Lawns: Animals in Herds, Plant Form, and Coevolution. *The American Naturalist,* vol. 6: 863–883.

S. J. McNaughton, M. B. Coughenour, and L. L. Wallace, 1982. "Interactive Processes in Grassland Ecosystems," in *Grasses and Grasslands: Systematics and Ecology* (Norman: University of Oklahoma Press).

S. J. McNaughton, F. F. Banyikwa, and M. M. McNaughton, 1997. "Promotion of the Cycling of Diet-Enhancing Nutrients by African Grazers," *Science,* vol. 278: 1798–1800.

CHAPTER 10. DEVELOPING A SENSE OF OWNERSHIP: ARE YOU SURE THAT'S WHAT YOU REALLY WANT?

1. Don Halladay and Randee Halladay, 1993. "In Developing Your Goal—Get Specific!" *Holistic Resource Management Quarterly,* no. 41: 2.

2. Ibid.

CHAPTER 12. WATER CYCLE: THE CIRCULATION OF CIVILIZATION'S LIFE BLOOD

1. P. A. Yeomans, *Water for Every Farm: Using the Keyline Plan* (Katoomba, Australia: Second Back Row Press).

CHAPTER 13. COMMUNITY DYNAMICS: THE EVER-CHANGING PATTERNS IN THE DEVELOPMENT OF LIVING COMMUNITIES

1. Roderick MacDonald, 1986. "Extraction of Microorganisms from the Soil," *Biological Agriculture and Horticulture,* no. 3: 361–365.

2. Chris Maser, 1988. *The Redesigned Forest* (San Pedro, Calif.: R & E Miles), 24–38.

3. Les Kaufman, 1992. "Catastrophic Change in Species-Rich Freshwater Ecosystems," *BioScience,* vol. 42, no 11: 846–858.

4. David Tilman, David Wedin, and Johannes Knops, 1996. "Productivity and Sustainability Influenced by Biodiversity in Grassland Ecosystems," *Nature,* vol. 379: 718–720.

5. Nyle C. Brady and Ray R. Weil, 1996. *The Nature and Properties of Soils,* 11th ed. (New York: Prentice Hall), 333.

6. Andre Voisin, 1988. *Grass Productivity* (Washington, D.C.: Island Press), 45.

7. Douglas H. Chadwick, 1995. "What Is a Prairie?" *Audubon,* vol. 97, no. 6: 36.

8. Robert van den Bosch, 1980. *The Pesticide Conspiracy* (Garden City, N.Y.: Anchor Books), 24.

CHAPTER 17. MONEY AND LABOR: ONE OR BOTH OF THESE TOOLS IS ALWAYS REQUIRED

1. Margrit Kennedy, with Declan Kennedy, 1995. *Interest and Inflation Free Money* (Okemos, Mich.: Seva International), 27.

2. Nicholas Hildyard, 1996. "Too Many for What? The Social Generation of Food 'Scarcity' and 'Overpopulation,'" *The Ecologist,* vol. 26, no. 6: 288.

CHAPTER 19. FIRE: THE MOST ANCIENT TOOL

1. Jean Michel Brustet, Jean Bruno Vickos, Jacques Fontan, Alain Podaire, and Francois Lavenu, 1992. "Characterization of Active Fires in West African Savannas by Analysis of Satellite Data: Landsat Thematic Mapper," in Joel S. Levine, ed., *Global Biomass Burning* (Cambridge, Mass.: MIT Press), 53–60.

2. J. Fishman, K. Fakhruzzman, B. Cros, and D. Nganga, 1991. "Identification of Widespread Pollution in the Southern Hemisphere Deduced from Satellite Analyses," *Science,* vol. 252: 1693–96.

3. Stein Mano and Meinrat O. Andreae, 1994. "Emission of Methyl Bromide from Biomass Burning," *Science,* vol. 263: 1255–56; Molly O'Meara, 1996. "The Next Hurdle in Ozone Repair," *World Watch,* vol. 9, no. 6: 8.

CHAPTER 20. REST: THE MOST MISUNDERSTOOD TOOL

1. David Sheridan, 1981. *Desertification of the United States* (Washington, D.C.: Council on Environmental Quality), 21.

CHAPTER 23. LIVING ORGANISMS: THE MOST COMPLEX TOOL

1. Masanobu Fukuoka, 1978. *The One Straw Revolution: An Introduction to Natural Farming* (Emmaus, Penn.: Rodale Press).

2. C. W. Gay, D. D. Dwyer, C. Allison, S. Hatch, and J. Schickedanz, 1980. *New Mexico Range Plants,* New Mexico State University Cooperative Extension Circular 3374: 43.

3. Paul R. Ehrlich, 1986. *The Machinery of Nature: The Living World around Us and How It Works* (New York: Simon & Schuster), 162.

CHAPTER 24. TECHNOLOGY: THE MOST USED TOOL

1. The "tragedy of the commons" concept was first expressed by the Rev. William Forster Lloyd in *Two Lectures on the Checks to Population, Delivered Before the University of Oxford, Michaelmas Term, 1832* (Oxford, England: Collingwood, 1933). This rare text was reprinted in 1968 by Augustus M. Kelly Economic Classics. American economist Garrett Hardin revived the idea and expounded on it in his famous essay, "The Tragedy of the Commons," which has been reprinted in numerous anthologies. Hardin's 1972 book *Exploring New Ethics for Survival: The Voyage of the Spaceship Beagle* (New York: Viking) is an elaboration of the essay.

2. Arnold Aspelin, 1994. *Pesticide Industry Sales and Usage: 1992 and 1993 Market Estimates.* Report issued by Environmental Protection Agency, Office of Pesticide Programs, Biological and Economic Analysis Division.

3. Robert Rodale, 1983. "Importance of Resource Regeneration," *Resource-Efficient Farming Methods for Tanzania* (Emmaus, Penn.: Rodale Press), 21.

CHAPTER 26. CAUSE AND EFFECT: STOP THE BLOWS TO YOUR HEAD BEFORE YOU TAKE THE ASPIRIN

1. *Insight on the News,* October 28, 1996, 38 (figures supplied by the U.S. Beverage Marketing Association).

2. Agenda 21, Chapter 12: Report on the Plan of Action to Combat Desertification, U.N. Conference on Environment and Development, Rio de Janeiro, 1992.

3. Tom Larson, 1996. "Swinging the 'Balance of Nature' in My Direction," *Nebraska Sustainable Agriculture Society Newsletter,* November: 4.

CHAPTER 29. GROSS PROFIT ANALYSIS: BRINGING IN THE MOST MONEY FOR THE LEAST ADDITIONAL COST

1. Information obtained from personal correspondence with David Wallace.

CHAPTER 30. ENERGY AND MONEY: USING THE MOST APPROPRIATE FORMS IN THE MOST CONSTRUCTIVE WAY

1. Stacy Perman, 1998. "Goodbye, Freebies–Hello Fees," *Time,* vol. 151, no. 1: 62.

2.   L. Hunter Lovins and Amory B. Lovins, 1989. "How Not to Parachute

More Cats: The Hidden Links Between Energy and Security," paper prepared for
the Center for a Postmodern World conference, *Toward a Postmodern Presidency:
Vision for a Planet in Crisis,* held at the University of California at Santa Barbara,
30 June–4 July. (Available from Rocky Mountain Institute, 1739 Snowmass Creek
Road, Snowmass, CO 81564.)

CHAPTER 31. SUSTAINABILITY: GENERATING LASTING WEALTH

1. Paul Hawken, 1993. *The Ecology of Commerce: A Declaration of Sustainability*
(New York: HarperCollins).

2. The four system conditions included in The Natural Step program are:

- Substances from the earth's crust must not systematically increase in
  nature.

- Substances produced by society must not systematically increase in
  nature.

- The physical basis for the productivity and diversity of nature must not
  be systematically diminished.

- Fair and efficient use of energy and other resources.

Source: John Holmberg, Karl-Henrik Robert, and Karl-Erik Eriksson, 1996.
"Socio-ecological Principles for a Sustainable Society," in R. Costanza, O. Segura,
and J. Martinez-Alier, eds., *Getting Down to Earth: Practical Applications of Ecological
Economics* (Washington D.C.: Island Press), 17–48.

CHAPTER 32. SOCIETY AND CULTURE: PERSONAL VALUES
AND SOCIAL RESPONSIBILITY

1. Chris Knippenberg, 1996. "Making the Testing Personal: Testing a Gift
Horse," *Holistic Management Quarterly,* no. 53: 6.

2. Bruce Gregory, 1996. "Making the Testing Personal: Filberts or Fencing This
Year?" *Holistic Management Quarterly,* no. 53: 6.

CHAPTER 35. LEARNING AND PRACTICE: SHIFTING YOUR PARADIGMS

1. David Irvine, 1994. "Building Management Clubs That Work," *Holistic
Resource Management Quarterly,* no. 44: 2.

CHAPTER 36. ORGANIZATION AND LEADERSHIP: CREATING AN ENVIRONMENT
THAT NURTURES CREATIVITY

1. Everett M. Rogers, 1983. *Diffusion of Innovations,* 3rd ed. (New York:
Macmillan), 7–8.

2. These beliefs are based on what I have observed in leaders I have served
under or worked with in one capacity or another. The following also document
the relationship between these leadership beliefs and an organization's ability to
function well:

Jay Hall, 1982. *The Competence Process.* The Woodlands, Tex.: Teleometrics
International, 226–229

Ed Oakley and Doug Krug, 1991. *Enlightened Leadership*. New York: Simon & Schuster.

CHAPTER 38. TIME: WHEN TO EXPOSE AND REEXPOSE PLANTS AND SOILS TO ANIMALS

1. My assertion that it was easy to double conventional stocking rates with planned grazing generated enormous controversy and condemnation of me in Rhodesia, South Africa, and America. To put the matter to rest once and for all, the then Rhodesian minister of agriculture publicly challenged me to demonstrate this in a controlled trial. The "Charter Trial," named after the company that provided the land and cattle, ran for eight years and was monitored by the University of Rhodesia and the Marandellas Research Station. We successfully ran double the conventional stocking rate without any deterioration of the land, as I had predicted. The conclusion was written up in "Results of the Botanical Analyses in the Charter Trial," by J. N. Clatworthy for the Rhodesian Branch of the South African Society of Animal Production, in 1976 and published in the *Zimbabwe Agricultural Journal*, in 1984, vol. 81, no. 2: 49–52.

No great change was measured on the ground despite vast man-hours spent in collecting data because only plant species composition, not ecological process, was considered by those doing the monitoring. However, as the effects on ecosystem processes were sufficiently pronounced, Clatworthy felt the need for additional comment on observations that were not reflected in species composition:

> Under the conservative stocking rate of the Charter system [the control] the grass grew tall and dead top hamper accumulated so that periodic burning was necessary to remove this. On the rotationally grazed plots (planned grazing) the heavier stocking rate kept the grass short and there was no build-up of dead material. This gave the sward a very healthy appearance.

Incidentally, this trial intended to end all controversy merely increased resistance among range scientists. Common sense suggests that a demonstration to sway public opinion will influence people. It does influence a few, usually when they are far removed from it. But to those closely involved, the underlying message of any successful demonstration is "look how clever we are and how stupid you are." Following the Charter Trial experience, I have consistently refused to be involved in similar demonstrations. Collaborating with others in mutual learning situations has proven far more effective as it does not create the psychological barriers that demonstrations of this sort can.

CHAPTER 39. STOCK DENSITY AND HERD EFFECT: USING ANIMALS TO SHAPE THE LANDSCAPE

1. D. M. Gammon and B. R. Roberts, 1980. "Aspects of Defoliation during Short Duration Grazing of the Matopos Sandveld of Zimbabwe," *Zimbabwe Journal of Agricultural Research*, vol. 18: 29.

When I visited the Matopos Research Station, where this study on my work took place, I found that only two steers were being used to constitute the herd. The researchers would not accept that two steers can never simulate the effects that a real herd of two hundred or more steers produced, and thus the research trial continued despite the defect, which rendered the results meaningless.

Chapter 40. Cropping: Practices That More Closely Mimic Nature

1. André Voisin, 1960. *Better Grassland Sward* (London: Crosby Lockwood & Son), 95–124.

2. Aldo Leopold, 1986. *Game Management* (Madison: University of Wisconsin Press), 124–136.

3. Clive Ponting, 1991. *A Green History of the World: The Environment and the Collapse of Great Civilizations* (New York: St. Martin's Press), 292.

Chapter 42. Population Management: Look to Age Structure Rather Than Numbers, Diversity Rather Than Single Species

1. Clive Ponting, 1991. *A Green History of the World: The Environment and the Collapse of Great Civilizations* (New York: St. Martin's Press), 103–6.

Chapter 49. Making Research Relevant

1. Cliff Montagne, 1997. "Orienting Research to Meet Human Needs," *Holistic Management Quarterly*, no. 56: 17.

Chapter 50. Creating Sound Policies

1. J. A. Onsanger, 1985. "An Ecological Basis for Prudent Control of Grasshoppers in the Western United States," *Proceedings of the Third Triennial Meetings, Pan American Acrididae Society*, 5–10 July, 1981. The Pan American Acrididae Society, 98.

2. K. J. Andrasko, D. R. Ahuja, S. M. Winnett, and D. A. Tirpak, 1995. "Policy Options for Managing Biomass Burning to Mitigate Global Climate Change," in S. J. Levine, ed., *Global Biomass Burning* (Boston: MIT Press), 445–456.

Index

About the Center for Holistic Management

The Center for Holistic Management was established in 1984 as an international nonprofit corporation to advance the practice of Holistic Management and to coordinate its continued development. The Center serves as the hub of an information exchange network that includes an association of educators certified to provide training in Holistic Management, individual practitioners, groups of practitioners who associate as management clubs/learning groups or more formally as state, regional, or national affiliates, and a sister organization, founded in 1992, the Africa Centre for Holistic Management, in Victoria Falls, Zimbabwe.

To facilitate the flow of information, the Center publishes a bimonthly newsletter, *Holistic Management IN PRACTICE*, which regularly updates the ideas presented in this book and provides a forum in which readers can share new insights or case studies of particular challenges they have overcome. The Center also hosts several conferences on the Internet that enable those with pressing questions to receive a variety of timely responses.

Each year we run training programs for up to twenty individuals who, on completion of the two-year program, are certified to provide Holistic Management training and follow-up support to people in their own communities or in the institutions they represent. Certified Educator training programs are currently run in the United States and in southern Africa and are planned in other countries in the near future.

To support the efforts of its certified educators the Center has engaged in a number of research projects that explore ways to introduce Holistic Management in a variety of forums, most recently within rural communities in the United States and in villages in developing nations that subsist entirely or largely on agriculture. In return, certified educators also work with Center staff to design educational materials and products for practitioners, such as planning and monitoring guides, charts and forms, Holistic Financial Planning software, and a number of other publications.

The Center provides management services and consultation to a variety of businesses, organizations, and government institutions. Through a for-profit subsidiary, Holistic Management International, the Center engages in commercial activity that makes it possible to introduce Holistic Management to new audiences while deriving revenue to help support our nonprofit efforts.

As this book was going to press, the Center's board and staff were in the process of changing the Center's name to Savory Center for Holistic Management in honor of its founder, Allan Savory.

For more information on any of our programs, products, or services, contact the Center for Holistic Management, 1010 Tijeras, NW, Albuquerque, NM 87102; tel: (505)842-5252; fax: (505) 843-7900; e-mail: center@holisticmanagement.org; website: www.igc.org/holisticmanagement.org.

HOLISTIC MANAGEMENT™ IN PRACTICE

Want to keep up-to-date on the latest developments in Holistic Management?

Subscribe now ...

to *Holistic Management IN PRACTICE*, a bimonthly publication of the Savory Center for Holistic Management.

In Every Issue ...

- ◆ **Featured topic** - Timely articles that put Holistic Management in the context of current issues and events.

- ◆ **Holistic Management Explorations** - Certified Educators and others offer practical tips and new insights into the challenges faced by beginning and seasoned practitioners.

- ◆ **Books in Brief** - A review of books that will enhance your practice of Holistic Management.

- ◆ **Land and Livestock** - A special supplement for natural resource managers that includes nuts-and-bolts features on the practical challenges faced by land managers, and a lively question and answer column.

- ◆ **Reader's Forum** - Made a new discovery? Gained a deeper understanding of some aspect of Holistic Management? Share it with others in this section.

- ◆ **Certified Educators** - A continually updated listing of Holistic Management educators and how to contact them.

- ◆ **Plus** information on how to order a variety of planning aids and materials and other Center-created products developed to enhance your efforts.

I WANT TO SUBSCRIBE TO *Holistic Management IN PRACTICE*

Name _____

Address_____

City & State/Prov. _____

Zip/Post Code _____ Country _____

Phone _____

❑ $30/yr (U.S.)

❑ $35/yr (International)

Mail to: **Savory Center for Holistic Management**
1010 Tijeras NW, Albuquerque, NM 87102, USA
Phone: 505/842-5252, Fax: 505/843-7900
email: center@holisticmanagement.org
website: www.holisticmanagement.org